THE CAMBRIDGE HISTORY OF
CAPITALISM

The second volume of *The Cambridge History of Capitalism* provides an authoritative reference on the spread and impact of capitalism across the world, and the varieties of responses to it. Employing a wide geographical coverage and strong comparative outlook, a team of leading scholars explore the global consequences that capitalism has had for industry, agriculture, and trade, along with the reactions by governments, firms, and markets. The authors consider how World War I halted the initial spread of capitalism, but global capitalism arose again by the close of the twentieth-century. They explore how the responses of labor movements, compounded by the reactions by political regimes, whether defensive or proactive, led to diverse military and welfare consequences. Beneficial results eventually emerged, but the rise and spread of capitalism has not been easy or smooth. This definitive volume will have widespread appeal amongst historians, economists, and political scientists.

LARRY NEAL is Emeritus Professor of Economics at the University of Illinois, Urbana-Champaign, Research Associate of the National Bureau of Economic Research, and Visiting Professor at the London School of Economics and Political Science. Specializing in financial history and European economies, he is author of *The Rise of Financial Capitalism: International Capital Markets in the Age of Reason* (Cambridge University Press, 1990), *The Economics of Europe and the European Union* (Cambridge University Press, 2007), and *"I Am Not Master of Events": The Speculations of John Law and Lord Londonderry in the Mississippi and South Sea Bubbles* (2012). He is co-editor of *The Origins and Development of Financial Markets and Institutions: From the Seventeenth Century to the Present* (Cambridge University Press, 2009).

JEFFREY G. WILLIAMSON is Emeritus Laird Bell Professor of Economics, Harvard University, and Honorary Fellow in the Department of Economics, University of Wisconsin-Madison. He is also Research Associate of the National Bureau of Economic Research, Research Fellow at the Centre for Economic Policy Research, and has been a visiting professor at seventeen universities around the world. Professor Williamson specializes in development, inequality, globalization, and history, and he is the author of around 230 scholarly articles and 30 books, his most recent being *Trade and Poverty: When the Third World Fell Behind* (2011), *Globalization and the Poor Periphery before 1950* (2006), *Global Migration and the World Economy* (2005, with T. Hatton), and *Globalization in Historical Perspective* (2003, edited with M. Bordo and A. M. Taylor).

Fundación **BBVA**

Cambridge University Press gratefully acknowledges the support of the BBVA Foundation in hosting and funding two workshops attended by contributors to the volume.

The BBVA Foundation expresses the BBVA Group's commitment to the improvement and welfare of the numerous societies in which it operates through the promotion of scientific research, innovation, and cultural creation, and their transmission to society using diverse channels and formats. Its work programs scrupulously respect the academic organization of knowledge and artistic creation and the principle of peer review, while facilitating the development of projects arising from the interaction of various fields and, particularly, emerging projects which move forward the frontiers of knowledge and thought. Among its multiple activities are the funding and co-organization of research projects, advanced training, lectures aimed at the general public, workshops, the endowment of special chairs, awards for researchers and creators (notably, the *Frontiers of Knowledge Awards* family, spanning eight categories and directed at the international community), publications under its own imprint and in partnership with academic publishers of excellence, and the recording and diffusion of classical and contemporary music.

Its areas of focus are Basic Sciences, Biomedicine, Environmental Sciences, Economics and Social Sciences, the Humanities and the Arts (particularly music and painting).

THE CAMBRIDGE
HISTORY OF
CAPITALISM

*

VOLUME II

The Spread of Capitalism:
From 1848 to the Present

*

Edited by

LARRY NEAL

and

JEFFREY G. WILLIAMSON

CAMBRIDGE
UNIVERSITY PRESS

Fundación **BBVA**

CAMBRIDGE
UNIVERSITY PRESS

University Printing House, Cambridge CB2 8BS, United Kingdom

Cambridge University Press is part of the University of Cambridge.

It furthers the University's mission by disseminating knowledge in the pursuit of education, learning and research at the highest international levels of excellence.

www.cambridge.org
Information on this title: www.cambridge.org/9781107583351

© Cambridge University Press 2014

First published 2014
3rd printing 2015
First paperback edition 2015

A catalogue record for this publication is available from the British Library

ISBN 978-1-107-58335-1 Paperback
ISBN 978-1-107-58459-4 Paperback set

Contents

Contents

Figures

vii

Tables

Contributors

ROBERT C. ALLEN Professor of Economic History, University of Oxford

GARETH AUSTIN Professor of International History, Graduate Institute of International and Development Studies, Geneva

KRISTINE BRULAND Professor of Economic History, University of Oslo

GIOVANNI FEDERICO Professor of Economic History, Department of Economics and Management, University of Pisa

JEFFRY FRIEDEN Stanfield Professor of International Peace, Department of Government, Harvard University

RON HARRIS Professor of Legal History and Dean, Faculty of Law, Tel-Aviv University

MARK HARRISON Professor, Department of Economics, University of Warwick, and research fellow at the Hoover Institution, Stanford University

MICHAEL HUBERMAN Professor of Economic History, Faculty of Economics and Social Sciences (SES), Université de Genève

HAROLD JAMES Professor of History and International Affairs, Princeton University

GEOFFREY JONES Isidor Straus Professor of Business History, Harvard Business School

PETER H. LINDERT Distinguished Research Professor of Economics, University of California, Davis

RANALD MICHIE Professor, Department of History, Durham University

RANDALL MORCK Stephen A. Jarislowsky Distinguished Chair in Finance and University Professor, Alberta School of Business

DAVID C. MOWERY William A. & Betty H. Hasler Chair in New Enterprise Development, Haas School of Business, University of Berkeley

LARRY NEAL Professor Emeritus of Economics, University of Illnois, Urbana-Champaign and London School of Economics

KEVIN H. O'ROURKE Chichele Professor of Economic History, All Souls College, University of Oxford

LEANDRO PRADOS DE LA ESCOSURA, Professor at the Economic History and Institutions Department, Carlos III University of Madrid

RONALD ROGOWSKI Professor of Political Science, University of California, Los Angeles

JEFFREY G. WILLIAMSON Laird Bell Professor of Economics, Emeritus, Harvard University, and Honorary Fellow, Department of Economics, University of Wisconsin-Madison

BERNARD YEUNG Stephen Riady Distinguished Professor and Dean, National University of Singapore Business School

Introduction: the spread of and resistance to global capitalism

KEVIN H. O'ROURKE AND JEFFREY G. WILLIAMSON

This second volume of the *Cambridge History of Capitalism* deals with capitalism's evolution within Western Europe and its offshoots, and its spread to the rest of the world after 1848. Throughout, capitalism increased in complexity as it overcame resistance and setbacks. Given that global capitalism is currently under severe stress and that world economic growth appears to be slowing down, it is easy to be distracted by these problems of the present. Indeed, the last chapter of this volume will focus mainly on those problems as they relate to the future. This introduction, however, will resist this presentist temptation and instead use the past to organize our thinking. Here we trace out capitalism's global historical road map since 1848 so that the details in the chapters that follow can be placed in context.

Capitalism and global capitalism: a roadmap

The spread of global capitalism has two dimensions, and they can be distinguished by means of an analogy that will appear again towards the end of the chapter. The gold standard was, strictly speaking, a *domestic* institution, linking a country's money supply to its gold reserves. The gold standard only became an *international* exchange rate system once several countries had independently decided to adopt the gold standard, and to allow free trade in gold. Similarly, the emergence of global capitalism as an *international economic system* required not only that the institutions of capitalism be introduced in the economies of all global participants, but also that those participants allowed a wide range of economic interactions to take place between them. If socialism had succeeded in embracing the planet, we would have had an international system that was certainly global, but not capitalist. And it has not been uncommon for capitalist economies to shield themselves from the global economy. A global capitalist system requires both the *domestic* capitalist institutions and the *international* interactions.

As long as individual nations retain control of their own destinies, it is unlikely that we will ever have a truly global capitalist system, certainly in our lifetimes. Nevertheless, it surely makes more sense to speak of a global capitalist system today than at any previous point in human history. It is also true that the domestic and the international dimensions of the transition to our twenty-first-century global capitalism have never been unidirectional: along the way, there have been many explosions of political backlash against globalization, and of rejections of the basic institutions of free markets (Chapter 12 by Jeffry Frieden and Ronald Rogowski). Some of these explosions arose endogenously, often as a response to some unequal distributional implication of capitalism (Chapter 13 by Michael Huberman; Chapter 14 by Peter Lindert). Others arose as a result of major shocks to the international system, some of which were endogenous and due to flaws in early capitalist institutions and some of which were arguably exogenous. Two notable examples of the latter were World War I and World War II, although this volume will explore ways in which these conflicts may have been produced by key features of the early and middle twentieth-century international economy (Chapter 11 by Mark Harrison). As Karl Marx suggested, other shocks may have been endogenously generated by the "inherent" instability of capitalism itself – most notably the Great Depression, or, more recently, the Great Recession. A key question is how different countries responded to these shared global shocks. After the Great Depression and World War II, for example, some countries reformed their financial systems, slowly opened their economies again to international trade (if not international capital flows), and constructed Grand Bargains between labor, capital, and government: this was the case in Western Europe, which experienced an economic growth miracle over the quarter-century from 1950 to 1973. Other countries, like many in Latin America, developed much more inward-looking, anti-global, and anti-market (import substituting industrialization, or ISI) policies during the same period, policies which were only abandoned in the 1980s or 1990s. Since the permanent abandonment in 1971–1973 of fixed exchange rates as an anchor for international monetary arrangements, a new surge of capitalism occurred within the context of renewed globalization. This sequence of events gives each chapter that follows three major episodes to consider: the nineteenth-century aftermath of the industrial revolution; the mid twentieth-century retreat from global capitalism; and the gradual resumption of global capitalism's spread and deepening after World War II.

The aftermath of the industrial revolution

The so-called long nineteenth century was largely defined by the industrial revolution. From the point of view of the development of global capitalism, the most important consequences were the following. First, there appeared the *Great Divergence* in per capita incomes between rich capitalist leaders and poor pre-capitalist followers. This Great Divergence went hand in hand with a decisive shift in military power that enabled the Western economies to dominate large areas of the globe via formal and informal imperialism (Chapter 10 by Gareth Austin). Imperialism facilitated the spread of a variety of legal systems (Chapter 5 by Ron Harris), corporations and other firm organizations (Chapter 6 by Geoffrey Jones; Chapter 7 by Randall Morck and Bernard Yeung), and financial institutions (Chapter 8 by Ranald Michie), as well as international economic integration. Second, the industrial revolution produced the *Great Specialization*, which gave the hegemonic power, the United Kingdom, a strong interest in an open international trading system, since that island economy relied so heavily on the exchange of manufactured exports for food and raw material imports from the poor periphery (Findlay and O'Rourke 2007; Williamson 2011). Third, the new industrial (and agricultural) technologies spread from the United Kingdom to the rest of northwestern Europe and the United States, and, with a lag, further afield to the European periphery, Latin America, and Asia (Chapter 2 by Robert Allen; Chapter 3 by Giovanni Federico; Chapter 4 by Kristine Bruland and David Mowrey). Fourth, new transportation technologies and the telegraph were both crucial in fostering trade and forging global commodity markets. Fifth, domestic money markets became more sophisticated, and financial capital flowed across borders in increasing waves, forming a world capital market (Chapter 9 by Harold James). Sixth, the fall in steerage costs, the rise in remittances to those who hadn't yet left for high-wage host countries, and the erosion of poverty traps in low-wage sending regions, all led to the emergence of mass migration. This mass migration fostered something like a gradually integrating Atlantic labor market. Finally, the industrial revolution was followed by the slow spread of democracy across the core countries, a process that would have major economic implications for twentieth-century global capitalism.

Domestic capitalist institutions

Most chapters in this volume have a great deal to say about the small sample of countries in which domestic capitalist institutions were relatively well-developed in 1848, as Volume 1 has shown so well. Almost all of these were in Western Europe and in their overseas offshoots, but very few were in the rest of the world. The chapters in this volume talk about both domestic capitalist institutional deepening and widening. By deepening, we mean the further development of capitalist institutions in the core countries during the late nineteenth century: for example, the continued development of increasingly sophisticated financial markets in countries like the United Kingdom and the United States; or the emergence of the modern corporate firm in the United States following the spread of the railroad and telegraph. By widening, we mean that more countries joined the capitalist club: for example, Japan's quick absorption of capitalist institutions during the Meiji and early Taisho periods, or the efforts of leading Latin American industrializers – like Mexico, Argentina, and Brazil – to do the same during their *belle époque*, or even the emergence of Asian centers of capitalism like Shanghai and Bombay.

Global interactions

The increased globalization across the nineteenth century was due to a combination of factors, especially the new transportation and information technologies referred to above. On the other hand, these technologies were able to have the impact they did because of favorable geopolitical conditions: the end of mercantilist competition in Western Europe, replaced by British dominance; the end of the great mercantilist trading monopolies, replaced by far more competitive conditions; the achievement of a durable peace in 1815 that made a century of world trade possible without disruptive intra-European conflict; and the rise of imperialism, which imposed free trade both on formal colonies (as opposed to the self-governing Dominions, which typically chose to erect substantial tariff barriers) and on only nominally independent countries such as China, Egypt, Japan, Siam, and the Ottoman empire – all forced to go open by gunboat diplomacy. In addition, Britain offered the military muscle to police the process (*pax Britannica*), just as America does today (*pax Americana*).

The international globalization of capitalism

What made it the first global century? Trade booms[1]

Four things happened to the world economy between the end of the Napoleonic Wars and World War I, four things that had never happened before and which would not happen again until after World War II. First, the richest and fastest-growing European economies went open, removing

---

1 This section relies heavily on O'Rourke and Williamson 1999; Findlay and O'Rourke 2007; and Williamson 2011.

long-standing mercantilist policies, lowering tariffs, and removing non-tariff barriers to trade. Their colonies in Africa and Asia did the same, and many others were forced by gunboat diplomacy to follow suit. In addition, much of the world integrated their currencies by adopting the gold standard or other international currency arrangements, lowering exchange risk. Thus, liberal commercial and exchange rate policy were one good reason for trade to boom. Second, led by new steam technologies, the world underwent a pro-trade transport revolution. As the cost of trade fell dramatically, the ancient barrier of distance was broken. The revolution was given added impetus by the appearance of the telegraph, another pro-trade technology that lowered uncertainty about prices in distant markets. Third, economic growth rose steeply as it was carried by industrial revolutions in Europe and its offshoots. As a consequence, the demand for everything soared, especially imports of intermediate inputs into manufacturing, fuel, and luxury foodstuffs. Fourth, the world was a much more peaceful place than previously. Frequent European wars in the past had impeded trade via embargoes, privateering, the draft of merchant marine bottoms for naval use, and the creation of market uncertainty. In the nineteenth century, *pax Britannica* reigned, creating a trade-stimulating peace.

After the wars with the French were over, Britain, the dominant hegemon, started dismantling its trade barriers. A series of liberal reforms in the 1820s and 1830s were followed by Robert Peel's momentous decision to abolish the so-called Corn Laws in 1846, which moved the United Kingdom unilaterally to free trade. This free trade movement did not happen as a one shot political event. Instead, it proceeded in four major steps over thirty years: between 1815 and 1827, the *ad valorem* tariff equivalent was about 70 percent; between 1828 and 1841, it dropped to 50 percent; between 1842 and 1845, it fell farther to 19 percent; and, finally, in 1846 Britain adopted free trade. Thus, Europe's biggest economy opened its markets to all comers. The rest of Western Europe followed Britain's liberal lead, and average tariffs on the continent fell throughout the 1850s and 1860s, accelerated by the presence of most-favored-nation clauses in their treaties.

Things changed in the late 1870s and 1880s, when cheap New World and Russian grain began to affect European markets, something that domestic landed interests did not like. The resulting late nineteenth-century European tariff backlash had little impact on exporters in the poor periphery, whose primary products did not compete with producers in European markets (except in the case of cane sugar, which competed with beet sugar). But the backlash was even more powerful in much of East Asia and Latin America, regions which were not at all interested in free trade. The English-speaking New World offshoots and the young Latin American republics had the highest tariffs in the world, protecting their infant industries and supplying revenue for the state. East Asia was also less than enthusiastic about free trade, but the naval muscle of the industrial leaders made it comply. Equally important for the poor periphery was the fact that European markets were open to their exports. Furthermore, the European leaders, their offshoots, and their colonies bound themselves more closely together by integrating currencies via the gold standard and other currency unions, adding more pro-trade policies to the mix.

Until well into the nineteenth century, overseas trade was too costly to allow much long-distance trade in bulky primary products. Thus, most food-stuffs, most industrial intermediate goods, and most fuels were not traded long distance on a regular basis. While wheat might be transported across the Atlantic in years of European scarcity, regular, large-scale, long-distance trade involved commodities with a high value-to-weight ratio: precious metals, spices, silk, porcelain and other consumption goods of the rich, slaves, and later 'colonial' commodities such as sugar, tobacco, or cotton, which could only be grown in Europe with difficulty, if at all. Things changed quickly in the nineteenth century as a transport revolution over both water and land took place. Investment in river and harbor improvements increased briskly in the European core following the French Wars. In the United States, comple-tion of the Erie Canal in 1825 reduced the cost of transport between Buffalo and New York by 85 percent. These transportation improvements began to destroy regional barriers to internal trade, and integrated national goods markets began to emerge within the United States, within Britain, within the German Zollverein, and within other countries on the continent.

Steamships made the most important contribution to nineteenth-century shipping technology. In the first half of the century, they were mainly used on important rivers, the Great Lakes, the Baltic, the Mediterranean, and other inland seas. A regular trans-Atlantic steam service was inaugurated in 1838, but until 1860 steamers mainly carried high-value goods similar to those carried by airplanes today, like passengers, mail, and gourmet food. The other major nineteenth-century transportation development was, of course, the railroad. The growth in railway mileage during the second half of the nineteenth century was phenomenal, particularly in the United States, where it played a major role in creating a truly national market. By the 1850s, every major port in the northwest of Europe was within relatively inexpensive reach of every small town in its rural hinterland. Atlantic freight rates dropped by almost 55 percent in real terms between the 1830s and 1850s. British freights dealing with the Liverpool and London trade fell by about 70 percent in the half-century after 1840. Furthermore, since the impact of railroads was probably even more important than transport improvements on ocean shipping, these big percentage point falls almost certainly understate the total decline in transport costs.

The transport revolution was not limited to the Atlantic economy. The decline in freight rates was just as dramatic on routes involving Black Sea and eastern Mediterranean ports. Over the fifty years after 1820, freight rates fell by 51 percent along routes connecting Odessa with England. And after 1870, the railroads had a big impact in Eurasia and Asia too: they tied the Ukraine interior wheat lands with Odessa, the Black Sea, and thus with world markets. The same was true of the American Midwest and the Latin American interior.

In many parts of the periphery, railroads were even more important than they were in the core. Where regions were fragmented by rough topography, poorly endowed with inland rivers, and isolated from coastlines, railroads had a spectacular market-integrating impact – in Argentina, the Brazilian southeast, Mexico, Spain, Turkey, and India. Railroads helped unlock the periphery's previously isolated interior, integrating it with world markets.

Late-twentieth-century growth rates by the East Asian tigers and then China have set a modern standard of 'growth miracles' hard to beat, making impressive growth spurts in the past look pretty modest. But the first growth miracle was unique by the standards of its time, carried by the industrial revolutions in Western Europe and its English-speaking offshoots: over the first global century up to 1913, growth rates increased by almost four times. Furthermore, this increase is understated to the extent that even these rich countries were largely populated by farms and families that were self-sufficient, and often barely connected with markets. Thus, the upward jump in the growth rate of the 'surplus' above subsistence must have been much bigger than four times. And it was that surplus which drove trade. Indeed, the world share of trade in GDP rose eight times between 1820 and 1913.

Finally, many of the exports from the poor periphery were essential intermediates for manufacturing. The canonical example is raw cotton to produce cotton textiles, but there are many more examples, like copper, hemp, hides, jute, nitrates, rubber, silk, tin, wool, and woods of all types. Trade in these intermediates and foodstuffs – what we call commodities today – were driven by the growth of industrial output in the rich core, which was much faster than the growth in total GDP. The world demand for commodities pulled the backward periphery into the world economy and forced it to learn about capitalist institutions.

The world trade boom across the first global century was impressive. In the six decades before 1913, it grew about 3.8 percent per annum, well above the growth rate in core GDP. Thus, the world trade share in GDP rose. The fact that world trade shares were rising steeply suggests that income growth, industrialization, transport revolutions, communication improvements, and more liberal policy were all playing a mutually supporting role. Which mattered most? The answer depends on whether the focus is on market integration, trade/GDP shares, or trade itself. If the focus is on trade, then income growth mattered most – which itself was driven by the deepening and widening of capitalism. If instead the focus is on trade shares in GDP and market integration, then falling trade barriers mattered most – which were lowered in part by pro-global policies initiated by the leading capitalist countries.

What made it the first global century? Mass migration[2]

During the few decades between about 1820 and the mid nineteenth century, global migrations changed dramatically. Emigration policies changed, from restricting outflows before (to keep military recruits and cheap labor home), to adopting *laissez-faire* policies thereafter. Magnitudes changed, long-distance world migrations soaring to levels never seen before 1848. Migrant composition changed. Most moved under contract or coercion before, while most moved unassisted and free thereafter. Most who moved free moved in families and were much less poor before, while most who moved as individuals were poorer thereafter. And while return migration was very uncommon before, it became increasingly common thereafter.

How and when did the European overseas countries, and North America in particular, switch from regions with modest to huge numbers of foreign-born? In the first three decades after 1846, European emigration averaged about 300,000 per annum; in the next two decades it more than doubled; and after the turn of the century it rose to over a million per annum. European emigrant sources also changed dramatically. In the first half of the century, the dominant emigration stream was from the British Isles, followed by Germany. A rising tide of Scandinavian and other northwest European emigrants joined these streams by mid century. Southern and eastern Europeans followed suit in the 1880s. This new emigrant stream accounted for most of the rising emigrant totals in the late nineteenth century. It came first from Italy and parts of Austria-Hungary, but from the 1890s onwards it swelled to include Poland, Russia, the Balkans, Spain, and Portugal.

2 This section draws heavily on Hatton and Williamson 2008: chap. 2.

The overwhelming majority of the European emigrants had the United States as their destination, but there were significant flows to South America after the mid 1880s, led by Argentina and Brazil, and to Canada after the turn of the century. A small but persistent stream also linked the United Kingdom to Australia, New Zealand, and South Africa. Still, the United States dominated: between 1846 and 1850, the years of the great Irish famine, the United States absorbed 81 percent of all emigration to the Americas; between 1906 and 1910, the years of peak migration before World War I, the United States still absorbed 64 percent of all emigration to the Americas, the main competitor being Argentina.

Cross-border migrations also took place *within* Europe. The earliest example is Irish migration into Britain between 1781 and 1851, by the end of which Irish-born accounted for almost a tenth of the population of British cities. A second example is the fact that more than half of all Italian emigrants in the 1890s went to European destinations, chiefly France and Germany. A third example is the movement from eastern Europe into Germany, a pattern repeated even today. These statistics almost always refer to gross rather than net migrations. The distinction is unimportant for most of the nineteenth century, since the cost of return migration was much too high. However, return migration became more important as time wore on. Thus, US authorities estimated that between 1890 and 1914 return migration had risen to 30 percent of the gross inflow, and the return rate was much higher for the decade before World War I (Bandiera, Rasul, and Viarengo 2012). Between 1857 and 1924, return migration from Argentina was 47 percent of the gross inflow. The high return migration rate represented a growing trend towards temporary, often seasonal, migration. And what was true of European emigration was also true of cross-border migration within Europe.

Since large countries send out and receive more migrants than small countries, we need some device to standardize the migration experience to judge its impact on labor markets. Thus, we want to measure the number who emigrate relative to all those in the sending country, and the number who immigrate relative to all those in the host country. The simplest approach is to divide the migrant flow by the sending or receiving country population or labor force. Rates exceeding 50 per thousand per decade were common for Britain, Ireland, and Norway throughout the late nineteenth century, and Italy, Portugal, and Spain reached those levels by the end of the century. Sweden and Finland recorded 50 per thousand rates in only one decade, but even the 10–50 per thousand rates achieved by the rest are very high by modern standards.

New World immigration rates were even larger than European emigration rates, an inevitable arithmetic consequence of the fact that the labor-abundant sending populations were bigger than the labor-scarce receiving populations. The immigration rates were high everywhere shortly before World War I, and high rates imply significant economic effects on sending and receiving labor markets. This is especially so when we recognize that migrations tended to self-select those who had most to gain from the move, namely young adult males. Thus, the migrants had far higher labor participation rates than either the populations they left behind or the ones they joined. It follows that the *labor* migration rates were even higher than the already-high population migration rates.

Undocumented migrants are not an issue when we look at the foreign-born reported in census documents. Just prior to World War I, the highest foreign-born shares were around 30 percent for Argentina and New Zealand, while they were about 15 percent for the biggest immigrant economy, the United States. These proportions are considerably higher than today.

The flows from labor surplus to labor-scarce parts of the periphery were often comparable to those recorded by the European mass migrations. About 50 million people emigrated from labor-abundant India and south China to labor-scarce Burma, Ceylon, Southeast Asia, the Indian Ocean islands, East Africa, South Africa, the Pacific islands, Queensland, Manchuria, the Caribbean, and South America. These migrants satisfied the booming labor force requirements in the tropical plantations and estates producing primary products. They also worked on the docks, and in warehouses and mills engaged in overseas trade. Most of these migrants were contract workers: their steerage was paid, and their contract was for a fixed set of years. This arrangement was effective for those from very poor families in India and China, which could not pay for their children's moves. In this sense, it was very much like eighteenth-century indentured servitude in the Americas.

Why the big boom in mass migration before World War I? First, the numbers "at risk" rose, as European demographic transitions produced lower child mortality and, with a 15- to 20-year lag, a rise in young adult population shares. Since young adults are always the most mobile, these demographic transitions pushed up European emigration, much like it did in the Third World after the 1950s. But there were also other positive forces at work. Most moved to escape poverty, and they did so using family resources, without government assistance, restriction or, in more modern terminology, special *guestworker* permission. As transportation and communication improved, the costs and uncertainty of migration fell, and overseas migration came within reach of an increasing share of the European poor for whom the move offered the most gain. Famine and revolution may have helped push the first great mass migration in the 1840s, but it was the underlying economic and demographic labor market fundamentals that made each subsequent surge bigger than the last. These fundamentals were: a demographic boom in sending countries, swelling the ranks of those most likely to move, young adults; the start of modern economic growth in the sending countries, increasing real incomes at home, thus making it possible for more families to finance the move; and the rising role of the foreign-born abroad, sending remittances, steerage tickets, and job market advice back home to potential emigrants. Most important, immigration into host countries remained unrestricted.

What made it the first global century? Financial capital markets[3]

The late nineteenth century also saw a large increase in the integration of international capital markets, and in the volume of international capital flows. Britain was by far the largest overseas investor during this period; the share of British wealth held overseas rose from 17 percent in 1870 to 33 percent in 1913, while the share of British savings invested overseas was enormous. At its peak, British foreign investment accounted for over 40, or even 50, percent of total British savings (Edelstein 1982; O'Rourke and Williamson 1999). While the empire took the lion's share of lending (42 percent between 1870 and 1913), this share was slowly falling over time, while the United States and Latin America absorbed an increasing share, 38 percent (Stone 1999). The key attraction for British capital was abundant land and other natural resources. Land offered the promise of elastic supplies of food at a time when an increasingly affluent British population was growing rapidly, and vast investments were required in order to realize this potential: transportation, other infrastructure, housing, and a variety of public utilities. British capital financed these investments, with governments and railway construction accounting for 40 and 30 percent respectively of total British overseas investments.

Other European countries also exported large amounts of capital, notably France and Germany, with both countries exporting somewhere around a fifth of domestic savings during peak years. Relative to Britain, they invested more in Europe, but they also tended to target land-abundant countries requiring large infrastructure investments, such as Turkey or Russia. Capital importers were in many instances extremely dependent on capital inflows

3 This section draws on O'Rourke and Williamson 1999.

during this period: foreigners owned almost half the Argentine capital stock in 1913, and a fifth of the Australian capital stock (Taylor 1992).

What explains these enormous flows? One tradition held that they represented, not capital market integration, but a dysfunctional financial system in Britain. According to this view, the City of London discriminated against domestic industry, preferring instead to lend to overseas borrowers. The evidence has not been kind to this hypothesis. During overseas investment booms foreign returns exceeded domestic returns, and during slumps the opposite was the case (Edelstein 1976). On average, foreign returns exceeded domestic returns, so no sign of dysfunctional irrationality there.

High and rising levels of British capital exports must therefore have been due to capital market integration (forces reducing the cost of transferring capital between economies); to outward shifts in the foreign demand for capital imports, due to increased investment demand overseas, or to falling foreign savings supply; or to outward shifts in the UK supply of capital exports, either due to increases in British savings, or reductions in British investment demand. Claims have been made on behalf of each of these five possible explanations.[4] Booming investment demand on the New World's frontiers is the most obvious explanation for British capital exports, and the destination of UK overseas investments is consistent with this interpretation. But the New World might also have demanded foreign capital because of a domestic savings shortfall: for example, high demographic dependency rates were associated with low savings rates during this period, and New World dependency rates were sufficiently high that this on its own could have accounted for a very large share of British capital exports (Taylor and Williamson 1994).

What about a decline in the frictions and costs associated with transferring capital internationally, forces which helped integrate capital markets internationally? This decline could have been driven by technology or politics. The technology that mattered most was the telegraph. The price gap for US Treasury bonds between London and New York fell by 69 percent immediately following the introduction of the transatlantic cable in July 1866 (Garbade and Silber 1978). Before the cable, it took ten days for news to cross the Atlantic. Thus, investors would only become aware of potential arbitrage opportunities with a lag, and would only have been able to instruct agents on the other side of the Atlantic to avail of this opportunity with another considerable lag. The result was that it was too risky to try to arbitrage away small price differences. With

4 And very similar claims were made about the sources of global imbalances in the 2000s.

the cable in place, information could cross the Atlantic in less than a day, allowing much more efficient arbitrage to take place.

Politically, the British empire (and other empires) could have facilitated overseas investment by providing investors with reassurance that their property rights would be respected. The other institution that the literature has stressed was, once again, the gold standard. The gold standard ruled out exchange rate risk by definition, but it also helped eliminate default risk as well, by obliging countries to pursue conservative fiscal and monetary policies (Bordo and Rockoff 1996).

There have been several econometric studies seeking to understand what was most important in lowering interest rate gaps in international capital markets, but these reach different conclusions (Ferguson and Schularick 2006; Flandreau and Zumer 2004; Obstfeld and Taylor 2004). But what happens when the determinants of British capital flows are explored, not interest rate gaps? While the gold standard and empire membership both lowered bond yields and increased capital exports, *ceteris paribus*, these "frictional" variables mattered a lot less for capital flows than variables determining the demand for and supply of savings, such as schooling, natural resource endowments, and demography (Clemens and Williamson 2004a).

In many parts of the world, imperialism was a by-product of global capitalism, and this would have important consequences in the twentieth century when these empires collapsed. As countries like China, Turkey, India, and the new countries of South and Southeast Asia and Africa regained their autonomy, they initially rejected globalization and capitalism as part of the system that colonized them. Decades later, decolonization continued when Eastern Europe regained its autonomy in the wake of the USSR's disintegration, but without the rejection of globalization and capitalism, since they were not part of the Soviet system that colonized them.

As we have pointed out, a key institution underpinning the extremely well-integrated late-nineteenth-century international financial system was the gold standard. But the gold standard was one important capitalist institution fatally undermined by the spread of democracy and increasingly inflexible domestic labor markets. Why? Because democracy gave ordinary citizens the voice to demand a reduction of unemployment during any aggregate demand slump, forcing authorities to adopt expansionary monetary policy, which meant going off gold. Aggregate demand could be increased by devaluing the currency, thus making exports more competitive, and imports less so. It could also have been increased simply by expanding the money supply, lowering interest rates, and inflating and stimulating economic activity, policies impossible under gold standard rules. These democratic forces became increasingly powerful after World War I when the first global century ended (Eichengreen 2008).

Interwar globalization retreat and postwar recovery

World War I brought the liberal international economy of the late nineteenth century to a sudden and dramatic end. Countries abandoned the gold standard, and started to micromanage all aspects of their economic relationships with the rest of the world, as belligerents sought to maximize those imports necessary for the war effort, and minimize other trade flows. The United States enacted a literacy test in 1917, which marked the symbolic end of the age of free migration into that country. After the war, the United States imposed quotas, and other New World host countries soon followed the US lead. The postwar landscape was bleak, with the Russian, German and Austro-Hungarian empires all collapsing, and with their successor states facing severe "transition" problems, leading in several cases to hyperinflation.

Nonetheless, with the important exception of the new communist leaders of the Soviet Union, policy-makers were generally committed to trying to reconstruct the international economy of the prewar era. They succeeded in gradually doing this over the course of the 1920s, although progress in dismantling tariffs and quantitative barriers to trade was often painfully slow. World trade flows recovered, exceeding their prewar peaks by 1924, and international price gaps between trading partners declined. Countries rejoined the gold standard, and international lending resumed. Unfortunately, the resumption of international capital flows proved to be a force for instability, and the Great Depression, which began in 1929 and culminated in the aftermath of a series of international banking crises in 1931, not only led to a catastrophic decline in output and employment in many core capitalist economies, but to a ferocious political backlash. In part this backlash was directed against the international economy, with countries imposing tariffs, quotas, and exchange controls, and abandoning the gold standard. In part it was directed against democracy, with the extreme right-wing vote increasing in many countries, and fascists coming to power in Germany (De Bromhead, Eichengreen, and O'Rourke 2012). Not surprisingly, many people concluded that the institutions of capitalism were fundamentally flawed, and that a completely new system was needed.

What is striking in retrospect is how flexible and resilient the institutions of capitalism proved to be in the core economies. New Deals, postwar welfare states, and mixed economies maintained the primary role of markets in producing and allocating output, while subjecting capitalists – especially but not exclusively in the financial sector – to a variety of controls designed to prevent a repeat of the interwar catastrophe, and nationalizing critical industries. Safety nets and tax and transfer systems designed to ensure a fairer and more politically sustainable distribution of income appeared. But it was in the developing world that the intellectual backlash against capitalism had the greatest influence, with many newly independent states adopting communist economic systems, or milder forms of central planning – which is perhaps ironic, since the Depression hurt the core economies more than it hurt the periphery. A consequence of this was that after 1945 much of the developing world turned its back on global-ization (and even the notion of unfettered domestic markets), pursuing a variety of development strategies. In the developed world, by contrast, domestic and international market liberalization resumed after World War II, although capital controls remained in place, as part of a macroeconomic policy mix that emphasized domestic stabilization policies coupled with fixed (but adjustable) exchange rates. These were only removed following the switch to floating rates in the 1970s, while much of the developing world would only move to pro-globalization policies in the 1980s and 1990s.

The available data on international trade and capital flows mirror this sequence of events, although international migration remained restricted and failed to recover pre-1914 levels until very recently. International trade had accounted for 8 percent of global GDP in 1913, and this had risen to 9 percent by 1929, reflecting the gradual reconstruction of the global economy. The ratio was down to 5.5 percent in 1950, but then recovered again, to 10.5 percent in 1973, 13.5 percent in 1992, and 17.2 percent by 1998, more than twice as high as in 1913 (Findlay and O'Rourke 2007: 510). Consistent with the data on trade flows, international trade costs fell by a third between 1870 and 1913, increased by 13 percent between 1921 and World War II, and fell by 16 percent between 1950 and 2000 (Jacks, Meissner, and Novy 2011). This U-shaped pattern also characterizes international capital flows, whether we focus on the size of these flows relative to GDP, or interest rate gaps, or correlations between savings and investment (Obstfeld and Taylor 2004): international capital markets integrated during the late nineteenth century, dramatically disintegrated between the wars, and gradually reintegrated after World War II. Net flows of capital, as measured by current account imbal-ances, are now of the same order of magnitude as before World War I, while gross capital flows, reflecting two-way short-run movements of speculative capital, are orders of magnitude higher. Finally, international migrations dis-play the same U-shape: just before World War I, the share of foreign born in the combined populations of Canada and the United States was about 15 percent; by 1965 it had fallen to 6 percent; and it then rose to 13 percent by 2000 (Hatton and Williamson 2008: 16 and 205, Tables 2.2 and 10.1). European migration presents the same U-shaped pattern, in an even more dramatic form.

Anti-market and anti-global backlash

Geopolitical factors

We saw above that the international economy has experienced a U-shaped pattern of late-nineteenth-century globalization, followed by deglobalization after 1914, and reglobalization in the aftermath of World War II. The causes of international economic integration are both technological and political, and we emphasized the technological drivers of nineteenth-century globalization earlier. So what explains the disintegration that followed? Certainly not technological regression, since the advances of the nineteenth century were retained and improved during the twentieth century. Indeed, the interwar period was one of unusually impressive technological progress (Field 2011), including transportation, where better motor vehicles, motorways, and much better airplanes offer the most obvious examples. The answer must therefore lie in the political sphere: while technology defines the maximum extent of international integration available at any one time, politics determines how close to that frontier the world economy actually comes.

The politics that matter are both domestic and international, and both were conspiring against globalization during the interwar period. Indeed, they had started to work against globalization even before the outbreak of World War I. In the international sphere, the very fact that economies were becoming more dependent on international trade became a source of tension. Britain had long been dependent on imports of food and raw materials, and hence on exports of manufactured goods, giving her a vital interest in maintaining an open international trading system. Naval hegemony was thus a strategic necessity for the United Kingdom, and the Royal Navy helped keep trade open for all nations. By the end of the century, however, German industrial and population growth was placing her in a similar position. Naval planners on both sides of the North Sea started to develop defensive plans to guard against potential aggression by the other side, and eventually they started developing offensive plans as well. The resulting naval arms race was a major source of tension in the lead-up to World War I (Offer 1989); while British naval commanders hoped that the prospect of blockade might deter the Germans from going to war, a Blitzkrieg strategy suggested itself to German military planners as a way of making any blockade redundant.

In fact, a blockade turned out to be an effective economic weapon during the war, and was used by the Allies even after the war ended, so as to focus German attention in the run-up to the treaty negotiations at Versailles. The lessons of this episode were not lost on German and Japanese nationalists, and while both countries participated in the moves to reconstruct the international economy in the 1920s, the Great Depression gave nationalists in both countries their chance to win resource security by using violence to construct self-sufficient imperial blocs. The 1930s saw a breakdown of the multilateral trading system of the late nineteenth century, with more and more trade being concentrated within formal and informal empires, diverting trade from between them. Indeed, the search for resource self-sufficiency was one of the major factors behind Japan's decisions to go to war in East and Southeast Asia, as well as Hitler's decision to invade the east, including the Soviet Union.

The quest for empire was one legacy of World War I, but the end of the Austro-Hungarian, Ottoman, and Russian empires was another. This led to the creation of new nation-states in Europe, which typically pursued nationalist economic policies after 1919. Most notable, of course, was the aftermath of the Russian Revolution of 1917, an event which cast a long shadow over the remainder of the twentieth century, spawning as it did communist regimes not only in the USSR but in many other parts of the world as well. Communist central planning was inconsistent with free markets domestically, and free trade internationally: communist regimes strictly regulated trade. Another wave of decolonization followed after World War II, as the British, French, and Dutch empires collapsed. Once again, in its wake the newly independent states often followed nationalist economic policies of autarky and market intervention.

The net postwar result of these trends was that while there was substantial trade liberalization after World War II, this was mainly a Western phenomenon, with much of the developing world moving in the opposite direction. It would take the jettisoning of traditional economic policies in nominally communist China, as well as in Asia, Latin America, and other developing regions, before the 'globalization' of the late twentieth century became genuinely global.

Economic factors

Economic factors also help to explain the anti-globalization backlash between the wars. Again, some of these factors had been at work even before the outbreak of that conflict (O'Rourke and Williamson 1999). Intercontinental trade in grain had sparked agricultural protection in much of continental

Europe from the 1870s onwards, and it was sufficient to seriously impede the further integration of the markets affected. Outside Europe, those countries able to choose their own tariff policies overwhelmingly opted for protection, so as to build up manufacturing sectors sheltered from foreign competition. This was the case in Latin America, the United States, eastern and southern Europe, and even in the self-governing Dominions of the British empire. And across the New World, immigration restrictions became increasingly common and accumulated more bite, as migrants from the poorer parts of Europe were thought to place downward pressure on unskilled wages, upwards pressure on unemployment, and thus created greater inequality. Or so it was thought.

These pressures persisted after the war, and were indeed heightened as a result of the conflict. The war had distorted international production patterns, with the European belligerents shifting resources out of peacetime activities and into the heavy industries needed for the war effort. European neutrals, and countries outside Europe, stepped in to replace the missing supplies of consumer goods and food. This led to increased competition in these sectors after the war, and consequently to protectionist pressures. These pressures were intensified by the economic difficulties caused by excess capacity in European heavy industry once the war had ended. As for migration, 1917 literacy tests in the United States had been replaced by far stricter quotas in the 1920s – favoring west Europeans and even excluding Asians – and these were still in place during the 1950s and until the liberal immigration reforms of the 1960s.

However, the biggest economic source of anti-globalization backlash during this period was the Great Depression. At one level this was the result of mistaken fiscal and monetary policies, but at a deeper level it was the result of a flawed international monetary system, the gold standard, which had been painstakingly put in place in an effort to revive the liberal international economy of the late nineteenth century. The gold standard transmitted contractionary monetary impulses from the United States to the rest of the world after 1929, and made it impossible for governments to respond adequately once their economies slipped into deep recession. Indeed, the gold standard *mentalité*, and fears about balance of payments constraints, led governments to pursue perverse pro-cyclical fiscal policies, most notably in Germany, with disastrous consequences. Another source of fragility was the international banking system, which led to bank panics spreading from Austria to the rest of central Europe, and ultimately to Britain, in 1931. The institutions which underpinned global capital markets were thus central in driving the crisis, and not surprisingly governments ended up abandoning these, leaving the gold standard, imposing exchange controls, or both. By the logic of the monetary *trilemma*, this allowed them to regain monetary policy autonomy, and to kick-start recovery.

Interwar governments threw out the baby of international trade as well as the bathwater of international capital flows. This was an understandable economic response on the part of those devaluing their currencies late in the 1930s, thus finding themselves losing competitiveness relative to those who devalued early in the decade (Eichengreen and Irwin 2010; Eichengreen and Sachs 1985). But it was an understandable intellectual response to the obvious bankruptcy of orthodox economic thinking, for which the gold standard was synonymous with a commitment to a liberal international economy. The economic costs of protection were lower once everyone else was doing it, and higher average tariffs may even have been good for growth in individual countries (Clemens and Williamson 2004b). Collectively, however, it fed into the nationalist spirit of the period, and into the dreams of imperial self-sufficiency in Germany and Japan highlighted earlier.

The disaster of the Great Depression helped to undermine the intellectual prestige of capitalism, as well as its attractions as a model of development. This, along with the existence of an alternative economic model – central planning and communism – which had performed so well during World War II, helped push postwar economic policies in the developing world towards state intervention and anti-market attitudes. The Western response was very different. Contrary to Marxist predictions, Western governments were able to reform the capitalist system sufficiently so as to meet the political demands for greater stability and fairness. When it came to the international economy, postwar governments drew their lessons from the 1930s: while international trade was something to be encouraged, international capital flows were to be controlled in order to promote domestic macroeconomic stability (and fixed exchange rates).

The potential for anti-globalization backlash survives today. Survey evidence shows that less skilled workers in rich countries are hostile to trade and immigration, just as Heckscher-Ohlin trade theory would predict. Indeed, international migrations remain strictly controlled (although not within the EU). While trade barriers are now low, the potential is always there for an anti-trade backlash to gather pace, international institutions notwithstanding: income distribution matters not just in its own right, but because of the policy responses to which it may give rise. And if today's economic and financial crisis is allowed to persist for too long, or get worse, this could also feed demands for another global retreat.

Widening and deepening domestic capitalist institutions along the global road

This then is the road that global capitalism has taken since 1848. The remaining chapters in this volume look at the long-term evolution of capitalist institutions over those 160 years, but now we have a global road map to which they can be related. Let us summarize them again. Two explore the spread of manufacturing (Allen, Chapter 2) and the performance of agriculture (Federico, Chapter 3). Two document the evolution of financial capitalism (Michie, Chapter 8), international capital markets, and international capital flows (James, Chapter 9). Three focus on changing technology (Bruland and Mowery, Chapter 4), the rise of multinational firms (Jones, Chapter 6), and the coexistence of different enterprise models (Morck and Yeung, Chapter 7). Five deal with political and intellectual responses to capitalism: the rise and decline of imperialism (Austin, Chapter 10); capitalism at war (Harrison, Chapter 11); the spread of political movements (Frieden and Rogowski, Chapter 12); the rise of labor's voice (Huberman, Chapter 13); and welfare capitalism and the welfare state (Lindert, Chapter 14). One chapter makes an assessment of the changing quality of life under capitalism and its competitors (Prados de la Escosura, Chapter 15). In the final chapter, the two editors conclude with a look to the future (Neal and Williamson, Chapter 16).

References

Bandiera, O., I. Rasul, and M. Viarengo (2012). "The Making of Modern America: Migratory Flows in the Age of Mass Migration," mimeo.

Bordo, M. D. and H. Rockoff (1996). "The Gold Standard as a 'Good Housekeeping Seal of Approval,'" *Journal of Economic History* 56: 389–428.

Clemens, M. A. and J. G. Williamson (2004a). "Wealth Bias in the First Global Capital Market Boom, 1870–1913," *Economic Journal* 114: 304–337.

(2004b). "Why Did the Tariff-Growth Correlation Reverse after 1950?" *Journal of Economic Growth* 9: 5–46.

De Bromhead, A., B. Eichengreen, and K. H. O'Rourke (2012). "Right Wing Political Extremism in the Great Depression," CEPR Discussion Paper 8876.

Edelstein, M. (1976). "Realized Rates of Return on U.K. Home and Overseas Portfolio Investment in the Age of High Imperialism," *Explorations in Economic History* 13: 283–329.

(1982). *Overseas Investment in the Age of High Imperialism*. London: Metheun.

Eichengreen, B. (2008). *Globalizing Capital: A History of the International Monetary System*. Princeton University Press.

Eichengreen, B. and D. A. Irwin (2010). "The Slide to Protectionism in the Great Depression: Who Succumbed and Why?" *Journal of Economic History* 70: 871–897.

Eichengreen, B. and J. Sachs (1985). "Exchange Rates and Economic Recovery in the 1930s," *Journal of Economic History* 4: 925–946.

Ferguson, N. and M. Schularick (2006). "The Empire Effect: The Determinants of Country Risk in the First Age of Globalization, 1880–1913," *Journal of Economic History* 66: 283–312.

Field, A. J. (2011). *A Great Leap Forward: 1930s Depression and U.S. Economic Growth*. New Haven, CT: Yale University Press.

Findlay, R. and K. H. O'Rourke (2007). *Power and Plenty: Trade, War and the World Economy in the Second Millennium*. Princeton University Press.

Flandreau, M. and F. Zumer (2004). *The Making of Global Finance 1880–1913*. Paris: OECD.

Garbade, K. D. and W. L. Silber (1978). "Technology, Communication and the Performance of Financial Markets: 1840–1975," *Journal of Finance* 33: 819–832.

Hatton, T. J. and J. G. Williamson (2008). *Global Migration and the World Economy: Two Centuries of Policy and Performance*. Cambridge, MA: The MIT Press.

Jacks, D. S., C. M. Meissner, and D. Novy (2011). "Trade Booms, Trade Busts, and Trade Costs," *Journal of International Economics* 83: 185–201.

Marx, K. and F. Engels (1848). *The Communist Manifesto*.

Obstfeld, M. and A. M. Taylor (2004). *Global Capital Markets: Integration, Crisis, and Growth*. Cambridge University Press.

Offer, A. (1989). *The First World War: An Agrarian Interpretation*. Oxford: Clarendon Press.

O'Rourke, K. H. and J. G. Williamson (1999). *Globalization and History: The Evolution of a Nineteenth Century Atlantic Economy*. Cambridge, MA: The MIT Press.

Stone, I. (1999). *The Global Export of Capital from Great Britain, 1865–1914: A Statistical Survey*. Basingstoke: Macmillan.

Taylor, A. M. (1992). "External Dependence, Demographic Burdens and Argentine Economic Decline after the *Belle Époque*," *Journal of Economic History* 52: 907–936.

Taylor, A. M. and J. G. Williamson (1994). "Capital Flows to the New World as an Intergenerational Transfer," *Journal of Political Economy* 102: 348–371.

Williamson, J. G. (2011). *Trade and Poverty: When the Third World Fell Behind*. Cambridge, MA: The MIT Press.

2

The spread of manufacturing

ROBERT C. ALLEN

The long-run record

We speak of the 'industrial West,' but before the industrial revolution, most of the world's manufacturing production took place in China and India. In 1500, the cost of shipping goods between continents was very high, so countries consumed what they produced. Since per capita income was similar across Eurasia, and since China and India each contained about one-quarter of the world's population, they produced similar proportions of the world's textiles, ceramics, metals, and other products. The situation was modified slightly in the next two centuries as the voyages of da Gama, Columbus, and Magellan showed that European ships could sail the seven seas, and improvements in their design cut the cost of the voyages, but changes were not substantial enough to seriously modify the late medieval situation, and China and India remained the world's great manufacturing centers to the eve of the industrial revolution. Other regions of the globe, including the Islamic world, for instance, had important manufacturing industries reflecting the size of their populations.

This state of affairs is shown in Figure 2.1, which plots the geographical distribution of world manufacturing output from 1750 to the early twenty-first century.[1] On the eve of the industrial revolution, China and India produced 33 percent and 25 percent of the world's manufactures. Manufacturing output soared in Britain after 1750 as her share of the world total rose from 2 percent to a peak value of about 23 percent in 1880. Over the same period, the Chinese and Indian shares dropped to 13 percent and 3 percent, respectively. (Their shares kept dropping in the twentieth century, bottoming out at 2 percent each in the 1950s.)

---

1 This chapter is based on Allen (2009, 2011). Detailed references can be found in those works.

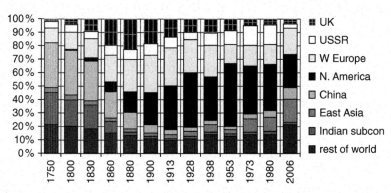

Figure 2.1. The geographical distribution of the world's manufacturing output
Source: Allen (2011).

While the traditional manufacturing centers declined in the nineteenth century, other centers developed and, indeed, joined Britain to form the "industrial West." The first was Western Europe. It produced far more of the world's manufactures in 1750 (11 percent) than Britain since it had a much larger population. The West European share never dropped like Asia's, but, instead, began to rise after 1800 as modern factories were established. By 1880, the West European share surpassed the British and continued to increase until World War I. Since then, it has slipped as other parts of the world have industrialized.

North America, in particular the United States, was another great success. It produced very few manufactures during the colonial period, which ended with the US Declaration of Independence in 1776. Since 1800, industrial output expanded almost without interruption, so that North America produced almost half of the world's manufactures in the 1950s.

The third region to industrialize was the Russian empire, which became the Soviet Union after the Russian Revolution in 1917, and which dissolved into fifteen independent states in 1991. Russia produced about 5 percent of the world's manufactures in the eighteenth and first half of the nineteenth centuries. After defeat in the Crimean War, the Imperial government began a series of development initiatives that boosted the manufacturing share to 9 percent in 1900. The Soviets commenced their first five-year plan in 1928, and their brand of economic planning performed impressively until the 1970s when growth slackened. At its peak in the 1980s, the USSR produced about 15 percent of the world's manufactures. Since the dissolution of the USSR, the successor countries have experienced extreme deindustrialization, and their combined share of world industrial output dropped to 3 percent in 2006.

The fourth region to industrialize was East Asia. Japan produced 3 percent of the world's manufactures in the eighteenth and first half of the nineteenth centuries. Following the Meiji restoration in 1868, economic development became a national priority. Manufacturing production rose to 5 percent of the world's total by 1940. World War II was a disaster for Japan and its economy, but growth rebounded in the 1950s. By the twenty-first century, Japan, along with South Korea and Taiwan, produced 17 percent of the world's manufactures. This dynamism has spread to China, whose share of world industrial output reached 9 percent in 2006 and has risen further since.

How can we explain industrialization, deindustrialization, and reindustrialization? Much discussion has turned on the roles of unfettered capitalism and the development state. At one extreme are those who argue that the state should limit its role to ensuring the security of private property and the rule of law while leaving economic decisions to private businesses. Policies along these lines were proposed by Adam Smith in his classic *The Nature and Causes of the Wealth of Nations*, and, more recently, by international agencies like the International Monetary Fund (IMF) under the rubric of the "Washington consensus." At the other extreme are those who think that the state should own and operate businesses and plan the economy to supersede market forces. In between are a range of options where the state intervenes in the economy to promote capitalist development. In this chapter, I will review the history of industrial development with this question in mind (see Frieden and Rogowski, Chapter 12 in this volume).

The British challenge and the policy response

The British economy grew slowly but steadily in the seventeenth and eighteenth centuries. On the eve of the industrial revolution in 1750, British GDP per head was considerably above the world average. Economic growth was driven by the expansion of international trade, but the policies of the British state were at some variance with the prescriptions of Adam Smith. The state did protect private property, but taxes were higher than in France, and commercial expansion was effected by chartered monopolies like the East Indies Company and was sustained through naval power, war, colonial expansion, tariffs, and mercantilism (see O'Brien, Chapter 12 in Volume 1). As a free trader, Smith took exception to these policies. The economy grew rapidly, however, and kept pace with the country's growing population with the result that English wages were high compared to those in most of Europe and Asia. The growth of London also led to a sharp rise in the price of fuel, which, at the end of the middle ages, was primarily charcoal and firewood, and, in turn, led to the expansion of coal mining in northeast England. Britain was the only country in Europe with a large coal industry in the eighteenth century, and the price of energy on the coalfields was the cheapest in the world (see Harley, Chapter 16 in Volume 1).

These factors help explain the trajectory of British invention during the industrial revolution: the new technology substituted capital and cheap energy for expensive labor. These technologies were invented in Britain since they were commercially successful there. At the outset, however, they were not cost-effective elsewhere since wages were lower and energy prices higher.

The new British technology was an opportunity and a challenge for other countries. To become rich, they needed to raise labor productivity, and they could do that if they adopted the new British technology. However, that technology was not cost-effective in view of their different input prices. What should they do?

This dilemma was sharpened by a second ramification of the new British technology. Since it increased productivity in British manufacturing without conferring the same advantage on other countries, Britain's comparative advantage in manufacturing increased, while the comparative advantage of other countries shifted towards agriculture. This was manifest as a heightened competitiveness of British manufacturing firms, which threatened to drive manufacturers out of business in other countries. At the same time, the other countries became more competitive in the production of agricultural products. British success, in other words, threatened to deindustrialize the rest of the world and turn other nations into primary product exporting "underdeveloped countries" (Williamson 2011).

This is exactly what happened in most of Asia. India is an important example. In the eighteenth century, it had one of the largest cotton textile industries in the world. Britain could only compete with India in producing the coarsest yarn and fabrics since these required less labor than finer yarn, and labor was much more expensive in Britain than in India. Machines cut costs in Britain by reducing the number of hours to process one pound of material and by allowing the substitution of low-paid women and children for high-paid men. The East India Company's trade monopoly with India expired in 1813, and a group of Manchester manufacturers opposed its renewal on the grounds that India was a great potential market if the cost of shipping fell. They pointed out that the cost of producing 40-count yarn (a common variety suitable for shirts) was 43 pence per pound in India in 1812 but only 30 pence in England. The manufacturers were right, but it is remarkable that they could not have made the same argument a decade earlier since in 1802 40 count yarn cost 60 pence in England. That is one measure of the speed of progress. Indeed, by 1826, the cost of 40-count yarn dropped to 16 pence, and British competition wholly destroyed the Indian cotton spinning industry. Weaving also contracted, although it was not entirely destroyed and was based on imported British yarn.

The United States and Western Europe faced the same threat but avoided India's fate with four policies that comprised the Standard Model of Economic Development (see Atack, Chapter 17 in Volume 1). This was first worked out in the United States and had four imperatives: create a large domestic market by abolishing internal tariffs and building transportation infra-structure; erect an external tariff to protect industries from British competition; charter banks to stabilize the currency and facilitate industrial investment; educate the population to equip people for commercial and technical work. The constitution implemented in 1790 marked a step forward in creating a large domestic market, for it did abolish state tariffs. The infrastructure investment, tariffs, and banks were outlined in Alexander Hamilton's *Report on Manufactures* (1791) and subsequently implemented. Education was already widespread in the colonial period, and states adopted universal primary education as a public responsibility in the first half of the nineteenth century, partly for economic motives.

The Standard Model created a policy environment that made manufacturing profitable, and British machinery was readily adopted since its high capital intensity was appropriate to the United States in view of the high wage level. Indeed, by the 1830s American wages were considerably higher than British, which had stagnated since the 1790s, and this induced Americans to invent even more capital-intensive technologies than the British. The foundation for American industrial preeminence was set.

The Standard Model in Europe

The Standard Model was promoted in Europe by Friedrich List in his *National System of Political Economy* (1841), although the application was well underway by the time he wrote. The adoption of British technology faced more impediments in Western Europe than it had in North America. Many historians believe that growth in the eighteenth century was held back by archaic institutions. These were swept away by the French Revolution and Napoleon, who introduced modernized French institutions into the countries he conquered. The changes included the abolition of serfdom, the expropriation of monastic property, a new legal code including equality before the law, the abolition of internal tariffs, the rationalization of taxes and external tariffs, universal primary education, the extension of advanced education and scientific institutions. Countries like Prussia, that were defeated by Napoleon but not annexed to his empire, also reformed their institutions along similar lines.

Germany is a good example of the Standard Model in Europe. Prussia established universal primary education in 1763, and the school system was strengthened over the next sixty years. Other steps were taken after Napoleon's defeat. After the Treaty of Vienna, Germany consisted of 38 states of which Prussia was the largest. The large domestic market and external tariff were features of the Zollverein or customs union created by Prussia in 1818 and gradually expanded to include most German states by 1866. Internal transport costs were also cut by building roads and canals, improving rivers, and constructing railways. Private investment banks operated in Germany in the first half of the nineteenth century. The Crédit Mobilier, founded in France in 1852, marked a breakthrough in continental banking, for it targeted investment to industrial projects and spun off the first great Germany investment bank – the Bank of Darmstadt – in 1853 and others followed by 1870. The Reichsbank, a central bank, was founded in 1876, five years after German unification. These banks helped finance Germany's rapid industrialization up to World War I, which underlies the rise in the Western European share of world manufactures in this period.

The Standard Model created an investment climate and labor supply conducive to capitalist development, but firms had to respond to the opportunities by erecting modern facilities. The incentive to do this was less in France or Germany than it was in the United States, since wages on the continent were lower (not higher) than in Britain. Factory spinning was less profitable in France before the Revolution than it was in Britain. British engineers, however, solved the problem for the French by continuously improving their spinning machinery, so that the real cost of coarse yarn dropped by 42 percent between 1775 and 1836. Productivity growth in fine yarn was even greater. At these higher levels of efficiency, it paid to spin with machines almost irrespective of the cost of labor or capital, and factory spinning was quickly introduced onto the continent after Waterloo. The productivity gain from power weaving was comparatively less, and the incentives to adopt the technology depended on the relative prices of capital and labor. As a result, the shift to the power loom on the continent was delayed until the late nineteenth century. The adoption of modern iron technology followed similar lines (Harley, Chapter 16 in Volume I).

Technological progress in today's rich countries

By the middle of the nineteenth century, the Standard Model was bearing fruit in the United States and Western Europe. All of the industries of the British industrial revolution were profitably established, and output boomed. By the beginning of World War I, the United States and Western Europe had overtaken Britain in industrial production (Figure 2.1). The locus of technological advance also shifted from Britain to the newcomers like Germany and the United States. Partly, this was a knock-on effect of their rapid growth. Iron and steel output, for instance, grew much more in Germany and the United States between 1870 and 1913 with the result that most of the world's new production facilities were built in these countries. This provided a tremendous opportunity for collective learning: firms exchanged information about the performance of new plants, so that they could build on each other's successes. There was an ascending spiral of progress in which rapid growth led to high investment which increased technical knowledge and pushed up productivity further. Since the investment was taking place in Germany and America, they became the world's technological leaders (see Bruland and Mowery, Chapter 4 in this volume).

The progress of technology was also accelerated by investments that Western Europe and North America made in their universities and scientific research. These investments yielded knowledge that led to technical advances in industries like chemicals and electricity in the nineteenth century and aircraft, nuclear power, and electronics in the twentieth.

Finally, economic incentives directed the evolution of technology in ways that reinforced divergent development. Wages in America, Britain, and Western Europe were higher than in the rest of the world by the middle of the nineteenth century, and this led inventors to embody their ideas in plant designs that economized on labor by increasing the use of capital. These designs further boosted labor productivity, and those advances were reflected in rising wages, that, in turn, led inventors to invent even more capital-intensive technologies. Not only did capital–labor ratios rise, but the scale of production increased as well. The technology that made rich countries rich became increasingly less appropriate for poor countries.

Colonialism and economic development

While today's rich countries pulled ahead, the rest of the world lagged behind. The obvious question is: Why didn't Asians, Africans, and Latin Americans adopt the Standard Model that had proved so successful in North America and

Western Europe? Colonialism is part of the answer (see Austin, Chapter 10 in this volume).

Indian nationalists thought that India needed the Standard Model. India did not get it, however. Economic policy reflected British interests rather than Indian needs. There was no national education program. Only 1 percent of the population was in school in the nineteenth century, and the adult literacy rate was 6 percent. Before World War I, tariffs were low and for revenue purposes. There was no banking policy aimed at economic development. The only part of the Standard Model to be implemented was the creation of a national market through the construction of a railroad network. Its main economic effect was to promote agricultural exports. Railroad building did not contribute to India's industrialization since rails, locomotives, and rolling stock were imported from Britain rather than being produced in India. Industrial development was limited. In the late nineteenth century a cotton spinning industry was established in Bombay and the jute industry in Calcutta. These industries were world players, but, in total, they employed less than 1 percent of the workforce in 1911. A more vigorous policy was necessary to transform the Indian economy.

Colonialism meant that sub-Saharan Africa did not get the Standard Model either. Africans responded positively to the opportunities that opened up in the nineteenth century. Falling shipping costs increased the prices at West African ports of staples like palm oil and cocoa beans. Africans responded by increasing harvesting and cultivation. This required them to work more per year, and they used the extra income to buy European cloth and iron goods.

Governments did little to capitalize on these advances in ways that benefitted Africans. Tariffs were not used to protect African industry, and indigenous production like the large handicraft cotton industry in the vicinity of Kano was driven out of business. Banks to finance African businesses were not created. Education was not publicly provided, and there was little of it. Some railways were built to connect the coast to the interior. Development efforts were otherwise limited to seizing mining sites and farm land and giving them to European settlers, as well as conscripting Africans for forced labor on railways and plantations.

Colonialism endowed Africa with particularly bad institutions. The hostile disease environment of the tropical forests meant that population growth was limited after the introduction of agriculture. There was much free land until well into the twentieth century. Land had no value since a new plot could be cleared without depriving anyone else. Consequently, governments could not be funded by farming, leasing, or taxing land. Tribes, which were collectives of the producers in an area, were a common form of political organization. More elaborate states emerged on the basis of slavery, since labor was a scarce and valuable input.

Colonial governments in many parts of Africa tried to propitiate the populace by devolving local administration on the "chiefs" of "tribes." These terms are put in quotes since they were legal constructs of the colonial government without any necessary connection to local conditions. Indeed, tribes and chiefs were created where they had not previously existed. The chiefs became the foremen of the empire, exploiting the populace by raising forced labor and allocating communal land, and extracting favors from the colonial rulers. Colonialism thus created a stratum of despotic petty rent-seekers to rule the countryside, and their presence continues in many places today.

Catching up with the Standard Model: Mexico

Independent countries had more control over their policies, but many made no effort to catch up with the West, while others made only halfhearted attempts to adopt the Standard Model. Only a few made sustained and vigorous efforts to develop their economies.

China is an important example of a country where development efforts were too little, too late. The Chinese Qianlong emperor had no use for the steam engine and other Western gadgets presented to him by Lord Macartney in 1792–4. Even defeat in the Opium Wars failed to cause the empire to modernize, perhaps because the emperor (mistakenly) believed that no foreign army could ever advance on Beijing. Between 1850 and 1864, the country was racked by the devastating Taiping Rebellion and, when it was finally suppressed, regional war lords had usurped control of most of the country. Reforms finally started in the second half of the nineteenth century with the Self-Strengthening movement, but it was limited in scope and not pursued vigorously.

The Mexican economy advanced in the eighteenth century by merging Spanish and indigenous technology (see Salvucci, Chapter 13 in Volume 1). Wheat was added to the local crop repertoire of maize, beans, and squash. The Aztecs lacked any large domesticated animals, so the introduction of sheep, cattle, horses, and mules revolutionized transportation as well as agriculture, and woollen cloth became a major new industry. Spanish mercantilism and the natural protection of bad roads from Vera Cruz to the Mexican plateau led to considerable manufacturing development in the colonial period. By the late eighteenth century, European imports were expanding as transportation costs fell. According to Alexander von Humboldt, who lived in Mexico in 1803, "the delf[t] manufactories [at Puebla] have fallen so much off, on account of the low price of the stoneware and porcelain of Europe imported at Vera Cruz, that of 46 manufactories which were still existing in 1793, there were in 1802 only sixteen remaining of delf[t] ware, and two of glass." Cotton textile production, which had boomed in Puebla in the 1790s as imports from Spain were cut off by warfare, was also threatened by renewed Catalan imports after 1804 and then by cheap British imports after Independence in 1821.

Mexico met this challenge with a truncated version of the standard development model. A tariff was imposed on foreign cotton cloth (although it may have been offset by another tariff imposed on raw cotton), and some of the tariff revenues were channelled to the newly chartered Banco de Avío, which lent them to cotton mills to buy equipment. Between 1835 and 1843, about thirty-five cotton spinning mills were established. This advance led to little further growth; in part, because all of the machinery was imported and the engineers to construct and manage the mills were foreigners. Mexicans only supplied the unskilled operators. The limited effects reflected the limited degree to which the Standard Model was implemented. No national market was created (the Mexican states continued to impose their own tariffs on interstate commerce), and there was no attempt to educate the bulk of the population. The white elite who governed Mexico were literate, but they only amounted to one-fifth of the population. The rest of the population was without schooling. This was a major difference with the United States and the industrializing countries of Western Europe.

The Standard Model of economic development was pursued somewhat more vigorously under the dictatorship of Porfirio Diaz between 1877 and 1911. A national market was created as state tariffs were suppressed and a national railway system constructed. Tariffs were used to protect Mexican industry, and the banking system was expanded. A notable policy innovation was an expanded role for foreign borrowing to finance investment (see James, Chapter 9 in this volume) – North America and Western Europe relied primarily on domestic savings to finance their industrial revolutions – and foreign-owned firms became the principal conduit for introducing modern technology to the country. Mass education was still neglected, however.

The Mexican economy grew at 2.2 percent per person per year during the Porfiriato. This was marginally faster than the United States (1.8 percent), but not enough to transform the economic structure or to catch up in a reasonable time frame. An important reason that Mexico did not do better was that it relied on the United States for its technology rather than inventing its own. The absence of any indigenous research and development (R&D) capacity was due to the restricted supply of educated citizens (80 percent of Mexicans were still illiterate, in contrast to the near-complete literacy among the white population in the United States). As a result, technological progress was limited to the branch plant economy (see Bruland and Mowery, Chapter 4 and Jones, Chapter 6 in this volume). Labor demand did not grow rapidly enough to tighten the labor market. As a result, real wages slid. The regime was overthrown in the revolution of 1911.

Catching up with the Standard Model: Russia

Imperial Russia followed similar policies with similar results. Peter the Great made the first efforts to modernize the country at the beginning of the eighteenth century. While he created a new city and some new factories, his policies reinforced serfdom and the related social hierarchy, and that may explain why his reforms did not lead to sustained growth. Modern development only began after Russia's defeat in the Crimean War when Tsar Alexander II abolished serfdom in an effort to transform the economy. Abolition did not lead to rapid growth, either, perhaps because ownership of the formerly servile lands was granted to the villages rather than to the individuals who farmed them, and the villages retained considerable powers over the movements and incomes of the former serfs. Provisions to let individuals and their land leave the communes were only introduced in the Stolypin Reforms of 1906. The effect of Russia's agrarian institutions on the pace of economic growth remains contentious.

Russia did, however, pursue most elements of the Standard Model in the late nineteenth century. First, a national market was created by building railways. By 1913 there were 71,000 kilometers of track that connected even remote farming regions like western Siberia to the global market. Second, tariffs and industrial procurement policies were used to promote the economic development of Russia. Cotton cloth, for instance, received a high tariff to promote investment in Russian mills. Raw cotton was also protected to encourage its cultivation in what later became Uzbekistan, but the tariff rate was kept sufficiently low, so that the manufactured cloth still enjoyed effective protection. Tariffs on steel, rails, and locomotives led to the establishment of modern smelting, refining, and engineering industries. Third, while efforts were made to create a modern banking system, progress was slow. Like Mexico, Russia relied much more on foreign savings than the United States, Germany, or Japan ever did. Also, like Mexico, Russia relied on foreign-owned firms as the vehicles for technological modernization. Finally, Russia promoted schooling more than Mexico. Schools were established by local authorities rather than the national government. By World War I, about two-fifths of the population was literate, and the percentage was rising rapidly.

As with Mexico, the Standard Model in Russia led to limited economic growth and only minor structural transformation. The greatest achievement was the creation of a heavy industrial sector, whose output jumped tenfold from 1885 to 1913 and whose share of GDP rose from 2 percent to 8 percent. The share of agriculture declined from 59 percent to 51 percent, but the increase in total farm output accounted directly for half of the growth in GDP and indirectly for much more once account is taken of the trade and transportation services involved in marketing the increase in farm output. The growth of agriculture was, in turn, due to the rise in the world price of wheat after 1896 and the construction of railways that linked farms to the markets of Western Europe. Nonetheless, the growth in GDP was weak (1.9 percent per year) and insufficient to tighten labor markets. As a result, real wages stagnated, and the gains in national income accrued to the owners of capital and land. Unequal development lay behind the revolutions of 1905 and 1917.

Catching up with the Standard Model: ISI in Latin America

After 1917, Soviet Russia adopted a radically different development strategy (to be considered shortly), but Latin America persisted with the Standard Model, which came to be known as ISI (Import Substitution Industrialization). Mexico remained a key player, but it was joined in the late nineteenth century by Argentina, Uruguay, and Chile. These countries had been too far from Europe to trade extensively in the age of the sailing ship, but transport costs fell with the introduction of steam shipping in the 1860s, and trade grew rapidly. Argentina and Uruguay became rich countries by exporting wheat and beef; Chile by exporting minerals. By the beginning of World War I, the population and income of Argentina, in particular, had become large enough for the state to promote industrialization. The state had already mandated universal schooling in 1884 (in this respect the Southern Cone was far ahead of the rest of the continent), and many railways had been built to bring wheat and beef to the coast. High tariffs protected the principal industries. Like Mexico and Russia, Argentina relied on foreign borrowing and foreign firms for finance and technology.

These efforts were redoubled after World War II and more countries embraced the Standard Model more completely. The first steps in expanding education, for instance, were made in Mexico after the 1911 revolution, but schooling was not made universal until after World War II. (Indeed, since 1950 universal education has become a universal strategy for economic development, but with only limited success.) Public investment and state-sponsored development banks boosted the supply of domestic savings across the continent. Foreign firms were still relied on to provide advanced technology and finance industry, but they worked within a framework set by the state. Most Latin American states used tariffs, procurement, and local content requirements to increase manufacturing in the continent. For example, Argentina's Automotive Decree of 1959 required that 90 percent of the value of autos sold in the country be manufactured domestically. Automobile production grew rapidly and accounted for 10 percent of the Argentine economy in the 1960s.

Import substitution industrialization was a mixed success in Latin America. On the plus side, GDP per head grew almost fourfold between 1914 and 1980. On the minus side, the industrial capacity that was created was remarkably inefficient. The real cost of manufacturing automobiles in Argentina, for instance, was 2.5 times higher than in the United States. The reason was that Argentina was too small to realize the scale economies achieved by large producers in the rich countries. In the 1960s, for instance, the minimum efficient size of an assembly plant was 200,000 vehicles per year, while the minimum efficient size of engine and transmission factories was 1 million units per year. The largest firm in Argentina only produced 57,000 cars per year. If the entire Argentine market had been supplied by one factory, vehicle assembly would have been carried out efficiently, but the manufacture of the engines, transmissions, and other major components would still have been done on an inefficiently small scale. This story was repeated in other industries like petrochemicals. The Standard Model resulted in gross inefficiency in Latin America in the second half of the twentieth century.

It is important to realize that technology was different in the nineteenth century when the Standard Model was first followed. In the 1850s, for instance, the market for cotton cloth in the United States was two thousand times greater than the minimum efficient size of a cotton mill. Likewise, the market for iron was 160 times greater than the minimum efficient size of a blast furnace. While the Standard Model may have imposed a burden on consumers in the nineteenth century by raising the prices they paid, it did not saddle countries like the United States and Germany with intrinsically inefficient industrial structures. That is a major reason why the Standard Model was successful in the countries where it was first applied but was increasingly unsuccessful in later would-be industrializers that tried to emulate their success by following the same strategy.

The Standard Model, as it came to be modified in the late nineteenth century, contained another weakness that governed the timing of its demise. The reliance on foreign borrowing meant that domestic capital accumulation was hostage to the fluctuations in international financial markets. The adoption of monetarist macroeconomic policies in the United States, the United Kingdom, and other rich countries around 1980 fixed central bankers' attention on the growth of the money supply rather than other indicators like interest rates. Attempts to limit money supply growth led to spiralling interest rates. As foreign debts were refinanced at higher and higher interest, the burden on Latin America became greater and greater, and Mexico defaulted on its foreign debt in 1982. Financial crisis engulfed the rest of Latin America as well. Western countries clamored for reform in Latin America, and the Washington consensus policies of stabilization, liberalization, and privatization were forced on the continent. These were supposed to kick-start growth by removing the efficiencies caused by ISI industrialization. The result, however, was several decades of lost growth.

Catching up through more directive state action in the nineteenth century: Egypt

While some peripheral economies tried to industrialize in the nineteenth century with incomplete applications of the Standard Model, other economies experimented with more direct forms of state intervention.

Egypt is an intriguing example that prefigured many features of the Soviet development model. In 1805, Muhammad-Ali was appointed Pasha of Egypt, nominally part of the Ottoman empire, after Napoleon's withdrawal which precipitated civil war between the Mamluks, who previously controlled the country, and Ottoman forces. Muhammad-Ali remained its absolute ruler until his abdication in 1848. In 1811, he murdered the leading Mamluks, destroyed their forces, and "nationalized" the land, which remained, however, in the hands of the cultivators. With the extermination of the previous aristocracy, Muhammed Ali usurped the agricultural surplus through a trade monopoly that paid producers low prices for food and cotton that were resold at higher prices to city dwellers and at even high prices in export markets. With this income, he established a modern army, extensive naval and ordnance production facilities, as well as a cotton textile industry that exported to the Middle East where it successfully competed against the British. Machinery production was initiated to free Egypt from dependence on foreign suppliers. Tariffs were not an option for promoting industry since they were limited to 3 percent by the Ottomans, so state ownership was used instead, and price manipulation replaced banks as the means of financing industry. Muhammad Ali also invested in canals and roads. Modern schools were established to train technical and administrative personnel, but mass education was not initiated.

Egypt's experiment, however precocious, did not succeed. Whether the cause was internal failings or British imperialism has long been debated. Lord Palmerston did write: "To subjugate Muhammad-'Ali to Great Britain . . . could be wrong and biased, but we are biased; the vital interest of Europe require that we should be so." Defeat of Muhammad-Ali's forces in the Levant by the British in 1840–1 led to the application of the Treaty of Balta Liman (1838) between the Ottoman empire and Great Britain. The treaty limited tariffs and, more important, abolished monopolies. Muhammad Ali's tax system was undone and with it the structure of his state and his development plans.

Catching up through more directive state action in the nineteenth century: Japan

Japan also used vigorous state action to boost growth after 1868, and it was considerably more successful than Egypt. Indeed, the Japanese economy was arguably the most successful of the twentieth century.

The burst of development was preceded by the so-called Tokugawa period (1603–1868) when power lay in the hands of the Tokugawa shogun rather than the emperor, who remained a figurehead. The polity was divided into several hundred "feudal" domains, while the society was divided into four castes (samurai, peasants, artisans, and merchants). In 1868, Japan had many hallmarks of an "underdeveloped country": most of its population was employed in agriculture, real wages were very low, and there was no factory industry. However, there were also important signs of modernity. In the seventeenth century, rice production and the population grew substantially. The feudal lords (daimyo) promoted rural and small-town manufacturing, which grew vigorously. Cities were large: Edo (modern Tokyo) had a population of one million while Osaka and Kyoto each had 400,000. Finally, literacy was unusually widespread for an agrarian society.

The administrative and technical competence of Tokugawa Japan was shown in the introduction of iron founding to the country. Since 1635, inbound ships were only allowed from China, Korea, and the Netherlands, and the Dutch were restricted to a tiny settlement in Nagasaki. Foreign contacts were rebuffed. It was a serious incident when *HMS Phaeton* entered the port of Nagasaki in 1808 to prey on Dutch shipping. *Phaeton* threatened to bombard the city when it refused to supply provisions. The Japanese were forced to back down since they had no cannon with which to defend themselves. Nabeshima Naomasa, who became the daimyo of Nagasaki, aimed to retrieve the situation by establishing an iron foundry to cast artillery. This had never been done in Japan, whose iron industry was limited to forges making wrought iron with charcoal. A team of savants and iron workers was assembled for the task. They translated a Dutch book which described an iron foundry at Leiden in the Netherlands and tried to replicate it. After many attempts, they succeeded in casting iron cannon.

The foreign peril to Japan increased dramatically in 1853–4 when US Commodore Perry threatened to attack Japan unless the shogun agreed to end the trade embargo, which he did. The Tokugawa shogun and some of the daimyo began to develop modern military forces to defend the country, but the reforms did not go far enough. The result was a virtual coup d'état: in 1867, Emperor Meiji ascended the throne, and the next year the Tokugawa shogun "voluntarily" surrendered his powers to the emperor.

Modern economic growth in Japan is often dated as beginning with the Meiji restoration which was followed by a blizzard of institutional reforms. In short order, the 1.9 million samurai surrendered their domains and were pensioned off with government bonds. Peasants were granted modern tenure to their farms and paid a land tax to the state (in lieu of the payments they had made to their feudal lords). This was the principal source of government income in the early years of the new emperor's reign. The four orders of Tokugawa society were abolished. A Western-style army based on universal conscription was established in 1873. Modern state structures were modelled on what the Japanese considered the best foreign practice.

Under the slogan "rich country, strong army," the Meiji state sought to boost economic development to meet its military objectives. The Japanese would have liked to follow the Standard Model, but initially could only adopt two of its four imperatives. First, a national market was created by abolishing the internal tariffs of the feudal domains and by constructing a railway system in the 1870s. Second, universal primary education was mandated in 1872 and was substantially achieved by the early twentieth century. A modest expansion of secondary education was undertaken, a substantial university sector created, and thousands of Japanese were sent abroad to study. Third, an external tariff to protect newly founded Japanese industries was precluded by the 1866 treaty, which was forced on Japan by the imperial powers, and which capped tariffs at 5 percent. This limit lasted until the early twentieth century, when Japan regained control over its tariffs and belatedly adopted this plank of the model. Fourth, efforts were made to establish a central bank and modern investment banks, but progress was slow until the 1920s.

Japan's response to these obstacles was to invent a highly effective alternative to the Standard Model. Instead of tariffs to promote industries, subsidies, procurement policies, and state ownership were tried as alternatives. These were the bases of "targeted industrial policy" that proved successful in the twentieth century. In contrast to Mexico and Russia, where foreign firms were the instruments for introducing modern technology, Japan nurtured its own firms. Rather than importing insulators for the telegraph lines along the first railways, the government gave contracts to local potters and in that way promoted an industrial ceramics industry. In 1905, the state established a modern steel industry by creating the Yawata Iron and Steelworks, which was a state-owned enterprise that was subsidized for years until it achieved efficient operation. During World War I, when it proved impossible to import hydroelectric generators from Germany, the order was given to Hitachi, which had never made such equipment, and the state paid for its learning experience. During the 1930s, the military subsidized the automotive and aircraft industries with a large stream of contracts. In these ways, the Japanese government built up the country's engineering and management capabilities, and nurtured the firms that were the basis of its postwar success.

The evolution of Japanese technology in the Meiji period was distinctive and reflected the country's strategy of building up its technical capabilities. In the 1870s and 1880s, the state imported modern machinery, which was installed in state-owned factories. Many of these proved unprofitable and eventually went out of business. One cause of failure was the inappropriateness of the technology to Japanese conditions. Foreign equipment was highly capital-intensive and Japan was a low-wage country, so the foreign designs were not cost-effective. Japanese firms redrew the foreign blueprints to make machinery that used more labor and less capital. The British mules imported by the state to spin cotton were costly, and the first commercially successful cotton mills relied instead on the rattling spindle, which was designed by Guan Tokimune and financed by a local development agency. While British (and Indian) firms operated one 11-hour shift per day, Japanese mills operated two 11-hour shifts, thereby cutting capital costs in half. Likewise, Japan quickly adopted ring spinning, which again increased capital productivity. In the interwar period, "just in time" delivery was a technique developed to limit investment in inventories. It has proved so successful that it is used where capital is cheap as well as where it is dear.

These policies were successful in promoting economic growth. By the beginning of World War II, an industrial, urban society had been created. Japan was the only Asian country to achieve such a breakthrough in the period.

Big Push industrialization: the Soviet Union

Japan made impressive progress between 1870 and 1940, but the rate of growth achieved (2 percent per head per year) was not enough for a rapid catch-up with the West. The trouble was that the leaders were also advancing, so the goal was a moving target. Between 1870 and 1940, per capita income in the United States grew at 1.5 percent per year. If those rates are projected forward from the income levels of 1950, it would have taken Japan 327 years to catch up. That was not fast enough, and Japan changed its development strategy after World War II to accelerate its growth rate.

This problem is a general one. Typically, per capita income in a poor country is 20 to 25 percent of the average income of a rich country. If the per capita income of the rich country grows at 2 percent per year, and the poor country wants to catch up with the rich country in two generations (sixty years), per capita income in the poor country must grow at 4.3 percent per year for the sixty years. Adding on the population growth rate implies that total GDP must grow 6 percent or more for sixty years to catch up to the leader.

Very few countries have sustained such rapid growth over a long period. Between 1955 and 2005, only ten countries averaged a growth rate of 4.3 percent per year in GDP per head. Oman, Botswana, and Equatorial Guinea are special cases in that large oil or diamond reserves were discovered during this period. Singapore and Hong Kong are city-states, and that makes them special since there was no peasant agricultural sector to swamp the city with migrants when investment rose. Wages could, therefore, increase in step with labor demand and prosperity could spread. The interesting cases are the large countries with large agricultural sectors – Japan, South Korea, Taiwan, Thailand, and China. In addition, the Soviet Union could be added since income per head grew at 4.5 percent per year from 1928 to 1970 if the decade of the 1940s is excluded.

These countries had to close three gaps with the West – in education, capital, and productivity. Mass schooling closed the education gap and one form or another of state-led industrialization closed the capital and produc-tivity gaps. Large-scale, capital-intensive technologies were adopted, even when they were not immediately cost-effective. These countries have avoided the inefficiencies that Latin America has endured in trying to shoehorn modern technology into small economies either because they were so large that they could absorb the output of efficient facilities or because they were given access to the American market at the expense of American production.

The large countries that have achieved high growth have done so with a Big Push. For GDP to grow at 6 percent or more per year, many investments have to be made concurrently that would have been made sequentially in an economy growing less rapidly. Cities must be built before the industries that provide employment are completed. Auto plants must be made before the steel mills that will supply them, and the steel mills must be under construction as the auto plants are built. Each investment requires confidence that the complementary investments will occur. Some form of planning or investment coordination is necessary to ensure that confidence. Countries have differed considerably in the forms that coordination has taken and in its effectiveness.

The Soviet Union is the paradigm of Big Push industrialization. The Bolsheviks won the civil war that followed the 1917 revolution, but the economy was in shambles. Lenin's New Economic Policy (1921–1928) revived it with a combination of state-owned industry and peasant agriculture. Lenin died in 1924, and Stalin emerged victorious in the ensuing leadership struggle. In 1928, the first Five Year Plan was adopted, and the Big Push was on. Thousands of factories and power plants had been built by 1941 when Hitler's armies invaded the country. Agriculture was collectivized to force the countryside to supply the cities with food, and millions of farm workers moved to the cities and remote construction sites. Many fled the terror of the state's attack on successful farmers, and millions more were deported through political purges.

During World War II around 25 million Soviet citizens were killed, and much of the country's capital stock was destroyed. By 1950, however, GDP and the capital stock had rebounded to their 1940 levels, and rapid growth resumed. Performance was so stellar that it looked as though the Soviet experiment might be the template for all poor countries to catch up to the West. In the 1970s, however, things started to go wrong. The growth rate gradually slackened – despite continued high investment. By 1985, expansion had ceased. President Gorbachev called for perestroika (reconstruction); central planning was ended. The changes were too late to save the Soviet Union, and it was dissolved in 1991.

Soviet history raises two questions about divergent development. The first is why growth was so rapid between 1928 and the 1970s. Soviet firms were state-owned, and the volume and allocation of investment was determined by the central planners. The economy was coordinated through "material balance planning," a system under which the planners determined the total production of most products and assigned firms output targets to realize the totals. Rapid growth was based on four legs. First, investment was channelled disproportionately to the metallurgical, construction, and machinery industries, so that the capital stock could be built up at a rapid rate. Second, firms were not guided by profit considerations; rather, they received output quotas from the central planners, and fulfilling those directives was their primary responsibility. Third, firms were not constrained to cover their costs, as that might have conflicted with achieving their quotas. Firms received bank loans to cover their costs, so they operated with "soft budget constraints" rather than the "hard budget constraints" of capitalist firms. Fourth, the educational system was rapidly expanded to train the population to design, manage, and operate an industrial economy.

GDP per head grew rapidly under this regime. Fast growth in per capita income was achieved both by accelerating the rate of growth of GDP and by reducing the rate of growth of the population. GDP grew rapidly because allocating investment to the producer goods sector led to a rapid growth in the physical capital stock and because expanding the educational system did the same for human capital. Giving firms output targets focussed the attention of management on increasing production, and soft budget constraints made it profitable to expanded employment in the context of structural unemployment in agriculture.

Per capita income also grew rapidly since the population expanded slowly. The decisive factors were neither Stalin's political terrorism nor the Nazi invasion; rather, the most important factor was the fall in the fertility rate. In the 1920s, the average Soviet woman had seven children, which was a typical value for women in very poor countries. By the 1960s, the average number of children had dropped to three. The causes of this decline were the same as those operating in other poor countries – educating women and providing them with paid work outside the home. These developments were the result of Soviet educational and employment policies.

The second important question about Soviet economic history is why the growth rate sagged after the 1970s. Economists have debated the explanation, and their answers range from the debilitating influence of dictatorship on free thought and innovation, to the allocation of research and development (R&D) resources to the military rather than civilian industry, to the impossibility of material balance planning, to the elimination of surplus labor as industry grew at the expense of agriculture, to perverse incentives of output targets and soft budgets which led firms to hoard labor and other inputs rather than releasing them to other firms in the economy. It will be instructive to consider this question in the light of Chinese history, which we shall do shortly.

Big Push industrialization: Japan

World War II was a shattering defeat for Japan. Not only was industrial capacity destroyed, but the national objectives that guided the country since the Meiji restoration were revised. Imperialism was abandoned, and the slogan "strong army, rich country" was truncated simply to "rich country." Japan has been singularly successful in achieving that goal. The rate of growth in per capita GDP was increased from the 2 percent per year achieved between 1870 and 1940 to 5.9 percent from 1950 to 1990. The peak years were 1953 to 1973 when per capita GDP increased at 8 percent per year. Rich country living standards have been achieved.

Japan achieved these results by reversing the technology policy it had pioneered during the Meiji period. Instead of re-engineering Western technology to accord with Japan's low wages (i.e. by reducing the use of capital and increasing the use of labor), Japan opted for the largest-scale, most capital-intensive technology available. An advanced industrial economy was built on the rubble of the war, and factor prices adjusted to the new capital-intensive factor proportions rather than the other way around.

At the outset, the choice of technique was not left to private firms but was guided by state institutions. The most famous was MITI, the Ministry of International Trade and Industry, although others played a role as well. These state structures were the outgrowth of prewar Japanese institutions.

In the 1950s, many Japanese manufacturing industries were too small to realize scale economies and achieve high productivity. The minimum efficient size of steel mills was 1–2.5 million tons. The Yawata steelworks, with a capacity of 1.8 million tons, was the only Japanese mill in this range. The capacity of other firms was less than 0.5 million tons per year with the result that the productivity of the Japanese steel industry was half that of the United States. MITI's objective was to restructure the industry so that steel was made in efficient-size mills. MITI's power came from its control over the banking system and the foreign exchange that was needed to import iron ore and metallurgical coal. By 1960, all steel was produced in mills of efficient size, and output had grown from 5 million to 22 million tons. In the 1960s and 1970s, MITI continued to guide investment in steel. New capacity was in plants that were large enough to achieve all scale economies and use the best modern technology. Japan led the United States in the adoption of the basic oxygen and continuous casting processes.

A large-scale, capital-intensive approach to technology was taken in other industries as well. Shipbuilding and automobiles are important examples. While car manufacture was a good example of the way ISI industrialization led to inefficiency in Latin America, it proved a source of high productivity in Japan. The firms that dominated postwar Japanese industry were established in the interwar period. In the 1920s, American firms built plants in Japan, but they were forced out of business by a 1936 law. Military contracts for vehicles supported Japanese firms, and the industry developed design and engineering capacities that underpinned later success. By the 1960s, the leading Japanese car firms had built vehicle assembly plants of minimum efficient size (at the time that was 200,000 vehicles per year), and by the 1970s, they pioneered on-site stamping and multiple line operation that pushed minimum efficient size to over 400,000 vehicles. By then Japanese facilities were more capital-intensive than American plants and produced at lower cost.

Finding markets for the output of Japan's large-scale industry was a key problem. Much of the production was absorbed internally. Automobile plants and shipyards consumed much of the steel output, for instance. As the capital stock expanded, the demand for labor rose sharply. As a result, the low-wage work that had characterized agriculture and small-scale manufacturing was eliminated. Japanese workers bought much of the increase in manufacturing output. However, their demand was not enough to absorb the production of Japan's very large factories, and the country relied on export markets. The United States was the most important. Access to that market raised issues that transcended MITI. The United States could have continued the high tariff policy the country had followed since 1816 and kept Japanese goods out of the country. However, the United States opted for multilateral free trade. Imports of Japanese steel, autos, and consumer goods generally caused large declines in production and employment in the American Midwest. The decline of the Rust Belt was the flip side of the East Asian Miracle. American production was sacrificed since Japan was the US bulwark against communism in East Asia.

Big Push industrialization: China

The economic development of China in the last half-century marks one of the great watersheds in world history. Before the industrial revolution, China was the world's greatest manufacturing country, but competition from British factories destroyed much of the traditional manufacturing. Political instability, civil war, and state weakness meant that no effective policy along Meiji lines was adopted. By the mid twentieth century, China, with an income of $448 per head, was one of the most impoverished "underdeveloped" countries in the world.

The communist victory in 1949 led to thirty years of central planning along Soviet lines. Per capita GDP grew at 2.8 percent – a respectable but not out-standing achievement and one that was substantially below the 4.3 percent need for rapid convergence with the leaders. Since 1978, growth has been much more rapid. Between 1978 and 2008, per capita GDP grew at 6.9 percent per year.

How did China do it? The usual answer is "free market reforms." After Mao's death in 1976, the new leader Deng Xiaoping began to increase price incentives and supplement central planing with market arrangements. The first reforms were in agriculture. In 1978, the communal operation of collective farms was replaced with the household responsibility system, whereby the land of the collective farms was leased to peasant families to operate individually. The collectives' delivery quotas were also divided among the farms. In 1979 and 1981, the state increased the price it paid for deliveries exceeding quotas, and this income accrued to the individual cultivators. Agricultural output, including rice in particular, grew very rapidly from 1978 to 1984 (although the growth rate has slackened considerably since then), and the acceleration is usually explained by the price incentives received by the farmers.

The second reforms also occurred in the countryside. Collective farms (like the peasants before them) had always engaged in processing and handicraft production. In 1978, local party officials were encouraged to expand small-scale manufacturing of consumer goods and sell the output on the free market. Employment in these "Township and Village Enterprises" increased from 28 million in 1978 to 135 million in 1996, when they accounted for 26 percent of China's GDP.

The third round of reform was focussed on the heavy industrial sector, which had been the showpiece of central planning. In the mid 1980s, the state froze its plan targets and let firms sell production beyond the quotas on the free market. As the economy has grown, the quotas have become increasingly superfluous, and material balance planning has become a dead letter. In 1992, the Fourteenth Communist Party Congress endorsed the "socialist market economy" as the goal of reform. Firms have been reorganized as state-owned corporations rather than government departments, and state-owned banks have been promoted to finance their investment. With markets have come profit and loss statements, and they provide a means of gauging performance. China has seen the closure of inefficient capacity – something the Soviet Union was never able to achieve.

The Chinese economy has grown rapidly as the reforms have come into effect, but the causal link from reforms to growth is problematic. Agriculture shows some of the difficulties. Under tropical conditions, three improvements are necessary to increase rice yields. The first is a large, regular supply of water. Throughout the 1960s and 1970s, China invested heavily in irrigation facilities, and they underpinned the post-1978 surge in output. The second is plants that respond to fertilizer by producing more grain. If indigenous Chinese rice was heavily fertilized, the rice stalks would have grown to a great height and then toppled over (lodging), preventing the formation of grain. This was a general problem in the tropics. What was necessary was dwarf rice with fibrous stalks. These varieties did not grow tall and lodge when fertilized, but instead produced more rice seeds. The Green Revolution in South Asia depended on IR-8, a dwarf rice produced by the International Rice Research Institution in the Philippines in 1966. The Chinese Academy of Sciences produced a similar dwarf rice in 1964, and that was the basis of the increased production post-1978.

The third necessary improvement was the nitrogen fertilizer to apply to the rice. China was not successful in building its own fertilizer plants in the 1960s, and in 1973–1974 the country contracted with foreign firms to build thirteen ammonia factories. These came on stream in the late 1970s, and provided the nitrogen for the expansion of rice production. The technology came together at the same time as the institutions were reformed, so it is difficult to say that the reforms caused the growth in output. Perhaps it would have happened anyway.

Reforms played a role in the growth of industrial output – particularly the production of consumer goods by Township and Village Enterprises – but it is unlikely that they are the whole story here either. Indeed, much of the economy is still planned, including heavy industry, energy, transportation, and technology. Steel, every planner's favorite industry, is a good example. In 2000, China made 127 million tons and was already the world's largest steel producer. By 2010, production had increased another fivefold, reaching 627 million tons. China now produces at least as much steel, on a per capita basis, as the rich countries consume. Little of this steel is exported – it is consumed domestically to build the modern society that China wants. The rapid expansion of the industry is driven by the state not the "market." While China does have markets in steel and its inputs, the firms are state-owned, new plants are financed by state-owned banks, and the timing of investment is laid out in the five-year plan.

What the Chinese have done is preserve the elements of central planning that were effective – planning the investment program and education – while avoiding the pitfalls that rendered planning counterproductive in the USSR. First, the Chinese do not plan all investment but only the investment in what used to be called the "commanding heights" of the economy. Second, material balance planning has been abandoned. Third, as a corollary, firms are guided by profit in the newly created markets. Fourth, in this environment, firms have an incentive to cut costs and eliminate inefficient facilities and unproductive labor. The Soviet Union never managed to do this, and, as a result, had too many resources locked up in unproductive enterprises. Of course, there is no guarantee that this recipe will always work well. It requires that investment be intelligently planned. That is not so hard for a poor country that is trying duplicate what rich countries already do. Thus, it is not hard to work out that China needs a steel industry that produces as much steel per head as rich countries consume. (This might not be true for a smaller country that could import its requirements, but China is too big for that to be feasible.) It will be intriguing to see how the Chinese modify their institutions as their income approaches that of rich countries and the technology challenge switches from replication to invention.

Conclusion

The causes of underdevelopment have been extensively debated in recent years, with most scholars emphasizing one or another of the so-called fundamentals – geography, institutions, and culture. In this chapter, I have indicated that these factors were the results of even more fundamental social processes. Africa's corrupt, rent-seeking institutions, for instance, were colonial constructions tailored to the low population density that was a consequence of the high mortality of the tropics. Likewise, popular culture – as manifest in fertility rates – has been powerfully affected by the education of women and their opportunities to work outside the home. Even the importance of geography is less than it seems, for the significance of location or disease environment depends on transportation and medical technology. Instead, I have argued that the decisive principles in explaining long-run economic history have been the evolution of the global economy, the inducement that factor prices and human needs more generally give to the invention of technology, and the role of state policy in guiding the role of these factors and assisting the population in successfully responding to the incentives they create. This is a more optimistic analysis for the future of humanity, since policy is an easier lever to pull than any of the "fundamentals."

References

Allen, R. C. (2009). *The British Industrial Revolution in Global Perspective.* Cambridge University Press.

(2011). *Global Economic History: A Very Short Introduction.* Oxford University Press.

Hamilton, A. (1791). *Report of the Secretary of the Treasury of the United States on the subject of manufactures, presented to the House of Representatives, December 5, 1791,* United States, Department of the Treasury.

List, F. (1974 [1841]). *National System of Political Economy.* New York: Garland.

Smith, A. (E. Cannan (ed.) 1937 [1776]). *The Nature and Causes of the Wealth of Nations.* New York: The Modern Library.

Williamson, J. G. (2011). *Trade and Poverty: When the Third World Fell Behind.* Cambridge, MA: The MIT Press.

3

Growth, specialization, and organization of world agriculture

GIOVANNI FEDERICO[*]

Introduction

Agriculture has been the main source of livelihood for the overwhelming majority of the world's population for thousands of years, from the first production of crops some 8,000 years ago to the start of worldwide industrialization in the nineteenth century. At the dawn of agricultural civilization, farms were self-sufficient production and consumption units, but the development of cities changed all that. Indeed, cities could not have developed without the commercialization of agriculture. They depended for their survival on a growing inflow of food and agricultural raw materials, and on the farmers' willingness to take manufactures in exchange. This exchange was made possible by the development of markets for agricultural products and credit, which, in turn, required the development of institutions to provide capital to farmers. It also required property rights which were secure enough to encourage farm investment. However, many cities did not trust the invisible hand to supply their needs and thus replaced it with market regulation, backed by political control of the countryside. In short, "capitalist" institutions and market intervention predated the industrial revolution. But the joint effect of the sixfold increase in the world population from 1800 to 2000, rising per capita incomes, and urbanization, all served to present a huge challenge for agriculture.

World agriculture met the challenge brilliantly. As detailed in the next section, total production and trade boomed, production per capita grew, and prices converged between locations, at least before the Great Depression. These changes had far-reaching consequences for the specialization of production and the allocation of resources. Then we discuss the proximate causes of the increase in production, the growth in land, labor, and capital inputs and the

---

[*] This chapter relies heavily on Federico (2005), where the interested reader will find all references to sources not quoted in this chapter.

efficiency gains. This sets the stage for the remainder of the chapter, which tackles the central question: To what extent was the spread of capitalism instrumental to this growth? We start by outlining the diffusion of modern (i.e. "capitalistic") property rights from Western Europe to almost the whole world. Then we show that large-scale, "capitalist" production units did not spread, unlike in other sectors, and argue that they were no more efficient than small-scale family farming. The next section deals with financing agricultural activity, focussing on the slow increase in the market share of "formal" institutions. The two last sections deal with state intervention, distinguishing between such "benign" policies as the funding of agricultural research and development (R&D), and the less "benign" ones such as the measures which directly affected farm income and resource allocation to, from, and within agriculture.

Setting the stage: the growth of agricultural production, 1800–2000

The available data on agricultural output in the first half of the nineteenth century are scarce and often only conjectural, but they are fairly consistent. All the country and area studies suggest that output grew at least as much as, and, in many cases, more than, the population, Portugal being a solitary exception. The data refer to Europe and Western Settlement countries, and thus the increase in these countries might have been offset by a decline in output per capita elsewhere in the world. This hypothesis is not, however, terribly plausible. In fact, the population was mostly employed in agriculture and, as we will detail in the next section, farmers could find new land to settle in almost every country of the world except Western Europe. Since 1870, it is possible to estimate a yearly series of "world" gross agricultural output, which covers twenty-five countries, accounting for about 50 to 55 percent of the world population.[1] The index can be linked in 1938 to the official series of world output by the FAO (Food and Agriculture Organization of the United Nations), which covers all countries, except the Soviet Union before 1948. Figure 3.1 compares this spliced index with series of population for the comparable set of countries (i.e. the twenty-five countries before 1938 and the world population after 1950). The accuracy of some series, especially for developing countries and for socialist countries before the 1990s, is somewhat

1 The sample includes all European countries (except Norway and the Balkans), Canada, the United States, Argentina, Chile, Uruguay, India, Indonesia, and Japan (Federico 2004).

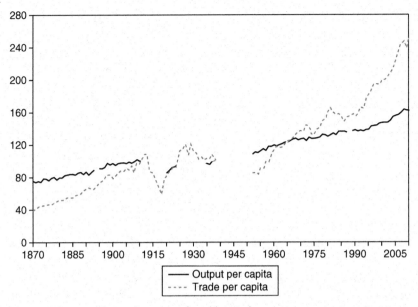

Figure 3.1. The performance of world agriculture, 1870–2010 (1938=100)

dubious. However, errors might compensate, and, anyway, no plausible aggregate bias can be so large as to question the conclusion about the outstanding performance of agriculture. For the twenty-five countries alone, the total production roughly doubled from 1870 to 1913 and, after the wartime shock, it increased by a further 20 percent from 1918–1919 to 1938. Output per capita had increased by a quarter before the war and then it remained roughly constant to 1938. If output per capita in the missing countries remained constant (a conservative assumption), world production per capita grew by about 10 percent from 1870 to 1938. The acceleration in the rate of growth of the world population after World War II was matched by an even sharper acceleration in the rate of growth of agricultural production, from about 1 percent per annum to over 2 percent. From 1938 to 2010, production per capita increased by 60 percent, and nowadays it exceeds the caloric needs of world population by far. Undernourishment, which, according to the latest data from the FAO, still affects about 1 billion people, is a consequence of waste and inefficiencies in distribution, rather than of absolute scarcity.

Over the whole period 1870 to 2000, per capita trade in agricultural products increased more than fivefold – less than total trade but decidedly more than agricultural output.[2] Trade grew faster than output before 1913, roughly as fast as output in interwar years, collapsed during the war, and recovered in the 1950s, to go on growing very fast until the end of the twentieth century. The increase of trade relative to output is strong evidence of a growing specialization of agricultural production.

Specialization both across countries and within each country ultimately depends on the movements in the relative prices of agricultural goods, which determine the allocation of productive factors. Unfortunately, the movement of world prices cannot be captured by a single series as total output or trade. In fact, trends may differ between countries and, within each country, between real prices (i.e. the ratio to an index of overall prices at the denominator) and domestic terms of trade (the ratio to industrial prices). Figure 3.2 presents both series for the United States.[3]

The two measures of relative prices tell a similar story. Prices increased, fairly steadily, until World War I, fluctuated hugely until the all-time peak during the Korean War, and then started a downward movement, interrupted only by a spike in the 1970s. Clearly, trends in the United States may not be representative, but the first impression is confirmed by the additional evidence of other countries. In the first decades of the nineteenth century, real prices and terms of trade increased in most advanced European countries, with the notable exception of the United Kingdom. Furthermore, many countries in the periphery experienced an improvement in their external terms of trade – i.e. the ratio of prices of their, mostly agricultural, exports to the prices of their, mostly industrial, imports (Williamson 2011). The improvement was very large in the European periphery (South Italy, Spain, Russia), the Middle East, and Southeast Asia (Indonesia), less impressive in Latin America and South Asia (India and Ceylon), while China had no change, and Japan remained close to world trade until 1859. Since 1870, the trends have been more mixed. Domestic terms of trade continued to improve in most

2 The series is obtained by splicing the series by Aparicio, Pinilla, and Serrano (2009) for the period to 1938 to the WTO data (www.wto.org, accessed March 13, 2012), assuming that trade of agricultural products was 13 percent higher in 1953 than in 1937. Trade in 1953, according to Yates (1959), was 96 percent of its 1937 level, but the figure excludes communist countries. In the same year, trade with communist countries was 18 percent of trade among market economies (United Nations 1952 and 1960). Population from Maddison (www.ggdc.net/maddison/maddison-project/home.htm, accessed July 22, 2013).

3 Series USA from Carter et al. (2006) extended to 2010 with data from the Federal Reserve Saint Louis (https://research.stlouisfed.org, accessed March 13, 2012). Unit values of exports of agricultural products and manufactures from WTO (www.wto.org, accessed March 13, 2012).

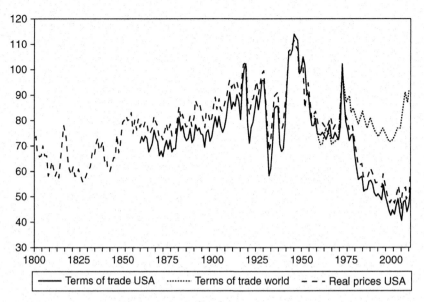

Figure 3.2. Agricultural prices (1950=100)

countries, but real prices remained flat or even decreased. As a rule, agricultural prices grew more in exporting countries – including the United States – than in Europe, and in the twenty years before World War I, than in the 1870s and 1880s. After the war, prices decreased in most countries, with some exceptions, but anyway short-term fluctuations, such as the collapse during the Great Depression, swamped long-run trends. Figure 3.2 reports, as a very crude proxy of "world" prices, the ratio of unit values of agricultural exports to unit values of manufactured exports. The series confirms the downward trend of American prices, but the decline is much less steep, and, above all, there is evidence of a rebound after the year 2000. Actually, trends in the world prices of primary products are the subject of a long-standing controversy, started in the 1950s by Prebisch and Singer (Spraos 1983). They argued that the relative prices of primary products were bound to decline in the long run and thus they declared specialization in commodity exports to be a dead end for development. This hypothesis has spawned a huge literature, with increasingly sophisticated statistical techniques. Unfortunately, scholars have not reached a consensus. Results depend on the type of price series that they use (individual commodities vs. indexes), on the product and country coverage (agricultural vs. all primary products, single country vs. all least developed countries [LDCs]), on the period (the whole twentieth century vs. only the post-World War 1 years) and on the techniques of estimation.

Although a detailed interpretation of price movements is beyond the scope of this chapter, it is possible to make some general statements. Prebisch and Singer predicted a decline in the prices of primary products because the demand was bound to grow less than the demand for manufactures. A very similar argument (renamed the farm problem) has been put forward to justify support for farmers in advanced countries (see "The benign state," below). This argument is not really convincing, however. If markets for factors are flexible enough and the adjustment is not hampered by state intervention, low prices would drive capital and labor out of agriculture, and the fall in supply would cause agricultural prices to rise. In the long term, movements in relative prices depend on relative productivity. *Ceteris paribus*, one would expect the relative prices of agricultural products to increase if productivity in agriculture grows less than in the rest of the economy (for real prices) or less than in industry (for the terms of trade). In a purely closed economy, relative prices would be determined by domestic relative productivity, while in a fully open economy with no barriers to trade, they would be determined by "world" relative productivity. Neither case is realistic: barriers to trade are product- and country-specific and also change in time as a consequence of trade policy and of technological progress in transportation. For instance, a fall in transportation costs causes commodity prices to converge, thus increasing in exporting countries and decreasing in importing ones. However, the convergence would affect prices of all traded commodities, not just agricultural products, and thus the effects on terms of trade or on real prices of agricultural products are impossible to predict a priori. What can be said is that the evidence is consistent with a moderate decline in relative productivity of agriculture until World War 1 and with a huge increase after 1950. This is quite an achievement.

How it was achieved: extensive growth

Tables 3.1 and 3.2 provide the essential information about trends in agricultural workforce (proxied by the number of workers) and in land endowment (measured as the sum of cropland and tree-crops) from 1880. Since 1938, the figures have been obtained from the FAO official statistics, which officially cover the whole world, although with widely different degrees of reliability of data by country. In contrast, earlier figures must be pieced together from country sources. The number of countries is growing over time and thus a

Table 3.1. *Workforce*

Continent	Circa 1880	Circa 1910	Circa 1938	1960	2000	2000 (mil)
Africa			31	51	100	197.1
Europe	392	392	359	309	100	17.6
Canada and USA	304	405	340	173	100	3.4
Latin America*	24	44	68	83	100	44.2
Asia	34	41	42	59	100	1031.8
Oceania	36	57	68	64	100	2.8
Former USSR			203	178	100	21.7
World				64	100	1318.6

Source: Federico 2005: Tables 4.16 and 4.17.
*including Mexico and Central America

simple sum would bias the growth rate upwards. Thus, for both land and labor, we extrapolate the 1938 figures backwards with the rates of change for homogeneous samples of countries and express the results as an index with base 2000=100. The implicit world total can be computed by multiplying the indexes by the absolute figures in 2000 (the last column on the right).

Table 3.1 adds an important qualification to the conventional wisdom about the effect of modern economic growth on employment by sector. The share of agricultural workers may have declined since the start of industrialization, but their absolute numbers only began to decline when industrialization was rather advanced. In the United Kingdom, the workforce in agriculture peaked around 1850, at least seventy years after the start of the industrial revolution. In other advanced countries, it continued to grow until the interwar years and shrank drastically only after World War II. A fortiori, the agricultural work-force must have increased in countries which had not yet started to develop, which, incidentally, account for almost all the missing figures in Table 3.1. Actually, according to the FAO data, the number of agricultural workers had been growing, although more and more slowly, until 2010.[4] One may wonder whether the number of workers accurately measures the input of labor accurately. Indeed, it is possible to list several sources of bias, such as changes in the gender ratio, the increase in the human capital of workers, the diffusion of part-time farming, and so on. However, arguably, they compensate each other, and, as a whole, the headcount can be considered a fairly accurate measure of total labor input.

4 Data from www.fao.org/corp/statistics/en, accessed March 1, 2010.

Table 3.2. *Acreage*

Continent	Circa 1880	Circa 1910	Circa 1938	1960	2000	2000 (mil ha)
Africa			86	77	100	201.8
Europe	110	112	112	114	100	133.2
Canada and USA	41	77	91	100	100	231.1
Latin America*		44	73	63	100	153.1
Asia	29	58	64	85	100	511.7
Oceania	7	22	34	66	100	53.0
Former USSR	48	52	55	110	100	217.5
World			81	90	100	1501.5

Source: Federico 2005: Tables 4.1, 4.3, and 4.5.
*including Mexico and Central America

Table 3.2 shows that worldwide acreage has been growing everywhere except in Western Europe and in some areas of Asia. By 1880, there was plenty of unexploited land on all continents, which has been settled since then. The public knows the story of the settlement of the American West thanks to many Hollywood movies, but the pattern has been repeated, albeit with some delay, in all the other countries of European immigration, such as Canada, South America, and Oceania. Cropland also increased in Asia and Africa, with little or no contribution by immigrants from Europe. Even in a supposedly overpopulated country such as China, there was a lot of new land to colonize: from 1860 to 1940, about 8 million Chinese settled in Manchuria. Worldwide acreage went on growing until it peaked in 2005, in spite of a (modest) decline in some advanced countries in the last decades of the twentieth century.

Although the table does not cover the period before 1880, there is very little doubt that acreage has been growing parallel to population in all areas, except perhaps Western Europe. If land was still abundant in 1880, *a fortiori* it was abundant one century before. One can doubt that the acreage in cropland and tree crop measures the total input of land accurately. In particular, it would overstate the increase in land if part of the new land had been formerly used as pasture (and thus had been producing something, rather than nothing) and/or if it had been qualitatively inferior. There is no evidence of a systematic quality bias against new land, while data on the extension of pastures until 1950 are scarce and hardly comparable between countries and across time. However, this problem should not affect the FAO series, and they show that acreage in permanent pasture and meadows has grown as much as cropland. We can conclude that land was not a constraint on agricultural growth, except perhaps in a few areas in Western Europe and China.

It is not possible to summarize changes in agricultural capital with a single measure, even a crude one. In fact, capital consists of a number of widely different items – livestock, buildings, machinery, irrigation works, trees, and so on, all of which must be summed together in monetary terms in order to obtain a meaningful total. The FAO provides an estimate of "world" capital stock which shows a 25 percent increase from 1975 to the year 2000 – i.e. much less than output. For the period before 1975, there are few series, which refer only to advanced countries and often cover only a subset of items. Most of them show an increase, which is, unsurprisingly, faster in the United States, Canada, and Russia than in more settled countries such as France, Germany, or the United Kingdom. This scarce information can be supplemented with item-by-item analysis of the available evidence on physical measures (e.g. the number of tractors, the extension of irrigated land). Such an analysis highlights four different patterns:

(a) In the Western Settlement countries, the initial capital stock was small, but grew fast during nineteenth- and twentieth-century settlement. After a (relative) lull, investments boomed from the 1930s after the start of rapid mechanization.

(b) The advanced, long-settled countries of Western Europe traditionally had a very substantial capital stock in building and land reclamation. Thus, it grew decidedly slower than in the Western Settlement countries until World War II, and boomed afterwards.

(c) In the "backward" long-settled countries, most notably China, the capital stock around the year 1800 was quite large, possibly even greater than in Europe, because rice-growing needed irrigation. It grew very slowly or did not grow at all until quite recently and then boomed, with the intensive use not only of fertilizers but also of machinery.

(d) In "backward" unsettled countries (i.e. Africa), the capital stock was initially minimal, and, with few exceptions in the production of cash crops for exports, it grew as much as population until World War II. Since 1950, the per capita stock of capital has increased, but much less than in Asia.

To summarize, all inputs have been growing throughout the whole period, but there is evidence of a slowdown after 1950, at least for labor and land. It seems highly unlikely that the acceleration in the growth of capital stock was

Table 3.3. *Change in total factor productivity before World War II*

	Before 1870		1870–1910		1910–1940	
	Number countries	Average rate	Number countries	Average rate	Number countries	Average rate
Europe	5	0.30	13	0.65	11	1.00
Europe (Van Zanden)			15	0.78		
Western Settlement*	1	0.40	2	0.74	2	0.56
Asia			3	1.24	6	0.08
Africa	1	3.41	1	0.83	1	−0.21
South America			1	−1.90	2	1.57

Sources: Van Zanden 1991; Federico 2005 Statistical Appendix Table IV; and Lains and Pinilla 2009.
*United States and Canada

large enough to compensate it. Therefore, the increase in inputs cannot account for the sharp acceleration in the growth of output after 1950.

How it was achieved: intensive growth

The conclusion of the last section implies that, at least after 1950, if not earlier, a substantial part of output growth reflects a more efficient use of existing inputs, or an increase in Total Factor Productivity (TFP). Table 3.3 uses the estimates available for the period up to 1938, as continent-wide averages.

Two stylized facts stand out. First and foremost, TFP grew in the overwhelming majority of countries/periods. The rates may seem low, but any growth is, by itself, a major break from the (alleged) stagnation of traditional agriculture. Furthermore, a low rate would deliver a substantial increase, if sustained for long enough: in forty years, a 0.5 percent yearly growth augments TFP by a quarter. Second, productivity growth has accelerated over time, at least in Western Europe and the United States, while performance elsewhere is more diversified. Productivity even decreased in Egypt, the Philippines, and the Soviet Union. The data are much more abundant after World War II, with literally hundreds of country estimates. It is possible to compute a "world" TFP growth, considering total world output and input for the period from 1960 to 2000 with the FAO data, using livestock and machinery as proxies for capital. Results differ slightly according to the method of computation, but vary between 1 percent and 1.25 percent per annum, corresponding to a 50 or 66 percent increase over forty years. An unweighted average of the country estimates for the post-World War II period comes out decidedly lower – "only" 0.7 percent. The figure is reduced by the very poor performance for most African and Socialist countries, which account for a tiny share of world output. In contrast, TFP growth was particularly fast in the advanced countries and in China. On average, growth in OECD countries was around 2 percent, double the prewar rate, confirming the acceleration already detected in interwar years. China's productivity had been stagnant or even negative under the Socialist system, and jumped to a 5–6 percent yearly rate of growth in the first half of the 1980s, only to slow down toward the end of the decade and in the 1990s. Contrary to widespread fears, there is no evidence of a slowdown in TFP growth in the late 1990s and early 2000s (Fuglie 2008).

TFP is often assumed to depend only on technology, but this is not necessarily true. It can grow (or decline), even without any technical change if resources are allocated more (or less) efficiently. Advanced statistical techniques can estimate separately pure technical progress (more precisely, the rate of shift of the technological frontier which describes the maximum feasible TFP given the factor endowment) and the change in efficiency (technically, changes in the distance between the frontier and the actual TFP). A negative value implies that the country is losing ground relative to its potential because it is not using its resources efficiently. This can happen if its institutions are not suitable or if it adopts the wrong policies, and these techniques do, indeed, sometimes return very negative figures, which depress the overall average.

We will discuss institutions and policies in the next sections. Here, we will focus on technical progress – i.e. on the development and adoption of innovations. We will not go into technical details – even a short description of the most important agricultural innovations would take several pages. Suffice to state that they can be classified in four main groups: new practices of cultivation; new plants and animals; chemical products (mostly fertilizers); and machines. The first three categories aimed mainly at increasing the productivity of land – i.e. at exploiting it more intensively. The change in practices of cultivation reduced the length of rest periods, the traditional method to restore soil fertility. In traditional agriculture, it ranged from twenty to thirty years in the most primitive slash-and-burn agriculture to one year out of two or three in Western Europe. Continuous cultivation without rest was possible only with irrigation – i.e. in few areas of Europe and in the rice-producing areas of China. Since the eighteenth century, European farmers started to substitute rest with soil-enriching plants (legumes and different types of grass) which served to feed humans and animals. However, plants had to be cultivated according to a specific sequence (rotation), constraining the farmers' choice of crops and thus reducing their capability to respond to changing demand. Further productivity gains could be achieved by using better varieties of plants or using artificial fertilizers, which became available from the mid nineteenth century. In advanced countries, their consumption increased steadily from the 1880s to a peak around 1980, and stagnated thereafter, while in LDCs it boomed from the 1950s. The very intensive use of artificial fertilizers makes it possible to grow rice up to three times a year in some areas of South and East Asia. The twentieth century also featured an impressive increase in the range of available varieties of plants or cultivars. In traditional agriculture, new cultivars could be obtained only via chance discovery or via imports from other areas. Transfers had been a major source of new varieties in the Age of Explorations, but by the late nineteenth century the pool of transferrable varieties was largely exhausted. New cultivars could be produced by hybridizing existing ones, but the first attempts were unsuccessful. Efficient techniques were developed only at the beginning of the twentieth century, after the (re-)discovery of the laws of genetics. Their first major success was the development of hybrid corn, which was adopted rapidly in the 1930s in the American Corn Belt. However, the epoch-making change was the production of new cultivars for cereals suitable for LDCs. Their adoption from the late-1950s boosted yields so much that they became known as High-Yielding-Varieties and their adoption during the Green Revolution. The fourth category of innovation, mechanization, differs as it aims mostly at increasing the productivity of labor. The tools for cultivation, such as the plow, had been improved in the early nineteenth century, and the first machine, the reaper, had been invented in 1843. However, the impact of these innovations was limited by the lack of a power source suitable for field cultivation. Thus, the mechanization of agriculture had to wait for the development of tractors powered by internal combustion engines at the beginning of the twentieth century. They were adopted quickly in the United States in the late-1920s and 1930s, in other advanced countries in the 1950s and 1960s, and in the rest of the world from the 1970s.

How can we explain differences in the rate of the adoption of innovations which account for most of the differences in rates of TFP among countries? As a general rule, adoption of innovations depends on the level of the development of the country and on its factor endowment. In general, the more the innovation saves on the scarce factor and uses the abundant factor intensively, the more likely its adoption becomes. With the possible exception of rotation, all the new techniques needed additional investments relative to traditional technologies, and thus they were not suitable for LDCs, where capital is scarce and the financial institutions to channel it to farmers are often not very effective (see "Financing agriculture, formally and informally," below). But factor endowment affected adoption also in capital-abundant advanced countries. Land is (or used to be) scarcer in Europe than in the countries of Western Settlement, where labor was the scarce factor. Thus, one would also expect Europe to be at the forefront of the adoption of fertilizers and new varieties of plants, and the Western Settlement countries to pioneer mechanization. Indeed, this was the case. The differences in the patterns of the adoption of new technologies between Europe and the United States were huge before World War II and, although somewhat smaller now, they are still sizeable. In a controversial book, Hayami and Ruttan (1985) go a step further to argue that factor endowments affect not only the adoption of innovations but also their production. Land-scarce countries invest more in research on land-saving innovations, and vice versa. However, Olmstead and Rhode (2008) disagree. They argue that, until World War II, the United States spent more on land-saving innovations than on labor-saving mechanical technologies, mostly to stave off the threat of new pests and diseases.

The level of development and factor intensity affect innovations in all sectors, but technical progress in agriculture has been shaped by three peculiarities to the sector.

(i) The productivity of plants in each given area depends on the environment – or, more precisely, on the difference between its ideal conditions (soil, rainfall, temperature, etc.) and those prevailing in the area. Olmstead and Rhode (2008) supply a lot of examples of environmental sensitivity, but the most striking is the case of wheat varieties in the United States. The varieties suitable for the East Coast could resist the climate of the northern states of the Great Plains, which became a world grain basket with varieties imported from Russia. This sensitivity implies that the adoption of a new plant or cultivar needs a lot of location-specific R&D. Selecting the best seed variety for North Dakota needs the testing of dozens or hundreds of cultivars in that specific environment, an expensive and time-consuming task conducted by specialized personnel in experimental stations. The same reasoning holds true for the right mixture of fertilizers, the ideal rotation, and so on.

(ii) Many so-called biological innovations are not fully appropriable – i.e. the inventors may not be able to obtain full returns from their investments in R&D. Fertilizers and machines are highly appropriable because they are difficult to replicate (only few firms can produce tractors) and can be patented. In contrast, any farmer can imitate the successful rotation of his neighbor, and produce as many seeds of a new natural variety as he wants from a single seed. The production of hybrid seeds does need scientific capabilities, which, however, can be built with very modest investments. Thus, investments in R&D in biological innovation would remain below the socially optimal level and technical progress would be slower than was feasible.

(iii) Last, but not least, the relation between factor intensity and the adoption of innovations is more complex than the simple model sketched above, for two reasons. First, the classification of innovations by factor intensity is less straightforward than it seems. Each innovation needs a combination of factors, rather than just one, and these need to be changed over time. Fertilizers required more labor when they had to be spread by hand, and early machines required land to feed the horses which pulled them. In both cases, the factor requirements change as a result of further innovations (the tractor, machines to spread fertilizers). Second, agricultural innovations are often complementary or interrelated – i.e. they only work if they are adopted together. The classic case is the high-yielding varieties, which do boost yields, but only if supported by very abundant supply of fertilizers and water. The failure to detect complementarities may cause farmers to discard potentially useful innovations and thus hamper technical progress. But detecting complementarities needs systematic location-specific testing.

The evidence from these two sections boils down to a simple conclusion: in the nineteenth century, agricultural production increased mainly thanks to more inputs, while efficiency growth, although not negligible, contributed relatively little. Its role progressively increased in the twentieth century, and will continue to grow. Arguably, in the future, efficiency growth will be the sole source of increase in agricultural production.

Modern property rights: an indispensable precondition?

Agriculture provides a lot of evidence to support the economists' belief in the superiority of private property rights over traditional ones (De Soto 2000). Full ownership of land, including the crucial right to sell and bequeath, prevents excessive exploitation of land for short-term gains (the so-called tragedy of the commons), stimulates location-specific investments in land improvements, irrigation, farm buildings, and tree crops, makes the reallocation of manpower within the sector and across sectors easier, and offers farmers collateral when seeking loans for farm investment.

By 1800, modern property rights on land existed only in Western Europe, in the already settled areas in the countries of Western Settlement, and in some areas in Asia, including most of China (Kishimoto 2011; Pomeranz 2008). In some areas, most notably Eastern Europe and parts of India, feudal lords or other powerful individuals had the right to claim a part of the product and/or workers' labor time (*corvée*). In many others, land was commonly owned by those who worked it. Even in Western Europe, village communities owned most forests and large swathes of arable land. The most primitive users, such as native Americans, hunted or gathered collectively, but, in most cases, land was allocated to households, who had exclusive rights to cultivation for a given period of time. The period could be very short, as in primitive slash-and-burn African agricultural systems, or fairly long, as in Russia after the 1861 emancipation of the serfs, but, at least in principle, at the end of the period the land was redistributed within the community. Furthermore, the community maintained some sort of control over agricultural practices, which often included the right to part of the product like the right to graze animals on land at rest. This control is said to have stifled technical progress, preventing innovative farmers from experimenting with new techniques. In this narrative, the prevalence of traditional rights explains, at least in part, the stagnation and backwardness in traditional agriculture, and suggests that property rights are an essential precondition for productivity growth.

There is no doubt that over the last two centuries property rights underwent a process of modernization, which, nonetheless, was slow, far from linear, and is not yet fully completed. The feudal systems of eastern Europe were the first to disappear, in the first half of the nineteenth century. The land was divided between the peasants (the former serfs) and the former landlords, who often also got financial compensation. The terms of the deal were particularly generous for the Prussian *Junkers*, who received substantial compensation *and* half of the land, and who then proceeded to hire former serfs as wage workers. In Russia, former serfs obtained about four-fifths of their holdings, but the ownership of land was transferred to the village (*obshchina* or commune) rather than to individual households. The Emancipation Act greatly improved the conditions of the former serfs, but it was not intended to extend modern property rights to peasant land. From this point of view, the Stolypin reform was a decisive step following the 1905 Revolution. The reform entitled peasants to reclaim the full ownership of the land which they culti-vated or to dissolve the commune altogether (with a two-thirds majority). However, farmers showed little enthusiasm for modern property rights: in 1916, only a quarter of them, with 15 percent of the land, had opted out from the commune. In many other countries, including Turkey and Indonesia, customary, albeit uncertain, rights to cultivation were gradually transformed into full ownership. The process was typically gradual and, in some cases, it occurred in steps stretching over long periods. For instance, the Turkish land code of 1858 recognized the hereditary usufruct to peasants for the land that they cultivated, but the right to sell was only granted to them in the 1940s.

The transition from traditional rights to full ownership was much less smooth when the ruling elite was not a native one. The Mexican landlords, mostly of Spanish descent, exploited the *Leyes de desamorticizacion* (1856) in order to seize most of the communal land and to reduce the native peasants to the status of workers in their *haciendas*. The European conquerors regarded the hunting grounds of the native American tribes or the African savannahs resting under a slash-and-burn system as idle land, which they could seize at will, ignoring the rights of the natives. The pattern of expropriation depended on the prospective European settlers' demand for land. The temperate climate of the overseas regions attracted many European settlers and thus the author-ities seized almost all the land, confining the natives to reservations. The method of distribution to farmers differed among countries and also within each country. For instance, in the United States, about 30 percent of the land was sold to farmers, 30 percent was granted to railway companies, which then sold it to prospective farmers in order to fund the cost of building the intercontinental lines, and the rest was distributed for free to anyone who promised to farm it (the so-called homesteads). In most tropical countries of Asia and sub-Saharan Africa, the demand by Europeans was comparatively modest and thus the natives continued to hold most land under traditional property rights. The colonial administrations started to register the ownership of individual farmers ("titling") in the 1940s, and the process has continued since then, with strong support from international organizations such as the World Bank. In 1990, according to the World census of agriculture, tribal land accounted for only 0.34 percent of the worldwide total, but still accounted for 14 percent of African land.

The forward march of modern property rights featured some notable reversals, which coincided with the victory of peasant revolutionary movements. In Mexico, from 1920 to 1964, about half of the total land was expropriated and transferred back to village communities (*eijidos*). After the revolution, the Russian Bolsheviks seized all the remaining estates,redistributing the land to cultivators. Eventually, in 1930, they went on to expropriate the land from the farmers and set up giant collective farms. The ensuing disruption of production and the repression of the peasants' opposition caused terrible famines with millions of deaths. The experience did not prevent the Soviet Union from imposing collective ownership in (most) countries of Eastern Europe after World War II, and the Chinese communists imitated the Soviet example at the beginning of its Great Leap Forward in 1958. In the long term, collective agriculture proved highly inefficient. It combined the monitoring problems of large-scale capitalist farming (see the next section, below), worsened by the prohibition of monetary incentives, with the defects of the central planning typical of the socialist system. Production increased only thanks to huge increases in the use of inputs – most notably fertilizers. The return to the market-based system has been long and, arguably, is not yet completed. After some local experiments, China returned to family farming (under the appropriately bureaucratic label of Household Responsibility System or HRS) nationwide in 1979–1980 and slowly liberalized the markets of agricultural products in the 1980s, finally abolishing all residual planning in 1992. However, farming households are still formally long-term tenants of state-owned land which they cannot sell (although they can sub-let or bequeath). The abolition of collective ownership in former socialist countries after 1992 offers a full range of solutions, from full privatization in Poland and Czechoslovakia, to the permanence of collective farming in Belarus.

How much are the expectations about the positive benefit of private property rights supported by evidence? China is the most impressive success story. The return to family farming in the 1980s was followed by a spectacular increase in TFP (see the previous section, above). However, in many other cases, including the former socialist countries in Europe, the benefits from the adoption of private property rights have been much less impressive. Some econometric estimates fail to detect any positive effect from titling, and in most cases the gains are not as large as expected. As argued by Deininger and Jin (2006), in some cases, the results may reflect the difficulty of designing a proper test, but in others the benefits might have been really small, because traditional rights were fairly efficient. For instance, scholars once deemed that the private enclosure of the remaining common land in Europe was a precondition for the adoption of modern rotation systems and releasing a workforce for the cities. Enclosures are no longer reckoned as important for the industrial revolution in England, but Olsson and Svensson (2010) find evidence of a positive effect of enclosures on output in South Sweden. Gerschenkron (1966) argued that common ownership was one of the major causes of Russian backwardness in the nineteenth century and thus ultimately of the Bolshevik Revolution. In his view, the Stoplyin reform was too little too late. In contrast, Gregory (1994) claimed that, in practice, peasants could easily circumvent the rules of the commune. Neither author based his argument upon quantitative evidence, which is provided by Nafziger (2010). He shows that factor markets existed and that households used them to react to shocks, such as a sudden death. However, the commune rules were not as irrelevant as posited by Gregory, as they slowed down the adjustment. Clearly, this result holds true only for the Moscow region. But it highlights a more general point: Traditional rights and modern private property are generic labels, which may conceal substantial differences. The latter are surely superior on paper, but, in many cases, farmers found ways to circumvent the shortcomings of traditional rights.

The capitalist organization of production in agriculture: a dead end

The diffusion of the factory system has been one of the pivotal innovations of the industrial revolution. Its agricultural counterpart was the "capitalist" farm – i.e. a large farm cultivated by wage workers and managed by the landlord or by tenants. Wage workers were, and still are, widely employed in agriculture as an additional source of labor, especially at harvest time. But a farm should be labeled as "capitalist" only if wage workers account for most of its permanent labor force. These farms were already widely diffused in the grain-producing southeast of England by the early eighteenth century, and spread throughout the rest of the country in the following decades, becoming the prevalent form of agricultural organization by 1851 (Shaw-Taylor 2012). Elsewhere in Europe, "capitalist" farms were quite rare and concentrated in certain areas, such as the Po valley in Italy, east of the river Elbe in Germany, and in some French wine-producing areas like Bordeaux. Large estates cultivated by wage workers (*latifundia*) did exist in South America and in the Mediterranean, but they are seldom classified as "capitalist," because they are deemed too technically backward (see Salvucci, Chapter 13 in Volume 1). It was assumed they could compete on the world market only by ruthlessly exploiting workers, who were shackled by quasi-feudal relationships. Thus, by 1850, the consensus view deemed "capitalist" agriculture almost exclusively a

British feature. But, by then, even the modern factory system was almost exclusively a British feature. Thus, Marxists predicted that England was leading both Europe and the world towards a new age of industrial agriculture, in which "capitalist" farms would match industrial companies in size, out-competing the inefficient family farms and the traditional *latifundia*.

Anyone with even a modest knowledge of world agriculture knows that the Marxist prediction has not materialized. However, proving this claim is less easy than it seems, because there are no data on the share of "capitalist" farms and its change in time. Many states had started to collect information on the size and management of farms in the nineteenth century, and the FAO has summarized this information in a series of censuses of world agriculture since 1930. Unfortunately, the country coverage differs from one census to another, and, above all, the censuses do not single out "capitalist" farms. They distinguish between tribal land, tenanted (i.e. rented-out) farms, and owner-operated farms, which accounted for about two-thirds of total acreage in 1950 and for three-quarters in the year 2000 (Federico 2006). This category also includes "capitalist" farms, which were bigger, *ceteris paribus*, than family farms. Thus, one would expect that their diffusion caused an increase in the average size of farm. But according to the censuses, from 1950 to 1990, farm size declined by 40 percent in Asia, where it had been quite small from the beginning, and by 30 percent in Latin America. The average acreage rose by 20 percent in Europe and more than doubled in North America. In theory, this increase might reflect the diffusion of "capitalist" farms, but this hypothesis is not confirmed by the situation of the United States, which, arguably, has the most advanced agriculture in the world. The 2007 agricultural census (US Department of Agriculture 2007, Table 64) distinguishes seven categories of family farms (ranging from "limited resources farms" to "very large" ones) from "non-family" farms (i.e. farms owned by a corporation). The latter accounted for about a fifth of the total sales, but hired – on average – only three permanent workers, and in any case about 90 percent of them were owned by a family. If one adds the "very large family farms" (with sales in excess of 1 million dollars and – on average – four permanent workers), the share on the total sales of the largest farms increases to 75 percent. They were substantial businesses compared to the peasant farms of traditional agriculture, but were still puny in relation to the whole agricultural sector. Only 5,584 farms (of any category) sold more than $5 million of produce, with an average of $14.9 million, a sum equivalent to 0.05 percent of the total sales of agricultural products.

Summing up, the evidence strongly suggests that large-scale "capitalist" farms have always been a rather marginal organization of agricultural production, and, if anything, that their worldwide share has been declining in the twentieth century. One might object that the data on acreage from world censuses undervalue the share of "capitalist" farms, and their growth over time, if they were more productive than other categories of farms. This assumption underlay the nineteenth-century views about their superiority, but it is not confirmed by the evidence. Gross output per acre is either not related to, or is inversely related to, farm size. Furthermore, the American data refer to sales, not to acreage. The substantial failure of the "capitalist" organization of production is a peculiarity of agriculture, which must be explained somehow. The simplest explanation of the success of family farming is that of state intervention. In the twentieth century, large farms, and, above all, the *latifundia*, did not enjoy a good reputation for ideological and political reasons. "The land to the tiller" had been a strong rallying cry for popular protest from the late nineteenth century and the success of the Mexican and, above all, the Russian Revolutions made this claim plausible. After the end of World War I, many newly established governments in eastern Europe implemented land reforms to gain consensus from their populations and to reduce the appeal of the Russian example (Jorgensen 2006). A similar fear of revolutionary contagion from communist China inspired land reform in Asia and in other developing countries after World War II. King (1977) lists twenty-three major land reforms before 1975. But the drive to reform was not confined to poor countries under threat of revolution. In Europe, the extension of the franchise to tenants and agricultural workers from the nineteenth century onward had gradually tilted the balance of political power away from landowning aristocracy. Some countries, such as Italy, forcibly divided the *latifundia*, while others, including the United Kingdom, forced landlords to sell their estates by imposing very high inheritance taxes or by capping agricultural rents in periods of high inflation (Swinnen 2002).

However, state intervention is only, at best, a partial explanation of the success of family farming. A reform could transfer land to tillers, but it could not ensure the long-term survival of household farms in a competitive market if they were not economically viable. In some cases, reform policies backfired as new farmers lost their land and their farms were consolidated in large units. In other cases, they survived barely, and only thanks to state subsidies. But, in most cases, family farms survived and prospered without much help from the state. The reason for their success can be summed up in one sentence: The cost of monitoring workers in "capitalist" farms exceeded the benefits of large-scale cultivation and economies of scale.

Monitoring workers is expensive in all sectors, but it is especially costly in agriculture for two reasons. First, agricultural workers are scattered across fields rather than concentrated under the same roof. Second, the damages from sloppy work in some tasks (e.g. pruning) can be serious, long-lasting, and, above all, difficult to detect in the short run. A careless worker could blame natural factors rather than his own shortcomings. In fact, wage workers were traditionally used for harvesting, a task which is concentrated in time and space, and is comparatively easy to monitor. But, for most operations, the best possible effort can be extracted only by giving workers a claim to part of the product. This condition is met by definition when farmers own the land, as they are the sole claimants of the product, net of taxes, and have a long-term commitment to the farm. Otherwise, the (non-cultivating) owner and the farming household have to enter into a suitable tenancy agreement. It is fairly easy to interest the worker in maximizing output, either by offering him a share of the total production (sharecropping) or the whole of the production, net of a predetermined sum (fixed-rent tenancy). It is more difficult to design an agreement which prevents a tenant from increasing production in the short run at the expense of the long-run value of the farm, and, at the same time, compensates him for his investments in the farm. Indeed, agriculture features an amazing variety of contracts, which some of the best minds in agricultural economics have examined in order to detect evidence of inefficiency and/or exploitation. The literature on sharecropping is huge and it is impossible to discuss here. Suffice it to stress that the combined evidence on farm size and type of tenure shows that renting land to farming households (tenanted family farms) has been the second most diffused form of organization of agricultural production, after family-owned farming. Thus, these contracts, although imperfect, have proven to be more efficient than individual contracts between the worker(s) and the manager/owner of the "capitalist" farm.

In industry, large factories are much more efficient than workshops (Allen, Chapter 2 in this volume), but this is not the case in agriculture. Almost all land-saving innovations (seeds, fertilizers, and new rotations) are scale-neutral – i.e. they work as well on a small farm as on a huge estate. In contrast, most agricultural machines are profitable only if the scale of production (e.g. the extension of fields to be harvested for a combine) exceeds a minimum threshold. In a famous and very controversial paper, David (1971) argued that, in the 1840s and 1850s, many American farms did not mechanize harvesting because the acreage to harvest did not reach the minimum to justify purchasing a reaper. In more recent years, a number of authors have investigated the existence of similar threshold effects for the adoption of tractors in the United

States and in other advanced countries (e.g Duffy-Martini and Silberberg 2006). Their approach and results differ, but, by and large, they do not show that the small size of farms was a major hindrance to mechanization. In the short run, farmers successfully tackled the problem by purchasing the machinery collectively or by renting it from specialized suppliers (contract labor). In the long run, the need for mechanization was one of the causes of the increase in farm size in OECD countries, alongside emigration to cities, the retirement of old farmers, and, in some cases, subsidies aimed at consolidating farms (most notably, the so-called structural policies of the European Union). However it is looked at, the optimal size of a fully mechanized farm remains very small when compared with the optimal size of plants in scale-intensive industries such as car making.

The statement holds true for fieldwork and, with some qualifications, for livestock rearing, but not for the processing of agricultural products. It is essentially an industrial operation and thus benefitted from scale-intensive technical progress from the nineteenth century onwards. The introduction of steam-powered machines reduced costs and, in some cases, such as wine making or cocoon reeling, improved the quality of the final product. However, it required far-reaching institutional changes in the organization of world agriculture. Only a few estates produced enough to operate modern machinery profitably. This was the case of the Cuban sugar estates, some of which built internal railways in order to transport the cane quickly, which must be crushed within a few hours of harvesting (Dye 1998). In the nineteenth century, the top-quality Bordeaux vineries purchased vineyards and rehired the former owners as workers with generous long-term contracts (Simpson 2012). They deemed that the control of all stages of the production process was necessary to produce a high-quality wine. However, these were exceptions; in the overwhelming majority of cases, the gains from economies of scale in processing were insufficient to overcome the transaction costs for concentration and the losses from insufficient monitoring. The minimum amount of product to be processed was reached either by selling products before processing, rather than selling processed products – for example, grapes rather than wine – or by setting up cooperatives of producers.

Selling on the market is a perfectly adequate solution if the quality of the product can be easily assessed *ex ante*. European farmers have sold cereals on the market and outsourced milling for their domestic consumption since the Middle Ages. This solution does not work well for perishable products because of coordination problems: good-quality milk or grapes are indispensable for producing good butter or wine, but checking their quality *ex ante* was (and still is) very difficult and too time-consuming. On the other hand, producing good-quality milk or grapes needs investments (e.g. in a herd of pure-bred cows), which farmers would undertake only if the processing firm credibly committed itself to recognize a premium for the quality of the product. This problem can be solved by signing a long-term supply contract between farmers and processing firms: The latter commit to purchasing the whole production, providing that it meets some predetermined quality standards, and to supply technical advice, seeds, and such. These contracts have been spreading in many advanced countries: in 2007, they accounted for about a sixth of total sales in the United States. However, this solution implies sizeable transaction costs, and needs efficient court systems to settle disputes. Furthermore, farmers may harbor a mistrust of the monopsonistic power of buyers (see "The benign state," below). Thus, the most popular solution to the coordination problem has been processing by farmers' cooperatives.

The first farmers' cooperatives date to the early nineteenth century, but the key institutional innovations were first adopted by Danish milk producers in the 1880s. The proximate cause was the invention of a machine to produce milk, the (centrifugal) cream separator, which, according to a recent estimate, was 10–20 percent more efficient than the traditional one (Henriksen, Lampe, and Sharp 2011). The members pledged to confer their entire production of milk to the cooperative, which could reject it if the quality was not up to standard. The very existence of a cooperative in a given area prevented the establishment of industrial companies, and the lack of an alternative outlet forced farmers to supply high-quality milk and not to cheat. On the other hand, the farmers shared the profits from the cooperative, and they were sure to earn full returns from their investments in pure-bred cows. Cooperative creameries were an instant success in Denmark. In a few years, their brand (Danish butter) became a household name, and the country became Europe's main exporter of butter, outcompeting Ireland on the British market. The Irish producers adopted the Danish cooperative model only belatedly and partially. Recent research explains this failure with the low density of cows within a feasible range (i.e. the insufficient supply of milk), the low share of medium-sized farms, and the intensity of social conflict (O'Rourke 2007). In the early twentieth century, the Danish model was adopted, albeit with some delay and less successfully, in the production of wine, meat products, and also fruit and vegetables. In the latter case, cooperatives select, package, and sell the product under their own brand (e.g. *Sunkist* in the United States). At the end of the twentieth century, cooperatives accounted for about half of total sales of milk in the European Union (up to 94 percent in Denmark) and for high shares of fruit and vegetables.

In the United States, the total sales of cooperatives increased eightfold in real terms from 1915 to 2002, up to 35–45 percent of gross output. Production cooperatives were much less successful in LDCs, where they are most needed, in spite of the official support from many governments. The literature quotes a long list of the potential causes for this failure: a high share of non-perishable, homogeneous goods on total output; the vulnerability to production shocks without outside relief; a high level of social and political conflict; and, last, but not least, the endowment of social capital (Beltran Tapia 2012). The importance of each of these factors should be assessed case by case.

Financing agriculture, formally and informally

In traditional agriculture, farmers needed credit mainly to fund their own consumption. Many of them needed short-term loans to bridge the period before the crop, and most of them needed long-term loans to avoid starving when crops failed, as public support was very often unavailable, except for the odd instance of "parish relief." The modernization of agriculture has changed, but it has not diminished the demand for credit. The increase in the wealth of farmers and the availability of national and international relief have greatly reduced the demand for distress credit, but technical progress has created new financial needs for the short term, to purchase fertilizers, and for the long term, to purchase machinery. In theory, agriculture should have benefitted hand-somely from the development of banks, insurance companies, and other credit institutions. In practice, the benefits have been reduced by a massive problem of asymmetric information, which plagues agriculture (Banerjee and Duflo 2011). As stated in the previous section, output, and thus the capacity to repay loans, also depends on circumstances that lie beyond the farmers' control, such as weather and prices. Thus, an unscrupulous borrower could cheat. Collecting the necessary information to check trustworthy clients is so expensive as to make lending non-profitable for a bank. It could reduce its risks by asking for real assets as collateral, but this option is available only to farmers with fully developed property rights. Thus, it excludes not only peasants with traditional rights but also tenants (if they are not backed by their landowner). Furthermore, a town bank might find the prospect of repossessing and managing a family farm rather unappealing, especially in years of generalized agricultural crisis. As a result, banks and other formal financial institutions would lend freely only to those who could pledge substantial and easily sellable assets – i.e. only to wealthy land-owners. Consequently, these institutions accounted for a very small share of total credit to agriculture in traditional agricultural societies – e.g. a mere

2.5 percent in China in the 1930s. Most farmers had to resort to informal lenders – landowners, community moneylenders, traders, and so on, who sometimes borrowed capital from "formal" institutions, gaining handsome profits from this intermediation. As late as 1970, according to an extensive survey by the World Bank, "informal" sources accounted for between 60 and 70 percent of total loans in Asia, the Middle East, and Africa. The "informal" lenders had much better information about the trustworthiness of each farmer and thus could discriminate among their clients. Hard evidence on the rates of interest they charged is scarce, but figures in excess of 100 percent per year are not uncommon. These rates have earned "informal" lenders a solid reputation as loan sharks, who ruthlessly exploited poor peasants. Ransom and Sutch (1977), in a famous book about the American South after the Civil War, argued that shopkeepers enjoyed a monopoly power as the only providers of credit and that they used it to put a "financial squeeze" on former slaves, thereby preventing them from escaping from abject poverty. The existence of such a monopoly is controversial, and, in a more general vein, high rates are not sufficient evidence of exploitation. Lending to peasants is very risky. They have little to pledge and are subject to the same idiosyncratic shocks, so an informal local lender had very little chance to diversify his portfolio. However, whatever their cause, high interest rates must have suppressed investments and technical progress.

The total amount of formal credit has been increasing, and it is likely that it has substituted, at least in part, for informal credit. In India, the share of formal in total credit rose from 7 percent in 1950 to 25 percent in 1970 and to 60 percent in 1981. This rise is a consequence of the growth of agriculture and also of the diffusion of farm ownership, but it has undoubtedly been helped by official support. From the late nineteenth century, governments set up institutions for both short-term and (especially) long-term credit to farmers, and the number of such institutions boomed after World War II. They proved to be quite effective in channeling funds to rural areas, although at high cost. Commercial, state-backed institutions have been plagued by a very high rate of default. Farmers' organizations have been more successful. Credit cooperatives had a long tradition in advanced countries, as the first such institutions had been established in Germany in the 1850s and 1860s. Since then, they have spread quite widely, although less than producer cooperatives. In contrast, their growth in LDCs has been rather disappointing, at least until the recent success of micro-finance (the so-called Grameen banks). The advantage of cooperative credit over "formal" institutions is clear: farmers in a village know each other well and thus they can assess the credit risk of other farmers in the same village much better than a bank clerk from the city. On the other hand, local credit cooperatives are highly vulnerable to shocks. If all members are stricken by the same shock like a drought, the cooperative can survive only with the help of outside lenders. Indeed, since the beginning of the movement, credit cooperatives have established regional and national organizations for mutual support. In more recent times, these private organizations have been given formal guarantees by governments.

The benign state: consumer protection and agricultural research support

Several of the new tasks which states have taken on in mature capitalist systems have deeply affected the development of agriculture. In this section, we will focus on three fields: consumer protection; competition policy; and the support given to scientific research.

The rulers of most advanced preindustrial societies had been protecting urban consumers well before the development of modern capitalism, albeit largely out of self-interest. In fact, they feared food riots and thus tried to guarantee city dwellers a supply of staple foods at reasonable prices. The Chinese emperors of the Qing dynasty set up an extensive network of state and local granaries (Will and Wong 1991). In Europe, central states and local authorities resorted to a wide range of measures – licensing markets or prohibiting them altogether, purchasing and selling grain on behalf of the city, setting quality standards and prices for bread and other foods. These pre-modern regulations disappeared in the nineteenth century. In Europe, they were discredited by the stinging criticism of the Enlightenment writers, and were slowly phased out in the second half of the eighteenth century and in the first decades of the nineteenth (Miller 1999; Persson 1999). In the same period, the increasing shortage of funds jeopardized the operation of Chinese granaries, which were indefinitely shut after the Taiping Revolt of the 1860s. The need for the protection of urban consumers resurfaced in the nineteenth century because slow transportation, insufficient preservation of perishables, and widespread fraud caused the quality of food to deteriorate, endangering public health. The United States approved a law to set minimum standards for the quality of milk as early as 1856, and passed the comprehensive Meat Inspection and Food and Drug Act(s) in 1906. These health regulations did not directly affect farmers, who, as a rule, sold milk and livestock in good condition. They could benefit indirectly, to the extent that a decline in the risk of adulteration increased demand and sales of agricultural fresh food.

Furthermore, producers could benefit directly from the extension of laws against fraud to their inputs, such as the acts against the adulteration of seeds in 1869 and of fertilizers in 1894 in the United Kingdom.

Since the market share of individual farms has always been negligible, agriculture has never been directly affected by anti-trust legislation. If anything, they asked the government to tame competition in product markets. They also asked for help in their struggle against the alleged monopsonist power of the processing firms, merchants, and railways as well as the monopolist power of producers over inputs like fertilizers and storage. To this aim, they lobbied and, in some cases, they entered into the political arena directly. Farmers were the main supporters of the People's Party in the United States, which, in the 1890s, asked for governmental control of railways. It failed, but farmers' interests remained strong both during the Progressive Era and beyond. In 1922, it succeeded in getting Congress to approve the Capper-Volstead Act, which exempted agricultural cooperatives from the anti-trust law. The French wine producers pioneered a different approach, which was to become very popular in Western Europe. In 1889, the Champagne *vignerons* obtained the right to reserve the name of *Champagne* for wines produced in the area (*appellation d'origine contrôlée*), and, in 1904–1905, this right was limited to those produced with local grapes (Simpson 2012). This exclusion was upheld by a British court in 1958–9, extending the protection for the first time outside the French borders. Geographical labeling is now also granted to products other than wine, and the rights of holders are actively defended by the European Union. The anticompetitive nature of the Capper-Volstead Act is obvious, while the effect of geographic labeling is more complex. It clearly reduces competition, as it prevents the producers of other areas from exploiting a successful brand name, but it gives consumers additional information about the designation of origin and hence the quality of the product.

Investment in R&D has been central to the state support of the agricultural sector in the twentieth century. The need to supplement private – for profit – investment in non-appropriable biological innovations had been clear for a long time, and some enlightened landlords tried to help. Gilbert and Boussingault decided to use their own estates at Rothamsted in England (1843) and Bechelbrom in France (1834) as experimental stations. Less unselfish landowners contributed by setting up learned societies, such as the *Académie d'Agriculture de France* (established, with a different name in 1761) or the "Royal Agricultural Society of England" (1838). These societies played an important and useful role, especially in diffusing knowledge about innovations, but their efforts were hindered by a typical freeriding problem: Why should a landlord commit time and money to organize field trials if he could obtain the information from the trials organized by someone else? This freeriding problem did not affect the American Ford and Rockefeller foundations, which funded the initial research in High Yielding Varieties in Mexico in the 1940s. However, their financial resources were limited. The real leap forward required the intervention of the public purse. Governments funded the agricultural R&D research indirectly via universities, and directly by setting up agricultural stations. The first one was established in Mockern (Saxony) in 1851, and, in the second half of the century, the United States and most European countries, with the notable exception of the United Kingdom, set up extensive networks of stations. Research in tropical agriculture started later, at the turn of the century, and was initially limited to cash crops for exports (cocoa and rubber). The research in food crops took off after World War II, following the early success of privately funded research. Since the 1950s, foreign aid donors and local governments have funded area- and product-specific stations, like CIMMYT in Mexico for wheat and IRRI in the Philippines for rice. The total investment in agricultural R&D was substantial. In the United States, it increased from $2 million (1993) in 1889, equivalent to 0.03 percent of gross output, to $50 million on the eve of World War II (0.7 percent) and exceeded $500 million (over 2 percent of output) in the late 1990s. According to the best estimates, worldwide public expenditure increased by 150 percent in the 1960s, by 50 percent in the 1970s, by 30 percent in the 1980s, and only by 15 percent in the 1990s (Federico 2005: Table 6.6 and Pardey, Alston, and Piggot 2006). By the year 2000, total expenditure was equivalent to 2.4 percent of gross output in advanced countries, but only to 0.53 percent in the developing countries (and to 0.8 percent worldwide). Expenditure for the diffusion of best practices among farmers (the so-called extension) doubled from 1959 to 1971 and increased by 25 percent in the next decade.

Was the taxpayers' money well spent? Following the pioneering work on hybrid corn by Grilliches (1958), many scholars have estimated the rates of return (the ratio of the benefits from the innovation to the expenditure) of specific R&D projects. A survey of almost 2,000 estimates, covering the period to the late 1990s, yields mean returns of 99.6 percent on R&D and of 81.3 percent on all investment, including extension. These figures are astonishingly high, but there are reasons to suspect that they overstate the actual returns. In fact, most estimates refer to successful projects, and thus they neglect the losses on failed attempts, as well as the fixed costs on research infrastructure. More accurate estimates of returns can be obtained from the literature on the causes of the TFP growth in agriculture, which considers the effect of R&D expenditure, together with other relevant variables like the environment, factor endowments, and macroeconomic policies. These works find a positive and significant effect of expenditure on productivity growth, with implicit rates of return on investment around 30–40 percent (see e.g. Arega 2010). These rates are quite impressive compared with other uses of public funds and thus more than justify the investment.

If the benefits of investment in R&D are so large and so widely recognized, why has public spending ceased to grow and, in some advanced countries, even declined in the 1990s and 2000s? To some extent, this stagnation reflects the recent generalized retreat of the state from the economy. However, there is also a more specific cause, the extension of patenting rights to living species, which allowed private firms to reap all the returns from their investments in R&D. This measure had been advocated by firms selling seeds and plants from the beginning of the twentieth century, and it was granted, for the first time, albeit only for trees, in the United States in the 1930s. In 1960, the European Union countries extended the right to all plants, and, in 1961, they signed an inter-country agreement, for the mutual recognition of patents, the "International Union for the Protection of New Plant Varieties" (UPOV). The United States followed suit in 1970. As of 2011, the UPOV has sixty-nine member countries. As a result, private investments have increased hugely. They had already overtaken public expenditure in the United States in the 1980s, and, by the year 2000, expenditure in agriculture-specific R&D (excluding mechanical or chemical research) accounted for about a third of the world total and for over half of the expenditure in advanced countries.

Away from free-market capitalism

Land reform, investment in R&D, and other policies described so far affected the income of farmers mainly indirectly or as by-products of measures which had different aims. For instance, the traditional market policies in pre-modern Europe aimed at fostering supply to urban markets: by prohibiting exports and fostering imports, they reduced domestic prices. Policies aimed at protecting farm incomes were therefore a novelty. The French Napoleonic war years had been a golden age for landowners and the prospect of a fall in wheat prices after their end prompted the United Kingdom to impose prohibitive duties (the so-called Corn Laws) in 1815 (Federico 2012). France and most countries of continental Europe followed suit in the next few years. However, this first wave of protectionism did not last for long. The United Kingdom reduced protection in 1828 and repealed it altogether in 1846, and other countries imitated it in the next two decades. By 1861, the grain trade in Europe was essentially free and remained free until the 1880s, when the threat of invasion by American wheat induced most European countries, with the notable exception of the United Kingdom, to reimpose duties. Conventional wisdom describes this change as a return to protection, but, at least for agriculture, this view is unwarranted. First, duties on wheat were not that high: in the main countries of continental Europe, they exceeded 50 percent of the Chicago price only for few years in the 1890s. Second, products other than wheat and rye were affected much less, if at all. The aggregate level of protection can be measured by the Nominal Rate of Assistance (NRA), which can be computed as an average of differences between domestic and world prices (as percentages of the latter) weighted by the composition of domestic agricultural output. The ratio remained very low or even negative in European countries until World War 1 (Swinnen 2009) and, after a short spell of wartime regulations, remained low also in the 1920s.

The real epoch-making change was triggered by the collapse of prices at the onset of the Great Depression (see Figure 3.2). European countries reacted by increasing duties and extending protection to all products. However, many governments feared that tariffs might not be sufficient and thus decided to supplement them with quantitative restrictions (e.g. mandatory minimum shares of home-grown wheat). Some countries, such as Germany and Italy, went as far as to establish full state control on the distribution of key products, such as cereals. Thus, the NRAs shot up well above 50 percent, with a peak of 160 percent in Germany in 1934. The main exception was the United Kingdom, which left imports from the empire free and compensated farmers with subsidies. The sudden increase in duties on their staples and the collapse of agricultural prices triggered a reaction by overseas producers. As early as 1924, the state of São Paulo in Brazil had set up a marketing board to finance coffee planters and to arrange collective sales of coffee, with limited success. In the 1930s, it was imitated by colonial administrations (e.g. the British in Kenya in 1933), independent countries in eastern Europe, and also by Western Settlement countries. The Agricultural Adjustment Act, one of the first New Deal laws, contained a series of measures to reduce supply and shore up farms, with the explicit goal of pushing prices up to their prewar levels (the so-called "parity"). The most important of these was the right to borrow from the Commodity Credit Corporation (CCC) by pledging the crops at a predetermined price. This apparently innocuous measure was the equivalent of a guarantee that domestic prices could not fall below the minimum.

After the end of World War II, these emergency measures were not abolished on either side of the Atlantic. The European Community adopted a Common Agricultural Policy (CAP), which aimed at keeping prices high and equal in all Member States. The Japanese government maintained the state monopoly of the rice trade, which had been created in 1942. According to a recent estimate by Anderson *et al.* (2009) the NRAs in the 1950s and 1960s come close to 100 percent in Japan, exceeded 50 percent in Europe, while they remained fairly low in exporting countries. Most newly independent countries in Asia and Africa inherited the marketing boards from their colonial past, but they drastically changed their role. Rather than fostering exports, they were used, jointly with direct taxation and other macroeconomic policies, such as double exchange rates, to keep the prices of agricultural products for urban consumers low and to squeeze as much tax as possible from farmers in order to fund industrialization. Thus, most LDCs featured an anti-agricultural bias. In fact, the NRA was negative (i.e. domestic prices were lower than world market prices) in at least two-thirds of the LDCs, and the average hovered around minus 10 percent, in spite of the presence of a small group of protectionist countries, such as South Korea.

Since the late 1980s, both OECD countries and LDCs have reduced their intervention. These latter started to liberalize markets, reduced taxes on farmers, and abolished the double exchange rate regime. Consequently, the domestic prices of agricultural commodities converged toward world market prices and the NRAs rose. In the early years of the twenty-first century, the average NRA, while still below zero in African countries, became positive in South America and in Asia in particular. The mid 1980s marked the heyday of policies of direct support to farmers in advanced countries. Since then, most countries have tried to reduce the burden for taxpayers and consumers. For instance, the MacSharry reform of the European Union (1992) shifted from indirect support via market policies to the direct subsidizing of farmers' income. The United States adopted a similar policy, with the FAIR Act (1996). As a result, the NRAs declined sharply in the early years of the new millennium, although the OECD average remains high, as the smaller European countries, such as Switzerland and Iceland, did not share the liberalizing zeal.

Economists reckon that state intervention is justified only when it can foster competition or can redress a market failure. Neither criteria apply to the agricultural policies described in this section. The threat to competition by agricultural producers was negligible, while state-funded investment in R&D did address one of the two main major market failures. The other main market failure was the environmental damage from irrigation and from the use of chemical products, and, arguably, from the agricultural policies in advanced countries which worsened, rather than alleviated, it. In fact, high guaranteed prices created a strong incentive to produce as much as possible, and this entailed a huge consumption of chemicals. On the other hand, the artificially high prices of agricultural products damaged consumers. In the 1980s, at its heyday, the support to agriculture was the equivalent of a tax of over 120 percent on the consumption of agricultural products. Notwithstanding this fact, this policy did not raise much opposition, in all likelihood because agricultural products, before processing, accounted for only a minor share of total consumption. According to some estimates, about three-quarters of these sums accrued to farmers, while the rest was a net loss for the whole economy (Federico 2009). The liberalization of the 1990s reduced consumer losses by about two-thirds. The effects of policies in the LDCs were the opposite: producers lost and urban consumers gained. Over the whole period, the tax equivalent of agricultural policies was negative in the majority of cases (i.e. consumers were subsidized), although the bias was decreasing in the 1990s and 2000s. These figures, as well as the NRAs quoted above, neglect all the secondary effects of agricultural policies on the prices of factors and the allocation of resources. These effects can be taken into account with a more sophisticated and data-intensive technique of estimation: CGE modeling. For instance, Cline (2004) and Anderson and Martin (2005) estimate that a complete liberalization of trade in agricultural products, without modifying other support policies, would have increased world GDP by about half a point – no small amount. Furthermore, poor countries would have benefitted the most, thanks to the abolition of barriers to their exports: their GDP would have increased by about 1–1.5 percent. Clearly, such a bold move is not on any political agenda.

Conclusion

In the last two centuries, the performance of world agriculture, in terms of the growth of output and, above all, total productivity has been at par with, if not superior to, that of industry. This achievement has been made possible thanks to modernization, which has had at least three distinctive features:

(i) Technical change has not caused massive changes in the organization of production: agriculture has remained dominated by small productive units managed by single households, not by giant corporations.

(ii) Traditional property rights and "informal" credit have survived much longer than in the rest of the economy. They were less inefficient than assumed by economists, but they may still have had a negative effect on growth.

(iii) State intervention has been more invasive in agriculture than in industry, for good (agriculture has needed more support for R&D than industry) and for bad. Agricultural trade has been heavily regulated for most of the twentieth century and agriculture is still resisting globalization.

In a nutshell, agriculture was, and still is, different.

References

Anderson, K. and W. Martin (2005). "Agricultural Trade and the Doha Development Agenda," *World Economy* 28: 1301–1327.

Aparicio, G., V. Pinilla, and R. Serrano (2009). "Europe and the International Trade in Agricultural and Food Products, 1870–2000," in P. Lains and V. Pinilla (eds.), *Agriculture and Economic Development in Europe since 1870*. London and New York: Routledge, pp. 52–75.

Arega, A. (2010). "Productivity Growth and the Effects of R&D in African Agriculture," *Agricultural Economics* 41: 223–238.

Banerjee, A. and E. Duflo (2011). *Poor Economics: A Radical Rethinking of the Way to Fight Global Poverty*. New York: PublicAffairs.

Beltran Tapia, F. (2012). "Commons, Social Capital and the Emergence of Agricultural Cooperatives in Early Twentieth Century Spain," *European Review of Economic History* 16: 511–528.

Carter, S., R. Sutch, S. Gardner, A. Olmstead, M. Haines, and G. Wright (2006). *Historical Statistics of the United States Millennial Edition*. Cambridge University Press.

Cline, W. R. (2004). *Trade Policy and Global Poverty*. Washington, DC: Institute for International Economics.

David, P. (1971). "The Mechanization of Reaping in the Ante-bellum Midwest," in R. W. Fogel and S. Engerman (eds.), *The Reinterpretation of American Economic History*. New York: Harper and Row, pp. 210–238.

De Soto, H. (2000). *The Mystery of Capital: Why Capitalism Triumphs in the West and Fails Everywhere Else*. London and New York: Bantam Press.

Deininger, K. and S. Jin (2006). "Tenure Security and Land-related Investment: Evidence from Ethiopia," *European Economic Review* 50: 1245–1277.

Duffy-Martini, D. and E. Silberberg (2006). "The Diffusion of Tractor Technology," *Journal of Economic History* 66: 354–389.

Dye, A. (1998). *Cuban Sugar in the Age of Mass Production: Technology and the Economics of the Sugar Central*. Stanford University Press.

Federico, G. (2004) "The Growth of World Agricultural Production, 1800–1938," *Research in Economic History*, 22: 125–181.

(2005). *Feeding the World*. Princeton University Press.

(2006). "The 'Real' Puzzle of Share-cropping: Why is it Disappearing?" *Continuity and Change*, 21: 261–285.

(2009) "Was the CAP the Worst Agricultural Policy of the 20th Century?" in K. Patel (ed.), *Fertile Ground for Europe? The History of European Integration and the Common Agricultural Policy since 1945*. Baden-Baden: Nomos, pp. 257–271.

(2012) "The Corn Laws in Continental Perspective," *European Review of Economic History* 16: 166–187.

Fuglie, K. (2008). "Is a Slowdown in Agricultural Productivity Growth Contributing to the Rise in Commodity Prices?" *Agricultural Economics* 39: 431–441.

Gerschenkron, A. (1966). "Agrarian Policies and Industrialization in Russia 1861–1917," in H. J. Habbakuk and M. Postan (eds.), *Cambridge Economic History of Europe*. Vol. VI.2. Cambridge University Press, pp. 707–800.

Gregory, P. (1994). *Before Command: An Economic History of Russia from Emancipation to the First Five-year Plan*. Princeton University Press.

Grilliches, Z. (1958). "Research Costs and Social Returns: Hybrid Corn and Related Innovation," *Journal of Political Economy* 66: 419–431.

Hayami, Y. and V. Ruttan (1985) *Agricultural Development*, 2nd edn. Baltimore, MD and London: Johns Hopkins University Press.

Henriksen, I., M. Lampe, and P. Sharp (2011). "The Role of Technology and Institutions for Growth: Danish Creameries in the Late Nineteenth Century," *European Review of Economic History* 15: 475–493.

Jorgensen, H. (2006). "The Interwar Land Reforms in Estonia, Finland and Bulgaria: A Comparative Study," *Scandinavian Economic History Review* 54: 64–97.

King, R. (1977). *Land Reform: A World Survey*. London: Bell and Sons.

Kishimoto, M. (2011). "Property Rights, Land and Law in Imperial China," in Debin Ma and Jan-Luiten Van Zanden (eds.), *Law and Long-term Economic Change: A Eurasian Perspective*. Stanford University Press, pp. 68–90.

Lains, P. and V. Pinilla (2009). *Agriculture and Economic Development in Europe since 1870*. London and New York: Routledge.

Lloyd Peter, J., J. Croser, D. Sandri, and E. Valenzuela (2009). "Agricultural Distortion Patterns since the 1950s: What Needs Explaining?" Agricultural distortion working paper 90 (May 2009).

Miller, J. A. (1999). *Mastering the Market: The State and the Grain Trade in Northern France, 1700–1860*. Cambridge University Press.

Nafziger, S. (2010). "Peasant Communes and Factor Markets in Late Nineteenth-century Russia," *Explorations in Economic History* 47: 381–402.

Olmstead, A. and P. Rhode (2008). *Creating Abundance: Biological Innovation and American Agricultural Development*. Cambridge University Press.

Olsson, M. and P. Svensson (2010). "Agricultural Growth and Institutions: Sweden 1700–1860," *European Review of Economic History* 14: 275–304.

O'Rourke, K. (2007) "Property Rights, Politics and Innovation: Creamery Diffusion in pre-1914 Ireland," *European Review of Economic History* 11: 395–417.

Pardey, P., J. Alston, and R. Piggot (2006). *Agricultural R&D in the Developing World: Too Little, Too Late?* New York: IFPRI.

Persson, G. (1999) *Grain Markets in Europe 1500–1900*. Cambridge University Press.

Pomeranz, K. (2008). "Land Markets in Late Imperial and Republican China," *Continuity and Change* 23: 101–150.

Ransom, R. L. and R. Sutch (1977). *One Kind of Freedom*. Cambridge University Press.

Shaw-Taylor L. (2012). "The Rise of Agrarian Capitalism and the Decline of Family Farming in England," *Economic History Review* 65: 26–60.

Simpson, J. (2012). *Creating Wine: The Emergence of a World Industry, 1840–1914*. Princeton University Press.

Spraos, J. (1983). *Inequalising Trade? A Study of Traditional North-South Specialization in the Context of Terms of Trade Concept*. Oxford: Clarendon Press.

Swinnen, J. (2002). "Political Reforms, Rural Crises and Land Tenure in Western Europe," *Food Policy* 27: 371–394.

(2009). "The Growth of Agricultural Protection in Europe in the 19th and 20th centuries," *World Economy* 32: 1499–1537.

United Nations, *Statistical Yearbook*. Published annually. New York: United Nations.

United States Department of Agriculture (2007). *US Census of Agriculture 2007 Summary and State Data*. Vol. 1. Updated December 2009 (www.agcensus.usda.gov, last accessed December 15, 2011).

Van Zanden, J. L. (1991) "The First Green Revolution: The Growth of Production and Productivity in European Agriculture, 1870–1914," *Economic History Review* 44: 215–239.

Will, P.-E. and R. Bin Wong (1991). *Nourish the People: The State Civilian Granary System in China 1650–1850*. Center for Chinese Studies Publications, Ann Arbor, MI: University of Michigan.

Williamson, J. (2011). *Trade and Poverty: When the Third World Fell Behind*. Cambridge, MA: The MIT Press.

Yates, P. L. (1959). *Forty Years of Foreign Trade*, London: Allen and Unwin.

4

Technology and the spread of capitalism

KRISTINE BRULAND AND DAVID C. MOWERY

Introduction

This chapter explores the interaction between technological innovation and the global spread of capitalism from 1848 to 2005. Our survey highlights three fundamental developments in the relationship between capitalism and innovation during this period. The first is the rise of industrialization, characterized by an extended transition toward large-scale production, the use of complex mechanized technologies within large enterprises, the building of management systems for such enterprises, and the expansion within these enterprises of distribution and marketing activities of unprecedented scale, complexity, and geographic reach. The second key development is the transformation of innovation itself: the emergence of a structured approach to innovation within capitalism, based on the systematic creation of knowledge. This was characterized by Whitehead as ". . .the invention of the art of invention" (Whitehead 1925: 98), and involved the growth of specialized institutions in education and science, firms dedicated to research and development (R&D), and capital goods industries focussed on the creation of new methods and techniques. The emergence of organized industrial research also affected the role of government in the innovation process, as public funding for research grew after 1945 and new public organizations were created to manage innovation for military and other government missions. Third, innovation catalyzed the global diffusion of capitalism, a development that involved the globalization of industry and trade, technology transfer, and the varying ability of nations to exploit international flows of capital, knowledge, and technology to achieve sustained economic growth (see also Jones, Chapter 6 and Allen, Chapter 2 in this volume, as well as Harley, Chapter 16 in Volume 1).

Capitalism first appeared in Europe, and technological change was essential to its global spread. Innovation was both a driving force behind industrialization and an increasingly important outcome of it. When Marx wrote in *The*

Communist Manifesto that "the bourgeoisie cannot exist without constantly revolutionizing the means of production," he was referring to a historically unique feature of capitalist economies, the constant innovation and adoption of new technologies. Innovation and the spread of new technologies have been distinctive parts of human society from its beginnings. But for long periods of human history, technological development was gradual, with important breakthroughs diffusing relatively slowly. Under capitalism, however, innovation became an integral part of production and the sustained productivity growth that arguably is the most important economic achievement of capitalism.

Early industrialization was characterized by a prolonged transition in which capitalist entrepreneurs first gained control of the flow and pace of work within production establishments from craftsmen and operatives who had formerly controlled production processes, and then used their new management power to change both techniques and organization. This assertion of control was associated with increased innovation in products and processes, culminating in two decisive changes. First, the factory became a prominent form of production organization, and second, production techniques were mechanized. The transition from craft to larger-scale production was gradual, and occurred across many sectors – spectacular developments occurred in steam power and textile production, but there were major changes in agriculture, food processing, small metals manufactures, shoes and clothing, glass, domestic implements, and a wide variety of other products. For the most part, the changes were small-scale, incremental, and based on trial-and-error methods. But by the early nineteenth century in Britain, mechanization produced an epochal change: the emergence in the 1820s of a specialized sector for producing tools, equipment, and machines that introduced a new dynamic into innovation (see also Harley, Chapter 16 in Volume 1).

Our historical analysis of the links between capitalism and technology is organized around a number of themes. The first of these themes concerns the ways in which technological change in the nineteenth century transformed the structure of capitalism, giving rise to new corporate forms. Second, these new corporate structures helped to transform the character of the innovation process itself, laying the foundations for the development of organized research and development in industry, universities, and government. Third, technological innovation had a powerful impact on the structure of capitalism, enhancing the role of government and changing the relations between firms and states. Finally, we examine the interaction of technological innovation, the global spread of capitalism, and the varied ability of nations to "catch up" with the technological and economic leaders in the world economy during this period of more than 150 years.

Defining technology and innovation

Technology is the integration of knowledge, organization, and technique (including tools, other equipment, and procedures for their use), directed towards material transformations. Innovation is the process through which some or all elements of technology are changed. Innovation may be *incremental*, making relatively small-scale improvements to an existing technology) or *radical*, which includes the replacement of an entire technology with a new one (such as the replacement of sail propulsion by steam in marine transport[1]), or the creation of entirely new technological and economic possibilities (the microprocessor).

Although radical innovation tends to receive the bulk of scholarly attention, incremental innovation is important to capitalist innovation in two ways. On the one hand there is incessant small-scale innovation in products that have existed for long periods, such as household appliances or agricultural implements.[2] These incremental improvements often have powerful long-term impacts, enhancing the quality and operating efficiency of existing technologies. But incremental innovation also influences the economic effects of radical innovations, which rarely work well when first introduced. Studies of improvements in the performance of such technologies (e.g. Enos 1962) have repeatedly demonstrated that the real productivity gains of "radical" innovations in fact result from innumerable incremental improvements, many of which originate in users. "Radical" innovations thus typically assume their economic importance as a result of numerous, individually modest but cumulatively significant, "incremental" improvements after the introduction of a new product.

The importance of incremental innovation also underscores the complex relationship between the appearance of a new technology and its adoption.

---

1 It should be noted that this shift, radical though it was, did not necessarily involve a specific new technological breakthrough – Mokyr (1990) points out that it involved a new combination of known technologies (steam power and steel hulls). Moreover, the development of steam-powered tugs benefitted both steam and sail transport, by enhancing the efficiency of port operations (see Harley 1988).

2 Philip Scranton (1997), for example, has shown the importance of product innovation in industries such as bread manufacture, boots and shoes, clothing, furniture, and saddlery in the nineteenth-century US economy, and Berg (1994) has highlighted the importance of small metal manufactures in the UK, including metal clasps, buckles and related devices, cooking equipment, hand tools, and domestic equipment.

Adoption of a new technology obviously is crucial for the realization of its economic benefits. But widespread adoption of innovations also can expand the possibilities for incremental advances in the performance of a new technology, by exposing more innovative users to the technology and supporting the collective learning that contributes to industrial innovation and productivity growth (see Allen 1983 and Chapter 2 in this volume). Moreover, the improvements in reliability, cost-effectiveness, and ease of use of a new technology that often result from incremental innovation may provide an additional impetus to the adoption of the innovation. Although this self-reinforcing dynamic is most apparent in the case of information technology, especially in the era of rapid adoption of low-cost desktop computers, it was also significant in the "tweaking" activities of eighteenth-century innovators examined in Meisenzahl and Mokyr (2012).

Chronological overview

Before turning to our discussion of the characteristics of capitalist innovation and the ways in which innovation influenced the global spread of capitalism, this section presents a chronological summary of the periods and technological innovations included in our subsequent thematic discussion.

There are no definitive lines that differentiate the phases of capitalist growth, but most scholars argue that innovation began to accelerate in Britain in the late eighteenth century across multiple sectors, with particularly important innovations in iron manufacture, cotton spinning, and steam power. Some of the innovations – such as the Watt steam engine, patented in 1775 – diffused slowly and had little impact until well into the nineteenth century. But beginning in agriculture,[3] and spreading to such activities as food preparation, clothing and footwear, construction materials and household implements, innovation raised productivity and supported the further reorganization of work. Expanding markets also provided an impetus to the development of specialized firms producing tools and machinery. The appearance of specialized producers of capital goods initially affected cotton spinning and weaving, and eventually had much broader economic effects.

The period between 1850 and 1870 was characterized by the acceleration of technology-enabled growth and industrialization in Great Britain, the

---

3 Harley, Chapter 16 in Volume I, emphasizes the pervasiveness of market relationships in agricultural factor and product markets in Great Britain dating back to the late middle ages as an important factor in the nation's early industrial development.

industrial "leader" of this period, and its subsequent diffusion to other countries. Exports of capital goods significantly expanded the flow of British technologies to other economies. In some geographic areas, as in the Benelux and Nordic regions of Europe and in the United States, imports of British capital goods in industries such as textiles and engineering products, along with creative imitation of British manufacturing technologies, were accompanied by the building of knowledge-related institutions such as technical societies and mass education systems. In other regions, however, including Brazil, India, and China, these complementary changes in domestic economic and political institutions, including public investments in education, were lacking, and the catalytic effects on industrial development of inward technology transfer through capital-goods imports were much less significant (see below, as well as Jones, Chapter 6 in this volume for further discussion). Indeed, this period was associated with growing economic divergence between a small group of advanced industrial economies in northwest Europe and North America, and the southern periphery of Europe as well as Latin America and Asia (Dowrick and DeLong 2003). The modest effects of inward technology transfer in both India and China also reflected the assertion by nascent European industrial powers of political control, enabled by these nations' technological superiority in military power.

The technological developments that transformed the structure of advanced industrial capitalism appeared in the period between 1870 and 1914 known as the "second industrial revolution." During the post-1870 period, improvements in transportation and communications technologies produced closer integration among national economies and commodities markets throughout the global economy. Advances in transportation and communications also benefitted from the appearance of a range of new technologies and industries.

At least three major clusters of innovations – the internal combustion engine, electric power and light, and organic chemicals – spawned new industries or transformed established ones. Moreover, the firms that came to dominate the industries that grew around these clusters of new technologies (including petroleum, synthetic materials, aircraft, and automobiles) also differed significantly from those in established industries. In most cases, these firms were larger, incorporated a broader range of functions, and often produced a diversified line of products. The technologies that first appeared in the second industrial revolution were major contributors to growth in income and productivity through at least the 1960s (Field 2011; Smil 2005). These and other innovations contributed to an expansion in the boundaries of industrial firms, and the new corporate entities that resulted from this transformation developed in turn new structures for managing innovation.

Innovation in transportation and communications technologies was essential to the growth of domestic and international commerce during the period between 1870 and 1914. For example, the growth of the US domestic rail network during this period had far-reaching economic and technological effects. Along with the domestic telegraph network that grew in parallel and enabled rapid communication and coordination of the rolling stock, the railways helped to integrate the US market, spurring the growth of large, continuous-process production establishments in food processing, machinery production, and metalworking. The development of reliable, all-weather transportation created important new economic opportunities for process innovation in manufacturing and distribution.

Railways also represented enterprises of unprecedented capital intensity and complexity, thereby stimulating major organizational innovations in the structure of corporate management, cost accounting, and industrial finance. The railways served as important training sites for many of the US entrepreneurs (e.g. Andrew Carnegie), who founded new industrial enterprises that pioneered new techniques of management, innovation, and coordination. Technological innovation in international commerce was equally significant during this period. The development of steam-powered, steel-hulled ships, combined with the international expansion of telegraph networks to coordinate international transactions in merchandise and finance, created global markets for agricultural and industrial commodities. As O'Rourke and Williamson (1999, and in Chapter 1 in this volume) show, the combined effects of improvements in railways and international shipping produced dramatic declines in transatlantic price differentials for agricultural commodities such as wheat and pork products.[4]

The quarter-century preceding World War 1 represented a high point of economic globalization in the development of capitalism, as international flows of goods, capital, technology, and people reached unprecedented levels (levels that in the case of international migration exceeded those achieved in the late twentieth century). Expanded international flows of capital during this period also supported the transfer of industrial technologies throughout the

---

4 Combined with higher levels of productivity in these and other commodities in North America or Latin America, these narrower price differentials put significant downward pressure on agricultural prices and incomes in much of Europe, contributing to large-scale migration from Europe to North America, Latin America, and the British Commonwealth.

global economy through foreign investment in offshore production facilities and resource-extraction activities.

The outbreak of war in Europe in 1914 initiated a period of more than three decades of war, genocide, and economic and political instability on a global scale. The large international flows of human migrants, technology, capital, and goods that had characterized the first decade of the twentieth century dried up and did not resume their former significance until late in the century. As Lindert and Williamson (2003) have emphasized, the "end of globalization" that characterized even the peacetime portion of this period resulted largely from the policy actions of governments – if anything, technological change continued to support closer integration among economies through flows of information, trade, and the like (see also O'Rourke and Williamson, Chapter 1 in this volume). The Russian Revolution created a major non-capitalist economic actor, the USSR, which utilized capital-goods imports from Europe and the United States during the 1920s and 1930s for industrialization and, eventually, rearmament. And in both capitalist and noncapitalist economies, the state became a major investor in private-sector R&D and a purchaser of the technological advances resulting from this investment.

During the period between 1914 and 1945, a significant diminution in international flows of capital, goods, people, and technology contributed to greater economic divergence among economies (such as those in North America and Western Europe) that formerly were highly interdependent (see Dowrick and DeLong 2003). The increased gaps among the economies in the "convergence club" of 1870–1914 were also manifested in the technological development of these economies, creating considerable potential for rapid growth based on technological "catchup" during the postwar period of renewed expansion in international trade and capital flows. Divergence was exacerbated (and the conditions for post-1945 "catchup" by Europe and Japan enhanced) by rapid productivity growth in the US economy during the 1930s that reflected the development of reliable highway transportation infrastructure and the expansion of industrial R&D investment during the decade (Field 2011).

The post-1945 decades through the global "oil shock" of 1973 were a period of high productivity growth throughout the industrial economies, a trend that benefitted from the restoration and growth of international flows of trade, capital, and technology as a result of political and economic institution-building during the immediate aftermath of the war (see O'Rourke and Williamson, Chapter 1 in this volume). The onset of the Cold War prevented the United States or the Soviet Union from full demobilization, and by the early 1950s, both nations had resumed high levels of investment in their military establishments, and high levels of public investment in R&D.

The economic convergence in per capita incomes among many of the economies of Western Europe and Japan that characterized the period between 1945 and 1972 was due in large part to the revival of international trade and capital flows that characterized this period and served as powerful channels for international technology transfer. Abramovitz (1989) and others (Nelson and Wright 1994) have pointed out that a substantial part of the observed convergence that characterized the period between 1945 and 1975 reflected economic reconstruction and the adoption by European and Japanese firms of technologies developed and adopted during the interwar period by firms in the United States. The expanded public investment in R&D in industry and universities in the United States and other OECD economies that developed after 1945 contributed to the rise of new technologies that in turn spawned new industries, including information technology and biotechnology.

Postwar convergence in incomes was initially focussed on the United States, European, and then Japanese economies, but important industrialization efforts were underway across the developing world. In some cases, such as Korea and Taiwan, success was spectacular. But industrialization also was underway in countries such as India, Indonesia, Brazil, Malaysia, Thailand, Mexico, and Turkey. As with Western Europe, such growth often depended on the industrial policies of governments that provided some protection for infant industries while promoting the adoption of foreign technologies, policies that (where successful, which was by no means uniformly the case) benefitted from these nations' status as technological "followers."[5]

The "golden age" of rapid growth in productivity and incomes, propelled in large part by revived trade and investment flows, largely ended with the collapse of the Bretton Woods system of international exchange rates and payments, and the oil-price shocks of 1973 and 1979. Although the precise links between higher oil prices and the period of lower productivity growth that followed remain surprisingly elusive in the face of an enormous body of empirical research, it seems likely that the unanticipated change in input costs imposed a productivity "tax" on the adoption

---

5 Amsden pointed out that "industry-level targeting in the context of late industrialization turned out to be a relatively straightforward task. For one, while targeted industries faced market uncertainty, they did not face the technological unknown, which complicated the targeting of science-based industries in advanced countries" (Amsden 2001: 138).

and operation of well-established industrial technologies. Just as time was required for industrial enterprises to exploit the productivity benefits of electricity in the 1920s and information technology in the 1990s, adjusting to the productivity tax associated with higher energy prices also required considerable time. The resurgence of productivity growth in the United States after 1990, at least, is consistent with this descriptive explanation of the productivity slowdown.

The political collapse of the Soviet Union and the political transformation of Eastern Europe between 1989 and 1991, along with the economic reforms that transformed the People's Republic of China (PRC) during the 1990–2005 period, represented a triumph of sorts of capitalism over socialist central planning. Although the period of "capitalist triumph" lasted for less than two decades before the financial crisis of 2008–2011 threatened the stability of the industrial economies of Europe and the United States, the 1990s in particular were characterized by a resumption of productivity growth in the United States that appears to have reflected a long-anticipated payoff to extensive investments (many of which drew on federal funds) in the development and deployment of information technology (see Jorgenson 2001). The Japanese economy, by contrast, faced a "lost decade" of poor economic performance, and the former Soviet Union and Eastern European economies confronted challenges in the wake of the collapse of central planning and state ownership.

This "triumph of capitalism" could not be described as a triumph of any specific type of capitalism (Hall and Soskice 2001; Whitley 2000). Both public policies and the institutions influencing the finance and governance of industry differed considerably among capitalist industrial and industrializing economies, and the forces that had contributed during earlier postwar decades to "convergence" in productivity and income levels affected these institutional and policy factors more slowly and indirectly. Although present in all advanced capitalist economies throughout the late nineteenth and twentieth centuries (and, by the end of the twentieth century, in a number of rapidly industrializing, formerly low-income economies), the interaction between technological innovation and the evolution of capitalism assumed very different forms in different national economies.

Innovation and the spread of capitalism: core themes

Innovation has shaped the dynamics of capitalism in many ways, but we focus here on four main themes: innovation's effects on the structure of firms and industrial economies, on the creation and use of knowledge, on the role of government, and on capitalism's global spread.

Innovation changes the structure of capitalism

A unique feature of capitalist economies is the emergence of a sector focussed specifically on innovation, including the machinery makers and capital goods producers of the early industrial economy in Britain. This sector drew on capabilities in toolmaking, clock-making, and instrument fabrication, all of which benefitted from improved precision in measurement and increased scale in production. By the 1840s, the managerial reorganization of British industry had increased demand for tools, implements, and machines as the technical bases of many production activities changed. The machinery and capital goods sector responded to this demand, contributing to productivity growth as well as exports. Competition between producers improved the performance and reliability of tools and equipment, while at the same time increasing the availability of precision tools and instruments for the manufacture of machinery.

Arguably, the most important development in mid-nineteenth-century Britain was not the amazing growth of the textile sector, but the growth of firms that supplied textile equipment and the power to run it. The products of firms such as Boulton and Watt dramatically increased the power supply to industry, while firms such as Platt's of Oldham supported growth in the output and functionality of textile spinning and weaving equipment. Following the repeal of government prohibitions on machinery exports in 1843, the value of exports of British industrial machinery to Western Europe and Russia nearly doubled by 1847. The economic and political turbulence that characterized the remainder of the 1840s in Europe were associated with a slowdown in machinery exports but after 1850, British machinery exports resumed their growth, increasing ninefold through 1875. Foreign markets accounted for 40 to 60 percent of overall sales through the 1860s of the leading British textile machinery firm, Platt Brothers of Oldham.[6]

The accelerated international diffusion of industrial technologies during the mid nineteenth century was not limited to textiles. Particularly spectacular growth occurred in steam power, which was a product of the early industrial revolution (although not a central technology within the British industrial revolution), and was widely and rapidly deployed in Europe after 1850. Growth in British machinery exports contributed to an acceleration in the

6 Bruland 1989: 149, 151.

rate and extent of global diffusion of a number of key technologies accelerated after the mid nineteenth century.[7]

Innovation during and after the middle of the nineteenth century favored growth in average firm size in the industrializing economies of Europe and the United States. Post-1850 innovation focussed in part on the development of scale economies, with substantial increases in the minimum efficient scale of production operations. Food products such as sugar and beer were among the first to scale up, but the scale of production operations also increased in chemicals, iron and steel manufacture, and later (via new process innovations such as extended production lines) in vehicles and metal manufactures generally. Increased production scale increased the throughput of materials, and this had impacts on materials supply technologies and transport innovation. The growth in the size of factories also relied on improvements in the marketing and distribution of products. Combined with innovations in sea and rail transportation, the growth of national and multinational distribution and marketing operations under the control of individual firms changed not only the industrial structure of capitalism but also its geographic spread.

Innovation in production and distribution technologies and communications during the mid nineteenth century thus created conditions for the creation of "modern" corporate structures characterized by separation of ownership and control, as well as the rise of professional managers. A key development was vertical integration: The drive for scale meant that these enterprises in many cases extended their boundaries to assert managerial control over transactions in distribution or the acquisition of production inputs that previously were organized through the market, and over time grew considerably in size and product diversification. Many of these firms extended their operations well beyond their "home" markets to produce and sell products, as well as obtaining inputs, on a global scale. These "new corporations" benefitted as well from improvements in communications and transportation technologies that enabled a smaller number of larger production establishments to serve national and global markets. In other words, innovation was one of a number of important influences on the emergence of new forms of industrial capitalism, exemplified by the large industrial

---

7 "Until the middle of the 19th century the British were unrivalled in machine tool making with their lathes for cutting revolving pieces of metal, planers and shapers for machining flat surfaces, boring machines for making cylinders and the gauges to ensure the desired accuracy. Along with these went machines such as Nasmyth's steam hammer, the epitome of power and delicacy, for precise forging of pieces of metal, large and small" (Milward and Saul 1973: 205–206).

corporations that appeared in the United States and Germany in the late nineteenth century.[8]

Capitalism transforms the process of innovation: the structured search for knowledge

The rise of industrial capitalism also changed the process of innovation itself. The increased salience of innovation during the industrial revolution that we highlighted earlier triggered greater engagement by capitalists in the creation of scientific and technological capabilities. Many early British industrial innovators had links to emergent "learned societies" in London and the Midlands (see Meisenzahl and Mokyr 2012). An even more far-reaching set of changes in the structure of the innovation process within capitalism occurred from the 1870s onward. What had been a trial-and-error undertaking became organized and formalized, in a process resting on advances in scientific knowledge about the physical and biological worlds.

The institutionalization of innovation that took root during this period both strengthened the links between scientific knowledge and technological innovation and benefitted from this stronger linkage. Equally important, however, was the establishment of R&D organizations within many large firms in the United States and Western Europe during the late nineteenth century. The development of "managed innovation," in which technological innovation relied on organized R&D that spanned both science and technology, also involved change in institutions external to the firm, including universities and government research facilities. The increased importance of innovation to the economic and political power of the state meant that many governments became more directly involved in financing innovation within firms and other supporting institutions.

Much of the recent research on this period from business historians has focussed on the large 'managerial enterprise' characterized by separation of ownership and control, and economies of scale in production and distribution. Schumpeter (1943) also saw these enterprises as central to a new economic environment in which innovation was the focus of competition among giant, oligopolistic firms. In-house R&D organizations first appeared in the large German chemical firms that had been established during the second half of the

---

8 As Atack (Chapter 17 in Volume I) notes, this transformation in the structure of industrial activity was a gradual process in the US and elsewhere. As late as 1900, no more than 41,000 of the 500,000 manufacturing establishments recorded in the 1900 US Census of Manufactures were incorporated. This small minority, however, accounted for more than half of the nation's output of manufactures.

nineteenth century. In both Germany and the United States, the development of corporate R&D was linked to the broader transformation of corporations in chemicals and electrical equipment (discussed in greater detail by Chandler 1977, 1990) that diversified their product lines, extended their boundaries into product distribution, finance, and marketing, and expanded the ranks of middle and senior management. As their in-house R&D organizations grew, these firms further extended and diversified their product lines.

But the in-house research facilities of large German and US firms were not concerned exclusively with the creation of new technology. Industrial R&D laboratories also monitored technological developments outside of the firm and advised corporate managers on the acquisition of externally developed technologies. Many of Du Pont's major product and process innovations during this period, for example, were obtained from outside sources, and Du Pont further developed and commercialized them within the US market (Hounshell 1996; Hounshell and Smith 1988; Mueller 1962).[9] In-house R&D in US firms developed in parallel with independent R&D laboratories that performed research on a contract basis (see also Mowery 1983). But over the course of the twentieth century, contract-research firms' share of industrial research employment declined.

Inventors operating outside of large corporate laboratories remained important well into the twentieth century's "transformation" of the process of innovation. But as Williamson (1975) and other scholars have argued (notably, Cockburn 2004 and 2006 in his discussion of vertical specialization in pharmaceuticals innovation), the contractual governance of a highly uncertain process such as innovation is fraught with difficulties. Indeed, many of the most celebrated independent inventors of Lamoreaux and Sokoloff's (1997) "golden age," including such giants as Elmer Sperry and Thomas Edison, sought to integrate "downstream" from invention into production. Although independent inventors who specialized solely in invention may indeed have been significant, a large share of the inventors cited by Lamoreaux and

---

9 The research facilities of AT&T were instrumental in the procurement of the "triode" from independent inventor Lee de Forest, and advised senior corporate management on their decision to obtain loading-coil technology from Pupin (Reich 1985). General Electric's research operations monitored foreign technological advances in lamp filaments and the inventive activities of outside firms or individuals, and pursued patent rights to innovations developed all over the world (Reich 1985: 61). The Standard Oil Company of New Jersey established its Development Department precisely to carry out development of technologies obtained from other sources, rather than for original research (Gibb and Knowlton 1956: 525). Alcoa's R&D operations also closely monitored and frequently purchased process innovations from external sources (Graham and Pruitt 1990: 145–147).

Sokoloff (Borden, McCormick, Tesla, Edison, Bell, Fessenden, and the Wright Brothers – see Lamoreaux and Sokoloff 1997: 2) as hallmarks of the "golden age" in fact sought to combine inventive activity with commercial production by enterprises in which they played prominent managerial roles.[10]

The evolution of industrial research in the United States was influenced by another factor that was absent in Germany during the late nineteenth and early twentieth centuries: competition policy. By the late nineteenth century, judicial interpretations of the Sherman Antitrust Act had made agreements among firms for the control of prices and output targets of civil prosecution. The 1895–1904 US merger wave, particularly the surge in mergers after 1898, was one response to this new legal environment. Since informal and formal price-fixing and market-sharing agreements had been declared illegal in a growing number of cases, firms resorted to horizontal mergers to control prices and markets.[11]

The development of industrial research, as well as the creation of a market for the acquisition and sale of industrial technologies, benefitted from late nineteenth-century reforms in US patent policy that strengthened patent-holder rights (see Mowery 1995). Although the search for new patents provided one incentive to pursue industrial research, the impending expiration of these patents created another important impetus for the establishment of industrial research laboratories.[12] Intensive efforts to improve and protect corporate technological assets were combined with increased

---

10 According to Millard 1990, "In Edison's view, a patent was hardly worth the trouble of inventing something. He knew from experience that selling patents to businessmen often left the inventor shortchanged. More often than not the returns from a new idea went to the financier or manufacturer, while the inventor struggled to protect his patent in the courts and obtain his share of the profits. A patent alone was not enough, nor was an invention. The original idea had to be developed into something more tangible than a patent; it had to be transformed, or 'perfected' into a working model of a prototype . . . This was essential to obtain financial support" (43). See also Hughes (1971) for an assessment of the inventive and commercial activities of Elmer Sperry.

11 See Stigler 1968. The Supreme Court ruled in the *Trans Missouri Association* case in 1898 and the *Addyston Pipe* case in 1899 that the Sherman Act outlawed all agreements among firms on prices or market sharing. Data in Thorelli (1954) and Lamoreaux (1985) indicate an increase in merger activity between the 1895–1898 and 1899–1902 periods. Lamoreaux (1985) argues that other factors, including the increasing capital-intensity of production technologies and the resulting rise in fixed costs, were more important influences on the US merger wave, but her account (109) also acknowledges the importance of the Sherman Act in the peak of the merger wave. Lamoreaux also emphasizes the incentives created by tighter Sherman Act enforcement after 1904 for firms to pursue alternatives to merger or cartelization as strategies for attaining or preserving market power.

12 Both American Telephone and Telegraph and General Electric, for example, established or expanded their in-house laboratories in response to the intensified competitive pressure that resulted from the expiration of key patents (Reich 1985; Millard 1990: 156).

acquisition of patents in related technologies from other firms and independent inventors. Judicial tolerance for restrictive patent licensing policies further increased the value of patents in corporate research strategies, since patents enabled some firms to retain market power without running afoul of antitrust law.

In contrast to the situation in the United States and Germany, British industrial firms appear to have been slower to expand their in-house R&D activities, in part because of the slower development of modern corporate structures in the United Kingdom (Chandler 1990). A late nineteenth-century merger wave in the United Kingdom affected a narrower range of industries, mainly brewing and textiles, and fewer firms were merged into larger successors. Through much of the twentieth century, according to Sanderson (1972) and Freeman (1962), the R&D intensity of British firms was roughly one-third that of US enterprises.

Capitalism, innovation, and government

Government policies exerted a direct and indirect influence on innovation in the post-1850 world. Regulatory policies, ranging from competition policy to financial regulation and intellectual property rights, shaped the path of corporate innovation. Another significant channel of government influence on innovation was the growing demand of the military for new technologies in the nineteenth and twentieth centuries, leading to funding for development and purchase of weapons and innovations in ships, aircraft, computing, and telecommunications. The post-1945 period saw growth in government funding of R&D within industry, intramural government laboratories, and universities for both civilian and defense-related R&D. But government funding for organized R&D in both military and nonmilitary technologies first appeared during the nineteenth century.

Beginning in the second half of the nineteenth century, public funding of organized R&D for civilian applications became significant in Germany, the United Kingdom, and the United States. In all three nations, the initial focus of publicly supported R&D was agriculture (see Federico, Chapter 3 in this volume, for a discussion of public support for R&D in agriculture). The first German agricultural research station supported with public funds opened in Saxony in 1851, and seventy-four more publicly funded agricultural experiment stations opened in what became Germany over the following twenty-five years (Ruttan 2001). Partly because of the growing strength of German university-based research in chemistry for industrial as well as agricultural applications,[13] this extensive network of agricultural research stations influenced the development of similar establishments in other industrial economies. What became the leading British publicly funded agricultural research establishment, at Rothamsted, was founded in 1843 by Lawes as a privately financed research facility, but by 1912 was funded largely from public sources.

In the United States, the 1862 Morrill Act established a foundation for publicly funded higher education, and (along with the 1887 Hatch Act) expanded federal and state government funding for research and extension activities in agriculture. Public funds, largely from state governments in the United States, also supported the development of new institutions for research and education in mining engineering, geology, and related fields that supported expansion in US output of minerals and related raw materials during this period (David and Wright 1997).

Other European economies began to invest in public research in the late nineteenth and early twentieth centuries. Publicly funded research in agriculture and fisheries expanded in Norway at the turn of the twentieth century (before Norway won full political independence from Sweden in 1905), with the establishment of a National Agricultural University in 1897 and the Fisheries Board in 1900. Publicly funded research in agriculture (primarily the dairy industry) in Denmark during the early twentieth century supported the adoption of advanced processing technologies for growing exports (Edquist and Lundvall 1993).

The expanded role of government in supporting innovation extended into military applications during the late nineteenth century. Reflecting their status as the most complex and costly military weapons systems of the era, naval vessels were the focus of an accelerating arms race between the United Kingdom and Germany in the late nineteenth and early twentieth centuries that was a catalyst for increased government investment in naval technology development that transformed the relationships among private firms, military customers, and state-owned production facilities in both nations (see O'Rourke and Williamson, Chapter 1 and Harrison, Chapter 11 in this volume). Although public armories and shipyards accounted for much of the output of weapons in the industrial nations of the mid nineteenth century, the

---

13 "The publication of *Organic Chemistry in its Relationship to Agriculture and Physiology* (1840) by Justus von Liebig is regarded by many as the dividing line in the evolution of agricultural research – a major step toward the development of a science-based agricultural technology" (Ruttan 2001: 208).

naval arms race expanded the role of private firms in supplying technologically advanced components and weapons.[14]

The large industrial firms that served the expanding government demand for advanced weapons in the United Kingdom and Germany operated during the late nineteenth and early twentieth centuries as important vehicles for international technology transfer in weapons design and manufacture, as well as advanced metalworking and fabrication techniques with broader civilian applications. According to Trebilcock (1973), the governments of Spain, Russia, Austria-Hungary, and other peripheral European economies contracted with leading British and German weapons firms to invest in shipyards and ordnance factories in their home economies, both to produce advanced weapons (primarily warships and the guns that they operated) and to train domestic engineers and workers in the advanced techniques necessary to equip and produce these weapons. Expanded government investment in weapons development and production in the most advanced European economies thus generated significant domestic and international economic spillovers.

Intellectual property rights

Although government-granted patents had extended temporary monopolies over the commercial exploitation of new technologies by inventors since the eighteenth century, by the mid nineteenth century, legal instruments for the protection of the intellectual property generated by individual and (eventually) corporate inventors had assumed greater economic and political importance. The US Congress insisted that the US Patent Office spare no effort or expense to diffuse information on granted patents, and inventors were allowed to submit applications without having to pay postage.[15]

The role of domestic patent systems in creating incentives for innovation was a topic of considerable debate in many European economies during the second half of the nineteenth century, reflected (among other things) in the relatively weak protection for patentholders afforded in the British courts' decisions in patent cases during this period. In Scandinavia the potential detrimental effects of patents on diffusion of innovations remained a topic

---

14 See Trebilcock (1969, 1973), McNeill (1982), and Cooling (1979), all of whom emphasize the role of the military services in Germany, the UK, and the US in supporting these technological advances through procurement contracts; little if any military-funded contract R&D was undertaken by private firms during this period.

15 The British patent system made no comparable effort to diffuse information on patented inventions within the UK, and, partly because of the limited availability of information, patent agents and brokers played a more prominent role in the British application process.

of debate for many years (Bruland and Smith 2010). Another indicator of the controversy over patenting was the decision of the Dutch Parliament in 1869 to abolish the patent system of the Netherlands. Both Denmark and Switzerland also enjoyed considerable growth in industry and innovation during this period despite having no domestic patent systems.

The Netherlands reinstated its domestic patent system in 1912, while Denmark adopted a domestic patent system in 1894, and Switzerland in 1888. A recent analysis of data from international industrial exhibitions (Moser 2005), concluded that the lack of a domestic patent system in these nations (all of which were small, open economies) did not depress the rate of inventive activity, but influenced the direction of inventive effort, as Danish, Swiss, and Dutch exhibitors at these industrial expositions all tended to focus their efforts on technologies for which the economic importance of patent protection was relatively modest by comparison with alternative mechanisms of protection such as secrecy.

The growth in economic significance and complexity of national patent systems, along with expansion in international trade, led to intergovernmental negotiations over international harmonization of domestic patent systems in the late nineteenth century. The US government supported such harmonization on terms it deemed acceptable largely because of concern over the potential for imitation by foreign inventors of US intellectual property displayed in international exhibitions such as the Vienna International Exposition of 1873 (Khan 2005: 298). These efforts at harmonization culminated in the Paris Convention of 1883, which enshrined the principle among signatories of "national treatment" for patentees (foreign patentees were to be treated identically to domestic patentees), in spite of US pressure for the Convention to adopt "reciprocity," whereby foreign governments would recognize the validity of US patents.[16] Similar harmonization efforts in the field of copyright produced the Berne Convention of 1886, which the United States signed only in 1988.[17]

16 Consistent with its long-standing hostility toward copyright protection, the US did not support international harmonization of copyright policy during this period, refusing to sign the Berne Convention of 1886 and joining it only in 1988 (Khan 2005: 302–303).

17 Copyright policy presented a sharp contrast to patent policy in the nineteenth-century United States. Senator Ruggles of Maine, the architect of the 1836 patent reform bill, viewed copyright as a welfare-decreasing tax on the public, restricting the diffusion of information. This attitude had found legislative expression in the Copyright Act of 1790, which denied copyright protection to foreign works. Although the scope of copyright protection was extended in successive Congressional statutes during the nineteenth century, US copyright remained far more limited than that of most other industrial nations throughout the period. Only in 1891 was US copyright protection extended to cover works by foreign artists.

World War I expands the role of the state in supporting and directing innovation

Britain's economic blockade of Germany in 1914 meant that exports from the dominant world supplier of organic chemicals, optics, and many of the ingredients for advanced explosives were severely curtailed to combatant and neutral nations alike. The need for these strategic products brought the government of the United Kingdom and, eventually, the United States, into a more direct role in supporting technological innovation in industry. The British government established British Dyestuffs Ltd. for the production of organic chemicals, although the firm encountered significant difficulties in expanding output rapidly. Although not a belligerent for the first three years of the conflict, the United States found its supplies of German dyestuffs severely constrained by the British blockade (submarine freighters proved insufficient to meet the needs of US firms). German-owned production facilities in the United States expanded output, but with US entry into World War I, these facilities and all German patents in chemicals and related fields were seized by the Alien Property Custodian. The patents eventually were licensed at nominal royalty rates to US chemicals firms. In spite of their access to the expropriated intellectual property of leading German chemicals firms, US firms failed to master the complexities of organic chemicals production based on coal-tar intermediates for years after the end of World War I.[18] Even technologically adept firms in a relatively advanced industrial economy thus were incapable of exploiting expropriated foreign intellectual property that was not accompanied by know-how and/or experienced practitioners, illustrating the challenges of inward technology transfer (see below for further discussion).

World War I triggered considerable expansion in the production (by both private firms and state-owned producers) of weapons systems, notably aircraft, in Germany, the United Kingdom, France, and the United States. State-owned armories remained significant suppliers of weapons in the United Kingdom, and in the United States, wartime R&D spending was limited in

18 "When Sterling Products had purchased the Bayer properties [in 1917], the American company had immediately sold the dyestuff part of the business to the Grasselli Chemical Company. Now, in the aftermath of the war, both Sterling Products and Grasselli Chemical needed German know-how and personnel so as to utilize successfully their new acquisitions ... The ownership of Bayer assets had moved to American hands – but key personnel remained German, as did the technology" (Wilkins 2004: 124). Similarly, the efforts of the US government to synthesize nitrates in the government-owned facility at Sheffield, Alabama during and after World War I were largely unsuccessful in spite of the expropriation of the BASF patents for the process.

scope, largely controlled by the uniformed services, and performed mainly in military arsenals and laboratories.[19] In Britain, new government research facilities in aeronautics (the Royal Aircraft Establishment) were created or expanded. In short, the state's role in supporting and guiding innovation expanded during World War I throughout the capitalist economies. This expanded state role diminished, but did not vanish, during the two decades of peace that followed the Armistice.

World War II: further expansion of the state's role in innovation

The global conflict that raged between 1939 and 1945 spanned a broader geographic area and involved many more capitalist and noncapitalist combatant nations than World War I. Partly because of its global scale, as well as the enduring political tensions that followed the surrender of the Axis powers, World War II had lasting consequences for the role and organization of technological innovation throughout the global economy. Although the technological capabilities of private industry had grown considerably since 1914 in the capitalist economies, even the advanced industrial nations, including the United Kingdom, Germany, and the United States, relied on an unprecedented level of government financing and direction of technology development and large-scale production for wartime.

Similarly to previous large-scale conflicts, much of the technological innovation associated with this war involved accelerated development and large-scale deployment of technological concepts already in existence at the inception of hostilities. Even the atomic bomb, after all, represented an engineering-driven development project of unprecedented scale and complexity that demonstrated the feasibility and incredible destructive potential of atomic fission, rather than undertaking the discovery of this natural phenomenon.

---

19 Sapolsky's history of the US Office of Naval Research characterizes US military R&D during World War I as follows: "... the military was initially reluctant to admit a need for outside assistance in the design of weapons, and then insisted on dominating the hurriedly created scientific effort that only began with the involvement of American troops in the fighting. Scientists who wished to contribute to the war by doing weapons-related research were required, with rare exception, to accept military command procedures. Research priorities were determined by the military, and no attention was paid to linking weapon development to operational experience. Although some major advances in weapons were achieved, their impact on the outcome of the war was negligible beyond contributing to its frightful cost in lives" (Sapolsky 1990: 13). Dupree (1986: chap 16) has a similar account, while arguing that the wartime experience itself served as a catalyst for the growth of private-sector investment in industrial R&D during the 1920s that laid the foundations for the very different government–industry relationship that characterized World War II.

Nevertheless, in technologies ranging from pharmaceuticals (large-scale production of penicillin) to electronics (microwave technologies, radar) and petrochemicals (synthetic rubber and aviation fuels production), World War II was associated with increased state funding and leadership of complex development projects of enormous scope. In the United States, many of these large-scale development projects accelerated interfirm flows of technological knowledge and ultimately contributed to fundamental change in industry structure and expanded international technology transfer.

For example, the US wartime synthetic-rubber development and production program required extensive sharing of technology among petrochemical firms, and arguably eroded the previous dominance of Standard Oil of New Jersey in this field. In addition, the development of a new group of specialized engineering firms (SEFs) in the chemicals and petrochemicals industry, firms specializing in the development and licensing of chemicals process technologies and the construction of production facilities, was spurred by the synthetic rubber and related wartime projects. Just as independent capital-goods producers had been important agents of international technology transfer in the global textiles industry of the nineteenth century, the SEFs would play a central role in the global diffusion of advanced chemicals process technologies during the 1950s and 1960s, accelerating the growth of petroleum-based chemicals production throughout the global economy (Arora and Gambardella 1998).

The expanded role of the state in wartime capitalist economies was a temporary phenomenon, but demobilization and conversion in victorious nations such as the United Kingdom took years, and state ownership expanded in sectors such as steel and coal. Even where demobilization was relatively swift and state ownership almost nonexistent after wartime, as in the United States, World War II vastly expanded the role of the central government in supporting technological innovation in defense-related and other areas defined as important to government missions (e.g. health).[20] As was true of other governments, much of the growth in US government investment in R&D after 1945 was devoted to national security missions. Defense-related R&D spending represented more than 80 percent of total US federal R&D spending for much of the 1950s (which itself accounted for roughly 1.3 percent of GDP in the early 1950s, almost four times the 0.35 percent reported by Bush

---

20 The US federal government before 1940 had accounted for a share of overall national R&D spending that only slightly exceeded that of state governments (National Resources Planning Board 1941).

1945 for 1940), and exceeded 50 percent of federal R&D expenditures through-out the 1949–1990 period.

Federal spending supported R&D activity in industry and universities, rather than being heavily concentrated in federal government laboratories. Substantial investments of defense-related R&D in university research during the 1950s and 1960s contributed to growth in both the scale and quality of an important institutional component of the postwar US research infrastructure (Leslie 1993; Lowen 1997).[21] Combined with large-scale military procurement programs, these unprecedented levels of US peacetime investment in military R&D contributed to important technical innovations that themselves spawned new industries with large civilian markets – the semiconductor, the electronic computer, and the computer networking technologies that eventually gave rise to the Internet (see Fabrizio and Mowery 2007; Mowery, 2011).

In other industrial economies with high levels of post-1945 defense-related R&D spending, including the United Kingdom and France, several factors may have diminished the military–civilian technological spinoffs that were important in at least some US industries.[22] The sheer scale of US postwar defense spending on both R&D and procurement, which exceeded the com-bined investment of Western European nations in these activities, meant that US defense-related R&D programs frequently were able to pursue multiple technical paths to a given objective, promoting a broader "frontier" of exploration and producing more knowledge of potential utility for other applications.

21 One important "knowledge spillover" from defense-related R&D that originated in part outside of the university was the funding by the US Air Force of research on the economics of R&D at the RAND Corporation, a nonprofit "think tank" established in 1946 as a subsidiary of the Douglas Aircraft Corporation and spun off as an independent, nonprofit organization in 1948. The Air Force's concern with management of its portfolio of complex development projects led to a series of projects that involved an extraordinary collection of economists, including Armen Alchian, Kenneth Arrow, Burton Klein, Andrew Marshall, Thomas Marschak, Richard Nelson, and Sidney Winter, who worked on issues related to defense R&D, producing a series of papers that laid the foundations for the modern study of the economics of technological innovation, including Nelson (1959, 1961), Arrow (1962), Marschak, Glennan, and Summers (1967), Marshall and Meckling (1962), and others. Hounshell (2000) describes RAND's early work on the economics of R&D.

22 Not all US industries benefitted from these infusions of defense-related R&D and procurement spending. Responding to US Air Force R&D contracts, the US machine-tools industry developed complex, highly sophisticated products to use in the aerospace industry that largely failed to find civilian markets (see Mazzoleni 1999). And the US civilian nuclear power industry, which enjoyed aggressive federal support for its efforts to utilize electricity-generation technologies that were derived from the US nuclear submarine program for "peaceful uses of the atom," went into eclipse by the late 1980s (Cowan 1990).

The differences in scale between most US postwar defense-related programs and those of major European powers also meant that competition among R&D performers and potential suppliers of components and systems could be maintained, resulting in greater competitive pressure on all participants in defense-related programs that may have been conducive to stronger performance. Nevertheless, the benefits for the US civilian economy resulting from the large postwar R&D and procurement programs of the federal government can hardly be characterized as "free," given the enormous scale of the federal investment in these activities.

Increased federal R&D investment in the United States was not confined to defense-related fields. The post-1945 period also witnessed growth in federal investment in biomedical R&D, through the National Institutes of Health (NIH), that by the 1990s represented by far the single largest federal program of support for academic R&D. This large federal R&D investment, growth in which accelerated with the announcement of the "War on Cancer" in 1973, contributed to important scientific advances in molecular biology that (along with other developments, including the Bayh-Dole Act of 1980 and the broader extension of intellectual property rights to cover life forms) expanded the role of US universities as sources of licensed intellectual property for commercial development by industry. No other industrial-economy government made a similarly massive investment in biomedical R&D during this period.[23] Moreover, the NIH R&D budget, which was dominated by extramural research, was largely allocated on a competitive basis among academic medical centers that combined scientific and clinical approaches and personnel in an institutional environment that again contrasts with research institutions in the United Kingdom or Germany (see Henderson, Orsenigo, and Pisano 1999 for further discussion).

The combination of expanded federal R&D investment in defense-related and biomedical R&D, along with military procurement policies that (in contrast to those in many European economies) did not discriminate against new suppliers of high-technology components and a much tougher US

23 Using OECD data that cover six large industrial economies (France, the UK, Germany, the Netherlands, Japan, and the US) for 1987, Henderson *et al.* (1999: Table 7.1) calculated that the United States devoted nearly one-half (48.9 percent) of total public spending on academic research to the life sciences, a substantially larger share than Germany's 36.7 percent and the six-nation average of 36.3 percent. The share of the aggregate public research budgets of these six nations also vary significantly, with the United States spending a total on academic research of nearly $15 billion (calculated at PPP), far more than the $4 billion accounted for by Germany, the next-largest public spender on academic research. In other words, US public funding of biomedical research accounted for a larger share of a much larger total public R&D budget during this and most other years during the post-1945 period.

competition policy during the 1945–1980 period, transformed the structure of new-technology commercialization in a number of the new postwar industries, such as computers, semiconductors, and biotechnology. In all of these industries, new firms played important roles in the commercialization of innovations. These postwar US industries differed in this respect from their counterparts in Japan and most Western European economies, where established electronics and pharmaceuticals firms retained dominant roles in the commercialization of these technologies.

The reconstruction of many Western European economies also was associated with a greater peacetime state presence in the operation of high-technology industries ranging from atomic power to aerospace and electronics. Many European governments increased investments in R&D during the postwar period, although a greater share of these publicly financed R&D activities was performed in public laboratories rather than in industry or universities, by comparison with the United States. By the 1960s, public commitments to "national champion" firms in military technologies, aerospace, computers, and other sectors had created quasi-monopolistic suppliers of high-technology products (some but by no means all of which were also state-owned) for governments in the United Kingdom, France, Germany, Italy, and Norway.

The "national champion" strategies for high-technology industrial development that many Western European nations had utilized during the 1960s and 1970s fell into disfavor during the 1990s, for several reasons. Their insulation from competitive pressures, as well as limited state budgets for support and procurement, ultimately impeded many of these "champions" from achieving commercial results that matched their often impressive technical capabilities. The spiraling costs of subsidizing national champions, combined with often disappointing commercial results, eroded political support for these strategies in nations ranging from Norway to the United Kingdom. Flat or declining military budgets in the wake of the Cold War also weakened a key policy lever for subsidizing domestic high-technology firms through R&D or procurement contracts. Finally, the economic integration of the European Union imposed constraints on the domestic subsidies for national firms and preferential procurement that had long been central components of national champion policies.

International technology transfer and the global spread of capitalism

The flow of technology from nations operating at the technological frontier to nations with lower productivity and incomes was critical to the ability of "follower" nations to catch up with and eventually overtake the United Kingdom in the late nineteenth century. The two initial sites of catching up industrialization were the United States and a set of continental European nations. These areas' successful "catchup" relied on the creation of indigenous knowledge-based capabilities, the international sale of technology and associated flows of knowledge, foreign investment, and the movement of skilled people. But other countries followed, with varied success, beginning in the late nineteenth century: first, Japan and, after the mid twentieth century, other economies in Asia and Latin America.

Cross-border flows of technology and knowledge are important for more than their purely economic significance. Understanding the circumstances in which follower nations can exploit inward technology transfer (meaning the acquisition and use of foreign technologies) for economic development forces a clearer characterization of the nature of both knowledge and technology, and also highlights the knowledge-intensive nature of the technology adoption process. Exploiting and applying both technologies from external sources requires a considerable level of knowledge on the part of the would-be adopter/exploiter, well illustrated by the failure of US chemicals firms to exploit German firms' expropriated organic chemistry patents after World War I. The need for such knowledge reflects the fact that much of the knowledge essential to technology adoption is not easily codified, as well as the idiosyncratic nature of the context in which it is being applied, which may differ in subtle ways from those associated with other applications. The history of technology and capitalism since the industrial revolution demonstrates that successful inward transfer and exploitation of foreign technologies rests on a foundation of domestic human capital formation that is the outcome of public and private investments in education and training.

At least three mechanisms for cross-border technology transfer are apparent during the period covered by our chapter. Although all three mechanisms have been significant throughout this period, their relative importance has shifted over time. The first mechanism, which was of great importance during the early nineteenth century, is the movement of individuals with expertise in these technologies. The development of specialized producers of capital goods who sold their products on global markets, a hallmark of the textiles industries of both the United Kingdom and the United States by the mid nineteenth century, served as a second important mechanism of cross-border technology transfer. In many cases, export of these capital goods was complemented by sales and support efforts that provided additional know-how. Far more was involved than simply selling machinery – imports of technology "packages" containing skilled workers, managers, after-sales service, and information characterized, for instance, such acquisition by Scandinavian textile and engineering firms (Bruland 2010). By the late nineteenth and twentieth centuries, a third important channel of technology transfer was the offshore production-related investments of US and European firms, an intrafirm channel of technology transfer that produced important spillovers in the host economies (see Allen, Chapter 2 and Jones, Chapter 6 in this volume, and Jones 2006 for further discussion).

These three mechanisms for cross-border technology transfer are not mutually exclusive, and by the late twentieth century, all three complemented one another. But the ability of recipient economies to exploit any of these three channels of technology transfer for domestic economic development typically required considerable indigenous technological knowledge and training.

By the end of the twentieth century, a fourth channel for technology transfer emerged: investment by multinational and other firms in offshore innovation-related activities. In many cases, this fourth channel relied on the establishment of a wholly owned R&D facility in a foreign market. In others, however, cross-border linkages in innovation operated through interfirm agreements and alliances. Much of this reported offshore R&D investment focussed on modifying product designs for foreign markets. In others, however, firms sought to locate R&D activities near offshore "centers of excellence" in specific types of knowledge production (often universities) or technological innovation; and in still others, firms used alliances to collaborate with foreign firms in the production or marketing of new products. Investment in offshore R&D obviously has considerable potential to transfer not just technology, but methods for managing and undertaking innovation.

Where and why did innovation and technology transfer catalyze capitalist development in the global economy?

This chapter and the larger study of which it is a part seek to illuminate the global spread of capitalism. A central issue for this chapter accordingly is the interaction between innovation, technology transfer, and the success or failure of capitalist (and noncapitalist) economies in utilizing new technologies for economic growth. Specifically, how have economies that initially lagged behind economic or technological leaders succeeded or failed in shrinking the gap between domestic incomes or productivity levels and those in leading economies? In other words, how (if at all) have technological change and cross-border flows of technology contributed to economic "catchup"? As we argue below, the ability of innovation to support economic catchup and growth has varied over time, and often has been affected by larger political and economic trends. But the ability of follower economies to narrow gaps between their levels of income and those of leading economies has also depended crucially on the development within these followers of institutions that support investment in knowledge creation and human capital.

New technologies and the extension of imperial control

Innovation was spurred by the growth of capitalism, but technology (including but not limited to military technology) had powerful effects on the global spread of capitalism. Innovations in guns, shipping, and communications facilitated expansion of European colonial empires, exploitation of offshore natural resources, and expansion of trade in agricultural commodities (Russia, North America, Australia) during the nineteenth century. Although the creation and improvement of new technologies in weapons gave European nations considerable advantages in extending their political control through the nineteenth century, the gradual diffusion of these technologies to other nations, including some initially challenged by mid-nineteenth-century imperial expansion, also shifted the balance of power. One of the most vivid illustrations of this shift was the defeat of the Imperial Russian fleet by Japan at Tsushima Strait in 1905. As we note below, Japan's rapid adoption and mastery of modern warship design and construction relied on a complex process of institutional transformation and inward technology transfer that triggered a process of economic catchup and accelerated Japanese industrialization.

Economic catchup and technology transfer in the nineteenth and early twentieth centuries

The nineteenth century was associated with the global diffusion of the new technologies of industrialization and the processes through which they were produced. Technology flowed in significant quantities throughout the world, but the outcomes of that flow differed radically. On the one hand major societies, notably India and China, which at the beginning of the eighteenth century had been at similar technological levels to Europe, declined sharply relative to Europe. Other former colonies such as Brazil imported technology but failed to achieve an accelerated pace of industrial development. On the other hand, independent nations in both Europe and Asia (Germany, France, the smaller European economies, and later, Japan) and settler colonial economies (the United States, Canada, and Australia) utilized international flows of technology to develop into industrial economies. A huge, independent, and resource-rich nation that largely failed to exploit significant inward technology transfer during this period was Russia.

Advanced industrial technologies thus diffused to all of these societies, yet technology alone was insufficient to catalyze development. The varying degrees of success with which follower nations were able to benefit from inward technology flows reflects the fact that both technology development and use rest on knowledge-based capabilities that are supported by knowledge-related institutions. These include mass education, technical training, scientific societies, and intellectual property protection. Taken together, they supported the acquisition, adaptation, and use of technologies. Broadly speaking, success was associated with the construction or strengthening of these capabilities and institutions, and failure with their absence.

Despite its autocratic political system and semi-feudal agricultural sector, Russia industrialized on an impressive scale from the 1840s, largely on the basis of machinery imports from Britain. By the 1860s and 1870s, Russian entrepreneurs were importing technology from Germany as well as Britain, and this trade in technology advanced the development of capitalism within Russia. State-financed railway construction expanded the domestic market for industrial goods, supported rapid growth in agricultural exports, and created strong demand for steel, rolling stock, and other capital goods. Imports of capital goods, along with a surge of private foreign investment from German, British, French, and Belgian sources, all served to introduce foreign technologies into Russian industry. In some cases, the combination of foreign technologies and higher-quality natural resources enabled Russian factories' productivity to exceed that of more advanced industrial production facilities in Western Europe. Nevertheless, the much lower levels of investment in public education at all levels, as well as the enormous size and backward status of Russia's agricultural sector, meant that these inward flows of investment capital and technology had a modest transformative effect.

Precapitalist China generated an extraordinary array of scientific and technological knowledge and technological achievements, including large-scale engineering projects of great complexity.[24] By the mid nineteenth century, however, China had developed a dual economy, with extensive use of

---

24 Needham's list of important inventions that had originated (contrary to popular belief) in China includes cast iron, clockwork mechanisms, the magnetic compass, printing with woodblocks and movable type, the plough, the stirrup, and gunpowder (Needham 1950–2004).

Western technologies in a few industrial sectors, mainly located in the coastal regions and focussed on exports, while the vast Chinese hinterland continued to depend on subsistence agriculture. Many of the coastal cities where industrialization was most advanced (e.g. Shanghai) were effectively colonies of various European powers, "treaty ports" that guaranteed favorable trading privileges to foreign nationals (Maddison 2007: chap. 3). Inward technology transfer to China during the nineteenth century, similarly to the Russian case, thus supported the growth of an industrial sector that was confined to few industries and regions, notably the coastal urban centers.

Like Russia, Brazil acquired industrial technologies from the United Kingdom and the United States during the nineteenth century, as industry grew within an economy dominated by agriculture and resource extraction.[25] During the nineteenth century, a small textile sector, iron foundries, rail transport, and the electricity supply industry all grew. There was little or no local knowledge involved, and "most industries" relied on foreign technology, especially in textiles, which remained economically significant until the 1930s.[26] Although Brazil was capable of absorbing and applying foreign technology in the development of new industries, this inward technology transfer had limited effects on the nation's industrial structure, which (like China and Russia) remained heavily oriented to primary commodities. Access to technology was not in itself sufficient to shift the developmental path of the Brazilian economy, even within its nascent industrial sector.

Finally, colonial India was a large recipient of foreign technology in the mid nineteenth century. During the early nineteenth century technologies in steam power, iron and steel manufacture, and textiles were imported from the United Kingdom. But the growth of the British colonial administrative apparatus was associated with increased British private investment in Indian textiles, mining and metallurgy, and then in steam power. By the early 1870s India accounted for 12 percent of the exports (by value) of the UK's biggest textile machinery producer, Platt Brothers. Despite India's long history of iron and steel manufacture, the British colonial administration sponsored technology transfer projects from a variety of sources, including Sweden: The Burwai iron works in Madhya Pradesh attempted to bring Swedish charcoal-based iron production to India, led by three Swedish engineers.[27] Nevertheless, as

---

25 Birchal 2001.
26 "Yet no indigenous textile technology emerged in Brazil during this period and textile entrepreneurs had to look for machinery/equipment and skilled labour abroad" (Birchal 2001: 50).
27 af Geijerstam 2004.

Headrick (1988) and others have noted, this extensive foreign investment and inward technology transfer had limited effects on Indian industrial development.[28] The limited effects of inward technology transfer on Indian economic development during the nineteenth century appears to have had less to do with the extent or types of technologies imported by Indian and British industrialists and administrators than with the influence of British colonial rule on the development of indigenous capabilities and the low-tariff policy for British textiles imports that lasted through the early 1920s (Headrick 1988; Maddison 2007).[29]

By contrast, nineteenth-century European industrialization was associated with rapid technological development of a number of small regional economies, which in most cases exploited channels of inward technology transfer similar to those that had limited effects in Brazil, India, and China. The Nordic area, Switzerland, Benelux, and regions such as Alsace (whose national status remained indeterminate through much of the twentieth century), all developed on the basis of technology imports, especially of metalworking machinery and textile equipment. The ability of these economies to utilize such inward technology transfer for industrial development, in contrast to the regions discussed immediately above, rested on change in domestic institutions of education and training. The Nordic area, which grew from poverty to wealth from the mid nineteenth century, illustrates the role of these institutional factors in industrialization based on inward technology transfer.

During the late nineteenth and early twentieth centuries, technological change, combined with growing demand for industrial materials, made the natural resource endowments of both Norway and Sweden economically attractive targets for investment by domestic and foreign firms. Such investment flows brought with them advanced technologies that in many cases were further modified by firms and entrepreneurs in the recipient economies. Innovations in electricity generation and industrial processes made the existing resource endowments of Scandinavia more valuable in export markets. Hydroelectric power became a valuable source of energy within Norway for applications in electrochemistry and aluminum production (Moen 2009). Norwegian exploitation of its abundant waterpower for electricity production

28 "[A]mong nations with large rail networks, India remains a special case for two reasons: it was the only colony among sovereign states; and it was the only one of them that failed to industrialize during the railway boom" (Headrick 1988: 56).
29 "If the British had been willing to give tariff protection, India could have copied Lancashire's textile technology more quickly. Instead, British imports entered India duty free..." (Maddison 2007: 128).

benefitted from substantial inward flows of capital and technology, as well as important indigenous innovations in electrochemistry from Kristian Birkeland, a professor at the University of Oslo, and Sam Eyde, who together founded Norsk Hydro, a producer of fertilizer and other electrochemical products.

Swedish industrial development similarly benefitted from the exploitation of domestic deposits of phosphoric iron that became valuable as a result of the Gilchrist-Thomas steelmaking process that appeared in the 1870s, and other natural resources, aided by foreign investment and a growing cadre of domestic inventors and entrepreneurs (Sandberg 1979). Swedish process innovations in pulp and paper production, as well as match manufacture, facilitated the exploitation of Sweden's extensive forests for profitable exports of processed lumber products. By the end of the nineteenth century, innovations in electrical and engineering process industries supported the foundation of large Swedish firms (Alfa-Laval, Ericsson, ASEA, and SKF) that became important exporters and early multinational corporations (Edquist and Lundvall 1993).

The ability of all three Scandinavian economies to exploit technologies from foreign sources, to rapidly adopt domestically developed innovations, and to develop new product and process technologies relied on an extensive infrastructure of primary and secondary education that had been established by the early nineteenth century throughout the region (see Sandberg 1979). By the early twentieth century, public investment in the primary and secondary educational system was supplemented by growing public support for technical training in universities and other post-secondary institutions, as well as increased investments of public funds in research on technical problems of industrial relevance in sectors of long-standing economic importance. In other words, among the most important resource endowments whose improvement and exploitation was advanced by investments of public and private funds during this period was Scandinavian human capital. But beyond education systems, these countries created a range of knowledge-related institutions. These institutions included technical societies, tertiary-level training focussed on specific industries (such as mining), intellectual property systems (including novel patent forms that permitted the appropriation of foreign patents), policies supporting the inward immigration of skilled labor, foreign travel (including government-sponsored industrial espionage), and participation in international exhibitions (Bruland 1989; Bruland and Smith 2010).

The first successful case of economic catchup by a large Asian economy occurred in nineteenth-century Japan. The coercive "opening" of Japan to foreign trade by Commodore Perry in 1853 underscored the considerable gap in military capabilities between Japan and nations such as the United States,[30] and following the 1868 Meiji restoration, Japan's political elites pursued a comprehensive strategy of industrial development that relied among other things on state support for inward technology transfer as well as education. Primary and secondary education expanded rapidly in the late nineteenth century and enrolment in primary school grew from 46 percent in 1874 to 99 percent for Japanese boys by 1904, and from 17 percent to 96 percent for Japanese girls during the same period. An important resource for industrial development, a literate workforce, thus benefitted from state investment. The Japanese government also enlisted foreign experts to establish a College of Engineering in 1874 that later became a central component of the Imperial University (forerunner of Tokyo University). This college and its successors trained many of the entrepreneurs who were active in Japan's industrialization of the late nineteenth and early twentieth centuries.

The Meiji regime invested directly in the establishment of production facilities in such "strategic industries" as shipbuilding, steel production, mining, and textiles, enlisting foreign experts to advise on the use of imported technologies in all of these fields. By the end of the nineteenth century, many state-owned production establishments had been sold to Japanese entrepreneurs, although steel production remained an area of substantial state involvement because of its military significance.[31] Reflecting the national security motives that underpinned much of its industrial development strategy during this period, Japan's military was a significant purchaser of the output of many of these early industrial establishments.[32] Military-owned production facilities were important importers of foreign technologies and served to train a substantial cadre of production workers and technicians, many of whom moved to privately owned establishments in the aftermath of the

---

30 The one-sided nature of the "opening" of Japan was further illustrated by the Tokugawa regime's signature in 1858 of the so-called "Unequal Treaties" with the United Kingdom, the Netherlands, the United States, France, and Russia, which severely constrained Japan's ability to raise import tariffs to levels comparable with those in such industrializing nations as the United States. The ability of Japan to pursue an "infant industry" industrialization strategy that relied on protective tariffs thus was limited until the renegotiation of the treaties in 1911.

31 The privatization of these government-owned factories, many of which were sold to former samurai who were embarking on industrial careers, served as the nucleus of a number of the *zaibatsu* that became major industrial conglomerates in pre-1945 Japan (Yamamura 1978).

32 By 1907, Japan's largest machinery production facility was the naval shipyard at Kure, with more than 20,000 employees (Odagiri and Goto 1993).

Russo-Japanese war of 1904–1905. In addition, a number of government research laboratories, including the Industrial Research Institution (founded in 1900) were established during the period before World War I, and Japan's government expanded the number of universities and vocational schools during this period.

Building on these nineteenth-century foundations, Japan's early twentieth-century industrial development benefitted from inflows of foreign technology through investments by large foreign firms (notable examples include General Electric and Western Electric from the United States) in Japanese firms in industries ranging from communications to electrical equipment. The record of Japanese economic development during the last decades of the nineteenth and early decades of the twentieth century is remarkable, possibly exceeded in Japan's modern history only by the nation's rapid growth after 1945. Japanese GDP more than doubled between 1885 and 1914, and growth in total factor productivity accounted for 70 percent of the growth in mining and manufacturing output. As noted earlier, Japanese economic catchup industrialization underpinned the nation's challenge to and naval defeat of Tsarist Russia in the Russo-Japanese War of the early twentieth century.

Although the industrialization of Tsarist Russia remained incomplete at best, the post-Revolution industrial development of the USSR during the 1920s and 1930s represented a "noncapitalist experiment" in economic catch-up, one whose mixed success was purchased at an exorbitant cost of human life and freedom. But the socialist economic development of the USSR relied heavily on imports of technology and technological know-how from North American and European sources, as Sutton (1968–1973) and others have pointed out. Although the USSR invested substantial resources in R&D (according to Lewis 1979, 0.6 percent of GDP in 1935, which compared favorably to the estimated 0.35 percent of GDP accounted for by US investment in R&D in 1940), the Soviet research effort was concentrated in centralized, independent research institutes, with weak links to either universities or industrial establishments. It is plausible that this substantial investment in domestic R&D aided in the inward transfer and application of imported technology, but Lewis (1979) argues that the lack of stronger connections between research performance and utilization, in contrast to the in-house R&D organizations of many large corporations in the Western economies during this period, weakened the innovative efficiency of Soviet R&D. These weak linkages between state-funded R&D and state-controlled production activities impeded innovation in the postwar Soviet Union and its Warsaw Pact allies.

We have emphasized the pervasiveness of international flows of technology, but unevenness in the growth outcomes. What differentiated between success and failure in catching up? The varying degrees of success with which follower nations were able to benefit from inward technology flows reflects the fact that both technology development and use rest on knowledge-based capabilities that are supported by specific institutions for the acquisition, adaptation, and use of technologies. Failure was associated with the absence or erosion of knowledge-based capabilities and their supporting institutions, and success was associated with the construction or strengthening of these capabilities and institutions.

Successful and unsuccessful economic catchup in the postwar "golden age," 1945–1973

Economic reconstruction in Japan and catchup in East Asia after 1945

Japanese industrial reconstruction during the post-1945 period once again relied on a distinctive pattern of state support for inward technology transfer and innovation. Although the Japanese central government contributed a smaller share of overall R&D investment than the US or many European governments, the government of Japan was able to use its large, sophisticated and (for much of this period) protected domestic market to import foreign technologies via license and through direct foreign investment by US and European firms, a strategy which proved to be effective in Japanese industries ranging from steel to semiconductors and computers. The Japanese government also supported collaborative R&D among erstwhile competitors that supported the inward absorption and domestic diffusion of technologies from foreign sources, and engaged in limited "indicative" planning (among other things, limiting the number of firms active in the automobile industry in the early postwar years), although the ultimate effectiveness of these efforts is less apparent. By the 1970s, the Japanese economy had undergone a remarkable reconstruction and transformation.

Although Japan's postwar economic "catchup" built on strong technological and institutional foundations (e.g. widespread primary and secondary education, discussed earlier) that dated back to the late nineteenth century, the speed and scale of Japanese industrial success during the postwar period, as well as its reliance on a complex mix of public and private investment in R&D and technology adoption, influenced the policies of a growing group of Asian economies that included South Korea, Taiwan, Singapore, and (eventually) the People's Republic of China.

By the 1980s, the economies of South Korea, Taiwan, and Singapore (two of which, South Korea and Taiwan, had been colonized by Japan for much of the twentieth century, while the former British colony of Singapore had broken away from Malaysia in 1965) had achieved high levels of economic growth that had transformed their former status as "low-income developing" economies during the 1950s. It is difficult to overstate the magnitude and significance of the economic "catchup" of the East Asian economies that occurred after 1960. One startling comparative benchmark is provided by Wade (1990), who notes that in 1962, South Korea's per capita GNP, reflecting the consequences of the destructive war of the early 1950s, ranked 99th in the world, placing this economy just behind Sudan and ahead of Mauritius. Taiwan's per capita GNP placed this economy at 85th place, just ahead of the nation now known as the Congo Republic.

The rapid growth of all three Asian economies was based in part on the inward transfer of technology from high-income economies, although the specific policies employed by each differed from one another and (in varying degrees) from those of Japan. In all three nations, government invested heavily in primary and secondary education to improve basic literacy and numeracy, while both Taiwan and South Korea rapidly expanded post-secondary education. Human capital formation, therefore, played a central role in the technology-based industrial strategies of all of these economies, just as had been the case in Japan and the Nordic countries of the nineteenth century.

Beyond this fundamental (and crucial) similarity, however, the policies of these three industrializing Asian economies toward inward technology transfer differed significantly, reflecting both economic and political influences. South Korea pursued a strategy of selective protection of domestic markets, technology licensing, and capital goods imports, combined with extensive government intervention in financial markets to support the growth of gigantic industrial conglomerates, the *chaebol*. The *chaebol* were in turn expected by policy-makers to achieve ambitious export goals, thereby enforcing some competitive discipline on their operations. Taiwan, on the other hand, pursued economic policies of financial liberalization that invigorated its domestic capital markets and supported the entry of numerous smaller manufacturing specialist firms. Both South Korea and Taiwan pursued broadly similar policies of government investment in domestic R&D institutions that bridged institutional gaps between domestic industrial firms and the sources of fundamental and applied research offshore, by establishing the

Korean Institute for Science and Technology and the Industrial Technology and Research Institute in Taiwan. Singapore was the most open of these three economies to direct foreign investment, which (combined with investments in domestic post-secondary education) served as an effective vehicle for the inward transfer of advanced industrial technologies.

The failure of economic catchup outside of East Asia during the "golden age"

The comparative statistics cited in the previous discussion of Asian economic "catchup" highlight both the remarkable growth of the East Asian economies during the subsequent decades and the failure of economic growth in sub-Saharan Africa. Indeed, the period between 1950 and 2000 was broadly characterized by a second "Great Divergence" that reflected lagging economic growth in Latin America, North Africa, eastern Europe, and sub-Saharan Africa (Dowrick and DeLong 2003). Nations that had begun to narrow the gap between their income levels and those of industrial economies during the interwar period fell behind, even as Western European nations whose incomes had fallen behind that of the United States during the interwar period displayed rapid growth and convergence.

What, if any, role did technological innovation play in the disappointing performance of so many nations included in the "Third World," a label that by the end of the twentieth century obscured significant contrasts in economic growth among these economies? As pointed out above, the contributions of technological innovation to economic catchup flow primarily from the ability of the "follower" economy to adopt (and adapt) technologies from external sources efficiently and effectively. In the nineteenth- and twentieth-century cases from Latin America, Europe, and Asia that were discussed above, substantial domestic investments in human capital, educational infrastructure, and competitive domestic firms were indispensable prerequisites for success-ful catchup. In varying degrees, the lack of these domestic investments and related policies contributed to the failures of economic catchup in the "Third World" outside of East Asia during the late twentieth century. The failures reflected unwise policy choices, especially the heavy emphasis on import-substitution economic strategies in much of Latin America and the establish-ment of state-owned enterprises in capital-intensive industries in many newly independent states of sub-Saharan Africa.

An equally significant policy failure, in view of the size of the agricultural sectors of many of the economies that failed to achieve economic convergence during this period, was the tendency for import-substitution and quasi-socialist economic planning policies to discriminate against productivity and innovation (based on indigenous innovation as well as inward technology transfer) in agriculture. And this discrimination often extended to reductions in public investment in agricultural R&D, particularly in Africa and Latin America (Brazil, India, and the PRC did not experience comparable declines in public investment during this period).[33] The agricultural research systems of newly independent nations such as Zaire and Uganda virtually collapsed during the 1980s and 1990s as a result of disinvestment and civil strife.[34]

By the end of the twentieth century, and during the first decade of the twenty-first, at least some of the disappointing trends in these economies had been reversed, and growth had accelerated. A portion of these welcome improvements reflected the surge in commodity prices resulting from rapid growth in large developing economies such as Brazil, India, and the PRC. Growing inflows of foreign investment from these economies also benefitted many formerly lagging nations in Africa and Latin America. And low-income economies "leapfrogged" a generation of communications technologies in their rapid adoption of Internet and wireless telecommunications technologies. By 2003, according to the World Bank, developing economies' level of adoption of wireless telephone technologies resembled that of high-income economies as of 1995.[35] The spread of these technologies within low-income economies supported important innovations in financial services and agricultural

---

33 According to Alston and Pardey (2006: 18–19), the rate of growth in public R&D investment in agricultural R&D in Africa shrank from 1.25 percent/year during the 1980s to 0.82 percent/year during the 1990s. When Nigeria and South Africa are excluded from the data, agricultural R&D investment in Africa shrank by roughly 2.5 percent/year during the 1990s.

34 "Civil strife and wars caused an exodus of scientific staff, or at least a flight from practicing science. Many of Uganda's scientific facilities, for example, were in shreds when its civil war ended in the early 1980s. It is hard to imagine that today's Congo once had perhaps the most sophisticated scientific infrastructure in colonial Africa, comparable to the facilities and quality of staff found in most developed countries at the time" (Alston and Pardey 2006: 23).

35 "For technologies discovered during 1950–75, only a quarter of the developing countries that have achieved at least a 5 percent penetration level have gone on to reach the 25 percent threshold, and all of these are upper-middle-income countries...The story is somewhat better for newer technologies. Not only have these technologies spread more quickly between countries, but also the share of countries that have achieved the 25 percent threshold is higher, at 33 percent. Indeed, developing countries have now reached the same average level of penetration of mobile phones as was observed in high-income countries in 1995" (World Bank 2008: 7). It is likely that the relatively rapid adoption of mobile telephone technologies within many of these low-income economies reflected the fact that state-owned enterprises were often less involved in the provision of these services.

marketing. But the lengthy period of poor economic performance was attributable in large part to the failures of governments to make the public investments necessary to support inward technology transfer, as well as related failures to support innovation and productivity in agriculture and a more competitive environment for industrial enterprises.

A noncapitalist catchup failure: the Soviet Union and Warsaw Pact, 1973–1989

The political, economic, and military influence of the Soviet Union arguably approached its zenith during the 1950s, in the aftermath of the Chinese Revolution and the detonation of the Soviet atomic bomb in 1949. The assertion by the USSR of political control over much of Eastern Europe, as well as technical assistance and advice to the new government of the PRC, led to the export of the R&D system associated with the Soviet Union to nations such as Poland and Hungary with established university and research institutions in industry and government. The basic model of government research institutes with limited links to universities or industry was widely adopted in both Eastern Europe and the PRC, with consequences for innovative performance in civilian industries that appear to have been similar to those observed in the USSR. Transferring technology and knowledge across the institutional boundaries dividing research institutes from production facilities had long been a serious problem in the Soviet R&D system, and these problems were significant in the nations influenced by the Soviet model.

The post-1973 global productivity slowdown had particularly significant consequences for the centrally planned economies of Eastern Europe, which had fallen behind the affluent consumer societies in the West. Although Western European governments and firms expanded financial support and investment in many Eastern European economies, the accompanying technology transfer was limited, and its effects on incomes modest. Economic and technological stagnation, combined with similar difficulties in the Soviet Union, ultimately contributed to the collapse of the Warsaw Pact and the end of the Cold War in Europe. In both the former Soviet Union and Eastern Europe, the post-Cold War challenges in reconstructing national R&D systems, which had been organized around centralized industry research laboratories and scientific academies that were not closely linked with either universities or individual firms, have taken more than a decade to address. Similar challenges of reorganization and reconstruction have been addressed with somewhat greater success in the PRC during its economic liberalization.

In all of these regions, central-government funding for R&D in the academies and research institutes has been reduced significantly, with limited growth in support for university- or firm-based R&D activities.

Conclusion

The interaction between technological innovation and the global spread of capitalism since 1848 is a complex historical process, and this chapter has presented an overview of some central themes rather than a comprehensive history. Central to our argument is the premise that the technological dynamism of capitalism reflects an interaction between market competition and government policy. Competition between firms has driven innovation, has facilitated the transfer of technology across borders (as firms seek markets and solutions to technical problems outside their own territories), and has promoted the diffusion of technologies among users. It has contributed to a central dimension of modern capitalism, namely the organized creation and use of knowledge. The development of formal R&D within the firm, involving specialized staffs in search of technological solutions to corporate problems, was an important change in the structure of the innovation process. The significance and role of this institutional innovation have only increased over time and have affected the growth of capitalist firms. The growth of organized R&D within the firm was paralleled by the expansion of research in supporting institutions, including universities and government laboratories.

But as the reference to "supporting institutions" suggests, the growth of innovation within capitalist economies involved more than simply firm-level search for knowledge. Capitalist economies are organized, shaped, and coordinated by national states, and since at least the nineteenth century, the state has played an important role in supporting and promoting innovation, both through financing innovation and supporting the development of regulatory policies and the broader institutional landscape noted earlier. In early capitalism, governments created economic institutions, procured new technologies, facilitated the appropriation of territory, rebuilt cities, and educated populations. These roles are so persistent through time, and so pervasive across countries, that it is insufficient to conceptualize capitalist economies, dating to the inception of industrialization, as simply market economies. In fact, they are market economies in which states exercise considerable influence over R&D and innovation in the public and private sectors. This influence was present at the inception of the industrial capitalist economy, but has expanded considerably since.

Indeed, the varied roles of the governments in supporting innovation within industrial and industrializing economies during the past 150 years have contributed to the emergence of a variety of capitalist approaches to innovation. The post-1989 "triumph of capitalism" was anything but the triumph of a single policy or institutional framework, instead reflecting the growth of very different institutional structures supporting competition and capitalist innovation. The global spread of capitalism has by no means erased enduring differences between the funding arrangements and numerous other institutional and policy features of the "national innovation systems" of industrial and industrializing economies.

The role of the state is closely linked to knowledge creation and diffusion. Every capitalist economy supports organizations to create and spread knowledge (especially universities, but also extensive systems of government-supported labs), and commits significant public funds to industrial R&D, education, and technology development and procurement. For much of the twentieth century, public investments in R&D, particularly within industry, were motivated by a central government mission, national defense. Other missions, such as public health, support for agriculture, and (more recently) space exploration, have also attracted significant public investments in knowledge creation and application. Indeed, the dominance of most OECD central-government R&D budgets by investments supporting government missions, rather than knowledge creation based on the "market failures" so prominent in the welfare economics of R&D (Arrow 1962; Nelson 1959), is as striking in the data on national patterns of R&D investment as is the widespread failure of economists to highlight this fact. Modern industries such as ICT, biotechnology, pharmaceuticals, and aerospace have been important beneficiaries of these mission-oriented public R&D programs. The role of the state, along with supporting institutions that have benefitted or been stifled by the state, also figures prominently in the ability of economies lagging behind a given period's technological and economic leaders to catch up with these leading economies.

We have argued that this process of technological and economic catchup has benefitted from cross-border flows of technology, capital, and people, but such flows are necessary rather than sufficient conditions. In addition to accessing nondomestic sources of knowledge and capital, economic catchup requires the development of indigenous institutions that can support the inward transfer, modification, and application of technologies from external sources. In most cases, political independence has been an additional necessary but insufficient condition to support the development of these indigenous institutions and the associated capabilities.

Where countries were able to create the institutional framework needed to support the growth of knowledge-based capitalism – as in the Nordic countries, the Anglo-Saxon periphery, or the small economies of Western Europe – they were able to participate in the extraordinary technological trajectory of modern capitalism. Where imperial penetration destroyed such institutions or prevented their creation, development was constrained and stunted. But the recent economic growth in much of what was formerly known as the less-developed world has benefitted from the rapid expansion of scientific and technological research and resources, as well as accelerated cross-border flows of knowledge, technologies, capital, and people. A new story of capitalism and technological innovation is now under way.

References

Abramovitz, M. (1989). "Rapid Growth Potential and its Realization: The Experience of Capitalist Economies in the Postwar Period," in M. Abramovitz, *Thinking about Growth*. New York: Cambridge University Press), pp. 3–79.

Allen, R. C. (1983). "Collective Invention," *Journal of Economic Behavior and Organization* 4: 1–24.

Alston, J. M. and P. G. Pardey (2006). "Developing-Country Perspectives on Agricultural R D: New Pressures for Self-Reliance?" in P. G. Pardey, J. M. Alston, and R. R. Piggott (eds.), *Agricultural R&D in the Developing World: Too Little, Too Late?* (Washington, DC: International Food Policy Research Institute, pp. 11–28.

Amsden, A. (2001). *The Rise of "The Rest": Challenges to the West from Late-Industrializing Economies*. New York: Oxford University Press.

Arora, A. and A. Gambardella (1998). "Evolution of Industry Structure in the Chemicals Industry," in A. Arora, R. Landau, and N. Rosenberg (eds.), *Chemicals and Long-Term Economic Growth*. New York: John Wiley, pp. 379–414.

Arrow, K. J. (1962). "Economic Welfare and the Allocation of Resources for R&D," in R. R. Nelson (ed.), *The Rate & Direction of Inventive Activity* (Princeton University Press, pp. 609–625.

Baba, Z. (1998). *The Science of Empire: Scientific Knowledge, Civilization and Colonial Rule in India*. New Delhi: Oxford University Press.

Beer, J. H. (1959). *The Emergence of the German Dye Industry*. Urbana, IL: University of Illinois Press.

Berg, M. (1994). *The Age of Manufactures 1700–1820: Industry, Innovation and Work in Britain*. London and New York: Routledge.

Birchal, S. de O. (2001). "The Transfer of Technology to Latecomer Economies in the Nineteenth Century: The Case of Minas Gerais, Brazil," *Business History* 43(4): 48–67.

Bruland, K. (1989). *British Technology and European Industrialization: The Norwegian Textile Industry in the Mid-nineteenth Century*. Cambridge and New York: Cambridge University Press.

(2010). "Reconceptualizing Industrialization in Scandinavia," in J. Horn, L. N. Rosenband, and M. R. Smith, eds., *Reconceptualizing the Industrial Revolution*. Cambridge, MA: The MIT Press, pp. 125–150.

Bruland, K. and K. Smith (2010). "Knowledge Flows and Catching-up Industrialization in the Nordic Countries: The Roles of Patent Systems," in H. Odagiri, A. Goto, A. Sunami, and R. R. Nelson, eds., *Intellectual Property Rights and Catch-Up: An International Comparative Study*. New York: Oxford University Press, 63–94.

Bush, V. (1945). *Science: The Endless Frontier*. Washington, DC: USGPO.

Cantwell, J. (1995). "The Globalization of Technology: What Remains of the Product Cycle?" *Cambridge Journal of Economics* 19: 155–174.

Chandler, Jr., A. D. (1977). *The Visible Hand*. Cambridge, MA: Harvard University Press.
    (1990). *Scale and Scope*. Cambridge, MA: Harvard University Press.

Cockburn, I. M. (2004). "The Changing Structure of the Pharmaceutical Industry," *Health Affairs* 23: 10–22.
    (2006). "Is the Pharmaceutical Industry in a Productivity Crisis?" in A. B. Jaffe, J. Lerner, and S. Stern (eds.), *Innovation Policy and the Economy*. University of Chicago Press for NBER. 7: 1–32.

Cockburn, I. M., R. Henderson, L. Orsenigo, and G. Pisano (1999). "Pharmaceuticals and Biotechnology," in D. C. Mowery (ed.), *U.S. Industry in 2000*. Washington, DC: National Academies Press, pp. 363–398.

Cooling, B. G. (1979). *Grey Steel and Blue-Water Navy*. Hamden, CT: Archon Books.

Cowan, R. (1990). "Nuclear Power Reactors: A Study in Technological Lock-In," *Journal of Economic History* 50: 541–567.

David, P. A. and G. Wright (1997). "Increasing Returns and the Genesis of American Resource Abundance," *Industrial and Corporate Change* 6: 203–245.

Dowrick, S. and J. B. DeLong (2003). "Globalization and Convergence," in M. D. Bordo, A. M. Taylor, and J. G. Williamson (eds.), *Globalization in Historical Perspective*. University of Chicago for NBER, pp. 191–220.

Dupree, H. (1986). *Science in the Federal Government*. Baltimore, MD: Johns Hopkins University Press.

Edquist, C. and B.-A. Lundvall (1993). "Comparing the Danish and Swedish Systems of Innovation," in R. R. Nelson (ed.), *National Systems of Innovation*. New York: Oxford University Press, pp. 265–294.

Enos, J. L. (1962). *Petroleum Progress and Profits*. Cambridge, MA: The MIT Press.

Fabrizio, K. and D. C. Mowery (2007). "The Federal Role in Financing Major Innovations: Information Technology during the Postwar Period," in N. Lamoreaux and K. Sokoloff (eds.), *Financing Innovation in the United States, 1870 to the Present*. Cambridge, MA: The MIT Press, pp. 283–316.

Field, A. J. (2011). *A Great Leap Forward: 1930s Depression and U.S. Economic Growth*. New Haven, CT: Yale University Press.

Freeman, C. (1962). "Research and Development: A Comparison between British and American Industry," *National Institute Economic Review* 20: 21–38.

af Geijerstam, J. (2004). *Landscapes of Technology Transfer: Swedish Ironmakers in India, 1860–64*, Jernkontorets berghistoriska skriftserie 42, Stockholm: Jernkontoret.

Gibb, G. S. and E. H. Knowlton (1956). *The Emergent Years: History of the Standard Oil Company (New Jersey), 1911–1927*. New York: Harpers.

Graham, M. B. W. and B. H. Pruitt (1990). *R&D for Industry: A Century of Technical Innovation at Alcoa*. New York: Cambridge University Press.

Hall, P. A. and D. Soskice (2001). *Varieties of Capitalism: The Institutional Foundations of Comparative Advantage*. New York: Oxford University Press.

Harley, C. K. (1988). "Ocean Freight Rates and Productivity, 1740–1913: The Primacy of Mechanical Innovation Reaffirmed," *Journal of Economic History* 48: 851–876.

Headrick, D. R. (1988). *The Tentacles of Progress*. New York: Oxford University Press.

Henderson, R., L. Orsenigo, and G. Pisano (1999). "The Pharmaceutical Industry and the Revolution in Molecular Biology: Interactions among Scientific, Institutional, and Organizational Change," in D. C. Mowery and R. R. Nelson (eds.), *Sources of Industrial Leadership*. New York: Cambridge University Press, pp. 267–311.

Hounshell, D. A. (1996). "The Evolution of Industrial Research in the United States," in R. Rosenbloom and W. J. Spencer (eds.), *Engines of Innovation*. Boston, MA: Harvard Business School Press, pp. 13–86.

    (2000). "The Medium is the Message, or How Context Matters: The RAND Corporation Builds an Economics of Innovation, 1946–62," in T. P. Hughes and A. Hughes (eds.), *Systems, Experts, and Computers*. Cambridge, MA: The MIT Press, pp. 13–86.

Hounshell, D. A. and J. K. Smith (1988). *Science and Corporate Strategy* New York: Cambridge University Press.

Hughes, T. P. (1971). *Elmer Sperry: Inventor and Engineer*. Baltimore, MD: Johns Hopkins University Press.

Jones, G. (2006). *The Evolution of International Business*. London: Routledge.

Jorgenson, D. (2001). "Information Technology and the U.S. Economy," *American Economic Review* 90: 1–32.

Khan, B. Z. (2005). *The Democratization of Invention*. New York: Cambridge University Press.

Lamoreaux, N. R. (1985). *The Great Merger Movement in American Business, 1895–1904*. New York: Cambridge University Press.

Lamoreaux, N. R. and K. L. Sokoloff (1997). "Inventive Activity and the Market for Technology in the United States, 1840–1920," NBER Working Paper No. 7107.

Leslie, S. W. (1993). *The Cold War and American Science*. New York: Columbia University Press.

Lewis, R. (1979). *Science and Industrialisation in the USSR*. London: Macmillan.

Lindert, P. H. and J. G. Williamson (2003). "Does Globalization make the World More Unequal?" in M. D. Bordo, A. M Taylor, and J. G. Williamson (eds.), *Globalization in Historical Perspective*. University of Chicago Press for NBER, pp. 227–271.

Lowen, R. S. (1997). *Creating the Cold War University*. Berkeley, CA: University of California Press.

Maddison, A. (2007). *Contours of the World Economy, 1–2030 AD*. Oxford and New York: Oxford University Press.

Marschak, T. A., T. K. Glennan, and R. Summers (1967). *Strategy for R&D*. New York: Springer.

Marshall, A. W. and W. H. Meckling (1962). "Predictability of the Costs, Time, and Success in Development," in R. R. Nelson (ed.), *The Rate and Direction of Inventive Activity*. Princeton University Press, pp. 461–476.

Mazzoleni, R. (1999). "Innovation in the Machine Tool Industry: A Historical Perspective on the Dynamics of Comparative Advantage," in D. C. Mowery and R. R. Nelson (eds.), *The Sources of Industrial Leadership*. New York: Cambridge University Press, pp. 169–216.

McNeill, W. H. (1982). *The Pursuit of Power*. University of Chicago Press.

Meisenzahl, R. R. and J. Mokyr (2012). "The Rate and Direction of Invention in the British Industrial Revolution: Incentives and Institutions," in J. Lerner and S. Stern (eds.), *The Rate and Direction of Inventive Activity Revisited*. University of Chicago Press for NBER, pp. 443–479.

Millard, A. (1990). *Edison and the Business of Invention*. Baltimore, MD: Johns Hopkins University Press.

Milward, A. and S. B. Saul (1973). *The Economic Development of Continental Europe*. Totowa, NJ: Rowman and Littlefield.

Moen, S. E. (2009). "Innovation and Production in the Norwegian Aluminum Industry," in J. Fagerberg, D. C. Mowery, and B. Verspagen (eds.), *Innovation, Path Dependency and Policy: The Norwegian Case*. New York: Oxford University Press, pp. 149–178.

Mokyr, J. (1990). *The Lever of Riches*. New York: Oxford University Press.

Mowery, D. C. (1983). "The Relationship between Contractual and Intrafirm Forms of Industrial Research in American Manufacturing, 1900–1940," *Explorations in Economic History* 20: 351–374.

  (1995). "The Boundaries of the US Firm in R&D," in N. R. Lamoreaux and D. M. G. Raff (eds.), *Coordination and Information: Historical Perspectives on the Organization of Enterprise*. University of Chicago Press, pp. 147–176.

  (2011). "Federal Policy and the Development of Semiconductors, Computer Hardware, and Computer Software: A Policy Model for Climate-change R&D?" in R. Henderson and R. Newell (eds.), *The Federal Government Role in Technological Innovation: Insights for the Development of Energy Technologies*. University of Chicago Press for NBER, pp. 159–188.

Mueller, W. F. (1962). "The Origins of the Basic Inventions Underlying Du Pont's Major Product and Process Innovations, 1920 to 1950," in R. R. Nelson (ed.), *The Rate and Direction of Inventive Activity*. Princeton University Press, pp. 323–346.

National Resources Planning Board (1941). *Research – A National Resource*. Vol. 2: *Industrial Research*. Washington, DC: National Research Council for the National Resources Planning Board.

Needham, J. (1950–2004). *Science and Civilisation in China*, 24 vols. Cambridge University Press.

Nelson, R. R. (1959). "The Simple Economics of Basic Research," *Journal of Political Economy*. 67(3): 297–306.

Nelson, R. R. and G. Wright (1994). "The Erosion of U.S. Technological Leadership as a Factor in Postwar Economic Convergence," in W. J. Baumol, R. R. Nelson, and E. N. Wolff (eds.), *Convergence of Productivity*. New York: Oxford University Press, pp. 129–163.

Odagiri, H. and A. Goto (1993). "The Japanese System of Innovation: Past, Present, and Future," in R. R. Nelson (ed.), *National Systems of Innovation*. New York: Oxford University Press, pp. 76–114.

O'Rourke, K. H. and J. G. Williamson (1999). *Globalization and History*. Cambridge, MA: The MIT Press.

Reich, L. S. (1985). *The Making of American Industrial Research*. New York: Cambridge University Press.

Robertson, P. and L. Alston (1992). "Technological Choice and the Organisation of Work in Capitalist Firms," *Economic History Review*, 45: 330–40.

Ruttan, V. (2001). *Technology, Growth, and Development*. New York: Oxford University Press.

Sandberg, L. (1979). "The Case of the Impoverished Sophisticate: Human Capital and Swedish Economic Growth Before World War I," *Journal of Economic History* 39: 225–241.

Sanderson, M. (1972). "Research and the Firm in British Industry," *Science Studies* 2: 107–151.

Sapolsky, H. M. (1990). *Science and the Navy*. Princeton University Press.

Scranton, P. (1997). *Endless Novelty. Speciality Production and American Industrialization 1865–1925*. Princeton University Press.

Schumpeter, J. A. (1943). *Capitalism, Socialism, and Democracy*. New York: Harper & Row.

Smil, V. (2005). *Creating the Twentieth Century*. New York: Oxford University Press.

Stigler, G. J. (1968). "Monopoly and Oligopoly by Merger," in G. J. Stigler (ed.), *The Organization of Industry*, Homewood, IL: Irwin, pp. 95–107.

Sutton, A. C. (1968–1973). *Western Technology and Soviet Economic Development*, 3 vols. Stanford, CA: Hoover Institution Press.

Thorelli, H. B. (1954). *Federal Antitrust Policy*. Baltimore, MD: Johns Hopkins University Press.

Trebilcock, C. (1969). "'Spin-Off' in British Economic History: Armaments and Industry, 1760–1914," *Economic History Review* 22: 474–490.

(1973). "British Armaments and European Industrialization, 1890–1914," *Economic History Review* 26: 254–272.

Wade, N. (1990). *Governing the Market: Economic Theory and the Role of the Government in East Asian Industrialization*. Princeton University Press.

Whitehead, A. N. (1925). *Science and the Modern World*. New York: Macmillan.

Whitley, R. (2000). *Divergent Capitalisms: The Social Structuring and Change of Business Systems*. New York: Oxford University Press.

Wilkins, M. (2004). *The History of Foreign Investment in the United States, 1914–1945*. Cambridge, MA: Harvard University Press.

Williamson, O. E. (1975). *Markets and Hierarchies*. New York: Free Press.

World Bank (2008). *Global Economic Prospects: 2008*. Washington, DC: World Bank.

Yamamura, K. (1978). "The Industrialization of Japan: Entrepreneurship, Ownership, and Management," in P. Mathias and M. Postan (eds.), *The Cambridge Economic History of Europe*. Vol. VII: *The Industrial Economies: Capital, Labor, and Enterprise*, Part II. New York: Cambridge University Press, pp. 215–264.

5

Spread of legal innovations defining private and public domains

RON HARRIS

The literature on law and the rise and spread of capitalism is consumed by two major tensions. The first is between the view of law as epiphenomenal to the rise of capitalism and of law as instrumental to its rise. The second is between a view of Western law as developing in two separate and distinct legal traditions, English common law and Roman civil law, and a view of the law as converging into a single capitalist enhancing model. This chapter is organized around the second tension.

It first surveys the literature and shows that much of it pays substantial attention to the unique features of each of the two European traditions, and to the different role played by each in enhancing capitalism. Much of the more recent literature upholds the common law side by asserting that Anglo-American common law and the British and American constitutional tradition facilitated faster and more sustainable growth.

The next part of the chapter surveys the development of the law in the core capitalist countries, in four fields of law that are postulated by economic theory as crucial for economic growth: the concept of freedom of contract; the establishment of land registries; patent law; and the formation of business corporations. This part of the chapter shows that, on the whole, the transformation of law in these fields into a capitalist mode was not based on legal traditions. Countries having similar legal origins, say Germany and France, or the United Kingdom and the United States, in some cases developed different models for dealing with similar problems, while countries of different origins sometimes adopted similar institutional-legal solutions.

The last part of the chapter accounts for the spread of European capitalist law in these four fields to the rest of the world. Here again a pattern of expansion along the lines of legal traditions does not hold well. In some cases, the law of the core of each empire indeed spread to its overseas colonies with settlers or trade. But transplantation throughout the empire was often affected by the local conditions in each colony and by contingencies. Furthermore, in the imperial peripheries, cross-empire influences sometimes resulted in borrowing models from rival empires. Countries that were not part of the formal empire of a European power were freer to borrow law from different European sources or to reject it, at least in some fields, in favor of local law. Last, a significant tool for spreading European capitalist law was through voluntary transnational organizations that promoted the harmonization of law.

The first theme, the role of law in economic development, is not directly addressed in this chapter. Yet the multiplicity of models of law that emerged in each of the four fields suggests that no single model of law was inevitable for the transformation to capitalism. There was no convergence into a single, most efficient, legal solution. Economies that adopted quite different legal models were able to develop. The question whether differences in legal tradition or in specific legal institutions and rules made a difference in terms of rate of growth or nature of growth is fiercely debated. The conclusion discusses the possibility that despite a multiplicity of legal designs, these were nevertheless functionally equivalent in a manner that suggests a second-order convergence.

Law and economic development

Max Weber was among the first to attribute a significant role to the law in the rise of capitalism. European law was developed by jurists on the basis of general legal rules that were shaped over centuries, from Roman times on, and embodied in codes. It was operated by independent judiciaries, academically spirited *jurisconsults*, and a distinct legal profession. These created a high level of separation between law and other realms of social life, such as religion or politics. European law combines a high degree of legal autonomy with a substantial reliance on preexisting general rules in the determination of legal decisions (Weber 1968: 641–901). Weber argued that the law of other civilizations, notably Chinese law, was not as formal and rational as European law. As a result, the law of these civilizations did not facilitate the rise of capitalism. His argument fails to explain why England's non-academic case-based law, which is the least formal and least rational in Europe, was the first to industrialize. What is known as the "England Problem" haunted Weber's thesis and gave rise to later explanations that privileged the common law (Likhovski 1999; Trubek 1972).

From Weber's time and until the 1970s, law was not viewed as a major factor in explaining economic development. Attention was mainly devoted to technology, capital accumulation, trade, and education. There were, however, two exceptions. In the 1920s and early 1930s, traditions that originated with Thorstein Veblen and Oliver Wendell Holmes eventually met in an institutional economics – legal realist interaction in the works of John Commons, Robert Hale, and their contemporaries, who viewed the law as a precondition to the functioning of the market (Fried 1998; Hovenkamp 1990: 993–1058; Pearson 1997). In the 1960s and early 1970s, the belief that the law can serve as the key to economic growth spread among lawyers. They believed that less formal and autonomous, and more instrumental and policy-oriented law could help Latin American and Asian economies grow faster. They worked in law school foreign aid programs and developmental agencies and collaborated with the Ford Foundation to promote the reform of legal rules and institutions, strengthen enforcement, and enhance the legitimization of the legal systems of developing countries (Trubek and Santos 2006).

The last three decades have witnessed an institutional turn in the social sciences and particularly in economics. Economists turned their attention from markets to institutions, including legal institutions. This institutional turn, mostly due to the influence of Nobel Laureate Douglass North, had historical tendencies. Attention turned to the development of impersonal exchange in pre-state settings, to the rise of states that credibly respect property rights, and to the evolution of market infrastructures. The sources of this change can be identified in the transaction costs and property rights adjustments of the neoclassical economic paradigm, which were first formulated in the theoretical economics discourse of the 1960s by Ronald Coase and later by Oliver Williamson and Armen Alchian, Harold Demsetz, and others. The application of neoclassical economic theory to non-market settings, notably public choice and economic analysis of law, also began during the same decade, in the work of James Buchanan, Ronald Coase, Gary Becker, and Richard Posner. Issues of collective action received attention from Kenneth Arrow, Mancur Olson, and others. These corrections, adjustments and extensions of the neoclassical paradigm drew economists' attention to institutions. The new turn to institutions in economics made inroads into economic history and into the study of the rise of capitalism in the 1970s and the early 1980s, and caused economic historians to divert more of their research from markets to institutions. Roughly speaking, the turn to institutions had three phases in terms of modeling the relationship between institutions and the economy. Initially institutions were viewed as exogenously endowed on the economy, and the focus was on their effect on economic performance. In the second phase, attention was given to the study of the ways in which economic development affects the creation and transformation of institutions. In the third phase, institutions were viewed as endogenous, affecting economic development and being shaped by it, and the study focussed on the details of the reciprocal causal relationships (Harris 2003: 297–346).

Douglass North (initially with Robert Thomas) was the first to argue that the rise of the West can be explained by its institutions. Institutions that developed in Europe were more effective than institutions of other civilizations in reducing transaction costs, protecting property rights, enforcing contracts, and facilitating the spread and management of risks and the monitoring of agents. More specifically, North discussed such institutional changes as bills of exchange, patent law, insurance, accounting methods, and joint-stock companies (North 1990; North and Thomas 1973).

Richard Posner, coming from a law-school tradition and applying to it price theory, argued that, due to litigation and judicial decisions, the common law constantly evolved towards efficiency and better supported economic growth than the code and legislation of continental legal systems (Posner 2002).

Douglass North and Barry Weingast argued that the British were the first to solve the credible commitments problem – the inability of the sovereign and unconstrained state to credibly commit towards its subjects not to expropriate them. The Glorious Revolution of 1688 epitomized a constitutional transformation, with the Bill of Rights, parliamentary supremacy in issues of taxation and spending, and the establishment of the Bank of England, and created an environment in which investors could rely upon the state to meet its financial promises. The solution to the credible commitment problem allowed Britain to increase government borrowing, lower the interest paid by the government on its debt, and expand the government bond market and private capital markets, resulting in Britain's ability to wage prolonged and successful wars, and to form the fiscal–military nexus (North and Weingast 1989).[1] The solution marked the beginning of a century and a half of continuous and unprecedented economic growth. Countries such as France, which were unsuccessful in solving the problem, dawdled. North and Weingast did not argue for the superiority of European institutions in general, they argued that some Europeans – the British – provided better institutional support for the rise of capitalism than others. The institutional support was connected to law, not to the common law, but rather to constitutional law.

---

1 But see also criticism of the argument: Munro 2003: 505–562; Sussman and Yafeh 2006; and Coffman, Leonard, and Neal (in press).

A team of four authors, La Porta, Lopez-de-Silanes, Shleifer, and Vishny, known as LLSV, developed a system for coding and measuring the legal rules governing the protection of outside investors in corporations. They then showed that legal rules protecting investors vary systematically among legal traditions or legal origins. Common law countries provide the most protection; German-based and Scandinavian civil law countries provide a medium level of protection; and French civil law countries provide the least protection (La Porta *et al.* 1997). They then correlated these levels of protection with economic outcomes. They found that legal origins explained the ownership structure of corporations, firm valuation, the extent and liquidity of the stock market, and, eventually, economic development. Previous econometric studies could not convincingly untangle the causation problem; namely, determine whether better law caused better economic performance, or whether more developed economies gave rise to better law. LLSV argued that because the law in most countries was transplanted by colonial powers, the causal direction is clear (La Porta *et al.* 1998). The law was exogenously determined at the stage of colonization and not endogenously in interaction with economic development. Developed economies did not adopt common law systems; common law countries developed sophisticated economies due to their legal origins. LLSV convinced non-legal scholars that law matters.

Another team of economists, Acemoglu, Johnson, and Robinson (hereafter AJR), tackled the causation problem in a different manner. Their theory was that mortality rates among early Europeans (soldiers, bishops, and sailors) in various colonies around the globe determined the feasibility of establishing long-term settlements and the type of early institutions in the colony, and these in turn, through inertia, shaped current institutions that determine current economic performance. Colonies which, due to the mortality of Europeans, could not be settled by Europeans, developed extractive institutions. Colonies that were settled by Europeans developed European-like institutions that protected private property rights and provided checks and balances against government expropriation. The theory is well supported by the empirical findings; a high correlation was found between mortality rates and institutions, and between institutions and economic performance variables such as income per capita (Acemoglu, Johnson, and Robinson 2001; Acemoglu and Robinson 2012). The mortality rate was exogenous to economic development. Further, the correlations hold up well when endowments and other variables are controlled for. The conclusion is that it was institutions, mostly the protection of property rights, that determined economic development.

To sum up, the understanding that law matters for the rise and spread of capitalism has expanded over the last three decades. Economists pay more attention to the law. Many of them attribute the effect of law on development to the legal tradition or the legal origin. In other words, much of the literature attributes to common law origins and to the Anglo-American constitutional tradition an advantage in enhancing economic performance. The role of law in economic development is very high on the research agenda these days (Dam 2006; Milhaupt and Pistor 2008).

The transformation into capitalist law in Europe

European law on the eve of the expansion of capitalism in the late eighteenth century was split. On the continent, civil law was based mostly on Roman law. Its core was the Justinian civil code. It was developed and adjusted to circumstances by university-based jurists that glossed, commented, and interpreted the code. Court procedures were inquisitorial and written. The jury and the lawyers were not central to the system. Legal education was academic. Judges were usually politically appointed and not independent, and tended to represent the ruler's interests. The civil law developed in detachment from constitutional law which tended to be authoritarian.

In the early modern era continental law underwent gradual divergence from a uniform *jus commune* to distinct national laws of the emerging nation-states. As the eighteenth century progressed, the law was increasingly inspired by Enlightenment and secular natural law ideas. After the turn of the nineteenth century, French Revolution influences and the Napoleonic codification changed it to better facilitate the rise of capitalism.

In England, common law and equity, as reflected in Blackstone's *Commentaries* (1765–1769), were still to a large extent based on institutions, procedures, and forms of action that were shaped in the formative era of common law around the thirteenth century. Roman law and university-level jurisprudence were rejected. The law was created by lawyerly trained judges who enjoyed a high level of independence. The court procedure was adversarial, relying on barristers. The jury was the fact finder. Legal education was in the form of apprenticeship in the Inns of Court. Private law and constitutional law, that embodied representative and later also liberal elements, developed hand in hand.

Later in the eighteenth century, Mansfield (Lord Chief Justice 1756–1788) led a judge-made reform mostly in the fields of mercantile law, and subsequently,

Bentham's inspired legislative reforms also contributed to making English law more amenable to capitalism.

In this section, the transformation of law into a more capitalism-enhancing framework will be examined in four legal fields postulated by economic theory as crucial for economic growth: the concept of freedom of contract; the establishment of land registries; patent law; and the formation of business corporations. They deal, in this order, with the facilitation of market transactions; the security of property rights; technological innovations; and the pooling together of capital for investment in firms.[2]

Freedom of contract

Contracts are the legal tools for conducting market transactions. Barter spot transactions can do without much law. Impersonal exchange relies more on law than personal exchange. Contract law becomes more important as transactions become more complex. Credit transactions, future transactions, multi-stage and relational transactions, and transactions in which quality cannot be observed by the buyer before payment, all need legal enforcement. Transactions that required contractual enforcement expanded with the rise of capitalism. Did contract law respond to the challenge?

Roman contract law recognizes and enforces a variety of forms of agreements including sale, hiring, mandate (agency), and partnership. This is one of the grounds for the assertion that Roman law is based on individualist and liberal values (Gordley 1993). But Roman law did not recognize the general conception of an agreement, divorced of specific form, which is legally binding based on the notion of free will. The French and German codification expanded the realm of contracts. But the process was gradual. The Napoleonic *Code Civil* (1804) still placed the book on "property" before the book on "acquiring property," in which sections on succession and donations featured before contracts. The German Civil Code, the BGB (1896), placed the book on "obligations" and the sections on contracts at its center, before the

---

2 These four fields are by no means the only fields of law which are relevant for economic performance. One could include other fields of law in the list, e.g.: constitutional law; bankruptcy law; tort law; banking law; bills of exchange law. Even within these four fields one could examine different doctrines than those examined here, say eminent domain law rather than land registries, contract enforcement rather the freedom to design contracts, or debt finance rather than equity finance of corporations. My selection is based on space constraints and personal inclinations. I will mention here two of the most intriguing recent examples that study relationships between legal traditions and economic performance in fields not covered here: bankruptcy (see Sgard 2006); and corporate debt finance (see Musacchio 2008).

book on "property." Pothier in *Traité des obligations* (1761) put forward a theory of contract that is based on the mutual assent of the parties rather than the unilateral promise of one or both parties. This theory was influenced by social contract philosophy and natural law jurisprudence. The French code followed Pothier and placed consent of the parties as the cornerstone of the validity of a legally binding agreement.[3] The French Revolution also freed land from the legal control of aristocracy and the Church and thus commodified it and made it a subject of contracts. In Germany, the commodification of land was still a contested issue when the BGB was drafted towards the end of the century (John 1989).

In England, things were altogether different. Contract was not recognized as a legal category until modern times. Some contracts that fitted forms of action devised during the formative period of the common law (twelfth to fourteenth centuries) were enforced. For example, the writ of covenant allowed claims of damages when promises made under seal were breached. The writ of debt allowed the recovery of a debt for a certain sum of money. Agreements that did not fit any preexisting writ could not be enforced. In the sixteenth and seventeenth centuries, judges gradually expanded the application of the preexisting writs to additional types of contracts. The application of the writ of assumpsit to executory contracts (in which performance of both parties was temporally separated from the agreement stage) in the case of *Slade v. Morley* (1602), is a notable example of this trend. Judges solved many of the practical problems that resulted from the rigidities of the archaic forms of action by granting discretion to the jury and by applying to the problems the commercial law device of bill of exchange and the equitable device of the trust. Blackstone still viewed contract as a mode for acquiring title in property and devoted to it only some twenty-odd pages in his four-volume survey of the laws of England. Common law jurists did not theorize much about the general principles of contract law until well into the nineteenth century.

Between Blackstone's account and Maine's famous observation a century later that the modern world had shifted from status to contract, the space and content of contract law were transformed. A series of contract law treatise writers, inspired by Pothier, gradually formulated an English contract theory. This theory was also based on the will theory. Common law finally marginalized promises and centralized agreements. Offer and acceptance were the

---

3 The French Civil Code, Clauses 1108–1122. Available at: www.napoleon-series.org/research/government/code/book3/c_title03.html#section6a.

mode by which contracts were made. Doctrinal developments dealt with the nature of contractual terms, the use of implied terms, the nature of mistakes that invalidate contracts, the assessment of damages. The just price doctrine died out. Implied warranties were more rarely read into contracts. The doctrine of caveat emptor reigned. The traditional requirements of consideration and privity of contract were narrowly read (Ibbetson 1999). According to some legal historians, English contract law underwent a transformation in first half of the nineteenth century, into an era of freedom of contract. But the economic and social effects of the transformation are disputed. While some historians believe that it enabled a release of entrepreneurial energy, the expansion of the market, a more efficient allocation of resources and economic growth, others view it as distributive, allowing the rising industrial capitalists to subsidize their activities and transfer wealth to their pockets at the expense of landowners and laborers (Horwitz 1979; Posner 1986: 229–238).

Late in the nineteenth century, the trend reversed. Dicey noticed the growth of intervening regulation and labeled the closing decades of the nineteenth century "the era of collectivism" (Dicey 1905). He referred particularly to legislation that protected labor and the poor. Atiyah's famous book *The Rise and Fall of Freedom of Contract* paid more attention to case law doctrines but also identified a turn away from the will theory late in the nineteenth century (Atiyah 1979: 681–777). One important example of this turn was backtracking from enforcement of contracts in restraint of trade, such as cartel agreements, and from giving full effect to contracts in monopolistic markets. The courts then followed the lead of the legislature and gave effect to intervention with freedom of contract in the context of consumer contracts, employment, predatory lending, and more. Next, courts developed doctrines that reviewed the free choice and consent of parties to contracts. Lastly, corporation law, property law, and tort law infiltrated some spheres that in the heyday of freedom of contract were considered within the exclusive realm of contract law.

So, while freedom of contract was on the rise both in England and on the continent, the tools that were used for promoting it were different: a reformed civil code on the continent and judge-made law in England. Furthermore, the heyday of freedom of contract was brief. Early capitalism emerged in its absence. Advanced capitalism expanded despite its retreat. Businesspersons were able to transact without resort to the grand doctrinal contractual rules using niches such as the stock exchange, the international arena, transactions that were carefully designed by shrewd attorneys, even before and after the epitome of contractual freedom.

Establishment of land registries

Lawyers pay a good deal of attention to the minute details of property law doctrines. They pay less attention to land registration, which they consider an administrative and technical matter. But when examined from the perspective of economic growth, such registries play an important role. The problem of recording property rights is common in today's less developed economies. Informal housing, in which land is first occupied and only years later, if at all, ownership titles are sorted out and registered, are commonplace in the rapidly growing urban centers throughout the developing world. As de Soto showed, a low level of definition and protection of property rights leads to less efficient informal economies (De Soto 1989). Referring specifically to land registries, Benito Arruñada argued that increasing certainty facilitates the use of land as collateral for credit, economizes transaction costs, and promotes efficient allocation of resources (Arruñada 2012; Arruñada and Garoupa 2005).

In France, notaries traditionally kept deeds of conveyances of land. These semi-public registries provided a good starting point on the way to establishing public registries in the modern era (Engerman *et al.* 2003: 9–10; Hofman, Postel-Vinay, and Rosenthal 2000). But this tradition also shaped a model of registries based on recording transactions and not on titles. Following the Revolution, calls for the formation of a national public inventory mounted. But only in the Napoleonic era did a law of 1807 provide the basis for the French parcel *cadastre*. The work was completed in 1850. In the *Code Civil*, there was no registration requirement for titles, but mortgages had to be registered. An act of 1855 required the recording of the full text of contracts for the sale of immovables. The register enrolled and kept title deeds and thus provided evidence for property claims. This evidence could be used by the courts to allocate property rights ex post – after litigation. Furthermore, courts apply a non-standard priority rule. When deciding on a conflict with third parties, they determine the priority of claims from the date of recording in the public office and not from the date of the contract.

The German tradition led to a different model of registration. Trading cities of the late Middle Ages (for example the Hanseatic cities of Hamburg and Bremen) were the first to create municipal registration systems. Such registries were further formalized in seventeeth-century statutes. At the beginning of the nineteenth century in some of the German states cadastral systems were established for taxation purposes. In some of the western provinces, they were based on the cadastres established by Napoleon. In the third quarter of the century, various German states established land registries for titles and mortgage guaranties, Prussia being one of the last in 1872. The Prussian statutes served as the basis of imperial legislation after the unification. In the BGB, a land registration system for the whole country was established. This system (*Grundbuch*) bases all rights of ownership and other rights on land and buildings. The German model contains information not on deeds or claims, but on the rights themselves. It thus requires a baseline of the complete allocation of property rights.

In England, land surveys for tax purposes were made only sporadically beginning with the Domesday Book (1086). Disputes about land titles were settled through cumbersome court litigation. In an action begun by writ of right, the losing party was deprived of all claims to the land, but that form of action was very slow and complicated. The alternative faster and less costly writ of *Novel Disseisin* was not a remedy for the recovery of land to which one is entitled; it was an action that could be employed by a person who has been turned out of possession, and against the person who turned him out. While the writ of right could set the strongest right of land ownership available in England, the writ of *Novel Disseisin* provided a step down the chain, a right of possession (Baker 2002; Maitland, Chaytor, and Whittaker 1909). There were several additional writs and levels of property rights in the labyrinth of traditional common law forms of action, and these produced much litigation, attorneys' fees, and economic uncertainties.

The burdensome system of settling property rights through litigation led to growing pressure in the eighteenth and early nineteenth centuries for reforms in property law, prominent among them the establishment of a land registry. The Real Property Commissioners Report of 1830 came down in favor of a general deeds of transfer registry. The idea that registration of titles, rather than transactions, would be possible grew after the Merchant Shipping Act 1854, which established a register of title to ships. Sir Robert Torrens, the Prime Minister of South Australia, piloted land registration in that colony in 1858, to which we shall return later. In England, land registration entered the statute books four years later through the Land Registry Act 1862. The flaws in the first registry were fixed by studying the German model and finally enacting compulsory registration in the 1897 Land Transfer Act (Offer 1981).

Patent law

Before the rise of capitalism, Western European states encouraged technological innovations in two ways, monetary payments and grants of monopoly. In *ancien régime* France, the former was the norm. Inventors and introducers of inventions could benefit from titles, pensions, lump-sum grants, bounties or subsidies for production, and exemption from taxes. They could also on some occasions be granted monopoly in the form of exclusive privileges. In England, the latter was the norm. Elizabeth and the early Stuarts used monopolies to encourage foreign craftsmen and innovators to settle in England and later extended the use of monopoly to inventions by Englishmen. The hostility of Parliament and of the common law judges to the use of monopolies by the Crown as a means of extracting independent income and increasing political power, led to the enactment of the Statute of Monopolies in 1624.[4] The statute prohibited the grant of monopolies by the Crown without parliamentary authorization. However, as part of a compromise, a number of exceptions were made to this rule. Section 6 of the Statute of Monopolies exempts the grant of monopoly by way of letters patent for "the true and first inventor" of "new manufactures" for "the term of fourteen years or under." This section created the statutory basis of English patent law for the next two centuries. It meant that the Crown could continue the practice of granting monopolies on inventions at the Crown's discretion. Such grants were not subject to any criteria or procedures. These monopolies were enforceable like any other Crown patent, charter, or franchise. The Crown employed the grant of patents ex post, at its discretion and for its own ends. Thus inventors could not rely on the grant of monopoly and the law did not create calculable ex ante incentives for investment of time and labor in inventive activity.

From the early eighteenth century, the system was redesigned as one of registration, involving time and money, but without an examination of the content of the patent or its value. After 1711, it became more common to ask inventors to append details of the method of their invention to their petitions. In some instances, the officers insisted on the inclusion of detailed drawings. By 1734, the request for specification became the standard practice, but it was only forty-four years later that this practice was embodied in the laws of England, not via legislation but as a result of Lord Mansfield's 1778 *Liardet v. Johnson* decision. In this case, Mansfield ruled that specification should be sufficiently full and detailed to enable anyone skilled in the general field to understand and apply the invention without further experiment (Adams and Averley 1986).

A plausible explanation for the emergence of the practice is that as patents accumulated – many of them centered on a limited number of fields such as carriages, bleaching, oil, and spinning – the task of the law officers of the

---

4 The discussion of England in this section follows Harris 2004.

crown became more complicated. They were obliged to grant patents only within the powers conferred to them by the Statute of Monopolies, that is, only to new manufacture. They found it more and more difficult to determine whether a petition submitted to them was indeed for a novel method or machine. By asking for specification, their aim was not to put the petitions under their own careful professional scrutiny; they continued to register them as before. The idea was to transfer the burden from themselves to other interested parties (Macleod 1988). In some circumstances, this also meant that the state was no longer a party to the ensuing litigation. An important implication of this shift was that the definition of the property rights of inventors was done ex post and not ex ante. Neither the crown officers nor the courts provided inventors with detailed rules regarding the submission of specifications. Inventors could go to the trouble of investing in experiments, specification, patenting, production, and marketing, only later to face a court suit that would void their patent.

The problem of patent law was wider and graver than the question of specification alone. It resulted from the fact that the statutory basis of intellectual property rights in inventions throughout the industrial revolution was one old clause, Clause 6 of the 1624 Statute of Monopolies. The rest had to be created by judges who could not do much to expound the law when they heard only one case between 1750 and 1769 and twenty-one cases between 1770 and 1799 (Dutton 1984: 69–85). Since judges, unlike legislators, cannot set their own agenda, they depend on the flow of cases into their courtroom. In this case, the flow was less than one case per year, and many of these cases were decided on evidence or on minor points of law. To this, one should add the fact that creating detailed rules in this field of law was exceptionally complicated, because judges could not apply legal doctrines borrowed from other fields of law since they had to deal with technical issues unfamiliar to lawyers, and because the nature of the innovations was changing rapidly.

A manifestation of the unsettled state of patent law can be found as late as 1795 in a note written by Watt himself listing "Doubts and Queries upon Patents." The eight queries on Watt's list can be classified into four main issues: What is patentable? What should be included in specifications? What is the relationship between newer and older patents? What kind of use of monopoly power will be considered illegal? Only well into the nineteenth century, with the increase in litigation and the formation of a series of parliamentary committees leading to the Patent Law Amendment Act of 1852, did more detailed and settled rules begin to emerge.

What the English system offered was ex ante incentives that sometimes only partly materialized ex post (Mokyr 1990: 247–252). Some patents were invalidated by the courts, others were not strictly enforced. Infringement was quite common. Though inventors did not always extract in full the profits they initially expected to gain from their monopolies, the incentives were sufficient for inventors to remain in business and to do well. The state was there to deal with the patent system when it led to undesirable results or when the inventor's lobby was strong enough. When the state had a strong or symbolic interest in an invention, as was the case with the water chronometer (from which accurate longitude at sea could be calculated for the benefit of the navy and of merchant shipping), a special prize was offered in advance to increase incentives.

The Patent Law Amendment Act, 1852, formalized and streamlined the application process. A Record and Commissioner's Office was established where applications could be easily filed and records of existing patents could be accessed by patentees and manufacturers. Costs were reduced. Patents were to apply to the entire United Kingdom. But the basic model of registration, without substantive examination and subject to future court review, was maintained.

The modern French patent system was established after the Revolution, according to the laws of 1791 and 1844. Patentees filed through a simple registration system. Unlike the *Liardet* requirement in England, there was no specification requirement in France as to the nature of innovation. Applicants could carry on in obtaining the grant even if warned that the patent was likely to be legally invalid. The validity of a patent was determined ex post when challenged and not ex ante when registered. In this sense, the French system was similar to the English.

US patent law developed along different lines and gave rise to a distinct model of examination. The Constitution gave Congress the power to "promote the Progress of Science and the useful Arts by securing for limited Times to Authors and Inventors the exclusive Right to their respective Writings and Discoveries." This federalized patent law prevented jurisdictional competition among states, assured uniformity, and provided inventors with monopoly over larger markets. The examination system was set in place in 1790, when a select committee consisting of the Secretary of State (Thomas Jefferson), the Attorney General, and the Secretary of War scrutinized the applications. Three years later, due to the time-consuming nature of the task, the examination of the validity of patents was delegated to the district courts. This created a registration system in which patents were registered unless an objection was filed. In case of objection, the court was to determine whether to uphold or repeal the patent. The 1836 Patent Law reformed the system and established the Patent Office (Bracha 2005; Khan 2005). The Office employed trained and technically qualified employees who were authorized to examine applications. Inventors whose applications were refused due to alleged conflict with a prior patent could petition the federal courts to review the decisions of the Patent Office. The ultimate right of appeal was to the Supreme Court of the United States. The examination system increased certainty with respect to the value of patents (Khan 1995; Lamoreaux and Sokoloff 2001). Registration fees were considerably lower than fees in England and continental Europe. Patent information was made public and accessible. Assignment of patents and licensing was allowed and made readily available due to the certainty of rights in patents.

Germany passed a unified Imperial Patent Act in 1877. The statute created a centralized administration for the grant of a federal patent for original inventions. The system was one of examination by expert Patent Commissioners. Registration of patents was made public and could be opposed by those affected. Patents were granted to the first applicant rather than to the "first and true inventor" (Seckelman 2002). After 1891, a parallel and weaker version of patent protection could be obtained through a *gebrauchsmuster* or utility patent (sometimes called a petty patent), which was granted through a registration system. Patent protection was available for inventions that could be represented by drawings or models with only a slight degree of novelty, and for a limited term of three years (renewable once, for a total life of six years). The German model was quite similar to the earlier American model with the exception of imposing considerably higher fees as a screening device.

A controversy over the desirability of patent systems of both models was at its height in Europe in the third quarter of the nineteenth century. Economists argued that the monopoly granted by any such system contradicts the principles of a free and competitive economy. In England, a bill was drafted in 1872 to weaken the monopoly, but the bill ultimately failed. In Germany, opposition to patents delayed legislation by a few years. In Switzerland, patent law was legislated for the first time in 1887 after earlier initiatives were rejected by the legislature and by referendum. In Holland, an existing patent law was repealed in 1869 and a new one was enacted only in 1910 (Machlup and Penrose 1950). It is interesting to note that at the height of the inventive burst of the second industrial revolution, one of the legal cornerstones of modern capitalism was under heavy attack. But it survived.

Khan and Sokoloff argue that US examination-based patent law was more effective in incentivizing technological innovation than the registration-and-litigation-based British law (Khan 2008; Khan and Sokoloff 1997). In the United States, eight federal patent acts were passed between 1790 and 1842 while in England the first act to be passed after 1624 was the 1852 act. As a result, US patent law encouraged a higher level of inventive activity among more varied social groups and in a wider array of industries. Measuring inventive activity and its impact on economic growth is a tricky business. Britain seems to have done quite well in terms of inventions and growth in the period discussed here. It is not clear that the United States did better. Furthermore, a patent law that would better define and more strictly protect property rights could have social costs. It could provide more incentives to inventors, but would also slow the rate of diffusion and increase the monopoly rent of inventors at the expense of manufacturers and consumers. There are notable examples of major inventions that were not registered as patents or whose registration was revoked by courts when disputed, and of patents that were successfully protected or prolonged and as a result, their application was more limited. Many contemporary Europeans envied the British spirit of invention and its patent system.

Corporations

The common early modern method of forming corporations was by way of individual charters granted upon application for a specific purpose and subject to specified terms. In time, the rising nation-states usurped the exclusive prerogative of incorporation at the expense of local and religious entities. The states exercised full discretion when considering petitions and utilized this discretion in order to promote their policies and increase their income in return for incorporation. This method was quite similar to the contemporary method of granting patents.

According to North, Wallis, and Weingast (2009), general incorporation is one of the central components of the transition from limited access to open access societies. This component of the transition took place in capitalist states quite rapidly and uniformly, around the middle of the nineteenth century. In the preceding decades, the number of petitions for incorporation grew dramatically and expanded to sectors beyond overseas trade. Entrepreneurs and firms in an array of new sectors, transportation, utilities, finance, and to a lesser extent manufacturing, sought incorporation. A combination of free market ideology, being overburdened by applications, the lack of a clear incorporation policy, and interest group lobbying drove England to be the first country to adopt general incorporation in 1844. The underlying principle was to replace the discretion exercised by state officials with one exercised by investors (Harris 2000). The new company law of 1844 conditioned incorporation, through registration with the Companies Registrar, on the filing and disclosure of documents that would provide potential stock buyers with legal and financial information. The English model was soon followed by France (1867), the German Reich (1871), and the United States. In the United States, the process was gradual, because incorporation was in state and not federal domain, and went through two stages: first the enactment of general incorporation for some or all sectors; and next the prohibition (in state constitutions) of incorporation through charters. By 1870, most US states had adopted general incorporation and prohibition of chartering. The shift to general incorporation converged on a quite uniform model.[5]

Limited liability was viewed by Easterbrook and Fischel (and others) as an essential precondition to the willingness of passive investors to invest in the equity of public corporations and diversify their investments, and to the development of a share market (Easterbrook and Fischel 1985). Hansmann, Kraakman, and Squire view asset partitioning, in the form of limited liability and entity shielding, as a device that increases efficiency by lowering monitoring and information costs, lowering agency costs, and ultimately reducing the costs of credit (Hansmann, Kraakman, and Squire 2006). Nevertheless, general limited liability was introduced even later than general incorporation. Some level of limited liability was attached to corporations in the chartering era. But its content was not always clear or uniform and not every corporation was granted limited liability. General limited liability was introduced in England in 1855–1856. But banking and insurance were subject to distinct liability arrangements. Significant uncalled capital balance was common and this allowed calls on shareholders at insolvency. In the United States, the trust fund doctrine died out only in the 1890s. In some continental jurisdictions, notably Germany, there were relatively high minimum capital and minimum share nominal value requirements, which forced shareholders to risk significant capital. Directors and officers could be exposed to personal liability for corporate debts. In most US states, double or even triple liability was imposed on shareholders by law until after the turn of the twentieth century. In California, pro-rata unlimited liability was abolished as late as 1931.

---

5 For further information concerning the history of corporations development in the US, see Atack, Chapter 17 in Volume 1.

Capitalism emerged and expanded without general limited liability. The latter became the norm only well into the twentieth century.

The evolution of the legal protection of outside investors against stealing or shirking is an essential precondition for the willingness of such investors to place their money, as equity or credit, in the control of managers or controlling stockholders. After the introduction of general incorporation and limited liability (which in one sense bounded investors' risk but in another sense augmented it), and with the growing use of joint-stock limited liability public corporation, the issue of the protection of investors became central. LLSV showed that the legal rules protecting investors vary systematically among legal traditions, or legal origins (La Porta *et al.* 1998). How exactly the basic tenets of Anglo-American law are more conducive to investors' protection, and when and why this protection developed, are questions that their methodology could not resolve. Others have argued that different investor protection mechanisms developed at least partly in response to different governance structures: widely dispersed ownership in the United Kingdom and the United States, controlling families or banks in France and Germany. Once different governance structures were in place, due to whatever causes, the law was adjusted efficiently to address the different agency problems (managers–shareholders or majority–minority) that each of the governance structures gave rise to. Alternately, path dependency led to the lock-in of some systems, not necessarily of French or German origins, in a suboptimal level of agency problems (Roe and Bebchuk 1999).

In the Anglo-American tradition, the organizational menu offered to entrepreneurs was narrow and included only corporations and general partnerships. On the continent, the menu was considerably wider. Limited partnerships were on the menu since the seventeenth century. In France, the *Code de Commerce* of 1807 also introduced the *commandités par action*, a limited partnership with tradable shares. Other European states followed France and introduced the share partnership. Germany was the first to introduce the private corporation, the GmbH, in 1892, allowing the use of an organizational form that better catered to the needs of small and medium-sized enterprises than the standard public corporation. A comparable form was introduced in France in 1925 as the SARL (Société à responsabilité limitée). In England in 1907, the law for the first time created a distinction between public and private companies, imposing lower disclosure requirements on the latter in return for restriction on the number of shareholders and on transferability of shares. The United States was the outlier. After an abortive attempt in some states in the 1880s to introduce the partnership association, a form somewhat similar to the private company, the form was abandoned for about a century (Guinnane *et al.* 2007). It was reintroduced only in the late 1970s as the LLC (Limited Liability Company). It seems that in terms of the menu of organizational forms, France and Germany offered firms more of a choice, while the US offered the most limited choice.[6] But it is not yet clear whether such a choice was an advantage as far as economic performance is concerned.

Conclusion

We have seen so far that legal institutions developed in the leading capitalist economies before or concurrently with the expansion of the market, the commodification of land, the burst of technological innovation, and the accumulation of capital in big business. In some fields, the leading economies converged on similar institutions; in some fields, different institutional models developed along the lines of legal traditions; and in some fields, countries clustered around distinct models across different legal traditions.

The spread of legal innovation

European law spread globally in several ways: with immigrants; through empire building and colonial administration; through informal imperialism, political pressures, and voluntary importation; and through the development of international organizations and treaties. The manner in which European law spread had an impact on how that law was perceived, implemented, and enforced effectively, and the extent to which it suited other components of the local law and ultimately contributed to economic development in the various jurisdictions.

Generally speaking, the continental legal tradition was better configured for spreading legal institutions than the common law tradition because since Roman times that tradition had expansionist and universalist tendencies. A law that originally applied to a town, expanded to relate to an empire. A law that originally applied to Roman citizens could be applied to all subjects of the empire. Similarly, the three components of the medieval *jus commune* were spread throughout Europe; canon law by the Church, Roman law by the universities, and merchant law through mercantile contacts in ports and fairs. Continental law expanded outside Europe with the Iberian conquests in America. On the other hand, common law for centuries was the law of the

---

6 For further discussion of the use of the corporation form, and specifically the formation of corporate groups, see Morck and Yeung, Chapter 7 in this volume.

English, tightly connected to the English Crown, the Constitution, and Anglo-Saxon customs. Another, more technical, reason for the difference is that continental law was better packaged for exportation. It was easier to transfer a legal code, packaged in a single volume, than judge-made law that relied on oral tradition and, insofar as it was recorded in writing, was scattered in dozens of case reports that were accessible only to trained barristers. But despite the differences in tendencies and techniques, both traditions spread outside Europe. European law, in its capitalist form, spread through two channels: first, within empires; and second, on a transnational and international level.

Expansion within the empires

The expansion of European law began with the expansion of the empires themselves.[7] The Spaniards carried their law to Muslim territories as part of the Reconquista and then to the Americas.[8] English law was carried to North America by settlers and to Asia with East India Company officials (Hulsebosch 2005; Stern 2011). This expansion reached its peak on the eve of World War I.[9] I will demonstrate this type of expansion through its prime example, the British empire, which, at its height, controlled a fifth of the world's population and a quarter of the earth's total land area.

English law, in its nineteenth- and early twentieth-century capitalist form, spread throughout the empire thanks to a number of legislative tools employed by three branches of the imperial governance: colonial governments; Britain's Parliament; and the Colonial Office. Colonial legislators throughout the empire were often British officials who were committed to English law and to harmonization. They had the authority to legislate within their colonies. The Parliament at Westminster was also an imperial Parliament and could pass legislation that would apply directly to the colonies. The Colonial Office was a pivotal player. One of the main tasks of the legal department of the Colonial Office, headed by John Risley in the years 1911 to 1931, was to promote harmonization. The Colonial Office had a dual capacity

7 For the wider contexts of European imperialism and the empires, with emphasis on the relations between the Imperial centers and their colonies, see Austin, Chapter 10 in this volume.

8 On the Imperial expansion of European law in general see: Whitman 2009; Benton 2002; Benton 2010. On the expansion of Spanish law and French law throughout their empires see Lobingier 1932: 153–161, 170–181. Regarding the expansion of Spanish Law to Latin America in particular see Mirow 2004: 11–18. For the formation of slavery law in the European empires in the Americas see Tomlins 2009: 389–422.

9 It should be noticed that the empires were a channel for the spread of economic policy to the colonies, just as they were a channel for the spread of law to colonies. See O'Rourke and Williamson, Chapter 1 in this volume.

with respect to the harmonization of commercial law. It directed and supervised legislation by local authorities in the colonies. In addition, it drafted Orders in Council, regulations which, once approved by the Privy Council and having received Royal Assent, through a formal but nominal procedure, were applied directly in the relevant colonies as part of their local law. Harmonization was required because the precolonial laws of the various colonies were obviously very different from each other and were often not suited for a capitalist economy, and because initiatives on the ground by officers in the colonies hampered harmonization. Non-uniform laws obstructed the flow of goods and capital between markets within the empire and reduced the advantage of trading within the empire compared to trade with foreign nations and empires. The Colonial Office, inspired by the Board of Trade, expected colonies to enact commercial legislation which closely followed the English model and could be updated in line with changes to that model. The subject matter of commercial law invited importation from England and consistency across the empire. Furthermore, English-based commercial law generally did not conflict with local traditions because it was not intended for the general population but, rather, for a commercial elite and for foreign investors.

On the other hand, uniformity in fields which were embedded in culture, customs, and religion was considered something that should be avoided. In relation to some fields of law, say family law, it was said that English law did not fit local religions or traditions and should not be transplanted. In relation to other fields, it was said that English law was too advanced for the colonies. And with respect to yet other fields, famously criminal law, and to new legal techniques such as the Benthamite codification of the common law, officials desired to use the colonies as a laboratory for experimenting with legal reform before applying it to the core of the empire. But the outcomes and their relevance to European civilization were debated and only rarely did law that was first experimented with in the colonies come to be applied back home.

The issue, however, was not only in which fields of law there was a demand in the empire for English law. On the supply side, in some fields, such as contract law, property law, the law of negotiable instruments, and (until 1890) the law of partnership, English law was wholly judge-made law and could not be readily packed and exported to the colonies. But in other more recently created fields of law, created by Acts of Parliament or through legislative reform by the mid nineteenth century, there was no need for the Colonial Office to prepare a code or a digest based on the English common law. New and relatively comprehensive acts existed, ready to use, on the shelves.

The transnational and international level

The idea of transnational law was not foreign to Europe. Roman law in its classical era, and *jus commune* around 1500, which contained Roman law, canon law, and law merchant, were uniform throughout vast territories, beyond their Italian place of origin. However, the rise of the nation-state, and with it of national law and national codes, not only led to legal divergence but also to hostility to universal law. The natural law school, in its Enlightenment form, and the post-revolutionary Napoleonic codes, allowed for the revival of legal unification. The codes were carried by French armies across Europe. In some localities, such as Germany, they were overturned with the withdrawal of the French, but in others, they were preserved. When the newly independent Latin American states looked for non-Spanish law in the 1820s and 1830s, they turned to France and adopted its codes. So did the Ottomans when they wished to modernize their law in the 1870s and beyond.

By the 1860s, a new movement that aimed to promote legal harmonization had emerged. The key players in the movement were not state officials but rather legal scholars and practicing lawyers. The creation of the Society for Comparative Legislation (1869) and of the International Law Association (1873) as well as comparative and international law journals indicated the return to aspirations for universal or at least more uniform law. The next practical measures were meetings at conferences, the formation of working committees, and the drafting of conventions (typically governments were called upon to join in only at this stage). Harmonization initiatives took place before World War 1 mainly in three general areas of law: international transactions including modes of payment, such as negotiable instruments; international transportation by sea, land (train), and air; and intellectual property. After the war, harmonization efforts gradually moved from the private realm to the newly created international organizations. Though the League of Nations Covenant (1919), which emerged from the Treaty of Versailles, and was signed by forty-four states, did not amount to a clear power to harmonize and universalize law, it came close and served as a basis for forming international organizations that came even closer to achieving this.[10] The International

---

10 Article 23 of the League's Covenant included among others the following aims: respecting international covenants; the maintaining of humane conditions for labor; the execution of agreements with regard to the traffic in women and children, and the traffic in opium and other dangerous drugs; and maintaining freedom of communications and of transit and equitable treatment for the commerce of all Members of the League.

Labor Organization (ILO) was set up in 1926 as an auxiliary organ of the League of Nations and promoted labor legislation. The International Institute for the Unification of Private Law (UNIDROIT) was established in the same year. Its declared purpose was: "to examine ways of harmonizing and coordinating the private law of States and of groups of States, and to prepare gradually for the adoption by the various States of uniform rules of private law."[11] More specifically, its aims were to prepare drafts of laws and conventions to promote uniform internal law; resolve conflicts of law in the field of private law; undertake studies in comparative private law; organize conferences and publish works in the field; and carry on preexisting activities in the field. Its activities mainly concerned the laws of sales of goods, transportation, arbitration, and negotiable instruments.

After World War ii, in the context of the formation of the UN, the Cold War, and the rise of the United States at the expense of Europe, some of the nineteenth-century and interwar institutions became less relevant, and new institutions connected to the UN or based on intergovernmental agreements, such as the International Monetary Fund (IMF), the World Bank, United Nations Commission on International Trade Law (UNCITRAL), and World Trade Organization (WTO), were created. To some extent, the agenda of each of these bodies includes the spreading of law that serves as infrastructure for markets and facilitates economic growth. The postwar period and these organizations and their legal activities are beyond scope of this chapter.[12]

Another central body that helped to promote the legal harmonization, with an emphasis on the convergence of the common law with the continental tradition, was the European Union (EU). The EU declared harmonization of law as one of its aims and policy objectives. The assignment of creating a harmonization across the two European legal traditions became part of the agenda upon the United Kingdom's and Ireland's joining of the EU in 1973. The most significant factor that contributed to the legal integration in Europe was the European Court of Justice (ECJ), which made use of Article 234 of the Treaty of Rome, the preliminary ruling procedure, in order to create increasing convergence between civil and common law procedures.[13]

---

11 Statute of UNIDROIT (1993), International Institute for the Unification of Private Law. Available at: www.unidroit.org/mm/statute-e.pdf.

12 The leading capitalist countries, who were the force driving those organizations, initiated pro-globalization policies which enabled the creation of an infrastructure for international and global markets and facilitate economic growth (see O'Rourke and Williamson, Chapter 1 in this volume).

13 For more about the large influence of the EU on harmonization see Gierczyk 2005–2006: 154–160; Curran 2001: 65–69; Heb 2002.

The spread of law on an international and transnational level was inhibited by several factors. On the legal level, scholars from different traditions, common law and civil law, German law and French law, could not agree on one model for uniform law. The French, whose jurisprudence was more universalist, supported the harmonization project. Germany invested its legal attention until the turn of the twentieth century in its own unification and national codification project. The United Kingdom did not view its common law as suitable for every civilization and focussed its attention on harmonization within the empire. Politically, the heyday of optimism with respect to the fate of globalization passed, with the scramble for Africa, the arms race, and the diplomatic maneuvers that led to the outbreak of World War I. After 1917, the USSR did not support the harmonization of law based on the capitalist model and aimed at spreading its socialist model of law. Following a short-lived revival in the 1920s, by the 1930s harmonization was again on the decline.

Retreat in face of Socialism and re-expansion

Before Socialism, the legal systems in Russia and Eastern Europe were influenced by the Roman-Germanic law both directly and indirectly (by the Byzantine law which was based upon the Roman law) (David and Brierley 1978: 148–152).

The Marxist ideology is based on the idea that law (of any kind) is a superstructure in the base and superstructure model of society, an instrument in the hands of the ruling class, landed aristocracy, or capitalist bourgeois, which makes use of it in order to strengthen and legitimize its class-based oppression (David and Brierley 1978; Pashukanis 1978). In the post-revolutionary transition to communism the law should be supportive of the abolition of private property, of the implementation of a more egalitarian society, and of the promotion of socialist ideology. An ultimate Socialist society is not supposed to be based on law but on a unanimous and harmonious agreement of the proletariat.

In canonic comparative law books, such as the first and second editions of David and Brierley's *Major Legal Systems in the World Today* (published in 1968 and 1978 respectively) and the first and second editions of Zweigert and Kotz's *An Introduction to Comparative Law* (published in 1977 and 1987 respectively), the socialist legal system was mentioned as a legal family for all intents and purposes alongside, and on equal status with the two Western legal families, common law and civil law (Zweigert and Kotz 1977: xii; Zweigert and Kotz 1987: xi; Zweigert and Kotz 1998). However, in the third edition of Zweigert and Kotz, published in 1998, the socialist legal system was left out. Hence, one could deduce that socialist law was seen by comparative law scholars, as long as the Eastern-Soviet bloc was held together by socialist ideology, as a separate legal system or legal family. After the 1989 revolutions, the fall of the Berlin Wall, and the dissolution of the Soviet Union, the notion of socialist law, as opposed to capitalist law, disappeared. Formerly socialist legal systems were mostly reclassified as Roman-Germanic civil law systems.[14]

The Socialist law began to develop in Russia following the 1917 Revolution. It supported nationalization, was hostile to private property and freedom of contract, subjected the court system to the Party and its ideology, downplayed the role of the legal profession, and criminalized counter-revolutionary activities. The Socialist legal system was supposed to be an answer to the common law and civil law traditions that were identified with capitalist, bourgeois, imperialistic, and exploitative societies. The practical reality in Russia has necessitated the creation of a legal system that would deal with everyday issues as well (De Cruz 1999: 184–185).

Socialist law had spread within the Soviet Union upon its formation. It spread with the expansion of Soviet dominance to Eastern Europe since 1945 and to China since 1949, to North Korea, North Vietnam, Cuba, and other states that turned to communism during the Cold War.[15] The Communist International (Comintern, 1919–1943) and Council for Mutual Economic Assistance (Comecon, 1949–1991) were among the facilitators of the voluntary expansion of socialist law globally next to the expansion by way of empire and military and political dominance (Zweigert and Kotz 1987: 312–317).

Starting in the middle of the 1960s, some of the states of Eastern Europe experienced changes in their laws, with an emphasis on civil legislature which was widely influenced by the BGB and by non-Socialist models (Ajani 1995: 99–102). In 1989 the law of Russia itself began stepping out of communism in favor of a more capitalistic law. In this context, Russia makes an enlightening example of the endogenous response of the law to the transition to capitalism. For example, the changes in Russia's company law occurred in accordance to the changing economic needs in Russia – from the decline of the USSR to the period following its fall. The origin of Russia's company law can be traced in "The Law of State Enterprise" from 1988, which was meant to support the beginning of the change from administrative control to greater enterprise

14 For more about the evolution of legal family taxonomies and the differences in classification of legal families, see Pargendler 2012: 1043–1074.
15 For more about the establishment of the People's Republic of China (PRC) and the triumph of Mao's communist regime, and about the legal experience under Mao's Leadership in China, see Chen 2008: 44–50.

autonomy. From the 1990s many changes have occurred in Russian company law, in order to align it with privatization and the market-oriented changes in the economy. The goal was to make Russian corporations more efficient and more suitable and opened to the global market (Grey and Hendley 1995: 21–26).

To conclude, the laws of Russia, Eastern Europe, and China were initially based on continental civil law, which was conducive to capitalism. This more capitalist-oriented law retreated, in the period from 1917 to 1949, in face of socialist political, economic, and legal order. But then again, starting in 1989, capitalist law re-expanded into these legal systems, reconnecting them with the civil law tradition.

Spread of contract law

French contract law, that embodied consensual and free market doctrines together with the ideas of the French Revolution, was carried to other countries in western and central Europe by the Napoleonic armies as part of the *Code Civil*. It was literally translated into Spanish and adopted by the newly independent Latin American states. It was implemented as is by French colonial administrators in Africa and Southeast Asia. The Ottoman empire, which imported other French codes (the commercial code, the criminal code, and procedural codes), did not import the French civil code. The Ottoman civil law that was based on the Shari'a was defended by conservative and religious circles among jurists. Nevertheless, the continental-Roman concept of codification as a framework for organizing legal rules was imported by the Ottomans from France. Ottoman-Islamic contract law went through a codification process that produced the *Mejelle*, which incorporated in it Shari'a-based contract law.

The English common law of contracts could not be exported as swiftly. In English settlement colonies, it was carried with the settlers but went through gradual adaptation that resulted from the level of communication and of legal expertise as well as from local conditions (Ross 2008; Nelson 1975). In Canada, for example, the idea of freedom of contract, a cornerstone of English mid-nineteenth-century common law, was imported into case law and not legislation. It was imported by jurists via a few importation channels. Many judges and legal scholars were educated in England. English contract law treatises were read in Canada. Canadian judges cited English cases. Appeals from Canada were decided by the Judicial Committee of the Privy Council in London, and its decisions were binding as precedents in Canada. The final outcome of importation through all these channels was that by the early twentieth century, Canadian contract law resembled English contract law, including its freedom of contract bent.[16]

While the importation of case law through a variety of channels well suited settler societies such as Canada, a contract law codification was especially prepared for the largest colony, the crown jewel, India. The Indian code was a hybrid, combining English law, Hindu law, Muslim law (also known as "Muhammadan Law"), and purposely drafted rules (Pollock and Mulla 1972: 1–2). Some of these served as laboratory experiments for possible future use in the core of the empire. In some of the other colonies, such as Palestine, the English made no effort to implement their contract law (Harris *et al.* 2002; Shachar 1995: 1–10).

China is an example of a country that introduced freedom of contract after a long period in which such was denied by the socialist-inspired concepts of law. In 1949, planned command economy was put in place by Mao's Communist Party. This economic system was supplemented by a legal system that justified state intervention in contractual relationships. No room was left for voluntary contractual relationships in the open market (Chen 2008: 39–76). Hand in hand with economic reforms, contract law received more space starting in 1982. Freedom of contract as a governing principle of contract law was legislated for the first time in the 1999 Contract Law. The principle was interpreted widely by scholars as encompassing freedom to choose parties, form, content, mode of dispute resolution and more (Zhang 2000: 241–246).

Spread of land registries

Land registries offer an interesting and complex pattern of expansion. The European continent offered two models, German and French. The English were latecomers in introducing land registries. Yet, the British empire was expanding fast and British settlers migrated to newly acquired colonies in North America, Australia, and South Africa in growing numbers. Were they to apply the medieval and by now outdated English model of defining titles in land, or adopt newer continental models?

The origins of the Torrens system of land registration introduced in South Australia in 1857–1858, which later spread to other parts of Australia and the empire, have been the subject of a great deal of debate over the years. Some scholars have put forward the view that the Torrens system is an entirely

---

16 *Grand Trunk Railway Co.* v. *Vogel*, 11 S.C.R. 612 (1886); *Saskatchewan Co-operative Wheat Producers Ltd.* v. *Zurowski*, 2 W.W.R. 604 (1926); Trakman 1985: 666–674.

indigenous South Australian invention, developed by Sir R. R. Torrens without any help from outside sources. Others argued for influences from the English Merchant Shipping Act of 1854. Yet others asserted that Torrens received significant help from Dr Ulrich Hübbe, a German lawyer from Hamburg who emigrated to South Australia in 1842. He had written a book that was published in Australia 1857 and promoted reform of the system of land transfer along the lines of the law of Hamburg. Torrens consulted him when preparing the original draft of his system in 1858. It is asserted that the chief features of the Hamburg system, as developed since the seventeenth century and which still functioned there in the mid nineteenth century, are all present in the South Australian system. Sometimes the resemblance is remarkable, as is the case, for example, with respect to the institution of register books, public maps, the use of predetermined formulae to effect transactions, and the mortgage. In addition, the principle of conclusiveness of the register, which is the crux of the system and did not exist in the British Merchant Shipping Act 1854, was adopted in South Australia as it existed in Hamburg (Esposito 2003).

South Australia was the first common law jurisdiction to establish a system of registration of title to land. Its success there was in vivid contrast to the failure in reforming the English land titles system throughout the nineteenth century, despite a succession of commissions, committees, and reports. The Torrens system was adopted in Queensland in 1861, in Tasmania, Victoria, and New South Wales in 1862, and in Western Australia in 1874. In 1870, New Zealand repealed the Land Registry Act passed in 1860, which was based on Report of the English Royal Commission of 1857, and replaced it with a land transfer act modeled on the Torrens system (Simpson 1976).[17]

By far the best known single Australian contribution to the law of Canada is the Torrens system (Finn 2002). The origins of land registration in Vancouver Island (1862) and British Columbia (1866, 1870) are debated, and may have been something of a hybrid combining Torrens principles and British proposals that were not implemented in the home country. It was not until later decades that pressure for the adoption of a true Torrens system grew sufficiently intense to produce legislative action. The first provinces to adopt a true Torrens system were Manitoba (1885), followed by New Brunswick, Saskatchewan, Alberta, and the Northwest Territories (Hogg 1920: 14). By 1920, there were no fewer than twenty-eight distinct land registration systems

---

17 Papua and Fiji are two other jurisdictions that adopted the Torrens system. See Hogg 1920: 8–10.

throughout the British empire. Some, though definitely not all, followed some variation of the Torrens system.[18]

The example of land registries is instructive. A law that facilitates a capitalist economy by better defining property rights did not spread from the center of an empire (Britain) to its peripheries. In Britain, the main issue was sorting out disputes over long-owned property. The needs in the colonies were different from those in Europe, mainly surveying lands and recording initial allocation to settlers in order to create a baseline of rights or a meaningful database of conveyances. A solution to these problems was designed in a colony (Australia), based on indigenous settlement needs, with some influences from a less developed capitalist system (Germany). This then spread from one periphery (Australia) to another (Canada). The colonies served as a lab for the center (Britain), which only later introduced its own registry.

The spread of European land registries to Latin America took place as part of the more general expansion of European law. The German, French, and Spanish statutes and regulations were among the most influential on the Mexican Civil Code for the Federal District and Territories of 1928. Mexico's land registry, a typical Latin American system, was based on Spain's system of registration in colonial times and after independence. Like Spain's, it was a hybrid system of rights and transactions. On one hand, it resembled the French or declarative system in its recognition of rights *in rem* created between the original parties outside of the registry. Accordingly, immovable property may be sold, transferred, or mortgaged without need of recording. On the other hand, it purports to follow the German system in protecting third parties' rights where an infirmity in their title does not appear clearly in the registry. Unlike German and Spanish law, however, Mexican law does not entrust the registrar with any significant powers of evaluation (Kozolchyk 1970).

But what is even more interesting with respect to Latin American land registries is the growing gap between the formal registration system as embodied in the law books and informal practices. The widening gap between the formal and the informal are best documented for Peru rather than Mexico, thanks to de Soto's studies. But the Peruvian experience is believed to be typical of Latin America. Early in the twentieth century, formally established businesses began constructing residential neighborhoods around Lima without obtaining permits, without completing public works as required by law, and without providing services. Such neighborhoods were initially built for

18 The Torrens system was also adopted by these jurisdictions in the British Empire: Jamaica; Trinidad-Tobago; East Africa; Uganda; and Sudan (Hogg 1920: 5, 17–18).

the middle class but later most were built for lower class residents. Municipalities tried to deal with this phenomenon by issuing decrees that prohibited the purchase of land, the initiation of construction, and the sale of apartments before formalities were met. But gradually, between the 1920s and the 1950s, the state gave up and began implicitly and informally recognizing the reality in these neighborhoods. By the 1960s, legislative recognition began. An alternative system of property rights emerged, rights that were not documented in the land registries but nevertheless provided some level of protection against further invasion of the same lands, some ability to obtain credit based on the informal right, some ability to sell the land, and some ability to benefit from urban services. This informal land regime, which had nothing to do with formal land registration institutions, was far from optimal economically (De Soto 1989: 17–57). The fact that European capitalist institutions such as land registries spread to Latin America on the formal law level clearly does not mean that they functioned in Latin America as they did in Spain, France, or Germany.[19]

Spread of patent law

Patent law reflects yet another pattern. The defining feature of this field was the desire of technological innovators in leading countries to implement it globally in order to protect their inventions and extract monopoly rent. Attempts at universalizing patent law took place both within the empires and internationally, and resulted among others in the Paris Convention for the Protection of Industrial Property of 1883. This convention required that its signatories, whose number grew rapidly, treat foreign nationals on equal terms with locals when applying for a patent. It did not adopt a principle, advanced by the United States, of reciprocity, which would allow inventors to register and enforce patents in host countries according to the law of their home country.

In the field of copyright law, the English law regime gradually expanded throughout the empire. The Statute of Anne, which had served as the basis for state protection of the rights of authors in their books since 1710 and was reformed in 1814, was gradually turned into "Imperial Law," an act that

---

19 The European capitalist institutions and the European law that supports them were also spread to Africa through the French empire and the British empire (Joireman 2001: 576–581). The law and institutions in the Middle East were influenced by the three ruling empires: the Ottoman empire, the French empire, and the British empire, in addition to the Islamic law, which was also dominant in the Middle East (Mallat 2007; Hill 1977–1978: 284–297).

protects rights throughout the British empire. In 1842, the Literary Copyright Act provided protection throughout much of the empire for books published in United Kingdom. No protection in Britain for books published in the colonies was offered. The 1862 Fine Arts Copyright Act did not protect British artistic work in the colonies, but did protect a work created in a colony in that colony. The 1886 International Copyright Act offered protection in the United Kingdom for books and artistic work produced in the colonies (subject to two conditions). The end result of this territorial expansion of English law was that books and fine arts produced in the colonies were protected in the United Kingdom and books produced in the United Kingdom were protected throughout the empire, but arts produced in the United Kingdom were not protected in the empire. Finally, in 1911, the Parliament in London exercised its power to enact for the empire as a whole, and passed the Imperial Copyright Act. This act offered reciprocal protection for works published in any dominion, colony or protectorate, throughout the empire. The general conception of rights in literary and artistic work roamed the empire throughout the second half of the nineteenth century and was ultimately uniformly applied on the eve of World War I.

Patent law, on the other hand, was not applied uniformly. The Patent Act of 1852 applied only in the United Kingdom, allowing the registration of a single patent for England, Scotland, and Ireland, but requiring separate registration in every colony in which the inventors wished to be protected. An imperial patent act, on the model of the copyright act, was discussed but never passed. Reactions in Australia to the idea of an imperial act well demonstrate the reasons for the failure to promote a single law for the entire empire. Until the mid nineteenth century, patents were not an issue in Australia. Only a handful of patents were claimed; some were secured through private bills and other applications were neglected along the way. Following the 1852 British Patent Act, the Colonial Office circulated a memorandum to the colonies. After drawing attention to the recent British act, it enquired as to the local patent law and the mode of proof of a British patent in each colony. The Colonial Office went on to suggest that it might be desirable to create a single system of patent law for the empire by extending the British law to cover the colonies as well. Local colonial officers in Australia were quick to respond, stating that they had no intention to privilege British inventors, that the costs imposed in Britain were too high for the colonies, and that the American patent law model should also be considered. Preemptive local patent laws were eventually enacted in several provinces (Finn 2000). For the next thirty years, the issue of an imperial patent act was periodically raised by London and repeatedly rejected in Australia.

In Australia and Canada, there was a shift from privately and specifically granted patents of monopoly to a general system of patent granting, a colonial adaptation of the British Patent Act of 1852 to allow the local grant of patents on examination. It seems clear that applications for patents increased markedly once this was possible. What prompted the system of local enactments? There appear to have been two quite different motivations for the legislation. The first was simply pressure by local inventors to simplify the procedure and reduce the costs of patent application. The second was colonial resistance to a unified imperial patent system (Finn 2000).

Parallel to the spread of patent laws within the British empire, laws also spread on the international level. A "unification of patent law" movement was initiated by a group of specialist patent lawyers who met at the Vienna World Fair in 1873 and decided to try to unify patent law on an international level. The project was taken up again and advanced at the Paris World Fair in 1878 and a commission was formed, which submitted the text of a preliminary draft to the governments in 1879. In 1880, an International Conference met in Paris, and in 1883 a second International Conference adopted the Convention for the Protection of Industrial Property ("Paris Convention"), in the field of copyright. Another private group, the International Literary and Artistic Association, started the movement for the unification of intellectual property law. This association was created in 1878 and, at its Congress in Rome in 1882 and in Berne the following year, drafted a convention that was approved by an international conference convened by the Swiss government in 1886, which became the Berne Convention on the Protection of Literary and Artistic Works. In the following years, conventions were also drafted for trademarks and patterns and designs. The Berne and Paris Conventions did not insist on a globally uniform intellectual property law. They aimed at a more modest goal: equality of treatment for nationals and foreigners; minimum protection to be provided for authors and inventors in every country; and coordination of the registration of patents. The Paris Convention was initially signed by eleven states in western and central Europe and Latin America. Common law legal systems joined gradually: the United Kingdom (1884); the United States (1887); Canada (1923); Australia (1925); and New Zealand (1931). Japan enacted a short-lived patent law in 1871, reintroduced in 1885 an act based on French and American influences, and finally another act in 1899 that was in line with the Paris Convention and was followed by the accession of Japan to the Convention that same year (Oda 1992). Japan thus represents the best example of the spread of European patent law beyond Europe by means of international harmonization rather than colonialism. China is a counter-example.

The Qing dynasty was reluctant to react to the harmonization movement. The first regulation relating to technology, Reward Regulations on the Development of Technology, was enacted in 1898 but was never effective. There was no concept of invention and no process of examination, and society at large was encouraged to use inventions and creations. During the Kuomintang era, a few patent laws were enacted but these were limited in scope and applicability. Only in 1944 was a more wide-scale reform introduced, which also allowed foreigners to apply for patents in China. With the rise of the communists in 1949, the law was suspended, and China accessed the Paris Convention only in 1985 (Yang 2003). After World War I, the Convention expanded to a few countries in North Africa, the Middle East, and eastern Europe.[20]

Spread of corporation law

As shown above and elsewhere in this volume, the development of corporation law made it possible for corporations to evolve in Europe and North America and those corporations had an unquestionable influence over the development of capitalism in these parts of the globe (Jones, Chapter 6 in this volume). Yet, the pressure for spreading corporation law globally was weaker than that for patent law. Less developed countries and countries in which business was organized in families and social networks were not in immediate need of it. Western capitalists could organize their corporations in their own countries and according to their domestic law even when doing business in their country's colonies or elsewhere overseas. As a result, there was no significant pressure for international conventions or imperial legislation. Nonetheless, the harmonization of company law in the British empire seemed more attainable when compared with other harmonization projects. The issue of harmonization of company law was on the agenda of the Imperial Conferences of 1907 and 1911, which were a meeting place for officials from London and from the colonies (primarily the white settlers' dominions). For each of these, the Board of Trade prepared a comparative survey, "Company Law in the British Empire." These surveys identified similarities and differences, particularly between the dominions and the United Kingdom, and served as a basis for discussion of further harmonization. The harmonization project received support from the legal profession and academia; for example, from the British Society of Comparative Legislation and its *Journal of the Society of Comparative Legislation* (established 1896). The journal published annual

---

20 WIPO website, available at: www.wipo.int/treaties/en/ip/paris.

surveys of legislation in numerous jurisdictions in the empire and in a few legal systems outside it. Local colonial officials could learn about trends throughout the empire from the journal and publicize their achievements in it.

Despite the institutional support and the importance of company law as perceived by jurists and politicians, in fact, company law throughout the British empire was a patchwork quilt of systems. There were colonies, such as Gibraltar, which had no company legislation. There were jurisdictions, such as Malta, the Seychelles, and Cyprus, in which the common law was not in force, and no attempt was made to enact English-based company legislation. In these jurisdictions, the company law in force was Ottoman or French-based. In many colonies, company law was based on one or another version of an English act. In some, it was based on the 1862 Act (Australian colonies and some Canadian provinces), in others on the 1908 Act (other Canadian provinces, South Africa, India, Hong Kong, Nigeria), and in still others, on the 1929 Act (Palestine). This was done either by literally copying the Act into a Colonial Ordinance or by making some adjustments for local conditions. Colonial Ordinance amendments were then based on amendments to the English legislation. In other colonies, the English legislation was imported through a single clause. For example, in Sierra Leone, the local statute imported the Companies Acts that were "in force in England at the commencement of the local statute." In the Falkland Islands, the importation was of "all laws, rules, and regulations for the time being in force." This created an open channel for importation. The Indian Companies Acts, which were based on the English acts with some adjustments, were in turn imported in full by colonial Iraq, North Borneo, East Africa, and Uganda.

Looking beyond the British empire, Japan constitutes an interesting example. During the Meiji restoration it drafted a German-inspired commercial code, promulgated in 1899, that included sections on company law. This law was in effect until the end of World War II. At that stage of the US occupation of Japan, the Supreme Commander for the Allied Powers was determined to change Japan's financial and commercial structure. As part of a wider New Deal-inspired legal reform, the Illinois Business Corporation Act of 1947 served as the basis for the new Japanese Commercial Code of 1950. So Japan initially adopted one capitalist corporation law model, the German, and with it made a huge leap forward in the first half of the twentieth century, and then switched to another model, the American, and with it achieved another economic leap forward in the second half of the century. But interestingly, though in 1950 the Japanese law was very similar to that of the State of Illinois, and to the American Model Business Corporation Act that was drafted in the same year based on the Illinois Act, Japanese corporation law diverged from American law in subsequent decades. The explanation suggested by West of the divergence is that different mechanisms of change operated in Japan and the United States. Different ability to respond to changing reality, different interest group politics, and different exogenous shocks led to a growing divergence despite globalization and integration of financial and goods markets (West 2001). Japanese corporate governance was not dramatically shifted due to the law from controlling shareholder or interlocking group model, akin to that of Germany, to widely dispersed ownership similar to the one most common in the United States. Chile provides a similar pattern. It borrowed in 1854 from France and from French-inspired Spain, its commercial code. This code allowed significant state intervention in the affairs of corporations. Only in 1981, during Pinochet's regime, Chile went through a major revision of its corporation law that borrowed heavily from the United States (Pistor *et al.* 2002).

China represents another kind of shift. Until the late nineteenth century, the private enterprise run as family or clan firms was the predominant form of business institution in China. The late Qing reforms were a moderate attempt by the government to introduce legal, institutional, and educational reforms in order to satisfy popular demands for change and modernization, in face of Western and Japanese dominance, while maintaining the political status quo of a conservative imperial monarchy. The 1904 Companies Act, part of this reform, was based on Japanese law, which was in turn recently influenced by German law and English company laws, but in much abbreviated form (Goetzmann and Koll 2005: 149–184). This Qing company law remained in force throughout the Republican period. In the 1950s, following the Communist Revolution, the 1904 Act that facilitated private ownership of companies was abolished. New socialist legislation complemented large-scale nationalization of enterprises and absorbed these now state-owned enterprises into the administrative apparatus of the state. Starting in 1984, the state-owned enterprises were gradually separated from the administration, were recognized as legal entities, as responsible for their own profits and losses, and enjoying managerial autonomy. The Corporate Law of 1993 was the first significant piece of corporate legislation since the founding of the People's Republic of China in 1949. In was an enabling legislation, regulating the formation of state-owned enterprises as well as closely held corporations and public corporations. China, thus exemplifies a pattern that combines the importation of European capitalist law, directly and via Japan, a reaction to capitalism that was manifested in the importation of a European-created

Soviet-Socialist model, and at a third stage a return to more capitalist law of corporations (Schipani and Liu 2002).

Interestingly, the LLSV law and finance literature does not deal with this diversity. They coded each country's quality of protection of shareholders and creditors based on the state of its company law in the mid 1990s. They classified legal systems into families of legal origins according to the perceived origins of their company law.[21] Countries with complex origins, even such that at some point were part of the British empire (such as Malta, the Seychelles, and Cyprus), seem to have been left out of the sample. They ignored the mode by which company law was introduced into each country. The transplant effect – that is, whether company law was introduced voluntarily or imposed – was later shown by Berkowitz et al. to make a difference (Berkowitz, Pistor, and Richard 2003). They also ignored the question of what exactly was imported from Europe. As we have seen above, there were significant differences in content and track of the importation of company law from England, France, or Germany. Their methodology could not account for countries such as Japan, Chile, and China that were for lengthy periods of time under the spell of company laws originating from different legal traditions within the capitalist world or, in the case of China, of capitalist, socialist, and again capitalist, law. These differences seem to only partly correspond with the mode of transplantation and also result from timing, interest group lobbying, administrative factors, personal issues, and contingencies.

Conclusion

All four examined fields of law went through a transformation in the nineteenth century. But the transformation was not uniform and neither was there convergence toward a single model. Furthermore, with respect to all fields, no consensus emerged as to the first best rules and institutions. In contract law, the idea of the freedom of contracts emerged in both common law and civil law jurisdictions. But it was packaged differently: in court cases in the former and in civil codes in the latter. Furthermore, the idea did not dominate contract law for long. Eventually a more interventionist, or collectivist, model replaced it. In land registries, two separate models, recording of transactions and recording of rights, emerged and prevailed in the capitalist

---

21 LLSV classified the following as common law countries: Australia; Canada; Hong Kong; India; Ireland; Israel; Kenya; Malaysia; New Zealand; Nigeria; Pakistan; Singapore; South Africa; Sri Lanka; Thailand; UK; US; and Zimbabwe.

economies, but not along the lines of legal traditions. In patent law, ex ante examination and ex post litigation developed. Again the two modes did not correlate with legal origins. Furthermore, abolishment of the entire system was seriously considered. In corporation law, the development both on the continent and in Anglo-American jurisdictions was based on statute law. Generally speaking, all the capitalist systems converged to a model of general incorporation, limited liability, joint stock, delegated management, and transferable shares. Differences were relatively marginal. The private company was added to the menu in Germany, the United Kingdom, and France in that order, and again, not based on legal traditions. Eventually, in the twentieth century, governance structures in the United States and the United Kingdom shifted toward widely dispersed ownership, while in France and Germany controlling shareholders prevailed. The debate as to whether convergence is taking place, and whether any of the models is more efficient, is still raging.

The spread of law beyond Europe did not reinforce the common law–civil law divide. A few of the above examples demonstrate this. The Torrens system of land registration is one example of a possible German influence that spread through part of the British empire. The non-enforcement of the European-Spanish-based land registration system and the rise of informality was another cause for divergence within a single legal tradition. Local resistance to the imposition of uniform imperial patent law that would serve the interest of British industrialists is another example of diverging dynamics. The Paris Convention is a further example of a force that works across legal traditions, but, in this case, leading to harmonization rather than hybrids.

The study of the four legal fields does not allow us to reach clear conclusions as to causality flowing from law to economic development. The recent aggregated econometric studies of LLSV and AJR definitely amount to a breakthrough in untangling the causation problem. But on the other hand, the detailed study of the four fields of law provides significant support for the thesis that the law in fields most relevant to economic growth did not converge to a single, efficiency superior, capitalist model, well into the twentieth century. This study thus leans on the side of persistence of legal divergence in the recent debates about convergence versus divergence. It backs those, in the old and still lively debate, who hold to the view that legal developments do not just respond instrumentally to demands from the outside but also to some internal autonomous dynamics. We may conclude that though the law creates some inertia and rigidity, these internal dynamics, for the most part, have nothing to do with ancient legal origins. Much more research is needed to explain in which legal institutions and rules the legal traditions manifested in a manner that affected economic growth rates. We can conclude that law mattered and facilitated the rise of capitalism but we still don't know enough on the extent to which it mattered. We now have a better understanding of how or why the two European legal traditions mattered in the rise and spread of capitalism. But we still have more questions than answers.

References

Acemoglu, D., S. Johnson, and J. A. Robinson (2001). "The Colonial Origins of Comparative Development: An Empirical Investigation," *American Economic Review* 91: 1369–1401.

Acemoglu, D. and J. A. Robinson (2012). *Why Nations Fail: The Origins of Power, Prosperity, and Poverty*. New York: Crown Publishers.

Adams, J. N. and G. Averley (1986). "The Patent Specification, the Role of Liardet v Johnson," *The Journal of Legal History* 7: 156–77.

Ajani, G. (1995). "By Chance and Prestige Legal Transplants in Russia and Eastern Europe," *The American Journal of Comparative Law* 43: 93–117.

Arruñada, B. (2012). *Institutional Foundations of Impersonal Exchange: The Theory and Policy of Contractual Registries*. University of Chicago Press.

Arruñada, B. and N. Garoupa (2005). "The Choice of Titling System in Land," *Journal of Law and Economics* 48(2): 709–727.

Atiyah, P. S. (1979). *The Rise and Fall of Freedom of Contract*. Oxford University Press.

Baker, J. H. (2002). *An Introduction to English Legal History*, 4th edn. Oxford University Press.

Benton, L. (2002). *Law and Colonial Cultures: Legal Regimes in World History, 1400–1900.* Cambridge University Press.

(2010). *A Search for Sovereignty: Law and Geography in European Empires, 1400–1900.* Cambridge University Press.

Berkowitz, D., K. Pistor, and J. Richard (2003). "The Transplant Effect," *The American Journal of Comparative Law* 51(1): 163–203.

Bracha, O. (2005). *Owning Ideas: A History of Anglo-American Intellectual Property, S.J.D. Dissertation*. Harvard Law School.

Chen, J. (2008). *Chinese Law: Context and Transformation*. Leiden and Boston: Martinus Nijhoff Publishers.

Coffman, D., A. Leonard, and L. Neal. (eds.) (2013). *Questioning Credible Commitment: Perspectives on the Rise of Financial Capitalism*. Cambridge University Press.

Curran, V. G. (2001). "Romantic Common Law, Enlightened Civil Law: Legal Uniformity and the Homogenization of the European Union," *Columbia Journal of European Law* 7: 63–138.

Dam, K. W. (2006). *The Law–Growth Nexus: The Rule of Law and Economic Development*. Washington, DC: Brookings Institution Press.

David, R. and J. E. C. Brierley (1978). *Major Legal Systems in the World Today*, 2nd edn. London: Stevens & Sons.

De Cruz, P. (1999). *Comparative Law in a Changing World*, 2nd edn. London: Cavendish Publishing Limited.

De Soto, H. (1989). *The Other Path*. New York: Basic Books.

Dicey, A. V. (1905). *Lectures on the Relation between Law and Public Opinion in England during the Nineteenth Century*. London: Macmillan and Co.

Dutton, H. I. (1984). *The Patent System and Inventive Activity during the Industrial Revolution, 1750–1852*. Manchester University Press.

Easterbrook, F. H. and D. R. Fischel (1985). "Limited Liability and the Corporation," *University of Chicago Law Review* 52: 89–117.

Engerman, S. L., P. T. Hoffman, J. Rosenthal, and K. L. Sokoloff (2003). "Financial Intermediaries in Europe," in S. L. Engerman, P. T. Hoffman, J. Rosenthal, and K. L. Sokoloff (eds.), *Finance, Intermediaries, and Economic Development*. Cambridge University Press.

Esposito, A. (2003). "A Comparison of the Australian ('Torrens') System of Land Registration of 1858 and the Law of Hamburg in the 1850's," *Australian Journal of Legal History* 7: 193–229.

Finn, J. (2000). "Particularism Versus Uniformity: Factors Shaping the Development of Australasian Intellectual Property Law in the Nineteenth Century," *Australian Journal of Legal History* 6: 113–133.

(2002). "Australasian Law and Canadian Statutes in the Nineteenth Century: A Study of the Movement of Colonial Legislation between Jurisdictions," *The Dalhousie Law Journal* 25: 169–214.

Fried, B. (1998). *The Progressive Assault on Laissez Faire: Robert Hale and the First Law and Economics Movement*. Cambridge, MA: Harvard University Press.

Gierczyk, Y. N. (2005–2006). "The Evolution of the European Legal System: The European Court of Justice's Role in the Harmonization of Laws," *ILSA Journal of International & Comparative Law* 12: 153–182.

Goetzmann, W. N. and E. Koll. (2005). "The History of Corporate Ownership in China: State Patronage, Company Legislation, and the Issue of Control," in R. K. Morck (ed.), *A History of Corporate Governance around the World: Family Business Groups to Professional Managers*. University of Chicago Press.

Gordley, J. (1993). *The Philosophical Origins of Modern Contract Doctrine*. Oxford University Press.

Grey, C. W. and K. Hendley (1995). *Developing Commercial Law in Transition Economies: Examples from Hungary and Russia*. The World Bank, Policy Research Department.

Guinnane, T. W., R. Harris, N. Lamoreaux, and J.-L. Rosenthal (2007). "Putting the Corporation in its Place," *Enterprise and Society* 8: 687–729.

Hansmann, H., R. Kraakman, and R. Squire (2006). "Law and the Rise of the Firm," *Harvard Law Review* 119: 1333–1403. Available at: http://papers.ssrn.com/sol3/papers.cfm?abstract_id=873507.

Harris, R. (2000). *Industrializing English Law: Entrepreneurship and Business Organization, 1720–1844*. Cambridge University Press.

(2003). "The Encounters of Economic History and Legal History," *Law and History Review* 1(2): 297–346.

(2004). "Government and the Economy, 1688–1850," in R. Floud and P. Johnson (eds.), *The Cambridge Economic History of Britain since 1700*. Cambridge University Press.

Harris, R., A. Kedar, P. Lahav, and A. Likhovski (2002). *The History of Law in a Multicultural Society: Israel 1917–1967*. Dartmouth: Ashgate.

Heb, B. (2002). "The Integrating Effect of European Civil Procedure Law," *European Journal of Law Reform* 4(3): 3–18.

Hill, E. (1977). "Comparative and Historical Study of Modern Middle Eastern Law," *The American Journal of Comparative Law* 26: 279–304.

Hofman, P. T., G. Postel-Vinay, and J. Rosenthal (2000). *Priceless Markets: The Political Economy of Credit in Paris, 1660–1870.* University of Chicago Press.

Hogg, J. E. (1920). *Registration of Title to Land throughout the Empire.* Toronto: The Carswell Company.

Horwitz, M. J. (1977). *The Transformation of American Law, 1780–1860.* Cambridge, MA: Harvard University Press.

Hovenkamp, H. (1990). "The First Great Law and Economics Movement," *Stanford Law Review* 42: 993–1058.

Hulsebosch, D. (2005). *Constituting Empire: New York and the Transformation of Constitutionalism in the Atlantic World, 1664–1830.* Chapel Hill: University of North Carolina Press.

Ibbetson, D. J. (1999). *Historical Introduction to the Law of Obligations.* Oxford University Press.

John, M. (1989). *Politics and the Law in Late Nineteenth-Century Germany: The Origins of the Civil Code* (Oxford Historical Monographs). Oxford University Press.

Joireman, S. F. (2001)."Inherited Legal Systems and Effective Rule of Law: Africa and the Colonial Legacy," *The Journal of Modern African Studies* 39: 576–596.

Khan, B. Z. (1995). "Property Rights and Patent Litigation in Early Nineteenth-Century America," *Journal of Economic History* 55: 58–97.

(2005). *The Democratization of Invention: Patents and Copyrights in American Economic Development, 1790–1920.* Cambridge University Press.

(2008). "An Economic History of Patent Institutions," in R. Whaples (ed.), *EH.Net Encyclopedia.* http://eh.net/encyclopedia/article/khan.patents.

Khan, B. Z. and K. L. Sokoloff. (1997). "Two Paths to Industrial Development and Technological Change," in M. Berg and K. Bruland (eds.), *Technological Revolutions in Europe, 1760–1860.* London: Edward Elgar.

Kozolchyk, B. (1970). "The Mexican Land Registry: A Critical Evaluation," *Arizona Law Review* 12: 265–389.

La Porta, R. L., F. Lopez-De-Silanes, A. Shleifer, and R. W. Vishny (1997). "Legal Determinants of External Finance," *Journal of Finance* 52: 1131–1150.

(1998). "Law and Finance," *Journal of Political Economy* 106: 1113–1155.

Lamoreaux, N. R. and K. L. Sokoloff (2001). "Market Trade in Patents and the Rise of a Class of Specialized Inventors in the Nineteenth-Century United States," *American Economic Review* 91: 39–44.

Likhovski, A. (1999). "Protestantism and Radical Reform of English Law: A Variation on a Theme by Weber," *Law and Society Review* 33: 365–391.

Lobingier, C. S. (1932). "Modern Expansion of the Roman Law," *University of Cincinnati Law Review* 6: 153–161 (Spain), 170–181 (France).

Machlup, F. and E. Penrose (1950). "The Patent Controversy in the Nineteenth Century," *Journal of Economic History* 10(1): 1–29.

Macleod, C. (1988). *Inventing the Industrial Revolution: The English Patent System 1660–1800.* Cambridge University Press.

Maitland, F. W. (1909). *The Forms of Action at Common Law.* Cambridge University Press.

Mallat, C. (2007). *Introduction to Middle Eastern law*. Oxford University Press.

Milhaupt, J. and K. Pistor (2008). *Law & Capitalism: What Corporate Crises Reveal about Legal Systems and Economic Development around the World*. University of Chicago Press.

Mirow, M. C. (2004). *Latin American Law: A History of Private Law and Institutions in Spanish America*. University of Texas Press.

Mokyr, J. (1990). *The Lever of Riches: Technological Creativity and Economic Progress*. London and New York: Oxford University Press.

Munro, J. (2003). "The Medieval Origins of the Financial Revolution: Usury, Rentes, and Negotiability," *International History Review* 25(3): 505–562.

Musacchio, A. (2008). "Can Civil Law Countries Get Good Institutions? Lessons from the History of Creditor Rights and Bond Markets in Brazil," *The Journal of Economic History* 68(1): 80–108.

Nelson, W. (1975). *Americanization of the Common Law: The Impact of Legal Change on Massachusetts Society, 1760–1830*. Cambridge, MA: Harvard University Press.

North, D. C. (1990). *Institutions, Institutional Change and Economic Performance*. Cambridge University Press.

North, D. C. and R. P. Thomas. (1973). *The Rise of the Western World: A New Economic History*. Cambridge University Press.

North, D. C., J. J. Wallis, and B. Weingast (2009). *Violence and Social Order: A Conceptual Framework for Interpreting Recorded Human History*. Cambridge University Press.

North, D. C. and B. R. Weingast. (1989). "Constitutions and Commitment: The Evolution of Institutions Governing Public Choice in Seventeenth-Century England," *The Journal of Economic History* 49: 803–832.

Oda, H. (1992). *Japanese Law*. London: Butterworths.

Offer, A. (1981). *Property and Politics 1870–1914: Landownership, Law, Ideology and Urban Development in England*. Cambridge University Press.

Pargendler, M. (2012). "The Rise and Decline of Legal Families," *The American Journal of Comparative Law* 60: 1043–74.

Pashukanis, E. B. (1978). *Law and Marxism: A General Theory*. London: Transaction Publishers.

Pearson, H. (1997). *Origins of Law and Economics: The Economist's New Science of Law*. Cambridge University Press.

Pistor, K., Y. Keinan, J. Kleinheisterkamp, and M. D. West (2002). "The Evolution of Corporate Law: A Cross Country Comparison," *University of Pennsylvania Journal of International Economic Law* 23: 791–871.

Pollock, F. and D. F. Mulla (1972). *The Indian Contract and Specific Relief Act*, 9th edn. Bombay: N.M Tripathi Private Ltd.

Posner, R. (1986). *Economic Analysis of Law*, 3rd edn. New York: Little, Brown and Company.

(2002). *Economic Analysis of Law*. New York: Aspen Law & Business.

Roe, M. J. and L. A. Bebchuk (1999). "A Theory of Path Dependence in Corporate Ownership and Governance," *Stanford Law Review* 52: 127–170.

Ross, R. (2008). "Legal Communications and Imperial Governance: British North America and Spanish America Compared," in C. L. Tomlins and M. G. Cambridge (eds.), *History of Law in America*. Cambridge University Press. pp. 104–143;

Schipani, C. A. and J. Liu (2002). "Corporate Governance in China: Then and Now," *Columbia Business Law Review* 2002: 1–69.

Seckelman, M. (2002). "Industrial Engineering and the Struggle for the Protection of Patents in Germany, 1856–1877," *Quaderns d'història de l'ingenieria* 5: 234–240.

Sgard, J. (2006). "Do Legal Origins Matter? The Case of Bankruptcy Laws in Europe 1808–1914," *European Review of Economic History* 10(3): 389–419.

Shachar, Y. (1995). "History and Sources of Israel Law," in A. Shapira and K. DeWitt-Arar (eds.), *Introduction to the Law of Israel*. The Hague: Kluwer Law International.

Simpson, S. R. (1976). *Land Law and Registration*. Cambridge University Press.

Stern, P. J. (2011). *The Company-State: Corporate Sovereignty and the Early Modern Foundations of the British Empire in India*. Oxford University Press.

Sussman, N. and Y. Yafeh (2006). "Institutional Reforms, Financial Development and Sovereign Debt: Britain 1690–1790," *Journal of Economic History* 66(4): 906–35.

Tomlins, C. L. (2009). "Transplants and Timing: Passages in the Creation of an Anglo-American Law of Slavery," *Theoretical Inquiries in Law* 10(2): 389–422.

Trakman, L. E. (1985). "Contract and Commercial Law Scholarship in Common Law Canada," *Osgoode Hall Law Journal* 43: 663–680.

Trubek, D. M. (1972). "Max Weber on Law and the Rise of Capitalism," *Wisconsin Law Review* 3: 720–753.

Trubek, D. M. and A. Santos (2006). *The New Law and Economic Development: A Critical Appraisal*. Cambridge University Press.

Weber, M. (1968). *Economy and Society*. New York: Bedminster Press Incorporated.

West, M. D. (2001). "The Puzzling Divergence of Corporate Law: Evidence and Explanations from Japan and the United States," *University of Pennsylvania Law Review* 150: 528–601.

Whitman, J. Q. (2009). "Western Legal Imperialism: Thinking about the Deep Historical Roots," *Theoretical Inquiries in Law* 10: 305–332.

Yang, D. (2003). "The Development of Intellectual Property in China," *World Patent Information* 25: 131–142.

Zhang, M. (2000). "Freedom of Contract with Chinese Legal Characteristics: A Closer Look at China's New Contract Law," *Temple International and Comparative Law Journal* 14: 237–262.

Zweigert, K. and H. Kotz (1977). *An Introduction to Comparative Law*. New York: North-Holland Publishing Company.

(1987). *An Introduction to Comparative Law*, 2nd edn. Oxford University Press and Germany: J.C.B, Mohr.

(1998). *An Introduction to Comparative Law*, 3rd edition. Oxford University Press and Tübingen: J.C.B. Mohr.

6

Firms and global capitalism

GEOFFREY JONES

This chapter examines the role of business enterprises as actors in the spread of global capitalism since 1848. Since the middle of the nineteenth century, firms have been the strongest institution to operate across national borders, with the possible exception of the Roman Catholic Church. Multinational firms, defined broadly as firms owning and controlling assets in more than one country, have been major drivers of the trade flows which characterized globalization waves. During the second half of the nineteenth century, they were the principal agents behind the discovery and exploitation of natural resources around the world. Large vertically integrated corporations controlled the value chains of many commodities. They were characterized by high levels of intra-firm trade, or trade flows across national borders but between affiliates of the same company, as when the same oil company drilled for petroleum, transported it along pipes and on ships, refined it into different products, and sold it to final consumers. As globalization intensified again during the late twentieth century, such intra-firm trade, now concentrated in manufacturing, was a dominant actor in the world trade system. Although global data are patchy for many countries, it is known that intra-firm trade accounted for 48 percent of US manufactured goods imports in 2009, and about 30 percent of US manufactured goods exports. The share of intra-firm trade is especially high in the automobile, pharmaceuticals, and transport equipment industries (Lanz and Miroudot 2011).

Multinational firms were more than creators and drivers of trade flows. They impacted the spread of capitalism in many other ways. As suggested by the quantitative measure most frequently used as a proxy for their size – foreign direct investment (FDI) – they transfer capital across borders, although this function has often been less important than it seems, as firms have often preferred to raise capital locally and plough back profits into subsidiaries. More significantly, as multinationals build factories and distribution networks, dig mines, and open plantations, they transfer technology and knowledge, and

Table 6.1. *World foreign direct investment as a percentage of world output 1913–2010 (%)*

1913	1960	1980	1990	2010
9.0	4.4	4.8	9.6	30.3

Source: UNCTAD 1994, 1997, 1999, 2011.

the managerial and organizational capabilities in which they are embedded. These capabilities are, in turn, embedded in cultural value-systems. As critics have complained and scholars have asserted, Coca Cola soda is not merely a consumer product, but in some sense, a symbol of American values (Giebelhaus 1994; Kuisel 1991).

The relative importance of multinational firms in the spread of capitalism was heavily influenced by the globalization waves which have characterized the last 200 years (Bordo, Taylor, and Williamson 2003). FDI represented a substantial proportion of the huge capital flows before World War I (see James, Chapter 9 in this volume). By 1914, estimated world FDI was equivalent to 9 percent of world output, a ratio which fell sharply, and was not to be reached again until 1990 (see Table 6.1).

The multinational strategies of firms, then, play an important role in the story of the spread of global capitalism. The historical record, however, shows that this role was not linear. Nor, given the multiple ways in which multinationals can impact countries, was it mono-dimensional. The following four sections review this role chronologically in different eras since 1848. A final section concludes.

Business enterprises and globalization 1848–1914

From the mid nineteenth century tens of thousands of firms, mostly based in Western countries which had experienced the industrial revolution, crossed borders and established operations in foreign countries. These firms drove the rapid increase in trade flows during this era. Latin America and Asia were especially important as host economies, attracting well over half of the total world stock of foreign direct investment. Possibly one-half of world FDI was invested in natural resources, and a further one-third in services, especially financing, insuring, transporting commodities and foodstuffs (Dunning and Lundan 2008; Jones 2005a; Wilkins 1970).

The global spread of firms rested crucially on the formal and informal institutions put in place during the nineteenth century, and sometimes earlier. In particular, the expansion of Western imperialism over much of Asia and Africa, the spread of an international legal system and legal norms which enforced contracts and private property rights (see Harris, Chapter 5 in this volume), numerous trade treaties, and the international Gold Standard, reduced the risks of doing business abroad, primarily for firms from the West (Lipson 1985; Magee and Thompson 2010). Yet the international growth of firms was not easy or automatic. While entrepreneurial opportunities were great, and access to capital was facilitated by the growth of large globally oriented capital markets in London and elsewhere, managerial execution remained a huge task. It was enormously challenging to build organizational structures capable of operating across borders. There needed to be constant experimentation with organizational design, and there were constant failures, as firms learned how to manage distance, and adjust to different market and factor conditions from their home countries.

The emergent petroleum industry provides one example of the nature of the challenges. The demand for petroleum products rose sharply from the late nineteenth century, as fuel oil began to be used as a substitute for coal, and the infant automobile industry originated a whole new source of demand. However, creating an oil business involved political, technological, transport, and marketing challenges. Outside the United States, a concession had to be negotiated with a local government. Once a concession was secured, finding oil when exploration techniques were primitive, and the use of geologists was in its infancy, was difficult. If an oil supply was found, the well had to be capped before it flooded neighboring lands, an all-too-regular occurrence. The oil then needed to be transported. This meant building pipelines and railroad tracks, ports and shipping terminals, refining facilities and storage tanks. Outside of the United States, it turned out that oil was frequently located in difficult geographical terrains, in countries with unstable or fragile political regimes, like Mexico and Iran. The pre-1914 oil industry, then, posed formidable challenges to firms which entered it (Bud-Frierman, Godley, and Wale 2010; Ferrier 1982; Jones 1981; Jonker and Zanden 2007).

The small minority of firms which survived long enough to build viable international businesses drove globalization by creating trade flows, constructing marketing channels, building infrastructure, and creating markets. By 1914 the production or marketing of most of the world's mineral resources was controlled by US and European firms. Foreign firms also dominated the production and marketing of renewable resources including rubber, tropical fruits, and tea. A high proportion of world trade in some primary commodities was intra-firm. The commodity chains created by these firms were fundamental actors in the process of world economic integration (Topik, Marichal, and Frank 2006).

Much of the infrastructure of the global economy – the telegraph, ports, railroads, and electricity and gas utilities – was put in place by international business enterprises (Ahvenainen 2004; Connolly 1999; Geyikdagi 2011; Hausman, Hertner, and Wilkins 2008; Hills 2002; McDowall 1988). International shipping companies carried the world's oceanic trade and moved millions of people (Harlaftis 1993; Harlaftis and Theokokas 2004; Munro 2003). Just as in the early United States, transportation improvements widened and deepened the emergent domestic market, so these investments in international transport and communications facilitated the emergence of a global market (Atack, Chapter 17 in Volume 1). Governments were less prominent actors than in the American story, although they were important as providers of concessions to build ports and operate utilities, and of mail contracts to oceanic shipping companies (Munro 2003).

Multinationals not only built the transport hardware of the first global economy, they also enabled the flows of trade along the new transport routes. Trading companies both facilitated and created trade flows between developed and developing countries, often investing in creating plantations and opening mines, and the processing of minerals and commodities (Jones 1998, 2000; Jonker and Sluyterman 2000). European overseas banks built extensive branch networks throughout the southern hemisphere and Asia, and financed the exchange of manufactured goods for commodities (Jones 1990, 1993). In east Asia, from the late nineteenth century, Japanese trading companies and shipping firms invested in China and other neighboring countries, facilitating the rapid regional integration seen before 1914 (Kuwahara 1990; Sugihara 2005).

Hundreds of manufacturing companies were also instrumental in transferring products and brands across borders during this era of fast globalization. The first instances of multinational manufacturing included small Swiss cotton textile firms in the 1830s (Schröter 1993a). The phenomenon intensified from mid century. Multinational manufacturing was stimulated by the spread of protectionism from the late nineteenth century. Firms were able to "jump" over the tariff barriers which blocked their exports by establishing local production. This strategy was prominent in industries such as chemicals, machinery, and branded consumer products. Alternative strategies such as licensing and franchising were discouraged because of the complexity of writing contracts for complex technologies and for brand names (Nicholas 1983).

Table 6.2. *World's largest host economies measured by stock of inward foreign direct investment, 1914, 1929, 1980, 2010*

1914[1]	1929[2]	1980[3]	2010[4]
United States	Canada	United States	United States
Russia	United States	United Kingdom	Hong Kong
Canada	India	Canada	United Kingdom
Argentina	Cuba	Germany	France
Brazil	Mexico	France	Germany
South Africa	Argentina	Netherlands	Belgium
Austria-Hungary	Chile	Brazil	Spain
India/China	United Kingdom	Australia	Netherlands
Egypt, Mexico, United Kingdom	Malaya	Indonesia	China
	Venezuela	Italy	Canada

[1] Wilkins (1994)
[2] Wilkins (1994)
[3] Dunning and Lundan (2008). The authors give a figure for Hong Kong ($138 billion) which is far higher than the United States ($83 billion) and far higher for the British colony a decade later. This is assumed to be a reporting error.
[4] UNCTAD 2011

The firms of different countries varied in their propensity to invest abroad. The United Kingdom alone was the home of nearly one-half of world FDI in 1914, and the United States and Germany accounted for a further 14 percent each. Firms from a number of small European countries, especially the Netherlands, Sweden, and Switzerland, were very active internationally (Schröter 1993b). Nationality influenced location also. Firms often reduced risks by investing in geographically or culturally proximate regions or in colonial empires. The United States was important as a host economy, both because of its market size and abundance of natural resources (Wilkins 1989).

Table 6.2 provides a ranking of the world's largest host economies over time using the measure of absolute stock of inward FDI. It reveals major historical shifts over time. Before World War II the fact that the majority of FDI was in natural resources and related services is reflected in the fact that the biggest host economies were countries of recent settlement and primary producers in the poor periphery. Well resource-endowed British colonies and protectorates such as India, Egypt, and Malaya also featured prominently.

The smaller amounts of manufacturing FDI were reflected in the position of the United Kingdom and the United States as leading host economies – much of that investment was cross-investment between the two countries (Jones 2005a; Jones and Bostock 1996; Wilkins 1989). As will be discussed in more detail later in this chapter, the post-World War II spread of communism, decolonization, and the subsequent growth of restrictions on foreign firms, and widespread nationalization of foreign-owned natural resource investments in the developing world, combined to dramatically reduce foreign investments in the periphery. The ranking of host economies in 1980 reflected the consequent concentration of postwar FDI flows into manufacturing, primarily in risk-free Western developed countries. The liberalization of governmental policies toward foreign multinationals during the recent era of globalization resulted in the re-emergence of China and some other emerging countries as major hosts, although the majority of FDI continued to be located in Western developed countries.

The importance of business enterprises in driving globalization has been in part obscured by the heterogeneity of the corporate forms they employed. There were large firms with managerial hierarchies, whose rise was the focus of attention of the iconic business historian Alfred D. Chandler (Chandler 1962, 1977, 1990). Many began as small entrepreneurial ventures, but a handful became global giants. Singer Sewing Machines was one example. By 1914 it accounted for 90 percent of the sewing machines built in the world. Singer's development of installment plans and direct selling enabled millions of relatively low-income consumers from Russia to Japan to purchase the machine (Carstensen 1984; Godley 2006; Gordon 2011).

Singer, and other large firms such as Standard Oil and Lever Brothers, coexisted with numerous small and family-owned firms. European firms, especially from smaller economies such as Sweden, made foreign investments at early stages of their corporate lives (Olsson 1993). Thousands of "free-standing" firms, which conducted little or no business in their home economies, were established in the United Kingdom and the Netherlands, especially, exclusively to operate internationally (Wilkins 1988; Wilkins and Schröter 1998).

Merchant networks established by *diaspora* communities were also important drivers of international business. The Greek *diaspora* spread over the Mediterranean and Russia was active in wide-ranging international commercial and shipping business, creating a cosmopolitan business network based on kinship ties extending over central Europe and even reaching France and the United Kingdom (Minoglou and Louri 1997). In Asia, Chinese and Indian commercial *diaspora* operated within and between European empires (Brown 1994, 2000). These merchant houses, built around language and ethnic communities, may have had fluid boundaries, but they were dynamic business enterprises.

The potential gains to welfare from multinational investment were high. Business enterprises operating across borders were, in theory at least, powerful agents for diffusing knowledge. They transferred products between countries: Bayer introduced the aspirin to the United States; Kellogg introduced breakfast cereals to the United Kingdom; and there were hundreds of other examples (Collins 1994; Jones 2005a; Wilkins 1989). Firms which built factories in foreign countries transferred new techniques and work practices. Beginning with a factory in Glasgow, Scotland, in 1867, Singer took mechanized sewing machine manufacture around the world. In Tsarist Russia, it built the largest modern engineering factory in the country, employing German and British managers to supervise both the production process and new methods of labor management (Carstensen 1984).

Nor was technology transfer limited to multinational manufacturing. The establishment and maintenance of mines, oil fields, plantations, shipping depots, and railroad systems involved the transfer of packages of organizational and technological knowledge to host economies. Given the absence of appropriate infrastructure in many countries, foreign enterprises frequently not only introduced technologies specific to their activities, but also social technologies such as police, postal, and education systems. This was evident in the giant tea plantations created by British firms like James Finlay in nineteenth-century India, and in the rubber plantations created by their counterparts such as Harrisons & Crosfield and Guthries in British Malaya (Jones 2000). The building of transport and distribution infrastructure was especially critical in enabling entrepreneurs to access world markets for the first time. Insofar as access to markets had been a constraint on capitalist enterprise in many parts of the world, this relieved it.

There appeared, therefore, considerable potential for multinational investment to facilitate the closing of the wealth gap which had opened up as Western Europe and North America underwent industrialization from the eighteenth century, whilst the rest of the world failed to follow or even, as in the case of India and China, transitioned over the course of the nineteenth century from giants of handicraft manufacturing to primary producing countries. In reality, this did not happen, except in isolated incidences, even as flows of FDI grew ever larger before 1914 (Allen, Chapter 2 in this volume).

It turned out that knowledge spillovers from multinational investment to the non-Western world were limited. Technological diffusion worked best when foreign firms went to a country with the institutional arrangements, human capital, and entrepreneurial values to absorb transferred knowledge, much of which was tacit and not readily codified (see Bruland and Mowery, Chapter 4 in this volume). Consequently, while the first global economy saw multinational firms become the conduits for significant technological and organizational transfers from the United States to Western Europe, and Western Europe to the United States, their role in transferring knowledge and capabilities from the West to the rest of the world appears more modest. In this respect, multinationals can be seen as part of the explanation for the convergence of technologies and incomes within the West, and the lack of convergence between the West and the rest (see Harley, Chapter 16 in Volume 1).

In addition to the absorptive capacity of host countries, both the strategies of multinationals and their management practices contributed to this situation. Most FDI in developing countries was in resources and related services. Such natural resource investments were highly enclavist. Minerals and agricultural commodities were typically exported with only the minimum of processing. This meant that most value was added to the product in the developed economies. Foreign firms were large employers of labor at that time. However, expatriates were typically employed in the higher-skill jobs. Training was only provided to local employees to enable them to fill unskilled or semiskilled jobs (Headrick 1988). The French-controlled Suez Company, which built and operated the Suez Canal in Egypt between 1854 and 1956, had a major stimulus on the Egyptian economy, yet until 1936 the Egyptian staff was almost exclusively unskilled workers (Piquet 2004).

The nature of such industries, and these employment practices, meant that the diffusion of organizing and technological skills to developing host economies was far less than to developed economies. Certainly some developing countries, such as Porfirian Mexico, experienced significant economic growth before World War 1, as foreign firms developed and exported minerals and commodities, and built the railroads and ports that allowed them access to foreign markets (see Allen, Chapter 2 in this volume) However on the whole, and with exceptions, the US and British firms in Mexico were not significant agents of technological diffusion into the domestic economy, given the formidable institutional, social, and cultural roadblocks in face of the transfer of technologies from advanced economies (Beatty 2003, 2009).

Western firms were not only the beneficiaries of the spread of Western colonialism over Asia and Africa, they were also part of the process of the spread of both formal and informal colonialism. During the mid-nineteenth-century Opium Wars with China, for example, Western governments actively supported the opium smuggling activities of firms such as Jardine Matheson. In West Africa, the activities of British shipping and trading companies such as Elder Dempster and the Niger Company preceded the extension of formal British colonial control (Jones 2000).

International companies were not transformers of the domestic institutions which often constrained growth in non-Western countries. While theoretically they may have been channels to transfer aspects of the institutional arrangements in their home countries to their hosts, for the most part they reinforced local institutions. This was evident especially in the concession system. In order to entice firms to make investments in mines, railroads, and so on, foreign firms were often given large, long-term, and tax-free concessions by governments in Latin America and elsewhere. These concessions turned Western companies into supporters of repressive governments, and associated Western capitalism with dictatorships and colonial regimes.

Guatemala provides a prime example of the role of foreign firms in strengthening growth-retarding institutional arrangements rather than challenging them. This country was one of the "banana republics" of the Boston-based United Fruit Company. From the late nineteenth century, this company built a shipping and distribution business which virtually created the mass market for bananas for the United States. Problems of quality control encouraged vertical integration into growing bananas. In Guatemala and elsewhere in Central America, the firm secured large land concessions, cleared land, and created plantations. General Manuel Estrada Cabrera, the Guatemalan dictator between 1898 and 1920, gave United Fruit large concessions in the hope that it could not only develop an export industry, but also modernize it through associated investments in railroads, telegraph lines, and other facilities.

The problem was that the Guatemala regime which gave such concessions was a dictatorship with no respect for the rule of law, which was a large part of the reason why the country was impoverished in the first place. The Spanish colonial legacy had resulted in a minority white population which owned the majority of the land, and a majority of the population, composed of Mayan descendants, who were impoverished, uneducated, and virtual slaves. United Fruit's plantation system in effect reinforced the unequal and repressive social structures in Guatemala, and then further froze the situation. The company supported the local regime, and the company was supported by the US government for strategic reasons. When, during the early 1950s, a democratic government sought to achieve agrarian and land reform, it was overthrown in a CIA-inspired coup and United Fruit reclaimed its lands (Bucheli 2005; Gleijeses 1991).

Meiji Japan, where a civil war had resulted in 1868 in a government that had ripped up the country's traditional institutions and replaced them with institutions and laws aimed at stimulating modern economic growth, turned out to be a rare non-Western exception in its absorptive capacity for such foreign knowledge. State policy to support industrialization was important in achieving this outcome (see Allen, Chapter 2 in this volume). The entrepreneurs who built businesses in these years, such as Yataro Iwasaki, the founder of Mitsubishi, and Sakiichi Toyoda, who built a textile machinery building which became the basis for Toyota automobiles, were beneficiaries of the new institutions of the Meiji state, but their success should not be seen as simply the result of supportive government policies including subsidies. Indeed, Yataro had to contend with repeated attempts by the government to set up rival Japanese shipping firms designed to challenge his business (Wray 1984; Yonekura and Shimizu 2010). Rather these entrepreneurs learned from foreign entrepreneurs and firms, with whom they sometimes collaborated, while building the capabilities to outcompete them. Although the amount of FDI going to Japan was small, there was an unusual amount of knowledge transfer to locally owned firms from multinational companies such as Western Electric (Mason 1992; Wilkins 1990).

In a broader sense, Western business enterprises became important agents during the decades before World War I in a significant, although patchy, homogenization of world cultures which has been one of the most significant outcomes of globalization. The "Coca-Colonization" of the post-1945 world had earlier precedents as American consumer culture began to diffuse internationally from the late nineteenth century (Grazia 2005). The international growth of the beauty industry, for example, drove a worldwide homogenization of beauty ideals. Whilst before the nineteenth century, societies differed widely in hygiene and beauty ideals and practices, the emergence of a modern beauty industry in the West over the course of the nineteenth century, and the international spread of French, US, and other firms, beauty ideals, assumptions, and routines which were prevalent in the West spread as global benchmarks. During the late nineteenth century, entrepreneurs such as Harley Procter in the United States, and Thomas Barrett and William Lever in the United Kingdom, used marketing and modern manufacturing to make soap a mass marketed product, and branded using emotional and romantic images. This transformed the age-old European soap industry, which was small, as Western people largely avoided washing with water until the nineteenth century. Defying all historical evidence, washing and using soap became associated with the virtues of Western and white people (Jones 2010). Crude racial stereotypes were used to advertise soap and other toiletries, which were presented as components of the Western contribution to "civilizing" colonized peoples (Burke 1996).

These emergent ideals included the status of Paris as the "world capital" of fashion and beauty. One of the peculiarities of the global economy was that country, or city, of origin assumed an ever-greater importance as an indication of quality and prestige. In the case of beauty, France and Paris became the symbolic world capital, joined later by New York (Jones 2010). The underlying assumptions of the beauty industry about ethnicity were most strikingly seen in the United States, where African-Americans represented over one-tenth of the population before World War I, but where the commercial beauty industry made no provision for their distinctive hair texture or skin tones (Peiss 1998).

Western beauty companies were interpreters, rather than creators, of the ethnic and cultural assumptions in their societies. While it was hardly surprising that at the high point of Western imperialism, Western people considered Caucasian features to be superior, along with everything else in Western civilization, adroit multinational marketing and branding strategies were effective in reinforcing such assumptions and diffusing them. As Western beauty was globalized, non-Western country ideals and practices were diminished in status, although at different rates and to different extents. This was a non-trivial impact, given that beauty norms exercise a profound influence on individual feelings of self-worth, and – as recent research has shown – on income and much else (Jones 2010).

The interwar years

The meltdown of the global economy during the interwar years is an important topic in economic history (see O'Rourke and Williamson, Chapter 1 in this volume). Global capital, trade, and labor flows fell sharply, especially after 1929, and the integrated markets constructed before 1914 disintegrated.

Firms operating across borders encountered numerous challenges during the interwar years as a result of wars, expropriations, exchange controls, and tariffs. If the management of geographical distance had been a major managerial challenge before 1914, the management of governments and their policies rose sharply up corporate agendas subsequently (Jones and Lubinski 2012). This represented a paradox. In terms of the CAGE framework of (Ghemawat 2001), technological advances in the interwar years continued to shrink "geographical distance" between countries. Telephones and automobiles became items of mass consumption, especially in the United States. Air travel became quite widespread, if costly. The advent of cinema and radio also provided unprecedented opportunities to see lifestyles real or imagined elsewhere, and facilitated the further diffusion of cultural influences (Grazia 2005). Yet as technology facilitated human beings to travel and observe one another as never before, so they disliked what they saw. Nationalism and racism proliferated during the interwar years. In Ghemawat's terms, "administrative distance" grew, and business enterprises were at the center of attention. For diverse reasons, governments sought to block foreign companies, alongside foreign imports and capital flows, and immigrants.

The nationality of firms rose rapidly up political agendas during World War I, as governments sequestrated affiliates of enemy-owned companies. Despite the rhetoric about "stateless firms" in the late twentieth century, if there was ever an era when the nationality of firms was not important it was before 1914, after which capitalism and business enterprises acquired and retained sharper national identities (Jones 2006). Thereafter, the sequestration of German-owned affiliates by US, British, and other Allied governments during World War I not only virtually reduced the stock of German FDI to zero, but also signaled the end of the era when foreign companies could operate in most countries on more or less the same terms as domestic ones. The Russian Revolution in 1917 resulted in France and Belgium losing two-thirds of their total foreign investment. Receptivity to foreign firms did not recover after the end of the war. Although the United States shifted from being the world's largest debtor nation to being a net creditor over the course of World War I, this was accompanied by a growing nationalism which resulted in major restrictions on foreign ownership in shipping, telecommunications, resources, and other industries (Wilkins 2002, 2004). The world became, and remained, much riskier for firms crossing national borders.

The restrictions on foreign firms formed part of the growth of critiques of unfettered capitalism which are considered in other chapters in this volume. However the spread of such ideas and subsequent policies should not be seen as entirely exogenous to global capitalism. In the broadest sense, many of the gains from the previous era of global capitalism had not been evenly shared. This was most clearly seen in the cases of the huge natural resource concessions which colonial regimes and assorted dictators had granted to Western firms. In the case of petroleum, the 1920s saw a failed attempt to renegotiate the vast oil concession held in Iran by the United Kingdom's Anglo-Iranian Oil Company, followed in 1938 by the successful expropriation of the oil concessions held by US and British oil companies in Mexico (Bamberg 1994; Maurer 2011).

Global capitalism had flourished within the context of Western colonialism, and became associated with the political and racial injustice of such regimes. In interwar India, for example, Gandhi's campaign against British imperialism encompassed a wider criticism of global capitalism as a whole. Key elements of Gandhi's alternative system included a critique of modern factory textile manufacturing and an argument instead for rural-based development designed to relieve rural poverty, the avoidance of industries considered immoral and damaging, such as alcohol, and the incorporation of ethical and religious values as central actors in business decision-making (Nanda 2003; Tripathi 2004).

The criticism, and restrictions, of global business form an important element of the narrative of deglobalization in this period. Yet multinational business did not disappear during these decades. Some rabidly nationalistic regimes, such as Japan in the 1930s, blocked new foreign investment, and squeezed existing foreign-owned businesses. However, Nazi Germany, while it used exchange controls to block profit remittances, exercised few restrictions on foreign businesses beyond requiring that they excluded Jews and others considered undesirable from the management of affiliates in Germany. As a result, US and other foreign firms such as General Motors and IBM were able to sustain growing businesses, albeit ones from whose profits they needed to plough back into their German operations, and as a result contribute to strengthening the Nazi state (Turner 2005; Wilkins 1974). Meanwhile consumers in Nazi Germany continued to watch the same Hollywood movies and purchase the same American cosmetic brands as their counterparts in the United States (Grazia 2005; Jones 2010). More generally, the ability of multinationals to finance their subsidiaries by ploughing back profits, or lending from local banks, meant that their businesses were much less impacted by the interwar collapse of capital flows than might have been expected (see James, Chapter 9 in this volume).

Business enterprises were more robust than an aggregate view of markets would suggest. From the perspective of firms, globalization was constrained rather than reversed after World War I. During the 1920s, German firms rebuilt international businesses (Jones and Lubinski 2012). In the interwar United Kingdom, as elsewhere, there were significant divestments as manufacturing multinationals closed down their affiliates, but there were at least as many new entrants (Bostock and Jones 1994; Jones and Bostock 1996). Firms in burgeoning consumer industries, such as automobiles, continued to invest heavily in producing in foreign markets (Bonin, Lung, and Tolliday 2003;

Wilkins and Hill 1964). Although international trade volumes fell sharply, commodity trading houses such as Bunge and Born and André grew rapidly, and consolidated their grip on wheat and other markets (Guez 1998; Morgan 1979). There were strong continuities, rather than massive disruption, in the global maritime world of shipping, trading, and ports (Miller 2012). Despite an era of falling commodity and mineral prices, multinational companies made vast investments developing new sources of supply, such as copper mines in East Africa and the Belgian Congo, and petroleum in Venezuela (Jones 2005a).

Numerous international cartels strove to regulate prices and output on a global scale. By the 1930s a high percentage of world trade was controlled by such international cartels. In manufacturing, the world electric lamp cartel controlled three-fourths of world output of electric lamps between the mid 1920s and World War II (Reich 1992). Commodities such as oil, tin, and tea saw wide-ranging and quite long-lasting international cartels. It is less straightforward to understand the place of these cartels in the narrative of global capitalism. While they may be seen as part of the story of growth-retarding institutions during this era, it is evident that most cartels were rarely able to control them for too long before new competitors appeared, unless they were strongly supported by governments. More importantly, however, they were often not agents of deglobalization. They often represented competition by another means rather than the elimination of competition altogether. They were sometimes powerful actors in the transfer of knowledge and intellectual property across borders. The cartel between Germany's IG Farben and Standard Oil of New Jersey during the 1930s resulted in a significant geographical diffusion of new chemical processes, and this was not an isolated example of widespread sharing of patent and knowledge inside such cartels (Fear 2008; Schröter 1988).

Global firms were less directly associated with the growth of capitalism in non-Western countries, but they were important as role models, competitive targets, and sometimes as partners. Much of the modern economic growth in these years was driven by local entrepreneurs who began to build businesses capable of competing with Western firms, although most also had a symbiotic relationship to such firms. There was a rapid growth, for example, of Indian-owned business from World War I. Modern industrialization spread from the small confines of parts of western and eastern India to many other regions of India. During the war, Ghanshyam Das Birla led the Marwari community into its first sustained manufacturing investments. He was offended by the racism he encountered from the British, but he also studied and learned from them about modern business methods. During the interwar years, the Marwaris and

entrepreneurs from other communities expanded their manufacturing investments, sometimes by buying the shares of British companies. Indian entrepreneurs invested in new industries such as sugar, paper, shipping, and
chemicals, and challenged the British incumbents in jute and coal (Timburg
1978; Tripathi 2004).

There was also a rapid growth of modern Chinese businesses. Some grew
in alliance with Western firms such as British American Tobacco, which
distributed cigarettes both through its own organization and through an
independent Chinese firm (Cox 2000). Between 1914 and 1922 the modern
textile industry capacity also tripled, and China became the most rapidly
expanding producer in the world. From the mid 1920s, rising Chinese nationalism expressed through foreign trade boycotts stimulated further growth led
by local entrepreneurs. These ventures developed hybrid organizational
forms combining Western and Chinese practices (Chan 2006, 2010; Koll 2003;
Zelin 2005). In the pharmaceutical and Chinese medicine industries, Chinese
entrepreneurs used innovative advertising and retailing strategies to build
not only domestic businesses, but regional businesses in southeast Asia
(Cochran 2006).

Business enterprises after World War II

After World War II ended, multinational firms made significant contributions
to the reconstruction of a global economy. Service firms such as management
consultants, advertising agencies, hotels, and film distributors served as
significant conduits for the international diffusion of American management
practices, values, and lifestyles (Quek 2012; West 1987). As US management
consultancies, such as McKinsey, globalized from the late 1950s, they both
created and served markets for consultancy services. They diffused managerial best practices from the United States, initially primarily to Western
Europe, where they opened branches (Kipping 1999; McKenna 2006).
Trading companies developed global networks exploiting information asymmetries. Japan's general trading companies (*sogo shosha*) survived their
dismantling by the Allied occupation after World War II to become the central
drivers of Japan's foreign trade and FDI (Yonekawa 1990).

Long-established European trading companies, many of which had had
their businesses devastated during the war, were also rebuilt and reinvented.
Jardine Matheson and Swire, for example, lost their substantial assets in China
after the 1949 revolution. However they developed new businesses in the
British colony of Hong Kong and elsewhere in the region, building and

operating ports, wharves, and shipping companies, and creating airlines. Swire's development of Cathay Pacific created, by the 1960s, a major airline which facilitated regional economic integration, and east Asian links to Europe and Australia (Jones 2000). In West Africa, Unilever-owned United Africa Company (UAC) withdrew from its long-established commodity trading business and created new manufacturing, distribution, and retail businesses. UAC grew as the largest modern business enterprise in postwar West Africa, and became a pioneer of modern manufacturing in the region (Jones 2005b; Fieldhouse 1994).

Shipping firms were especially important actors in the postwar growth boom. They carried the bulk of international trade, including much of the energy, raw materials, and food that the Western world and Japan required. A new generation of Greek ship-owners, headed by Aristotle Onassis and Stavros Niarchos, built new bulk shipping companies, taking advantage of regulatory arbitrage opportunities by, for example, registering ships using flags of convenience. Employing financial innovations such as charter-backed finance, these companies built the supertankers which carried the petroleum which fuelled postwar economic growth. The share of world shipping held by Greek shipping companies rose from 3 percent in 1949 to 15 percent in 1973 (Harlaftis 1993).

Multinational banking also assumed a new importance (Jones 1993). As British overseas banks such as the Bank of London and South America and US banks such as Citibank took advantage of the Bank of England's liberal policies toward foreign exchange markets during the late 1950s, the development of the Eurodollar markets in London provided a dynamic new source of funding for global capitalism. In the interests of financial stability, governments had sought to tightly regulate their financial markets since the Great Depression, and had separated them from each other by exchange controls. The new unregulated Eurocurrency and Eurobond markets soon began to capture a rising share of financial intermediation from regulated domestic markets. The new financial markets were global in scope, but physically located in a small number of financial centers, of which London stood at the apex, and in offshore centers where the primary attraction was not the size of domestic markets, but a combination of regulations and fiscal conditions, and political stability (Jones 1992; Michie 1992; Roberts 1994; Schenk 2001, 2011).

The commercial and investment banks in the new Euro markets innovated financial products on an accelerating scale with the tacit, and later explicit, support of the British and US governments (Helleiner 1994). However the financiers who created these markets also subverted the strategies of governments to closely regulate their financial markets. In some instances, such as the British merchant bank Warburg, they were explicitly motivated by political and economic ambitions to erode national sovereignties and foster European integration (Ferguson 2009).

The physical location of international financial markets in a few geographies formed part of a wider pattern of the concentration of business activity in certain cities and regions during the postwar decades. The advantages of proximity and agglomeration drove such patterns. While such clustering had always been a feature of the world economy, the growing importance of knowledge, and knowledge workers, intensified the trend. This was evident in the origins of the Silicon Valley technology cluster during the 1950s and 1960s, where an unusual convergence of technological skills, educational institutions, and venture capital led to the creation of multiple entrepreneurial firms which were to dominate innovation in many parts of the IT industry for the remainder of the century (Lécuyer 2005). Luxury consumer industries, where access to skills, related industries, and country of origin effects were strong, also clustered. In Italy, which had a long history of comparative advantage in silk, Milan emerged as an international fashion hub during the 1970s through its accumulation of resources and the ability to harness creative and managerial capabilities (Merlo and Polese 2006).

During the 1950s, most of the international cartels of the interwar years were dismantled, while US manufacturing companies invested on a large scale in Western Europe, initially in response to the "dollar shortage," which encouraged US firms to establish factories to supply customers in countries that lacked the dollars to buy American products (Wilkins 1974). There was initially little rationalized production, and intra-firm trade was low. However, from the 1960s, firms began to seek geographical and functional integration across borders. The process of building integrated production systems was difficult. While a European company such as Unilever was a prominent proponent of European economic integration from the 1950s, it struggled to achieve regional integration of their own production and marketing facilities (Jones and Miskell 2005).

The postwar decades were the classic era of the Chandlerian large corporation managed by professional managers, which served as powerhouses of innovation in many manufacturing industries, especially in the United States. US-based firms were preeminent in new technologies, and they sought to maintain innovation and other value-added activities within firm boundaries. In the computer industry, for example, it proved impossible for Western European firms, let alone those from developing countries, to build sustainable businesses. Advanced knowledge was locked within the boundaries of such large Western corporations, as well as geographical clusters such as Silicon Valley.

Yet global capitalism seemed a restricted affair during the postwar decades. The communist states of the Soviet Union, Eastern Europe, and China excluded capitalist firms from their borders (see Allen, Chapter 2 in this volume). After the 1949 revolution, China expropriated foreign enterprises over a number of years (Thompson 1979). The communist world resembled an "alternative" global economy, but one without capitalist firms, at least until the deterioration of political relations between China and the Soviet Union halted attempts at economic integration (Kirby 2006). Yet, even here, global capitalism maintained a role. At the height of Mao Zedong's Cultural Revolution in China, the regime made considerable use of financial institutions and financial markets in Hong Kong (Schenk 2011). In consumer products such as hair care, Western firms sold ingredients to Soviet and other Eastern European state-owned firms from at least the 1970s, and sometimes licensed their technology also (Jones 2010).

Even leaving aside the communist countries, much of the world restricted or banned foreign companies in some or all industries. In European and many other developed countries, tight exchange controls enabled governments to vet or sometimes prohibit investments from other firms. In major European economies such as France, the United Kingdom, and Italy, large swathes of industry were nationalized and taken out of capitalist control, domestic or foreign. The United States was broadly more open to foreign firms, although they were blocked from sectors considered strategic, including defense, airlines, and broadcasting (Wilkins 2002).

In the postcolonial world, the restrictions on global capitalism were much greater. In both Africa and Asia there was widespread restriction and expropriation of foreign firms. Entrepots and colonial outposts which remained open to foreign multinationals, such as Singapore and Hong Kong, experienced rapid economic growth, although their equally successful Newly Industrializing Countries (NIC) counterparts, South Korea and Taiwan, adopted Japanese-style restrictions on wholly-owned foreign companies. During the 1970s Western firms lost ownership of much of the world's natural resources, as Middle Eastern and other governments expropriated assets. In 1970 the seven major Western oil companies owned 69 percent of world crude petroleum. By 1979 their share had fallen to 24 percent. By 1980 two-thirds of world multinational investment were located in Western Europe and North America. The United Kingdom alone hosted more foreign direct investment than the whole of Africa and Asia combined. Within the non-Western world, there was enormous concentration of FDI flows. In Asia, there was no FDI in China, and almost none in Japan and India. Most investment was in a handful of southeast Asian countries, where firms such as Intel had started to place assembly operations requiring cheap labor, while higher value-added activities were located in developed countries (Jones 2005a).

The interventionist policies and import substitution regimes prevalent in much of the non-Western world between the 1950s and the 1980s have been widely, and appropriately, criticized for causing slow economic growth, low productivity, and corruption, but it is striking that the origins of many non-Western multinationals lay precisely in these decades. Protection provided local manufacturing and service firms, if they were well managed, with the opportunity to achieve scale within their national markets. Cemex, now the world's third largest cement company, was founded in Mexico in 1906, and was able to grow in a sheltered environment, slowly becoming a regional player and then, in the 1970s, a national player. In India, the departure of IBM and other US computer firms during the high point of government intervention and protectionism during the 1970s enabled local firms such as Tata Consulting Services to gain scale in software services, laying the foundation for India's successful software outsourcing industry (Athreye 2005; Tripathi 2004).

Global business also often changed its form, rather than disappearing, and resilience remained a prominent feature. Whilst foreign ownership of natural resources vastly declined, especially during the 1970s, foreign orchestration of commodity trade flows and dominance of higher-value-added activities did not. World trade in commodities was increasingly handled by giant commodity trading firms such as Cargill, the grain trader and largest private company in the United States (Broehl 1992, 1998). While large integrated oil companies lost control of their oil fields in many countries, they kept control of refineries, tankers, and distribution facilities. New forms of independent trading companies emerged as key players in the global economy. The trading house of Marc Rich, founded in 1974, had revenues of $15 billion by 1980. It flourished as the world's largest independent oil trader (Ammann 2009).

Firms proved adept at pursuing strategies to respond to anti-foreign sentiments or critical governmental policies. They assumed local identities. In 1947 Sears, the US department store chain, started a successful business in Mexico, a country which only a decade earlier had expelled foreign oil companies and was widely regarded as highly nationalistic. Sears carefully crafted its strategy to appeal to Mexicans, representing policies such as profit sharing, pensions, and low-priced meals as in the traditions of the Mexican Revolution (Moreno

2003). Unilever retained its large consumer goods business in India, and other emerging markets such as Turkey, by means of employing local nationals in senior management positions, selling equity shares to local investors, and investing in industries deemed desirable by governments, such as chemicals in India (Jones 2005b, 2007).

Multinationals also learned that interventionist government policies could work in their favor. In Latin America, postwar governments imposed high tariffs to achieve import substitution manufacturing, but they did not prohibit ownership of industries by foreign firms. As shown in Table 6.2, Brazil was among the ten largest host economies for FDI in 1980. The Brazilian and other Latin American governments offered incentives to attract foreign firms to build manufacturing facilities. Although such import substitution strategies have since been widely derided, in part as they became associated with the chronic macroeconomic mismanagement which resulted in hyperinflation in Brazil and elsewhere during the 1970s and 1980s, they resulted in the building of much new industrial capacity.

A striking example was the creation of a large automobile industry in Brazil from the late 1950s. While the US automobile giants Ford and General Motors initially refused to respond to the government's desire to start local production, the upstart German car maker VW began local manufacturing, benefitting from exchange rate subsidies. It was able to rapidly overturn the large market share of the US firms which had relied upon importing knock-down kits for assembly. By 1980 VW, eventually joined by the leading US and other firms, had given Brazil an annual production of over one million vehicles a year, making the country the world's tenth largest automobile industry. The downside was excess capacity and low productivity, but VW and the other firms had also laid the basis for the subcontinent's largest automobile industry (Shapiro 1994).

Business enterprises and contemporary globalization

As the world spectacularly reglobalized from the 1980s, among the most dramatic changes was the worldwide policy embrace of global capitalism. State planning, exchange controls, and other instruments of interventionist policies were abandoned. Instead, practically every government on the planet eventually came to offer incentives for global firms to invest. In some federal systems, such as the United States, individual states competed with one another to attract foreign investors. It was not until the world financial crisis

Table 6.3. *FDI inward stock as a percentage of GDP 1990–2010*

Region/Country	1990	2010
World	9.6	30.3
All Developed	8.7	30.8
US	9.3	23.5
UK	20.1	48.4
All Developing	13.4	29.1
Brazil	9.2	22.9
Russia	0.0	28.7
China	5.1	9.9
India	0.5	12.0

Source: UNCTAD 2011.

in 2008 that voices arguing that unfettered global capitalism had some evident downsides as well as positives began to be heard.

The role of global business in the growth and dynamics of the contemporary global economy is considerable. As Table 6.3 shows, the relative importance of FDI rose sharply in the world between 1990 and 2010.

Foreign multinationals were important components of the economic growth which accelerated as governments relaxed controls and liberalized markets. China embraced FDI during the 1980s, initially almost certainly at the expense of the indigenous private entrepreneur. Western firms drove the initial growth of export-oriented industries in China (Huang 2003). India made a mirror-image choice, with much growth driven by powerful business groups such as Tata (Khanna 2008), although both in India and Russia inward FDI has assumed a significant role in the economy.

As during the fast globalization during the late nineteenth century, business enterprises were drivers of economic integration. Multinational investment grew far faster than world exports or world output. International production systems developed within which firms located different parts of their value chain across the globe. In some industries international production systems became highly externalized through outsourcing. This was sometimes interpreted as signaling the end of the Chandlerian integrated corporation (Lamoreaux, Raff, and Temin 2003). In reality, large corporations typically continued to control key functions, including brand management and product definition, and the setting of quality standards. In many industries there was consolidation and concentration. The dominant mode of multinational investment became mergers and acquisitions. During the 1990s, and again during the middle years of the following decade before the outbreak of the financial crisis in 2008, there were large cross-border merger waves, especially in pharmaceuticals and food, beverages and tobacco, and automobiles.

The global significance of firms based beyond North America, Western Europe, and Japan also rose. During the 1960s and 1970s, some manufacturers from South Korea and Taiwan began to invest abroad, typically in other emerging markets. They were usually small-scale and used labor-intensive technology. A second wave of firms, based in both Asia and Latin America, began to expand globally from the 1980s, often after they had built scale and corporate competences in their protected domestic markets. They were prominent in assembly-based and knowledge-based industries including electronics, automobiles, and telecommunications. These investments often originated from firms embedded in the business groups which characterized emerging markets, including the Korean *chaebol* and the *grupos economicos* in Latin America (Amsden 2003; Khanna and Palepu 2006; Kosacoff 2002).

The ability of firms from emerging markets to become significant actors in global capitalism rested on several factors. They were sometimes able to piggyback on incumbent Western or Japanese firms as customers through subcontracting and other linkages (Mathews 2002). The spread of management education, as well as the growing number of international students at leading US business schools, provided firms outside the developed core with well-trained and globally minded managers. Finally, there was a new generation of state-owned, or partly owned firms, which could invest in building global businesses without the constraint of having to deliver private shareholder returns.

The growth of state-owned firms was particularly evident in China, where state support enabled highly competitive local firms to emerge even in high technology sectors. A prominent example was the rapid global growth of Huawei as a manufacturer of Internet routers and wireless networking devices, an industry created and developed by high technology US firms such as Cisco. Huawei was founded in 1987 by Ren Zhengfei, a former officer in the Chinese army, and was widely believed to have benefitted from close links to the Chinese military, as well as credit from the state-owned development bank. However, Zhengfei also developed an aggressive corporate culture, which rewarded talent, and made heavy investments in innovation, which included creating research centers in multiple locations around the world including Silicon Valley and Bangalore. By 2012, Huawei had revenues of US$32 billion and sold its products and services in more than 140 countries. Chinese state-owned firms also grew rapidly against powerful Western incumbents in sustainable energy sectors such as solar and wind power. State-owned Goldwind, the second-largest Chinese wind turbine company, was established in 1998 in northwest China, Goldwind acquired its technology through alliances with second-tier Western firms, and then grew rapidly in its domestic market because the Chinese government enforced strict local content requirements, which enabled its rapid growth as it could meet them more quickly than the European companies, which needed to build capacity in China. By 2012 it was among the top ten largest wind turbine manufacturers in the world (Buckley *et al.* 2011; Lewis 2007; Yueh 2011).

The dynamic growth of global firms, drawn from a widening range of home countries, was apparent. It was less evident that the optimism of many policy-makers concerning the positive impact on their economies of foreign multinationals was supported by empirical evidence. There remained little or no aggregate evidence of spillovers from multinational firms to local firms in the same sector, especially in developing countries, although there was evidence of positive linkages between multinationals and suppliers. Foreign affiliates were often more demanding in their specifications and delivery targets, while more willing to provide assistance and advice to local firms. Multinationals continued to have no incentive to encourage knowledge leakages to competitors. In many developing countries, local firms also still lacked the capabilities to compete with large multinationals, and the greater the technology gap, the more difficult this gap was to fill (Alfaro and Rodriquez-Claire 2004).

It turned out that while it was possible for governments to attract foreign firms and create whole industries as designated free trade areas or export processing zones, it was less easy to capture knowledge spillovers, as had been the case of enclaves in previous eras. For example, Malaysia attracted numerous Western and Japanese electronics firms to a number of export processing zones, such as the island of Penang. The country became one of the world's largest exporters of electronic components. However four-fifths of the intermediate products used in the manufacturing were imported. Local firms primarily supplied low-value-added products such as cardboard boxes. Foreign firms undertook little design or research and development in Malaysia. By 2000, electronics provided over a quarter of Malaysia's manufacturing employment, but this employment was overwhelmingly female and low-skilled (Rasiah 2001). Malaysia was not an outlier: most export processing zones, whether in Asia, Africa, or Latin America, have failed to attract more than the low-value-added, low-skill segments of industry value chains (Cling, Razafindrakoto, and Roubaud 2005; Steinfield 2004).

There is also contradictory evidence regarding whether multinationals have become more effective agents for changing growth-restricting institutions and cultures in host economies. The development of capitalism in many of the world's poorest countries remains handicapped by high corruption levels. Historically, multinational companies had probably contributed to such corruption, at least until Western governments adopted measures such as the Foreign Corrupt Practices Act, passed in the United States in 1976 (Safarian 1993). More recently, multinationals have usually been less willing than local firms to engage in bribery and tax evasion, in part because of the threat to corporate reputations, but they do not have the capacity to change societal norms for the most part. In important markets, multinational firms have lent support to institutional norms, as seen in the willingness of US firms such as Cisco and Google to assist the Chinese government's censorship of the Internet and curbing of political dissent. Indeed, as in the case of Cisco's supply of the sophisticated networking equipment which has enabled Chinese government filtering of the World Wide Web, multinational firms continued to be as much shapers of as responders to their political environment.

As large firms moved resources across borders in pursuit of profitability opportunities, they also continued to reinforce trends more than counter them. They were more agents of "spikeness" than "flatness" in the global economy (Florida 2005; Friedman 2005). As the Chinese economic boom took hold during the 2000s, they facilitated the relocation of resources out of Mexico, southeast Asia and other once-favored low-cost production sites. In knowledge industries such as pharmaceuticals and IT, the United States had long sucked knowledge from everywhere else. Despite the availability of technologies which permit the dispersal of economic activities, multinational firms served as major actors in the clustering of higher-value-added activities in "global cities" and regions such as Silicon Valley and Bangalore. A significant difference with earlier eras may have been that US firms started to "outsource" domestic jobs to foreign countries, although the evidence on domestic employment loss and hollowing out was not straightforward. Longitudinal research has not generally been supportive of rhetoric on the major threats to domestic employment (Harrison, McMillan, and Null 2007).

A final feature of this contemporary period of globalization has been a shift in corporate rhetoric, some of which has translated into actual policies. From at least the 1970s, when criticism of multinational corporations rose to a fever pitch, corporations began to articulate far more explicitly than in the past their responsibilities to the communities in which they operated, and to the environment. Unilever was among the pioneers in implementing policies of corporate responsibility in the many developing countries in which it operated. By the 1970s it was already engaged in rural development schemes in India, sending its managers to work with local farmers to improve their skills, and facilitating access to capital and modern medicine (Jones 2005b). Unilever was favorably cited in Prahalad's influential study on how multinational companies could both find a profitable business and help the world's poor by developing businesses aimed at consumers at the "bottom of the pyramid" (Prahalad 2004). Although contemporary capitalism has been most frequently associated with the kind of corporate scandals, the gaming of regulations, and unethical behavior seen in the case of the US energy company Enron (Salter 2008), as striking has been the articulation by some corporations, and business school professors, of their responsibility toward the communities in which they operate, and global capitalism as a whole.

Conclusion

Business enterprises have been powerful actors in the spread of global capitalism after 1848. Emerging out of the industrialized Western economies, multinational firms have created and co-created markets and ecosystems through their ability to transfer a package of financial, organizational, and cultural assets, skills, and ideologies across national borders. They have been major drivers of trade growth, which they often organized within their own boundaries. They have been shapers of, as well as responders to, globalization waves. Multinational business enterprises, which have always been highly heterogeneous, have been highly resilient, frequently changing organizational form in response to major political and economic shifts and shocks which have characterized the global world over the last two centuries. During the interwar years, while global capital and trade flows fell sharply and levels of market integration receded back to mid-nineteenth-century levels, multinational firms continued to span borders, developing new strategies and adopting new organizational forms in response to the changed environment.

Multinationals had, at least in theory, the potential to become major agents in overcoming the constraints to modern economic growth faced by follower countries. Capitalism proved much better than political leaders in building institutions which coordinated activities across national borders. Firms built, often in challenging conditions, the telegraph lines, ports, shipping, and airline networks which were the sinews of globalization. They created, intermediated, and orchestrated trade flows. They transferred knowledge across geographical locations. They sometimes transferred industries, whether machinery manufacturing in late nineteenth-century Russia or automobile manufacturing in Brazil after World War II, between countries.

Yet the historical evidence also points to often disappointing and sometimes negative outcomes in knowledge and technology transfer. Before the interwar years, in particular, multinational resource and related investments were highly enclavist, and embedded in the institutional arrangements of Western imperialism and autocratic dictators. Western firms reinforced rather than disrupted institutional and societal norms which restricted growth in many countries. They often functioned, as a result, as part of the problem, rather than part of the solution.

Whilst business enterprises have been important drivers of international economic growth, then, they were also significant agents in the divergent patterns of wealth and poverty which have characterized the last two centuries. By exploring for minerals and creating plantations, Western firms helped turn the South and Asia into the suppliers of primary commodities to the developed world. In turn, the perceived unfairness of tax-free concessions and racist employment practices, and the inability of enclavist investments to diffuse wealth creation to host economies, stoked resentment, and provided the background for the growth of socialist and populist ideologies in many parts of the world. In the more recent past, the strategies of Western corporations have moved far beyond the practices of the colonial past, but linkages and spillovers to local economies have often been disappointingly low. Their ability, and motivation, to locate value-added activities in the most attractive locations means that they strengthen clustering rather than encourage dispersion of knowledge. It turns out that the outcomes from multinational investments depend heavily on the institutions and societal values of the host economies, as well as on corporate strategies themselves. However, what was also evident in the era of contemporary globalization was that there were major shifts under way in the world of global business. On the one hand, there were, at least but not only in the West, rising expectations concerning the responsibility of corporations to their societies and the environment. On the other hand, the era when Western and Japanese corporations dominated global markets and innovation was rapidly giving way to one in which they competed as equals, with firms whose homes were in China, India, Brazil, and elsewhere.

References

Ahvenainen, J. (2004). *The European Cable Companies in South America before the First World War*. Helsinki: Finnish Academy of Science and Letters.

Alfaro, L. and A. Rodriguez-Clare (2004). "Multinationals and Linkages: An Empirical Investigation," *Economía* 4(2): 113–69.

Ammann, D. (2009). *The Secret Lives of Marc Rich*. New York: St. Martin's Press.

Amsden, A. H. (2003). *The Rise of "the Rest": Challenges to the West from Late-Industrializing Countries*. Oxford University Press.

Athreye, S. S. (2005). "The Indian Software Industry and its Evolving Service Capability," *Industrial and Corporate Change* 14(3): 393–418.

Bamberg, J. H. (1994). *The History of the British Petroleum Company*. Vol. II. Cambridge University Press.

Beatty, E. (2003). "Approaches to Technology Transfer in History and the Case of Nineteenth Century Mexico," *Comparative Technology Transfer and Society* 1(2): 167–200.

(2009). "Bottles for Beer: The Business of Technological Innovation in Mexico, 1890–1920," *Business History Review* 83: 317–348.

Bonin, H., Y. Lung, and S. Tolliday (2003). *Ford: The European History 1903–2003*, 2 vols. Paris: P.l.a.ge.

Bordo, M. D., A. M. Taylor, and J. G. Williamson (2003). *Globalization in Historical Perspective*. University of Chicago Press.

Bostock, F. and G. Jones (1994). "Foreign Multinationals in British Manufacturing, 1850–1962," *Business History* 36(1): 89–126.

Broehl, W. G. (1992). *Cargill: Trading the World's Grain*. Hanover, NH: University Press of New England.

(1998). *Cargill. Going Global*. Hanover, NH: University Press of New England.

Brown, R. A. (1994). *Capital and Entrepreneurship in South East Asia*. London: Macmillan.

(2000). *Chinese Big Business and the Wealth of Asian Nations*. London: Palgrave.

Bucheli, M. (2005) *Bananas and Business: The United Fruit Company in Columbia, 1899–2000*. New York University Press.

Buckley, P. J., H. Voss, A. R. Cross, and L. J. Clegg (2011). "The Emergence of Chinese Firms as Multinationals: The Influence of the Home Institutional Environment," in R. Pearce (ed.), *China and the Multinationals: International Business and the Entry of China into the Global Economy*. Northampton, MA: Edward Elgar, pp. 125–157.

Bud-Frierman, L., A. Godley, and J. Wale (2010). "Weetman Pearson in Mexico and the Emergence of a British Oil Major, 1901–1919," *Business History Review* 84(2): 275–301.

Burke, T. (1996). *Lifebuoy Men, Lux Women*. Durham, NC: Duke University Press.

Carstensen, F. V. (1984). *American Enterprise in Foreign Markets: Singer and International Harvester in Imperial Russia*. Chapel Hill, NC: University of North Carolina Press.

Chan, K. Y. (2006). *Business Expansion and Structural Change in Pre-War China*. Hong Kong University Press.

Chan, W. K. K. (2010). "Chinese Entrepreneurship since Its Late Imperial Period," in D. S. Landes, J. Mokyr, and W. J. Baumol (eds.), *The Invention of Enterprise*. Princeton University Press, pp. 469–500.

Chandler, A. D. (1962). *Strategy and Structure*. Cambridge, MA: The MIT Press.

(1977). *The Visible Hand*. Cambridge, MA: Harvard University Press.

(1990). *Scale and Scope*. Cambridge, MA: Harvard University Press.

Cling, J., M. Razafindrakoto, and F. Roubaud (2005). "Export Processing Zones in Madagascar: A Success Story under Threat?" *World Development* 33(5): 785–803.

Cochran, S. (2006). *Chinese Medicine Men. Consumer Culture in China and Southeast Asia.* Cambridge University Press.

Collins, E. J. T. (1994). "Brands and Breakfast Cereals in Britain," in G. Jones and N. J. Morgan (eds.), *Adding Value. Brands and Marketing in Food and Drink.* New York: Routledge, pp. 237–258.

Connolly, P. (1999). "Pearson and Public Works Construction in Mexico, 1890–1910," *Business History* 41(4): 48–71.

Cox, H. (2000). *The Global Cigarette.* Oxford University Press.

Dunning, J. H. and S. M. Lundan (2008). *Multinational Enterprises and the Global Economy,* 2nd edn. Northampton, MA: Edward Elgar.

Fear, J. (2008). "Cartels," in G. Jones and J. Zeitlin (eds.), *The Oxford Handbook of Business History.* Oxford University Press, pp. 268–292.

Ferguson, N. (2009). "Siegmund Warburg, the City of London and the Financial Roots of European Integration," *Business History* 51(3): 364–382.

Ferrier, R. W. (1982). *The History of the British Petroleum Company.* Vol. 1. Cambridge University Press.

Fieldhouse, D. K. (1994). *Merchant Capital and Economic Decolonization.* Oxford: Clarendon Press.

Florida, R. (2005). "The World is Spiky," *Atlantic Monthly* 296(3): 48–51.

Friedman, T. L. (2005). *The World is Flat.* New York: Farrar, Straus and Giroux.

Geyikdagi, V. N. (2011). "French Direct Investments in the Ottoman Empire before World War I," *Enterprise & Society* 12(1): 525–561.

Ghemawat, P. (2001). "Distance Still Matters: The Hard Reality of Global Expansion," *Harvard Business Review* 79(8): 137–147.

Giebelhaus, A. W. (1994). "The Pause that Refreshed the World: The Evolution of Coca-Cola's Global Marketing Strategy," in G. Jones and N. J. Morgan (eds.), *Adding Value: Brands and Marketing in Food and Drink.* London: Routledge, pp. 191–214.

Gleijeses, P. (1991). *Shattered Hope: The Guatemalan Revolution and the United States, 1944–1954.* Princeton University Press.

Godley, A. (2006). "Selling the Sewing Machine around the World: Singer's International Marketing Strategies, 1850–1920," *Enterprise & Society* 7(2): 266–314.

Gordon, A. (2011). *Fabricating Consumers: The Sewing Machine in Modern Japan.* Berkeley, CA: University of California Press.

Grazia, V. De (2005). *Irresistible Empire. America's Advance though 20th-century Europe.* Cambridge, MA: Harvard University Press.

Guez, S. (1998). "The Development of Swiss Trading Companies in the Twentieth Century," in G. Jones (ed.), *The Multinational Traders.* London: Routledge, pp. 150–172.

Harlaftis, G. (1993). *A History of Greek-owned Shipping.* London: Routledge.

Harlaftis, G. and J. Theotokas (2004). "European Family Firms in International Business: British and Greek Tramp-Shipping Firms," *Business History* 46(2): 219–255.

Harrison, A. E., M. S. McMillan, and C. Null (2007). "U.S. Multinational Activity Abroad and U.S. Jobs: Substitutes or Complements?" *Industrial Relations: A Journal of Economy and Society* 46(2): 347–365.

Hausman, W. J., P. Hertner, and M. Wilkins (2008). *Global Electrification. Multinational Enterprise and International Finance in the History of Light and Power, 1878–2007.* Cambridge University Press.

Headrick, D. R. (1988). *The Tentacles of Progress: Technology Transfer in the Age of Imperialism, 1850–1940*. Oxford University Press.

Helleiner, E. C. (1994). *States and the Re-emergence of Global Finance*. Ithaca, NY: Cornell University Press.

Hills, J. C. (2002). *The Struggle for Control of Global Communications: The Formative Century*. Urbana, IL: University of Illinois Press.

Huang, Y. (2003). *Selling China: Foreign Direct Investment During the Reform Era*. Cambridge University Press.

Jones, G. (1981). *The State and the Emergence of the British Oil Industry*. London: Macmillan.

ed. (1990). *Banks as Multinationals*. London: Routledge.

(1992). "International Financial Centres in Asia, the Middle East and Australia: A Historical Perspective," in Y. Cassis (ed.), *Finance and Financiers in European History, 1880–1960*. Cambridge University Press, pp. 405–428.

(1993). *British Multinational Banking 1830–1990*. Oxford: Clarendon Press.

ed. (1998). *The Multinational Traders*. London: Routledge.

(2000). *Merchants to Multinationals*. Oxford University Press.

(2005a). *Multinationals and Global Capitalism: From the Nineteenth to the Twenty-First Century*. Oxford University Press.

(2005b). *Renewing Unilever: Transformation and Tradition*. Oxford University Press.

(2006). "The End of Nationality? Global Firms and 'Borderless Worlds,'" *Zeitschrift für Unternehmensgeschichte* 51(2): 149–165.

(2007). "Learning to Live with Governments: Unilever in India and Turkey, 1950–1980," *Entreprises et Histoire* 49: 79–101.

(2010). *Beauty Imagined: A History of the Global Beauty Industry*. Oxford University Press.

Jones, G. and F. Bostock (1996). "U.S. Multinationals in British Manufacturing before 1962," *Business History Review* 70(1): 207–256.

Jones, G. and C. Lubinski (2012). "Managing Political Risk in Global Business: Beiersdorf 1914–1990," *Enterprise & Society* 13(1): 85–119.

Jones, G. and P. Miskell (2005). "European Integration and Corporate Restructuring: The Strategy of Unilever c1957–c1990," *Economic History Review* LVII: 113–139.

Jonker, J. and K. Sluyterman (2000). *At Home on the World Markets*. The Hague: Sdu Uitgevers.

Jonker, J. and J. L. Van Zanden (2007). *History of Royal Dutch Shell*. Vol. 1: *From Challenger to Joint Industry Leader, 1890–1939*. Oxford University Press.

Khanna, T. (2008). *Billions of Entrepreneurs: How China and India Are Reshaping Their Futures–and Yours*. Boston, MA: Harvard Business School Press.

Khanna, T. and K. G. Palepu (2006). "Emerging Giants: Building World-Class Companies in Developing Countries," *Harvard Business Review* 84(10): 60–69.

Kirby, W. C. (2006). "China's Internationalization in the Early People's Republic: Dreams of a Socialist World," *China Quarterly* 188: 870–890.

Kipping, M. (1999). "American Management Consulting Companies in Western Europe, 1920–1990: Products, Reputation and Relationships," *Business History Review* 73(2): 190–220.

Koll, E. (2003). *From Cotton Mill to Business Empire*. Cambridge, MA: Harvard University Press.

Kosacoff, B. (2002). *Going Global from Latin America: The ARCOR Case*. Buenos Aires: McGraw-Hill Interamericana.

Kuisel, R. F. (1991). "Coca-Cola and the Cold War: The French Face Americanization, 1948–1953," *French Historical Studies* 17(1): 96–116.

Kuwahara, T. (1990). "Trends in Research on Overseas Expansion by Japanese Enterprises prior to World War II," *Japanese Yearbook on Business History* 7: 61–81.

Lamoreaux, N., D. Raff, and P. Temin (2003). "Beyond Markets and Hierarchies: Toward a New Synthesis of American Business History," *American Historical Review* 108: 404–433.

Lanz, R. and S. Miroudot (2011). "Intra-Firm Trade: Patterns, Determinants and Policy Implications," *OECD Trade Policy Working Papers*, No. 114, OECD Publishing. http://dx.doi.org/10.1787/5kg9p39lrwnn-en.

Lécuyer, C. (2005). *Making Silicon Valley: Innovation and the Growth of High Tech, 1930–1970.* Cambridge, MA: The MIT Press.

Lewis, J. I. (2007). "A Comparison of Wind Power Industry Development Strategies in Spain, India and China." http://q.investorideas.com/research/PDFs/L_Wind_I_Dev_I_S_C_July2007.pdf.

Lipson, C. (1985). *Standing Guard: Protecting Foreign Capital in the Nineteenth and Twentieth Centuries.* Berkeley, CA: University of California Press.

Magee, G. B. and A. S. Thompson (2010). *Empire and Globalization: Networks of People, Goods and Capital in the British World, c 1850–1914.* Cambridge University Press.

Mason, M. (1992). *American Multinationals and Japan.* Cambridge, MA: Harvard University Press.

Mathews, J. A. (2002). *Dragon Multinational: A New Model for Global Growth.* Oxford University Press.

Maurer, N. (2011). "The Empire Struck Back: Sanctions and Compensation in the Mexican Oil Expropriation of 1938," *Journal of Economic History* 71(3): 590–615.

McDowall, D. (1988). *The Light: Brazilian Traction, Light and Power Company Limited, 1899–1945.* University of Toronto Press.

McKenna, C. D. (2006). *The World's Newest Profession. Management Consulting in the Twentieth Century.* Cambridge University Press.

Merlo, E. and F. Polese (2006). "Turning Fashion into Business: The Emergence of Milan as an International Fashion Hub," *Business History Review* 80(3): 415–447.

Michie, R. C. (1992). *The City of London.* London: Macmillan.

Miller, M. (2012). *Europe and the Maritime World.* Cambridge University Press.

Minoglou, I. P. and H. Louri (1997). "Diaspora Entrepreneurial Networks in the Black Sea and Greece, 1870–1917," *Journal of European Economic History* 26(1): 69–104.

Moreno, J. (2003). *Yankee Don't Go Home.* Chapel Hill, NC: University of North Carolina Press.

Morgan, D. (1979). *Merchants of Grain: The Power and Profits of the Five Giant Companies at the Center of the World's Food Supply.* New York: Viking Press.

Munro, J. F. (2003). *Maritime Enterprise and Empire.* Woodbridge: Boydell.

Nanda, B. R. (2003). *In Gandhi's Footsteps: The Life and Times of Jamnalal Bajaj.* Oxford University Press.

Nicholas, S. (1983). "Agency Contracts, Institutional Modes, and the Transition to Foreign Direct Investment by British Manufacturing Multinationals before 1939," *Journal of Economic History* 43: 675–686.

Olsson, U. (1993). "Securing the Markets: Swedish Multinationals in a Historical Perspective," in G. Jones and H. G. Schröter (eds.), *The Rise of Multinationals in Continental Europe.* Aldershot: Edward Elgar, pp. 99–127.

Peiss, K. (1998). *Hope in a Jar.* New York: Henry Holt.

Piquet, C. (2004). "The Suez Company's Concession in Egypt, 1854–1956: Modern Infrastructure and Local Economic Development," *Enterprise & Society* 5(1): 107–127.

Prahalad, C. K. (2004). *The Fortune at the Bottom of the Pyramid: Eradicating Poverty Through Profits*. Upper Saddle River, NJ: University of Wharton Press.

Quek, M. (2012). "Globalizing the Hotel Industry 1946–1968: A Multinational Case Study of the Intercontinental Hotel Corporation," *Business History* 54(2): 201–226.

Rasiah, R. (2001). "The Importance of Size in the Growth and Performance of the Electrical Industrial Machinery and Apparatus Industry in Malaysia," in C. T. Nyland, W. Smith, R. L. Smyth, and M. Vicziany (eds.), *Malaysian Business in the New Era*. Cheltenham: Edward Elgar, pp. 89–107.

Reich, L. S. (1992). "General Electric and the World Cartelisation of Electric Lamps," in A. Kudo and T. Hara (eds.), *International Cartels in Business History*. University of Tokyo Press.

Roberts, R., ed. (1994). *International Financial Centres*. Vol. 1. Aldershot: Edward Elgar.

Safarian, A. E. (1993). *Multinational Enterprise and Public Policy*. Aldershot: Edward Elgar.

Salter, M. S. (2008). *Innovation Corrupted: The Origins and Legacy of Enron's Collapse*. Boston, MA: Harvard Business School Press.

Schenk, K. (2001). *Hong Kong as an International Financial Centre: Emergence and Development 1945–65*. London: Routledge.

(2011). "The Re-emergence of Hong Kong as an International Financial Centre, 1960–1978," in L. Quennouëlle-Corre and Y. Cassis (eds.), *Financial Centres and International Capital Flows in the Nineteenth and Twentieth Centuries*. Oxford University Press, pp. 199–253.

Schröter, H. G. (1988). "Risk and Control in Multinational Enterprise: German Businesses in Scandinavia, 1918–1939," *Business History Review* 62(3): 420–43.

(1993a). "Swiss Multinational Enterprise in Historical Perspective," in G. Jones and H. G. Schröter (eds.), *The Rise of Multinationals in Continental Europe*. Aldershot: Edward Elgar, pp. 49–64.

(1993b). *Aufstieg der Kleinen: multinationale Unternehmen aus fünf Kleinen Staaten vor 1914*. Berlin: Duncker und Humbolt.

Shapiro, H. (1994). *Engines of Growth. The State and Transnational Auto Companies in Brazil*. Cambridge University Press.

Shiba, T. and M. Shimotani, eds. (1997). *Beyond the Firm: Business Groups in International and Historical Perspective*. Oxford University Press.

Steinfeld, E. (2004). "China's Shallow Integration: Networked Production and New Challenges for Late Industrialization," *World Development* 32(11): 1971–1987.

Sugihara, K., ed. (2005). *Japan, China, and the Growth of the Asian International Economy, 1850–1949*. Oxford University Press.

Thompson, T. N. (1979). *China's Nationalization of Foreign Firms: The Politics of Hostage Capitalism, 1949–57*. Baltimore, MD: School of Law, University of Maryland.

Timburg, T. A. (1978). *The Marwaris, from Traders to Industrialists*. New Delhi: Vikas.

Topik, S., C. Marichal, and Z. Frank, eds. (2006). *From Silver to Cocaine. Latin American Commodity Chains and the Building of the World Economy, 1500–2000*. Durham, NC: Duke University Press.

Tripathi, D. (2004). *The Oxford History of Indian Business*. Oxford University Press.

Turner, H. A. (2005) *General Motors and the Nazis* New Haven, CT: Yale University Press.

UNCTAD, *World Investment Report*, various years.

West, D. C. (1987). "From T-square to T-plan: The London Office of the J. Walter Thompson Advertizing Agency, 1919–1970," *Business History* 29: 467–501.

Wilkins, M. (1970). *The Emergence of Multinational Enterprise*. Cambridge, MA: Harvard University Press.

(1974). *The Maturing of Multinational Enterprise*. Cambridge, MA: Harvard University Press.

(1988). "The Free-Standing Company, 1870–1914: An Important Type of British Foreign Direct Investment," *Economic History Review* XLI(2): 259–285.

(1989). *The History of Foreign Investment in the United States before 1914*. Cambridge, MA: Harvard University Press.

(1990). "The Contributions of Foreign Enterprises to Japanese Economic Development," in T. Yuzawa and M. Ugudawa (eds.), *Foreign Business in Japan before World War II*. University of Tokyo Press.

(1994). "Comparative Hosts," *Business History* 36(1): 18–50.

(2001). "The History of Multinational Enterprise," in A. M. Rugman and T. L. Brewer (eds.), *The Oxford Handbook of International Business*. Oxford University Press, pp. 3–35.

(2002). "An Overview of Foreign Companies in the United States, 1945–2000," in G. Jones and L. Gálvez-Muñoz (eds.), *Foreign Multinationals in the United States*. London: Routledge, pp. 18–49.

(2004). *The History of Foreign Investment in the United States 1914–1945*. Cambridge, MA: Harvard University Press.

Wilkins, M. and F. E. Hill (1964). *American Business Abroad: Ford on Six Continents*. Detroit, MI: Wayne State University Press.

Wilkins, M. and H. Schröter,, eds. (1998). *The Free-Standing Company in the World Economy, 1836–1996*. Oxford University Press.

Wray, W. D. (1984) *Mitsubishi and the N.Y.K., 1870–1914: Business Strategy in the Japanese Shipping Industry*. Cambridge, MA: Harvard University Press.

Yonekawa, S. (1990). *General Trading Companies: A Comparative and Historical Study*. Tokyo: United Nations University Press.

and H. Shimizu (2010). "Entrepreneurship in Pre-World War II Japan: The Role and Logic of the Zaibatsu," in D. S. Landes, J. Mokyr, and W. J. Baumol (eds.), *The Invention of Enterprise*. Princeton University Press, pp. 501–526.

Yueh, L. (2011). *Enterprising China: Business, Economic and Legal Developments since 1979*. Oxford University Press.

Zelin, M. (2005). *The Merchants of Zigong*. New York: Columbia University Press.

7

Enterprise models: freestanding firms versus family pyramids

RANDALL MORCK AND BERNARD YEUNG*

Introduction

Business enterprises are organized very differently in different countries, and neoclassical economics is built around only one such model. Limited liability firewalls, limited partnerships, and other such legal niceties aside, "firm" and "corporation" are approximately synonymous in modern America and Britain; and whole fields of "corporate" finance, "corporate" governance, and "corporate" strategy model decision-making at the level of the corporations. However, this synonymy is both historically recent and geographically exceptional, leaving these major branches of economics oddly disconnected in other countries and historical eras.

Big business in many countries is organized as business groups (La Porta, Lopez-de-Silanes, and Shleifer 1999): constellations of seemingly distinct separately listed corporations, each with its own CEO, board of directors, creditors, and public shareholders, but all controlled by a single decision-maker, usually a wealthy old-moneyed business family, less commonly a single powerful tycoon. For simplicity, we define a "business group" as two or more listed firms under common control.[1] The largest business groups in some countries encompass dozens, or even hundreds, of distinct listed and

* The authors thank Kristine Bruland, Larry Neal, Jeff Williamson, and participants at the Cambridge History of Capitalism Conference, hosted by the BBVA Foundation in Madrid, for numerous suggestions – all exceptionally helpful. This chapter draws heavily from Morck, Stangeland, and Yeung 2000; Morck 2005, 2009, 2011; Morck and Yeung 2004, 2007; and Morck, Wolfenzon, and Yeung 2005. To avoid clutter, we do not cite these articles each time we draw from them. However, ambient cites to these works prevail throughout the entire chapter.
1 This definition, introduced by La Porta, Lopez-de-Silanes, and Shleifer (1999), is now standard in the finance literature. Other definitions stretch business groups to include Japan's keiretsu groups, connected by networks of small intercorporate equity stakes, and even firms connected by their CEO's networks of friends and acquaintances (Khanna and Yafeh 2007). While each definition has its merits, ours is uniquely useful in the present context.

unlisted firms, and comprise sizeable fractions of national economies. Their ubiquity in today's successfully emerging markets and their historical prominence in late industrializers' peak growth periods suggest that business groups are far more than chance configurations. They may well play a pivotal role, for good or ill, in deciding the wealth of nations.

Business group basics

Both historically and across modern economies, business groups are usually organized as pyramids (La Porta, Lopez-de-Silanes, and Shleifer 1999). A family firm controls a first tier of listed companies by holding a dominant equity block in each. A majority block in each is often unnecessary, as small shareholders seldom vote in annual general meetings; however control can be assured by allocating multiple votes to each share held by the family firm, by reserving a majority of seats on the board for family representatives, or by allocating enough shares to family-controlled financial institutions – mutual funds, pension funds, and the like – to raise the family's total voting power above 50 percent.

Through like mechanisms, each first-tier firm, in turn, controls several listed firms in the pyramid's second tier, and each of these, in turn, controls yet more listed firms in a third tier. The pattern can be replicated through as many tiers as are needed to leverage the family's private wealth into control over a business empire containing corporate assets worth vastly more. The strategic insertion of unlisted firms throughout the structure can help disguise the actual chains of control. Thus, although hundreds of firms might trade on a country's stock exchanges, most might belong to ten, five, or even one huge pyramidal business group. A façade of pluralism and competition can thus disguise a monolithic concentration of corporate control.

The control leverage equity-financed pyramiding provides can be startling (Morck, Wolfenzon, and Yeung 2005). For example, Högfeldt (2005) finds Sweden's two largest pyramidal groups, together, control firms comprising over half the country's total stock market capitalization. The largest of these is controlled by the Wallenberg family, with family wealth below one billion dollars. A pyramidal business group controlled by one branch of Canada's Bronfman family in the 1990s contained sixteen tiers and over 500 corporations, listed and unlisted, again with relatively modest family wealth sufficient to control the structure's apex sufficing to lock in control over the whole structure. Another group, controlled by the Naboa family, encompassed essentially all of Ecuador's large-scale private-sector businesses. Li Ka-shing,

Asia's richest man, controls a vast business group that not only dominates the economy of Hong Kong, but encompasses a huge array of operating companies around the world. Throughout Europe, Latin America, and Asia, a handful of such structures constitutes the greater part of each nation's private big business sector.[2]

History lessons

Business groups figure prominently in economic history, especially in late industrializers. America's post-Civil War industrialization, especially its era of most rapid development around the turn of the twentieth century, occurred largely under the auspices of its robber barons – tycoons, such as John D. Rockefeller and John Pierpont Morgan, whose business empires each included numerous distinct companies.[3] At the height of Canada's industrialization, the so-called Laurier boom surrounding the turn of the twentieth century, over 40 percent of the assets of the county's 100 largest businesses were held within 12 pyramidal groups (Tian 2006). Japan's high-growth period, from the 1880s through its successful industrialization by the 1920s, saw its economy almost entirely organized into pyramidal business groups, called *zaibatsu* (Shiba and Shimotani 1997). Similar structures, called *chaebol*, dominated South Korea as it developed rapidly in the 1970s and especially the 1980s

---

2 Similar pyramidal groups, usually controlled by business families, predominate in the economies of Argentina (Fracchia, Mesquita, and Quiroga 2011); Brazil (Aldrighi and Postali 2010); Chile (Khanna and Palepu 2000a, 2000b); Colombia (Trujillo *et al.* 2012); East Asia in general (Claessens *et al.* 2002); Lefort 2011); India (Khanna and Palepu 2005; Sarkar 2011); Israel (Kosenko and Yafeh 2011; Kosenko 2007); Italy (Aganin and Volpin 2005); Mexico (La Porta and López-de-Silanes 1999; Hoshino 2011); Russia (Guriev 2011); Pakistan (Haque and Kabir 2001); Singapore (Tsui-Auch and Yoshikawa 2010); South Africa (Goldstein 2011); South Korea (Bae *et al.* 2002; Kim 2011); Taiwan (Chung and Mahmood 2011); Thailand (Charumilind, Kali, and Wiwattankantang 2006; Suehiro and Wailerdsak 2011); Turkey (Colpan 2011); Western Europe in general (Barca and Becht 2001; Faccio and Lang 2002); and the global economy in general (La Porta, Lopez-de-Silanes, and Shleifer 1999; Masulis, Pham, and Zein 2011).

3 America's late nineteenth- and early twentieth-century business groups were structured as voting trusts: a unique organizational form necessitated by legal restrictions proscribing corporations from owing shares in corporations located in other states (Becht and DeLong 2005). This makes American business history less generally useful as a background against which to study other countries in this specific context. This chapter consequently draws heavily on Canadian examples on the grounds that Canada is similar to the United States in many ways, but exhibits more typical business groups throughout its history as an industrializing and industrialized economy (Morck *et al.* 2005). We beg the indulgence of American readers, who might reasonably expect more examples from their country's history. The political economy forces that caused American states to establish and retain these restrictions, until New Jersey broke ranks near the turn of the twentieth century, are incompletely understood (Becht and DeLong 2005).

(Bae, Kang, and Kim 2002). Large, initially predominantly equity-financed pyramidal business groups also play important roles in the industrialization eras of Germany (Fohlin 2007), Italy (Aganin and Volpin 2005), Sweden (Högfeldt 2005), and other European countries; and played a role in US (Berle and Means 1932) and British (Jones 2000) economic development too.

This pattern suggests that such groups might have features that are especially useful during very rapid industrialization, and might constitute optimal second-best solutions amid incomplete markets and imperfect institutions. But the prevalence of similar groups in Latin America, South Asia, and other regions that have long failed to attain first world status (Colpan, Hikino, and Lincoln 2011) – the Brazilian adage, "This is, and always will be, the country of the future" comes to mind – also suggests that they sometimes become a hindrance, or even an explicit liability, in later stages.

Business groups in Japan's industrialization

Japan, an industrial power by the 1920s, was the first non-Western country to industrialize successfully.[4] Admiral Perry's mid-nineteenth-century gunboat diplomacy abruptly ended Japan's hermetic isolation, and exposed its relative impotence and poverty. Concluding that foreigners could only be beaten back with foreign technology, Japan sent the best of its youth abroad for education and reconnaissance, and grew more dismayed as Japan's true situation grew clearer. Resolved to jumpstart industrialization, Japan's government hired foreign experts and returning students to establish new state-owned enterprises (SOEs) in each sector deemed essential to modernization in the 1870s. These soon bled money profusely, triggering a budget crisis, and collapsing both the yen and Japan's credit in London. A liberal government took over, organizing the world's first mass privatization in the 1880s to sell off virtually all the SOEs. Thus stung, Japan embraced a classical liberal vision of government until the 1930s military takeover.

The mass privatization ultimately transferred most former SOEs to wealthy merchant families, and a high-growth era commenced. The families rapidly assembled large pyramidal business groups as a growing middle class took to investing in shares. The business groups diversified widely, the largest each controlling a firm in virtually every industry. Pyramid members produced inputs for other member firms, bought each other's outputs, and made complementary goods to each other's products. By the 1920s, the industrial structure of Japan's economy resembled those of other developed countries.

4 This section is a vastly simplified synopsis of Morck and Nakamura (2005, 2007).

While historians of the Japanese economy debate the ethics of the *zaibatsu* families, especially amid the military takeover in the 1940s and the ensuing war, the overwhelming predominance of a few very large family-controlled pyramidal groups over the country's economy during its rapid industrialization is uncontroversial.[5]

Business groups in late industrializers

Variously called business groups, pyramids, *zaibatsu*, *chaebol*, robber baronies, and terms yet less flattering, structures akin to *zaibatsu* loom large in the economic histories of many countries. The structures generally appear as financial markets develop sufficiently to let their controlling shareholders leverage their wealth with public investors' money, though not always.

The first developed economies – the United Kingdom, Flanders, the Netherlands, and perhaps a few others – apparently managed without large pyramidal groups, though more detailed examination of shareholder records may yet challenge this. But these countries were beating paths through the wilderness, and took centuries to do what Japan did in decades. As noted above, other successful late industrializers – Canada, Germany, South Korea, Sweden, etc. – all developed large pyramidal groups very similar to Japan's *zaibatsu* in structure, scope, and scale. America's robber barons used trusts to control their vast business groups in the late nineteenth and early twentieth centuries, only switching to pyramiding after anti-trust laws and other developments shifted the legal landscape (Becht and DeLong 2005; Bonbright and Means 1932), rendering trusts inoperative and pyramiding viable.[6] Despite these differences, some evidence suggests American business group firms were also star performers in this era (DeLong 1991). Countries now associated with bank-based financial systems, such as Germany (Fohlin 2005) and Japan (Morck and Nakamura 2005), all relied primarily on stock markets to capitalize large business groups in the nineteenth and early twentieth centuries; and only shifted towards bank financing after their industrializations were complete.

A second common feature of large business groups is their sweeping industrial diversification (Khanna and Yafeh 2007). For example, Canada's

---

5 Bruland and Mowery, Chapter 4 in this volume, discuss the role of the *zaibatsu* in product and process quality improvement, and their ties to the education system.

6 See n. 4 above re trusts. Becht and DeLong (2005) describe these legal changes in detail. In brief, criticism of trusts for organizing monopolies gave rise to anti-monopolies laws aimed specifically at trusts. Business lobbying induced New Jersey to amend its laws to allow pyramiding as a substitute mechanism with which a single tycoon or business family might control a large number of seemingly distinct firms. Many US groups became unusually focused, notably in public utilities or railroads, by the 1930s.

largest late nineteenth-century pyramidal business group, run by Max Aitken, a.k.a. Lord Beaverbrook, spanned the full array of modern industries – from steel to cement to insurance; and the others were scarcely less diversified (Morck *et al.* 2005). These groups were not restricted to manufacturing, but encompassed all manner of service, trade, and even agriculture-related firms. The Beaverbrook Group and others like it transformed the country, still largely agrarian in the early 1890s, into a predominantly industrial economy by World War I. A second wave of pyramiding in the 1920s capitalized lighter industries – automobiles, electrification, power and water, traction, and the like. Large business groups in nouveaux riches Asian economies are also supremely diversified, as are their likenesses in the still emerging economies of Israel, Turkey, South Asia, and Latin America. Khanna and Yafeh (2007) show pyramidal groups in today's developing economies to be diversified extraordinarily widely – the largest having member firms in virtually every sector.

A third common feature of large pyramidal business groups is their tight connections to government. Japan's prewar Parliament featured a major party associated with each of its largest pyramidal business groups. In Canada, Arthur Meighen, the controlling shareholder of Canada General Investment, the country's largest pyramidal group in the 1920s, twice served as Prime Minister in that decade. Sweden's largest pyramidal business groups, especially the largest, controlled by the Wallenberg family, developed tight links with the country's Social Democratic party by simplifying tripartite agreements. A simple conversation between the Prime Minister, a national union leader, and a few business family patriarchs could produce an accord on industrial subsidies, labour peace, entry, taxes, and tariffs (Högfeldt 2005).

Another intermittent theme is an inflow of foreign capital. Lord Beaverbrook's lower-tier firms were usually cross-listed in London, whose financial markets were by then accustomed to financing national development schemes organized as pyramidal business groups; and during Canada's high-growth period – roughly 1896 to 1913 – more British capital flowed into Canada than into any other country. Nonetheless, other pyramidal business groups, usually headquartered in Britain and with member companies' shares trading largely in London, but with their operating companies physically located in far-flung corners of the nineteenth- and early twentieth-century British empire, undertook to develop the economies of Australia, Britain's Chinese concessions, Hong Kong, India, and the British West Indies (Jones 2000; Allen, Chapter 2 in this volume). Similar groups operated constellations of businesses outside the empire – most notably in Argentina.

Business groups in perpetually developing economies

Many Latin American countries seemed ready for economic takeoff in the late nineteenth century, and again in the 1920s, and again in the 1960s, and seem similarly poised today. India seemed ready for takeoff through the 1950s, and then stagnated for decades. Egypt, Indonesia, the Philippines, Turkey, and numerous other middle-income countries, likewise cleared for takeoff by investors, development economists, and the business press, returned to their terminals.

Firms affiliated with business groups in poor economies tend to be the star performers (Khanna and Yafeh 2007). In successfully developed economies, this finding is typically reversed (Morck, Wolfenzon, and Yeung 2005). The former result invites several explanations, which lead into explanations for the latter result that are detailed in the next section.

Why should business group firms be star performers in low-income economies? Low-income economies typically have weak institutions. High transactions costs constipate their labour, capital, and product markets. Corruption undermines the rule of law and the viability of business contracts. Weak investor protection undermines trust in financial markets and institutions. Business groups may well be second-best solutions to these problems. Absent good institutions, member firms in business groups can reduce transaction costs by hiring personnel from each other, investing in each other, and doing business with each other. A common ultimate controlling shareholder prevents group firms from cheating each other, and a family's good name can engender trust among outside investors, customers, and suppliers. This credibility can also commend family group member firms to state-owned enterprises, or government agencies and banks that would otherwise risk large non-performance costs. Large family-controlled business groups may well possess a genuine economic advantage over freestanding professionally run firms in such economies.[7]

---

7 Empirical evidence pertinent to these points is primarily from present-day economies (Leff 1978; Khanna and Palepu 2000; Khanna and Fisman 2004; Khanna and Yafeh 2007). More specifically, Khanna and Palepu (2005) present evidence that firms in a major Indian business group, that are controlled by the Tata family, have a major advantage over independent firms in innovation, and Morck, Stangeland, and Yeung (2000) estimate Canadian business group member firms' costs of capital to be lower than those of their independent peers.

A rite of passage?

These considerations suggest that large pyramidal business groups might enhance efficiency – at least under some conditions and in some phases of economic development. An era of oligarchs, robber barons, and the like might even be a rite of passage into the ranks of high-income countries.

Insiders and outsiders

The historical importance of business groups confounds students of corporate governance, who associate pyramiding with aggravated agency problems (Berle and Means 1932; Bebchuk, Kraaakman, and Triantis 2000). Microeconomics associates efficient resource allocation with firms maximizing their value, specifically the expected present value of their future profits. But firms are run by utility-maximizing top executives. Agency problems arise where these top executives, who are supposed to be faithful agents acting for the firm's owners, its shareholders, instead maximize their own utility (Jensen and Meckling 1976). Agency problems are shown by a broad empirical literature to exert a first-order effect on returns to capital, and agency cost minimization is thought to drive mergers, divestitures, and business organization in general (Shleifer and Vishny 1997).[8] Given this, the historical ubiquity and persistence of business groups requires explanation.

What follows is a brief overview of why pyramidal business groups seemingly ought to magnify agency problems. This done, we turn to explanations of their popularity and persistence.

Agency problems (Jensen and Meckling 1976) arise from an internal contradiction in microeconomics: Individuals are presumed to maximize their utility, firms are presumed to maximize their profits, but CEOs are individuals who run firms and might well run them to maximize their own utility. Where agency problems are worse, public investors pay less for firms' shares in initial public offerings (IPOs) by an amount called an *agency cost*. A pervasive

---

8 Higher agency costs leave a firm's shares trading at lower prices. Corporate raiders are posited to buy the shares of such firms, delist them, restructure them to reduce agency problems with credible new constraints on managerial utility maximization at the expense of profits, and refloat the firms' shares in the stock market at a higher price than that paid in the takeover. Economies in which takeovers are commonplace, such as those of the US and UK, thus exert a constant pressure on firms towards minimized agency costs (Shleifer and Vishny 1997). Franks, Mayer, and Rossi (2005) argue that raiders finance their takeover activity with continual issues of new shares, diluting their stakes in their own firms, and posit that more extensive takeover activity is responsible, partly at least, for the greater importance of widely held firms in those countries.

misapprehension in much recent work is that agency costs reflect insiders expropriating public shareholders' wealth. In an efficient stock market, agency problems reduce the value of a firm's shares to account for the expected behavior of its insiders when the shares are first issued. Public shareholders buy in at low prices, and get (on average) exactly the returns they expected. The social cost of agency problems is not the expropriation of shareholders' wealth, but the depressed return to entrepreneurs for founding new firms and selling out in IPOs – the venture capital cycle Gompers and Lerner (2006) find central to the financing of continual innovation. Higher agency costs mean entrepreneurs glean lower returns, all else equal, from founding and listing new firms.

A huge literature on corporate governance (Shleifer and Vishny 1997) examines how laws, regulations, corporate charters, etc. affect agency problems. This corporation-level focus is reasonable in the United Kingdom and the United States, where business decisions are indeed made by firms' CEOs and boards of directors, but loses traction elsewhere, where important decisions are often made at the level of the business group. Business group governance, though obviously related to corporate governance, raises new and different issues (Morck 2011).[9]

First, pyramidal business groups hugely magnify the separation of ownership rights from control rights that underlies agency problems. The family controls the firm at the apex of its pyramid, and usually owns much of it too. Any misallocation of the family firm's resources directly diminishes the family's wealth, and is thus likely to be avoided. But the fortunes of individual firms in lower tiers can have scant effect on the controlling family's wealth. Consider Imperial Windsor, a member firm in a 1990s Canadian business group described in Morck, Stangeland, and Yeung (2000). The Bronfman family's Broncorp Inc. controlled HIL Corporation with a 19.6 percent equity block. HIL controlled 97 percent of Edper Resources, which controlled 60 percent of Brascan Holdings, which controlled 5.1 percent of Brascan, which controlled 49.9 percent of Braspower Holdings, which controlled 49.3 percent of Great Lakes Power Inc, which controlled 100 percent of First

---

9 What follows pertains to pyramidal business groups because these are by far the predominant structure of large business groups, both across countries and historically. The issues raised also pertain to nineteenth-century American business groups organized as voting trusts, with minor variations. State-controlled business groups, such as attained importance in fascist Italy (Aganin and Volpin 2005) and comprise most of the "private sector" in modern China (Fan, Wong, and Zhang 2012), potentially bestir radically different agency problems associated with political agendas compromising economic efficiency.

Toronto Investments, which controlled 25 percent of Trilon Holdings, which controlled 64.5 percent of Trilon Financial, which controlled 41.4 percent of Gentra, which controlled 31.9 percent of Imperial Windsor Group. Multiplying the chain of ownership stakes reveals that a one million dollar drop in the value of Imperial Windsor would cost its controlling family about $300. Assuming public shareholders owned all other shares in each firm along the control chain, Imperial Windsor is 99.97 percent financed with public shareholders' money and only 0.03 percent financed with wealth provided by the family. Consequently, the separation of ownership from control is precisely equivalent to that in a widely held company whose top managers owned a 0.03 percent stake.

If the controlling family, or managers, spent a million additional dollars of their firm's money on unnecessary executive jet flights they valued at over $300, the insiders' utility would rise as the firm's value fell. If the managers of the widely held firm went too far down this path, their firm's depressed share price might attract a hostile takeover by a raider intent on replacing them with less epicurean top managers. The business group member firm is, however, not at similar risk. The business family controlling the group's apex firm controls every firm in the pyramid utterly, by dint of controlling its parent company, its parent's parent, and so on. As long as managers and directors throughout the structure please its controlling family, their positions are secure: they and the controlling family are entrenched. Should the family patriarch be senile or a venal patriarch, neither he nor the cronies he places in charge of his group firms can be ousted by a raider, a shareholder rebellion, or an institutional investor. Indeed, the institutional investors in many countries are themselves pyramidal group member firms.

In America or Britain, both currently economies of freestanding firms, bereft of business groups, widely held firms endure agency problems associated with insiders spending public shareholders' money and narrowly held firms bear agency problems associated with entrenched insiders (Morck, Shleifer, and Vishny 1988; Stulz 1988). Pyramidal groups neatly allow both problems in the same firms.[10]

---

10 Negative effects of concentrated voting control on firm-level performance correlate with the extent to which the controlling shareholders' voting power exceed their cash-flow rights – that is, their actual ownership of the firm's shares (Claessens et al. 2002; Edwards and Weichenrieder 2004; Faccio and Lang 2002). Attig et al. (2006) also show this gap to correlate with lower liquidity for the firm's public float – that is, the shares not part of the pyramidal control structure and owned by public investors.

Moreover, pyramiding allows a third agency problem, dubbed tunneling (Johnson, Lopez-de-Silanes, and Shleifer 2000), in which net worth is transferred from low- to high-tier pyramid group firms to augment the controlling family's private wealth. This is typically accomplished with transfer pricing, intragroup intercorporate transactions at non-market prices of the same sort that multinationals use to move taxable income from country to country.[11] Understandably, the public shareholders of wealth-contributing firms view tunneling as a corporate governance problem; and empirically, laws and regulations against tunneling are found to matter most in explaining variation in financial development across countries.

Oligarchs and peons

Cross-country studies correlate a preeminence of large family-controlled business groups with all manner of institutional deficiencies. Inefficient capital, labour, and product markets; poor transportation, communication, power, and water infrastructure; deficient public education; interventionist government, high inequality, and low incomes all correlate with larger or more dominant family business groups (Fogel 2006).

This does not appear to be a cross-sectional photograph of early-stage very rapid development featuring large business groups and mature industrialization featuring more atomistic business sectors. Overall, a predominance of large old-moneyed family-controlled business groups correlates with slower, not faster growth (Fogel 2006; Morck, Stangeland, and Yeung 2000).[12] On the surface, this seems paradoxical: the firms in family business groups are the best performing firms in developing economies (Khanna and Yafeh 2007), so one might think more of them would be better for the economy. This might indeed be so, but what is good for Tata Motors need not be good for India. To understand why, we must look at some examples.

---

11 Bonbright and Means (1932) posit that overpriced or underpriced intragroup services fees, harder to detect than mispriced goods, are a preferred method of tunneling. For example, an engineering services or financial firm might sell overpriced services to another group firm as a way of tunneling funds out of that firm, and might provide services at cut rates as a way of tunneling funds into another group firm in need of subsidies.

12 The direction of causality cannot be directly inferred from correlations. A predominance of large family-controlled business groups might keep an economy from developing, or countries in the early stages of development might be preferential environments for large family-controlled business groups, or both. The preponderance of empirical evidence, much of it admittedly circumstantial, suggests "both." Thus, bidirectional causality is central to the arguments below.

Country studies of seemingly interminably developing economies reveal remarkably old and stable family business groups dominating their economies (Colpan, Hikino, and Lincoln 2011). While smaller new business groups wax and wane through India's economic history, those of the Birla and Tata families remained overwhelmingly dominant from the Raj, through most of India's history as an independent nation (Khanna and Palepu 2005). Only in the past few years has a third group challenged their diarchy. Roughly one-third of Argentina's large business groups are controlled by their founders' sons, another third are controlled by their founders' grandsons, and the remaining third are controlled by their founders' great-grandsons (Fracchia, Mesquita, and Quiroga 2011). Further cross-country evidence reveals rapid growth in economies dominated by self-made tycoons' business groups, but much slower growth in economies dominated by old-moneyed families' business groups – or business groups controlled by political leaders (Morck, Stangeland, and Yeung 2000). Of course, the very poorest countries lack stock markets, and hence business groups.

These findings suggest that countries might become trapped in a "middle income trap," a stable and prolonged situation in which a few large business groups dominate an institutionally deficient economy, and protect their dominance by preventing further institutional development. The last can be accomplished by capturing regulators or even whole governments, or by controlling a country's banks and thus potential entrants' access to capital (Rajan and Zingales 2003, 2004). If business group firms achieve their profits primarily from political rent-seeking, findings that business group firms' profits surpass those of independent firms in low-income countries (Khanna and Yafeh 2007) need not imply that the group firms are better managed; rather, group firms' profits may have major negative externalities for their economies (Morck, Wolfenzon, and Yeung 2005).[13] Thus, that firms controlled by Russian oligarchs are the country's best performers (Guriev and Rachinsky 2005) need not imply that oligarchs ought to control more firms.

---

13 *Political rent-seeking* (Krueger 1974) occurs when firms invest in political connections, as opposed to productive assets. Baumol (1990) argues that large, invasive, and corrupt governments can make political rent-seeking the highest-return investment available to most firms, and that this can stall economic development. This can be a stable situation in which the rent-seeking firms do well – their investments in government connections yield high returns in subsidies, trade protection, tax breaks, and protective barriers to entry; as do the politicians who favor them; but the economy suffers from a lack of genuine investment in productivity-improving assets and thus stagnates (Morck, Wolfenzon, and Yeung 2005). We refer to this as a "middle income trap."

Robber barons, oligarchs, and the like are roundly blamed for many countries' economic injustices. While the corporate governance literature stresses agency problems associated with pyramids, country histories tend to stress broader problems. The predominance of a few very large pyramidal groups evokes broader political economy concerns. Where a handful of very large business groups comprise much of an economy's big business sector, capital allocation can depend more on the controlling shareholder's preferences than on market forces. This could enhance efficiency if the controlling shareholder has superior information, judgment, and appropriately aligned incentives; but might also misallocate resources severely.

Long-run sustainable economic growth is thought to require creative destruction, wherein innovative, high-productivity, upstart firms continually arise and displace established lower-productivity firms. King and Levine (1993) show that creative destruction requires financial development because the creative entrepreneurs with potentially disruptive new ideas are unlikely to get financing from the large existing firms or business groups that stand to be destroyed. Those who are already rich and powerful tend to prefer the status quo. Indeed, they might divert capital to lower-return projects within their established firms rather than to far more profitable ventures that would be controlled by outsiders (Almeida and Wolfenzon 2006). Similar considerations work against groups financing competitors to their established firms, allowing concealed cartelization despite an appearance of numerous competing corporations (Morck, Wolfenzon, and Yeung 2005). Economies dominated by large business groups might thus depend critically on established firms' cautious application of foreign innovation for productivity growth, and on trade openness for competitive pricing. The same reputation, information, and coordination advantages that let group firms do business with lower transactions costs in institutionally weak economies also render groups' controlling shareholders better able to influence government officials, evoking the possibility that group firms' superior economic performance might arise, in part at least, from advantages in political rent-seeking, rather than resource allocation (Morck and Yeung 2004). More fundamentally, where too few control too much, a family patriarch's error in judgment can become a macroeconomic crisis.

Commissars and cadres

Central planning is usually thought of as a government function. Paul Rosenstein-Rodan (1943), one of the twentieth century's most influential economists, argued that "the problem of economic underdevelopment" is one of financing and coordination. Each firm in a modern market economy depends critically on the simple existence of sufficient populations of firms to sustain competitive prices throughout its vertical supply chains and those of makers of relevant complementary goods, as well as the existence of infrastructure public goods. In rapid development starting from a low level, many nodes in this network are missing. Filling in these missing pieces has huge benefits for the rest of the economy, but the first firms to do so cannot readily capture these returns. Indeed, hold-up problems (Williamson 1975) can deter first movers and development stalls. To overcome these problems, Rosenstein-Rodan called for a Big Push: a foreign aid-financed government-coordinated industrial policy in which large state-owned enterprises would coordinate the development of all sectors of the economy. Only a state-led Big Push, he argued, could overcome the multitudes of hold-up problems, externalities, and incomplete network problems that stymie investment by private enterprise and lock poor countries into low-level equilibriums.

Rosenstein-Rodan's characterization of the problem stands unrefuted, and remains a central theme of development economics (Murphy, Shleifer, and Vishny 1989). His solution, however, aged poorly. Like its better-known cousin, the natural resources trap (Sachs and Warner 2001), a foreign aid trap can undermine the quality of recipient countries' governments (Djankov, Montalvo, and Reynal-Querol 2008; Easterly 2006). Just as plenteous natural resources royalties plump politicians' budgets without any real attention to genuine development, huge aid inflows fixate politicians' attention on pleasing donors. In both, genuine development is at best unnecessary to the political elite, and may even seem undesirable for empowering troublesome upstarts. Massive state-led industrial policies are even more thoroughly discredited (Ades and di Tella 1997). Political rent-seeking (Krueger 1974), regulatory capture (Stigler 1971), and corruption (Shleifer and Vishny 1993) are now widely accepted as first-order problems in developing economics, and few policy options provide them a broader invitation than does Rosenstein-Rodan's state-led Big Push.

Through the 1950s and 1960s, Rosenstein-Rodan and his London School of Economics students organized state-led Big Push industrializations in scores of newly independent African, Arab, and Asian countries; and even found followers in the long-independent, but economically stagnating economies of Latin America. Half a century later, most economies that took his medicines remain mired in poverty, bound by seemingly intractable corruption, rent-seeking, and elite capture. The handful of Asian economies that successfully developed into high-income economies in the later twentieth century – Hong Kong, Malaysia, Taiwan, and South Korea – entrusted their economies to powerful tycoons and business families, whose fortunes rose with development, not Rosenstein-Rodan's central planners. Rosenstein-Rodan erred in not anticipating the rent-seeking, capture, and other government failure problems that ensued, though so did virtually all mainstream economics of his era.

Rosenstein-Rodan (1943) felt state-control was essential because finance concerned individual corporations:

> Financial markets and institutions are inappropriate to the task of industrialization of a whole country. They deal with too small units, and do not account for externalities. Capital goes to individual firms ... There has never been a scheme of planned industrialisation comprising a simultaneous planning of several complementary industries.

Rosenstein-Rodan was right (more or less) about the problem, but wrong about the solution. Large pyramidal business groups are fully capable of the "simultaneous planning of several complementary industries." Indeed, their primary function may well be internalizing network externalities, circumventing hold-up problems, and privately providing public goods: precisely the tasks Rosenstein-Rodan's Big Push assigns to governments. Japan's development is widely cited as a successful state-run Big Push (e.g. Ohkawa and Rosovsky 1973), but its economy staggered until its *zaibatsu* took charge (Morck and Nakamura 2007). South Korea's government largely abandoned direct intervention, except in sectors related to military supply lines, in the 1970s; and by the 1980s had overtly neoliberal government policies (Lim and Morck 2013). The economy rose from third to first world levels from the late 1970s through the 1990s. Even during the 1960s, arguably the period of heaviest government intervention, subsidies were dependent on exporting success (see Bruland and Mowery, Chapter 4 in this volume). It seems likely that business groups served as private-sector central planners in both the distant economic histories of developed economies and present-day rapidly developing economies.

China may or may not fit this pattern. Virtually all large firms classified by the government as privately owned are, in fact, member firms in pyramidal groups with state-owned enterprises, rather than business families, at their apexes (Fan, Wong, and Zhang in press). Such structures were prominent in fascist Italy (Aganin and Volpin 2005). However, state control may veil de facto control by powerful families of "princelings" – the direct descendants of the communist revolutionaries who founded the People's Republic. After documenting the top state-owned enterprise positions of 103 descendants of the "eight immortals" – all now dead and revered in communist lore as transcendent revolutionary figures – a Bloomberg analysis concludes:[14]

> Twenty-six of the heirs ran or held top positions in state-owned companies that dominate the economy . . . Three children alone – General Wang's son, Wang Jun; Deng's son-in-law, He Ping; and Chen Yuan, the son of Mao's economic tsar – headed or still run state-owned companies with combined assets of about $1.6 trillion in 2011. That is equivalent to more than a fifth of China's annual economic output.

Free-market analogs of Soviet central planners, the controlling shareholders of such business groups – by coordinating investment in numerous diverse sectors, by controlling the major decisions of all the firms in their groups, and by tunneling funds from one member firm to another – can internalize externalities, prevent hold-up problems, and even organize the private provision of public goods – at least in theory (Morck 2009). But unlike Soviet central planners, the tycoons who orchestrated the successful development of Canada, Japan, South Korea, and Sweden (and perhaps China too) used markets and public capital, and built personal fortunes that grew with development. Incentives were aligned.

Morck and Nakamura (2007) document evidence of Japan's *zaibatsu* families behaving in this way in that country's high-growth era – the late nineteenth and early twentieth centuries. Turkey's major business groups each operate a private university – investments perhaps made profitable by the very high likelihood that graduates will ultimately end up working for a group company, there being few other choices.

In an admirably complete explanation of how a business group can naturally find itself organizing a Big Push across multiple sectors, Koo Cha-Kyung, Chairman of Korea's LG pyramidal business group, explains how business groups overcome Rosenstein-Rodan's litany of coordination problems thus (Kim 2011):

> My father and I started a cosmetic cream factory in the late 1940s. At the time, no company could supply us with plastic caps of adequate quality for cream jars, so we had to start a plastics business. Plastic caps alone were not sufficient to run the plastic molding plant, so we added combs, toothbrushes, and soap boxes. This plastic business also led us to manufacture electric fan blades and telephone cases, which in turn led us to manufacture electrical and

---

14 Oster *et al.* 2012. The eight immortals – Deng Xiaoping, Wang Zhen, Chen Yun, Li Xiannian, Peng Zhen, Song Renqiong, Yang Shangkun, and Bo Yibo – play a near-mythical role in official Chinese history akin to that of Washington, Jefferson, Hamilton, or Lincoln in the United States.

electronic products and telecommunications equipment. The plastics business also took us into oil refining, which needed a tanker shipping company. The oil refining company alone was paying an insurance premium amounting to more than half the total revenue of the largest insurance company in Korea. Thus, an insurance company was started. This natural step-by-step evolution through related businesses resulted in the Lucky-Goldstar (LG) group as we see it today.

Graduation exercises

Once the Big Push phase of industrialization is complete, and the institutions allowing low-cost arm's-length transactions fall into place, the business groups' *raison d'être* fades and their litany of agency problems and political economy concerns loom large. Like institutions favoring any powerful vested interest, family-controlled pyramidal business groups tend to persist until a major crisis disturbs the status quo, erodes the wealth of entrenched elites, undermines the faith of the general populace in existing institutions, and creates what Olson (1984) calls a "clean institutional slate." The twentieth century's greatest economic shocks – the European hyperinflations of the 1920s, the Great Depression of the 1930s, World War II, and ideologically polarized Cold War economic policy flips – affected different countries' great pyramidal business groups in very different ways.

Business groups at the end of history?

Large pyramidal business groups persist in some highly developed economies. But they are housebroken. Their controlling families strive to be seen as good citizens, and are often keen to cooperate with popular governments.

Sweden serves as a prime example of this path (Högfeldt 2005). Two large pyramidal business groups control firms amounting to roughly half of the stock market capitalization of all listed Swedish businesses. How Sweden's business groups reacted to the Great Depression and how they adapted to an ideologically driven social democratic economic experiment thereafter cast much light on political economy issues concerning such groups. Sweden's late nineteenth- and early twentieth-century "catchup" industrialization featured business groups similar to Japan's *zaibatsu*. In discussing the latter decades of this era, Dahmen (1950) highlights *development blocks* – interdependent sectors developed in concert.

A wave of bankruptcies left Sweden's largest banks holding huge inventories of industrial firms' nonperforming loans. The two largest creditors, the Wallenberg family's group of financial institutions and Svenska Handelsbanken, accepted equity control blocks in lieu of debt repayment and assembled these into pyramids of control blocks. Swedes reacted to the Great Depression by voting in an almost back-to-back succession of Social Democratic governments over the next several decades. Social Democratic prime ministers and business family patriarchs initially got on poorly. But over time, the Social Democrats came to appreciate the convenience of "doing deals" with big business with a few phone calls, and the patriarchs came to appreciate the barriers to entry inherent in high taxes, dense regulations, and industrial policy subsidies. Strong labour laws and penetrating disclosure requirements arose to preclude tunneling. A symbiosis developed that many Swedes, including ardent Social Democrats, view as highly practical and beneficial.[15]

Italy's economy featured several very large pyramidal business groups in the early twentieth century (Aganin and Volpin 2005). Amid a 1920s bank crisis, Benito Mussolini seized power and nationalized the problem banks. The SOE banks then accepted equity blocks in industrial firms in lieu of debt repayment, and assembled large pyramidal groups with state-owned enterprises, rather than family firms, at the apexes. These structures helped promulgate Fascist Party control across a still nominally private-sector economy of listed firms with distinct CEOs and boards of directors. But the pyramidal control blocks ensured that each member firm's board had a solid Party majority. These structures appeared useful to postwar governments, and persisted until a 1990s mass privatization program; whereafter family controlled business groups staged a comeback. The country's largest business group today, that of the Agnelli family, was also its largest before fascism.[16]

Canada perhaps provides the best examples of pyramids dying of natural causes (Morck et al. 2005). No radical political transformation upset that

15 One commonly perceived benefit of pyramidal business groups in Sweden is the insulation of group member firms from the short-term performance pressures exerted by public shareholders, allowing business–government cooperation in the development of new technologies. For example, the Wallenberg pyramidal group firm L. M. Ericsson developed a state-financed digital technology to achieve prominence in telecoms. However, evidence that public shareholders exert short-term pressures on managers is largely anecdotal, and empirical studies point to the opposite: firms' share prices rise abruptly on news that they are increasing R&D spending in the US (Jaffe 1986; Chan, Martin, and Kensinger 1990; Doukas and Switzer 1992; Chan, Lakonishok, and Sougiannis 2001), Canada (Johnson and Pazderka 1993), and Europe (Hall and Oriani 2004). While a role for the state in financing basic research persists in successful developed economies throughout the world, state-financed commercialization tends to increase returns to political rent-seeking (Gompers and Lerner 2004, chap. 13).

16 Aganin and Volpin (2005) document family-controlled pyramidal business groups being somewhat overshadowed by state-controlled pyramidal groups from the 1920s until a privatization drive in the 1990s; after which family-controlled business groups regained their early twentieth-century dominance.

country's old-line parties in the Great Depression, and its postwar politics remained largely centrist. Its early twentieth-century business groups simply persisted. Some groups dissolved amid 1930s bankruptcies; others grew by buying up bankrupt families' dismembered subsidiaries. A steep inheritance tax, in effect until the 1970s, forced heirs to sell companies and pared down older groups even as new ones formed.[17] Business groups resurged dramatically in the 1970s as the country adopted a Social Democratic model, and then fell away again amid post-1980s liberalizations. It seems plausible that competition from more efficient firms in the United States and elsewhere may have had a role in this.

Nonetheless, Canada has never sought to banish pyramidal business groups. Rather, the country seeks to domesticate them. A central pillar of Canada's business law is its Oppression Remedy. This lets shareholders, and other designated stakeholders, reach up through successive tiers of control blocks to sue personally a firm's ultimate controlling shareholder for acts deemed oppressive. Though seldom used, this shareholder right is thought far more important than shareholder rights deemed important in the United States. Djankov *et al.* (2008), in a cross-country study, show laws of the Canadian ilk to be the most important constraints on agency problems in most countries. As explained below, the United States forged a unique path away from a business group dominated economy, and consequently has unique institutions.

How business groups should be governed remains an open question. Different countries have developed very different bodies of fully articulated business group law. For example, Belgian law requires officers and directors of group member firms to act in the best interests of the business group, not their specific firm (Johnson, Lopez-de-Silanes, and Shleifer 2000). Economists, focussed on the governance of singleton corporations, have barely scratched the surface (Morck 2011).

---

17 Political economy aspects of these reforms are complicated, but almost certainly very important. Pierre Trudeau, whose father Charles Trudeau controlled a small business group, abolished the estate tax in 1972. The replacement, capital gains realization on death, was amended in 1974 to allow family trusts to postpone this for a generation or more. Political pressure from wealthy business families nonetheless persisted. In 1986 and 1991, a branch of the Bronfman family sought permission to move $2.2 billion, in such a trust, out of the country without triggering a realization, effectively avoiding all taxes on the estate. Allegedly, Revenue Canada denied permission, but was overruled by the Finance Ministry and the funds were transferred. See Peter C. Newman "The soft touch of an ace tax collector," *Maclean's*, June 10, 1996; Diane Francis (2000) "The crusade to know what went on at Revenue Canada" *National Post*, August 26, 2000.

The end of history for business groups?

A high-income economy's Big Push commencement exercise can be traumatic for the graduating class of business group controlling shareholders. Successful development brings efficient markets and high-quality public goods, such as education and public health, all of which highlight the problems of inherited corporate governance: a regression to the mean in talent, blunted incentives for non-kin and excessive job security for kin in family firms, and disruptive feuds between quarrelsome princes and princesses. Chandler (1977, 1990) associates economic development with a waning of family-controlled business and a waxing of professionally managed firms. As evidence, he documents such transformations in four major economies: the United States, the United Kingdom, Japan, and Germany. While family firms persist in all four, and comprise much of Germany's vaunted Mittelstand of small and medium-sized enterprises, Chandler's observation is essentially valid. In each case, major economic shocks wrought this transformation.

In the United States, the shock was the Great Depression (Morck 2005). In the late 1920s, pyramidal business groups attracted increasing criticism for avoiding taxes through opportunistic tunneling, concealing cartels, destabilizing the economy, and entrusting too much economic power to too few people. President Roosevelt's New Deal, launched in the mid 1930s, took direct aim at business groups, applying double taxation to intercorporate dividends, banning large pyramids from public utilities sectors, and dangling tax incentives to families that broke up their pyramids. By the late 1930s, the pyramidal groups previously evident across most sectors of the US economy had all but vanished.[18] Most large US firms are now widely held, lacking any single dominant shareholder; and virtually all are freestanding. Listed US firms do not hold control blocks in other listed US firms, except when a takeover or divestiture is in progress.

---

18 Mahoney (2012) notes that many US pyramidal groups contained public utility firms, with regulated cost-plus pricing, making them not only cash cows (sources of subsidies for other group firms), but mechanisms for turning high costs into high profits (cost-plus pricing sets rates so that profits are always a given figure times costs). Concerns that other firms in groups with public utility operations were unfairly advantaged at the expense of public utility rate payers led to the 1935 Public Utilities Holding Companies Act, which limited public utility pyramiding to two tiers. This act was almost certainly paramount in forcing the dismantling of pyramids whose main edge was the regulated profits of their utilities affiliates. Although many US pyramids were indeed involved largely in public utilities (Bank and Cheffins 2010), many others contained railroad, financial, and industrial firms (Morck 2009). The importance of regulated utilities with cost-plus pricing as pyramidal group cash cows in other countries is incompletely investigated.

In Germany, a hyperinflation and the Great Depression brought Adolf Hitler's National Socialist Party to power (Fohlin 2005, 2007; Weitz 1997). The families that controlled Germany's great pyramidal business groups often used control chains containing dominant, but not majority equity blocks. To extend Party control over the country's private-sector businesses, the Nazis altered shareholder voting rules, vesting public investors' votes with the banks that served as custodians for their shares. Aryanizing the country's largest few banks then left Party loyalists with voting power over combined equity blocks sufficient to control the boards of most large German firms. Directors' duty to shareholders was replaced by a duty to all stakeholders: shareholders, creditors, workers, the community, and most importantly, the Reich and its Führer.

With minor modifications, this system remains in place today. Most large German firms have professional managers primarily loyal to the country's most powerful bankers, whose voting power determines their careers. Since the large banks are widely held, the bankers jointly control elections to their own boards.

Japan endured a series of devastating crises in the twentieth century (Morck and Nakamura 2005). A 1923 earthquake destroyed much of its industrial base, and the Great Depression's trade barriers idled more. With popular support for liberal democracy waning, the military slowly assumed power with a policy of selective assassination. A series of reforms inserted military personnel into companies and onto boards, and military planners soon dictated investment, payout, and production decisions.

Japan's surrender and postwar occupation was, if anything, an even bigger crisis. The economy the American military took charge of in 1945 was so tightly controlled by the military that it resembled a centrally planned Soviet economy. Roosevelt New Dealers, charged with rebuilding Japan, saw no reason to return firms to the families whose pyramidal groups dominated the prewar economy. Instead, family and intercorporate control blocks were seized and either sold or allocated to workers. When the Americans departed in 1952, Japan's corporate sector looked much like America's now: Most large firms were freestanding and widely held.

Two waves of hostile takeovers ensued, with raiders buying control blocks in underperforming firms and threatening their managers with dismissal. This ended with Mitsui Bank's invention of a new anti-takeover defense: the *keiretsu* business group. The tactic assembled a dozen or two firms, each of which created new shares numbering more than their public shares outstanding. These shares were then traded among the participating companies so each ended up holding one or two percent of the stock in every other member firm in the group. The resulting configuration left each firm without any single controlling shareholder, yet insulated its managers from the threat of a hostile takeover because all managers pledged never to sell their stakes, which when summed constituted a majority of every group firm's stock (Lazonick 2004).

Keiretsu business groups, though never substantially more than anti-takeover devices, attracted the favorable attention of outside experts amid Japan's 1980s boom. *Keiretsu* member firms' long-standing financial under-performance now attracts criticism from investor groups, and many large *keiretsu* appear to be dissolving. Former *keiretsu* firms are now enthusiastically adopting poison pills.

The United Kingdom, devastated by the Depression and war, elected a series of radical Labour governments in the postwar era (Cheffins 2009; Franks, Mayer, and Rossi 2005). These organized trade-based pension funds, which soon became major shareholders in large British firms. Unhappy with the laggard performance of the public floats of pyramid group member firms' shares, the pension funds successfully lobbied the London Stock Exchange for a change in its takeover rules. The new 1968 Takeover Rule requires any shareholder who acquires a 30 percent stake in a listed firm to bid for 100 percent. Hurried along by raiders and pension fund activism, pyramidal groups largely disappeared.

Elsewhere, Chandler's prediction that economic development heralds professional management remains unfulfilled (La Porta, Lopez-de-Silanes, and Shleifer 1999). But it may be slow in coming rather than wrong. Tested techniques for dissolving pyramidal business groups are attracting public policy interest in many countries whose self-made tycoon-run business groups are about to pass to heirs or less certain talent. South Korea's *chaebol* are taking increasingly heavy fire (Albrecht *et al.* 2010; Kim 2006); and Israelis are reflecting on the power of their pyramids (Kosenko 2007). Conflicts between princelings over inheritances and succession may be weakening the power of business groups in these countries and elsewhere (e.g. Bertrand *et al.* 2008).

Is there a future in resisting history?

If large pyramidal business groups are valuable because they can coordinate Big Push development, but become net drags on economic growth once an economy attains first world status, their unwanted persistence becomes a public policy problem. Large business groups, by facilitating successful Big Push development, undermine their *raisons d'être*. The powerful families, whose economic and social status depends on the continued importance of their business groups, might thus come to see developmental success as a problem, rather than an objective.

Rajan and Zingales (2003, 2004) show that many countries experienced a spurt of financial liberalization, but then reversed this once an initial set of entrepreneurs obtained capital to build business groups. They suggest that this first generation of successful business families pressed for financial atavism to lock in a favorable (to them) status quo. By slowing the pace of development, or even bringing it to a halt, they retain their economic and social prominence. But their countries remain stuck partway through the process of economic development.

A growing literature documents how many countries become stuck in a "middle income trap" (Eichengreen, Park, and Shin 2011). Once they have taken control of the commanding heights of an economy, as they must to coordinate Big Push development, large business groups may be very hard to dislodge. Their vast resources and reach make them all but irresistible political lobbyers (Morck and Yeung 2004). They can divert free cash flows from their resources firms, regulated utilities with guaranteed rates of return, government-guaranteed financial institutions, and so on to sustain their other firms, and even engage in bouts of predatory pricing to deter competition. As long as their controlling shareholders value the social and economic benefits of staying in control more than the wealth they might obtain from continued development, the situation persists.

Stalled development is more than a local problem. First world economies have come to rely on rising demand from emerging economies, most notably China and India. Economic distortions emanating from these increasingly globally insignificant economies can thus have global costs. More generally, stalled development in the developing world means sagging demand for developed economies' exports. And perhaps most importantly, stalled development squanders the potential talents of millions of people and slows the overall progress of the species. We have too many problems in urgent need of solutions to waste minds and talent.

Conclusion

Business groups can play an important role in early-stage development of a capitalist economy. Every firm in a developed capitalist economy depends implicitly on a huge network of institutions and other firms that set input, output, and complementary good prices efficiently. Without these, a host of network externalities, hold-up problems, and other market failures can retard industrialization. Arguably, early industrializers took centuries to develop – in part at least because these problems were overcome slowly by trial and error. Suspending market forces and entrusting government central planners to allocate resources works poorly because another host of even more development-retarding government failure problems arise. Business groups can be private-sector mechanisms for internalizing network externalities, preventing hold-up problems, and overcoming other institutional deficiencies – and for promoting rapid development envisioned by advocates of Big Push industrialization. Large business groups thus feature prominently in the histories of successful late industrializers and in today's rapidly industrializing economies. Pyramiding was perhaps invented too late to coordinate rapid industrialization in pioneer economies, such as Britain.

After a successful Big Push, business groups' inherent potential for governance problems and ability to transcend market forces can become a net liability (Morck, Wolfenzon, and Yeung 2005). Of course, they need not do so: many developed economies retain large business groups, subject to potent transparency, anti-self-dealing, and other legal and regulatory constraints. Others, most notably the United States and United Kingdom, adopted tax and regulatory policies explicitly designed to dissolve business groups into independent corporations. Especially tumultuous economic and political histories left still others, notably Japan and Germany, with uniquely structured business groups and more limited rosters of traditional family-controlled pyramids. As Olson (1984) shows, major institutional changes tend to follow major crises that dislodge vested interests. Consistent with this logic, the different ways different countries reorganized corporate control in reaction to major crises played major parts in the development of different "flavors" of capitalism (Morck and Yeung 2009).[19] Similar choices now confront today's newly developed economies, or soon will. Economic history weighs against the continued unfettered dominance of a few large business groups, but provides several seemingly viable alternative policy options.

Economies that are always developing, but never developed, may be caught in a "middle income trap" because of a time inconsistency problem: Large family-controlled business groups may *ex ante* favor rapid development, but stymie development ex post.[20] Large family-controlled business groups

---

19 Although sociologists have developed a rich literature on "varieties of capitalism" (Hall and Soskice 2001), many finance and economics issues remain open. Further research into these issues is clearly warranted.

20 Time inconsistency problems (Kydland and Prescott 1977) occur throughout economics – wherever a naïvely optimal strategy, if successful, changes conditions to render itself suboptimal.

can lead a developing economy into the first world: they have done so in Japan, South Korea, and elsewhere. But by doing this successfully, they render themselves economically unnecessary. Where this prospect threatens a status quo favorable to their controlling shareholders, we suggest that a developing economy's business elite might react by slowing, or even stopping the pace of development.

References

Ades, A. and R. di Tella (1997). "National Champions and Corruption: Some Unpleasant Interventionist Arithmetic," *Economic Journal* 107: 1023–1042.

Aganin, A. and P. Volpin (2005). "The History of Corporate Ownership in Italy," in R. Morck (ed.), *A History of Corporate Governance around the World: Family Business Groups to Professional Managers*. University of Chicago Press, pp. 325–361.

Albrecht, C., C. Turnbull, Y. Zhang, and C. Skousen (2010). "The Relationship between South Korean Chaebols and Fraud," *Management Research Review* 33(3): 257–268.

Aldrighi, D. M. and F. Postali (2011). "Business Groups in Brazil," in Colpan *et al.*

Almeida, H. and D. Wolfenzon (2006). "Should Business Groups Be Dismantled? The Equilibrium Costs of Efficient Internal Capital Markets," *Journal of Financial Economics* 79(1): 99–144.

Attig, N., W. M. Fong, Y. Gadhoum, and L. H. P. Lang (2006). "Effects of Large Shareholding on Information Asymmetry and Stock Liquidity," *Journal of Banking & Finance* 30: 2875–2892.

Bae, K. H., J. K. Kang, and J. M. Kim (2002). "Tunneling or Value Added? Evidence from Mergers by Korean Business Groups," *Journal of Finance* 57: 2695–2740.

Bank, S. and B. Cheffins (2010). "The Corporate Pyramid Fable," UCLA School of Law Working Paper.

Barca F. and M. Becht, eds. (2001). *The Control of Corporate Europe*. New York: Oxford University Press.

Baumol, W. (1990). "Entrepreneurship: Productive, Unproductive, and Destructive," *Journal of Political Economy* 98(5): 893–921.

Bebchuk, L. A., R. Kraakman, G. G. Triantis (2000). "Stock Pyramids, Cross-Ownership, and Dual Class Equity: The Mechanisms and Agency Costs of Separating Control from Cash-Flow Rights," in *Concentrated Corporate Ownership*. Chicago and London: University of Chicago Press, NBER Conference Report series, 295–315.

Becht, M., J. B. DeLong (2005). "Why Has There Been So Little Block Holding in America?" in R. K. Morck (ed.) *A History of Corporate Governance around the World: Family Business Groups to Professional Managers*. Chicago and London: University of Chicago Press, 613–660.

Berle, A. and G. Means (1932). *Modern Corporation and Private Property*. New York: Commerce Clearing House.

Bertrand, M., S. Johnson, K. Samphantharak, A. Schoar (2008). "Mixing Family with Business: A Study of Thai Business Groups and the Families Behind Them," *Journal of Financial Economics* 88: 466.

Bonbright, J. C. and G. C. Means (1932). *The Holding Company: Its Public Significance and its Regulation*. New York: McGraw-Hill Book Co..

Chan, L. K. C., J. Lakonishok, and T. Sougiannis (2001). "The Stock Market Valuation of Research and Development Expenditures," *Journal of Finance* 56(6): 2431–2456.

Chan, S. H., J. Martin, and J. Kensinger (1990). "Corporate Research and Development Expenditures and Share Value," *Journal of Financial Economics* 26(2): 255–276.

Chandler, A. (1977). *The Visible Hand: The Managerial Revolution in American Business*. Cambridge, MA: Belknap Press.

   (1990). *Scale and Scope: The Dynamics of Industrial Capitalism*. Cambridge, MA: Belknap Press.

Charumilind, C., R. Kali, and Y. Wiwattankantang (2006). "Connected Lending: Thailand before the Financial Crisis," *Journal of Business* 79: 181–218.

Cheffins, B. (2009). *Corporate Ownership and Control: British Business Transformed*. Oxford University Press.

Chung, C.-N. and I. P. Mahmood (2011). "Business Groups in Taiwan," in Colpan *et al.*

Claessens, S., S. Djankov, J. P. H. Fan, and L. Lang (2002). "Disentangling the Incentive and Entrenchment Effects of Large Shareholdings," *Journal of Finance* 57(6): 2741–2771.

Colpan, A. M. (2011). "Business Groups in Turkey," in Colpan *et al.*

   T. Hikino, and J. R. Lincoln (2011). *The Oxford Handbook of Business Groups*. Oxford University Press.

Dahmen, E. (1950). *Entrepreneurial Activity and the Development of Swedish Industry 1919–1939*. Homewood IL: American Economic Translation Series, Irwin.

DeLong, J. B. (1991). "Did J. P. Morgan's Men Add Value? An Economist's Perspective on Financial Capitalism," in Peter Temin (ed.), *Inside the Business Enterprise: Historical Perspectives on the Use of Information*. University of Chicago Press for NBER, pp. 205–236.

Djankov, S., J. Montalvo, and M. Reynal-Querol (2008). "The Curse of Aid," *Journal of Economic Growth* 13: 169–194.

Djankov, S., R. La Porta, F. Lopez-de-Silanes, and A. Shleifer (2008). "The Law and Economics of Self-Dealing," *Journal of Financial Economics*. 88(3): 430–465.

Doukas, J. and L. Switzer (1992). "The Stock Market's Valuation of R&D Spending and Market Concentration," *Journal of Economics and Business* 44(2): 95–114.

Easterly, W. (2006). *The White Man's Burden: Why the West's Efforts to Aid the Rest have done so much Ill and so little Good*. New York: Penguin Press.

Edwards, J. S. S. and A. Weichenrieder (2004). "Ownership Concentration and Share Valuation," *German Economic Review* 5: 143–171.

Eichengreen, B., D. Park, and K. Shin (2011). "When Fast Growing Economies Slow Down: International Evidence and Implications for China," NBER Working Paper No. 16919.

Faccio, M. and L. H. P. Lang (2002). "The Ultimate Ownership of Western European Corporations," *Journal of Financial Economics* 65(3): 365–395.

Fan, J., T. J. Wong, and T. Zhang (in press). "Institutions and Organizational Structure: The Case of State-Owned Corporate Pyramids," *Journal of Law, Economics, & Organization*.

Fogel, K. (2006). "Oligarchic Family Control, Social Economic Outcomes, and the Quality of Government," *Journal of International Business Studies* 37: 603.

Fohlin, C. (2005). "The History of Corporate Ownership and Control in Germany," in R. Morck (ed.), *A History of Corporate Governance around the World: Family Business Groups to Professional Managers*. University of Chicago Press, pp. 223–277.

(2007). *Finance Capitalism and Germany's Rise to Industrial Power*. Cambridge University Press.

Fracchia, E., L. Mesquita, and J. Quiroga (2011). "Business Groups in Argentina," in Colpan *et al.*

Franks, J., C. Mayer, and S. Rossi (2005). "Spending Less Time with the Family: The Decline of Family Ownership in the United Kingdom," in R. Morck (ed.), *A History of Corporate Governance around the World: Family Business Groups to Professional Managers*. University of Chicago Press, pp. 581–607.

Goldstein, A. (2011). "Business Groups in South Africa," in Colpan *et al.*

Gompers, P. and J. Lerner (2004). *Venture Capital Cycle*. Cambridge, MA: The MIT Press.

(2006). *The Venture Capital Cycle*. 2nd edn. Cambridge, MA: The MIT Press.

Guriev, S. (2011). "Business Groups in Russia," in Colpan *et al.*

Guriev, S. and A. Rachinsky (2005). "The Role of Oligarchs in Russian Capitalism," *Journal of Economic Perspectives* 19(1): 131–150.

Hall, P. and D. Soskice, eds. (2001). *Varieties of Capitalism: The Institutional Foundations of Comparative Advantage*. Oxford University Press.

Haque, M. and H. M Kabir (2001). "Diversification as a Corporate Strategy for a Family-controlled Business Group in a Frontier Market *Journal of Social, Political, and Economic Studies* 26(4): 719–758.

Högfeldt, P. (2005). "The History and Politics of Corporate Ownership in Sweden," in R. Morck (ed.), *A History of Corporate Governance around the World: Family Business Groups to Professional Managers*. University of Chicago Press, p. 62.

Hoshino, T. (2011). "Business Groups in Mexico," in Colpan *et al.*

Jaffe, A. (1986). "Technological Opportunity and Spillovers of R&D: Evidence from Firms' Patents, Profits, and Market Value," *American Economic Review* 76: 984–1001.

Jensen, M. C. and W. H. Meckling (1976). "Theory of the Firm: Managerial Behavior, Agency Costs and Ownership Structure," *Journal of Financial Economics* 3(4): 305–360.

Johnson, L. and B. Pazderka (1993). "Firm Value and Investment in R&D," *Managerial and Decision Economics* 14: 15–24.

Johnson, S., F. Lopez-de-Silanes, and A. Shleifer (2000). "Tunneling," *American Economic Review* 90: 22–27.

Jones, G. (2000). *Merchants to Multinationals: British Trading Companies in the Nineteenth and Twentieth Centuries*. Oxford University Press.

Khanna, T. and R. Fisman (2004). "Facilitating Development: The Role of Business Groups," *World Development* 32(4): 609–628.

Khanna, T. and K. Palepu (2000a). "Is Group Affiliation Profitable in Emerging Markets? An Analysis of Diversified Indian Business Groups," *Journal of Finance* 55(2): 867–893.

(2000b). "Emerging Market Business Groups, Foreign Investors, and Corporate Governance," in R. Morck (ed.), *Concentrated Corporate Ownership*. National Bureau of Economic Research Conference Report. University of Chicago Press, pp. 265–294.

(2005). "The Evolution of Concentrated Ownership in India: Broad Patterns and a History of the Indian Software Industry," in R. Morck (ed.), *The History of Corporate Governance around the World: Family Business Groups to Professional Managers*. University of Chicago Press, pp. 283–320.

Khanna, T. and Y. Yafeh (2007). "Business Groups in Emerging Markets: Paragons or Parasites?" *Journal of Economic Literature* 45(2): 331–372.

Kim, E. (2006). "The Impact of Family Ownership and Capital Structures on Productivity Performance of Korean Manufacturing Firms: Corporate Governance and the 'Chaebol Problem,'" *Journal of the Japanese and International Economies* 20(2): 209–233.

Kim, H. (2011). "Business Groups in South Korea," in Colpan *et al.*

King, R. and R. Levine (1993). "Finance and Growth: Schumpeter Might Be Right," *Quarterly Journal of Economics* 108: 717–737.

Kosenko, K. (2007). "Evolution of Business Groups in Israel: Their Impact at the Level of the Firm and the Economy," *Israel Economic Review* 5(2): 55–93.

Kosenko, K. and Y. P. Yafeh (2011). "Business Groups in Israel," in Colpan *et al.*

Krueger, A. O. (1974). "The Political Economy of the Rent-Seeking Society," *American Economic Review* 64: 13.

Kydland, F. and E. Prescott (1977). "Rules Rather than Discretion: The Inconsistency of Optimal Plans," *Journal of Political Economy* 85(3): 473–492.

La Porta, R. and F. Lopez-de-Silanes (1999). "The Benefits of Privatization: Evidence from México," *Quarterly Journal of Economics* 114(4): 1193–1242.

La Porta, R., F. Lopez-de-Silanes, and A. Shleifer (1999). "Corporate Ownership around the World," *Journal of Finance* 54(2): 471–517.

Lazonick, W. (2004). "The Innovative Firm," in J. Fagerberg, D. C. Mowery, and R. R. Nelson (eds.), *Oxford Handbook of Innovation*. Oxford University Press, pp. 29–55.

Leff, N. (1978). "Industrial Organization and Entrepreneurship in the Developing Countries: The Economic Groups," *Economic Development and Cultural Change* 26(4): 661–675.

Lim, W. and R. Morck (2013). "The Long Shadow of the Big Push," Alberta School of Business working paper. Edmonton: University of Alberta.

Mahoney, P. G. (2012). "The Public Utility Pyramids," *Journal of Legal Studies* 41: 37–66.

Masulis R., P. Pham, and J. Zein (2011). "Family Business Groups around the World: Costs and Benefits of Pyramids," *Review of Financial Studies* 24(11): 3556–3600.

Morck, R. (2005). "How to Eliminate Pyramidal Business Groups: The Double Taxation of Inter-corporate Dividends and Other Incisive Uses of Tax Policy," in J. Poterba (ed.), *Tax Policy and the Economy*. Vol. XIX. Cambridge, MA: The MIT Press, 135–179.

(2009). "The Riddle of the Great Pyramids," in A. Colpan and T. Hikino (eds.), *Oxford Handbook of Business Groups*. Oxford University Press.

(2011). "Finance and Governance in Developing Economics," *Annual Review of Financial Economics* 3: 375–406.

Morck, R. and M. Nakamura (2005). "A Frog in a Well Knows Nothing of the Ocean: A History of Corporate Ownership in Japan," in R. Morck (ed.), *A History of Corporate Governance around the World: Family Business Groups to Professional Managers*. University of Chicago Press, pp. 367–459.

(2007). "Business Groups and the Big Push: Meiji Japan's Mass Privatization and Subsequent Growth," *Enterprise and Society* 8(3): 543–601.

Morck, R., M. Percy, G. Tian, and B. Yeung (2005). "The Rise and Fall of the Widely Held Firm: A History of Corporate Ownership in Canada," in R. Morck (ed.), *A History of Corporate Governance around the World: Family Business Groups to Professional Managers*. University of Chicago Press, 65–140.

Morck, R., A. Shleifer, and R. Vishny (1988). "Management Ownership and Market Valuation: An Empirical Analysis," *Journal of Financial Economics* 20(1/2): 293–315.

Morck, R., D. Stangeland, and B. Yeung (2000). "Inherited Wealth, Corporate Control, and Economic Growth: The Canadian Disease?" in R. Morck (ed.), *Concentrated Corporate Ownership*. University of Chicago Press, 319–369.

Morck, R., D. Wolfenzon, and B. Yeung (2005). "Corporate Governance, Economic Entrenchment, and Growth," *Journal of Economic Literature* 43: 655–720.

Morck, R. and B. Yeung (2004). Family Control and the Rent-seeking Society. *Entrepreneurship: Theory and Practice* 28, 18.

(2009). "Never Waste a Good Crisis: An Historical Perspective on Comparative Corporate Governance," *Annual Review of Financial Economics* 1: 145–179.

Murphy, K. M., A. Shleifer, and R. Vishny (1989). "Industrialization and the Big Push," *Journal of Political Economy* 97(5): 1003–1026.

Ohkawa, K. and H. Rosovsky (1973). *Japanese Economic Growth Trend Acceleration in the Twentieth Century*. Oxford University Press

Olson, M. (1984). *The Rise and Decline of Nations*. New Haven, CT: Yale University Press.

Oster, S., M. Forsythe, N. Khan, D. Lawrence, and H. Sanderson (2012). "Heirs of Mao's Comrades Rise as New Capitalist Nobility," *Bloomberg News*, December 26, 2012 at www.bloomberg.com/news/2012-12-26/immortals-beget-china-capitalism-from-citic-to-godfather-of-golf.html.

Rajan, R. and L. Zingales (2003). "The Great Reversals: The Politics of Financial Development in the Twentieth Century," *Journal of Financial Economics* 69(1): 5–50.

(2004). *Saving Capitalism from the Capitalists: Unleashing the Power of Financial Markets to Create Wealth and Spread Opportunity*. Princeton University Press.

Rosenstein-Rodan, P. N. (1943). "Problems of Industrialisation of Eastern and South-Eastern Europe," *Economic Journal* 53: 202–211.

Sachs, J. and A. Warner (2001). "The Curse of Natural Resources," *European Economic Review* 45: 827–838.

Sarkar, J. (2011). "Business Groups in India," in Colpan *et al.*

Shiba, T. and M. Shimotani (1997). *Beyond the Firm: Business Groups in International and Historical Perspective*. Oxford and New York: Oxford University Press.

Shleifer, A. and R. Vishny (1993). "Corruption," *Quarterly Journal of Economics* 108(3): 599–617.

(1997). "A Survey of Corporate Governance," *Journal of Finance* 52(2): 737–783.

Stigler, G. J. (1971). "The Theory of Economic Regulation," *Bell Journal of Economics* 3: 3–18.

Stulz, R. M. (1988). "Managerial Control of Voting Rights: Financing Policies and the Market for Corporate Control," *Journal of Financial Economics* 20(1/2): 25–54.

Suehiro, A. and N. Wailerdsak (2011). "Business Groups in Thailand," in Colpan *et al.*

Tian, G. (2006). *Three Essays on Corporate Control in Canada*. University of Alberta doctoral thesis in finance.

Trujillo, M. A., A. Guzman, M. G. Ferrero, and C. P. Vejarano (2012). *Family Involvement and Dividend Policy in Listed and Non-Listed Firms*. Galeras de Administracion Facultad de Administracion Universidad de Los Andes.

Tsui-Auch, L. S., T. Yoshikawa (2011). "Business Groups in Singapore," in A. Colpan and T. Hikino (eds.), *Oxford Handbook of Business Groups*. Oxford University Press.

Weitz, J. (1997). *Hitler's Banker: Hjalmar Horace Greeley Schacht*. Boston, MA: Little, Brown.

Williamson, O. (1975). *Markets and Hierarchies*. New York: The Free Press.

8

Financial capitalism

RANALD MICHIE

Introduction

Through a combination of external forces and its inner dynamics financial capitalism has been transformed over the last 250 years. The death of distance through the revolution in communications has both intensified competition between financial centers, and integrated all those engaged in the provision of financial services into global networks. The growth and operation of multinational and multidivisional businesses have internalized functions once performed by banks and financial markets. Governments have molded the structure and composition of financial systems through laws and controls while both promoting and hindering the process of globalization. Financial capitalism has also constantly evolved. Though the basics of financial capitalism remain constant, the products and processes involved changed, as did the structures through which they were delivered and the controls they were subjected to. This inner dynamism of financial capitalism made it the dominant economic system in the nineteenth century and provided it with the resilience to cope with two world wars, a world economic crisis, and antagonistic governments in the twentieth century. However, this dynamism also created periodic bouts of speculative excesses and bank failures, as well as ongoing tensions between the providers and users of capital, while generating solutions to these problems. Financial capitalism constantlyreinvented itself with the result that there is no single type of financial capitalism, as it has adopted many different forms both over time and in different countries (see O'Rourke and Williamson, Chapter 1 in this volume).

Financial innovation

Central to financial capitalism is financial innovation. It is through innovation that financial capitalism responds to external challenges and opportunities while generating its inner dynamics. This innovation was not confined to new financial products, markets, and organizations but also extended to regulation. Underlying financial innovation was the attempt to improve the match between the opposing demands of lenders/borrowers and buyers/sellers so as to generate a profit for the intermediary. Lenders sought the highest rate of interest while borrowers demanded the lowest. Buyers looked for the lowest price while sellers searched for the highest. Though price was the key variable, there were others related to amount, type, location, and time. The process of financial innovation could involve all five of these variables or simply one. Whatever the cause or focus of financial innovation, it involved four basic forms, namely product, market, organization, and regulation. Product innovation was the design of a financial instrument to meet a specific need. Market innovation was the creation of a trading system through which these financial products could be bought and sold. Organizational innovation involved the grouping of separate financial activities together in such a way as to be greater than the sum of their parts. Regulatory innovation was a response to the need to reduce the risks involved and so increase the use made of the product, market, or organization. None of these innovations occurred in isolation but as components of an evolving financial system. Each was designed to meet a precise need and so was dependent upon the financial system already in existence and, in turn, was influential in determining its future direction and shape.

Despite financial innovation possessing a long pedigree, major advances were made during the nineteenth century, generated by a vast increase in both wealth and trade. This was especially in terms of the use made of financial products, the sophistication of financial markets, the role and importance of financial organizations, and the progress made in self-regulation. This dynamic period for financial innovation was brought to an abrupt end in 1914. During the two world wars, the operation of financial markets was subjected to a high degree of government intervention to ensure that all national resources were directed to the single object of achieving victory. Between the wars, many banks ended up under state control, having been brought to actual or near collapse because of the fragile economic conditions, while international financial transactions were greatly restricted as governments sought to limit the contagion created by financial and monetary instability. Even after 1945, the process of financial innovation remained subdued for the next twenty-five years because of government prohibitions and restrictions on those financial products, markets, or organizations believed to be responsible for past economic chaos. Nevertheless, both before and after World War II, financial innovation continued to take place driven by the need to cope with instability or evade government controls. From the mid 1970s onwards, financial innovation flourished once again in an era when governments relaxed or abolished controls. The Global Financial Crisis of 2007/2008 can thus be seen as the first serious interruption to the new age of financial capitalism (Rajan and Zingales 2003).

Financial innovation tends to be generated in a small number of financial centers. Trading in money, securities, derivatives, and foreign exchange clusters in a small number of centers possessing the densest markets, as it was there that global reference prices were constantly being set. Even the smallest advantage to be gained in terms of access to the market or receipt of news is of value in the race to be the first to profit from rapidly changing buying and selling opportunities. It was also only in a very few locations that the range and depth of talent existed to devise highly sophisticated financial products or arrange and manage complex deals and businesses. To undertake these financial activities required regular and intense personal interaction among people who knew and trusted each other. However, in opposition to these centripetal forces that attracted financial activity to centers such as London and New York, the very cost of doing business there, whether measured by salaries or office rents, created centrifugal forces, which drove financial activity to cheaper locations. Though the combination of centripetal and centrifugal forces produced a constant reordering of the location of financial activity, the overall effect was to integrate all into a global network, unless prevented by government-imposed barriers (Carlos and Neal 2011; Cassis 2006). One effect of this combination of clustering and integration was to identify financial capitalism with a very few global cities, particularly the financial districts located in the heart of London (the City) and New York (Wall Street). The result of this physical clustering was to make financial capitalism remote from most people (Von Peter 2007).

Aiding that perception was financial innovation itself. This created products that the public could not understand which were then traded in markets where the turnover was beyond human comprehension. In the global financial crisis of 2008 the causes were believed by many to lie in the introduction of a bewildering array of complex financial derivatives. In the wake of that collapse, the costs and benefits of financial innovation were widely debated. In the debate led by two eminent US economists, the majority opinion sided with Joseph Stiglitz, who argued against financial innovation because of the risks it posed, rather than Ross Levine, who stressed the positive contribution it made (see the debate on financial innovation in *The Economist* between February 23,

2011 and March 5, 2011). In all areas of innovation, progress is made through a continuous process of trial and error, involving both success and failure. Over time ways have been devised to test the results of innovation in medicine, science, and technology before they are generally applied, though not all risks can be eliminated. However, in the case of financial innovation no such tests are available. For financial innovation, the choice remains one of either preventing it taking place or allowing its introduction and awaiting its consequences. The problem here is that, given the dynamic nature of financial capitalism, restrictions placed on one type of financial innovation have a displacement effect. If blocked, financial innovation will change direction and shape so as to bypass any obstacles placed in its way. This may result in a financial system that is neither as efficient nor as stable as the one that would have evolved if no intervention had taken place. As no financial system is free from intervention, not only from governments but also from those controlling banks and markets, it is almost impossible to reach a definite conclusion on whether the eventual outcome is the best possible one. All outcomes are sub-optimal because all reflect the influence of those who want to promote their own interests and restrict those of others (Beck *et al.* 2012).

Financial products

One of the earliest financial products devised was the bill of exchange. It simultaneously provided temporary credit and a means of making payments. The huge expansion of international trade in the nineteenth century relied upon the use of bills of exchange redeemable ninety days after issue. During and after World War I, commercial bills faced great competition from the treasury bills issued by the UK government to finance its military expenditure. Finally, in the 1930s the collapse in world trade, and the restrictions placed on access to foreign currency, largely killed off the commercial bill, and it never revived after World War II. Instead, it was US treasury bills that became the most popular short-term financial instrument in use. Short-term bills allowed governments to bridge the gap between expenditure, which was often continuous throughout the year, and income, which varied from month to month due to when taxes were paid. To replace commercial bills, business relied increasingly on short-term credit provided directly by banks. The growing scale of the business corporation after 1945 also allowed much short-term financing to be internalized. By the twenty-first century, an estimated one-third of world trade took place between the subsidiaries of multinational corporations.

New financial products were also devised in the nineteenth century to exploit the fact that information, beginning with the telegraph, flowed faster than physical trade. The result in commercial centers such as Chicago for wheat and Liverpool for cotton was the emergence of standard contracts that allowed buyers and sellers to cover their exposure to fluctuations in supply and demand and the impact these had on prices. Such contracts provided a high degree of certainty to those businesses reliant on producing commodities for the world market, encouraging them to invest so as to expand output. Major consumers of these products also gained from this certainty of supply and price and so, likewise, they could scale up their operations. These contracts were of two kinds. One was an option to buy or sell a fixed amount at a fixed price at a fixed date in the future. These could be allowed to lapse if not required. The other was a futures contract that offered the same guarantees but had to be exercised, though it could be closed by purchasing a reverse contract at the required time.

Though regarded as little more than speculative counters, these option and future contracts played a vital role in reducing the risks associated with business, especially those involving interregional and international trade. The result was a huge expansion in the volume of trade that took place both within and between countries before 1914. In the economically troubled interwar years, governments intervened to stabilize prices and even provide guarantees to producers. This continued after World War II, building on the experience that governments had gained managing production and distribution. However, from the 1970s onwards, governments were unable to maintain either stable prices or fixed exchange rates and this generated a demand for new contracts that would reduce exposure to the risks caused by volatility. Many of these were created in Chicago based on experience in the commodity trade. Such was the success of these contracts that they fostered a belief that all risks could be calculated and a financial instrument devised that would eliminate them. The result was the growing reliance upon complex mathematical formulas to underpin new financial instruments whose properties were poorly understood by those buying and selling them. It was those products that were exposed in the global financial crisis of 2007/2008, with a number proving deficient.

One reason for the high degree of trust placed in new financial instruments prior to the global financial crisis was the success of stocks and bonds. Bonds represented a long-term loan on which interest was paid and was normally repayable on a stated date in the future. Stocks represented a permanent stake in a business and on which dividends were paid if profits were generated. By issuing securities such as stocks or bonds, the vendor obtained funds for immediate use in return for future payments. By buying such securities, the purchaser received a promise of future payment incorporating interest and repayment in the case of a bond, or dividends and capital gain in the case of stocks. The advantages of securities over a direct loan or a stake in a business were *divisibility* and *transferability*. Divisibility expanded the absolute amount that could be raised at any one time, through the ability to access the pool of passive investors. Divisibility also mobilized funds for high-risk ventures through the ability to spread the investment among numerous individuals. Transferability changed the time horizon associated with an investment, as repayment was replaced by regular interest payments or a share in annual profits. This encouraged long-term investment. Transferability also permitted a better matching between investor and investment, as investors could exit or enter according to personal preferences and changing circumstances. This lowered the cost of capital. Transferability of stocks also meant that control of a business was divorced from the way it was financed. This permitted the employment of professional management and eased the creation of new business units, whether through mergers or subdivisions. The combination of divisibility and transferability also meant that these securities generated constantly changing prices which transmitted important signals to investors and the wider financial community. Finally, the divisibility and transferability that securities possessed made them highly flexible financial instruments, as ownership could be easily changed both over time and between countries, without affecting the management and operation of a business.

What was to make securities central to financial capitalism was the growing importance of the joint-stock company (see Jones, Chapter 6 in this volume) It was in the nineteenth century that joint-stock companies began to play a central role in economic activity. The major breakthrough came with the railways, as their scale required both a huge investment of capital and the services of an extended managerial hierarchy. Railways could not be built incrementally, as an entire system needed to be in place for any single component to be viable, unless it was the short connection between a mine and a port because of the constant freight traffic carried. Operating a railway system was also highly complex and required a large and diverse staff that had to be actively managed. To raise the capital and manage the business, railways drew on the precedents set by governments and the early forms of joint-stock business organization. Railways copied governments by issuing bonds and earlier joint-stock companies in issuing stocks. With the addition of limited liability, those who bought the stocks issued by these railway companies acquired the right to control the management and share in any profits, in proportion to the investment made, but escaped the obligation to meet any losses beyond the stock that they held. What corporate enterprise brought to business was extended longevity for success, and growth was no longer dependent on a single person or even family but on the collective input of numerous investors and managers from one generation to the next. This did not mean that any single business now enjoyed a permanent existence and immunity from competition. Instead, a business organized as a joint-stock company could metamorphose over time in response to challenges and opportunities, rather than simply disappear and be replaced by another.

The relationship between corporate capitalism and financial capitalism was not always a supportive one, as the two parties involved had competing objectives. In corporate capitalism, the company was center stage with everything directed towards furthering its success. In financial capitalism it was the investment that was center stage, with everything directed towards maximizing the returns obtained. Though the two objectives had much in common, they were not always perfectly aligned when ownership and management were split. Those owning stocks had to weigh up such considerations as the need to reduce risks by rebalancing a portfolio, the opportunity to make alternative investments, or the requirement to access funds to meet repayment commitments. In contrast, those managing a company were driven by such desires as personal gain, beating competitors, or responding to public pressure. What intensified the conflict between the two groups in the twentieth century, and especially after 1945, was the changing nature of corporate capitalism and the switch from investors holding bonds to owning stocks. When the typical company was a railway or a utility, as it was before 1914, the difference between owning stocks or bonds was limited. Each tended to generate a steady return because of the nature of the business, while changes in control were rare as each operated largely as a monopoly.

That was to change markedly after 1950, beginning in the United States and the United Kingdom, as institutional investors chose to invest increasingly in corporate stocks as a way of generating returns that kept pace with inflation. That had not been a concern earlier because prices had fallen for much of the half-century before World War I and was only in limited evidence between the wars as the individual ownership of stocks was still widespread. In contrast, the years after World War II saw a steady build-up in inflation, which eroded the real value of fixed interest investments like corporate bonds. In contrast, the ability of companies to pass on price rises to customers meant that they could increase their profits and so deliver higher payouts to stockholders. A strong two-way relationship then developed in which a growing appetite among institutional investors for corporate stocks encouraged the conversion of businesses into joint-stock companies. Taxation also favored this trend. High levels of personal taxation encouraged investors to channel their savings through financial institutions which were able to utilize tax breaks and exemptions. In turn, these financial institutions favored the stocks of large companies, as these were better able to smooth out fluctuations in dividend payments than smaller companies. That provided institutional investors with a steady but growing income, so placing them in the position of being better able to meet future insurance and pension payments. It also encouraged mergers and acquisitions among companies as there was now a premium attached to size. From that emerged the battles for corporate control that became such a feature of the post-World War II world in the United States and the United Kingdom in the 1950s and 1960s and then spread worldwide in the late twentieth and early twenty-first centuries (Jones 2005).

As early as the 1930s, this divorce between ownership and control had been identified by John Maynard Keynes in his General Theory as creating problems for business (Keynes 1936). With ownership of large companies increasingly concentrated in the hands of a small number of financial institutions, collectively managing the savings of millions, it became easier to mount successful takeover bids as the calculation of whether to sell out was one based on financial returns. The behavior of stockholders thus became similar to bondholders whose commitment had always been a financial one. One consequence of this was to make managements very focussed on delivering regular returns rather than building up a business that would succeed in the long run. Such a position worked well in the case of railways and utilities, as these required care and maintenance rather than risk taking and vision, and also applied to many other areas of business that were converted into joint-stock companies after 1945. However, there were also types of business that required managers and owners to share a common purpose if it was to succeed, as was the case with the long-term development of a new technology or service. In those cases the separation of owners and managers could be detrimental if both were not equally familiar with the nature of the business and did not share the same time horizon.

It is for that reason that the relationship between financial capitalism and corporate capitalism has varied both over time and between countries. The continuous search for attractive investments has encouraged the conversion of businesses into joint-stock companies but not all of these have been successful because of the mismatch between the objectives of the owners of the stock and the managers. Financial capitalism of the type identified with joint-stock companies has shown itself ideal for certain types of economic activity, especially those where scale was of major importance, as in financial and retailing services, as well as those able to offer relatively predictable returns, as with many regulated services. It also suited the needs of many high-risk activities such as mining, where risks could be spread over many investors. In contrast, joint-stock companies have been found not to be ideal where a strong and continuous bond between owners and managers was necessary for success and where there were few benefits to be derived from scale. It is also recognized that the principal sources of long-term business finance were reinvested earnings, not issues of stocks and bonds.

Financial markets

Unlike stocks and bonds, many financial products did not require an organized market where they were actively bought and sold. This was the case when trading took place between a few counterparties, who either dealt directly with each other or through trusted intermediaries. One such market was the money market which, in the nineteenth century, largely dealt in bills of exchange. Once a bill of exchange was made transferable, it could be traded many times until it was redeemed. As such it provided a convenient investment for those with temporarily idle funds as well as collateral to support lending and borrowing. For these reasons, bills of exchange were used extensively by banks to either borrow from or lend to each other. When a bank sold a bill it was borrowing and when it bought one it was lending. Banks constantly faced positions in which they were temporarily short of funds to lend to customers or possessed surplus funds for which they had no immediate use. The existence of an interbank market allowed banks to make up the shortfall or employ the excess without the need to keep a large balance idle in case of withdrawals or borrowing requests. As such, it simultaneously maximized the supply of credit while increasing stability, as temporary funds could be easily and quickly accessed in a liquidity crisis. Conversely, the existence of the interbank market tempted banks to finance long-term lending through short-term borrowing from other banks, and so increase profitability. In the event of those short-term loans not being renewed or replaced, the bank faced a liquidity crisis that would force it to suspend doing business. In turn, the collapse of a single bank could spread fear throughout the interbank market, leading it to freeze, creating a liquidity crisis, with severe consequences for the entire financial system.

In the nineteenth century, London developed rapidly as the world's most important money market, attracting banks from all over the world to either open offices or authorize banks already established there to operate on their behalf (Furniss 1922). This market survived World War I, as the disappearance of the commercial bill coincided with the rise of the UK treasury bill, which fulfilled the same role. Nevertheless, the war did create opportunities for other money markets to grow, as in New York, where there had long existed one based on short-term borrowing from banks by members of the New York Stock Exchange with securities as collateral. New York thus attracted bank connections from around the world wanting to make use of its market. The only new risk to these international money markets was currency fluctuations, and this was met by the development of an almost entirely new interbank market, namely that for foreign exchange. In this market the UK pound and the US dollar were the main currencies traded, as this allowed banks to cover their exposure to exchange risks. In this way, financial markets provided a solution to the collapse of the fixed exchange rate era that had prevailed before World War I, under the gold standard (see James, Chapter 9 in this volume). Both the interbank money and foreign exchange markets were then rendered almost obsolete during World War II, as governments stepped in to control both domestic and international financial flows in the interests of a wartime economy. Nor did these markets rapidly revive after World War II, as governments, often operating through central banks, continued to exercise strong controls over both money and foreign exchange as they pursued national objectives.

Such was the value of money and foreign exchange markets to the international banking community that they did begin to recover in the 1950s despite the controls imposed by governments, especially those of the US government on the interest that could be paid on deposits. Once again, financial innovation came to the fore. The development of the Eurodollar market in London provided a forum in which banks could borrow from and lend to each other on the basis of US dollars, the international currency of choice, but bypass New York. Another was the emergence of Hong Kong as an international financial center, as it could provide a forum for trading the UK pound against the US dollar, and so evade UK exchange controls. With the collapse of the era of fixed exchange rates in the 1970s, international money and foreign exchange markets regained their importance, especially those for foreign exchange and the interbank money market.

Whereas the interbank markets operated on the basis of trust between a few participants, some financial products were of a bespoke nature, being used to solve a particular problem, and so did not require a market of any kind. These included a large number of derivative contracts as well as securities held to maturity. However, there was always an incentive to create standardized products which could be easily bought and sold, as these attracted interest from investors who valued them solely for the returns they could generate. This meant that the existence of a market was essential if these standardized financial products, whether securities or derivative contracts, were to have a value greater than the assets or income stream they represented. Those who bought securities, particularly, expected to be able to sell them if required, and that required a market in which they could be easily, quickly, and cheaply traded. This made securities and the market in which they were traded highly interdependent, with the growth in the use of the former being dependent upon the development of the latter. By World War I, these markets were provided by the stock exchanges that were to be found in every major city in the world. Most of these provided a market for the stocks of local companies, as these were largely held by local investors. A few of these stock exchanges attracted international interest, as with Johannesburg for gold mining stocks. Finally, a few became regional hubs, as New York did for North America, while London and Paris played a global role because British and French investors had such extensive holdings of foreign stocks and bonds (see O'Rourke and Williamson, Chapter 1 and James, Chapter 9 in this volume).

These stock exchanges made an essential contribution to the increasing use made of securities in advanced economies over the course of the nineteenth century. To explain this, it must be recognized that securities markets served two masters. On the one hand, they provided a market for those who issued securities, whether they were governments or business. On the other hand, securities markets served those who bought and sold securities once they had been issued. This meant that securities possessed a life independent from that which had led to their creation. By providing an interface between borrowers and lenders and between credit and capital, the securities market ensured that the needs of all could be met in a way that maximized the returns on savings and minimized the risks involved. The securities market imparted flexibility and mobility to the operations of banks, businesses, and individual investors, for they could employ temporarily idle funds in holding securities or switch the ownership of such assets at will. Increasingly, for example, the existence of an active market for securities became an essential tool in the way that banks balanced assets and liabilities while maximizing the use they made of their capital and deposits.

This transferability of ownership also lent itself to market manipulation, while the constant fluctuation of stock prices induced short-term horizons among management as they strove to produce immediate returns, and so avoid a predatory takeover, rather than devising a long-term business strategy. This trading of stocks could also degenerate into a speculative frenzy, where values became divorced from the underlying reality regarding the prospects for future growth. The outcome was windfall gains for the lucky few, but the loss of savings for the many, accompanied by the destabilization of the financial system and the distortion of financial flows, none of which was conducive to the finance of long-term economic growth. It is these negative aspects of securities markets that have helped fuel criticism of financial capitalism among economists such as Robert Schiller (Schiller 2000). However, the existence of an active securities market did contribute to the increasing stability of financial systems, as they permitted a continuous adjustment of positions. In a speculative bubble, investors increasingly bought illiquid assets as prices rose because these offered the most attractive returns while cheap credit was available to finance their purchase. Conversely, when the bubble burst and prices fell, investors sold the most liquid assets to repay loans, because they were the ones that could be disposed of. Securities with liquid markets were the shock absorbers of the financial system, but were perceived to be the causes of financial crises as their rising and falling prices were the most visible. In contrast, it was the legacy of physical property that could not be sold, because of the lack of an active market, which lay behind the financial problems left in the wake of a financial crisis (Reinhart and Rogoff 2009).

The unstoppable advance of stock exchanges from the mid nineteenth century onwards was brought to an abrupt end by World War I, as virtually all of them were closed within days of the outbreak of hostilities. Without closure the dramatic collapse in prices would have bankrupted many of the members of the exchanges and, in turn, would have brought down banks that had lent them money with securities as collateral. Some of these stock exchanges never reopened, as in Russia, while for others the conditions under which they operated were radically different after the war. Those in Germany had to cope with postwar hyperinflation, while those in the United States were now located in the wealthiest economy in the world, and so boomed as a result. For all stock exchanges, however, the 1920s proved a difficult period, as they all had to cope with much greater financial and monetary instability as a legacy of the war. Out of this instability was born the speculative boom in the United States that eventually culminated in the Wall Street Crash of 1929. In its aftermath, stock exchanges were subjected to closure or control, and that was completed during World War II and the immediate postwar years. Even where stock exchanges still operated, as in Western Europe, the nationalization of so many companies and the defaults by so many governments on their debts deprived the remaining stock exchanges of the business that had once taken place on their trading floors. Even in the United States, which was relatively immune from either nationalization or defaults, the controls imposed in the 1930s remained and so restricted the operations of stock exchanges.

It was not until the 1970s that stock exchanges began to recover the position they had once occupied. Beginning in the United States and then spreading across Western Europe and finally reaching Japan, the controls imposed on stock exchanges were relaxed, allowing them to flourish as active securities markets. Coinciding with growing investor interest in corporate stocks, this made stock exchanges once again an important feature of financial capitalism. In addition, the collapse of centrally planned economies created a need for stock exchanges in which the stocks issued by state enterprises, after conversion into companies, could be traded. Finally, emerging economies also embraced the idea of corporate capitalism and so required stock exchanges. The result was an explosion of stock exchange formation in the late twentieth century, along with greatly increased trading activity. Speculative bubbles even reappeared, as with the Dot.com boom around 2000.

However, this flourish in new stock exchange formation also coincided with the disappearance of many long-established ones. The dominance of business by large companies and the dominance of investment by institutions had the effect of concentrating trading on a single national exchange, so removing the need for local ones. The same phenomenon was also beginning to appear between countries, as with the formation of Euronext, as that combined the exchanges of France, Belgium, Portugal, and the Netherlands. In turn, Euronext merged with the New York Stock Exchange. Thus, over the course of the last 250 years the world has moved from a position at the beginning in which stock exchanges hardly existed to a peak in numbers and importance on the eve of World War I to one today where only a few exist. Standardized contracts were also created for a small number of commodities, such as coffee, cotton, wheat, copper, and later oil, that led to the formation of exchanges, as with the London Metal Exchange. Though initially these exchanges arranged for physical delivery of commodities, increasingly they existed to produce reference pricing for numerous related products. Some, like the Chicago Mercantile Exchange, reinvented themselves as markets for complex financial derivatives, such as those based on exchange rates, interest rates, and stock indexes. For that reason there was a steady convergence among exchanges in the late twentieth and early twenty-first centuries so that a single institution covered the whole range of those financial products that were most actively traded.

The value of the market provided by exchanges was made apparent during the global financial crisis of 2008. Prior to that crisis, mortgage and other loans had been repackaged as securities, which were then sold to investors, so increasing the supply of funds available to finance the purchase of houses, automobiles, and other products. This was made possible because those who bought these securities wanted an investment which could be subsequently bought and sold, rather than commit themselves to making a long-term loan. What had been omitted in this process was the need to create a public market in which these securities could always be bought and sold. As a result, the subsequent marketability of these securities was dependent upon the willingness of the investment bank that had issued them to ensure that they could be sold when required. This worked well when demand was buoyant and the value of such securities was not in doubt, but lacked the resilience found in exchanges. What happened in the global financial crisis was that these securities could neither be sold nor valued, converting them back into illiquid long-term loans. The effect was to magnify the crisis, as the creation of such products had generated a belief that a way had been found to match the supply of short-term credit to the demand for long-term finance while eliminating the risks such a process normally involved. One way that risk had been reduced in the past was the formation of exchanges on which such products were constantly bought and sold at prices that were known to all.

Financial organizations

The most important organizational innovation in finance was the bank. A bank is a financial intermediary whereas a moneylender is a capitalist. The essence of a bank is that it employs the savings of others when lending to borrowers. The bank obtained these savings in two ways. It could attract deposits by promising to pay interest or by exchanging them for notes that could be used as a convenient means of payment. Successful banking thus involves a constant compromise between the opposing needs of savers and borrowers. Savers want low-risk products that could be instantly converted into cash but yield a high rate of return. Borrowers want long-term loans at low rates of interest. A balance must always be struck between the two, which also generates sufficient income for banks to cover their costs, particularly staff remuneration, and pay out profits to their owners, whether partners or investors. Doing so involved a degree of risk. Default was always possible on a loan, making the bank insolvent, as its liabilities to depositors were now greater than the assets it possessed. Conversely, the demand by savers to withdraw their deposits could exceed the funds currently available, making the bank illiquid. It was thus vital for a bank to maintain the trust of those who deposited money with it or used the notes it issued. Otherwise the depositors would rush to withdraw their savings and those holding its notes would convert them into another currency. For that reason, a bank had to operate in such a way that it could meet withdrawals and conversions. That required it to have capital of its own, which could be called on to meet losses, and so always remain solvent, and to balance its assets and liabilities in such a way as to be always able to meet withdrawals, and so remain liquid.

During the nineteenth century, banking moved from being the preserve of the individual banker to become a business undertaken by large companies that employed numerous highly trained staff and were linked together through extensive branch or correspondent networks. Increasingly, the individual banker operating alone or in a partnership was relegated to niche areas, such as investment banking, or continued to be found only in less economically advanced areas, such as inland parts of India and China. This did not mean that all banking was the same. The degree to which earlier forms of banking survived, the intervention of governments, and the interaction with other components of the financial system, along with the nature of the demand for specialist services, combined to ensure that a wide variety of banks existed. Though expatriate Europeans formed banks to operate across Africa and Asia, these exhibited marked differences between the practices followed back in countries such as the United Kingdom and France, as success depended upon adapting to local conditions. The banks formed by expatriates focussed on meeting the short- and long-term needs of colonial governments, expatriate businesses, and international trade, while native bankers serviced the requirements of the local population for short-term credit. This was to pose problems after the end of colonial rule, for expatriate banks had to reorientate themselves to meet the needs of the whole population and independent governments, as was the case in both Ghana and India (Jones 1991).

In contrast, where European migrants dominated the economy, as in Australia, Argentina, Brazil, Canada, New Zealand, and even South Africa, there was little in the way of traditional banking and so the form it took was very similar to what was developing in Europe at this time. One exception to that was the United States, which developed its own unique form of banking in the nineteenth century, largely molded by national legislation passed in the 1860s. This legislation reflected the enduring tensions between the individual states and the Federal authorities since independence in 1783. The main effect of this legislation on the structure of US banking was to prevent the formation of nationwide banking companies. Whereas Canadian banking was dominated by a small number of large joint-stock banks with head offices in such centers as Montreal and Toronto, the United States remained a country of thousands of small banks that were locally owned and conducted a local business.

While noting the exception of US experience during the nineteenth century, two main models of banking emerged. One was the creation of banks that spread risk through the use of extensive branch networks. By focussing on collecting deposits from numerous savers and short-term lending to numerous borrowers, such banks avoided excessive risk taking. At the same time, experience taught those running them how best to monitor the activity taking place in the branches and to balance assets and liabilities. Such banks could distribute funds internally to meet demand, and so minimize the risks that could come from a liquidity crisis, though also exposing themselves to problems occurring in any of their branches. These banks became very stable and so were able to economize on the capital and deposits they had to keep available to meet sudden withdrawals or defaults (Grossman 2010). Though largely associated with the United Kingdom, banks of this kind were found throughout the world. The conservative nature of the branch banking model did create opportunities for other financial intermediaries to develop in order to meet the areas they neglected at both ends of the spectrum. Savings and mortgage banks offered more attractive rates of interest to long-term savers and lent the funds to governments and property owners. Investment banks specialized in issuing securities on behalf of governments and companies, selling them to investors, and then handling subsequent trading in the market.

The other model that developed from the mid nineteenth century onwards, especially in continental Europe, was that of the universal bank. A universal bank offered the full range of financial services, ranging from collecting deposits and providing short-term loans to making long-term investments and issuing and trading securities. The demand for such banks was greatest in countries that were rapidly industrializing but lacked the accumulated savings within the business community to finance major investment in mining and manufacturing. Hence the importance of such banks in Germany, Switzerland, Austria, Italy, and also Russia in the second half of the nineteenth century. Long-term investment exposed a universal bank to liquidity problems if deposits were suddenly withdrawn. In response universal banks maintained large capital reserves, restricted long-term investment to a few carefully monitored high-quality borrowers, and held a portfolio of securities that could be sold if required. Nevertheless, even these universal banks did not dominate all financial activity in the countries in which they operated. With few branches, for example, such banks lacked a retail network and so relied on a large number of locally based banks to provide them with deposits and generate business.

Though two distinctive models of banking did develop in the century before 1914, the position was somewhat fluid. Financial crises encouraged universal banks to adopt a more risk-averse lending policy and to open branches as a way of engaging more directly with customers. In contrast, branch banks sought to expand the range of business they conducted by engaging in longer-term lending, which was more profitable. The result was an increasing convergence between the branch banking model and the universal banking one before 1914, as was evident in both Germany and Britain (Fohlin 2007). The one unique development that did take place in banking before 1914, that was to become of major significance during the course of the twentieth century, was the emergence of highly specialized investment banks in the United States. The restrictions placed on branch banking in the United States kept the size of US banks small, even those based in New York. This meant that it was difficult for these banks to provide the finance required by large businesses. Though a number of the New York banks did move towards the universal banking model before 1914, as was the case with National City Bank, this was not as easy as in Germany because, unlike in that country, US stock exchanges denied joint-stock banks direct access to their trading floors. Thus it was not possible to create a joint-stock bank in the United States that covered the entire field from collecting deposits to trading securities. However, the New York Stock Exchange did permit partnerships to become members, such as J. P. Morgan, which remained privately owned. However, as they could not become companies, and thus match the scale of a universal bank like Deutsche Bank, they specialized in the issuing, retailing, and trading in stocks and bonds, though also accepting deposits and making loans (Carosso 1970). As British merchant banks, also organized as partnerships, were denied stock exchange membership, they could not trade securities. Instead, they concentrated on issuing stocks and bonds and left the retail side to those banks with extensive branch networks. A slightly different pattern also developed in France, where the Paris Hautes Banques could actively participate in the large securities market that operated outside the jurisdiction of the Paris Bourse, but they faced competition from a number of French universal banks.

It was World War I and subsequent events that were to make the US investment bank the most visible symbol of financial capitalism. The two world wars considerably diminished the importance of all European banks. Prior to 1914, Western Europe was the principal source of international finance but by the end of World War II it had become considerably impoverished compared to the United States. The result was to undermine the international role of European banks, while events in the United States cemented the position of the New York investment banks. During the 1920s, US deposit banks had built up an investment banking business in response to growing demand from US investors for stocks and bonds. Their appetite for securities had been fuelled by the huge debt issues made by governments, including their own, during the war. In the 1920s, the US government began to pay off its debts, while low interest rates and economic prosperity fuelled a rising stock market. That ended with the Wall Street Crash of 1929 and the US banking crisis of the early 1930s. The response of the US government was to impose further restrictions on US banks, including the separation of deposit and investment banking with the Glass-Steagall Act of 1933. Though that legislation forced J. P. Morgan to choose commercial over investment banking in 1934, it left the remaining Wall Street investment banks as masters in their own field.

After World War II conditions gradually favored the US investment banks, leaving them without peer in the world. Rising inflation turned investors, both individual and institutional, towards assets that would maintain their value in real terms over time, and US corporate stocks offered that possibility as their price was linked to the ability of businesses to grow their earnings. Thus the services of investment banks were in growing demand, both from investors wanting to buy stocks and companies wishing to issue them. With US deposit banks blocked from entering this field it was left to the New York investment to exploit, using their freedom to open branches nationwide and membership of stock exchanges. Finally, two constraints were removed that had limited the further growth of investment banks. One was the relaxation by the New York Stock Exchange on corporate membership, so allowing investment banks to convert into joint-stock companies. The other happened in 1975 when the New York Stock Exchange ended the rule that forced members to charge minimum commissions. When that was done the largest Wall Street investment banks were able to compete aggressively for the available business using their scale and nationwide reach to undercut their rivals. The result was the emergence of a small number of New York investment banks, namely Merrill Lynch, Morgan Stanley, Lehman Brothers, and Goldman Sachs.

What brought these banks onto the world stage was the combination of the removal of barriers between countries and internal deregulation of financial activity after the 1970s. Throughout the world, exchange and other controls were removed, so allowing the creation of global money and capital markets. In addition, national governments ended the protection given to national stock exchanges that had allowed them to exclude US investment banks from membership. Britain abandoned exchange controls in 1979 and the London Stock Exchange ended its restrictions on membership in 1986, so opening up London, the second most important financial center in the world, to the full force of competition from Wall Street investment banks. Others were soon to follow. The consequence was that these US investment banks were able to replicate their US model internationally, offering their brand of financial capitalism to companies throughout the world. The privatization of state assets from the 1980s onwards, and their replacement with corporate enterprise, created a booming global demand for the services of these US investment banks, whether it involved investment decisions, trading stocks and bonds, mergers and acquisitions, or providing governments and business with imaginative solutions to problems of finance. In this they faced limited competition. New York investment banks had the inbuilt advantage of being based in the United States, which was the location for so many of the world's major companies, the greatest number of investors, the most active stock markets, and the dominant international currency. This generated a huge amount of domestic business that stimulated financial innovation and placed these investment banks at the forefront of the business they were conducting.

However, the direction of travel among the world's banks was not towards specialist institutions like these Wall Street investment banks. Instead, it involved the convergence of the branch banking and universal banking models, as had been the case before World War I and was again evident in both Western Europe and Japan after World War II. Events between the wars had cast doubt on the viability of the universal banking model because of its exposure to corporate failure. Both in the 1920s and, especially, in the early 1930s, banking systems where universal banking prevailed had to be rescued through government intervention, as in Germany, Austria, and Italy. The US model of unitary banks had also proved highly vulnerable to collapse and, again, was only saved by the government, and the introduction of deposit insurance accompanied by further restrictions on competition. In contrast, the branch banking model had proved itself resilient. However, the events between 1914 and 1945 were very peculiar, involving two world wars with devastating consequences and an economic collapse of unparalleled magnitude between 1929 and 1932. In the more settled conditions that followed World War II, universal banking was, once again, able to re-emerge as a model that delivered benefits and could cope with risks. In contrast, the branch banking model was deemed to be overly risk averse as it focussed on short-term lending to business. As a result, universal banks grew by expanding their branch network and branch banks grew by expanding the variety of business that they did.

Even in the United States, the forces leading to a convergence of financial activity within a single bank had an impact, forcing the relaxation and then the abolition of the restrictions placed on both branch banking and the separation of deposit and investment banking operations in the 1990s. This convergence was taking place throughout the world. The growing size of business enterprise, with joint-stock companies becoming increasingly dominant, forced banks to also grow in scale if they were to provide the financial services now required. A similar development was taking place with the growing importance of institutions that managed savings and investment on a collective basis, as they also required banks to be bigger and more diversified. Finally, the emergence of an increasingly integrated global economy drove banks to expand internationally, not only to participate in the new opportunities but also to protect the business they did domestically from those who had access to a wider range of services.

The banking crisis that took place globally over the years between 2007 and 2009 has suggested to some that the trend towards a few universal banks created a less resilient financial system (Haldane and May 2011). Hence the intervention of governments to prevent the collapse of major banks because of the threat that posed for entire national financial systems. From a longer term perspective, what is evident is that banking has long been in a state of flux. At times circumstances favored a branch banking model, while at others universal banking appeared to offer the greatest advantages. In the period before World War I, banks of all kinds evolved in different ways, but each type worked out a model for itself that proved reasonably resilient in the face of financial crisis. There was also a process of convergence at work. All banks then faced testing times between 1914 and 1945. Following World War II, banks were closely monitored by national governments and operated in an environment largely free from financial crises. Following the global financial crisis of the 1970s, banks have had the opportunity to evolve under more market-oriented conditions. It was this evolving banking system that was severely tested in the global financial crisis of 2007/2008 and found wanting in a number of respects. The exposure of the flaws in a number of banking systems does not necessitate a return to some golden age of banking, as no such time existed. Instead, the necessity is for banking to move on, having learnt the lessons of the crisis it has passed through.

Financial regulation

Almost from the inception of financial innovation in products, markets, and organization, attempts were made to minimize the risks that they posed for all users. These risks were often beyond what could be covered by national legal systems. In terms of financial products there were risks associated with both design and sale, and the one guarantee that many buyers of financial products valued was the reputation of those who provided them with the product or service, such as the name of the banker. What changed in the nineteenth century was the appearance of banking, insurance, and other financial companies that were large, stable, and permanent. Companies of this kind became trusted and so had reputations to lose if they defaulted on payments. This made them behave more conservatively over time, which was bad for product innovation. However, as long as barriers to entry were low, this left scope for newer and more innovative rivals. The result was a combination of conservative and competitive behavior that simultaneously emphasized both stability and innovation.

One way in which this balance was maintained was the growing importance of gatekeepers (Coffee 2006). Gatekeepers such as auditors evolved in the nineteenth century to provide protection for investors in companies where ownership was widely dispersed. Especially for those auditors who belonged to professional bodies, such as the chartered accountants, their reputation was at stake when they signed off company accounts. As such, they had a vested interest in presenting a 'true and fair' balance sheet, even though it was the management of the company that both appointed and paid them on behalf of the shareholders. Though the presence of auditors did not prevent fraud taking place, they did restrain the behavior of managers. Acting in a more general capacity were the credit rating agencies that also appeared in the nineteenth century. These judged the ability of businesses to meet the commitments they had entered into, such as paying for goods bought on credit. That service was later extended to bonds and other financial products. Though not infallible, these rating agencies did provide investors with some guidance in differentiating between the various bonds being issued and so encouraged investment. As with auditors, rating agencies were also exposed to reputational risk if their judgments proved to be wrong. The collapse of Enron brought down the accountancy firm, Arthur Andersen, while the global financial crisis revealed that a too close relationship existed between those issuing securities and those providing a rating for them. Nevertheless, in the case of both auditors and rating agencies, regulatory innovation did provide a means of coping with many of the informational asymmetries that arose when investment became impersonal. In addition, both in the nineteenth and twentieth centuries there emerged a number of professional bodies that exercised a degree of control over those working in the financial sector, as with bankers. These had the power to censure and expel members, as well provide practical training and advice regarding accepted behavior.

Compared to the high degree of self-regulation that developed, prior to World War I governments played a very limited role in protecting investors from the choices they made when buying stocks and bonds or depositing money in a bank. That was to change after World War I as Western democracies became more responsive to public opinion and the demand for action in the wake of any scandal or loss. Increasingly after 1945, governments provided implicit or explicit guarantees for a growing range of financial products. There was an expectation that the state would intervene to prevent misselling and compensate victims. In turn, that responsibility gave governments the authority to supervise a diverse range of financial activities, and so dictate the direction of travel. One major effect of that was to encourage financial innovation so as to evade the restrictions imposed by governments.

The sequence can be traced in the case of US banking. The failure of numerous banks in the financial crisis of the early 1930s led to depositors rushing to withdraw their savings, so precipitating a wave of closures. In response the US federal government introduced mandatory deposit insurance in 1934, which promptly stopped the epidemic of bank runs. Accompanying deposit insurance was a ceiling on the rate of interest that a bank could pay. This was to prevent competition between banks, as any failure would involve the Federal Deposit Insurance Corporation compensating depositors. However, against a background of rising post-World War II inflation, these interest rate ceilings made bank accounts unattractive to savers. One response was the introduction of financial products that replicated bank accounts but were not covered by the interest rate ceiling. These money market funds became increasingly popular in the United States from the mid 1970s, being provided by brokerage houses such as Merrill Lynch, which were able to operate nationwide as they were not covered by the restrictions placed on interstate banking. The success of these money market funds forced the US authorities to relax the controls imposed on banks. Eventually the interest rate ceilings were removed, as were the restrictions on the activities that banks could engage in, creating an environment in which banks and others actively competed to attract deposits and make loans. The eventual outcome was a financial crisis in 2007/08 which threatened the value of these money market funds, forcing the government to extend protection to them.

Regulatory innovation was also found in financial markets, though much again was left to the reputation of the participants. All markets involved counterparty risks, as either the seller or the buyer could default on a deal. Markets also lent themselves to price manipulation through the spread of false information or orchestrated buying and selling. Where a limited group of participants was involved, control was exercised through restrictions placed on those with whom deals were made. Interbank markets were of this kind. For others it was necessary to create formal markets because of the number of participants and the individuality of the financial products being traded. Specialist exchanges were of this kind because they incorporated sets of rules and regulations governing admission, behavior, and expulsion. What exchanges provided was that third element that was a vital ingredient in the successful trading of many financial products. Governments were important in introducing and upholding the law of the land. Businesses were responsible for policing the actions that took place in their name. That left exchanges to control trading behavior and so provide a certainty to buying and selling and a guarantee that prices accurately reflected the balance of supply and demand.

However, there was a conflict of interest at the heart of every self-regulated exchange which was evident throughout the nineteenth century. An exchange faced a financial cost in providing not only the trading floor but the supervisory regime. This cost was borne by those who paid to access the market an exchange provided and accepted the rules and regulations governing behavior there or faced expulsion. The problem with that situation was that those paying for access obtained privileged information regarding current prices. Such a position was anticompetitive, as those excluded were disadvantaged as a result. Exclusion was justified when it involved those who refused to abide by the rules and regulations, but not when it was a device used to limit competition. However, as long as the possibility existed of forming an alternative exchange, a balance was maintained between the need to limit access so as to create an orderly market and the importance of widening participation so as to include all those who wanted to trade. That was the case before World War I.

What undermined this equilibrium was the intervention of governments, which greatly increased during and after World War I. Governments became much more involved in the oversight of exchanges, once they reopened, because of fears that speculation would undermine the ability to raise finance. The involvement of government then intensified in the wake of the Wall Street Crash of 1929 and subsequent collapses in other financial markets around the world. This intervention took the form of either direct government control, as had long been the case with the Paris Bourse, or the formation of a separate statutory agency, as with the Securities and Exchange Commission set up in 1934 to supervise all US stock exchanges. Increasingly it was the US model of a separate authority policing exchanges that was adopted internationally after World War II. The result was to convert the self-regulation of markets into state regulation with exchanges acting as instruments of government policy. In return, exchanges were given a monopoly over trading, as only in that way could they effectively police the market. However, this monopoly was then open to abuse, with members of exchanges able to restrict new entrants into the business, impose high fixed charges on users, and prevent changes that would undermine their business.

The effect was to force trading away from the exchanges and into other avenues, which was apparent with the growth of over-the-counter markets. In the United States, much of the trading in bonds and the stocks of smaller companies gravitated away from the floor of the New York Stock Exchange, while the main product innovations, such as the development of financial derivatives, took place on the commodity exchanges, which were not regulated by the Securities and Exchange Commission. In response to complaints from users of exchanges, governments began to intervene to force exchanges to drop anticompetitive practices. This began first in the United States in 1975 and then spread worldwide in the following twenty-five years. The outcome was to return exchanges to the self-regulating bodies they had once been, but with the added dimension of external scrutiny and supervision imposed by statutory authorities. However, governments continued to view exchanges as anticompetitive and so forced them to disseminate current prices to all, so undermining their ability to provide a regulated market. This altered the balance between governments, businesses, and exchanges in favor of the first two and away from the last. Encouraging such a move was the increasing dominance of trading by an ever-smaller group of banks who had the reputation and financial strength to stand behind every deal that they made. It was this belief that rendered it unnecessary for many of the new financial products created prior to the global financial crisis of 2007/2008 to be quoted on exchanges, where an active regulated market could be developed. Thus there were no signals from the market about what was happening to these products, allowing adjustments to be made, and when a crisis did occur these products could not be sold, even at a loss.

Thus, in both financial products and financial markets the increased role played by governments in regulating activity had negative as well as positive outcomes, especially when the long view is taken. It was not possible for governments to intervene in one area without having consequences for others because it was impossible to isolate one component of a financial system from another. However, a degree of government intervention was, at times, essential, as in the case of bank collapses that could threaten an entire financial system with serious long-term economic consequences. In the nineteenth century, a mechanism was created that ensured that the banking system as a whole would be able to continue functioning, through the provision of additional liquidity, even when insolvent banks were allowed to fail. The solution that developed in London from the middle of the nineteenth onwards was a bank that acted as a lender of last resort to the banking system, not only during a crisis, but on a daily basis, as long as the problem was liquidity not solvency. Confidence that such a bank existed and would act in this way ensured that banks would continue to lend to each other even under the most extreme conditions, including war or a major financial crisis. The Bank of England developed this role and so helped to make the British banking system one of the most stable in the world and enhanced the attractions of the London money market. Through connections to those banks with an office in London, banks from around the world were able to access this lender-of-last-resort facility. In addition, the establishment of central banks elsewhere in the world by 1914, such as Germany and France, provided their banking systems with the same facility, though more directly (Singleton 2011).

As the support provided by these central banks to individual banks was conditional rather than guaranteed, the problem of moral hazard was either avoided, as in the United Kingdom, or, at least, minimized, as in France and Germany. Moral hazard existed when a bank was so confident that it would receive support in any crisis that it indulged in excessive risk taking, which could then destabilize the entire banking system. As with banking in general, the United States again proved to be an exception among advanced economies before 1914. It was not until 1913 that a central bank, the Federal Reserve, was finally established in the United States, after yet another major financial crisis in 1907. Until then the US banking system was dependent on actions linked to bankers' clearing houses to provide emergency liquidity. Actions by the US government also contributed to the absence of a single lender of last resort to the world money market emerging after World War II. Prior to World War I, the Bank of England had acted in this position and continued to do so until the 1960s, to a greater or lesser degree. However, from the 1970s onwards it was no longer in a position to do so because the United Kingdom was now a relatively small economy compared to the United States and increasingly Japan and Germany, and the currency used for international transactions had become the US dollar, not the UK pound. Despite that, because of the actions taken by the US authorities, the international money market remained in London rather than New York, where it would have been able to call upon the direct support of the Federal Reserve. Thus, when the crisis of 2007/2008 occurred, it was national central banks, either alone or collectively, that acted as lender of last resort to the international money market, rather than a single institution that had maintained direct and daily contact (Kindleberger and Aliber 2011).

After World War II, government-controlled central banks became key features of all national financial systems, but they were given numerous and often conflicting roles. Nevertheless, one of their main tasks was to provide the financial system with the stability it required. This did appear to be very effective for the first twenty-five years after World War II because there were virtually no banking crises around the world during these years, with Brazil being a rare exception. However, these were not testing times for banks, being years of rapid economic growth sustained by government intervention. In the years since 1970, financial crises returned, becoming both more frequent and severe, eventually culminating in that of 2008. Central banks appeared powerless in preventing these crises despite both a high degree of cooperation and international agreements setting minimum capital levels for banks. It was in 1974 that the Committee on Banking Regulation and Supervisory Practices was established in Basel with responsibility for drawing up rules and making recommendations about the way banks should operate. By then there already existed a number of international organizations that coordinated action among the world's banks, especially the central banks, including the Bank for International Settlement, dating from 1930, and the International Monetary Fund and the World Bank, which had both been formed in 1944. These organizations did assist central banks in making a coordinated response to a crisis, so avoiding any repetition of the financial and monetary chaos that had prevailed in the 1930s.

The reason for the failure of central banks to prevent crises lies in the growing importance of both markets and globalization from 1970 onwards (see James, Chapter 9 in this volume). These exposed a fundamental trilemma involving markets and government policy (see James, Chapter 9 in this volume). The legacy of the years between 1914 and 1945 was an enormously enlarged role for government. This meant that the policies pursued by all governments had a major influence over their national economies, contributing to divergent performance. This situation worked well between 1945 and the early 1970s, when national economies were compartmentalized through restrictions on financial flows. Those conditions even made it possible to maintain fixed exchange rates, though regular balance-of-payments crises did occur, but they eventually collapsed in the mid 1970s. What emerged then was an era without exchange and capital controls but one in which governments still wanted to pursue independent economic policies and maintain fixed exchange rates. Achieving all three of these was not possible, as the policies pursued put pressure on the fixed exchange rate. If free financial flows were to be maintained, the choice was either not to pursue independent economic policies or abandon fixed exchange rates. Few governments were willing to do the former and many were reluctant to do the latter, so creating problems for national banking systems as they tried to cope with a combination of destabilizing financial flows, fixed exchange rates, and excessive government expenditure financed by borrowing. The result was a series of financial crises around the world, with that of 2008 being the most serious to date but unlikely to be the last. The creation of the euro, a single currency covering very divergent economies, indicates that governments continue to believe that it is possible to combine independent economic policies, free financial flows, and fixed exchange rates.

The emergence of a much greater degree of government regulation of financial services after 1945 exposes another fundamental trilemma. The first objective that governments had in regulating financial services was to achieve such a degree of control that they would be able to implement their policies. The problem was that governments could only exercise control over selected components of the financial system. One component was the banks, as they looked to the central bank for support in any crisis and were thus responsive to its wishes. The second were exchanges, as they were formally organized markets with rules and regulations that could be used to influence the behavior of members. However, the more restrictions that were imposed on these, the more financial activity drifted into the hands of shadow banks and unregulated markets, so depriving governments of the control they wanted to exercise. The second objective of government regulation of financial activity was stability. By acting as a lender of last resort or guaranteeing bank deposits governments could foster stability. However, such actions created a moral hazard. Banks could operate in the belief that whatever risks they took, the government would intervene to save them from collapse. Savers could pursue the best terms and conditions on offer, secure in the knowledge that any losses would be covered by the government. Thus the pursuit of stability in the short run could generate instability in the long run. The third objective of governments was to stimulate competition in the financial sector. Through competition savers would get higher rates of return, borrowers would obtain larger loans at less cost, and investors would pay less to buy and sell. However, with increased competition, banks and other financial intermediaries were driven to take greater risks in order to maintain or gain market share, such as operating on less capital and keeping lower reserves. That meant that in a crisis they were less able to withstand defaults among borrowers and withdrawals among depositors, so increasing the likelihood of collapse.

The trilemma for governments was how to, simultaneously, achieve control, stability, and competition within the financial system. Before 1914, control was sacrificed and the financial system did become both more stable and more competitive, though the United States was something of an exception because of the structure of the banking system. After 1945, control was the priority and that was achieved at the expense of competition before the 1970s and stability afterwards. The switch from a highly regulated financial system, whether involving either banks or exchanges, to one that promoted greatly increased competition, created instability as it transformed the basis upon which both had been operating. The stability that had existed from 1945 to 1970 had lulled all governments into a false sense of security, and it was only in those countries where a crisis did occur that lessons were learnt about what was required to minimize the impact of such events in the future. A similar position prevailed for banks in those countries where collapses were a distant memory, as a belief was fostered that stability could be assumed, rather than action being required to preserve it. It was thus in the United States and Western Europe that the global financial crisis of 2007/2008 had its twin epicenters, as it was there that competition between banks had become most intense. Further evidence for the failure of regulation, whether externally by governments or internally by banks, comes from the revelations regarding abuses at the retail and wholesale level. Lax controls allowed those employed by banks to sell flawed financial products to consumers and to manipulate key interest rates. This suggests that regulation cannot be left to the self-interest of either individual governments or businesses, but also needs to operate at the industry-wide level.

Financial sector

As S. E. Thomas observed in his 1930 book, *Banking and Exchange*, "The greater the civilization of a community and the higher its development, the more efficient usually is its system of credit and method of cancelling indebtedness." As he was writing at a time of global economic crisis, he was well aware of the negative consequences created by this sophisticated financial system, but he remained positive on the long-term benefits it had provided (Thomas 1930: 52–53).

Evidence certainly exists to suggest there is a strong correlation between a country's per capita income and financial sector development, judged by such measures as bank deposits and holding of securities (Goldsmith 1985). The function of the financial sector is to match the supply and demand of savings and to do so in a way that lenders and borrowers are appropriately rewarded and charged in order to allocate scarce resources as efficiently as possible. It is those countries with high per capita incomes and complex economic structures that generate demands for financial intermediation, whether in the collection and use of savings or the continuous buying and selling in markets. In turn, those savings were then available for reinvestment, so generating further increases in productivity. Similarly, the creation of banks and financial markets also served the needs of those with idle funds which they wanted to invest, whether through deposits or the purchase of securities. By doing so, the financial sector encouraged additional saving and investment to take place (Bordo, Taylor, and Williamson 2003; Levine and Zervos 1988; Rajan and Zingales 1988).

However, that did not mean that financial sectors were identical, even in countries at the same level of economic development. Comparisons reveal major differences in their nature and composition. In no case was the financial system of one country identical to that of another, due to the influence of historical experience, government legislation, and the pattern of economic development. This diversity existed because the financial sector covers such a wide spectrum of activities, ranging from retail and investment banking to wholesale markets trading in money, securities, derivatives, and foreign exchange. Out of this has come the debate on the relative merits of a bank-based versus a market-based financial system. What this debate ignores is that in each country the financial sector as a whole found a means of delivering the products, markets, organization, and regulation required. The same criticism applies to comparisons over time, as events such as wars and revolutions all affected the relative standing of banks and markets. Both before 1914 and after 1970 there was a growing convergence of national financial systems, as all were developing both universal banks and stock markets. Within that, some countries emerged in which the financial sector outgrew their economy through serving the needs of the entire world. This was the case for the United Kingdom, and later countries such as Switzerland or city-states like Hong Kong and Singapore. Through the process of globalization that has gathered pace since the removal of government controls began in the 1970s, certain financial activities have gravitated to these countries and are then provided from there to the international community. This makes their financial sectors different from those located in countries such as the United States, Germany, Japan, or China, as these largely serve their domestic economy with the full range of services required.

The financial sector is also in a state of constant flux, which can be seen in terms of its relationship with the corporate sector. Though there is an inextricable link between the growth of the financial sector and corporate capitalism, they are also rivals. The greater the size of the business unit, the more it was able to internalize financial activities. Big companies were often able to finance the entire chain linking production and consumption from their own resources and so eliminate the services provided by banks. Similarly, internal systems of debits and credits could reduce the need for externally provided payments networks. Large companies were also able to mobilize finance from retained earnings in one sector of the business and direct these to an area of activity requiring large inputs of capital. As a result, the need to form new companies and raise capital from outside investors was not required. Through these means companies generated organic growth and so reduced their dependence on the financial sector. With the growth of multi-divisional and multinational companies, the degree to which business could free itself from the financial sector was greatly magnified. Internal accounting procedures could cope with transactions between branches of the same business located in different countries and currency zones, with the added advantage that the most tax efficient structure could be adopted. The consequences for the financial sector of these changes in business organization were far-reaching. They had the effect of eliminating many of the most basic services that the financial sector provided, such as the provision of short-term credit, the raising of long-term capital, and access to global payments networks. Instead, businesses organized as multinational companies looked to the financial sector for ways of reducing risks created by currency volatility, supplying the funds required to arrange management buy-outs, or providing the means to mount aggressive takeover bids. In each case these demands required a creative response from the financial sector.

A similar relationship exists between the financial sector and government. On the one hand, the financial sector both serves governments and benefits from the business that it generates. Governments need loans, whether to cover the fact that everyday expenditure and income are not always aligned, or because they face the need to finance expensive projects or wage wars. Governments also need access to networks through which taxes can be collected and payments made. Thus, in many different ways both banks and markets have long been valued by governments. On the other hand, governments can either bypass the financial sector or dispense with it altogether. Through the ability to levy taxes and employ staff, governments are able to access income and arrange expenditure for themselves. Thus, when focussing solely on the contribution made by the financial sector to the mobilization and use of savings, it is relatively easy to speculate on alternatives, whether in the form of large-scale business units or governments and other public bodies. However, when examining the financial sector, what needs to be recognized is that it serves two masters, not one. Important as is the ability of the financial sector to provide business or government with the credit and capital they require, of equal importance is the service provided to savers and investors. This aspect is often overlooked, as the focus is on what the financial sector contributes to an economy, both through the employment, incomes, and taxes generated and the assistance it provides to such activities as agriculture, mining, manufacturing, and services in general. Providing finance was only half what the financial sector did, because it also met the needs of those looking for a temporary or permanent home for savings, so allowing these to be used for the future benefit of society, as in the payment of pensions, pay-outs on insurance policies, and the ability to draw on bank deposits when required. In achieving these ends, the financial sector operates at the local, national, and international level, and both now and for the future. Without a sophisticated financial sector, an advanced global economy would cease to function.

Conclusion

Over three centuries financial capitalism has moved far beyond a division between those who lent money to a business and those who used it. Nevertheless, central to financial capitalism throughout is the separation between lenders and borrowers and between the suppliers and users of capital. It was that separation that made financial capitalism a distinctive form of capitalism. However, the increasing size and complexity of economic activity increased the degree of separation as businesses grew from small enterprises producing goods and providing services for immediate consumption and run by owner/managers to become multinational corporations controlling extended global supply chains. This had consequences for both those who lent money to businesses of that kind and those who provided the capital upon which they operated. The result was a constant interaction, as changes in business produced a response among lenders and investors which, in turn, drove change in business, and then a subsequent reaction among lenders and borrowers. The consequence of this dynamic relationship was a situation in which financial capitalism increasingly came to characterize capitalism itself, rather than referring simply to the use of capital provided either by the owners of a business or borrowed from their immediate circle of family, friends, and business associates.

None of this would have been possible without financial innovation, as this continually created new products, markets, organizations, and regulations through which the process of lending and borrowing, or the raising and using of capital, was transformed. Financial innovation from at least the twelfth century onwards had produced all the basic elements required by a modern financial system by the eighteenth century. However, it was developments in the subsequent centuries that were to fuse these elements together to make financial capitalism into a force possessed of enormous creative and destructive power. When unleashed, that power was able to support such a sustained period of economic growth that the world economy has been completely altered over the last 250 years, despite the reverses inflicted by such man-made events as two world wars as well as natural catastrophes. Conversely, financial capitalism also possessed seeds of its own destruction, resulting in successive crises which had the effect of destroying many of the gains made in previous years, and some of these were of such magnitude that their consequences were both deep and prolonged. Financial capitalism involves both risk and resilience. A short-term verdict based on the aftermath of a financial crisis stresses risk and the need for regulation. A long-term verdict based on the interplay between the financial sector and the global economy stresses resilience and the need for deregulation. Both verdicts matter as they each contribute to the evolution of financial capitalism and its ability to balance the creative and destructive forces that are inherent within it.

References

Beck, T., T. Chen, C. Li, and F. M. Song (2012). "Financial Innovation: The Bright and Dark Sides," SSRN: http://ssrn.com/abstract=1991216

Bordo, M. D., A. M. Taylor, and J. G. Williamson, eds. (2003). *Globalization in Historical Perspective*. University of Chicago Press/NBER.

Carlos, A. M. and L. Neal (2011). "Amsterdam and London as Financial Centers in the Eighteenth Century," *Financial History Review* 18: 1–26.

Carosso, V. P. (1970) *Investment Banking in America: A History*. Cambridge, MA: Harvard University Press.

Cassis, Y. (2006). *Capitals of Capital: A History of International Financial Centres, 1780–2005*. Cambridge University Press.

Cassis Y. and E. Bussiere, eds. (2005). *London and Paris as International Financial Centres in the Twentieth Century*. Oxford University Press.

Cassis, Y., G. D. Feldman and U. Olsson (eds.) (1995). *The Evolution of Financial Institutions and Markets in Twentieth Century Europe*. Aldershot: Scolar Press.

Casson M. (ed. (1992). *International Business and Global Integration*. London: Macmillan Press.

Coffee, J. C. (2006). *Gatekeepers: The Professions and Corporate Governance*. Oxford University Press.

Fohlin, C. (2007). *Finance Capitalism and Germany's Rise to Industrial Power*. Cambridge University Press.

Forsyth, D. J. and D. Verdier, eds. (2003). *The Origins of National Financial Systems*. London: Routledge.

Furniss, E. S. (1922). *Foreign Exchange: The Financing Mechanism of International Commerce*. New York: Houghton Mifflin.

Goldsmith, R. W. (1985). *Comparative National Balance Sheets: A Study of Twenty Countries, 1688–1978*. University of Chicago Press.

Grossman R. S. (2010). *Unsettled Account: The Evolution of Banking in the Industrialized World since 1800*. Princeton University Press.

Haldane, A. G. and R. M. May (2011). "Systemic Risk in Banking Ecosystems," *Nature* 469: 351–355.

Jones, G., ed. (1991). *Banks and Money: International and Comparative Finance in History*. London: Frank Cass.

(2005), *Multinationals and Global Capitalism: From the Nineteenth to the Twenty-first Century*. Oxford: Oxford University Press.

Keynes, J. M. (1936). *The General Theory of Employment, Interest and Money*. London: Macmillan Press.

Kindleberger C. P. and R. Z. Aliber (2011). *Manias, Panics, and Crashes: A History of Financial Crises*. London: Palgrave Macmillan.

Lamoreaux, N. R. (1994). *Insider Lending: Banks, Personal Connections and Economic Development in Industrial New England*. New York: Cambridge University Press.

Levine, R. and S. Zervos (1998). "Stock Markets, Banks, and Economic Growth," *American Economic Review* 88: 537–558.

Michie, R. C. (2006). *The Global Securities Market: A History*. Oxford University Press.

Nishimura, S. T. Suzuki, and R. Michie, eds. (2012). *The Origins of International Banking in Asia: The Nineteenth and Twentieth Centuries*. Oxford University Press.

Rajan, R. and L. Zingales (1998). "Financial Dependence and Growth," *American Economic Review* 88: 559–586.

(2003). "The Great Reversals: The Politics of Financial Development in the Twentieth Century," *Journal of Financial Economics* 69: 5–49.

eds. (2004). *Saving Capitalism from the Capitalists: Unleashing the Power of Financial Markets to Create Wealth and Spread Opportunities*. New York: Random House.

Reinhart, C. M. and K. S. Rogoff (2009). *This Time is Different: Eight Centuries of Financial Folly*. Princeton University Press.

Schiller, R. J. (2000). *Irrational Exuberance*. Princeton University Press.

Singleton, J. (2011). *Central Banking in the Twentieth Century*. Cambridge University Press.

Thomas, S. E. (1930). *Banking and Exchange*. London: Gregg Publishing.

Von Peter, G. (2007). "International Banking Centres: A Network Perspective," *BIS Quarterly Review*, December: 33–45.

9

International capital movements and the global order

HAROLD JAMES

What is the relationship between the phenomenon of globalization and the free movement of capital? Is the world held together by capital flows, or do they produce such instability as to generate backlashes against global interconnectedness? Economists are divided on these questions. Whereas there is a broad agreement among economists about the beneficial consequences of trade flows, some of the most prominent and articulate voices in defense of free trade, Jagdhish Bhagwati and Joseph Stiglitz, have also been among the skeptics on capital liberalization (Bhagwati 2004). Capital flows, in the view of Stiglitz, generate such large waves as to upset the delicate rowing boats of small countries afloat on the sea of globalization (Stiglitz 1998).

In order to answer these questions, this paper distinguishes the varieties of cross-border capital movements in the two modern eras or waves of globalization, from the mid-nineteenth century to World War I, and then again from the 1970s to 2007, as well as the capital market and financial developments that contributed to the catastrophic unraveling of globalization in the intervening period. The core of the paper is thus a chronology of the succession of phases: first, substantial and increasing movements – largely through the expansion of the bond market – in the interconnected global economy of the late nineteenth century (the era often characterized by its monetary arrangement: the gold standard); second, an attempt to revive the flows of the gold standard era but one which was more and more dominated by volatile hot money flows (the interwar era); third, a period in which there was relatively little (and relatively state-controlled or state-directed) international capital movement (again, usually named after its monetary arrangement, the Bretton Woods era); and fourth and finally, a loosening of controls and a return to substantial international capital mobility, without much of a formal monetary system or mechanism, the era in which the term "globalization" in its modern meaning was coined (modern globalization).

A priori, it seems likely that free and abundant capital movements should facilitate worldwide and balanced economic growth, because – in the absence of obstruction – capital is employed where it can be used most efficiently, i.e. generate the highest returns. Capital is thus assumed to flow from countries with advanced technologies to poorer countries, which use imported capital in a process of catchup. This process can be observed and documented, especially in the two eras of substantial global interconnectedness. Mature industrial economies, above all the United Kingdom and France, exported capital and experienced high living standards but relative decline as fast-growing capital-importing countries such as Argentina, Australia, Canada, and the United States caught up and even surpassed them in terms of per capita income. But this process is much less common than might be supposed, and its rarity has produced the formulation of the Lucas paradox: that enough capital does not flow downhill to facilitate a beneficent catchup process.

In principle, mechanisms that allow societies to finance their investment in the absence of adequate sources of domestic saving might be thought of as substantially identical: but alternative instruments and mechanisms carry very different implications for domestic institutional development as well as inter-nationally for the sustainability of the financial system. In particular, the mediation by large financial institutions of capital movements became pro-foundly destabilizing in the late phases of each globalization push: both in the early twentieth century and in the new millennium.

Cross-border capital movements were also subjects of political controversy – even when they were entirely private in nature. Consequently, in both global-ization epochs, demands appeared for greater political control or direction, especially when diplomatic, strategic, or military aspects became prominent. The more, too, that the capital movements were concentrated via financial intermediation, the more intense became the political aspects of capital flows and the likelihood of backlashes when capital movements are regulated or controlled.

The current account

The easiest – and most superficially attractive – way to grasp the working of capital movements comes from an accounting identity in National Income methodology. The current account is the result of change in resident holdings of foreign assets (the gross outflow) minus change in resident liabilities to non-residents (the gross inflow), or the net capital outflow. But it is also arithmetically defined as saving minus investment. National Income accounting thus offers a convenient way of summarizing the overall outcome of a myriad individual decisions about the allocation of resources to savings, consumption, and investment. The current account is often in consequence treated as a proxy for the extent of global interconnectedness, or a measure of the extent of globalization. The basic framework was provided by Feldstein and Horioka (1980). According to their elegant reasoning, in a world in which capital did not move, savings would be equal to investment in each country or economic entity. A current account imbalance therefore reflects the ability of a country to export excess or import scarce capital. That ability in turn depends on the availability of security instruments that embody claims on capital, and of market mechanisms that allow the trading of such instruments.

The twentieth century – viewed through the current account – shows a U-shaped development, with more capital flowing at the beginning and end of the century, and substantially less in the middle. The flows of the early years of the twentieth century also looked more steady, and were less prone to reversals or sudden stops than in the middle years, but also than at the end of the century (see Figure 9.1).

Though there is widespread agreement on the existence of the U-shape, the interpretation of its significance and its explanation are problematical. Is the rise of capital flows (and current account imbalances) a consequence of removing barriers to capital movement? Is it a consequence of financial

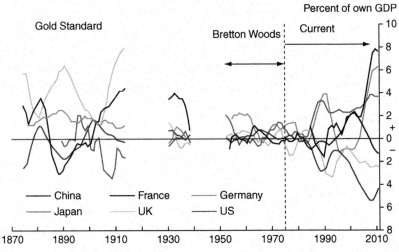

Figure 9.1. Current account positions 1870–2010 (five-year averages)
Source: Bank of England 2011

innovation, and in what ways is that innovation measurably beneficial? Or, thirdly, is it rather a response to greater levels of income and wealth, and thus indirectly to the institutional and intellectual developments that produced greater wealth? Finally, fourthly, is it a consequence of macroeconomic policy choices that alter the relationship between saving and investment and thus are fundamental determinants of the current account position?

In the first thesis, government policy (or rather its absence) holds the key. Capital markets are first driven by economic and political liberalism in the sense of an absence of governmental intervention; and subsequently intervention is shaped by a backlash against global connectedness. Obstfeld and Taylor suggest that "the construction of the first global marketplace in capital, as well as in goods and labor, took hold in an era of undisputed liberalism and virtual laissez faire" (Obstfeld and Taylor 2004: 23). In the absence of governmentally imposed obstacles, capital flows freely and efficiently to where it can be used most effectively – as shown by a price mechanism, where flows occur to uses which generate the highest returns.

According to the second thesis, specific types of innovation increase the propensity of capital to move. The innovation may be a new type of instrument, or an institutional guarantee that makes instruments more credible (such as a commitment to the gold standard, which plays a prominent part in some interpretations [Bordo and Rockoff 1996; Ford 1960, 1962]). The monetary order became so attractive because of the lure of the diffusion of particular innovations in finance. The nineteenth century was dominated by the bond (mostly the sovereign bond, usually denominated in a foreign currency, and often in British pounds), a promise to repay credit in a regular income stream, and by the bill (mostly a commercial bill, relating to a specific trade transaction in which the buyer/importer promises to pay the seller/exporter, and usually in a three-month or ninety-day version which was the basis for trade finance). The success of the bond and the bill encouraged further financial innovation in the form of emulation: Sub-sovereign and parastate and private-sector borrowers began to imitate states and issue bonds; and financiers thought of using bills as a convenient way of borrowing short-term, even when there was no underlying trade transaction. The language of the time distinguished between "trade bills" which were good and "accommodation bills" or "finance bills" which were frowned on as speculative and demonized in countless fictional portrayals of profligacy and disgrace. Large cross-border banking deposits began to play a role only at the end of the first era of globalization, but are a key element in global capital movements in the second era.

In the third interpretation, laissez faire and financial innovation are not the key drivers that push capital across frontiers. There is no quick fix to be obtained through a single policy stance. Macroeconomic fundamentals and a much broader mix of policies that drive sustainable development are the key to the rise of capital (Flandreau and Zumer 2004). Sustainable capital flows depend on a deep web of propitious circumstances.

Finally, in the fourth interpretation the accent is placed on adjustment strategies, and the problems of unstable capital flows diagnosed as problems of adjustment in the international system – most frequently as the failure of surplus countries to expand demand so as to reduce saving and thus bring the current account to balance (see e.g. Wolf 2008).

A further issue related to innovation complicates the long-term picture of how globalized capital ties the world together. Much of the older literature on capital movement was driven by an interest in net capital movements, as reflected in current account positions; and often carries echoes of seventeenth- and eighteenth-century mercantilist writing on the undesirability or unsustainability of trade deficits. The intensified financialization of the late twentieth century produced very much larger gross capital movements. As a result, some observers began to reflect whether the current account no longer mattered (Borio and Disyatat 2010; Obstfeld 2012). Very large movements were mediated through the financial system, and the complexity of that intermediation produced a systemic vulnerability.

Many analysts have attempted to distinguish long-term capital movements, which reflect long-term judgments about differing productive potential and are often thought to be beneficial in their effects, from short-term and easily reversible movements, which are speculative and destabilizing. They depend on different institutional arrangements: long-term movements generally occurred by means of financial instruments or securities: bonds, but also equity participations. But even long-term flows are subject to trends and fashions, and there may be surges or bonanzas that increase the likelihood of misallocation and crisis (Reinhart and Reinhart 2008). Short-term movements occurred much more via the banking system. The mix (or mismatch) of maturities differed from country to country. Some countries, especially financial centers, resemble banks in that they transform maturities, taking in short-term deposits (which are vulnerable to sudden reversals) and undertaking longer-term investment.

Short-term movements respond very quickly to interest rate differences. They were thus more directly affected by the actions of central banks than longer-term flows. The late nineteenth century saw the emergence of a new doctrine of central banking that emphasized the role of bank policy and of interest rates in guiding capital flows. The gold standard did not necessarily require such action (and indeed some gold standard countries did not have central banks), as the adjustment occurs through an automatic mechanism that is not dependent on policy decisions. In the simplest (Humeian) model of adjustment, flows of precious metal generate price effects that produce adjustment to trade imbalances. In theory, an analogous model can be constructed in which the purchase of securities is equivalent to the purchase of goods. When there are substantial short-term flows, the picture changes. Attracting inflows of money through the sale of short-term securities at higher interest rates leads to an expansionary monetary effect with higher prices at the same time as interest rate pressure is expected to reduce demand and lower prices. The action of central banks often produced higher levels of short-term liabilities, and potentially thus created a situation in which there might be sudden stops or reversals of capital flows. The institutional innovation of central banking in the gold standard added a new level of complexity, but also made for greater potential volatility, especially when the large short-term positions are held in the banking system.

Central banks were often newly established after financial crises – after 1873 for the German empire, or after 1907 for the United States – and then they were thought to play a role in stabilizing markets. That might require using the interest rate tool either to attract or ward off short-term capital movements, and consequently the encouragement of short-term movements became a central feature of the international monetary system. This evolution contained potential dangers. With expectations of long-term or sustained differences in interest rates, so-called carry trades become attractive or popular, with companies and individuals funding themselves abroad at lower interest rates, in order to buy securities or other assets that promise higher yields. The carry trades are subject to quick reversals when policy conditions alter, and such alterations occur quite dramatically in managed currency regimes. The question of whether the current account matters then becomes primarily an assessment of the way in which political and monetary authorities react to current account imbalances.

Before World War I, it was generally supposed that there was not enough participation in the political system, or not enough extension of the democratic order, for there to be much political resistance to the costs of adjustment as carried out by central banks. After World War I, much greater adjustments were required, because of the extent of the profound shocks that followed the war, and there was also more democracy. The influential interpretation of

Polanyi (1944) suggests that the changed political circumstances made the gold standard unworkable. There are thus some paradoxes in the politics of capital movement: Some measure of accountability, it will be suggested, is vital to generating the security and credibility on which international capital movements depend; but democracy also interrupts the application of the rules on which the international system depended.

The gold standard

From the middle of the nineteenth century to World War 1, both gross and net capital flows increased. As capital markets became more connected, yields converged. But that development was not a smooth one-way process. Integration rose in the 1870s and 1880s, but then was interrupted after a severe financial crisis in Argentina (1890), one of the heaviest capital importing countries. The trend toward integration resumed in the 1900s.

The core members of the gold standard had absolutely credible fixed exchange rates. In the 1860s and 1870s, as the world moved to a general adoption of the gold standard, there were even discussions about the creation of a world currency. Part of the set of intellectual assumptions on which the gold standard was constructed included the belief that convertibility might be suspended in the case of major military conflict between great powers, but would be restored again with the resumption of peace. These countries experienced a substantial convergence, though not a complete equalization, of short- and long-term interest rates. But a substantial convergence also took place between the core and the periphery, and provided the incentives for peripheral countries to take policy measures that would align them with the core. Many policy figures in the periphery believed that the adoption of an increasingly universal currency standard would guarantee access to financial markets and lower borrowing costs. At the same time there were still differences in return that provided the incentive for capital to move.

The surpluses of the first era of globalization were concentrated in two countries, the United Kingdom and France. In both cases, capital export was often associated with the rhetoric of national decline. By 1914, half of British savings went abroad. The decline discussion was stimulated by the chronological coincidence of the acceleration of capital export in the 1870s with declining growth (the Victorian climacteric). France was not as advanced an economy as the United Kingdom, but it had an exceptionally high savings rate. Many contemporaries explained the high French proclivity to save through demographics, with low fertility meaning a need for higher savings as individuals contemplated the financing of their old age. France and the United Kingdom were the major financial centers of the *belle époque*, with major markets in Paris and London that intermediated capital movements (see Michie, Chapter 8 in this volume).

For both Britain and France a substantial debate has taken place about whether the flows were rational in that they corresponded to higher ex post yields (Edelstein 1982). Since defaults became increasingly rare in the early twentieth century, the ex ante yields began to converge with ex post returns. The British and French discussions raised the question: Did capital flow downhill, to more productive uses in developing countries? Was there a push generated by high savings that could find no adequate domestic employment?

In fact, most foreign investment very evidently did not go to countries with large and poor populations. British capital in particular went to resource-abundant countries that also attracted large migrations from the United Kingdom and elsewhere in Europe: about two-thirds of prewar British foreign investment was in the western hemisphere and Australasia. The best explanation for the destination of British capital lay in education and schooling, in natural resources, and in the extent of immigration (Clemens and Williamson 2004). French lending had a very strong political dimension.

A great deal of the capital flows involved either public borrowers, sovereigns, provinces, municipalities, or railway and other transportation companies. The bond purchasers believed that their money was being used to make investments that would then generate a secure and constant revenue stream that would be used to service the bond. In some instances, the public borrowers were financing current expenditure, and taking a bet that they would be able to raise the revenue needed for debt service. An absolutely clear-cut distinction between revenue and development borrowers is harder to make than theory would indicate (see Fishlow 1985 for such an attempt). The modern discussion of the phenomenon hinges around the problem of asymmetric information, in that distant lenders find it hard to really know what the likely returns on their investment will be. Institutions that reduce or correct asymmetries then lead to greater as well as more sustainable capital flows (Bordo, Eichengreen, and Irwin 1999).

Creditors engaged in attempting to provide systematic judgments about the capacity of their borrowers to repay and thus on the credibility of the fundamental promise that constituted the bond. Should the creditors do this as individuals, each making choices about which instrument to purchase? How could they get reliable information? As individual investors as well as banks flooded into the market, demand for financial advice also developed. For some periods of time, particular countries became the favorites of the capital markets, with a sort of herd behavior following hot tips. In the 1830s, there had been a flood of British lending to the western hemisphere, followed by a series of defaults, and *Fenn's Compendium* then started up as a handbook on the character-istics of borrowing countries. From 1869, the periodical *The Economist* published an *Investors' Monthly Manual* (Flandreau and Zumer 2004). In continental Europe, capital flows were channeled much more through financial institu-tions. Characteristically, it was a French bank, the Crédit Lyonnais, that developed in the 1890s the first systematic approach to the credit rating of foreign investments (there had been rating of the US domestic market: Olegaria 2006). At the beginning of the twentieth century, in the United States a market developed for separate rating agencies (Gaillard 2012).

Some judgment as to the sustainability of development is the key to determining the credibility of a debt contract. Capital inflows responded to opportunities for growth – as did flows of migrants. In the mid nineteenth century, the fact that capital was free to move was at first viewed simply as part of a generally shared consensus about the virtues of an open or liberal economic order. Indeed, movements of people were initially more con-strained (the United Kingdom, for instance, prohibited the emigration of skilled workers until 1827), and in the early nineteenth century there were heavy import duties on goods.

Argentina in the late 1880s experienced a major boom, with substantial inflows of European migrants (largely from Italy) as well as capital, and provides a powerful case of the linkages between flows of humans and flows of money. From 1880 to 1890 the population increased from 2.5 to 3.4 millions. A modern calculation suggests that Argentina imported capital amounting to 18.7 percent of its GDP between 1870 and 1889 (the other big importers of capital were Australia, 9.7 percent, and Canada, 7.2 percent, over this period) (Flandreau and Zumer 2004). By the 1880s, Argentina accounted for almost half of British foreign lending (Ford 1962; Mitchener and Weidenmier 2008). By the end of the 1880s, Argentine public finances were increasingly strained, with the cost of financing the federal deficit amounting to 68 percent of government expenditure by 1889. Subsidiary government institutions continued to borrow even when the federal government promised not to borrow more without the consent of the bankers. All Argentine short-term borrowing became much more expensive, and long-term bond issues impossible. Bank credit creation, which had been regulated under an 1887 Law of National Guaranteed Banks in which banks issued notes backed by gold-denominated government debt, represented another weak point of the

Argentine structure. The crunch came when the largest and most prestigious London merchant bank, Barings, which had been handling the Argentine debt issue since 1824, failed to sell the bonds of the Buenos Aires Water Supply and Drainage Corporation, and faced a substantial loss on its underwriting that threatened the solvency of the bank. The government was unable to make gold payments, and paid instead in depreciated paper. Without access to more finance, the economy collapsed, and political unrest brought down Juarez Celman, the President of the Republic, in 1890. It was only in 1893 that the Argentine debt was restructured (in the *arreglo Romero*), with a deferral of most payments for ten years and a reduction of interest payments for five years; and only in the new century that capital flows to Argentina really resumed.

The 1890 Argentine crisis (or Baring crisis) had major international ramifications. The Argentine collapse had an immediate effect on the ability to borrow and on yields of other Latin American borrowers. As borrowing rates surged, other countries too defaulted: Greece and Portugal in Europe, and in 1898 Brazil required a restructuring through a funding loan raised by the major London houses. The effects of the credit tightening were felt as far away as Australia, where the problem lay in private-sector banking rather than in government borrowing. Capital had also flowed into Australia, with an explosion of mortgage lending. By 1892, there were clear signs of financial strain, and the Mercantile Bank of Australia failed. By 1893, there was a general banking crisis.

The most immediate or most obvious lesson of the Argentine crisis was that the creditworthiness of public borrowers depended not merely on the fact of potential growth or a powerful export sector, but on the fiscal soundness of a regime, on its ability to raise a stream of revenue in taxation in order to allow the regular servicing of debt. The attention of creditors, and of those who tried to cater to their lust for information, now shifted from the question of general development potential (which suggested the downhill flow of capital from rich to poor countries) to the estimation of fiscal effectiveness. In that respect, rich and developed countries were likely to be better and more credible than poor and politically volatile countries. Hence the Lucas paradox. The original fiscal compact of eighteenth-century England, in which the government promised to pay bondholders who voted for a Parliament that in effect controlled the government; but with foreign lending there was much more uncertainty about the nature of the promise (Macdonald 2006). Flandreau and Zumer document how the critical variable for investors now became the share of government revenue needed for interest rate service, with a consensus emerging that the danger level lay between 33 and 40 percent of the annual budget (Flandreau and Zumer 2004, 41). Probabilities of default started to rise very steeply once the 40 percent threshold was reached.

In a domestic setting, fiscal effectiveness was often judged by the sophistication of political development, and in particular the extent of the development of representative institutions and of Parliaments. The theory was that if the creditor classes were politically represented, and their consent required for fiscal measures, then they would not agree to any measure that threatened the creditworthiness of the government. Thus the promise to repay became more credible, and the default risk decreased. That perspective was then reflected in the pricing of debt, with the result that the cost of borrowing fell for countries with strong representative institutions. They could then afford more debt, which at that time was used mostly to pay for military commitments. Hence in a sort of competitive evolution, representative governments were more likely to be powerful and impose their will on their authoritarian rivals. This model was associated, especially for British commentators at the time and later (Brewer 1989; Ferguson 2001), with the rise of British naval hegemony and of British economic power (which benefitted from the low cost of credit). The success of the model was finally confirmed by the British victory over Napoleon, and in the first half of the nineteenth century, bankers such as the Rothschilds actively urged borrowing countries to introduce assemblies and constitutions in order to reduce financing costs (Ferguson 1998).

The problem behind a high level of external debt is that the creditors are obviously not represented in any Parliament, and the political representatives of debtor classes (or those who have to pay taxes in order to service debt) may well have a powerful incentive to default. The substitute for the domestic political credibility in the case of the domestic market lay for the international market in some sort of strong diplomatic commitment, in which a security relationship underpinned the financial and economic relationship. The strongest form of such association was empire, in that countries which were the subject of imperial rule were not expected to vote about external debt but were perfectly aware that the metropole could impose harsh sanctions in the case of non-compliance. Some other forms of political imposition looked similar, and could be described as "informal empire."

For those borrowers, diplomatic and political calculations played a much greater role than for Argentina. The Ottoman empire was a major part of the European power system. A default in 1875 brought major upheaval. The debt was restructured in 1878 following the Russo-Turkish war, with a debt administration imposed by the creditors (the *dette ottomane*) administering customs and tobacco revenues directly. In this particular setting, sovereign bankruptcy was relatively easy to manage because the international political system accepted and even encouraged intrusion into the sovereignty of the debtor country. The inability to service debt was interpreted by more powerful countries as a symptom of a broader failure of a state.

Other rival states learnt lessons from the Ottomans: that survival as a Great Power depended on a strengthening of not just military but economic fundamentals. The Russian autocracy, too, sought foreign money, but mixed military and administrative demands with an increased interest in economic development. In the 1890s, the innovative finance minister, Count Sergei Witte, viewed foreign money as a way of overcoming economic backwardness, while persuading the conservatives around the tsar that economic development was a necessity for Russian standing as a Great Power (von Laue 1963). By 1914, almost half of the 1,733 million ruble Russian government debt was held abroad, and four-fifths of that was in French hands, with the United Kingdom holding 14 percent. The diplomatic, military, and financial calculations were intricately tied together, and were skillfully used by Russia as a way of locking in the creditors politically and economically.

The beginning of the diplomatic rapprochement of Russia with France in 1891 was accompanied by a French bond issue, which the supporters of the new diplomacy celebrated as a "financial plebiscite" on the Franco-Russian alliance. The Witte boom was the outcome of a long period of rapprochement with the international financial order, and would have been unthinkable without a painful period of preparing Russia's entry into the gold standard (under Witte's predecessor, Vishnegradski). On the face of it, the Russian experience could be read as a case of the gold standard as a "good housekeeping seal of approval," since it limited the possibility of adopting the Argentine approach of the 1880s with government operations in both paper and gold. Russia survived a sharp contraction in 1900–1901, as well as a political crisis with war and revolution in 1905, with no default.

In the Russian case, the official sector clearly influenced the capacity of the private sector to borrow. Sub-sovereign debt – such as loans to the city of Moscow – as in Argentina were an alternative route to obtain finance when sovereign lending was subject to political conditions and limits. But foreign investors had even greater hopes in the capacity of the state to enforce their interests. The Russian central bank, instituted as part of Russia's convergence on the gold standard, was seen as the "Red Cross of the bourse," ready to intervene if bond or stock prices fell and new foreign investors might be warned off (Crisp 1976). Japan provides an equally convincing case of how reforms and strong state structures reduced rick perceptions and thus encouraged capital inflows (Sussman and Yafeh 2000).

At the beginning of this period, private-sector investment was dwarfed by the large market for state debt. In 1867, British investment in joint-stock banks was estimated at £85 million, and in other joint-stock enterprises at £100 million, while investments in foreign states was £2,566 million (Fenn 1869). By the end of the century, the balance was shifting to the private sector, and the Russian case is revealing. Substantial direct private investment in Russian enterprises followed in the wake of the official flows. Foreign direct investment (FDI) appeared as a good route for developing economies to gain technical and managerial skills. Some companies began to appear as multinational corporations (MNCs): Vickers or Shell (Jones and Trebilcock 1982), or most strikingly the US sewing machine company Singer (a pioneer of multinational marketing) in 1905 also set up a Russian plant (Godley 2006) as well as a small facility in Germany. German companies began to invest extensively in France in the years before World War I, as did French companies in Germany. By the eve of World War I, FDI had reached 9 percent of world output, a figure unsurpassed until the 1990s (see Jones, Chapter 16 in this volume).

Some financial institutions internationalized themselves, above all the big central European joint-stock banks. The Austro-Marxist economist Rudolf Hilferding in 1910 interpreted the result as *Finanzkapital*, or what he would in subsequent work name organized capitalism, in which massive concentrations of financial power controlled industry and stabilized prices (Hilferding 1981). Hilferding saw these nationally rooted concentrations of financial power as inevitably in competition with each other – and as a source of the growing international tension. In his interpretation, they made national crises less likely, but international crises more probable.

What role did central banks play? While at the beginning of the nineteenth century, the Bank of England had been the dominant – indeed the only – British joint-stock bank, by the end of the century, its balance sheet was dwarfed by the big clearing banks produced by a series of joint mergers facilitated by the legalization of the joint-stock form. The gold standard required sometimes quite dramatic changes in short-term rates, in response to external drains. Central banks were in a position to simply reverse carry trades when they experienced outflows of gold, but only in conditions when the market was tight (otherwise their increase in interest rates would not be "effective"). In 1889, the Bank of England's policy was the immediate precipitant of the Argentine sudden stop, as the bank rate, which had not been above 3 percent in the mid 1880s at the period of the big Argentine boom, was increased from 2.5 percent to

6 percent. At these rates, there was no longer any attraction in foreign lending. The same pattern recurred in another big international crisis, following from turbulences in New York in 1906 and 1907. As the Bank of England lost gold, it needed to increase bank rate in October 1906 from 4 to 6 percent, then eased, but in a response to a new panic put up the rate in November 1907. That had its consequences for other central banks, and for the periphery. The Reichsbank rate rose from 5.5 percent in April to 6.5 percent at the end of October and then 7.5 percent at the beginning of November. Some of the economies most badly hit by the panic of 1907 were very remote from New York, and had no direct financial linkages: Italy, or Egypt. The crisis of 1907 posed questions about monetary management in the face of unstable capital flows that anticipated the policy problems of the late 1920s.

The interwar experience

World War I revealed just how politically important capital movements had become. In the first place, war finance depended in large part on mobilizing foreign as well as domestic resources. A large part of the UK war effort was paid through selling off the accumulations that had resulted from the prewar creditor position. Citizens were encouraged and then (from 1917) obliged to sell their US and Canadian assets to the government (Taylor 1963: 42).

Second, governments borrowed directly from other governments with which they were allied. The tsarist regime in Russia borrowed from France and the United Kingdom. France and the United Kingdom also borrowed from the United States. As before World War I, large-scale official borrowing necessitated a convergence of foreign policies – and a sort of community of fate, sometimes between improbable allies. An extreme solution to the question of continued financial support between military allies, that was briefly proposed and debated in 1915, involved a full fiscal and political union of France, the United Kingdom, and Russia (*Economist*, 1915; Siegel, in press): the United Kingdom in particular wanted to mutualize the substantial Russian gold stock and use it as a basis to stabilize the currencies of the Allied group, collectively against the dollar (Neilson 1984: 65–66). On the other side of the conflict, by 1917 Germany was virtually in control of its Austro-Hungarian ally, using its control of economic resources to stop any independent Austrian peace initiatives. Such relationships between unequal allies raised the question of default in a highly political form. The Russian revolutions of 1917 in particular, culminating in the Bolshevik decision not to service the tsarist debt, launched a new era in global finance. It was no longer safe to assume that political reform would ensure creditworthiness; on the contrary, radical populist governments were likely to see a powerful attraction in expropriating foreign creditors. The Bolsheviks then portrayed Allied intervention in the Civil War as an attempt to impose financial claims on the Russian people.

Countries that were defeated militarily also lost their credit standing. The success and the attractiveness of the prewar order, however, convinced many investors that peacetime "normalcy" would quickly resume. As a result, there were major speculative inflows to Germany in the immediate aftermath of the armistice and the peace treaty, in 1919 and 1920, as foreign creditors expected a reversal of the currency depreciation and bought German assets in the hope of large exchange rate gains. German reconstruction and the initial political stabilization of the Weimar Republic thus benefitted from substantial capital inflows (Holtfrerich 1986). Those inflows stopped abruptly in 1921, in the aftermath of the assassination of the German Finance Minister (and signatory of the Versailles Treaty) which made it clear that Germany was not quickly re-establishing normalcy. The absence of capital inflows and the real cost of adjustment in 1921 and 1922 in turn intensified the political crisis and the government funding problem, and inflation turned into hyperinflation.

The overhang of wartime international government debt had a considerable effect on the postwar order. Both the United Kingdom and France were badly hit by the default that followed the Russian Revolution. For France, the repayment of wartime debt was unthinkable without reparations payments by the defeated powers, above all Germany.

The principle of reparations was set out in the 1919 Versailles Treaty, but the amount owed by Germany was not settled until 1921. In the face of Germany's failure to pay reparations in 1923, French and Belgian troops occupied Germany's industrial heartland in the Ruhr valley in an abortive attempt to extract physical reparations. The outcome of the subsequent political crisis was a new schedule of reparations payments, agreed at the London Conference of 1924 and generally known as the Dawes Plan. The innovative aspect of the Dawes Plan lay in a coupling of the political payments with a major loan to Germany floated on the US and British markets, which also promised to restore Germany to the international market and give German governments at the state and local level as well as German corporations access to foreign credit. When Germany's schedule was readjusted in 1929 under the terms of the Young Plan, reparations were accompanied by a new foreign loan. There now existed a flow of payments, in which private citizens in the western countries bought German bonds from the big investment houses. The proceeds flowed directly or indirectly (via German corporate borrowers and the taxes they paid) to the German government, which then made the reparations payments to the French and Belgian governments, and the French government could then service the war loans from World War I and repay the US government. The US taxpayer thus became the ultimate recipient of funds raised largely on the US domestic market. Supposing that this flow of new credit stopped, there would be a competition or struggle between the US taxpayer (the creditor of the interallied debt contracts) and US private investors (the creditors of the 1920s loan operations). Some German politicians made exactly this calculation, and deduced that pressure on the US government from wealthy American creditors might lead to an agreement of the US government to cancel war debts and also reparations payments.

The terms of the 1929 agreement changed the calculation. By instituting a new mechanism for transfer protection – in response to fears that the transfer of the reparations might put Germany in an impossible situation, the official payments were in effect prioritized over the private payments. Private creditors saw that they were pushed back in the line for repayment by the German sovereign borrower, and accordingly became more nervous (Ritschl 2002).

The calculations of the Allied governments in the reparations settlements of 1924 and 1929 can be explained in political terms. In both cases, diplomats and politicians worried that continued flows of credit to Germany, and other central European countries, were essential to further the consolidation of democracy and peace, and that without such flows there would be a heightened risk of radical revolution or bolshevization.

The 1920s struggle over reparations also led to a theoretical debate about how the balance of payments adjusted to capital flows. On the one side, the Cambridge economist John Maynard Keynes, who from the beginning had been a stern critic of the reparation settlement, argued that the adjustment process could only occur through relative price changes and a deterioration of the terms of trade of the paying country. The prices of German products would fall in order to make the transfer (Keynes 1929). The Swedish economist Bertil Ohlin responded with a demonstration that the payments were financed through the tax system: German taxes would rise, demand would fall, and imports would also fall; in the recipient countries, taxes could be lowered, and there would be a greater demand for German goods. Ohlin's argument is theoretically more convincing, but in practice there were real limits to the extent to which the tax screws could be applied in debtor countries (Ohlin 1929). Germany is an exemplar of a general problem. The rich – organized through politically powerful lobby groups – demanded subsidies and resisted tax rises, while popular political parties of the center and left resisted attempts to increase indirect and consumption taxes. By the time of the depression, it became impossible for governments to pass fiscal measures with a majority in Parliament (James 1986).

The political payments and debts occurred in a world in which "normal" capital flows of the prewar kind had resumed. Raw material and commodity-producing countries, especially in Latin America and in eastern Europe, borrowed for the same reasons as in the era of the classic gold standard. So did new countries, especially in central Europe, which wanted to invest in new infrastructure. All paid an interest rate premium, which reflected risk perception: Thus in Germany, by far the largest single borrower, the yield on ten-year government bonds at the beginning of 1926 was almost 4 percent over that on US bonds, with the difference falling to 1.8 percent in February 1927, but then increasing again as the world slid into the Great Depression. In general, the slow fall of commodity prices from the mid 1920s and a much more rapid collapse after 1929 made the debt levels unsustainable and debt service impossible (Kindleberger 1973). In these circumstances there were powerful elements that made for a contagious crisis and a dramatic reversal of capital flows: both in similarities between commodity producers, and in the shocks generated by the appearance of losses for creditors, which required the liquidation of other assets. There was also a general reaction to risk, with a new emphasis on safety and security.

The duality of a large structure of private credits and the official-sector debt intensified the confidence crisis. The debt crisis that had virtually been programmed by the nature of the reparation settlement and by the 1929 modification of payments priorities broke out in 1931. The key to keeping the flows of money moving from the US and the United Kingdom had lain in a yield differential that made the servicing of debt expensive and ultimately impossible.

The extent of the debt crisis was further amplified by the character of the financial system. One flaw was in the international currency system. A key part of the assumption about returning to normalcy had involved the restoration of a credible currency commitment. In returning to the gold standard in the 1920s, most countries adopted a fractional reserve system, with the aim of economizing on the need for monetary gold. A typical rule was that adopted by the German Reichsbank in the new legislation of 1924, which aimed at currency stabilization. The central bank was required to hold a reserve of 40 percent of its note issue in gold and foreign exchange. When the reserve ratio approached the 40 percent limit, the central bank needed to contract its note issue by a much greater factor (100/40) than the loss of reserves.

A second flaw lay in the structure of banking in many continental European countries. Unlike the United States, where banking was highly localized, continental European economies were dominated by financial systems in which a small number of very large banks – with big international exposures – dominated the economy. In Austria, where the crisis began in May 1931, the Creditanstalt controlled some 60 percent of Austrian firms through ownership stakes (Nötel 1984). The failure or potential failure of very large financial institutions thus posed a major policy problem. The banking problems and central banking issues were interrelated, nowhere more obviously than in Austria, which provided the epicenter of the currency and banking crisis. The Austrian National Bank had kept its reserves in large part in London in the form of bills or short-term deposits, which were then used to make deposits in the large private bank, the Creditanstalt. This system of cross-deposits enhanced the interdependence of banks and the central banking regime.

Bank collapses followed from the price shocks of the international depression imposed upon bank weakness in countries that had been wrecked by the aftermath of bad policies that produced inflation, hyperinflation, and a destruction of banks' balance sheets. The intrinsic financial-sector vulnerability made for a heightened exposure to political shocks, and disputes about a central European customs union and about the postwar reparations issue were enough to topple a house of cards. Central European banks in 1931 were additionally vulnerable as a result of a monetary policy subject to gold standard constraints, and they were victims of monetary deflation (Ferguson and Temin 2003). But there were plenty of specific issues which long antedated the collapses of the early 1930s (James 1986). They are the result of specific design features of the financial system that could not simply be corrected by macro-economic policy, whether monetary or fiscal. US banking was highly localized, and thus vulnerable to geographically limited shocks (such as the agricultural depression); while larger nationwide banking in Canada was much more resilient. Banks in many debtor countries in South America and central Europe accumulated mismatches between assets (in local currency) and liabilities (in dollars or other key currencies), that made for a vulnerability to currency turmoil. Universal banks suffered large losses on their shareholdings, and as their capitalization fell, cut back on their lending. Some British banks (the so-called merchant banks) had heavy overseas exposures that made them vulnerable to foreign crises (Accominotti 2009; James 2001).

The aftermath of 1931 was a reversal of capital flows, with flight capital moving to "safe havens": above all the neutral countries of World War I, the Netherlands and Switzerland, and the United States. These flows were also

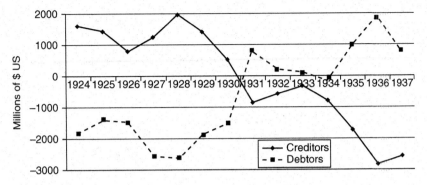

Figure 9.2. Capital flow reversals 1924–1939 (aggregated capital flows)
Source: James 2001

described at the time as "hot money," that was very sensitive to interest rate differentials, but also to changes in the security situation. The extent and the rapidity of the inflows to these remaining gold standard countries threatened banking stability there.

As the capital flows reversed, the gold standard was destroyed (see Figure 9.2). Countries with high external debts ended convertibility (as a devaluation would have balance sheet effects for borrowing banks, corporations, and governments). Central European and Latin American countries thus imposed exchange controls. Countries without substantial foreign liabilities could more easily move to a floating exchange rate. The United Kingdom and the Scandinavian countries followed this course after September 1931.

Staying on the gold standard at first generated very significant capital inflows (so-called "hot money"), but at the same time also the potential for future attacks should the possibility of outflows emerge. Even the US was subject to such outflows. US banks lost deposits internationally between September 1931 (the date of the British abandonment of the gold standard) and April 1933, when the gold convertibility of the dollar was suspended; and from April 1933, French banks lost deposits (much of these funds initially went to Switzerland). Some of the largest flows into Switzerland came out of France at the time of the fascist demonstrations of 1934 and the formation of the Popular Front government of 1936. An examination of flows into the United States and of flows from Switzerland to the United States shows peaks above all during the political and economic crises of France (in September 1936, November 1936, February 1937), but also smaller spikes coinciding with political crises in Germany (the German pogrom of November 1938; the invasion of Czechoslovakia in March 1939) (Wilkins 1999). Possible returns or outflows of flight capital posed a double threat: to the banks who held the deposits, but also to the Swiss National Bank which would be required to make the conversions from francs into foreign exchange.

At first the most obvious course for dealing with this problem was for central banks to deny absolutely that there would be any parity change. Even the strongest countries became vulnerable (Straumann 2010). Immediately after the sterling crisis in September 1931, the Swiss franc looked relatively secure, and the major speculative attacks against the remaining gold standard countries affected the United States and France. But it became increasingly clear that the flood of short-term deposits that had moved into the Swiss financial system during the crisis years was not necessarily tied to Switzerland, and that an outflow would weaken both the banking system and the currency, or in other words provoke exactly the same combination of banking and currency crisis that had brought down central Europe in 1931. The outflow might originate in security or Europe-wide political worries, but of course it might also be set off by worries about the stability and the credibility of Swiss policy. Policy-makers were aware of the bind that they were in: The situation was becoming increasingly fragile, but any action they might undertake held the risk of being destabilizing rather than stability-promoting.

The Bretton Woods era

In 1944 and 1945, the Allied makers of the postwar order wanted to draw lessons from the disasters of the interwar period. Their collective preference can be formulated in terms of a response to the "trilemma" that was explicitly formulated later: the mutual incompatibility of free capital movements, autonomous monetary policy, and fixed exchange rates. Control of national monetary policies was a politically powerful demand. The trade wars of the 1930s had been furthered through competitive currency devaluations, and trade was believed to benefit from the certainty of fixed exchange rates. There was nothing at all attractive to the new designers of global order about capital flows.

A new consensus on the causes of the Great Depression had shifted the emphasis away from the favorite villains of the 1930s literature – the uneven distribution of gold and the sterilizing policies of the Banque de France and the Federal Reserve System, or the allegedly excessive monetary inflation of the 1920s, or structural weaknesses in major industrial centers. Rather the new view looked at the transmission process of depression, and came to the conclusion that the large short-term capital flows of the 1920s and 1930s had led to disaster. These movements had made it impossible for states to pursue stable monetary policies, they threatened exchange rate stability, and they made fiscal stabilization counterproductive.

This approach to the interwar economy, oriented towards the diagnosis of capital movements as the fundamental ill had been developed by League of Nations economists in the 1930s. The most influential academic statement was Ragnar Nurkse's *International Currency Experience* (1944). His approach appealed to Keynes, who had repeatedly asserted his skepticism about the benefits of both capital exports and capital imports. Keynes fully shared the belief that capital flight had been the major international interwar problem:

> There is no country which can, in future, safely allow the flight of funds for political reasons or to evade domestic taxation or in anticipation of the owner turning refugee. Equally, there is no country that can safely receive fugitive funds, which constitute an unwanted import of capital, yet cannot safely be used for fixed investment. (Horsefield 1986: III, 31; Moggridge 1992)

It is true that Keynes added that the new controls, which might become a "permanent feature of the post-war system," should not bring an end to the "era of international investment": but it would need states and international agreements to define (in accordance with national priorities) what constituted desirable investment and what was unwanted capital movement. Many Americans also shared this view.

The Bretton Woods scheme depended on a worldwide agreement on the control of capital movements, which was presented as a "permanent feature" of the postwar system (Horsefield 1986: III, 13). The consequences of general deflation during the Great Depression were so severe that devising mechanisms to prevent a recurrence were at the heart of postwar institutional designs. The necessity of tackling the problem was central to the design of the International Monetary Fund (IMF). IMF facilities would be used to smooth adjustment in deficit countries; but there was also a "scarce currency clause" that required action by a country running a persistent surplus. Such calculations occurred not simply on the global level, however. The Treaty of Rome (1957) establishing the European Economic Community also specified in Article 104:

> Each Member State shall pursue the economic policy necessary to ensure the equilibrium of its overall balance of payments and to maintain confidence in

its currency, while ensuring a high level of employment and the stability of the level of prices.

In practice, the idea of devising institutional mechanisms for changing policy and correcting surpluses was very difficult to realize. The "scarce currency" clause was never used, as at the beginning it would have required actions against the United States, the largest member of the IMF and clearly the most powerful country in the world. IMF rulings that currencies were underappreciated were made against Sweden and Korea in the 1980s, but never against the major countries that were at the center of discussions of adjustment in the 1970s and 1980s, Germany and Japan.

When capital movements recommenced in the second globalization wave after 1945, they came in a different order than that of the nineteenth century wave.

The initial flows were official credits, in the framework of the Marshall Plan and other official reconstruction programs. FDI was the first private-sector type to assume a major importance after World War II. It is associated with major flows of skills, technology, and management. It often responded to trade protection and closed off good markets, in that production moved to markets that would otherwise have been inaccessible. The MNC was thus a major bearer of the initial dynamic of the second globalization wave. MNCs play a large part in the transformation of European production, but also in development in Latin America.

Other forms of capital flow started to reappear in the 1960s, despite extensive capital controls. Notwithstanding extensive capital controls, there could be substantial short-term movements – occurring, for instance, through channels intended for trade finance, with early or late foreign exchange payments (leads and lags). An offshore bond market (Eurobonds) developed, and some big US banks helped to redevelop London as a financial center for offshore finance. But banks remained largely national (and old-fashioned or unadventurous or "retro" in Amar Bhide's terminology) in their orientation (Bhide 2010).

Modern globalization

The term globalization was first used in its modern meaning in 1970 but it still carried something of its older diplomatic meaning of a connection or linkage or interaction between disparate issue areas. The 1970s was the decade when internationalization really took over banking, and international banking and political calculations were now linked in a way not seen since the interwar period. Capital movements – through the banking system – were the response to the emergence of significant current account imbalances in the aftermath of a general commodities boom and, in particular, substantially politically driven manipulations of the petroleum market. The 1970s financial revolution can be thought of as an outcome of:

(1) Changes in domestic finance, above all in the United States. The development of a capital market made bond financing available for large corporations. As a consequence, US bank lending to industry diminished, and banks felt a need to look for alternative or new borrowers. There was thus a substantial push element to the growth of foreign lending.

(2) An international imbalance issue, in the aftermath of the two oil price shocks, with oil producers unable to spend the greatly enhanced revenues that followed the oil price rises. The petroleum exporters suddenly had very large current account surpluses, the counterparts of industrial and developing country importers who saw immediate adjustment as catastrophically deflationary.

(3) Encouragement by Western governments (in particular the United States) for oil producers to "recycle" the surpluses through the banking system (rather than say through the official sector: though the IMF came up with an Oil Facility that was intended to allow the funds of oil producers to ease the adjustment in non-oil developing countries). On occasion, National Security Adviser Henry Kissinger spoke directly about how the inclusion of Middle Eastern oil producers into an economic and political "West" through the international banking system was a better way of securing an alignment of their interests with those of the large industrial countries than any sort of openly confrontational course.

(4) A belief by some bankers that the encouragement of their governments of the recycling process amounted to an implicit guarantee on the part of governments. In the case of US banks, bankers, when asked about the security of their syndicated lending to Latin America, referred to views in the State Department about the desirability of political and economic stability in the western hemisphere; German banks that lent considerable amounts to Warsaw Pact (Soviet satellite) countries, in particular Hungary and Poland, also liked to refer to their government's interest in the new phenomenon of *Ostpolitik*. Sometimes bankers formulated their new confidence in absurdly overstated slogans, as when Citibank's Walter Wriston opined that countries could not go bankrupt.

(5) A lack of any detailed knowledge about the extent of total exposure of banks through loans to developing countries, and a general regulatory

failure. Both the Federal Reserve System and the Bank for International Settlements (the central bankers' principal global institution) tried to collect statistical information, but largely failed because of bank resistance. It is not even clear that individual debtor countries had information about the total indebtedness of their public sector (because a multiplicity of state and para-state institutions was involved in the lending process).

(6) The low interest rate environment prevailing until the dramatic shift in the policy orientation of the Federal Reserve in October 1979. With often negative real interest rates, debt service appeared unproblematical.

(7) Nearly ubiquitous cross-default clauses in syndicated loan agreements made an isolated individual default impossible, and a collective default triggered by such clauses would have such impossibly dangerous consequences that it was also unthinkable.

(8) Competition within different national banking sectors for the lucrative activities associated with recycling or relending oil surpluses and other deposits. Newcomer institutions that wanted to expand quickly would be prepared to take greater risks.

(9) Competition between national banking sectors, with Japanese and continental European banks gradually displaying increasing eagerness to catch up with British and American lenders.

(10) Within the lending banks, there may also have been agency problems. The individuals responsible for making loans saw their (highly profitable) activity as a channel for rapid career advancement, and assumed that if there were to be problems regarding borrowers' capacity to pay in the future, they would no longer be in their old positions.

The outbreak of a debt crisis in August 1982 with the possibility and threat of Mexican default created the threat of a repetition of a 1930s-style contagious and general debt and banking crisis. A Mexican default alone would have wiped out almost all the capital of almost all the substantial New York lending banks.

What followed was a seven-year play for extra time. The initial approach was to link policy improvement in the borrowing countries with help from international institutions, but also extra lending from the banks. The latter element seemed to defy the most elementary canons of sensible bank behavior. The aftermath of the Latin American debt crisis produced the first systematic attempt at international regulatory coordination, culminating with the 1988 Basel Agreement (with its notorious weighting system, under which OECD country debt was assessed as risk free).

Three years after the outbreak of the Latin American crisis, US Treasury Secretary James Baker announced a systematization of the initial response. It was not very imaginative. Banks and multilateral development institutions should all lend more, and the debtors should continue their efforts to improve their policy. The Baker Plan was a universal disappointment. Growth faltered again, and the IMF actually reduced its lending.

More than three years passed before a new Treasury Secretary, Nicholas Brady, set out a more satisfactory program, in which banks would be given a menu of options that included lower interest rates on the debt and selling back the debt to the debtor at a hefty discount. If the banks were unwilling to accept some form of restructuring, they would have to put in new money. The lending of the international institutions might also be used for buying back discounted debt. The Brady plan was a great success. Confidence returned, capital flight from Latin America was reversed, and the capital markets began to be willing to lend again.

Why did it come so late? The most obvious answer is that at an earlier stage in the Latin American saga, the banks simply could not have afforded to take such losses on their capital. They needed the seven years of faking the position in order to build up adequate reserves against losses. It is also important to recognize that the initiative for the Brady Plan really did not come from the official sector at all. It was the willingness of some big financial institutions to trade in discounted debt that established a market that would clear out the legacy of past policy mistakes. In particular, two institutions took a lead: Citicorp in the United States, and Deutsche Bank in Europe. Their CEOs at the time presented their actions as motivated by a far-sighted benevolence and a concern for the well-being of the world as a whole. That may have been plausible, but these two banks also were playing in a competitive field and wanted to demonstrate very publicly that they had a better balance sheet than their weaker rivals. In Germany, the relatively weaker Dresdner Bank and the publicly owned Landesbanken could not afford to take such a hit.

The aftermath of the Latin American debacle was quite long-lived in that banks learnt an immediate lesson about avoiding developing country debt. The Brady bond solution also introduced securitization to emerging market finance, with the consequence that in the next surge of investment (in the 1990s), risk was much more widely distributed. Pension and mutual funds were not principals in any kind of restructuring negotiation, and thus the bail-in solutions of the 1980s could no longer be used. The internationalization of bond debt, and the breaking down of insulated or isolated domestic markets (financial repression), is thus a relatively late development that took off in the intensive wave of financial globalization in the 1990s and 2000s.

In the 1990s, in the wake of the collapse of Soviet-style planned economies, capital account liberalization seemed more desirable. The IMF actively discussed an amendment of its Articles of Agreement to require capital as well as current account convertibility. Before such a Third Amendment of the Articles could be agreed, however, a new crisis blew up which made the case for capital account liberalization more problematical.

Especially in Asia, many emerging market economies encouraged large capital inflows that fueled an investment boom. There was a widespread belief among investors that a new economic miracle was occurring, and the World Bank published an influential study of the *East Asian Miracle* (1993). The inflows took different forms. From 1993 Thailand encouraged offshore deposits via the new Bangkok International Banking Facility. For Korea, most of the capital inflows occurred to the big industrial holding companies, the *chaebols*. The borrowing was used to finance large current account deficits, with Thailand running a deficit of nearly 8 percent in 1995 and 1996 (the Korean figure was much lower). Since the deficits were used to finance private-sector investment and not government spending, it was thought to be sustainable for long periods (as such flows had been in some nineteenth-century borrowers). The distinction between private (good) and public (bad) origins of current account deficits had been formulated in the 1980s by the British Chancellor of the Exchequer, Nigel Lawson, and was consequently sometimes called the Lawson doctrine; an academic version of the same theory applied to Australia (which also ran large deficits) is called the Pitchford Thesis (Pitchford 1990). In fact, the UK experience in the early 1990s, with a dramatic exchange rate crisis in 1992, indicated the limits of the Lawson doctrine as the private sector inflows suddenly reversed. Asia learnt the same lesson: dependence on short-term capital inflows is not just a problem for government borrowers.

The capital inflows to Asia fueled rises in prices and wages, and the real exchange rate of the borrowing countries deteriorated. But by this stage, the borrowing countries were caught in an impossible dilemma. The exchange rate adjustment that would have been needed to deal with the real appreciation problem would destroy the balance sheets of corporations and banks that had assets mostly in the domestic currency but liabilities in foreign currencies. The restructuring of the banking systems then involved expensive public support, and private debt in effect became the responsibility of public authorities. When the Asia crisis blew up in 1997–1998 and capital flows reversed, the Asian governments faced a large fiscal cost.

Although the immediate aftermath of the Asia crisis of 1997–1998 looked similar to the Latin American debt crisis of 1982, the long-term implications were quite different. The Asian economies returned to growth relatively rapidly, in part on the basis of very orthodox adjustment policies (for instance in Korea), and in part on the basis of unorthodox policies aimed at controlling capital movements (most dramatically in Malaysia, where Prime Minister Mahathir Mohamed built himself up as the enemy of international finance). China, with a controlled capital account, was scarcely affected by the dramatic regional crisis. But all the Asian countries learnt one lesson: that current account deficits were dangerous because the capital flows could easily be reversed. As a consequence, reserve accumulation and current account surpluses became the default policy choice. In the aftermath of the Asia crisis, global capital flows increased even more dramatically, but the direction of net flows changed. Gross capital flows constituted 10 percent of world GDP in 1998, but over 30 percent by 2007. While savings rates rose in developing countries, they fell in industrial countries, and many industrial countries became net borrowers. In an apparently perverse movement, surpluses from poor but rapidly growing emerging market countries flowed into rich and mature industrial countries, above all the United States and the United Kingdom, as well as some fast-growing countries in the European periphery (see Figure 9.3).

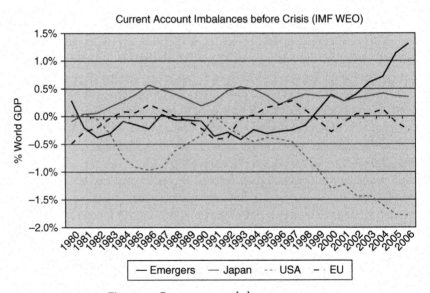

Figure 9.3. Current account balances 1990–2010

Those who continued to advocate capital market liberalization concluded that there was a problem in sequencing, and that large inflows to countries with inadequately developed domestic financial institutions were destabilizing.

A great deal of attention focussed on the high savings rates of Asian countries. But the phenomenon was a more general one. In the 1990s, the pool of world savings increased dramatically, leading some influential policy-makers to speak of a global savings glut that was likely permanently to depress the cost of borrowing (Bernanke 2005). The Asian NICs (Taiwan, Singapore, Korea) saw a reduction in savings rates in the 2000s, although this was compensated by lower investment levels, so that funds continued to flow out. For the NICs, the saving rate 1990–2000 had been 33.5 percent of GDP; by 2006 it was 31.3 percent. But lower-income countries ("developing Asia") had big increases in savings: from 32.9 percent to 42.2 percent. Especially quickly growing but politically unstable and insecure countries experienced dramatic rises in the savings rates, as citizens felt unsure about their future and unable to rely on state support mechanisms. China provides a paradigmatic case. Although in absolute terms Chinese consumption rose, consumption *rates* fell as incomes rose: By 2005, Chinese households consumed less than 40 percent of GDP, and Chinese households moved to very high savings rates (of around 30 percent). With simultaneous high saving by the government and by enter-prises, the outcome is a large amount of capital in search of security. But the savings surge, and the accompanying positive current account balance is not just a Chinese peculiarity, but can be found in most Asian, South Asian, and Middle Eastern economies. For the Middle East, the savings rate rose from 24.2 percent in the 1990s to 40.4 percent in 2006. In the latter case, the surge in oil prices has been responsible for the growth in savings, but in Asia it reflects the combination of stronger growth and increased precautionary saving (Horioka and Terada-Hagiwara 2011; Kraay 2000).

Why did capital flow to the United States and other mature economies? The best explanation lies not in higher returns, but in the greater security that the United States offers. One apparently odd fact makes the deficits more sustain-able than most analysts believed they should be: the yield on US assets for foreigners, the price paid by the United States for its borrowing, is substantially lower than the yield for Americans on their foreign holdings. This is the reason why the balance on investment income continues to be so surprisingly resilient and large. Gourinchas and Rey (2005) calculate that for the whole period 1960 to 2001, the annualized rate of return on US liabilities (3.61 percent) was more than two percentage points below the annualized real rate of return on US assets (5.72 percent), and that for the post-1973 period the difference is significantly larger (3.50 and 6.82 percent respectively) (Congdon 2002; Haussmann and Sturzenegger 2006). The yield difference reflects not miscalculation or stupidity on the part of foreign investors, but a calculation in which they buy security in return for lower yields. The primary attraction of the United States as a destination for capital movement is the unique depth of its markets (which generate a financial security) and the political and security position of the country. Only a very few other countries share the US reputation as a stable and secure haven in which property rights are powerfully protected. This is why inflows to the United States increased after global security shocks (as, for instance, after the terrorist attacks of September 11, 2001).

The United Kingdom had similar characteristics to the United States, with a substantial difference between high returns on external assets and lower yields on external liabilities. Australia has similar returns on assets and liabilities, while in Spain (another country with a large current account deficit that needs to be financed by external inflows) the assets yield less than the liabilities. It might thus be concluded that the British and American position was fundamentally more sustainable than that of Spain, which became one of the most vulnerable economies in the post-2008 era.

Europe had its own version of the imbalances problem. Until 2009–10, the European flows were sometimes portrayed as being more sustainable and less perverse than the international flows. Capital was flowing in the "right" direction, and not "uphill" from poor to rich countries. Northern European surpluses corresponded to south European deficits. Like the Asian borrowers of the 1990s, the south European borrowers had problems in a real appreciation, but this time the real appreciation occurred within the framework of a currency union, and thus could not simply be corrected by devaluation. European governments as well as private borrowers increasingly financed themselves from abroad – but from within the eurozone. In the wake of the transition to monetary union, debt holding became internationalized. This is what distinguishes the European experience from that of another country that has also built up a high debt burden. Japan, despite a horrendously high proportion of debt to GDP, is usually thought to be very stable because the lenders (debt holders) are domestic. They are also aging, and thus need to hold investments to pay for their retirement. In consequence, there is an overwhelming home bias. Up to the late 1990s and the advent of monetary union, most EU government debt was domestically held: in 1998 the overall ratio of foreign-held debt was only a fifth. That ratio then climbed rapidly in the aftermath of the introduction of the euro. In 2008, on the eve of the financial crisis, three-quarters of Portuguese debt, and half of Spanish and

Greek debt, as well as over two-fifths of Italian debt was held by foreigners. A significant proportion, especially in the case of Greece, Portugal, and Italy, was held by banks.

Was the deterioration of fiscal positions merely a European phenomenon, driven by a relaxation of market discipline on fiscal policies that followed from the apparent logic of monetary union? And is it macroeconomic policy (fiscal policy) or the structure and institutions of the financial system that is responsible? The same trajectory occurred in the United States, from fiscal responsibility in the 1990s (under President Clinton) to persistent and high deficits in the 2000s under Bush. So other explanations are that the United States also provided a bad example, or (more plausibly) that the markets were apparently willing to finance almost limitless amounts of government debt, as they perceived the debt of industrial countries to be an entirely risk-free asset. Bank regulators, pushed by governments desperate for cheap financing, then embedded this conventional wisdom in their regulatory codes.

The greater relative size of financial transactions and new financial instruments, coupled with a great ability of large banks to tap into one national source of funds and pass them on to users of capital elsewhere, contributed to what was seen in the 2000s as a "frictionless" global financial system. These large financial institutions became central mediators of international capital movements because in practice they alone could provide "markets" for their customers – pension and trust funds – who required counterparties for dealings with complex financial products in which there was no obvious or natural market. In practice, a relatively small number of institutions (termed SIFIs, Systemically Important Financial Intermediaries after 2008) became central in market making. It later emerged that some of the critical signals on which the market depended – notably the widely used interest rate LIBOR (London Inter-Bank Offer Rate) had been set not by a normal market process but rather by collusion between a handful of key players.

The internalization of international banking activity can be seen in the activities of domestic affiliates of foreign banks. From 2000 to 2008, intra-bank assets grew in all countries by approximately 20 percent per annum. In Iceland and Australia, they grew by over 100 percent per year, and the United Kingdom was not far behind with 80 percent, followed by France, Germany, and the United States with around 40, 20, and 20 percent respectively. Between 2000 and 2007 the outstanding stock of banks' foreign claims grew from $10 trillion to $34 trillion. On an ultimate risk basis (including guarantees), the domestic claims of foreign banks' affiliates make up a huge percentage of total international claims (cross-border and domestic of foreign-owned entities). In March

2008 in the United States, for example, they amounted to 110 percent of total international claims excluding the guarantees. A substantial part of the foreign bank claims represented both a currency and a maturity mismatch: The extent of the maturity mismatch was estimated at between $1.1 and $6.5 trillion (McGuire and Peter 2009).

After 2008, a consensus emerged – analogous to that which developed in response to the 1930s Great Depression – that there was too much capital moving. There are two alternative tracks for dealing with the problem: one lies in limiting the global risks built up in the financial sector. But that is a complex issue, and pressure to increase the safety of the banking system by increasing capital ratios in the short run risks contracting bank lending and forcing the world into deflationary adjustment. In addition, pressure on big financial institutions to reduce risk and increase capitalization is also often linked with pressure on banks to provide more facilities to their home economies. As a result, the Great Recession after 2008 has produced a renationalization of banking.

The other alternative policy lies in addressing the question of international imbalances by means of macroeconomic adjustment strategies (monetary and fiscal expansion in surplus countries, and correspondingly contraction in countries with deficits). Such adjustment became a major part of the IMF's attempt to reform its mission of providing surveillance of the international monetary system. The main critique lies in the way surplus countries try to achieve trade surpluses. The big current account surpluses of China – in the global system – or Germany – within the eurozone – are interpreted as a mercantilist act in which a currency is deliberately undervalued for the purpose of increasing export competitiveness.

The major test cases that people regard as precedents for the problem of Chinese surpluses concern the two countries whose strategy of growth through the development of a powerful export sector is widely regarded as providing a model for development elsewhere, especially in Asia. The surpluses look smaller than those of China today (Germany's current account surplus reached a peak of 4.8 percent in 1989; and Japan's stood at 4.3 percent in 1986); but they posed substantial problems for other industrial countries, which believed that both the major export economies were deliberately undervaluing their currencies in order to achieve export advantages. In the late 1970s and again in the late 1980s, substantial pressure was applied on the surplus countries to bear more of the responsibility for global adjustment, and to act as a "locomotive" for the world economy. The most dramatic of these interventions – with heavy international pressure on Japan and Germany to take action against surpluses – occurred in the framework of the G-5/G-7 Finance Ministers' meetings in the mid 1980s, between the 1985 Plaza and the 1987 Louvre agreements. The package involved exchange rate correction, since calculations showed a considerable currency undervaluation, but also a combination of fiscal and monetary measures. Again, as in the late 1960s, the international pressure pushed Germany into looking for more European ways of dealing with its imbalances. The German surplus quickly disappeared after 1989, and not because of international coordination, but rather from 1990 in the aftermath of the massive costs of the unpredicted reunification of East Germany with West Germany.

The bitterest legacy of the mid 1980s coordination experience was felt in Japan, where there was a large fiscal expansion after 1986 and a monetary easing. The currency appreciated very rapidly after the Plaza agreement, and GDP growth fell off. In order to respond to the slowing of the Japanese economy, and in line with continued international pressure, government deficits continued. The aftermath of the experience of intensified "international cooperation" was seen as first the bubble economy of the late 1980s, and then the collapse of the bubble and the "lost decade" of the 1990s.

Clearly the "bubble" and its bursting in Japan have a more complex explanation than simply the monetary and fiscal mix of 1985–1987, but the fact that this is the most dramatic instance of international engagement to tackle persistent current account surpluses overshadows current debates about what the appropriate response to Chinese surpluses should be.

The IMF's *World Economic Outlook* (April 2010) presented a substantial number of cases of adjustment in order to derive the conclusion that "policy-induced current account surplus reversals were not typically associated with lower growth" (see also Blanchard and Milesi-Ferretti 2011). But the list of specific examples, from Japan in 1973, Germany in 1970, Japan in 1988, to Switzerland in 1978, involve experiences that are considered in the domestic debates and literature of the countries concerned to be disastrous experiences, or at least precedents that should not easily or thoughtlessly be emulated. In that sense, the history of policy-induced current account reversal looks like a poisoned chalice.

In fact, the financial crisis of 2008 was followed by some adjustment, as private-sector flows underwent a sudden stop, and capital flight by domestic residents as well as foreign creditors ravaged debtor countries (Milesi-Ferretti and Tille 2011). But that dramatic development is not completely reflected in net figures on capital flows, as public-sector and central banking credit replaced the private money that was fleeing. Within large banking groups, currency mismatches needed to be resolved by central bank lending: Thus the Federal Reserve expanded its swap network in 2008 to provide dollar funding to large foreign (and especially European) banks. As private money fled out of south European government debt, more was bought by domestic financial institutions, which in turn refinanced themselves through borrowing from the European Central Bank. The stabilizing action of central banks, international institutions, and governments inevitably raises the same sort of question as in the 1920s as to the relative priorities given to service and amortization of private- and public-sector debt.

The debate between debtors and creditors in the international economy swings dangerously between two different ways of assessing legitimacy: power and morality. What irritates debtors is often that the creditors present their position as being fundamentally more virtuous: The Greeks are said to have excessively high pensions, excessively early retirement ages, and too may extra months' salaries, while the Americans engage in consumer binges on the never-never, financed in ever more ingenious ways. The creditors point to generations of Confucian or Protestant teaching on the virtues of thrift.

Conclusion

The problems of the international monetary system in this period are often analyzed in terms of a trilemma (or impossible trinity) of free capital movements, fixed exchange rates, and monetary autonomy. In the nineteenth century, capital moved freely and exchange rates were fixed, but there was no possibility of adopting nationally different monetary policies. The attempted restoration of this order in the 1920s foundered because extreme monetary policy was needed in order to make adjustment in a world that had suffered numerous severe economic shocks. That monetary policy triggered extreme volatility in capital movements. In the 1930s a consensus emerged that capital movements should be limited, and that provided the intellectual groundbed of the postwar monetary order. But it soon became clear that some types of capital flow might be regarded as desirable because they solved financing gaps. The Bretton Woods era ended in the early 1970s, as the world moved to greater exchange rate flexibility. But in practice, the continued presence of Bretton Woods-like elements means that the trinity problem persists. First, many Asian countries pegged to the dollar and thus created what is sometimes referred to as Bretton Woods Two (Dooley, Folkerts-Landau, and Garber 2003). Second, Europe introduced a monetary union. Once the imbalances become a focus of concern, and seem to require unbearably disruptive adjustment strategies in deficit countries, the result – increasing pressure to restrict capital movements, and to renationalize finance – comes to resemble the reaction of the interwar period. Both demands have become more prominent in the wake of the 2007–2008 sub-prime crisis and the post-2010 eurozone debt crisis.

Rodrik (2007) added a political trilemma to the monetary one, presenting democracy, national sovereignty, and global economic integration as mutually incompatible. In particular, democratization (with representative institutions) in an early phase was linked to greater creditworthiness, as long as finance was primarily national; but it leads to an articulation of demands for debt cancellation when finance is largely internationalized and a large part of debt is external. The compensatory mechanisms used in the past to establish greater credibility were imperialism in the late nineteenth century, but also alliance systems and enhanced political cooperation. That political cooperation sometimes seems to require an overriding of national sovereignty. The solution that political theorists sometimes come up with – increased democratic accountability of international coordination mechanisms – has been tried with some success in the European case. Faced with a crisis – and the challenge of differing creditor and debtor claims across national frontiers – that sort of coordination is looking increasingly fragile.

At this point, it is possible to revert to the initial question of why it is that capital does not always flow in the beneficent way that theory assumes. There is a powerful institutional incentive to build structures and devise policies that are compatible with larger capital imports because they produce an institutional umbrella or carapace. Another way of describing this phenomenon is as a political concentration of risk. But how strong or how resilient are the protective devices? Their structures are really quite fragile, and the policies subject to reversal, because of the volatilities produced by large concentrations of risk, sometimes in the form of large financial institutions, and sometimes also in the form of agglomerations of power in the shape of large states.

References

Accominotti, O. (2009). "London Merchant Banks, the Central European Panic and the Sterling Crisis of 1931," *The Journal of Economic History* 72(1), 1–43.

Bernanke, B. S. (2005). "The Global Saving Glut and the U.S. Current Account Deficit," Richmond speech, www.federalreserve.gov/boarddocs/speeches/2005/200503102/default.htm

Bhagwati, J. (2004). *In Defense of Globalization.* New York: Oxford University Press

Bhide, A. (2010). *A Call for Judgment: Sensible Finance for a Dynamic Economy*. New York: Oxford University Press.

Blanchard, O. and G. Maria Milesi-Ferretti (2011). "(Why) Should Current Account Balances be Reduced?" IMF Staff Discussion Note SDN 2011/03.

Bordo, M. D., B. Eichengreen, and D. A. Irwin (1999). "Is Globalization Today Really Different than Globalization a Hundred Years Ago?" NBER Working Paper No. 7195.

Bordo, M. D. and H. Rockoff (1996). "The Gold Standard as a 'Good Housekeeping' Seal of Approval," *Journal of Economic History* 56: 389–428.

Borio, C. and P. Disyatat, (2010). "Global Imbalances and the Financial Crisis: Reassessing the Role of International Finance," *Asian Economic Policy Review* 5(2): 198–216.

Brewer, J. (1989). *The Sinews of Power: War, Money, and the English State, 1688–1783*. London and Boston, MA: Unwin Hyman.

Bush, O., K. Farrant, and M. Wright (2011). "Reform of the International Monetary and Financial System," Bank of England Financial Stability Paper No. 13.

Clemens, M. and J. Williamson (2004). "Wealth Bias in the First Global Capital Market Boom," *The Economic Journal* 114: 304–337.

Congdon, T. (2002). "The Analyses of Unsustainability, and Total Unsustainability, Based on the Familiar Theory of Debt Dynamics Have Been Dumbfounded," Lombard Street Research Ltd. *Monthly Economic Review*, November–December: 5.

Crisp, O. (1976). *Studies in the Russian Economy before 1914*. New York: Barnes & Noble Books.

Dooley, M. P., D. Folkerts-Landau, and P. Garber (2003). "An Essay on the Revived Bretton Woods System," NBER Working Paper No. 9971, September.

Economist (1915). "Financial Arrangements and the War Debts of Europe," February 13: 262–263.

Edelstein, M. (1982). *Overseas Investment in the Age of High Imperialism*. New York: Columbia University Press.

Feinstein, C. and K. Watson (1995). "Private International Capital Flows in Europe in the Inter-War Period," in C. Feinstein (ed.), *Banking, Currency and Finance in Europe Between the Wars*. Oxford University Press, pp. 94–130

Feldstein, M. and C. Horioka (1980). "Domestic Saving and International Capital Flows," *Economic Journal* 90: 314–329.

Fenn, C. (1869). *Fenn's Compendium of the English and Foreign Funds*. London: E. Wilson.

Ferguson, N. (1998). *The House of Rothschild: Money's Prophets 1798–1848*. New York: Viking.
(2001). *The Cash Nexus: Money and Power in the Modern World 1700–2000*. New York: Basic Books.

Ferguson, N. and M. Schularick (2006). "The Empire Effect: The Determinants of Country Risk in the First Age of Globalization, 1880–1913," *Journal of Economic History* 66/2: 283–312.

Ferguson, T. and P. Temin (2003). "Made in Germany: The German Currency Crisis of 1931," *Research in Economic History* 21: 1–53.

Fishlow, A. (1985). "Lessons from the Past: Capital Markets during the 19th Century and the Interwar Period," *International Organization* 39(3): 383–439.

Flandreau, M. and F. Zumer (2004). *The Making of Global Capital 1880–1913*. Paris: OECD Development Centre Studies.

Ford, A. G. (1960). "Notes on the Working of the Gold Standard before 1914," *Oxford Economic Papers* New Series 12(1): 52–76.

(1962). *The Gold Standard 1880–1914: Britain and Argentina* Oxford University Press.

Gaillard, N. (2012). *A Century of Sovereign Ratings*. New York: Springer.

Godley, A. (2006). "Selling the Sewing Machine Around the World: Singer's International Marketing Strategies, 1850–1920," *Enterprise and Society* 7(2): 266–314.

Gourinchas, P.-O. and H. Rey (2005). "From World Banker to World Venture Capitalist: US External Adjustment and the Exorbitant Privilege," NBER Working Paper No. 11563, August.

Haussmann, R. and F. Sturzenegger (2006). "Global Imbalances or Bad Accounting? The Missing Dark Matter in the Wealth of Nations," Harvard Center for International Development WP 124, January 2006.

Hilferding, R. (1981) (transl. M. Watnick and S. Gordon). *Finance Capital: A Study of the Latest Phase of Capitalist Development*. London and Boston, MA: Routledge & Kegan Paul.

Holtfrerich, C.-L. (1986) (transl. T. Balderston). *The German Inflation, 1914–1923: Causes and Effects in International Perspective*. Berlin and New York: De Gruyter.

Horioka, C. Y. and A. Terada-Hagiwara (2011). "The Determinants and Long-term Projections of Saving Rates in Developing Asia," NBER Working Paper No. 17581.

Horsefield, K. (1986). *The International Monetary Fund, 1945–1965: Twenty Years of International Monetary Cooperation*. Washington, DC: International Monetary Fund.

International Monetary Fund (IMF) (2009). *World Economic Outlook* (April).

(2010). *World Economic Outlook* (April).

James, H. (1986). *The German Slump: Politics and Economics 1924–1936*. Oxford University Press.

(2001). *The End of Globalization: Lessons from the Great Depression*. Cambridge MA: Harvard University Press.

Jones, G. and C. Trebilcock (1982). "Russian Industry and British Business: Oil and Armaments," *Journal of European Economic History* 11(1): 61–103.

Keynes, J. M. (1929). "The German Transfer Problem"; "The Reparation Problem: A Discussion. II. A Rejoinder"; "Views on the Transfer Problem. III. A Reply," *Economic Journal* 39, March: 1–7; June: 172–178; September: 404–408.

Kindleberger, C. P. (1973). *The World in Depression, 1929–1939* Berkeley, CA: University of California Press.

Kraay, A. (2000). "Household Saving in China," *World Bank Economic Review* 14(3): 545–570.

Macdonald, J. (2006). *A Free Nation Deep in Debt: The Financial Roots of Democracy*. Princeton University Press.

McGuire, P. and G. von Peter (2009). "The US Dollar Shortage in Global Banking and the International Policy Response," *BIS Working Paper*, no. 291.

Milesi-Ferretti, G. M. and C. Tille (2011). "The Great Retrenchment: International Capital Flows during the Global Financial Crisis," *Economic Policy* 26(4): 285–342.

Mitchener, K. J. and M. Weidenmier (2008). "Trade and Empire." *Economic Journal* 118: 1805–1834.

Moggridge, D. (1992). *Maynard Keynes: An Economist's Biography*. London and New York: Routledge.

Neilson, K. (1984). *Strategy and Supply: The Anglo-Russian Alliance 1914–17*. London: George Allen & Unwin

Nötel, R. (1984). "Money, Banking and Industry in Interwar Austria and Hungary," *Journal of European Economic History* 13(2).

Nurkse, R. (1944). *International Currency Experience: Lessons of the Interwar Period*. Geneva: League of Nations.

Obstfeld, M. (2012). "Does the Current Account Still Matter?" *American Economic Review* 102 (3): 1–23.

Obstfeld, M. and A. M. Taylor (2004). *Global Capital Markets: Integration, Crisis and Growth*. Cambridge and New York: Cambridge University Press.

Ohlin, B. (1929). "The Reparation Problem: A Discussion," *Economic Journal* 39: 170–178.

Olegaria, R. (2006). *A Culture of Credit: Embedding Trust and Transparency in American Business*. Cambridge, MA: Harvard University Press.

Pitchford J. (1990). *Australia's Foreign Debt: Myths and Realities*. Sydney: Allen & Unwin.

Polanyi, K. (1944). *The Great Transformation*. New York: Farrar & Rinehart.

Reinhart, C. and V. Reinhart (2008). "Capital Flow Bonanzas: An Encompassing View of the Past and Present," in J. Frankel and C. Pissarides (eds.), *NBER International Seminar on Macroeconomics 2008*. University of Chicago Press, pp. 9–62.

Ritschl, A. (2002). *Deutschlands Krise und Konjunktur 1924–1934: Binnenkonjunktur, Auslandsverschuldung und Reparationsproblem zwischen Dawes-Plan und Transfersperre*. Berlin: Akademie Verlag.

Rodrik, D. (2007). "The Inescapable Trilemma of the World Economy," at http://rodrik.typepad.com/dani_rodriks_weblog/2007/06/the-inescapable.html.

Siegel, J. (in press). For Peace and Money: International Finance and the Making and Unmaking of the Triple Entente.

Stiglitz, J. (1998). "Boats, Planes and Capital Flows," *Financial Times*, March 25.

Straumann, T. (2010). *Fixed Ideas of Money: Small States and Exchange Rate Regimes in Twentieth-century Europe*. New York: Cambridge University Press.

Sussman, N. and Y. Yafeh (2000). "Institutions, Reforms and Country Risk: Lessons from Japanese Government Debt in the Meiji Era," *Journal of Economic History* 60(2): 442–467.

Taylor, A. J. P. (1963). *English History 1914–1945*. Oxford: Clarendon Press.

Von Laue, T. (1963). *Sergei Witte and the Industrialization of Russia*. New York: Columbia University Press.

Wilkins, Mira (1999). "Swiss Investments in the United States 1914–1945," in S. Guex (ed.), *La Suisse et les Grandes Puissances, 1914–1945: Relations économiques avec les Etats-Unis, la Grande Bretagne, l'Allemagne et la France*. Geneva: Droz, pp. 1–139.

Wolf, M. (2008). *Fixing Global Finance*. Baltimore, MD: Johns Hopkins University Press.

World Bank (1993). *The East Asian Miracle*. Washington, DC: World Bank.

10

Capitalism and the colonies

GARETH AUSTIN[*]

The history of empire is longer than the history of capitalism. It is also wider: In the mid twentieth century, while capitalist empires still extended across the oceans, the communist Soviet Union included the major land empire of the time. Yet the nearly 500-year continuous history of overseas, transcontinental colonial rule has very often been seen as having strong causal relations to capitalism, in both directions: in the imperial ("metropolitan") countries themselves, and in their colonies. A succession of theorists suggested systematic links between the evolution of capitalism at home and the extent and form of empire abroad. Scholarly critics of both capitalism and empire have viewed the possession of colonies as a means of accumulating wealth and securing political stability in the metropoles; advocates of empire, in their own times, hoped they were. Above all, colonial rule by capitalist countries has often been seen as the primary vehicle for the spread of capitalist institutions worldwide.

This essay reviews a specific era in the complicated interactions of capitalism and colonialism, one defined by the consequences of industrial development: of the industrial revolution that had already occurred in Britain and was, as of 1850, spreading rapidly but unevenly within the West; of its even more uneven spread elsewhere, starting with Meiji Japan; and of the continuous changes in the structure and technologies of industrial economies throughout the era. The history of colonialism after c.1850 is distinguished from earlier patterns by five key features.

First, this relatively late era in the history of overseas empires took place in the context of a broad-based, largely cumulative, divergence in wealth and military technology between the West and the "Rest." Whatever gap existed in 1780 between incomes per head in Western Europe and North America on the one hand, and the economic "cores" of Asia and the rest of the world on

* I thank Tony (A. G.) Hopkins for very helpful comments on the draft, and for the suggestions of the editors and other contributors. The mistakes are mine.

the other (Gupta and Ma 2010; Parthasarathi 2011; Pomeranz 2000), the industrialization of the West turned it into a gulf. The enhanced logistical capacity created by economic expansion combined with the naval and military application of industrial technology to give Western armed forces, relatively suddenly, an edge over the Rest unparalleled in the centuries since the Portuguese inaugurated the era of overseas empires early in the fifteenth century. Hence the Chinese emperor could no longer dismiss a British request to open diplomatic relations, as happened as late as 1793, adding the much-quoted barb, "I set no value on objects strange and ingenious and have no use for your country's manufactures." Instead, his successors could be bullied into opening their markets under the well-named "unequal treaties." Thus the opportunities for Western countries to impose their interests by force were increased and the costs of doing so decreased.

Second, the first industrial revolution generated a historic transformation of commercial relations between Europe and Asia. Instead of European countries running a permanent trade deficit with India, southeast Asia, and China, having to pay for Asian goods – which included the products of handicraft industries such as Indian cotton textiles and Chinese porcelain – with bullion because the Asians did not want European goods, the advent of the power loom in Manchester led to a European invasion of Asian consumer markets. It also enabled British ships to sell British factory-made cotton cloth into Africa, instead of re-selling the products of Indian handlooms. Further, by enormously increasing the supply of manufactured goods, the British industrial revolution triggered a prolonged shift in the barter terms of trade worldwide in favor of primary producers. This combination of increasing competition from imported manufactures and increasing positive incentives to specialize in primary products stimulated a partial "deindustrialization" of the Rest. Thus the steadily widening gap between the West and the Rest in income per head was accompanied by the emergence of a new international division of labor, with the former exporting manufactured goods, while the latter specialized in the export of primary products (Williamson 2011). This Western-dominated pattern was first effectively challenged by Japan's industrialization following the Meiji restoration of 1868. By 1914, significant industrial growth, albeit falling short of industrialization, had occurred in the larger Latin American republics. A crucial question for this essay is how far European rule reinforced the development of the new division of labor in the colonies, and whether it aided or obstructed the beginnings of modern industry there.

Third, the nature of the empires of trade (as opposed to settlement) had been changing: By the nineteenth century, seaborne mercantilist empires had evolved into territorial empires with huge subject populations, epitomized by the Netherlands Indies and British India, and followed by later-created colonies in Africa, Indo-China, and Malaya. When new chartered companies were created after 1850, their responsibilities began with establishing or maintaining territorial control. Conversely, when the "imperialism of free trade" of the middle and late nineteenth century again used guns to enter markets, it did so increasingly in the name of multilateral or universal free trade, rather than mercantilism.

Fourth, by 1850 the period of founding new "settler-monopoly" colonies or "neo-Europes," territories which became mostly populated and almost entirely led by the descendants of European settlers (in the case of the United States, populated also by African slaves imported by the settlers), was over. The process of dispossessing the indigenous populations and extending European settlement continued, however; as did its eventual corollary, the trend for European settlers and their descendants to assert independence from the metropole. The United States, Argentina, and Uruguay had already rebelled and become independent republics; Canada was en route to autonomy and eventual independence, to be followed in due course by the much younger neo-Europes of Australia and New Zealand.[1] The trend for settlers to assert independence was to be re-run in the twentieth century, in a different form and with different results, in the "settler-elite" colonies of South Africa and Southern Rhodesia, where the population of European origin were very much minorities.

Finally, the old European empires were joined by the neo-Europes and Japan. The United States acted as an "informal" free trade imperialist in east Asia, and in 1898 took over, in one form or another, most of the remnants of the Spanish empire. Japan established itself as a major colonial power through its victories over China in 1894–1895 and Russia in 1905, annexing Korea and Taiwan. Australia, New Zealand, and the settler-elite state of South Africa (which became independent as a "dominion" within the British empire in 1910) took over the administration of former German colonies after World War I.

Capitalism's most famous critic had two theories of the origins of the system: an endogenous one, which he applied to Europe; and an exogenous one, for the rest of the world. Writing in 1853 on British India, Marx argued

---

1 Though Belich (2009) argues for a series of economic "recolonizations" from the mid nineteenth century into the early twentieth century, accompanied by a stronger sense by the settlers that they were equal partners in the British empire. Hopkins (2008) argues that the final moves to independence from Britain came significantly later than has usually been supposed, in Australia, New Zealand, and even Canada.

that colonialism was the means by which capitalism, propelled by what he considered to be its unique intrinsic dynamism, was imposing itself beyond its native continent (Marx 1853, 1867; re-stated by Warren 1980). Some nationalist intellectuals, and later especially Dependency theorists, concluded that Marx overestimated the depth of the imperialist diffusion of capitalism. What the foreign rulers and firms imposed in the colonies, they argued, was merely an inferior form of the system that Marx credited with the conquest of nature (Frank 1978). Specifically, what Amin called "peripheral capitalism" reduced vast additional populations into dependence on the market, but without establishing within the colonies the virtuous cycle of accumulation and reinvestment, often accompanied by technical innovation, that characterized metropolitan capitalism (Amin 1976).[2] This position has been restated by some rational-choice institutionalist economists, contrasting the remarkable economic growth of countries of recent European settlement (North America and Australasia) with the decline in relative economic standing of the countries which the Europeans colonized but did not settle (Acemoglu, Johnson, and Robinson 2001, 2002).[3]

This chapter is organized around these debates over colonialism in the era of industrialization. The first section summarizes the metropolitan (imperial) side.[4] On the causes of empire, it outlines the connections from the workings of capitalist economies to the motives for seeking and maintaining colonies. Within the era under review, the biggest worldwide outburst of new territorial annexations occurred in the late nineteenth century, epitomized by the European partition of Africa. We will outline the controversy over the relationship between the uneven industrialization of Europe and the motivation of this "new imperialism."

On the consequences of empire, the section reflects briefly on the famous question of the importance of colonies in the origin of industrialization, and then sketches the economic balance sheets of empire: the gains and losses

2 For a survey of left-wing theories of the relationship between capitalism and imperialism, see Brewer 1990. For an acerbic review of the origins and development of the Dependency and World Systems tradition, see Warren 1980.
3 The irony, of course, is that the "good" colonizations in this sense were based on the dispossession of the indigenous inhabitants (cf. Guha 2012: 30). The "reversal" of fortune applied to the territory only (Acemoglu, Johnson, and Robinson 2002: 1232n1).
4 It is important to note that the imperial ("metropolitan") and colonial ("peripheral") sides of the history of the relationships between capitalism and empire have different literatures, addressing different questions. Very few scholars have emulated A. G. Hopkins in making major contributions to both (Falola and Brownell 2011). The subject of this section merits a chapter in itself; some of its themes, however, are examined in other contexts elsewhere in these volumes.

from the possession of colonies for the imperial powers. It also considers the argument that changes in the nature of industrial capitalist economies reduced their interest in retaining colonies, and therefore facilitated the relatively sudden decolonization during the generation after World War II.

The subsequent sections explore the impact of the imperialism of capitalist countries on capitalism in the colonies themselves: on the spread of capitalist institutions; the proliferation of capitalists; and the achievement of "capitalist" forms of economic development. The section on the political economy of capitalism in the colonies introduces the range of types of colonial rule during the period under consideration, elucidating this in the context of the territories' respective factor endowments and preexisting forms of capitalism. This is followed by sections which, respectively, ask how far colonial rule promoted or retarded the development of capitalism in the colonies, evaluate economic development in the colonies including industrial growth, if any, and discuss the respective roles of pro- and anti-"capitalist" forces in the opposition to colonial policies and to colonial rule as such.

In this chapter, "empires" are large political units, "expansionist or with a memory of power extended over space ... that maintain distinction and hierarchy as they incorporate new people" (Burbank and Cooper 2010: 8). A "colony" is a territory whose material assets and political decisions are largely controlled by the subjects or citizens of an outside state, whether sovereignty has been ceded in law or only in fact – "informal empire," in the phrase of Gallagher and Robinson (1953).[5]

"Capitalism" has multiple senses, which for present purposes may be reduced to two. The broader equates it with the market, or more precisely with markets in which prices are determined by the interaction of supply and demand. The narrower links it with private property rights. Price-forming markets, and the "rational" economic behavior associated with them, turn out to have been widespread in economies that are usually considered "precapitalist" (Braudel 1982: 227–228; Hoffman, Postel-Vinay, and Rosenthal 1999; Law 1992). They have thus been much more widespread historically than

---

5 A key case for the informal empire thesis is Latin America. Gallagher and Robinson's view that Britain established this kind of control over the Latin American republics between their establishment and World War I was challenged by Platt (e.g. Platt 1972). The British government rarely intervened in support of British business in the region, but British commercial and financial dominance in the region was such as to make it unrealistic to see the "interdependence" of the UK and Latin American economies as a relationship between equals (Cain and Hopkins 2001: 243–274).

regimes enforcing individual property rights. While the extension and integration of markets are facilitated by private property rights, it is the latter rather than the former that is distinctive of the kinds of economies that people usually have in mind when applying the label "capitalist." Accordingly, in this chapter "capitalism" means an economic (and social and political) system based on legally enforced private property rights.

Marx thought the corollary of private property rights was the progressive separation of workers from the ownership of the means of production. The human product of this process is the (archetypally male) proletarian, free to sell his labor, and "freed" from owning other assets. This view is endorsed in Fox-Genovese and Genovese's remark that "capitalism . . . rested on free labor and had no meaning apart from it" (Fox-Genovese and Genovese 1983: vii). In global perspective this conception of commodified labor mistakes a species for the genus (Van der Linden 2008). Economies founded on private property have variously had laborers as commodities (slavery), labor power as a commodity (wage labor), and self-employed and family laborers producing commodities (and depending for their livelihood on their capacity to do so).

Imperialism in the metropoles

Causes: "capitalist" elements in imperial expansion

The causes of individual acts of gunboat diplomacy or territorial annexation are usually complex and disputed, making generalization difficult. Two general propositions will be advanced here. Probably the less contentious is that the causes were often at least partly non-economic. Notions of national prestige and identity, and military and naval planning, were just two of the non-economic (or at least, far from directly economic) considerations that mattered in some cases. This statement is put forward here simply as context for the next, which is more directly important in the history of capitalism, and probably more contentious. This further proposition is that, once industrialization was under way, the propensity of imperial powers to use force against foreigners overseas, either to make them open their markets or to seize their territory, was related to the unevenness of the spread of industrialization in time and space. This claim has five elements.

First, the earlier observation that the cost of coercion was reduced by the advances in knowledge and logistics associated with, and driven further by, industrial development, has implications for imperial decision-making.

Military productivity was increased and European casualty rates reduced by a range of innovations: from steam warships to repeating rifles and machine guns and, not least, the adoption of quinine. This helps to explain the readiness of Britain, the United States, and other Western powers to threaten or apply force against East Asian empires in the mid nineteenth century, a method about which they were much more reticent in earlier centuries. Again, when we puzzle over the reasoning behind the conquest of (then) seemingly resourceless terrain such as the Sahara, it is important to consider that for European governments in this era, the incremental cost of territorial expansion was often relatively low.

Second, the most advanced industrial economies of the time – those that were most competitive internationally – had least economic incentive to engross territory. What they needed was access to markets, to sell their products and buy raw materials. This was the practical logic behind the British shift from mercantilist to free trade imperialism, though it is important to recognize also the ideological charge that "free trade" acquired in Britain by 1846: its advocacy went beyond material expediency. Free trade imperialists sought treaties with local elites who were, or could be made to be, willing to collaborate; they sought to avoid the costs and risks of administrating territory and subject populations (Gallagher and Robinson 1953; Robinson 1972; Robinson and Gallagher 1961). Two of the leading industrial powers, Belgium and Germany, had relatively little involvement with the tropics, whether as producers or consumers, before they acquired colonies. Britain was the largest trading partner of tropical Africa but, until the "Scramble for Africa," had managed this with minuscule claims on territory. Indeed, it was not the most advanced industrial countries in Europe, Britain, Belgium, and Germany, who started the Scramble for Africa. Rather, it was the French, beginning to march eastwards from Senegal in 1879, who obliged the British and others to stake their claims or lose them. The least industrially advanced of the imperial powers, Portugal, was an eager participant, but effectively had to wait for the more powerful states to give the green light to participate in full. The debate about colonial expansion in Portugal was less about whether expansion was economically desirable than about how to make it pay: whether by neo-mercantilist means to help metropolitan industries, or by leasing territory to foreign companies (Clarence-Smith 1979). In contrast, Bismarck initially sought to keep Germany aloof from the Scramble, hoping it would turn into an Anglo-French conflict. He changed tack in 1884, convening the Congress of Berlin, the object of which was to enable the Europeans to avoid fighting each other over Africa. At the Congress, Germany successfully claimed four colonies in Africa. To minimize their cost to the government, however, Bismarck delegated their administration to chartered companies. For the same reason, Britain later relied on "indirect rule" in its African colonies, ruling through the chiefs in the hope that this would be cheaper and more effective than direct administration by European officials. The United States, too, adopted forms of indirect rule in its colonies. Meanwhile the Belgian Parliament avoided involvement in the Congo until 1908, when embarrassment at the international scandal over the extreme brutality of King Leopold's kleptocracy obliged the government to "nationalize" what had been the monarch's personal domain. A case could be made for treating the Japanese annexation of Korea and Taiwan within this framework of the less advanced industrial economies having the greater need to initiate contests for territory. For Japan, like Portugal, was a latecomer to industrialization, albeit a much faster mover once the process began (and with military reasons for trying to advance its frontiers beyond the Japanese islands).

Third, this does not mean that the most industrialized economies had nothing to gain from territorial expansion: simply that the manufacturers themselves were unlikely to be leading the charge. In West Africa, it was the merchants, and their chambers of commerce in Marseilles, Bordeaux, London, Liverpool, Manchester, and Hamburg, who called on their respective national governments to reduce the risks and costs they faced by removing, for example, the power of independent African polities to tax European imports (Hopkins 1973: 135–166). Again, Cain and Hopkins (2001) argue that British imperialism was propelled, not by the new industrialists, but rather by the "gentlemanly capitalism" of landowners and – increasingly, in our period – financiers. It remains unclear how far this thesis can be applied to other imperial powers.

Fourth, like the remaining aristocracies (and in so far as one can distinguish them by this period), the capitalist classes of the newly industrialized and industrializing countries of the West had an interest in calming the discontent of the growing proletariats. The French philosopher Ernest Renan wrote in 1871, "A nation that does not colonize is bound irrevocably to socialism, to the war between rich and poor" (quoted in Brocheux 2012: 75). Such thinking has been given particular attention in the case of Germany, with Wehler arguing plausibly that Wilhelmine *Weltpolik* was intended in part to give both psychic and material benefits to the workers (as well as the middle classes), in the hope of countering the growth of the Marxist Social Democratic Party (Wehler 1975).

Fifth, regarding the industrial growth of Japan and, indeed, parts of south China in the interwar years, Sugihara links the role of the City of London as "a vital facilitator of technological transfer from the West to East Asia" with the Cain and Hopkins thesis (Sugihara 2002) that British imperialism was driven by the needs of finance rather than manufacturing. Sughiara's argument, elaborated further by Akita, suggests a counterintuitive degree of complementarity between British imperialism and Japanese economic development (Akita 2011), rather than the former consistently defending the postindustrial revolution international division of labor.

Finally, it will be noted that these suggested links from the uneven spread of industrialization to the motivation of new acts of overseas imperialism do not include the best-known such hypothesis: The idea, put forward by J. A. Hobson and adapted by Lenin, that colonies were acquired as an outlet for surplus capital accumulated in the leading industrial countries of the late nineteenth and early twentieth century, has been refuted (e.g. Warren 1980: 57–70). For example, the hypothesis looks weak, given that the major outflows of capital from the leading imperial powers, Britain and France, went not to their new colonies but to countries which were either the more autonomous of their existing colonies (such as Australia), or were former colonies (the United States), former colonies of another European country (as with Argentina), or had never been colonized (Russia). Decisively, several of the expansionist imperial powers of the period were themselves net importers of capital: the United States, Japan, Portugal, and Italy.

Effects on metropolitan economies

Even the briefest discussion of the effects of colonies on the metropolitan economies in the age of industrialization should take note of the fundamental debate on the contribution of "the periphery" to the launch of the process of industrialization in the first place. Clearly, as Germany showed in the mid nineteenth century, it was possible to industrialize early without having colonies or a great trans-oceanic trade. But the importance of the colonial contribution to the original industrial revolution is not a matter of merely British interest. Allen has shown how the British industrial revolution enabled the cost of power looms and the rest of the new capital-intensive technology to be reduced to the point where its adoption became profitable in the lower-wage economies of continental western Europe (Allen 2009). So, did colonies make an important, even essential, contribution to the demand and supply sides of the original industrial revolution? Williams's thesis that the reinvested profits of slave trading and slave ownership made a vital contribution to financing the British industrial revolution (Williams 1944) was generally rejected by subsequent research. This showed that the first industrial revolution did not require as high a capital/GDP ratio as later industrializations, and that profits from slavery and slave trading were much too small for their absence to have prevented industrialization (Engerman 1972; Eltis and Engerman 2000; more generally, O'Brien 1982).[6]

This revisionist interpretation has been challenged by recent work, however, in different but complementary ways. Inikori argues that British industrial precocity was made possible by British participation as increasingly the leading player in an emerging Atlantic (South as well as North) economy based on slavery and slave trading (Inikori 2002). While in principle it makes sense to see the ultimate determinants of a process rooted in technological innovation as on the supply rather than the demand side (O'Rourke, Prados de la Escosura, and Daudin 2010: 118–119), Inikori bridges the supply-demand duality by pointing to markets for specific products, for example particular kinds of cloth for sale in West Africa, as stimulants to specific technological innovations by British manufacturers (Inikori 2002). Again, Berg emphasizes the importance of Chinese and Indian designs, embodied in porcelain and cloth mainly imported via the East India Company, as stimuli to technical innovation in England (Berg 2009, 2012). Moreover, larger markets contribute to the profitability of innovations, and therefore to the incentives to make them (O'Rourke, Prados de la Escosura, and Daudin 2010: 120). Finally, it is necessary to remember the importance of cotton manufacturing to the industrial revolution in England, which for raw cotton was totally dependent on imports. Without the combination of cheap – African slave – labor and free land on which to grow cotton in America, the industrial revolution would have faced a major supply constraint, as the demand it created for raw cotton bid up the price of this basic raw material (O'Rourke, Prados de la Escosura, and Daudin 2010: 119–120; see Pomeranz 2000, especially at 264–269, 274–285, for an important more general argument).

Thus there is a strong case that colonial trade made an important, perhaps even necessary, contribution to the British origins of global industrialization. This is not to say that this was sufficient to explain the cluster of technological advances whose application defined the industrial revolution, nor why it was Britain, rather than another of the major European participants in the Atlantic

---

6 One should distinguish the issue of causality of the industrial revolution from the fact that various specific industrial investments were indeed made with profits from slave ships or slave estates, as Williams documented. In a reasonably competitive capital market, the provenance of particular savings may well not affect the overall level or even composition of investment. But that does not mean that particular firms were not tainted by "slave money."

and Asian trades, which derived so much industrial benefit from them. But once industrialization was underway, and spreading in continental Europe and the United States, did imperialism pay for the imperial powers?

Disaggregating by region or colony suggests mixed results. By using or threatening force to open the markets of China and Japan, Britain, the United States, and their French and German allies clearly made some gains from the resultant trade, while India was a major contributor to the British balance of payments. On the fiscal side, colonial administrations were generally expected by their metropolitan superiors to at least balance the books in the long term. The Dutch went further in the mid nineteenth century. The Netherlands Indies was supposed to deliver a net annual tribute to the metropole. Under the Cultivation System in Java from 1830 to 1870, the local population was forced to grow selected export crops on a large scale. Its most successful decade, in fiscal terms, was the 1850s, when it contributed more than one-third of the budget of the Dutch state, and 3.8 percent of Dutch GDP (Van Zanden and Marks 2012: 50–51). This was probably the largest single example of extraction from the colonies in the post-1850 era, and it could not be sustained. The costs to the population were high, in extended hours of labor and, arguably, reduced food security. Following domestic criticism, but also the emergence of a colonial administration with a degree of autonomy and a desire to promote development, the system was gradually dismantled later in the century (Van Zanden and Maarks 2012: 76).[7] Ironically, when the Netherlands eventually lost Indonesia in 1949, the Dutch economy grew much faster afterwards than before. France seems to have made modest net gains from colonies in Algeria and Indo-China, but net losses from her colonies in tropical Africa – at least until the abolition of forced labor in 1945 spurred economic expansion, especially in Ivory Coast. The Portuguese economy probably made net gains from empire, thanks to the more systematic exploitation introduced after an economics professor became dictator in 1926. But in the 1960s and early 1970s any gross gains were surely swallowed by the costs of fighting independence wars.

It has been suggested that, in the early and mid twentieth century, the possession of captive markets diverted metropolitan firms and governments from the task of meeting the challenge of remaining competitive with the new industrial leaders, especially the United States and Germany, whose colonial empires were at most a tiny part of their national economies. This thesis has

---

7 For a systematic examination of the concept of "extractive" colonies in two classic cases, see Frankema and Buelens 2012.

some applicability to protectionist France. But it works least well for the largest empire, because of British commitment to free trade between 1846 and 1931. Indeed, concentrating on captive markets was precisely the option forgone when successive governments in London stood firm against the campaign of Joseph Chamberlain, a former industrialist from Birmingham who was colonies minister from 1895 to 1903, to replace free trade by "imperial preference." For the post-1931 period, the thesis has a superficial plausibility. From the 1930s to the 1970s, and especially during the postwar "Golden Age" of European economic growth, the United Kingdom's rate of growth of productivity was indeed poor relative to her industrial competitors. However, this was mainly the result of British firms being shielded from competition at home and in trade with other industrial countries. Thus the slow productivity growth persisted until after the United Kingdom joined the European common market in 1973, long after the independence of India and indeed of most of the other British colonies (Crafts 2012).

The most detailed attempt to quantify the balance sheet of a major empire as a whole remains Davis and Huttenback's (1986) exercise for the British case, 1860–1912. They concluded that the metropolitan economy was the poorer for empire, though they also found that private investors, especially concentrated in London and the southeast, were net beneficiaries. Thus the British empire was an economic success during that half-century for at least one major part of the ruling classes, even it was not as a national venture. Subsequent research has extended the skepticism about metropolitan gains to the other European empires (O'Brien and Prados de la Escosura 1999). Again, a distinction can be made between national and sectional – capitalist – interests. Until the last few years before decolonization, Belgian firms operating in the Congo generated much higher returns on capital than their counterparts active in the metropolitan economy (Buelens and Marysse 2009). More so, it seems clear that the biggest economic benefits of empire were captured not in the metropoles, but in the four "neo-Britains" (Belich 2009). On the other hand, national economies do not survive by their economic activities alone. Davis and Huttenback's finding of a net loss to the British economy turns on the question of how much the defense of Canada cost the British treasury. If the calculation was adjusted to allow for the imperial contributions to the British war efforts in 1914–1918 and 1939–1945, the balance sheet would look very different (Offer 1993).

End of empire

An interesting literature argues that the British and French retreat from empire was in part a strategic withdrawal in response to a shift in the balance sheet of empire: rising costs and falling gains, each related to a different aspect of the international development of capitalism. Before exploring these ideas, however, it is necessary to set this debate in a wider picture: It was nationalist pressure, whether exerted through violent or non-violent methods, that swept away the biggest of the colonies in the European empires that survived or sought to resurrect themselves after World War II. The British accepted that they could no longer hold on to India, withdrawing in 1947 (and from Burma, 1948); the Dutch fought, ultimately unsuccessfully, to restore their control over Indonesia (1945–1949); the French lost protracted wars of independence in Indochina (1946–1954) and Algeria (1954–1962). The Portuguese faced wars of independence in all their African colonies from 1961 onwards. The increasing strain of these wars on metropolitan society and economy, and the conversion of some Portuguese officers to radical left-wing ideologies learned in part from their African opponents, led to the revolution of 1974 which ended the dictatorship in Portugal. The revolution precipitated recognition of the independence of the remaining Portuguese colonies the following year.[8] Elsewhere, especially in tropical Africa, the colonial regimes, though under increasing – but usually unarmed – pressure from the street, might have lingered longer than they did. Instead, there was something of a scramble out of Africa by Belgium, the United Kingdom, and France in the late 1950s and early 1960s, with the Belgian Congo, Nigeria, and a dozen French colonies all receiving independence in 1960 alone.

The sudden willingness of the West Europeans to haul down their flags may be seen as in part a response to a general reorientation of business in the metropoles, notably in France, from colonial markets to the markets of fellow industrial economies. The "colonial" firms themselves did not necessarily participate in this reorientation – for as long as they had the chance to stay put. In the French empire, for instance, the long-established French enterprises in Indochina recognized the inevitable, staff cuts after 1945 being followed by general disengagement from North Vietnam in the early 1950s. The big French firms in Algeria were willing to "play on" after independence, only to be confronted with nationalizations in the 1960s. In the rest of Africa, French firms, which had already participated in the imperial government's post-1945 scheme for industrial development, adapted with much greater success in the context of the continuation of a strong French political and military presence in many of the former French colonies (Hodeir 2003).

---

8 Except for Macau, whose return to China was delayed until 1999 at the wish of the latter.

Ironically, the colonies concerned had never been more useful to the metropolitan economies than in the years of postwar reconstruction in Europe, when exports of tropical produce earned dollars that the recuperating imperial powers badly needed. Trade with Africa as a share of British and French trade reached record levels (Austen 1987: 277–228). Exports to the franc zone as a share of all French exports peaked in 1952, at 42 percent (Marseille 2005: 51). But the longer-term trend was downwards (Lipietz 1983; Marseille 2005). Perhaps this helps a little to explain the otherwise puzzling lack of interest shown by the British authorities in the future of British commercial interests during the process of decolonization in Burma, Malaya, the Gold Coast, Nigeria, and Kenya (Brown 2011; Stockwell 2000; Tignor 1998; White 1998).[9]

A related but more general reason why the governments in London and Paris became willing to withdraw formally from tropical Africa was that in the 1950s, having audited the economic costs and gains from these colonies to the metropolitan economies, they concluded that the balance was at best neutral – hardly worth the political costs of continued imperialism in the context of Cold War competition (Cooper 1996: 392–406, 596–602; cf. Ferro 1994). A particular reason for official anxiety about the likely future costs of government in Africa arose from a major ideological change that, as Cooper has shown, had been underway since the late 1920s. This was the increasing acknowledgment that African wage-earners were not subsistence farmers temporarily resident in town, but rather were workers in the same sense as their counterparts in the West – with the expensive corollary, as the International Labour Organization and African political and union leaders urged, that they ought to receive the same kinds of rights and benefits as workers in Europe (Cooper 1996).

Conclusion

From early modern mercantilism to the end of empire, there seems to have been something of a reversal in the economic effects of colonies on the metropoles. Whereas colonial trade helped unleash the process of global industrialization in the late eighteenth century, by the mid 1950s colonies appear to have been redundant for the much more advanced capitalist economies that had now developed in the metropoles.

9 This attitude contrasted with the anxieties displayed a few years later by the British government over the oil, as well as political aspects of Biafra's attempted secession from Nigeria (Uche 2008). Perhaps it was the strategic importance of oil, or the exceptional size of the companies involved, that made the difference.

The political economy of capitalism in the colonies

Typology of colonies after 1850

There were major differences between (and in some cases, within) the political economy of different colonies. Even a fivefold categorization is insufficient, but it gives the flavor. We can distinguish the following, each with a distinctive combination of demographic, political, and economic characteristics:

(1) "settler-monopoly" colonies, where settlers from the imperial metropolis took virtually complete control of the territory, its resources. and government: North America, Argentina and Uruguay, Australasia;

(2) "settler-elite" colonies, where the settlers became either the sole rulers, as in South Africa and eventually Rhodesia, or constituted a very powerful pressure group, as in Algeria and Kenya. The Japanese colonies were a variation on this theme, with much larger numbers of settlers;

(3) "plantation" or "concession" colonies (and especially, parts of colonies), where much land was allocated to European estates or plantations: upper Malaya, central Ceylon, Assam in India, and much of German, Belgian, and French-ruled equatorial Africa;

(4) "peasant" colonies where land remained mostly in indigenous ownership and mainly under small-farmer cultivation;

(5) city-ports, therefore with a mainly urban, non-agricultural population, notably Singapore, Hong Kong, and Macau.

The fourth category, "peasant" colonies, was particularly well populated and heterogeneous. Within it there were cases where the colonial administration, perhaps temporarily as it turned out, sought to impose a high degree of control over the composition and scale of production. The extreme example was the Cultivation System in mid-nineteenth-century Java. Again, particularly for India, one should distinguish areas where the peasants were largely free of lords with superior rights over the land (whether as the landowners or as holders of a right to a share in any land tax), from areas where they were not, as in Bengal. There is a case for a further distinction, between genuinely peasant-dominated agricultural colonies such as Tanganyika, where most labor on African farms came from family members, and those in which much of the output was in the hands of indigenous capitalists, usually small-scale but reliant on the market for most of their labor, as in the cocoa belts of southwestern Nigeria and of what is now Ghana.

This variety was shaped above all by colonial responsiveness to two kinds of prior conditions: factor endowments and elements of indigenous capitalism.

Factor endowments and colonial strategies

Factor endowments (factor ratios and land quality) mattered for colonial strategies. They especially affected the use of various means of securing labor for European users, or for obliging or encouraging colonial subjects to apply their own labor power to the production of commodities. The Nieboer-Domar hypothesis maintains that forced labor is profitable as an economic system where land is abundant in relation to labor and capital, in the absence of technologies offering significant economies of scale (Domar 1970; Nieboer 1900/1910). Until well into the colonial era in the region concerned, this situation applied in much of the Americas, Australasia, most of sub-Saharan Africa and southeast Asia, and even in corners of the otherwise more populated Indian subcontinent. In this context, the hypothesis captures the basic economic logic behind what Fox-Genovese and Genovese (1983: vii) considered the "anomaly" that "capitalism . . . conquered, absorbed, and reinforced servile labor systems throughout the world." However, the hypothesis is conditional upon prospective users of labor having the necessary coercive capacity and the will to apply it. There was an alternative: economies based on family labor, with hired labor minimal or non-existent. The hypothesis also leaves undetermined what form any labor coercion would take. Thus it provides, not a sufficient explanation for slavery anywhere, but a framework within which the economic logic can be combined with political and cultural elements to account for the changing variety of systems of labor coercion that characterized much of the colonial world. In a context where, as will be emphasized below, markets were an important element in the organization even of most non-capitalist economies around the world, it is not surprising that slavery was the form of coercion that was most widespread in the eighteenth and, often, in the mid nineteenth century. For slavery is the most market-oriented form of labor coercion, in that – by the standard definition – slaves could be bought and sold. A slave trade was a labor market, albeit not directly in labor services but in people compelled to supply them. Slavery and slave trading was a particularly efficient form of labor coercion when the labor was required by individuals or firms rather than by the state – which, for occasional tasks, might be better served by the obligatory but temporary service of free subjects.

The Nieboer-Domar framework can be formulated most succinctly as a "trilemma": only two of free land, free peasants, and non-laboring landlords could exist together. Where the colonial state presided over territory where land was relatively scarce for demographic and commercial reasons, as in much, though not all, of later nineteenth-century India, the direct producers tended to be free peasants rather than slaves, and there was a sizeable agricultural surplus available to tax, even if it had to be shared with (often non-laboring) landlords. Denser populations made dispossession much more difficult: It is no coincidence that wholesale demographic displacement, as in North America and Australia, was largely confined to colonies where the indigenous population was thin. Denser populations – short of Geertzian or Malthusian levels, which were indeed rare if not non-existent until well into the twentieth century – also tended to offer greater commercial opportunities, albeit ones potentially or already handled by indigenous traders and regional merchant diasporas, rather than being easily available to European merchants.

The contrasting situation arose where the incoming colonial state encountered an abundance of cultivable land in relation to the available supply of labor, with free farmers having little incentive to produce a substantial agricultural surplus. Here, the government's problem of ensuring that the population produced something taxable was compounded by the likelihood that working for someone else would be unattractive to most of the inhabitants. In this setting, the government had three basic options: to permit a free farming population; to make land artificially scarce (creating or facilitating landlords); or to use some form of forced labor. All these scenarios can be found in the colonial empires of the industrial era. The abolition of slavery in the West Indies created a free peasantry, to the frustration of European planters and government officials who would have preferred the laborers to have continued working on the plantations.[10] Conversely, Edward Gibbon Wakefield, the leading proponent of settlement in New Zealand, the last-to-be-occupied of what became the "settler-monopoly" colonies, proposed (in writings and agitation from 1829 onwards), in effect, the creation of an artificial market in land.[11] His idea was that prices should be set high enough to deny poorer immigrants the chance to farm for themselves, rather than sell their labor. In the "settler-elite" colonies of southern Africa, the state's strategy was to restrict African land rights (whether as owners, or even as tenants on European-owned land) in the hope of driving the majority of the population

10 An experience which explicitly concerned French thinkers later, in the context of the mobilization of labor in African colonies (Cuvillier-Fleury 1907).
11 His long, rambling, but in places brilliant *A Letter from Sydney, the Principal Town of Australasia: Together with the Outline of a System of Colonization*, was actually written while in jail in England (Wakefield 1829).

out of the produce market and into the labor market (Arrighi 1970; Palmer and Parsons 1977). The policy was much more effective in South Africa than in Southern Rhodesia, where, as in Kenya, the white population remained much smaller than in South Africa, and African agricultural production for the market proved more resilient (Mosley 1983). The settler-elite colony in North Africa, Algeria, followed a different course from those to the south. It was more densely populated, which reduced the "need" for the colonial state to apply coercion, direct or indirect, to coerce the indigenous labor force into working for Europeans. Partly as a result, the area of land under European ownership was built up relatively gradually, with land appropriations being more incremental and piecemeal than in South Africa (Lützelschwab 2013).

Large-scale land appropriations, intended to provide European employers simultaneously with both land and labor, occurred south of the Sahara in plantation as well as settler-elite colonies, though in the former it was strongly supplemented with direct forced labor (Northrup 1988). Even in India, relatively low-populated but fertile land existed, albeit on the northeastern periphery. There, in Assam, land was appropriated by the English East India Company to enable the establishment of tea plantations operated with labor forces whose recruitment owed much to direct or indirect coercion. The Dutch Cultivation System in mid-nineteenth-century Java was the most systematic example of forced labor in situ, forcing peasants to cultivate specific crops in stipulated quantities. The same approach was applied in German, French, and Portuguese colonies in Africa, notably with respect to cotton (e.g. Isaacman and Roberts 1995; Likaka 1997); but the pressure was generally less sustained than during the relevant decades in Java.

In most of what became the "peasant" and "indigenous capitalist" colonies in Africa, the incoming authorities found that indigenous ruling elites had already tackled the Domar problem: by acquiring captives (through regional slave trades) as slaves, and to a lesser extent through debt bondage. By this time all the European colonizers were officially committed to ending slavery. Indeed, the British abolition of 1834 applied to such African territories as Britain already ruled at the time: principally the Cape, where slavery was initially converted to "apprenticeship," under which the "emancipated" slaves were still obliged to work for their masters (Dooling 2007). In partial contrast, when the area of Africa under European rule was multiplied nearly tenfold between 1879 and c.1905, the new colonial regimes responded, in most though not all cases, by initially tolerating the continuation of slavery, though usually not the slave trade. This permitted the institution a notoriously "slow death" (Lovejoy and Hogendorn 1993). Because Domar conditions still generally prevailed, many colonial administrations, notably the French until 1945, resorted to extracting some degree of forced labor from "free" subjects, for the government or private expatriate employers (Fall 1995). The exception was areas where the emergence of a lucrative export market (especially in the cases of cocoa beans, which could be grown in parts of the forest zone of West Africa) enabled African farmers to offer terms sufficient to attract seasonal migrant labor from less favorably endowed areas, often replacing slaves who had left to become free peasants or free labourers themselves (Austin 2009). The combination of African-owned export agriculture and laborers who retained land rights in their home areas resulted in relatively high real wages for African unskilled laborers in the "indigenous capitalist" colonies of British West Africa. They were higher than in the settler-elite colonies further south (Bowden, Chiripanhura, and Mosley 2008). They were also higher than in British India and (until at least the 1940s) in East Asia, in both of which land was, on average, markedly less abundant (Frankema and van Waijenburg 2011).

Natural resources and location also influenced colonial strategies. For port-cities the latter was crucial, as Huff emphasizes in the case of Singapore, which was perfectly situated for shipping routes and became an outlet for the staple products of a highly productive hinterland (Huff 1994). In settler-elite colonies, the reservation of land for Europeans often exceeded their appetite for cultivation, because the primary aim of the policy was to deprive the indigenous population of an alternative to selling their labor to European employers (e.g. Feinstein 2005: 32–46). But soil fertility and access to markets were central to the economic development of all agricultural colonies, whatever their political economy. Again, a major feature of colonial rule over the centuries was mineral extraction. Traditional precious metals mattered as much or more than ever. The discovery of diamonds and, especially, of gold in South Africa, in the 1860s and 1880s respectively, ultimately multiplied the value of the region's exports and output. This surely made it much more worth fighting for: while the causation is complex, contrast the willingness of the British to accept the independence of the Boer republics after one military defeat in 1881, before the gold finds, compared to their relentless determination to prevail in the Anglo-Boer war of 1899–1902. The last century and a half of the history of overseas empires, however, was distinguished by an intermittent but fundamental lengthening of the list of natural resources with market value, as a result of successive innovations in industrial technology. Among these, the single most important, economically and militarily, was the creation of demand for petroleum and rubber as a result of the invention of the internal combustion engine. These markets were the basis of the mid-twentieth-century prosperity of British Malaya and the Netherlands Indies, and made both into major targets of Japanese invasion in 1941. Oil also greatly enhanced the attraction of the Middle East to Western investors, partly motivating and certainly rewarding the British policy of establishing a mixture of informal and formal rule in much of the former Ottoman empire, after the collapse of the latter in 1918.

Indigenous capitalism and the limits of colonial strategies

The impact of the colonizers needs to be approached with an awareness of the capacity of colonized people, in spite of the obstacles they faced, to contribute to the making of their own histories (Austin 2008b). In this context we need to qualify the assumption that capitalism was entirely exogenous. In important senses, capitalism had native as well as exotic roots in what became the European colonies. Defined, as here, as a system of private property rights, capitalism existed only in partial forms at the time of European colonization. But crucial elements of, and prerequisites for, capitalism were already widespread: price responsiveness by producers in general; capital investments for private gain; and communities of specialist merchants. The extent to which the inhabitants of precolonial economies were already oriented towards the market, and especially towards external markets, shaped the problems and opportunities facing colonial policy-makers and the form of colonial rule to which they were eventually subjected.

Marx's notion that capitalism was invented in Europe and then spread – or, outside settler-monopoly colonies, was imposed – elsewhere has been echoed to varying degrees in much of the non-Marxist literature. In Marx's own sense of "capitalism," he remains correct: Specialists still agree that it was in England that a class of people first emerged who depended for their sustenance on selling their labor services. But the last half-century of research in Asian and African economic history has revealed that the other basic features associated with capitalism – whether as prerequisites or attributes, depending on definition – were far from unique to Europe. At micro level, economizing behavior – maximizing the ratio of output to inputs – and price-making markets and general-purpose currencies seem to have been more the norm than the exception around the early modern world (contrary to Polanyi's romantic fable [Polanyi 1944, 1966]).[12] It was indeed, in important ways, a world of "surprising resemblances," in the words of Pomeranz (2000) (see,

---

12 Among a large literature, a particularly systematic empirical refutation of Polanyi's argument, for the case to which he devoted his last book, is Law 1977, 1992.

further, Wong 1997 and Chapter 6 in Volume I). To be sure, supply-response was constrained by the necessity to ensure that the producer lived to harvest the profit. Food security was always a concern with rain-fed agriculture and non-mechanized transport – and remained so in many areas during and after the colonial era (Lipton 1968; Tosh 1980). But such pressures had often constrained production for the market in Europe too. Merchant capitalist communities operated, and risk-taking entrepreneurship could be found, in many regions of the Old World besides Europe (see Volume I). Hence colonial rulers and foreign firms faced the prior existence of market behavior and of certain kinds of market institutions among most, probably all, of the populations colonized by overseas empires. Thus, in considering capitalism in the colonies, a fundamental set of issues include the ways in which capitalistic propensities among the colonized structured the choices available to the colonizers, obliged alien rulers and firms to cooperate with them, and variously enabled or limited the latter's access to local markets.

First, to a considerable extent, indigenous and/or regional trading networks, helped by a comparative advantage in information, succeeded in defending their markets throughout the colonial era. British merchants were never able to gain much of a share of the biggest market in India, the internal grain trade and related credit transactions (Morris 1979). In the interregional commerce of south, southwest, and southeast Asia, merchant communities from south Asia endured and thrived[13] (Brown 1994; Markovits 2008). In the last decades of the Raj, Indian entrepreneurs increasingly had the upper hand in competition with their British counterparts (Misra 2000; Tomlinson 1981). Similarly in Niger, French merchants never made an impression on their African counterparts' domination of the cattle trade (Baier 1980: 164–166). Even with raw cotton, which French manufacturers had assiduously sought to obtain from West Africa from the days of the Scramble onwards, with the help of varying degrees of state coercion in production and marketing, French merchants in Mali were regularly out-competed for the cotton harvest by African traders buying for the indigenous handicraft industry (Roberts 1996).

Second, the fact that the main British acquisitions in West Africa, the Gold Coast and Nigeria, became "indigenous capitalist" rather than plantation colonies, was a function of the relatively high market orientation of their economies before colonial rule, which provided the foundation for the continued competitiveness of African producers and traders during the British

---

13 In the case of Burma and Thailand, they thrived until the 1930s, when xenophobic reactions to the Depression drove many to return to the subcontinent (Baker 1981).

period (Hopkins 1973).[14] The colonial administration in the Gold Coast initially experimented with the plantation route. It permitted Europeans to take out 99-year agricultural leases, and a number of European plantations were established, growing cocoa and rubber. By the 1910s, however, it was clear that they were failing in competition with African farmers whose methods of production were better suited to the prevailing factor ratios and environmental conditions (Austin 1996). Thereafter the administration discouraged further European enterprise in agriculture. In Nigeria, the colonial administration rejected repeated applications from W. H. Lever for a huge oil palm concession (Phillips 1989). In defense of this decision, the government pointed to the superior performance of African farmers compared to European planters in the production of the crops grown in West Africa. The decision also enjoyed the support of European import-export merchants whose interests lay in trading with African brokers and, thereby, with African producers who exported crops and thereby earned the means to buy imported consumption goods (Hopkins 1973: 213–214).

Third, in India, British firms and officials found themselves in a more far-reaching pattern of cooperation and rivalry with indigenous entrepreneurs. Some of the latter operated on a much greater scale than their West African counterparts, which was epitomized in their pioneering role in the development of modern manufacturing in the subcontinent, from the 1850s. While Scottish firms developed the jute trade, it was Indians who first successfully pioneered, and thereafter maintained a majority share in, the growth of mechanized cotton weaving, both large-scale and eventually small-scale (Roy 2006: 232–235, 2013). Iron and steel making was pioneered by Tata, from 1907. The British government benefitted from Indian manufacturers' contributions to employment and revenue, albeit at the expense of a declining market share for imports from Britain. The colonial administration repeatedly found it worthwhile to support the Indian firm, from changing the rules on mining concessions to help it in 1899, to introducing differential tariffs protecting the steel industry (Tata) from British and "foreign" imports, albeit the tariffs were higher on the latter (Markovits 2008: esp. 158–161). There is an evident continuity from Indian industrial enterprise during the colonial period to Indian ownership, in the early twenty-first century, of what remains of the steel industry of the former colonial power.

14 See further, a book manuscript in preparation for Cambridge University Press: Austin, "Markets, Slaves and States in West Africa, 1500–2010."

Finally, both the famous port-city economic successes of the second half of the twentieth century, Singapore and Hong Kong, owed much to their respective states but certainly also to Chinese entrepreneurship and labor. For instance, Singapore expanded considerably in the late nineteenth and early twentieth centuries as an outlet for the tin mining industry of Malaya, which was developed in the late nineteenth century by Chinese entrepreneurs who established small-scale open-cast operations, while their circulating capital was supplied as credit from Chinese traders based in Singapore (Huff 1994: 57–60). The crucial role of Chinese business in the development of Hong Kong is generally acknowledged, and the economic success of this capitalist enclave was such as to persuade the government in Beijing to tolerate colonial rule there until the British concession expired in 1997.

Colonialism, pioneer of capitalism?

Did colonial rule protect and promote, or attack and retard, the development of capitalism in the two basic senses defined above, markets and private property? The closest any empire has ever come to combining the pursuit of free and integrated markets with the establishment and entrenchment of individual private property rights was surely mid-nineteenth-century Britain. British gunboat diplomacy imposed free treaties on, among others, the Ottoman empire (including Egypt) in 1838, on Persia in 1841, and on China in 1842. Strikingly, the principle of free trade, advocated by the Lancashire liberals Richard Cobden and John Bright, was adopted at home in 1846 with the abolition of the Corn Laws. Thus, unlike the late twentieth-century hegemonic champion of free trade, the United States, in the nineteenth century the British commitment to free trade went as far as ending protection for its own agriculture. Whereas Cobden and Bright thought free trade made empire redundant, Palmerston as foreign secretary or prime minister for much of the period 1836–1865, readily applied force to open markets. Albeit, the 1842 Treaty of Nanking, which followed the First Opium War, secured British rather than universal access to Chinese markets; whereas the treaties imposed on China in 1858 and 1860, by British and French arms (and signed also by Russia and the United States), opened the treaty port system internationally.

Besides free trade, mid-Victorian imperialists sought to export such quintessentially capitalist institutions as individual ownership of land. Accordingly, the acquisition of Lagos (with the declaration of a protectorate in 1851, and annexation in 1861) was a response to a demand from British (and some African) merchants for the establishment of an administration that would introduce a system of property rights that would permit loans to be secured on land and buildings (Hopkins 1980, 1995). To a degree, this move revived the spirit of Cornwallis's reform of the Bengal land revenue system in 1793, which was supposed to turn the zamindars from holders of a share of the land tax into English-style landlords with an incentive to invest in increasing productive capacity. Yet the twin projects of promoting markets and private property came to be often separated, and pursued only with much restraint, in the remaining decades of British rule in Asia and Africa. They were still less firmly characteristic of late modern imperialism as a whole.

Late nineteenth-century imperialism was notable for a tendency toward the multilateral imposition of free trade. Major examples were the Congo Free Trade Area and the multilateral treaties imposed on China and Japan. But Britain's rival empires remained generally protectionist (in the French case, with the partial interlude of 1860–1892, following the Cobden–Chevalier treaty with Britain). With the onset of the Great Depression, Britain abandoned free trade (in 1931) and its rivals raised their tariffs higher. World War II saw the creation of new instruments for state intervention in colonial economies. In particular, the British introduced statutory government export marketing boards in many colonies, with a monopoly of the export of agricultural produce. Though initially intended to enable the government to avert a collapse of producer prices, export marketing boards soon turned out to be effective means of taxation, by keeping the producer price well below that received by the board on the world market. Hence they were retained after the war, and in many African countries were the principal source of revenue in the years following independence. Again, the exigency of war led Britain to introduce a range of controls over imports as well as exports. In the largest colony, India, this extended into a degree of planning. Some of the Indian officials who worked on the post-independence five-year plans had received their initial experience of planning working for the British government. Thus, though the image of British rule, especially, somehow retained an association with *laissez-faire*, the institutional legacy contained tools for state-led development policies (Bauer 1954).

Internally, each capitalist empire did something to integrate markets, by investing in mechanized transport, standardizing currencies, and abolishing internal tolls. However, colonial administrations frequently tolerated the concentration of ownership and the formation of price-setting and even quantity-fixing agreements between firms. Admittedly, the full details of the latter were not always shared with government, and in Europe itself, collusion between suppliers was frequently tolerated at the same time. The extent and effectiveness of anticompetitive practices by European firms varied between colonies. In the 1920s to 1940s, for example, banking in the British West Indies was more competitive than in British West Africa, thanks to the intervention of Canadian banks (Austin and Uche 2007; Montieth 2000).

Compared to the Victorian zeal for free trade, the project of exporting individual private property rights was compromised much more quickly. It ran into a range of administrative and political obstacles, epitomized by the 1857 revolt in India, which was interpreted by some officials as a warning against further British interference in agrarian systems of property, taxation, and markets. Further colonial interventions in India tended to be at most ambiguous with respect to the promotion and integration of markets. The 1879 Deccan Agriculturalists Relief Act, which sought to prevent the alienation of land to moneylenders from non-agricultural castes, may be seen as mitigating the welfare consequences of monopolistic local credit markets. But it was hardly a step towards unimpeded markets in land and capital.[15]

Policies varied between colonies even within the same empire. During the inter-world-war period the British government in Mandated Palestine imposed a land reform on Arab cultivators, to replace the *mushā'* system of communal land ownership with periodic redistribution of plots, with consolidated farms with individual title (Nadan 2006: 212–260). In British Africa individual officials, such as R. H. Rowe, who served as surveyor-general of the Gold Coast between 1920 and 1927 and then lands commissioner in Nigeria until his death in 1933, continued to argue within the colonial administration for the introduction of compulsory registration of farms, in the names of individual owners. Rowe argued that individual property in land was a natural outcome of social evolution, and thought it the duty of British rule to accelerate the fulfillment of this teleology (Phillips 1989: 118–135). After all, we have noted that Lagos had been annexed partly in order to create such titles. But, by the time of the Scramble for Africa, the policy changed. Even in the 1920s and 1930s, and indeed through to independence, the arguments of the likes of Rowe were ultimately rejected. This was for a combination of reasons. There was a belief that a land registration exercise would provoke a storm of litigation, even if it would reduce legal and other transactions costs in the longer term. In British West Africa, the rapid growth of agricultural exports under the existing land tenure systems made reform unnecessary in economic terms. The so-called "communal" land tenure system of the Gold Coast, for example, distinguished between the ownership of land and the

---

15 For a nuanced analysis of the Act see Charlesworth 1985.

ownership of crops and buildings that stood on it, and actually protected (during their lifetimes) the individual ownership of the investors who created those assets. Evidently, this rule – supported by the colonial government – provided sufficient security for investors to permit the high rates of capital formation, through the planting of cocoa trees, that enabled Gold Coast cocoa exports to rise from zero in 1890 to overtake Brazil in 1910–1911, and multiply a further five times to reach over 200,000 tons in 1923. Finally, there was official concern that, by facilitating a free market in land, individual land ownership would be socially polarizing and destabilizing, with the poorer farmers ultimately selling out and joining the urban unemployed (Austin 2005: 339–347, 531–533).

Wage labor grew, absolutely and relatively, in most if not all colonies during the century and more discussed here. This was true, for example, of south and southeast Asia and, in the twentieth century, also sub-Saharan Africa. Meanwhile, obligatory labor, of various forms (customary as in India; slavery and debt bondage in Africa), declined, as, to some extent, did family labor. Whether this process involved growing landlessness varied. In the many land-scarce districts of south Asia, it did; whereas in Africa male migrant laborers, whether on the gold mines of the Witwatersrand or the cocoa farms of Ghana, continued to retain rights to land back in their home areas, where their wives and older children grew food crops (Austin 2005; Roy 2005; Sender and Smith 1986).

Colonial rule contributed to this fundamental transition in labor relations in various ways, for example by encouraging export agriculture. In Indochina, taxation drove the poorest peasants to give up their farms, contrary to the French government's intentions (Brocheux and Hémery 1995: 151, 270). Actually, it is probably fair to say that in the twentieth century, in contradiction of Marx's prediction, no colonial regime deliberately sought "proletarianization," the separation of the laboring population from the ownership of land. On the contrary, as we have seen, in Africa, colonial officials generally adopted a distinctly gradualist approach to the ending of slavery. Where wage labor was encouraged, as for the southern African mines, it was in migrant form, the workers retaining land rights in their home areas. The stabilization of wage labor, requiring employers to pay family rather than "bachelor" wages, was begun in the 1920s by a Belgian copper-mining company in Katanga, in the Congo. It was adopted in the British-controlled part of the same copperbelt, in what is now Zambia, only in the 1950s, having been delayed by opposition from white trade unionists and the British administration (Austen 1987: 165–168; Berger 1974). By then the change in official attitudes, French and British alike, towards the recognition of wage labor and urban settlement as a permanent and acceptable feature of African life was well underway. For example, the strikes and disturbances in the British West Indies between 1935 and 1938 attracted the attention of the labor movement in Britain and concentrated minds in the Colonial Office, leading the latter to pressure governors in Africa and elsewhere to create labor departments charged with improving the conditions of employment and to encourage "responsible" trade unionism (Cooper 1996: 58–65). This still did not mean the adoption of policies calculated to dispossess rural populations of access to subsistence plots.

At least in part, it was precisely in order to avoid proletarianization that colonial administrations tended to discourage the sale of land among the indigenous population almost wherever they could: deciding against the introduction of compulsory land registration, which would have facilitated a land market, and upholding an interpretation of customary law as prohibiting land alienation in any case. The general motive was probably the hope of preventing the appearance of a landless class, which would have been hard for the colonial authorities to control, socially and politically. In British West Africa, the decisive consideration was probably that the economy was doing well anyway. In contrast, settler-elite economies were characterized by individual land tenure – *except*, for the most part, in the "native reserves" (e.g. Legassick 1977: 180–182). This refusal to implement a throughgoing system of individual land tenure lasted to the end of European rule in most of the territories that remained under indigenous occupation. A significant exception, right at the end of the era, was in Kenya. Faced with the crisis of the Mau Mau revolt, under the Swynnerton Plan of 1953, the British strengthened the position of the most prosperous Kikuyu peasants by giving them individual titles to consolidated plots (including, in some cases, land confiscated from rebels) (Branch 2009: 120–125). This politically conservative strategy was as far as colonial promotion of African agrarian capitalism went in colonial Africa.

Development in the colonies

Some overviews of the extent of economic development under colonial rule see it in binary terms: a story of either "extraction" or economic growth, in the language of the rational-choice institutional economists Acemoglu, Johnson, and Robinson; a position similar to Dependency theory. As briefly referred to above, Acemoglu and colleagues made a pioneering and highly ingenious attempt at a quantitative comparison of the relative prosperity of all the former European colonies in 1995, compared to the relative prosperity of the equivalent territories around 1500. They argue that those that were comparatively wealthy in 1500 were comparatively poor in 1995, and vice versa (Acemoglu, Johnson, and Robinson 2001, 2002). Their work has done more than any other to direct the attention of economists to very long-term patterns of change, and thereby has stimulated much productive debate and further research. But their analysis takes it as axiomatic that impulses towards economic rent and economic growth are opposites. Yet rents may be reinvested productively, and the prospect of rent may be an incentive to market entry and technical innovation. Economic history is not only about contrary tendencies, but also about unexpected syntheses. Their argument also seems to have no room for the colonized populations, including indigenous capitalists, making their own economic history. Finally, it also compresses history, in that they assume that the same causal relationships operate across the half-millennium gap between the two cross-sections, which seems highly unlikely (Austin 2008b). Two subsequent quantitative reassessments argue that the "reversal of fortune" that can be seen in the evidence is essentially confined to the four "neo-Britains" of North America and Australasia (Fails and Krieckhaus 2010; Olsson 2004). If there are reasons for suspecting that a binary view of the developmental consequences of colonialism since 1500 is too simple, what broad observations can be made regarding colonialism in the age of industrialization?

An important preliminary remark is that most colonies received very little investment, public and private, per head of population. During the heyday of foreign direct investment from Western Europe, c.1870–1914, French capital exports went primarily, not to the colonies, but to Russia. Meanwhile, the biggest exporter of capital was the country with the biggest empire, but the prime recipients of British investment were continuing or former settler-monopoly colonies (whether of Britain or, in the case of Argentina, of Spain). This investment helped the development of temperate, land-abundant, and generally resource-rich territories from primarily agricultural to much more diversified, increasingly wealthy economies (Argentina was well within the richest ten countries in the world in the 1920s). Within the tropical colonies, on the other hand, very little private, and not much public, foreign investment went into the main economic activities of the subject populations. Large concentrations of capital were attracted mostly by extractive industries – mining or petroleum. For instance, Frankel estimated that for the period c.1870–1937, total (foreign) investment per head was £55.8 in South Africa, with its gold and diamond mines, compared to £3.3 in France's African colonies,

and only £4.8 in the category representing what are called here the "indigenous capitalist" colonies of British West Africa (Frankel 1938: 158–160, 169–170).
The reasons for the mere trickle of capital into the territories occupied by the
vast majority of colonial subjects include the difficulties of making profits in
competition with local producers, and difficulties in embodying capital
in tools and techniques of production that would actually be very profitable
in the physical conditions (Austin 1996, 2008a).

Colonial administrations generally spent most on facilitating import-export
trade, through transport infrastructure and a bit of agricultural research.
Generally, they went with the grain of such economies' existing comparative
advantage in primary product exports, and sought to develop it further, rather
than trying to move the country's site of comparative advantage higher up the
value-added table. Colonial states constructed ports, railways, and, especially
after 1918, relatively durable motor roads. Many of the railways were financed
by government bonds raised in the European markets. It has been argued that
these would have been impossible or more expensive for independent Asian
and African countries to raise. The interest rates paid by colonial administrations tended to be lower than those paid by independent countries (Ferguson
and Schularick 2006).

Within the British empire, however, it was the self-governing (settler-
monopoly) colonies who captured most of this benefit, because they were
free to borrow, untrammeled by the requirement placed on dependent
colonies to balance their budgets (Accominotti, Flandreau, Rezzik, and
Zumer 2010).[16] Likewise, taking advantage of their democratic legitimacy
and relatively strong states, they were able to command a higher share of
national income in tax than the rest of the colonies (Frankema 2010), and even
had some freedom to impose tariffs on goods from the metropolis.

Strong criticisms have been made of the costs, intentions, and execution of
colonial investment in agricultural colonies. In many cases the railway map
reflected military priorities and gave priority to imperial politics over economic logic. Thus the French railway ran laterally across the West African
savannah, entailing a much longer distance to port for agricultural exporters in
the interior than if the railway had linked to the ports in coastal British
colonies. At least that railway can be exempted from the usual criticism of
colonial transport networks, that they facilitated import-export trade over the

---

16 On the role of imperial power in liberal international financial arrangements, see
Balachandran 2008.

balanced development of the domestic economy. Colonial agricultural research was often misconceived, especially at the start, because of taking insufficient notice of the constraints facing farmers, and of what they could learn from the farmers themselves (Richards 1985).

On the positive side, even railways built for military reasons, such as that from Lagos to Kano in northern Nigeria, opened more lucrative markets to colonial producers: in that case, making possible northern Nigeria's spectacular entry into peanut exporting the year after the railway was completed (Hogendorn 1979). Rail "networks" that initially comprised a set of unconnected lines from the interior to ports, as in India, assisted market integration in the internal grain trade – as was demonstrated by price convergence between regions (Hurd 1975). Agricultural research in tropical colonies became more effective by the 1940s, discovering things useful to producers that the latter could not have found by themselves, such as the viral origin of the swollen shoot cocoa disease. Even so, the most successful agricultural developments (unless we include the first decade of the Cultivation System in Java) were primarily the result of indigenous initiative, as with the expansion of rice growing in mainland southeast Asia during the nineteenth century (Adas 1974; Brown 1997: 114–125, 141), and the willingness of West African farmers to invest heavily in the production of an exotic tree-crop, cocoa, which took several years before beginning to yield (Hill 1997 [1963]). Colonial agricultural stations did some research on food crops, and colonial officials in agricultural-exporting areas themselves tended to complain that farmers took excessive risks with food security. But the "Green Revolution" was a postcolonial phenomenon.

Overall, colonial investment, and institutional reforms, delivered relatively little in the productivity of food growing, whether in Asia or Africa. Again, both the agricultural and mining export economies were subject to the fluctuations of international commodity prices, and the disruptions to international trade brought about by the two world wars. The chronic blight on the colonial record in developing agricultural economies was the general tendency to neglect those areas that were not suited by soils and location for profitable export production; a tendency which reflected the combination of lack of fiscal resources and a concentration on existing areas of comparative advantage. Such neglected areas were integrated – partly by colonial policy and pressure, in some cases also by choice – into larger markets mainly by the export of labor: often indentured in the later nineteenth century, usually seasonal thereafter, and mainly male (see, for example, Fall 1995; Harries 1994; Northrup 1995; see further, Balachandran 2012).

The worst part of the agricultural record was the famines in India in the later nineteenth century. The death toll from two temporally overlapping famines in 1876–8 totaled 5.55 million, while a single mega-famine in 1896–7 cost 5.15 million lives (Visaria and Visaria 1983: 530–531). If average annual famine mortality was higher than in earlier periods (on which data are lacking), it may well (as has often been argued) reflect the risks entailed in increasing the market orientation of a largely rain-dependent economy supporting a large population with highly unequal incomes. The colonial government made detailed investigations of the causes, which were the basis of the now generally accepted view that these were failures of "entitlement" rather than production (Sen 1981). In the words of a British observer in 1861, they were "rather famines of work than of food" (quoted in Drèze 1988: 8). After the 1876–8 disaster, the British administration moved away from *laissez-faire* toward providing food relief to people who provided public work. The post-1900 fall in famine mortality (the wartime Bengal famine of 1942 apart) suggests amelioration of some of the institutional constraints. For example, the positive side of market integration included the stimulation of higher output in areas with the capacity to provide it.

Census figures show rising populations, evidently made possible by declining mortality, beginning at different times in different colonies, and owing something – it is hard to determine how much – to government policy. A major example was Java's transformation from labor-scarcity to labor-abundance, underpinned by population growth which began in the earlier nineteenth century. Boomgaard (1989) emphasizes the contribution of colonial vaccination programs to the falling mortality rates. Colonial censuses are harder to interpret in sub-Saharan Africa, where they are thought to have become progressively more comprehensive, thus exaggerating the eventual population take-off (Manning 2010). The population of the Indian subcontinent is estimated to have grown from 250 million in 1881 to 389 million in 1941 (Visaria and Visaria 1983: 488–489), accelerating (as in much of sub-Saharan Africa) from the 1920s.

We have much to learn about general trends of physical welfare during the last century or so of European rule in most of the colonies. Perhaps the most promising approach is the study of the changing heights of the populations, which (when handled with sufficient care) is a remarkably good indicator of physical welfare. Moradi has pioneered anthropometry in the study of colonial Africa, using the large samples available from military recruitment methods. The initial results, for Kenya and what is now Ghana, show a general rise in the heights of people born during the colonial period (Moradi 2009; Moradi,

Austin, and Baten 2013). This is doubly striking. In Kenya, it is perhaps surprising that this should apply to people born in all regions of that settler-elite colony notorious for the European appropriation of much of the most fertile land, and for the increasingly harsh treatment of the African "squatters" who constituted the main labor force on the European farms. That there was a general improvement in African living standards in Ghana is more predictable, as we know that peasant and, especially, "indigenous capitalist" colonies saw earlier and greater improvements in African real incomes than did the "settler-elite" colonies (Bowden, Chiripanhura, and Mosley 2008; Frankema and van Waijenburg 2011). What is more noteworthy is that, while the timing of the birth of taller cohorts was correlated with higher cocoa incomes, the improvement in physical welfare was far from confined to the cocoa-growing areas (Moradi, Austin, and Baten 2013). In other words, living standards in the neglected hinterland, supplying migrant labor to the cocoa economy, rose as well – thanks to a free labor market, following the end of slavery in 1908, which enabled migrant laborers to obtain increasingly good terms of employment (Austin 2005).

Let us turn to manufacturing under colonial rule. Some readers may suspect this is a contradiction in terms. Many scholars would argue, in the tradition of Alexander Gerschenkron and more recently Alice Amsden, that "late development" – industrialization with borrowed technology, in Amsden's definition (Amsden 1992; Gerschenkron 1962) requires leadership from the state;[17] and only an independent government would have the motivation to pursue industrialization. Indeed, a colonial administration was unlikely to have the fiscal and political capacity to embark on a project likely to entail major sacrifices from taxpayers and consumers, as the country defied its existing comparative disadvantage in manufacturing. In any case, colonial industrialization might threaten profits and jobs in the metropole, given the division of labor characteristic of empires and the world as a whole after the industrial revolution.

Yet mechanized textile production was introduced to southeast Asia by French investors in North Vietnam in the 1890s, starting with a spinning mill in Hanoi in 1894, followed by other spinning, and weaving, factories. These investments, protected by tariffs from British and Indian competition, complemented the import of finer, more expensive cloth from France

---

17 To be precise, Gerschenkron (1962) thought that countries without the prerequisites for a spontaneous industrialization could industrialize only by substituting for the absent elements. If the absences were greater than they were, for instance, in mid-nineteenth-century Germany, then the state had to be the leading agent of substitution.

(Brown 1997: 210–211). Several colonies, including the most populous ones, had substantial manufacturing sectors by the time World War II ushered in the period in which most of them achieved decolonization. In the American colony of the Philippines, manufacturing accounted for about 21 percent of gross value added in 1938. In French-ruled Vietnam, manufacturing employed over 11 percent of workers. Manufacturing and mining together comprised about 24 percent of Taiwanese net domestic product in 1938. In the same year the proportion was about 24 percent in Korea, and, according to Booth, probably about the same in the Netherlands Indies, where (because of greater labor-intensity) it would have accounted for a higher share of employment (Booth 2007b: 526–528).

Given the pessimistic theoretical expectations about manufacturing under colonial rule, these figures seem surprising. Both the theory and the figures require context and qualification. Some of the industrial growth achieved by 1938 reflected changes during the 1930s which shifted the usual parameters of colonial political economy, enlarging the scope for manufacturing (Booth 2007a; Brown 1997: 312–314). In southeast Asia, colonial administrations feared that the international depression was breeding poverty among their subjects, endangering the achievement of the welfare goals sought by some, and increasing the risk of political unrest. As a means of insulating the colonies against world market shocks, asserted a contemporary specialist, "Among the solutions offered none was seized upon with more enthusiasm than industrialisation."[18] Political opposition from metropolitan industrialists was presumably reduced by the fact that Japanese goods, especially textiles, were already conquering what had been "captive" markets for metropolitan exporters. In the Netherlands Indies, government promotion of manufacturing was a continuation of the "Ethical Policy" adopted after the abandonment of the Cultivation System, designed to increase income and employment (Brown 1997). There the state encouraged foreign investment, and factories were established not only by "Dutch but also American, British and other European firms" (Booth 2007a: 261). It is instructive to consider much the same variables in a different context. In the 1940s the Colonial Office in London was seized with similar enthusiasm for industrialization as an antidote to reliance on primary product exports on uncertain world markets. But they were unable to win over the more powerful department, the Treasury, which was more concerned with the scantiness of resources available to the postwar British state, and about the likely loss of markets for British

---

18 Jack Shepherd, *Industry in South East Asia* (New York: Institute of Pacific Relations, 1941), p. 4, quoted in Booth 2007b: 5.

exporters (Butler 1997). Returning to the 1930s, the industrial expansion in Korea was largely the result of investments in heavy industry by Japanese *zaibatsu* (Booth 2007b: 4–6). Conversely, in Taiwan manufacturing expanded in that decade more slowly but from a broader base.

Meanwhile, in India the growth of large-scale manufacturing had been continued, albeit slowly, since the 1850s. It was joined by a revival of small-scale industry. Factory employment outside the princely states rose from 317,000 in 1891 to 1,266,000 in 1938, to which should be added 299,000 in the princely states in 1938, up from 130,000 in 1921 (Roy 2013: 112). Roy argues that both large and small-scale sectors improved their labor productivity, nineteenth-century "deindustrialization" having eliminated the least efficient of the handicraft producers, and both sectors showing income outpacing employment in the early twentieth century (Roy 2005, 2013). Industry as a whole accounted for only 8.9 percent of employment in 1931, compared to 10.5 percent in 1901. But its contribution to income rose in the same period from 11.8 to 14.3 percent (Roy 2005: 122). Important changes in the composition of the sector included the establishment of a steel industry (as noted above), the entry of Hindu capitalists to the sector during the interwar period, partly in response to depressed agricultural prices which also reduced the profitability of their established business in lending money to farmers (Baker 1978), and improved productivity in handloom weaving, related to the increasing use of hired labor (Roy 2013).

A comparison between African economies in the same period will help to restore the importance of state intervention as a variable in the analysis. In sub-Saharan Africa in 1960, three economies had manufacturing sectors large enough to account for more than ten percent of GDP: South Africa, Southern Rhodesia (now Zimbabwe), and the Belgian Congo (Kilby 1975: 472). The relatively large size of these manufacturing sectors – by the then standards of the region – was made possible, at least indirectly, by the lucrative mining revenues around which these economies had grown. But in the two settler-elite colonies it owed much to the fact that the settlers had become self-governing: South Africa from 1910, and Southern Rhodesia from 1923, when an assembly with a white electorate took over power from the chartered company that had established the colony. Their governments could exercise this autonomy to embark on import-substituting industrialization even within the sterling area.[19] South Africa did so from 1924 and, partly in defensive response to the South African initiative, Southern Rhodesia followed in the 1930s (Feinstein 2005: 113–127; Phimister 2000).

19 Though it was only in 1930 that the government of Southern Rhodesia got the power to introduce tariffs.

Finally in this section, let us turn from colonial-period manufacturing to the question of how far the legacies of colonial rule facilitated postcolonial industrialization. The most successful such industrializers were South Korea and Taiwan. The direct legacy of manufacturing capacity was small, at least in South Korea, because of wartime destruction and the fact that most of the Japanese factories had been in the north of the peninsula. Some foreign authors have argued that this is no coincidence, and that Japanese rule, oppressive as it was, created conditions that favored industrialization, for example by improving the efficiency and discipline of the bureaucracy, and by widening access to education (Cumings 1984; Kohli 2004). Booth has provided a quantitative examination of the developmental outcomes of both colonies up to 1938, in comparison with the other colonies of eastern Asia. She found a rather mixed picture. In education provision, the Japanese colonies were behind the US colony of the Philippines in 1938. In GDP per capita, they were behind both the Philippines and British Malaya at that time, while Malaya had slipped from the richest colony in eastern Asia in 1929 to fall between the two Japanese ones. In industrial employment (including mining) as a proportion of the total, Taiwan and Korea were behind Malaya, Burma, Netherlands Indies, and the Philippines (in that order). So Booth is skeptical of the claims for the benefits of Japanese colonialism (Booth 2007b), though her measures do not directly address, in particular, the claim by Kohli (2004) that the Japanese left state bureaucracies that were particularly suited to playing the role that would be required of them in state-led industrialization.

Indeed, much may turn on the nature of the states that the departing colonizers left. Myrdal (1968) maintained that the post-independence states of south and southeast Asia were "soft," and thereby unsuited to leading development. More so, the very modest average economic growth rates of sub-Saharan Africa as a whole from the independence of most of its component countries concerned, c.1960, until at least 1995 is often attributed, at least in part, to weak state capacity and a weak sense of national identity (on which see Herbst 2000). The parallel has been drawn with Latin America in the equivalent period after independence, which was also characterized by often violent struggles to establish effective state legitimacy and control.[20] In this perspective, the colonial legacy may be unhelpful, but it can be overcome after

20 Albeit, Prados argues that Latin America improved its economic position relative to the rest of the world, apart from North America, between 1820 and 1870 (Prados de la Escosura 2009). The now classic debate about why the former British colonies of North America grew much faster than the former Iberian colonies of Central and South America in the decades after their respective independence is outside the remit of this post-1850 chapter. The debate originated between economic historians of the US, and

a couple of generations, leading to much greater development (Bates, Coatsworth, and Williamson 2007). There may well be something in this, though Prados notes that Latin American countries grew faster over their first half-century after independence than Asian and African countries did during theirs (Prados de la Escosura 2009). India, to take the most populous of all former colonies, had much more modest economic growth during the first thirty or so years after independence than it has had during the subsequent thirty or so years. However, whether the latter difference can be attributed to a strengthening of the state in the interim is questionable. While the shift in the 1980s toward a more liberal and export-oriented policy built on capacity established during the era of import-substituting industrialization, excessive protectionism and regulation during the earlier decades of independence owed something to an unintended ideological legacy of colonial rule: the Nehruvian perception that colonial *laissez-faire* had retarded Indian development, a view widely shared by both economists and historians at the time, even more than since (Roy 2005: 15–16, 27).

Capitalism and anti-capitalism in the opposition to colonialism

Capitalism, in one or more senses, was an element in various campaigns of opposition to foreign firms or specific colonial government policies, and for independence. The focus here is thus specific: it does not include, for example, resistance to colonial taxation or conscription, or to foreign rule as such. In pursuing the theme of capitalism, it is important to distinguish between anti-colonial movements opposed to the spread of market relations, and anti-colonial movements fighting to improve access to market for indigenous capitalists and peasants in the face of foreign cartels and imports.

According to Scott, in southeast Asia opposition to colonial rule was inter-woven with opposition to markets. His focus was the peasant revolts during the 1930s depression against the French in central Vietnam and the British in Burma. In his view, peasants were moved to rebel, not simply by unwill-ingness to pay the taxes imposed by the colonial authorities, or even because the combination of direct taxation and food markets threatened their food

focussed on whether institutional differences were decisive, or whether the institutional differences were themselves the outcome of differences in resource endowment. Interested readers may consult Engerman and Sokoloff (1997), North, Summerhill, and Weingast (2000), and later contributions by Grafe and Irigoin (2006); also Mahoney (2010).

security. Rather, Scott argued, colonial policies had caused profound offence because they violated a peasant "subsistence ethic," under which everyone has a moral right to survive (Scott 1976). Popkin challenged this analysis, insisting that Vietnamese peasants sought not restrictions on markets but better terms on the markets (Popkin 1979). It may be that both are right, but for different districts, according to variations in the balance between food security and profit opportunity that faced peasants in different local ecological and agrarian regimes (Baker 1981: 348).

Scott's story, though not Popkin's, stands in contrast to the struggles of extra-subsistence producers and traders in the "peasant" or "indigenous capitalist" colony which became Ghana. During the colonial period there was a repeated pattern – eventually, a conscious tradition – of African cocoa farmers and brokers staging "hold-ups," collective refusals to sell the produce to European firms, reinforced by partial boycotts of European imports. The hold-ups sought not only to oblige the firms to raise the price they offered for cocoa beans, but also to force them to dissolve whatever cartel they had formed in order to depress prices (Miles 1978). A further example of indigenous capitalist anti-colonialism was the self-consciously nationalist challenge to the European banking monopoly by the movement to create independent African banks in Nigeria, from the 1930s onwards (Hopkins 1966). While neither the Ghanaian hold-ups nor the Nigerian banking movement directly called for the departure of the colonial governments – that would have seemed unrealistic at the time – they were major challenges to the European cartelization of their respective colonial economies. In no sense did they reject the market; rather, they fought for unobstructed access to it. In the settler-elite colony of Kenya, on the other hand, the British benefitted from the opposition of cash-crop-growing peasants and chiefs to the Mau Mau guerrillas, many of whom were evidently recruited from landless former squatters on European-owned lands (Bates 1989: 11–40).

Indigenous capitalism did play a role in overt independence movements, though less so in Africa than in India. There, Congress had strong participation and financial support from from Indian merchants and industrialists (Markovits 2008). In the interwar period, Bombay millowners became more effective in influencing tariff policy in India than their rivals in Lancashire, thanks to their influence on Congress, and the latter's success in winning concessions from the British authorities (Dewey 1978). A board to introduce protection for specific infant industries was established in 1924 – seven years before Britain's general renunciation of free trade. In the 1930s, Lancashire cotton piecegoods were largely banished from Indian markets, partly because of a 25 percent tariff (albeit, they were outsold by Japanese competitors, who faced a 50 percent tariff). In 1938–9 Indian mills had 86 percent of the Indian market (Dewey 1978: 36). A particularly notable moment occurred in 1944, when a group of the largest Indian entrepreneurs met Congress representatives to formulate a plan for government policy after independence, towards the economy in general and the private sector. The Bombay Plan was – for better and worse – a milestone on the way to the protectionist policy of the state toward the larger firms in the 1950s to 1980s, against competition in domestic as well as international markets. Conversely, in Nehru's India and in Nkrumah's Ghana, among other cases, the rulers of newly independent states believed in the primacy of politics; the economics would follow.

Conclusion

This chapter has considered colonialism and capitalism in the context of the continuing spread of industrialization. There remains a strong case that the earlier history of overseas empire contributed to the origins of industrialization. British participation as the leading player, thanks to naval power, in the expansion of Atlantic trade during the seventeenth and eighteenth centuries – an expansion based on African slaves producing for the market within European colonies in the Americas – contributed to the combination of capital, markets, and incentives for specific kinds of technical innovation that facilitated the industrial revolution. Following the latter, some critics within the imperial metropoles thought that empire was now an anachronism. But the late nineteenth century and the beginning of the twentieth saw one more major spasm of territorial expansion of overseas empires – which itself took some of its impulses, variously motivating or facilitating, from the unevenness of the spread of industrialization in the West and in east Asia. By the mid 1950s, however, structural change in the industrial capitalist economies of the leading colonial powers minimized the economic costs of (according to the case) their withdrawal or expulsion from empire. Perhaps one can trace a dialectic: colonies helped industrialization begin, but as industrial economies evolved further, they had less need for colonies.

This chapter has emphasized the importance of indigenous capitalism in the colonies. Capitalism as a system did not exist in territories the Europeans colonized, but such elements in it as responsiveness to market opportunities (where food security permitted), price-forming markets, and merchant capitalist communities were already widely established. Indeed, the extent of prior market orientation was an important influence on the forms that colonialism took in different parts of the world making it more difficult for European firms to penetrate some markets, and creating incentives for colonial states to cooperate with indigenous enterprise in others. Indigenous farmers, traders, and industrialists lobbied and struggled for better access to markets, especially when confronted with European cartels and denied state protection. While the postcolonial states were not generally dominated by local capitalists, the latter had played a key role in financing the Indian Congress, the largest of all the independence movements.

We have considered how far colonial administrators fulfilled the historic mission identified for them by Marx, of uprooting precapitalist institutions and installing capitalist ones. In the age of industrialization, their actual role proved much more ambiguous.[21] Though much of the colonial world, including the "peasant" colonies, experienced a major rise in wage labor, relatively as well as absolutely, the role of government in this was often indirect and unintended; with notable exceptions, administrators often wished to constrain land markets, and thereby avert or limit proletarianization.

Colonialism contributed importantly to deepening the international division of labor between Western (and later Japanese) exporters of manufactures and "Third World" exporters of primary products. In the mid nineteenth century this was done partly through the use of force from outside: Free trade imperialism enabled the terms-of-trade shift in favor of primary producers to have more effect in China and other independent states than it would otherwise have done. Colonial administrations themselves invested in ways that reinforced the development of a comparative advantage in export agriculture, for example in southeast Asia and West Africa (Austin 2013). Yet, perhaps counterintuitively, there was a considerable growth of manufacturing, especially in the 1930s. Governments' role in this was particularly strong in settler economies with self-governing elites, but was also positive in south and southeast Asia. Colonial states were never going to be Gerschenkronian drivers of industrial catchup, but in important cases they became gradually more favorable towards manufacturing, partly in response (notably in India) to pressure from the entrepreneurs and political movements of the colonized.

Having long since shaken off the unequal treaties imposed during the heyday of Western technical supremacy, Chinese industrialization was underway by the time the return of Hong Kong and Macao, in 1997 and 1999 respectively, more or less concluded the European project of overseas empire (Darwin 2007), which the Portuguese had initiated with the capture of Cueta in Morocco back in 1415.

---

21 Etemad (2012) uses this word generally in his careful assessment of colonial legacies.

References

Accominotti, O., M. Flandreau, R. Rezzik, and F. Zumer (2010). "Black Man's Burden, White Man's Welfare: Control, Devolution and Development in the British Empire, 1880–1914," *European Review of Economic History* 14(1): 47–70.

Acemoglu, D., S. Johnson, and J. A. Robinson (2001). "The Colonial Origins of Comparative Development: An Empirical Investigation," *American Economic Review* 91(5): 1369–1401.

(2002). "Reversal of Fortune: Geography and Institutions in the Making of the Modern World Income Distribution," *Quarterly Journal of Economics* 117(4): 1231–1279.

Adas, M. (1974). *The Burma Delta: Economic Development and Social Change on an Asian Rice Frontier, 1852–1941.* Madison, WI: University of Wisconsin Press.

Akita, S. (2011). "The British Empire as an 'Imperial Structural Power' within an Asian International Order," in T. Falola and E. Brownell (eds), *Africa, Empire and Globalization: Essays in Honor of A. G. Hopkins.* Durham, NC: Carolina Academic Press, pp. 417–431.

Allen, R. C. (2009). *The British Industrial Revolution in Global Perspective* (Cambridge University Press).

Amin, S. (1976 [French original 1973]). *Unequal Development: An Essay on the Social Formations of Peripheral Capitalism.* Hassocks, Sussex: Monthly Review Press.

Amsden, A. H. (1992). "A Theory of Government Intervention in Late Industrialization," in L. Putterman and D. Rueschemeyer (eds.), *State and Market in Development.* Boulder, CO: Lynne Reinner, pp. 53–84.

Arrighi, G. (1970). "Labour Supplies in Historical Perspective: A Study of the Proletarianization of the African Peasantry in Rhodesia," *Journal of Development Studies* 3: 197–234.

Austen, R. A. (1987). *African Economic History: Internal Development and External Dependency.* London: James Currey.

Austin, G. (1996). "Mode of Production or Mode of Cultivation: Explaining the Failure of European Cocoa Planters in Competition with African Farmers in Colonial Ghana," in W. G. Clarence-Smith (ed.), *Cocoa Pioneer Fronts: The Role of Smallholders, Planters and Merchants.* Basingstoke: Macmillan, pp. 154–175.

(2005). *Labour, Land and Capital in Ghana: From Slavery to Free Labour in Asante, 1807–1956.* Rochester University Press.

(2008a). "Resources, Techniques and Strategies South of the Sahara: Revising the Factor Endowments Perspective on African Economic Development, 1500–2000," *Economic History Review* 61(3): 587–624.

(2008b). "'The Reversal of Fortune' Thesis and the Compression of History: Perspectives from African and Comparative Economic History," *Journal of International Development* 20(8): 996–1027.

(2009). "Cash Crops and Freedom: Export Agriculture and the Decline of Slavery in Colonial West Africa," *International Review of Social History* 54(1): 1–37.

(2013). "Labour-Intensity and Manufacturing in West Africa, c.1450–c.2000," in G. Austin and K. Sugihara (eds.), *Labour-Intensive Industrialization in Global History.* London: Routledge, pp. 201–230.

Austin, G. and C. U. Uche. (2007). "Collusion and Competition in Colonial Economies: Banking in British West Africa, 1916–1960," *Business History Review* 81: 1–26.

Baier, S. (1980). *An Economic History of Central Niger*. Oxford University Press.

Baker, C. (1978). "Debt and the Depression in Madras, 1929–1936," in C. Dewey and A. G. Hopkins (eds.), *The Imperial Impact: Studies in the Economic History of Africa and India*. London: Athlone Press for University of London, pp. 233–242, 370–371.

(1981). "Economic Reorganization and the Slump in South and Southeast Asia," *Comparative Studies in Society and History* 23(3): 325–349.

Balachandran, G. (2008). 'Power and Markets in Global Finance: The Gold Standard, 1890–1926," *Journal of Global History* 3(3): 313–335.

(2012). *Globalizing Labour? Indian Seafarers and World Shipping, c.1870–1945*. Delhi: Oxford University Press.

Bates, R. H. (1989). *Beyond the Miracle of the Market: The Political Economy of Agrarian Development in Kenya*. Cambridge University Press.

Bates, R. H., J. H. Coatsworth, and J. G. Williamson (2007). "Lost Decades: Postindependence Peformance in Latin America and Africa," *Journal of Economic History* 67(4): 917–943.

Bauer, P. T. (1954). *West African Trade*. Cambridge University Press.

Belich, J. (2009). *Replenishing the Earth: The Settler Revolution and the Rise of the Anglo-World, 1783–1939*. Oxford University Press.

Berg, M. (2009). "Quality, Cotton and the Global Luxury Trade," in G. Riello and T. Roy (eds.), *How India Clothed the World: The World of South Asian Textiles, 1500–1850*. Leiden: Brill, pp. 391–414.

(2012). "Luxury, the Luxury Trades and the Roots of Industrial Growth," in F. Trentmann (ed.), *The Oxford Handbook on the History of Consumption*. Oxford University Press, pp. 173–212.

Berger, E. L. (1974). *Labour, Race and Colonial Rule: The Copperbelt from 1924 to Independence*. Oxford University Press.

Boomgaard, P. (1989). *Children of the Colonial State: Population Growth and Economic Development in Java, 1795–1880*. Amsterdam: Free University Press.

Booth, A. (2007a). "Night Watchman, Extractive, or Developmental States? Some Evidence from Late Colonial South-East Asia," *Economic History Review* 60(2): 241–266.

(2007b). "Did It Really Help to be a Japanese Colony? East Asian Economic Performance in Historical Perspective," *Japan Focus*, 7 May 2007.

Bowden, S., B. Chiripanhura, and P. Mosley (2008). "Measuring and Explaining Poverty in Six African Countries: A Long-Period Approach," *Journal of International Development* 20(8): 1049–1079.

Branch, D. (2009). *Defeating Mau Mau, Creating Kenya: Counterinsurgency, Civil War, and Decolonization*. Cambridge University Press.

Braudel, F. (1982 [1979]). *Civilization and Capitalism 15th–18th Century*. Vol. II, *The Wheels of Fortune*, transl. S. Reynolds from French original. London: William Collins.

Brewer, A. (1990). *Marxist Theories of Imperialism: A Critical Survey*, 2nd edn. London: Routledge & Kegan Paul).

Brocheux, P. (2012). "Reflections on Vietnam" (interview), *New Left Review* 73: 73–91.

Brocheux, P. and D. Hémery (1995). *Indochine la colonisation ambiguë 1858–1954*. Paris: Éditions La Découverte.

Brown, I. (1997). *Economic Change in South-East Asia, c.1830–1980*. Oxford University Press.

(2011). "The Economics of Decolonization in Burma," in T. Falola and E. Brownell (eds.), *Africa, Empire and Globalization: Essays in Honor of A. G. Hopkins*. Durham, NC: Carolina Academic Press, pp. 433–444.

Brown, R. A. (1994). *Capital and Entrepreneurship in South-East Asia*. London: Macmillan.

Buelens, F. and S. Marysse. (2009). "Returns on Investment During the Colonial Era: Belgian Congo," *Economic History Review* 62(1): 135–166.

Burbank, J. and F. Cooper (2010). *Empires in World History: Power and the Politics of Difference*. Princeton University Press.

Butler, L. J. (1997). *Industrialisation and the British Colonial State: West Africa, 1939–1951*. London: Frank Cass.

Clarence-Smith, W. G. (1979). "The Myth of Uneconomic Imperialism: The Portuguese in Angola, 1836–1926," *Journal of Southern African Studies* 5(1): 165–180.

Cain, P. J. and A. G. Hopkins (2001). *British Imperialism 1688–2000*, 2nd edn. Harlow: Longman [Pearson Education].

Charlesworth, N. (1985). *Peasants and Imperial Rule: Agriculture and Agrarian Society in the Bombay Presidency, 1850–1935*. Cambridge University Press.

Cooper, F. (1996). *Decolonization and African Society: The Labor Question in French and British Africa*. Cambridge University Press.

Crafts, N. (2012). "British Relative Economic Decline Revisited: The Role of Competition," *Explorations in Economic History* 49(1): 17–29.

Cumings, B. (1984). "The Legacy of Japanese Colonialism in Korea," in R. H. Myers and M. R. Peattie (eds.), *The Japanese Colonial Empire, 1895–1945*. Princeton University Press.

Cuvillier-Fleury, R. (1907). *La main d'oeuvre dans les colonies françaises de l'Afrique occidentale et du Congo*. Paris: Société du Recueil J.-B. Sirey.

Darwin, J. (2007). *After Tamerlane: The Rise and Fall of Global Empires, 1400–2000*. London: Penguin.

Davis, L. E. and R. A. Huttenback with S. G. Davis (1986). *Mammon and the Pursuit of Empire: The Political Economy of British Imperialism, 1860–1912*. Cambridge University Press.

Dewey, C. (1978). "The End of the Imperialism of Free Trade: The Eclipse of the Lancashire Lobby and the Concession of Free Trade to India," in C. Dewey and A. G. Hopkins (eds.), *The Imperial Impact: Studies in the Economic History of Africa and India*. London: Athlone Press for University of London, pp. 35–67, 331–338.

Domar, E. D. (1970). "The Causes of Slavery or Serfdom: A Hypothesis," *Journal of Economic History* 30(1): 18–32.

Dooling, W. (2007). *Slavery, Emancipation and Colonial Rule in South Africa*. Scotsville: University of KwaZulu-Natal Press.

Drèze, J. (1988). "Famine Prevention in India," World Institute for Development Economics Research, Working Paper No. 45 (Helsinki).

Eltis, D. and S. L. Engerman. (2000). "The Importance of Slavery and the Slave Trade to Industrializing Britain," *Journal of Economic History* 60(1): 123–144.

Engerman, S. L. (1972). "The Slave Trade and British Capital Formation in the Eighteenth Century: A Comment on the Williams Thesis," *Business History Review* 46(4): 430–443.

Engerman, S. L. and K. L. Sokoloff (1997). "Factor Endowments, Instititutions, and Differential Paths of Growth among New World Economies: A View from Economic Historians of the United States," in S. Haber (ed.), *How Latin America Fell*

Behind: Essays on the Economic Histories of Brazil and Mexico, 1800–1914. Stanford University Press, pp. 260–304.

Etemad, B. (2012). *L'héritage ambigu de la colonisation: économies, populations, sociétés.* Paris: Armand Colin.

Fails, M. D. and J. Krieckhaus (2010). "Colonialism, Property Rights and the Modern World Income Distribution," *British Journal of Political Science* 40: 487–508.

Fall, B. (1995). *Le travail forcé en Afrique Occidentale française (1900–1945).* Paris: Karthala.

Ferro, M. (1994). *Histoire des colonisations: des conquêtes aux indépendances XIIIe–XXe siècle.* Paris: Éditions du Seuil.

Falola, T. and E. Brownell, eds. (2011). *Africa, Empire and Globalization: Essays in Honor of A. G. Hopkins.* Durham, NC: Carolina Academic Press.

Feinstein, C. H. (2005). *An Economic History of South Africa: Conquest, Discrimination and Development.* Cambridge University Press.

Ferguson, N. and M. Schularick (2006). "The Empire Effect: The Determinants of Country Risk in the First Age of Globalization, 1880–1913," *Journal of Economic History* 66(2): 283–312.

Fox-Genovese, E. and E. D. Genevese (1983). *Fruits of Merchant Capital: Slavery and Bourgeois Property in the Rise and Expansion of Capitalism.* New York: Oxford University Press.

Frank, A. G. (1978). *Dependent Accumulation and Under-Development.* London: Macmillan.

Frankel, S. H. (1938). *Capital Investment in Africa.* Oxford University Press.

Frankema, E. (2010). "Raising Revenue in the British Empire, 1870–1940: How 'Extractive' were Colonial Taxes?" *Journal of Global History* 5(3): 447–477.

Frankema, E. and F. Buelens, eds. (2012). *Colonial Exploitation and Economic Development: The Belgian Congo and the Netherlands Indies Compared.* London: Routledge.

Frankema, E. and M. van Waijenburg (2011). "African Real Wages in Asian Perspective, 1880–1940," Center for Global Economic History Working Paper No. 2 (Utrecht).

Gallagher, J. and R. Robinson (1953). "The Imperialism of Free Trade," *Economic History Review*, 2nd series 6(1): 1–15.

Gerschenkron, A. (1962). *Economic Backwardness in Historical Perspective.* Cambridge, MA: Harvard University Press.

Grafe, R. and M. A. Irigoin (2006). "The Spanish Empire and its Legacy: Fiscal Redistribution and Political Conflict in Colonial and Post-Colonial Spanish America," *Journal of Global History* 1(2): 241–268.

Guha, R. (2012). "Perfidy, Villainy, Intrigue," *London Review of Books,* 20 December.

Gupta, B. and D. Ma (2010). "Europe in an Asian Mirror: The Great Divergence," in S. Broadberry and K. H. O'Rourke (eds.), *The Cambridge Economic History of Modern Europe.* Vol. I: *1700–1870.* Cambridge University Press, pp. 264–285.

Harries, P. (1994). *Work, Culture, and Identity: Migrant Labourers in Mozambique and South Africa, c.1860–1910.* Portsmouth, NH: Heinemann.

Herbst, J. (2000). *States and Power in Africa: Comparative Lessons in Authority and Control.* Princeton University Press.

Hill, P. (1997 [1963]). *The Migrant Cocoa-Farmers of Southern Ghana,* 2nd edn with preface by G. Austin, Hamburg: LIT; 1st edn. Cambridge University Press).

Hodeir, C. (2003). *Stratégies d'empire: le grand patronat colonial face à la décolonisation.* Paris: Éditions Belin.

Hoffman, P. T., G. Postel-Vinay, and J.-L. Rosenthal (1999). "Information and Economic History: How the Credit Market in Old Regime Paris Forces us to Rethink the Transition to Capitalism," *American Historical Review* 104(1); 69–94.

Hogendorn, J. S. (1979). *Nigerian Groundnut Exports: Origins and Early Development*. Nigeria: Ahmadu Bello University Press.

Hopkins, A. G. (1966). "Economic Aspects of Political Movements in Nigeria and the Gold Coast, 1918–39," *Journal of African History* 7(1): 133–152.

(1973). *An Economic History of West Africa*. London: Longman.

(1980). "Property Rights and Empire-Building: Britain's Annexation of Lagos, 1861," *Journal of Economic History* 40(4): 777–798.

(1995). "The 'New International Economic Order' in the Nineteenth Century: Britain"s First Development Plan for Africa," in R. Law (ed.), *From Slave Trade to "Legitimate" Commerce: The Commercial Transition in Nineteenth-Century West Africa*. Cambridge University Press, pp. 240–264.

(2008). "Rethinking Decolonisation," *Past and Present* 200: 211–247.

Huff, W. G. (1994). *The Economic Growth of Singapore: Trade and Development in the Twentieth Century*. Cambridge University Press.

Hurd II, J. (1975). "Railways and the Expansion of Markets in India, 1861–1921," *Explorations in Economic History* 12(3): 263–288.

Inikori, J. E. (2002). *Africans and the Industrial Revolution in England*. Cambridge University Press.

Isaacman, A. F. and R. L. Roberts, eds. (1995). *Cotton, Colonialism, and Social History in Sub-Saharan Africa*. Portsmouth, NH: Heinemann.

Kilby, P. (1975). "Manufacturing in Colonial Africa," in P. Duignan and L. H. Gann (eds.), *Colonialism in Africa 1870–1960* Vol. IV, *The Economics of Colonialism*. Cambridge University Press, pp. 470–520.

Kohli, A. (2004). "The Colonial Origins of a Modern Political Economy: The Japanese Lineage of Korea's Cohesive-Capitalist State," in *State-Directed Development: Political Power and Industrialization in the Global Periphery*. Cambridge University Press, pp. 27–61.

Law, R. (1977). "Royal Monopoly and Private Enterprise in the Atlantic Trade: The Case of Dahomey," *Journal of African History* 18(4): 555–577.

(1992). "Posthumous Questions for Karl Polanyi: Price Inflation in Pre-Colonial Dahomey," *Journal of African History* 33(3): 387–420.

Legassick, M. (1977). "Gold, Agriculture, and Secondary Industry in South Africa, 1885–1970: From to Periphery to Sub-Metropole in a Forced Labour System," in R. Palmer and N. Parsons (eds.), *The Roots of Rural Poverty in Central and Southern Africa*. London: Heinemann, pp. 175–200.

Likaka, O. (1997). *Rural Society and Cotton in Colonial Zaire*. Madison, WI: University of Wisconsin Press.

Lipietz, A. (1983). "Towards Global Fordism?" *New Left Review* 132: 33–47.

Lipton, M. (1968). "The Theory of the Optimizing Peasant," *Journal of Development Studies* 4: 327–351.

Lovejoy, P. E. and J. S. Hogendorn (1993). *Slow Death for Slavery: The Course of Abolition in Northern Nigeria, 1897–1936*. Cambridge University Press.

Lützelschwab, C. (2013). "Settler Colonialism in Africa," in C. Lloyd, J. Metzer, and R. Sutch (eds.), *Settler Economies in World History*. Leiden: Brill, pp. 141–167.

Mahoney, J. (2010). *Colonialism and Postcolonial Development: Spanish America in Comparative Perspective*. New York: Cambridge University Press.

Manning, P. (2010). "African Population: Projections, 1850–1960" in K. Ittmann, D. D. Cordell, and G. Maddox (eds.), *The Demographics of Empire: The Colonial Order and the Creation of Knowledge*. Athens, OH: Ohio University Press, pp. 245–275.

Markovits, C. (2008). *Merchants, Traders, Entrepreneurs: Indian Business in the Colonial Era*. Basingstoke: Palgrave Macmillan.

Marseille, J. (2005). *Empire colonial et capitalisme français: histoire d'un divorce*, 2nd edn. Paris: Albin Michel.

Marx, K. (1853). "The British Rule in India," New York Daily Tribune, 3804, June 25. Reprinted in K. Marx and F. Engels (1959). *On Colonialism*. London: Lawrence & Wishart, pp. 35–41.

(1867). *Das Kapital: Kritik der politischen Oekonomie*. Vol. 1. Hamburg. English translations include that by S. Moore and E. Aveling, ed. F. Engels (London 1970), reprinted many times, e.g. New York: International Publishers, 1967.

Miles, J. (1978). "Rural Protest in the Gold Coast: The Cocoa Hold-Ups, 1908–1938," in C. Dewey and A. G. Hopkins (eds.), *The Imperial Impact: Studies in the Economic History of Africa and India* (London: Athlone Press for University of London), pp. 152–170, 353–357.

Misra, M. (2000). "Business Culture and Entrepreneurship in British India, 1860–1950," *Modern Asian Studies* 34(2): 333–348.

Montieth, K. E. A. (2000). "Competition Between Barclays Bank (DCO) and the Canadian Banks in the West Indies, 1926–45," *Financial History Review* 7(1): 67–87.

Moradi, A. (2009). "Towards an Objective Account of Nutrition and Health in Colonial Kenya: A Study of Stature in African Army Recruits and Civilians, 1880–1980," *Journal of Economic History* 69(3): 719–754.

Moradi, A., G. Austin, and J. Baten (2013). "Heights and Development in a Cash-Crop Colony: Living Standards in Ghana, 1870–1980." Lund: African Economic History Working Paper Series, 7.

Morris, M. D. (1979). "South Asian Entrepreneurship and the Rashomon Effect, 1800–1947," *Explorations in Economic History* 16: 3.

Mosley, P. (1983). *The Settler Economies: Kenya and Rhodesia 1900–1963*. Cambridge University Press.

Myrdal, G. (1968). *Asian Drama: An Inquiry into the Poverty of Nations*, 3 vols. London: Allen Lane.

Nadan, A. (2006). *The Palestinian Peasant Economy under the Mandate*. Cambridge, MA: Harvard Center for Middle Eastern Studies.

Nieboer, H. J. (1910 [1900]). *Slavery as an Industrial System*. 1st edn The Hague: Nijhoff; revd. edn. Free Library of Philadelphia.

North, D. C., W. R. Summerhill, and B. R. Weingast (2000). "Order, Disorder, and Economic Change: Latin America versus North America," in B. Bueno de Mesquita and H. L. Root (eds.), *Governing for Prosperity*. New Haven, CT: Yale University Press, pp. 17–58.

Northrup, D. (1988). *Beyond the Bend in the River: African Labor in Eastern Zaire, 1865–1940*. Athens, OH: Ohio University Press.

(1995). *Indentured Labor in the Age of Imperialism, 1834–1922*. Cambridge University Press.

O'Brien, P. K. (1982). "European Economic Development: The Contribution of the Periphery," *Economic History Review* 35(1): 1–18.

O'Brien, P. K. and L. Prados de la Escosura (1999). "Balance Sheets for the Acquisition, Retention and Loss of European Empires Overseas," *Itinerario* 23(3–4): 25–52.

Offer, A. (1993). "The British Empire, 1870–1914: A Waste of Money?" *Economic History Review* 46: 215–238.

Olsson, O. (2004). "Unbundling Ex-Colonies: A Comment on Acemoglu, Johnson and Robinson 2001," Working Papers in Economics No. 146. Göteborg University.

O'Rourke, K. H., L. Prados de la Escosura, and G. Daudin (2010). "Trade and Empire," in S. Broadberry and K. H. O'Rourke (eds.), *The Cambridge Economic History of Modern Europe*. Vol. I: 1700–1870. Cambridge University Press, pp. 96–122.

Palmer, R. and N. Parsons, eds. (1977). *The Roots of Rural Poverty in Central and Southern Africa*. London: Heinemann.

Parthasarathi, P. (2011). *Why Europe Grew Rich and Asia Did Not: Global Economic Divergence, 1600–1850*. Cambridge University Press.

Phillips, A. (1989). *The Enigma of Colonialism: Briitsh Policy in West Africa*. London: James Currey.

Phimister, I. R. (2000). "The Origins and Development of Manufacturing in Southern Rhodesia, 1894–1939" and "From Preference to Protection: Manufacturing in Southern Rhodesia 1940–1965," in A. S. Mlambo, I. R. Phimister, and E. S. Pangeti (eds.), *Zimbabwe: A History of Manufacturing 1890–1995*. Harare: University of Zimbabwe Publications, pp. 9–50.

Platt, D. C. M. (1972). "Economic Imperialism and the Businessman: Britain and Latin America Before 1914," in R. Owen and B. Sutcliffe (eds.), *Studies in the Theory of Imperialism*. London: Longman, pp. 295–311.

Polanyi, K. (1944). *The Great Transformation*. New York: Rinehart.

(1966). *Dahomey and the Slave Trade: An Analysis of an Archaic Economy*. Seattle: University of Washington Press.

Pomeranz, K. (2000). *The Great Divergence: China, Europe, and the Making of the Modern World Economy*. Princeton University Press.

Popkin, S. L. (1979). *The Rational Peasant: The Political Economy of Rural Society in Vietnam*. Berkeley, CA: University of California Press.

Prados de la Escosura, L. (2009). "Lost Decades? Economic Performance in Post-Independence Latin America," *Journal of Latin American Studies* 41(2): 279–307.

Richards, P. (1985). *Indigenous Agricultural Revolution: Ecology and Food Production in West Africa*. London: Hutchinson.

Roberts, R. L. (1996). *Two Worlds of Cotton: Colonialism and the Regional Economy in the French Soudan, 1800–1946*. Stanford University Press.

Robinson, R. (1972). "Non-European Foundations of European Imperialism: Sketches for a Theory of Collaboration," in R. Owen and B. Sutcliffe (eds,), *Studies in the Theory of Imperialism*. London: Longman, pp. 117–142.

Robinson, R. and J. Gallagher with A. Denny (1961). *Africa and the Victorians: The Official Mind of Imperialism* London: Palgrave Macmillan.

Roy, T. (2005). *Rethinking Economic Change in India: Labour and Livelihood*. London: Routledge.

(2006). *The Economic History of India 1857–1947*, 2nd edn. New Delhi: Oxford University Press.

(2013). "Labour-Intensity and Industrialization in Colonial India," in G. Austin and K. Sugihara (eds.), *Labour-Intensive Industrialization in Global History*. London: Routledge, pp. 107–121.

Scott, J. C. (1976). *The Moral Economy of the Peasant: Rebellion and Subsistence in Southeast Asia.* New Haven, CT: Yale University Press.

Sen, A. (1981). *Poverty and Famines: An Essay on Entitlement and Deprivation.* Oxford University Press.

Sender, J. and S. Smith (1986). *The Development of Capitalism in Africa.* London: Methuen.

Stockwell, S. (2000). *The Business of Decolonization: British Business Strategies in the Gold Coast.* Oxford University Press.

Sugihara, K. (2002). "British Imperialism, the City of London and Global Industrialisation," in S. Akita (ed.), *Gentlemanly Capitalism: Imperialism and Global History.* London: Palgrave Macmillan.

Tignor, R. L. (1998). *Capitalism and Nationalism at the End of Empire.* Princeton University Press.

Tomlinson, B. R. (1981). "Colonial Firms and the Decline of Colonialism in Eastern India 1914–47," *Modern Asian Studies* 15(3): 455–486.

Tosh, J. (1980). "The Cash-Crop Revolution in Tropical Africa: An Agricultural Reappraisal," *African Affairs* 79(314): 79–94.

Uche, C. (2008). "Oil, British Interests and the Nigerian Civil War," *Journal of African History* 49(1): 111–135.

Van der Linden, M. (2008). *Workers of the World: Essays Toward a Global Labor History.* Leiden: Brill.

Van Zanden, J. L. and D. Marks (2012). *An Economic History of Indonesia 1800–2012.* London: Routledge.

Visaria, L. and P. Visaria (1983). "Population (1757–1947)," in D. Kumar and M. Desai (eds.), *The Cambridge Economic Hitory of India.* Vol. II: *c.1757–c.1970* Cambridge University Press, pp. 463–532.

Wakefield, E. G. (1829). *A Letter from Sydney, the Principal Town of Australasia: Together with the Outline of a System of Colonization*, R. Gouger (ed.). London: Robert Cross.

Warren, B. (1980). *Imperialism: Pioneer of Capitalism*, ed. J. Sender. London: NLB.

Wehler, H.-U. (1975). "Industrial Growth and Early German Imperialism," in R. Owen and B. Sutcliffe (eds.), *Studies in the Theory of Imperialism.* London: Longman, pp. 71–92.

White, N. J. (1998). "Capitalism and Counter-Insurgency? Business and Government in the Malayan Emergency, 1948–57," *Modern Asian Studies* 32(1): 149–177.

Williams, E. (1944). *Capitalism and Slavery.* Chapel Hill, NC: North Carolina University Press.

Williamson, J. A. (2011). *Trade and Poverty: When the Third World Fell Behind.* Cambridge, MA: The MIT Press.

Wong, B. (1997). *China Transformed: Historical Change and the Limits of European Experience.* Ithaca: Cornell.

11

Capitalism at war

MARK HARRISON[*]

"Capitalism means war." Béla Kun, cited by Daniel Guérin. (1938)

The nineteenth century witnessed the triumph of capitalism (O'Rourke and Williamson, Chapter 1 in this volume); the twentieth century saw the bloodiest wars in history. Both war and society were transformed; what was the link? In what ways did capitalism transform warfare? Was the capitalist system responsible for spreading or facilitating war, or for the rising toll of war deaths?

To some, the causal link is so obvious that it has required only illustration. The Marxist demographer of war and peace Boris Urlanis (1960/1994: 404–405) carefully estimated premature deaths in European wars and allocated them to different stages of the rise of capitalism. He found an accelerating rate. Under early capitalism there were 33,000 war deaths per year (1600 to 1699), rising to 44,000 per year (1700 to 1788). With the onset of "industrial capitalism" (1789 to 1897) the annual rate rose further to 62,000; with "imperialism" (1898 to 1959) it exploded to more than 700,000. What more needed to be said?

Modern scholarship would qualify this picture in three ways. First, warfare captures only a narrow band in the overall spectrum of violence in society. This spectrum runs all the way from ordinary homicide through the violence associated with organized crime to social and political strife, civil

* Earlier versions of this chapter were presented at the German Historical Institute in Moscow as one of "Ten Lectures about the War," June 17 and 18, 2011, the xvith World Economic History Congress, Stellenbosch University, South Africa, July 9 to 13, 2012, and a conference on the Economic History of Capitalism, BBVA, Madrid, November 14 to 16, 2012. I thank Hein Klemann, Sergei Kudriashov, Andrei Markevich, Richard Overy, Leandro Prados de la Escosura, James Robinson, and other participants for discussion; Sascha O. Becker, Michael S. Bernstam, Nick Crafts, Erik Gartzke, and Vasily Zatsepin for comments and advice; Jari Eloranta for access to data; Larry Neal and Jeff Williamson for inspiration and guidance; the University of Warwick for research leave and financial support; and the Hoover Institution for generous hospitality.

war, and interstate conflict. Deaths in war omit a large part, and possibly the larger part of this spectrum. Estimates of the incidence of deaths from violence of all types in society over the last 10,000 years are suggestive of a great decline that continues to the present day. If more people died of violence in the age of imperialism, it was not because there was more violence at that time, but because more people lived in that era than ever before (Gat 2006; Pinker 2011).

Second, if we limit our focus to conflicts among states, the two world wars of the first half of the twentieth century continue to be recognized as the greatest wars in history. In contrast, the second half of the century was more peaceful on a variety of measures (K. Gleditsch 2004; N. Gleditsch 2008; Goldstein 2011; Hewitt 2008; Pinker 2011). The annual number of wars involving fatalities and the number of military fatalities in each year declined. Despite conflicts associated with the breakup of the Soviet and Yugoslav states in the early 1990s, these downward trends continued through the turn of the century.

Third, not all indicators have been pointing in the same benign direction. While the intensity of conflict appears to be in decline, the global number of interstate disputes involving the use or display of force has been rising (Harrison and Wolf 2012). The probability that any pair of countries in the world would find themselves in conflict in a given year may have fallen slowly (Martin, Mayer, and Thoenig 2008), but there has been a great increase in the number of countries and, with that, the number of country pairs. More countries have meant more state actors claiming sovereignty over the use of force in global society, and more borders over which to quarrel. Conflict has become less cataclysmic but more endemic. Perhaps we are living in an era of "new wars" (Münkler 2005).

What does all this have to do with capitalism? The question is more complicated than would appear at first sight. First, it raises important issues of identification: what is "capitalism" and what can it mean to say, as some once claimed, that "capitalism means war"? In the second part of the chapter I will ask whether capitalism has affected our choices over war and peace by changing opportunity costs. Specifically, have we had more wars, not because we wanted them, but because we could? In the third part I will ask whether the structure of the capitalist economy has motivated the owners of capital to show some systematic preference for war by comparison with the elites of other systems. Having considered the influence of capitalism on war, the fourth part considers the influences of war on capitalism. The fifth part concludes.

Capitalism, anti-capitalism, and war

Ricardo (1817) used the word "capitalist" to distinguish the owners of capital from landowners and laborers. But the mere existence of capitalists falls short of implying "capitalism," an entire economic and social system with private capital ownership at its foundation. In fact, the identity of capitalism was created by its critics, Proudhon (1861) and Marx (1867). Marx, before anyone else, argued that capitalism's defining features allow us logically to infer distinct and general attributes of capitalism (such as alienation) and propensities (such as the declining rate of profit). In this sense, to inquire into whether "capitalism" as such has a propensity for anything, let alone something as emotive as war, is to enter a debate on conceptual territory chosen by the enemies of capitalism.

Second, the histories of capitalism and warfare are certainly intertwined, but not uniquely. War is as old as history; capitalism is not. All societies that have given rise to organized government have engaged in warfare (Tilly 1975). The slave and serf societies and city-states of the ancient, classical, and medieval eras made war freely. Turning to modern times, the socialist states of the twentieth century were born in wartime, prepared for war, and did not shrink from the use of military power to achieve their goals. Thinking comparatively, it will not be easy to identify any causal connection between capitalism and war. At most, we will look for some adaptation or propensity for war under capitalism, relative to other systems.

Third, if there is a story here, who are the actors? Capitalism is an economic structure; war is a political act. War can hardly be explained by structure alone, for there is no war without agency, calculation, and decision. Given this, our search must be for aspects of capitalism that may have created incentives and propensities for the political actors to choose war with greater frequency, and made them more willing to impose the increasing costs of war on society than under alternative conditions, real or counterfactual.

From the outset, I will follow the definition of capitalism set out by Larry Neal (Chapter 1 of Volume 1): "(1) private property rights, (2) enforceable contracts, (3) markets with prices responsive to supply and demand, (4) supportive governments." Here, "supportive" means supportive of the first three features, not supportive of wealthy individuals, rich corporations, or other special interest groups. Borrowing terms from Rodrik and Subramanian (2005), the first three conditions are most likely to be met when government is "pro-market," not "pro-business." What if that condition is not met? It's a matter of degree. A pro-business government that favors incumbent firms and receives their loyalty weakens competition, contracts, and property rights. At some point we would move into the territory of "crony capitalism." Thus, capitalism has varieties.

To define capitalism implies both pre-capitalism and anti-capitalism. In nearly all countries before the seventeenth century, private property and markets existed, but much production was not marketed and many prices were not free. Contracts were insecure. Rulers tended to be more concerned with their own prerogatives than with accepting and upholding the rule of law. Whatever you call it, this was not capitalism.

In the nineteenth century we had anti-capitalist ideologies and, in the twentieth century, anti-capitalist systems (Frieden and Rogowski, Chapter 12 in this volume). Notably, there was communism: Where they could, the communists abolished private business ownership, suppressed markets, and imposed dictatorship over the law. Communism, also, was clearly not capitalism.

The case of fascism is contested. Was fascism somewhere within the spectrum of capitalisms, or outside it and antithetical to it? "Fascism is war," wrote Georgi Dimitrov (1936/1972: 176). If fascism is capitalism, and fascism means war, then capitalism means war. It is important, therefore, to get this right. Under fascist rule there was dictatorship. The courts upheld the interests of the state, not the rights of the citizen or the rule of law. Private property existed, but property rights were maintained if the government allowed, not otherwise (Overy 1994). Often the government did wish it, viewing contracts with capitalist proprietors as creating the right incentives for efficient procurement (Buchheim and Scherner 2006). Whether this was a deep conviction or an instrumental motivation is debated; Hitler himself declared on one occasion that family property was a productive institution but joint-stock shareholders were parasites whom the state should expropriate (Trevor-Roper 2000: 362–363). As we will discuss below, the national socialist government was neither pro-market nor pro-business in any general sense. It favored those businesses that conformed to its policies, while others, such as businesses owned by Jews, and the aircraft interests of the anti-Nazi Hugo Junkers, were confiscated or driven out. There were markets, but many prices were regulated and the government often rationed goods to producers and consumers.

Was fascism closer to socialism or communism than to capitalism? In Italy, the fascist Mussolini came out of the Socialist Party. In Germany, Hitler called his followers National Socialists. When they railed against capitalism, brawled in the streets, and promoted mass mobilization, a politicized and militarized economy, and dictatorial rule, the fascists did not look very different from the communists, who struggled to differentiate themselves. Left socialists and communists emphasized fascism as an extreme variant of capitalism to cover the resulting embarrassment. The canonical example is Stalin's infamous *Short Course* (CPSU 1941: 301–302), according to which fascism was "the dictatorship of the most reactionary, most chauvinistic, most imperialistic capitalist elements," taking the name of national socialism only "in order to hoodwink the people."

The communists portrayed fascism as pro-capitalism in disguise. I do not find this convincing. The Nazis did not try to disguise anything else; they were not ashamed to advocate racial hatred and war, for example. Compared with these, being in favor of capitalism would seem a small thing; why would they have wished to hide it? Perhaps we should take them at their word: if this was still capitalism, it was captured by an anti-capitalist political agency. Fascism made property, prices, and contracts conditional on the will of the government. This does not mean that fascism and communism were the same. But the superiority of the state over private interests was something they held in common.

As for capitalism and war, there is already a large literature, so we do not start from a blank page. I will mention some highlights as we proceed. I will organize the discussion in the following order. Has the existence of capitalism, in some morally neutral and quite general sense, promoted the capacity for war in global society? Then, does the structure of the capitalist economy exhibit some systematic preference for war in comparison to other systems? I will focus on capitalism in the interstate wars of the twentieth century. In the background of this chapter are the experiences of eighteenth-century mercantilism and nineteenth-century imperialism (O'Brien, Chapter 12 in Volume I; Austin, Chapter 10 in this volume).

The capacity for war

Has capitalism promoted the capacity for war? Before 1914, many observers of the rise of international business would have answered this question decisively in the negative. Writers like Norman Angell (1911) and Ivan Bliokh (de Bloch 1914) believed that modern capitalism had driven up the opportunity cost of war to a point where the industrial and commercial powers would no longer fight major wars. They were both right and wrong. In the twentieth century, the costs of war were unprecedented. As it turned out, however, the costs of not being prepared for war and of not fighting had risen even more rapidly. Moreover, the heavy costs of warfare proved to be unexpectedly sustainable; it turned out that major industrial economies could bear them for years on end without collapsing. How did this come about?

Military innovation

The relative price of destruction has been falling for centuries. The headlines we pay most attention to may be the rising prices of big-ticket items like interceptor aircraft and warships; when we do that, we may forget that their destructive power has risen more rapidly than the price. Today, you can destroy a city in a flash, and the means will fit in a suitcase. Two generations ago you could do it in a night, but it required not less than a thousand bombers. A few generations before that, to ruin a city took an army weeks or months of unceasing effort, with uncertain results.

It is almost too obvious to say that capitalist industry has hugely affected this process, primarily through mechanization. Capitalism mechanized the weaponry, the production and projection of weapons, and the transportation of armies. This is so obvious that it may seem impossible to overstate. Yet, it can be overstated, for several reasons.

First, the long-term decline in the real price of weaponry did not start with industrial capitalism; the industrial revolution prolonged and speeded up a tendency that was already in place. Philip Hoffman (2010, 2012) has shown that the real price of weapons was falling in the late Middle Ages, long before capitalism. It fell faster in Europe than elsewhere. Its driver was the battlefield rivalry of princes, not the market competition of capitalist firms. Europe's lasting comparative advantage in what Hoffman calls the "gunpowder technology" was conditioned on its political divisions, its lack of natural frontiers, and princely competition. Capitalism continued this trend, and was well suited to accelerate it. But capitalism did not start it.

Second, the mechanism of improvement under capitalism was largely the competition of private producers, but government provided the market, and in the few countries that maintained large defense industries, competition was (and remains) highly imperfect. Military-technical innovation is subsidized. Pre-contract lobbying and collusion, among firms and between buyer and seller, and post-contract renegotiation are normal (Rogerson 1994). These standard features of capitalist defense markets were largely replicated under both national socialism and communism (Buchheim and Scherner 2006; Harrison and Markevich 2008a, 2008b; Markevich and Harrison 2006; Milward 1965; Overy 1994).

If we limit ourselves to the qualitative improvement of military technologies in the twentieth-century competition between different social systems, it would appear that the capitalist economies had the edge. But it is hard to tell whether this was a systemic bias (capitalism was better than other systems at this specifically), or an income effect (capitalist economies were richer and so better than other economies at everything, including military-technical innovation).

Fiscal capacity

A more original contribution of capitalism was enormously to enhance the fiscal capacity of the state. This innovation arose from the commercial revolution of the seventeenth and eighteenth centuries. Spreading from the Dutch Republic to England, this revolution separated the economy from politics, and public finance from the money of the king; it subjected property rights, contracts, and exchange to the rule of law, even when one of the contracting parties was the king. The result was a dramatic increase in the willingness of the wealthy to pay taxes and in the ability of the government to borrow (Bonney 1999; Ferguson 2001; Gelderblom and Jonker, Chapter 11 in Volume 1; Hoffman and Rosenthal 1997; O'Brien, 2005, 2011, Chapter 12 in Volume 1).

Fiscal revolution gave unprecedented power to governments to extract resources from the economy. The rapid issuance of large amounts of debt on credible promise of repayment added speed to power. This power grew to the point where, during World War 1, it could put the viability of the "home front" at risk. For the first time, a relatively developed economy such as Germany's might exhaust itself because the government spent too much on the war (Feldman 1966).

Fiscal revolution was delayed, in contrast, in the agrarian states of central and southeastern Europe (Karaman and Pamuk 2010). In World War 1, a clear gap emerged between the French and German economies, with half of GDP allocated to the war or more, and Austria-Hungary and Turkey, which struggled and failed to reach one-third (Broadberry and Harrison 2005). The inability of the Habsburg and Ottoman rulers to tax, borrow, centralize revenues, and spend them on the war was an important factor in their eventual defeat (Pamuk 2005; Schulze 2005).

The fiscal advantage of liberal capitalism, clearly marked at the beginning of the twentieth century, proved temporary. The 1930s saw the rise of states intent on promoting industrial power where property was less private, contracts less enforceable, prices less responsive to supply and demand, and governments more intent on supporting their own geopolitical agendas than the rule of law and free enterprise. In short, these states were less "capitalist"; we know them as varieties of fascism and communism. During World War 11, Britain and America could once again drive their fiscal ratios to half of national income or more, but Germany, Japan, and the Soviet Union could go higher, to 60 or even 70 percent for short periods (Harrison 1998) This was a second fiscal revolution.

If the first fiscal revolution was based on transparency and the rule of law, the second revolution was based on modern nationalism and modern repression. A nationalist police state proved an effective substitute for transparent legal regulation. Nationalism and repression gave Hitler, Stalin, and the Japanese military a coercive power to mobilize society and centralize resources not only far beyond the traditional bureaucracies that they succeeded, but even greater than liberal capitalism. Fascism and ultra-nationalism did not survive 1945, but communism did. The capacity to pour resources into a privileged and prioritized defense sector was the basis of the Soviet Union's postwar superpower status, achieved despite mediocre economic performance (Harrison 2001: 81).

There was another way in which capitalism promoted fiscal mobilization. This was by transforming agriculture. Agriculture was an important source of rents for traditional agrarian bureaucracies, but collecting and centralizing direct revenues from small-scale subsistence farmers generally involved high transaction costs and payoffs to intermediary landlords and tax-farmers. Urbanization and the spread of urban–rural exchange created the possibility of taxing farmers indirectly by turning the terms of trade against them. In fact, such a shift in the terms of trade was an inevitable result of war mobilization, which diverted the production capacities of industry to the supply of war and curtailed supplies to the countryside. Faced with this, pre-capitalist or proto-capitalist farmers retained an "inside" option: to retreat into autarky and feed themselves alone, leaving the food needs of the industrial workers and soldiers unmet (Broadberry and Harrison 2005; Offer 1989). In much of central and eastern Europe in two world wars, a large part of the domestic economy proved able to withhold resources from the grabbing hand of the state. There were local famines and spreading general hunger.

In Britain and America capitalist farms, fully integrated into the economy as a whole, no longer had the inside option. They proved to be as responsive as any other business to wartime incentives and controls. Agricultural production was quickly expanded (in the British case) and restructured to increase the calorie yield per hectare. There was less butter and meat, and more cereals and potatoes; nobody starved.

The dictators, governing countries with large peasant populations, arrived at contrasting solutions. The Axis powers aimed to avoid having to squeeze their own farmers by imposing starvation on the foreign territories they occupied. Starvation followed, but with disappointing results for domestic food availability (Collingham 2011). Stalin found a more durable solution in collective farming, which was designed to rule out the Soviet peasant's inside option (Harrison 2011). To enforce collectivization required violence of the level of a civil war, leading to millions of famine deaths. The result was an agricultural system that was less productive but more amenable to government control. It did not prevent further famine deaths in wartime, but it did ensure that the Soviet wartime economy did not disintegrate.

In short, capitalism proved to have advantages in mobilizing resources for warfare. These advantages arose, paradoxically, from the ability of the government to bind itself by the laws of the state, just like a private person. The advantage was temporary, and was lost when modern dictators learned to break traditional constraints on authoritarian rule.

Managing war risks

Angell (1911) and his followers, such as Hull (1948), expected globalized capitalism to inaugurate lasting peace because of the interdependence it enforced upon trading states. International trade, they believed, created complementarities in the world economy, powerful enough to turn national rivals into international partners in a global network of stable, durable supply chains. The closing of borders in times of conflict threatened modern economies with breakdown; global war would bring global collapse. This was an aggregate risk that could not be hedged or laid off. Risk-averse governments would therefore back away from war.

The real historical relationship between war and trade is different. Since the eighteenth century, the economies that were most open to multilateral trade proved also to be strategically more secure. Far from being a source of war risk, long-distance trade turned out to be an instrument for managing it. In two world wars, the alliances that were better placed to maintain external economic integration also better managed food resources across countries and fighting power across the theatres of combat (Broadberry and Harrison 2005; Harrison 1998). The countries that had resisted globalization in peacetime suffered local famines and generalized hunger in wartime (Collingham 2011). In short, the "commercial" capacity for war deserves to be ranked alongside the technological and fiscal capacities that made modern mass warfare possible (Harrison and Wolf 2012).[1]

Martin, Mayer, and Thoenig (2008) show how globalization has helped to manage war risks. Using data from 1970 to 2000, they show that trade has a double effect on the propensity for war. Consider any pair of countries. The more a country traded with its pair, they show, the more likely were the two to remain at peace. But as trade increased with third countries, the less likely was peace to persist. Bilateral trade reduced the frequency of bilateral war; multilateral trade increased it.

At the root of the historical process was falling trade costs (Jacks, Meissner, and Novy 2008). Suppose the leaders of a country have some reason to fight their neighbor. Under high trade costs, the adversary is the only trading partner. There is no substitute for the food and fuel previously imported, so war leads to autarky. The peacetime supply chain is broken; the home prices of food and fuel must rise. The duration of autarky is uncertain, since it depends on how quickly the war can be concluded, which is a matter of chance. As a result, the risk of persistent trade disruption and economic losses is high. When trade costs are low, in contrast, the home country can lay off its war risks in the rest of the world; for example, it can easily substitute away from the neighbor for the source of its imports. The broken supply chain can be replaced with others. Thus, low trade costs enable the home country to fight its neighbor while continuing to trade with the rest of the world.

Falling trade costs, the economic aspect of globalization, reduced the market risks that countries faced as they contemplated war. Did capitalism do this? The modern era is not the first in which trade costs have fallen. Long before modern capitalism, Mediterranean trade was repeatedly transformed by innovations in agriculture, shipping, and contractual institutions. The greatest revolution in global trade, the opening up of the Atlantic economy,

---

1 The strategic advantage that goes along with being able to trade across the world is still not well understood in public policy debate. This is shown by the discussions that our societies continue to have about "food security" and "energy security." Despite two centuries of evidence to the contrary, many people continue to identify security with self-sufficiency. In a bipartisan spirit, here are two recent examples. On December 19, 2007, US President George W. Bush signed into law the Energy Independence and Security Act, which aims to "move the United States toward greater energy independence and security." And, in a widely cited speech on United Nations World Food Day, October 16, 2008, former US President Bill Clinton said: "Food is not a commodity like others. We should go back to a policy of maximum food self-sufficiency. It is crazy for us to think we can develop countries around the world without increasing their ability to feed themselves." In fact autarky and security are unrelated or even inversely related. It was long-distance trade based on specialization that made the major capitalist economies rich, and trade also made them secure – even in wartime.

came on the eve of the capitalist era (Acemoglu, Johnson, and Robinson 2005). The most that may be said is that the rise of capitalism continued a process that was already under way.

War as a free lunch

There is a persistent view that, without wars, capitalism would fall into depression (e.g. Baran and Sweezy 1966; Steindl 1952). The philosophy of "military Keynesianism" maintains that capitalist economies tend to suffer from a deficiency of demand, and will stagnate without frequent injections of demand into the circular flow of income. The deficiency can be made up by debt-financed military spending combined with the Keynesian multiplier. If so, it does not follow that "capitalism means war." Rather, it implies one more way in which capitalism has reduced the costs of war. In this case, supposedly, capitalism can supply war free of charge. If the weapons and armies were not bought up by the government, the resources they represent would be unused; this would make war a free lunch. The lunch will then be eaten, not because we are hungry, but because it is free.

Three historical examples are frequently cited. One is the German recovery from the Great Depression under Hitler's four-year plans; there, unemployment fell from 29.9 percent of the working population in 1932 to 1.9 percent in 1938. Joan Robinson (1972: 8) started the legend of a Keynesian recovery by proposing that "Hitler had already found how to cure unemployment before Keynes had finished explaining why it occurred." Another was the vast war boom that followed US entry into World War II; US unemployment fell from 9.5 percent in 1940 (or 14.6 percent, if we include those on "emergency government employment") to 1.2 percent in 1944. So strong was the connection that afterwards Paul Samuelson (in 1948, cited by Rockoff 1998: 196) likened fiscal policy to the atomic bomb: "Too powerful a weapon to let men and government play with." And third is the generally higher level of NATO countries' military spending at the height of the Cold War compared with previous norms, illustrated in Table 11.1.

More detailed investigations of these episodes have given little support to the Keynesian interpretation. In the German case, recovery had already begun when Hitler took power. Reconstructing fiscal aggregates from the German archives, Ritschl (2002) shows that full-employment budget deficits were modest until 1936, and too small to account for recovery. Multiplier effects cannot be identified with any confidence because (as modern macro would predict) current household income was one of the least important determinants of consumer spending. Rather than exploiting the multiplier to promote

Table 11.1. *Military spending, 1870 to 1979, percent of GDP, in four countries*

Country	1870 to 1913	1920 to 1938	1960	1970	1979
USA	0.7	1.2	8.9	7.9	5.2
UK	2.6	3.0	6.5	4.8	4.8
France	3.7	4.3	6.3	4.2	3.9
Germany/West Germany	2.6	3.3	4.0	3.5	3.2

Sources: 1870–1913 and 1920–1938 from Eloranta and Harrison (2010); later years from Murdoch and Sandler (1984).

recovery, National Socialist policies repressed consumption to make room for public investment and rearmament.

As for the US experience, Robert Higgs (1992) pointed out that between 1940 and 1944 the Federal government pulled the equivalent of 22 percent of the prewar working population into the armed forces. "No one needs a macroeconomic model," he wrote, "to understand this event." What happened after the war is of greater interest. Between 1944 and 1947 US military outlays fell by 37 percent of GDP, yet in the same period 3.9 million civilian jobs were created (Rockoff 1998: 83, 101). In the same way, the postwar demilitarization of western Germany did not lead to stagnation but was the prelude to the Wirtschaftswunder.

More generally, the hypothesis that postwar capitalism has stabilized itself by means of military spending finds no support in the data. In the 1960s, military spending shares across NATO countries were strongly correlated with overall GDP, and not at all with GDP per head (Olson and Zeckhauser 1966; Smith 1977). In other words, defense allocations reflected security spillovers and butter–guns trade-offs, not underconsumption. During the "great moderation" that began in the 1970s, Western economic growth became smoother, and unemployment fell, but this owed nothing to military spending, national shares of which continued to decline (Smith 2009: 99–102) along the trend already visible in Table 11.1. In the recent global recession, conservative voices (e.g. Feldstein 2008) called for military spending to be used countercyclically, but there is no sign that they were heard.

As for theory, modern macroeconomics has tended to the conclusion that, in a competitive capitalist economy, a stable inflation target (for the central bank) and stable tax-and-spending rules (for the fiscal authority) will assure full employment in the medium term. Whatever the implications of the recent recession, it is hard to find anyone who seriously thinks capitalism cannot recover without a boost from military spending. There is nothing military spending can do for capitalism that cannot be done more efficiently by civilian spending, tax cuts, or monetary easing.

Preferences for war

Up to this point, we have considered whether capitalism lowered the costs of going to war. Preferences for war have been left outside the story so far. Even if preferences were strongly biased towards peace, and were stable, and had not changed, lower opportunity costs could be expected to make war more frequent. Beyond this point lie more radical questions. Motivating them is the possibility that capitalism – or capitalists – might have derived specific benefits from war, such that war became the systematically preferred means of resolving internal or external problems.

Lobbies for war

On the face of it, capitalism and war would seem to be a surprising association. It was of the era before capitalism that Charles Tilly (1975: 42) wrote, "War made the state and states made war." As late as the eighteenth century, Prussia was "not a country with an army, but an army with a country" (Friedrich von Schrötter, cited by Blackbourn 2003: 17). The rise of capitalism separated the economy from politics and decentralized economic power. The accumulation of mobile industrial, financial, human, and social capital reduced the importance of immobile natural resources and the territories to which they were confined. And modern commerce gave the state so much more to think about than soldiers and guns. These are all visible reasons why one might expect capitalist societies to have lost the taste for war.

The idea that capitalism not only means war but *wants* war persists on two main foundations. One is a simple post-hoc-propter-hoc argument: first, global capitalism, then global war. The other is a dark view of the world that disputes what is visible on the surface: that capitalism decentralizes economic decisions, and that democratic government truly governs. Instead, it views the separation of business from the state as a façade behind which lobbying and conspiracies go on invisibly, to the detriment of both property rights and democracy.

Writing during the Great War, Vladimir Lenin (1916) thought he observed the first transnational companies competing with each other for shares of the world market, while colluding to drive governments to re-divide the world's colonial spheres to private advantage. Between the wars, radical commentators in both Germany and America accused national business elites of promoting war as a source of war profits (for the charge sheet against the "merchants of death," see Engelbrecht and Hanighen 1934). In the postwar period, US President Dwight D. Eisenhower (1961) warned of the political danger arising from a large peacetime "military-industrial complex." More recent variants of this tradition include the "oil wars" of Pelletière (2004) and Naomi Klein's (2007) "disaster capitalism."

We will go step by step through this complex topic. Does the corporate sector expect to profit from war? Does it actually profit from war? Do corporate owners value connections to power? Do they use these connections to lobby for war contracts? Do such activities have analogues under anti-capitalist and non-capitalist regimes?

To start with profit expectations: If war is a capitalist conspiracy, it turns out that the capitalists were generally not too happy when the conspiracy worked. As Niall Ferguson and others have documented, on the outbreak of World War I, European bond prices fell and unemployment rose in London, Paris, and Berlin (Ferguson 1998: 186–197; Lawrence, Dean, and Robert 1992). The panic on Wall Street was so great that the New York Stock Exchange was closed for the rest of the year.

More generally, think of stock prices as embodying the probability-adjusted profit expectations of the owners of capital. There is no evidence that stockholders see the realization of war probabilities in a positive light. Figure 11.1 shows closing values of the Dow Jones Industrial Average in New York for the ten working days before and after eight twentieth-century onsets of war (the value on the day itself is omitted). Only two events saw stock prices climb; in five they fell, and in two cases the stock market was closed (for more than four months after the outbreak of World War I in Europe, and for four days after 9/11). The median change in stock prices over the eight crises was a 5.3 percent decline.

After realized war come realized war profits. Have wars provided private business with direct benefits? Before we can understand whether or not business is pro-war, we need to know whether war is pro-business. Many have thought so. The Great War saw widespread discontent in both Britain and Germany over industrial war profits and war profiteers (Carsten 1982). In most countries, major wars reduced incomes and weakened the family-based or social safety net, so that poor and vulnerable people suffered harm. It was a short step from this to the idea that the rich had exploited the opportunity of war in order to tilt the distribution of income in their own favor (and another short step to the proposal that the rich had promoted the war with this in mind).

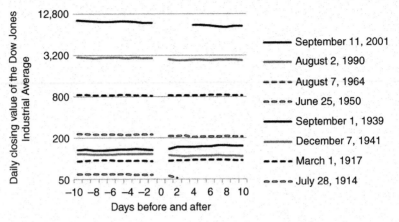

Figure 11.1. Daily closing values of the Dow Jones Industrial Average
Source: http://measuringworth.com/datasets/DJA/ (accessed on June 8, 2011).
Key:
July 28, 1914: Russia mobilizes against Germany.
March 1, 1917: The Zimmermann telegram published.
September 1, 1939: Germany invades Poland.
December 7, 1941: Japan attacks Pearl Harbor.
June 25, 1950: North Korea invades South Korea.
August 7, 1964: Gulf of Tonkin Resolution.
August 2, 1990: Iraq invades Kuwait.
September 11, 2001: Al-Qaeda attacks American cities.

With regard to World War I, it was Gerd Hardach (1977: 106–107) and
Jürgen Kocka (1984) who originally made the case that war profits destabilized
the distribution of income among the German social classes. Hardach concluded: "These findings point, not so much to the harnessing of big business to
the machine of state, as to the reverse." Baten and Schulz (2005) and Albrecht
Ritschl (2005) have re-examined these claims. Baten and Schulz found that the
appearance of rising inequality is explained by two errors, a failure to account
for inflation in measuring profits, and a selection bias in the profits reported. A
wider sample of big businesses shows the real profits of German large-scale
industry declining *pari passu* with returns to labor, so that the labor share in
national income, after initial improvement, was more or less the same in 1917
as it had been in 1913. Ritschl reached similar results independently by
comparing real wage and real output data. What this meant for top incomes
can be judged directly from the historical cross-country data of Atkinson,
Picketty, and Saez (2011). These show sharp wartime declines in the personal

income shares of the very rich in every belligerent country for which wartime data are now available.

It was not necessary to go to war to make war profits. In neutral Netherlands, for example, the outbreak of war in 1914 immediately relieved competitive pressures on Dutch corporations; real wages fell and national income was temporarily redistributed in favor of profits (Klemann 2007). In neutral Argentina, similarly, between 1940 and 1943 the top 1 percent increased their share of personal incomes from one-fifth to more than one quarter (Atkinson, Picketty, and Saez 2011: 44). Despite this, no one has tried to blame World War I on Dutch corporations such as Philips or Unilever, or World War II on the Argentinian beef complex.

The claim that corporate owners were able to exploit war conditions to increase their profit incomes acquired its hold on the popular imagination in association with the image of an organized, secretive, military-industrial lobby at work behind the scenes. Therefore, we turn to consider corporate political action, on which there is a large literature. Adam Smith 1776) remarked on the propensity of "people of the same trade" to meet and conspire against the public. In fact, do corporate owners lobby politicians and make self-interested political donations? Yes, all the time (Hillman, Keim, and Schuler 2004). Do they value these connections? Again, yes. In countries that are relatively corrupt, such as Indonesia and Malaysia, connections to the ruling party add market value to the firm (Fisman 2000; Johnson and Mitton 2003). In the 2000 US presidential election, when Bush beat Gore, oil and tobacco firms gained value and legal firms lost (Knight 2007). And German firms that were linked to the Nazi Party before 1933 by donations or open support gained value when Hitler took power (Ferguson and Voth 2008).

In capitalist societies there is lobbying behind the scenes. Who holds the initiative in this relationship: the corporate owners looking for influence, or venal politicians looking for money? Evidence on this can be found in historical narratives. It was a meeting of German industrialists, for example, that provided Hitler's March 1933 election fund. But it was Hitler that decided whom to invite to the meeting, and he opened it with a blackmail threat to those present (Tooze 2006: 99–106) if they failed to support him. In other words, his corporate sponsors seized an opportunity, but Hitler created the opportunity and conditioned the incentives to take it up.

Two world wars left German capitalism with a bad press, much of it deserved. Even so, the relationship between the industrialists and war aims was more complex than is commonly assumed. The German industrialist Hugo Stinnes, for example, was a militarist and imperialist in the Great War, but an economic liberal and a free trader before and after. The reason, Feldman (2000) argued, was circumstances:

> The war had created a new situation for Stinnes and, like strikes, which he would also just as soon have seen disappear, one had to adjust to them and to their periodic reappearance . . . this meant placing oneself in the best position for the next occurrence, and that was the goal, exaggerated and uncontrolled as it was, of Stinnes's war-aims policies.

Studies of German industry and industrialists under the Third Reich point us in the same direction. Until 1930, big business showed little interest in the Nazi party or Hitler, who aimed only to reassure the business interest and neutralize opposition from that quarter (Turner 1985). After that, many business leaders were converted to "willing partners" in the expansionist plans of the Third Reich (Tooze 2006: 134). As Hitler unfolded his plans, step by step, the compliant majority adapted easily to new perspectives, such as the idea that foreign forced labor would become a permanent resource (Mommsen 2005: 182). In this way they accepted the growing inevitability and then the fact of war. As for the plan for war and the decision to execute it, this belonged to the political actors, who were reticent on the subject before business audiences until their authority was assured.

Gustav Krupp, whose furnaces forged Hitler's victories and whose facilities exploited up to 100,000 slaves, was an early adherent to the Hitler regime. But until 1933, Richard Overy (1994: 119–143) has shown, he was a traditional conservative. His chief aim was to keep his firm intact under family control, avoiding the fate of Hugo Junkers whose opposition to Nazi plans led to a state takeover. Like Hugo Stinnes, he accommodated to the realities that he could not alter. Peter Hayes's history of I.G. Farben tells "not why bad men do evil but why good men do" (Hayes 2001: xxi): Business leaders who feared and shunned national socialism beforehand were captured morally and became complicit in its most terrible crimes, including the Holocaust.

Not all fell into line. A few, like Junkers, resisted on grounds of the public good. On a more practical plane, Hjalmar Schacht, a banker who became Hitler's economics minister, resigned in 1937 over the cost of rearmament; he became a resister only later.

Still, open opposition to Nazi plans in business circles was rare. This makes Hermann Göring's confrontation with the steel industrialists in 1937 all the more revealing. In the pursuit of autarky, Göring wished to reorient the steel industry away from imported iron ores. In December 1936 he demanded investments in facilities to exploit inferior domestic deposits. The Ruhr industrialists resisted for a variety of reasons, including the fear that, once they had committed the investments, the National Socialist state would hold them up for lower steel prices. While their united front was quickly broken, the outcome was a state-owned steel giant, the Reichswerke Hermann Göring (Overy 1994: 93–118). Schacht's resignation followed Göring's victory (Schweitzer 1964: 537–547). RHG later became the major conglomerate vehicle for German investments in occupied Europe (Overy 1994: 144–174).

In prewar Japan, the business class was conservative and patriotic but not reckless. Its leaders were embedded in the political system through both party representation and networks (Von Staden 2008). In the 1930s, however, their influence was threatened and increasingly limited by the rise of Japanese "ultra-nationalism," which was hostile to private property and industrialization. Radical militarists established a political base in the countryside on plans to colonize East Asia, and mounted attacks on those conservative leaders that preferred financial orthodoxy to paying for military adventures (Collingham 2011). Representatives of the armed forces increasingly took over the government.

While the *zaibatsu* ("money cliques," the leading Japanese conglomerate corporations) were afterwards reviled for supporting Japanese militarism, the range of their behaviors under this threat is consistent with that of their German counterparts. Japanese business leaders took the opportunities that seemed profitable, shouldered the obligations to support the war that they could not refuse, and accepted the government funding that aligned their incentives with the war effort. As Takao Shiba (1994) has shown, for the Mitsubishi Corporation in the 1930s this meant repeatedly postponing plans to expand civilian automotive engineering in favor of instructions for war production received from the army. Kawasaki, in contrast, was ready to build ahead of military demand, but was relieved of the risk after the event by government capital. As all-out war approached, the army and navy took legal measures to bring privately owned industrial facilities under direct supervision. These measures were resisted until it became clear that only firms that accepted military supervision would receive allocations of supplies and labor. While cooperating fully with Japan's war effort, both Mitsubishi and Kawasaki took steps to preserve the basis of postwar independence.

The common feature of these stories is the "primacy of politics" (Mason 1968). In Japan and Germany, the political leaders held the initiative. Corporate behavior was reactive, defensive, and opportunistic. It is not a pretty picture, but it does not show a capitalist lobby for war. Overy (1994: 94) concludes the Krupp story: "Nazi political hegemony in the end prevented

German capitalists from acting as capitalists." From this we learn not about how big business changed government, but how big government diverted business from competitive profit-seeking to rent-seeking and dependence on government contracts and subsidies.

Interwar evidence on the influence of military-industrial lobbies in other countries is thin. Wilson and Eloranta (2010) have carefully examined the military procurement practices of four interwar democracies (the United Kingdom, the United States, Sweden, and Finland). They show that democratic institutions created effective barriers to profiteering from rearmament. Edgerton's (2006) revisionist history finds the first exemplar of a modern military-industrial complex in interwar Britain's "warfare state," but this one was led by efficient technocrats, not greedy capitalists or venal politicians. Robert Higgs (1993) has shown that, on the eve of World War II, US business-people were distrustful of the Roosevelt administration, reluctant to undertake war investments, suspicious of the government interference that would follow if they did, and fearful that they would not be allowed to make money on them.

If corporate money has observable influence on politics anywhere, it must surely be in the postwar United States. Robert Higgs has modelled the strategic interaction among US voters, defense producers, and politicians in the Cold War (Higgs and Kilduff 1993; Higgs 1994). Defense firms provided jobs for voters and campaign funding for politicians seeking election. They were rewarded by a swollen military budget that overprovided both national defense and private profit. The losers were the taxpayers and the armed forces, whose budget was diverted to purchasing lines of equipment that they did not want and could not use. The gains to defense corporations and labor were concentrated and obvious; the efficiency losses were diffuse and opaque, a recipe for status-quo bias, as defined by Fernandez and Rodrik (1991).

Even in this model, the carousel did not go round forever. In the end, voter opinion could still bring it to a halt. Empirically, the balance of public sentiment on whether defense spending should rise or fall was the single most important factor in whether it did so. Successive generations of politicians worked to persuade the public to accept the existence of security threats and shortfalls, but ultimately they could not control voter sentiment. In an open society, two things limited public support for the military and kept the defense budget in check: the tax increases necessary to pay for defense resources, and the war casualties that followed from using them in war. "Deaths and taxes," Higgs argues, set the ultimate constraints on the power of the military-industrial complex.

How do such outcomes compare with those of non-capitalist arrangements? The Soviet defense market differed from the US defense market
most obviously in the lack of transparency and public accountability. The
postwar Soviet defense sector took a consistently larger share of national
resources than the US one (Firth and Noren 1998). If American corporations
lobbied for development funding, so too could Soviet weapon designers; they
did have to be more careful, knowing Stalin's capacity for suspicion (Harrison
2008; Harrison and Markevich 2008b). The Stalin-era state agencies responsible for the construction of defense plants were prolific and willing users of
forced labor (Harrison 1994; Simonov 2000). These rough comparisons do not
point to a moral deficit in capitalism. Rather, the transparency and accountability of democratic political processes placed limits on the power of
American military-industrial interests that did not exist under communism.

David Holloway (1980: 158) once considered the proposition that: "The
Soviet Union does not *have* a military-industrial complex, but *is* such a
complex. This is too sweeping a statement," he commented, "but it does
make the point that the history of the Soviet Union is so bound up with
military power that it seems wrong to speak of a separate military-industrial
complex acting within the state."[2] More recently Kontorovich and Wein
(2009) have asked: "What did the Soviet rulers maximise?" Based on revealed
preferences in resource allocation ("a high share of military spending in GNP,
a low share of consumption, and a high share of investment directed primarily
into heavy industry"), their answer is not "socialism" or economic growth or
even modernization but military power. In other words, no one needed to
lobby for it; it was a fundamental preference of the communist regime.[3]

To summarize: Are capitalist corporations interested in politics? Yes,
unquestionably. Do they lobby politicians and make self-interested political
donations? Yes, all the time. Do they push for external confrontation or

2 In the same spirit the appointment of former defense minister Raúl Castro as President of
   Cuba, where the armed forces control as much as 60 percent of the economy (Gershman
   and Gutierrez 2009: 68), prompted Christopher Hitchens (2006) to comment: "As was
   once said of Prussia, Cuba is not a country that has an army but an army that has a
   country."
3 While Stalin undeniably placed high priority on rearmament and military power, it was
   still possible to overstate the case. According to Viktor Suvorov (1990), Stalin's rearmament was motivated by a plan for aggressive war (see also Raack 1995; Weeks 2002). On
   this view, in 1941 Stalin intended to use Hitler as his "icebreaker" to the West; the Soviet
   plan was to exploit the opportunity presented by Germany's war with the Anglo-French
   alliance by launching an aggressive war to occupy Europe; Hitler struck first to preempt
   this plan. This idea, if true, had far-reaching implications, because it would have transferred political (and moral) responsibility for the opening of the Eastern front from Hitler
   to Stalin. For refutations see Glantz 1998; Uldricks 1999; and Gorodetsky 1999.

conflict? Examples are hard to find. Are they ready to take the profits offered by war preparations? Yes, although competitive pressures and an open society appear to limit this in various ways. Do they willingly exploit the spoils of conquest or enslavement? Yes, if the opportunity to do so presents itself. Do they do these things systematically? There is no evidence of that. In fact, the character of the state and the agency of politicians appear to be the decisive factors. Communism, not capitalism, has been more conducive to a militarized economy and the accumulation of military power.

Diversionary wars

Bill Pritchard (the prime minister's press secretary):	"May I suggest that instead of trying to butter up the press, we distract them? Let's give them a story."
Jim Hacker (the prime minister):	"Such as?"
Bill Pritchard:	"Start a war, that sort of thing."
Jim Hacker:	"Start a war?"
Bernard Woolley (the prime minister's private secretary):	"Only a small war."[4]

In the concept of diversionary wars, political leaders seek and exploit conflict with external adversaries in order to rally domestic support. The idea is well established in the literature, perhaps because the theoretical case is quite intuitive, and narrative support is not hard to find. In fact, it may be too easy. As Jack Levy (1989) pointed out, few wars have *not* been attributed to political leaders' desire to improve domestic standing.

The idea of diversionary wars is directly relevant to a discussion of capitalism only if it can be shown that capitalist polities are more likely to exploit foreign adventures. One reason might be advanced from a Marxist perspective: perhaps capitalist societies, being class-divided, are more likely to give rise to wars intended to divert the workers from the cause of socialism. A long-standing interpretation of the origins of World War I in domestic German politics conveys exactly this message (Berghahn 1973).

This view does not sit well with the equally traditional idea that a class-divided society is less able to go to war. The official Soviet histories of World War II used to claim that, under capitalism, divided class interests made the working people reluctant to fight for the nation. Because of this, the workers

---

4 "Official Secrets," the tenth episode of the BBC TV series "Yes Prime Minister," was first broadcast on December 10, 1987.

could be motivated to take part only by "demagogy, deception, bribery, and force" (Grechko *et al.* 1982: 38; on similar lines see also Pospelov *et al.* 1965: 80–82).

It is also true that governments of capitalist societies have found many ways to hide the true costs of war from the electorate, as Hugh Rockoff (2012: 24–27) has argued in the case of the United States. These include price controls, the rationing of goods, conscription, and the omission of future liabilities to veterans and their families from the public accounts. These instruments, however, are not peculiar to a capitalist economy; if anything they reflect methods of managing shortage and mobilization that would be more familiar in a customary economy.

Quantitative empirical work has lent little support to the idea of diversionary war (Levy 1989). Exceptions include studies of the use of force by US and British postwar governments by Morgan and Bickers (1992) and Morgan and Anderson (1999). They conclude that the use of force is more likely when government approval is high but the government's supporting coalition is suffering erosion. They also suggest that force is unlikely to be used at high intensities under those circumstances ("only a small war") because the higher expected costs of larger wars will erode political support, and because any degree of foreign conflict will be polarizing rather than consolidating support when domestic conflict is already high.

Another line of research suggests that new or incompletely established democracies are particularly vulnerable to risky adventures in nation-building (Mansfield and Snyder 2005). One inspiration for this view was the record of the new democracies born out of the former Soviet Union and Yugoslavia. More recently, Georgia seems to have provided out-of-sample confirmation.

Suppose diversionary wars exist. Is capitalism somehow more internally conflicted than other societies, and so disproportionately likely to externalize conflict? As a comparator, the case of fascism seems straightforward. Fascism did not produce diversionary wars because, for fascists, war was not a diversion; it was the point.

The more interesting case is that of communism. Communists do not seem to have pursued diversionary wars. At the same time, the domestic legitimacy of Soviet rule visibly relied on the image of an external enemy, and thrived on tension short of military conflict. Soviet leaders used external tension to justify internal controls on movement, culture, and expression, and the associated apparatus of secrecy, censorship, and surveillance. When they began to tolerate trends toward détente in the 1970s, they subverted their own controls. An East German Stasi officer told his boss, repeating it later to Timothy Garton Ash (1997: 159):

> How can you expect me to prevent [defections and revelations], when we've signed all these international agreements for improved relations with the West, working conditions for journalists, freedom of movement, respect for human rights?

If Soviet foreign policy was sometimes expansionist, it sought expansion only up to the point where the desired level of tension was assured. Bolsheviks of the 1917 generation knew well that too much conflict abroad encouraged defeatist and counter-revolutionary sentiments at home. As Oleg Khlevniuk (1995: 174) noted:

> The complex relationship between war and revolution, which had almost seen the tsarist regime toppled in 1905 and which finally brought its demise in 1917, was a relationship of which Stalin was acutely aware. The lessons of history had to be learnt lest history repeat itself.

Stalin did all he could to avoid war with Germany in 1941 (Gorodetsky 1999). Postwar Soviet leaders risked war by proxy, but avoided direct conflict with the "main adversary." Faced with unfavorable odds, they tended to withdraw (from Cuba) or do nothing (in Poland) or accepted them with great reluctance (in Hungary, Czechoslovakia, and Afghanistan).

Diversionary tension must fall short of diversionary war. From this follows an acceptance that capitalism, because of its tendency to give rise to democratic structures and political competition, has been more open to diversionary wars than other systems. But the empirical research and analysis that underpin this conclusion also imply that such wars would generally be small-scale and short-lived, and the circumstances that give rise to them would be exceptional or transient.

We should place this in the wider context of the "democratic peace." As Levy (1988) wrote: "Liberal or democratic states do not fight each other . . . This absence of war between democracies comes as close as anything we have to an empirical law in international relations." Since all liberal democracies have also been capitalist on any definition, it is a finding of deep relevance.

Capitalism's wars

The United States is the world's preeminent capitalist power. According to a poll of more than 21,000 citizens of 21 countries in the second half of 2008, people tended on average to evaluate US foreign policy as inferior to that of their own country in the moral dimension.[5] While this survey did not disaggregate respondents by educational status, many apparently knowledge-able people also seem to believe that most wars in the modern world have been caused by America; this impression is based on my experience of presenting work on the frequency of wars to academic seminars in several European countries.

According to the evidence, however, these beliefs are mistaken. We are all aware of America's wars, but they make only a small contribution to the total. Counting all bilateral conflicts involving at least the show of force from 1870 to 2001, we find that that the countries that originated them come from all parts of the global income distribution (Harrison and Wolf 2012). It is not the countries that are richer (measured by GDP per head) that tend to start more conflicts. It is the countries that are economically larger (measured by GDP). The United States is both large and rich, but it turns out that sheer size is what matters. In fact, controlling for size, the United States has been less warlike than some other countries. We rank countries by the numbers of conflicts they initiated over the period. The United States, with the largest economy, comes only in second place. Third place belongs to China. In first place is Russia (the USSR between 1917 and 1991).

What do capitalist institutions contribute to the empirical patterns in the data? Erik Gartzke (2007) has re-examined the hypothesis of the "democratic peace" based on the possibility that, since capitalism and democracy are highly correlated across countries and time, both democracy and peace might be products of the same underlying cause, the spread of capitalist institutions.

It is a problem that our historical datasets have measured the spread of capitalist property rights and economic freedoms over shorter time spans or on fewer dimensions than political variables. For the period from 1950 to 1992, Gartzke uses a measure of external financial and trade liberalization as most likely to signal robust markets and a *laissez-faire* policy. Countries that share this attribute of capitalism above a certain level, he finds, do not fight each other, so there is capitalist peace as well as democratic peace. Second, economic liberalization (of the less liberalized of the pair of countries) is a

---

5 Specifically, 24 percent of respondents rated their own country's foreign policy as morally above average, and 21 percent rated it below average; the equivalent ratings for US foreign policy (with US respondents excluded) were 20 percent (above average) and 32 percent (below). "Most People Think Their Nation's Foreign Policy Is Morally No Better Than Average," January 22, 2009, available from www.WorldPublicOpinion.org (accessed on October 18, 2011).

more powerful predictor of bilateral peace than democratization, controlling for the level of economic development and measures of political affinity.

Why, then, with more capitalism and more democracy, do we have more wars? Possibly we have more wars because the quality of war is changing. Münkler (2005) suggests that "new wars" are more like the Thirty Years War (1618–1648) than the great-power territorial conflicts of the twentieth-century world wars. Behind the new wars, he argues, lie deep forces of globalization, including world markets awash with cheap Kalashnikov rifles and unemployed young men. The new wars are small-scale and protracted; the opposing forces may prefer maintaining a state of conflict over victory, so that new wars smoulder without coming to a definite conclusion, a point also made in relation to civil wars by David Keen (1998). In new wars, as Münkler sees them, conflict is exploited by private causes for private ends. New wars lose the distinction between combatants and civilians; they substitute massacre for battle; they erode rather than build state capacity. By implication, modern states are losing control of violence.

Münkler's vision can be compared with the perspective of Harrison and Wolf (2012). In both perspectives, trends in globalization and the relative cost of means of destruction are underlying forces. For Harrison and Wolf these forces are changing the number of wars, not their quality. "If the frequency of conflict has been increasing," they conclude, "it may be not because we want it; more likely, it is 'Because we can'."

Effects of war

In whatever ways capitalism has changed war, war has also changed capitalism. But the nature and persistence of the changes are energetically debated. In the world before 1913, war promoted the transition to modern fiscal systems and this in turn promoted productivity. Based on a nineteenth-century sample of 96 countries, Dincecco and Prado (2012: 172) find that, as a result, "states in the top decile of past war casualties are 80% more productive today than states with no recorded casualties." For those that prefer narrative, the British story (O'Brien, Chapter 12 in Volume 1) points in the same direction.

It does not follow, however, that war has had the same beneficial effect after the transition to a modern state was complete. Münkler (2005) has argued to the contrary that the "new wars" of the late twentieth century, like the Thirty Years War of the seventeenth, have tended to undermine state capacity rather than promote it.

Since Adam Smith, it has been recognized that capitalism does not work without law, taxes, and public goods (Cardoso, Chapter 18 in Volume 1), and most of these are provided by nation-states. At the same time, too much taxation and regulation are stifling. There is a right amount. In the twentieth century, capitalism worked best under a touch that was light, but not non-existent, when borders were open and the world was more cosmopolitan than nationally minded.

It is hardly surprising that in wartime most national stories diverged from this receipe. Everywhere warfare closed borders, limited private enterprise and market access, mobilized the people around the identity of the nation in battle, and built the authority and legitimacy of the state. Government took charge of economic life and imposed a command economy, borrowing business personnel and "businesslike" methods of management, monopolizing markets for goods and credit, discriminating in favor of government contracts, overriding private property rights, and replacing the high-powered incentives of market competition with administrative enforcement and low-powered artificial incentives (Broadberry and Harrison 2005; Harrison 1998; Higgs 1993).

Some countries went to war while others remained neutral, but all countries experienced large reallocations. Belligerents repressed consumption, withdrew from export markets, and prioritized war production and military services. Neutrals experienced large increases in demand from the belligerents for food and raw materials. Some were too close to the fighting for comfort and had to balance uneasily between the two sides (Golson, in press). Others reaped the short-term profits they could, or seized the time to industrialize, aiming to fill the gap in the world market for civilian manufactures (Findlay and O'Rourke 2007). These reallocations also created large rents, appropriated domestically or (in the case of colonial occupation) captured by the occupier (Klemann and Kudriashov 2012).

War redistributed power and reallocated resources; did these changes persist when peace was restored? When the war was over, some countries experienced dramatic reversals. For the aggressors, defeat was generally salutary, although this came at terrible cost. A number of democracies were born from the wreckage of empires in central and eastern Europe after 1918, but not in Russia, and within two decades most poor countries (and a rich country, Germany) had reverted to dictatorship (Eloranta and Harrison 2010). The Atlantic Charter of 1941 placed self-determination at the heart of World War II. The defeat of the aggressors in 1945 was more complete and more lasting. In Germany, Italy, and Japan, defeat discredited the politics of aggression, broke the existing ties between wealth and power, and destroyed the slave and serf empires that had grown up around the war. Freed of burdensome pretensions to great-power status, these countries were enabled to experience unprecedented prosperity (Olson 1982).

For some other countries, the two world wars had effects that were highly persistent and often negative. Most obvious was the return of communism to the Baltic and its advance into Eastern Europe, which postponed full realization of the goals of the Atlantic Charter until the Cold War ended half a century later.

More generally, the politicians that found themselves leading their nations into the unfamiliar territory of the postwar world faced every temptation to use the levers at their disposal to shield the economy and protect old and new vested interests. In addition to redistribution and welfarism (Lindert, Chapter 14 in this volume), the quarter-century after 1945 saw fixed exchange rates, capital controls, industrial interventionism, and widespread (though declining) tariff barriers, the main purpose of which was to protect the "strategic" industries of the old powers and the "infant" industries of the emerging ones (Foreman-Peck and Federico 1999). As a result, globalization did not return to the level of 1913 until the 1970s (James, Chapter 9 in this volume; O'Rourke and Williamson, Chapter 1 in this volume).

Since the 1970s, capitalism has changed again (and is continuing to change), but the effects of the world wars, which once seemed so decisive, are no longer clearly identifiable. The gloss that wartime experience put on government controls and industrial plans has faded. Other trends are still present, but it is not convincing to continue to ascribe them to the legacies of warfare. The point is made by Figure 11.2, which compares the Swedish and British shares of government purchases in GDP over more than a century. Taking the British case in isolation, what strikes us is the seemingly permanent leaps in the share of government outlays occasioned by two world wars. The Swedish case shows how wrong this could be. Over the same period, Sweden was consistently neutral, yet Sweden's share starts and finishes with Britain's. Sweden's neighbors were frequently at war, but the Swedish series shows no noticeable response even to warfare among neighboring states. Based on study of a wider sample, Eloranta and Andreev (2006) fail to identify war as a significant long-run influence on the scope of government economic activism. What mattered, they find, was extension of the franchise.

Since the eighteenth century, international institutions have provided a growing array of global public goods. International arrangements help to explain why, twice in two centuries, major conflict was followed by an era

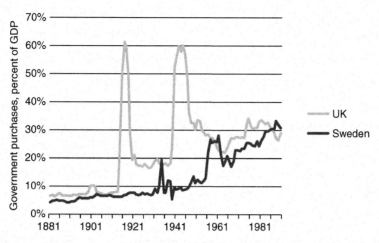

Figure 11.2. Government purchases, percent of GDP: Sweden and the United Kingdom, 1880–1990

Source: Eloranta and Andreev (2006).

of liberalization and international capitalist integration. One was the Congress of Vienna, which ended the Napoleonic Wars in 1815; the other was the ensemble of measures from the Bretton Woods conference in 1944 to Marshall Aid in 1947 that ended World War II. In contrast, the treaties that ended World War I and inaugurated the League of Nations failed abjectly to promote economic stability and integration (Findlay and O'Rourke 2007). It seems that a modicum of international security was needed for national elites to cooperate in the virtuous circles of policy reform and sustained growth (Broadberry 1994; Eichengreen 1996).

An important lesson from history is that no one institutional framework is good forever. This seems to apply to national and international arrangements alike. The vicissitudes of capitalism since the 1970s have shown again and again that the challenges of growth are continuous. To meet these challenges, policy reform must also be uninterrupted (Aghion and Howitt 2006; Crafts and Magnani 2013). Consciously or unconsciously, we continue to periodize the history of capitalism using brackets defined by warfare: 1815 and 1914; 1918 and 1939; 1945 and 1991 when the Cold War ended. The true history of capitalism is a seamless story of challenge and response. The historical discontinuities of wartime command our attention because in war there is agency, adventure, triumph, tragedy, and a struggle that engulfs many societies at once. It would be a mistake, however, to conclude that war will necessarily be more important than peace as the source of the challenges that capitalism will face tomorrow.

Conclusion

I have compared capitalism and its historical alternatives. Has capitalism helped to lower the costs of war? Yes, but not uniquely. The technological and trade costs of war began to fall before the capitalist era; capitalism certainly continued this trend. A distinctive contribution of capitalism came from the fiscal revolution of the eighteenth century that opened the way for mass warfare in the twentieth. By the twentieth century, however, the capitalist fiscal revolution had been all but overtaken by the repressive mobilization capacities of fascism and communism. As for the idea that capitalism reduced the costs of war by making it a Keynesian "free lunch," I reject it.

Does capitalism prefer war; that is, is war in the private interest of big business? Yes – conditionally. History shows the government can put in place incentives that align the private interests of big business with war, but this is a politically (not economically) determined outcome. The interest of business in war is opportunity, not strategy. There is no evidence that private business has had any greater interest in war, conquest, exploitation, or enslavement than the private or bureaucratic interests that have operated in other forms of society.

Are capitalist polities particularly liable to undertake foreign wars to divert attention from conflicted issues at home? Yes, but only weakly: the circumstances under which this happens are narrowly defined and the level of conflict is likely to be low. Moreover, there is strong evidence that since 1945 capitalist democracies have formed a "peace club" among themselves.

The determinants of wars involve both structure and agency. Agency must have a role, because wars are conceived, planned, declared, and waged by human actors. On the historical evidence, capitalism has gone to war only when captured and driven by a determined political enterprise. The fact remains that of all social systems, liberal capitalism seems to have least in common with war. This is because of the primary emphasis that capitalism gives to private interests, decentralized decisions, and personal freedoms. It is true that even liberal capitalism has allowed the temporary subordination of the individual to the interests of the state in wartime. In communist and fascist societies, in contrast, the supremacy of the state over the individual was a permanent condition. Thus, communism and fascism seem to have had more in common with states at war than with capitalism.

References

Acemoglu, D., S. Johnson, and J. Robinson (2005). "The Rise of Europe: Atlantic Trade, Institutional Change, and Economic Growth," *American Economic Review* 95(3): 546–579.

Aghion, P. and P. Howitt (2006). "Appropriate Growth Theory: A Unifying Framework," *Journal of the European Economic Association* 4(2–3): 269–314.

Angell, N. (1911). *The Great Illusion: A Study of the Relation of Military Power to National Advantage*, 3rd edn. London: Heinemann.

Atkinson, A. B., T. Piketty, and E. Saez (2011). "Top Incomes in the Long Run of History," *Journal of Economic Literature* 49(1): 3–71.

Baran, P. A. and P. M. Sweezy (1966). *Monopoly Capital: An Essay on the American Economic and Social Order*. New York: Monthly Review Press.

Baten, J. and R. Schulz (2005). "Making Profits in Wartime: Corporate Profits, Inequality, and GDP in Germany during the First World War," *Economic History Review* 58(1): 34–56.

Berghahn, V. R. (1973). *Germany and the Approach of War in 1914*. London: Macmillan.

Blackbourn, D. (2003). *History of Germany, 1780–1918: The Long Nineteenth Century*. Oxford: Blackwell.

Bonney, R. (ed.) (1999). *The Rise of the Fiscal State in Europe, 1200–1815*. Oxford: Oxford University Press.

Broadberry, S. (1994). "Why was Unemployment in Postwar Britain so Low?" *Bulletin of Economic Research* 46(3): 241–261.

Broadberry, S. and M. Harrison, eds. (2005). *The Economics of World War I*. Cambridge University Press.

Buchheim, C. and J. Scherner (2006). "The Role of Private Property in the Nazi Economy: The Case of Industry," *Journal of Economic History* 66(2): 390–416.

Carsten, F. L. (1982). *War Against War: British and German Radical Movements in the First World War*. Berkeley and Los Angeles, CA: University of California Press.

Collingham, L. (2011). *The Taste of War: World War Two and the Battle for Food*. London: Allen Lane.

CPSU (1941). *History of the Communist Party of the Soviet Union: Short Course*. Moscow: Foreign Languages Publishing House.

Crafts, N. and M. Magnani (2013). "The Golden Age and the Second Globalization in Italy," in G. Toniolo (ed.), *The Oxford Handbook of the Italian Economy, 1861–2011*. Oxford University Press.

De Bloch, J. (I. S. Bliokh). (1914). *The Future of War*. Boston, MA: World Peace Foundation.

Dimitrov, G. (1972 [1936]). *Selected Works*. Vol. ii. Sofia Press.

Dincecco M. and M. Prado (2012). "Warfare, Fiscal Capacity, and Performance," *Journal of Economic Growth* 17(3): 171–203.

Edgerton, D. (2006). *Warfare State: Britain, 1920–1970*. Cambridge University Press.

Eichengreen, B. (1996). "Institutions and Economic Growth: Europe after World War ii," in N. Crafts and G. Toniolo (eds.), *Economic Growth in Europe Since 1945*. Cambridge University Press, pp. 38–70.

Eisenhower, D. D. (1961). "Farewell Address to the Nation," January 17, 1961. Available at http://www.h-net.org/~hst306/documents/indust.html (accessed June 9, 2011).

Eloranta, J. and S. Andreev (2006). "Democratization, Legitimization, and Central Government Spending, 1870–1938," Paper to the CEPR/NBER Workshop on European Growth and Integration since the Mid-Nineteenth Century, 13 to 15 October, Lund, Sweden.

Eloranta, J. and M. Harrison (2010). "War and Disintegration, 1914–1945," in S. Broadberry and K. O'Rourke (eds.), *The Cambridge Economic History of Modern Europe*. Vol. II: *1870–2000*. Cambridge University Press, pp. 133–155.

Engelbrecht, H. C. and F. C. Hanighen (1934). *Merchants of Death: Study of the International Armament Industry*. New York: Dodd, Mead & Co.

Feldman, G. D. (1966). *Army, Industry and Labor in Germany, 1914–1918*. Princeton University Press.

(2000). "War Aims, State Intervention, and Business Leadership in Germany: The Case of Hugo Stinnes," in R. Chickering and S. Förster (eds.), *War, Total War: Combat and Mobilization on the Western Front, 1914–1918*. Cambridge University Press, pp. 349–368.

Feldstein, M. (2008). "Defense Spending Would Be Great Stimulus: All Three Service Branches are in Need of Upgrade and Repair," *Wall Street Journal*, December 24.

Ferguson, N. (1998). *The Pity of War*. London: Allen Lane.

(2001). *The Cash Nexus: Money and Power in the Modern World, 1700–2000*. London: Allen Lane.

Ferguson, T. and H.-J. Voth (2008). "Betting on Hitler – The Value of Political Connections in Nazi Germany," *Quarterly Journal of Economics* 123(1): 101–137.

Fernandez, R. and D. Rodrik (1991). "Resistance to Reform: Status Quo Bias in the Presence of Individual-Specific Uncertainty," *American Economic Review* 81(5): 1146–1155.

Findlay, R. and K. O'Rourke (2007). *Power and Plenty: Trade, War, and the World Economy in the Second Millennium*. Princeton University Press.

Firth, N. E. and J. H. Noren (1998). *Soviet Defense Spending: A History of CIA Estimates, 1950–1990*. College Station, TX: Texas A & M University Press.

Fisman, R. (2000). "Estimating the Value of Political Connections," *American Economic Review* 91(4): 1095–1102.

Foreman-Peck, J. and G. Federico, eds. (1999). *European Industrial Policy: The Twentieth-Century Experience*. Oxford University Press.

Garton Ash, T. (1997). *The File: A Personal History*. London: Atlantic.

Gartzke, E. (2007). "The Capitalist Peace," *American Journal of Political Science* 51(1): 166–191.

Gat, A. (2006). *War in Human Civilization*. Oxford University Press.

Gershman, C. and O. Gutierrez (2009). "Can Cuba Change? Ferment in Civil Society," *Journal of Democracy* 20(1): 36–53.

Glantz, D. M. (1998). *Stumbling Colossus: The Red Army on the Eve of World War*. Lawrence, KS: University Press of Kansas.

Gleditsch, K. S. (2004). "A Revised List of Wars Between and Within Independent States, 1816–2002," *International Interactions* 30(3): 231–262.

Gleditsch, N. P. (2008). "The Liberal Moment Fifteen Years On," *International Studies Quarterly* 52(4): 691–712.

Goldstein, J. (2011). *Winning the War on War: The Decline of Armed Conflict Worldwide*. New York: Penguin.

Golson, E. B. (in press). "Swedish Trade in the Second World War," in J. Scherner and E. N. White (eds.), *The Short and Long-term Economic Effects of German Exploitation in the Occupied Territories*. Cambridge University Press.

Gorodetsky, G. (1999). *Grand Delusion: Stalin and the German Invasion of Russia*. New Haven, CT: Yale University Press.

Grechko, A. A., chief ed. (1982). *Istoriia vtoroi mirovoi voiny*. Vol. XII. Moscow: Voenizdat.

Guérin, D. (1938). "Fascism and Big Business," *The New International: A Monthly Organ of Revolutionary Marxism* 4(10): 297–300. Available at www.marxists.org/history/etol/writers/guerin/1938/10/fascism.htm (accessed on June 9, 2011).

Hardach, G. (1977). *The First World War, 1914–1918*. Berkeley, CA: University of California Press.

Harrison, M. (1994). "The Soviet Defense Industry Complex in World War II," in J. Sakudo and T. Shiba (eds.), *World War II and the Transformation of Business Systems*. Tokyo: University of Tokyo Press, pp. 237–262.

(2001). "Providing for Defense," in P. R. Gregory (ed.), *Behind the Facade of Stalin's Command Economy: Evidence from the Soviet State and Party Archives*. Stanford, CA: Hoover Institution Press, pp. 81–110.

(2008). "The Market for Inventions under Stalin: Experimental Aircraft Engines," in M. Harrison (ed.), *Guns and Rubles: The Defense Industry in the Stalinist State*. New Haven, CT: Yale University Press, pp. 180–209.

(2011). "Stalinizm i ekonomika voennogo vremeni," in E. I. Kondrashina (chief ed.), *Istoriia stalinizma: Itogi i problemy izucheniia*. Moscow: Rosspen, pp. 546–565.

ed. (1998). *The Economics of World War II: Six Great Powers in International Comparison*. Cambridge University Press.

Harrison, M. and A. Markevich (2008a). "Hierarchies and Markets: the Defense Industry under Stalin," in M. Harrison (ed.), *Guns and Rubles: The Defense Industry in the Stalinist State*. New Haven, CT: Yale University Press, pp. 50–77.

(2008b). "The Soviet Market for Weapons," in M. Harrison (ed.), *Guns and Rubles: The Defense Industry in the Stalinist State*. New Haven, CT: Yale University Press, pp. 156–179.

Harrison, M. and N. Wolf (2012). "The Frequency of Wars," *Economic History Review* 65(3): 1055–1076.

Hayes, P. (2001). *Industry and Ideology: IG Farben in the Nazi Era*, 2nd edn. Cambridge University Press.

Hewitt, J. J. (2008). "Unpacking Global Trends in Violent Conflict, 1946–2005," in J. J. Hewitt, J. Wilkenfeld, and T. R. Gurr (eds.), *Peace and Conflict 2008*. Boulder, CO and London: Paradigm, pp. 107–118.

Higgs, R. V. (1992). "Wartime Prosperity? A Reassessment of the U.S. Economy in the 1940s," *Journal of Economic History* 52(1): 41–60.

(1993). "Private Profit, Public Risk: Institutional Antecedents of the Modern Military Procurement System in the Rearmament Program of 1940–41," in G. T. Mills and H. Rockoff (eds.), *The Sinews of War: Essays on the Economic History of World War II*. Ames, IA: Iowa State University Press, pp. 166–198.

(1994). "The Cold War Economy: Opportunity Costs, Ideology, and the Politics of Crisis," *Explorations in Economic History* 31(3): 283–312.

Higgs, R. V. and A. Kilduff (1993). "Public Opinion: A Powerful Predictor of U.S. Defense Spending," *Defence and Peace Economics* 4(3): 227–238.

Hillman, A. J., G. D. Keim, and D. Schuler (2004). "Corporate Political Activity: A Review and Research Agenda," *Journal of Management* 30(6): 837–857.

Hitchens, C. (2006). "The Eighteenth Brumaire of the Castro Dynasty: Cuba's Military Coup Marks the End of the Revolutionary Era," *The Slate*, August 7. Available at www.slate.com (accessed on October 11, 2011).

Hoffman, P. T. (2010). "Prices, the Military Revolution, and Western Europe's Comparative Advantage in Violence," *Economic History Review* 64(S1): 39–59.

(2012). "Why Was It Europeans Who Conquered the World?" *Journal of Economic History* 72(3): 601–633.

Hoffman, P. T. and J.-L. Rosenthal (1997). "The Political Economy of Warfare and Taxation in Early Modern Europe: Historical Lessons for Economic Development," in J. N. Drobak and J. V. Nye (eds.), *The Frontiers of New Institutional Economics*. San Diego, CA: Academic Press, pp. 31–55.

Holloway, D. (1980). "War, Militarism, and the Soviet State," in E. P. Thompson and D. Smith (eds.), *Protest and Survive*. London: Penguin Books, pp. 129–169.

Hull, C. (1948). *The Memoirs of Cordell Hull*. 2 vols. New York: Macmillan.

Jacks, D. S., C. M. Meissner, and D. Novy (2008). "Trade Costs, 1870–2000," *American Economic Review* 98(2): 529–534.

Johnson, S. and T. Mitton (2003). "Cronyism and Capital Controls: Evidence from Malaysia," *Journal of Financial Economics* 67(2): 351–382.

Karaman, K. K. and Ş. Pamuk (2010). "Ottoman State Finances in European Perspective, 1500–1914," *Journal of Economic History* 70(3): 593–629.

Keen, D. (1998). *The Economic Functions of Violence in Civil Wars*. Adelphi Papers No. 320. London: Routledge.

Khlevniuk, O. (1995). "The Objectives of the Great Terror, 1937–38," in J. M. Cooper, M. Perrie, and E. A. Rees (eds.), *Soviet History, 1917–1953: Essays in Honour of R. W. Davies*. New York: St. Martin's, pp. 158–176.

Klein, N. (2007). *The Shock Doctrine: The Rise of Disaster Capitalism*. London: Allen Lane.

Klemann, H. (2007). "Entwicklung durch Isolation. Die niederländische Wirtschaft 1914–1918," *Jahrbuch Zentrum für Niederlande-Studien* 18: 131–157.

Klemann, H. and S. Kudriashov (2012). *Occupied Economies: An Economc History of Nazi-Occupied Europe, 1939–1945*. London and New York: Berg.

Knight, B. (2007). "Are Policy Platforms Capitalized into Equity Prices? Evidence from the Bush/Gore 2000 Presidential Election," *Journal of Public Economics* 91(1): 389–409.

Kocka, J. (1984). *Facing Total War: German Society, 1914–1918*. Leamington Spa: Berg.

Kontorovich, V. and A. Wein (2009). "What did the Soviet Rulers Maximise?" *Europe-Asia Studies* 61(9): 1579–1601.

Lawrence, J., M. Dean, and J.-L. Robert (1992). "The Outbreak of War and the Urban Economy: Paris, Berlin, and London in 1914," *Economic History Review* 45(3): 564–593.

Lenin, V. I. (1952 [1916]). "Imperialism, the Highest Stage of Capitalism," in V. I. Lenin, *Selected Works*. Vol. 1 (part 2). Moscow: Foreign Languages Publishing House.

Levy, J. S. (1988). "Domestic Politics and War," *Journal of Interdisciplinary History* 18(4): 653–673.

(1989). "The Diversionary Theory of War," in M. I. Midlarsky (ed.), *Handbook of War Studies*. Boston, MA: Unwin Hyman, pp. 259–288.

Mansfield, E. D. and J. Snyder (2005). *Electing to Fight: Why Emerging Democracies Go to War*. Cambridge, MA: The MIT Press.

Markevich, A. and M. Harrison (2006). "Quality, Experience, and Monopoly: The Soviet Market for Weapons under Stalin," *Economic History Review* 59(1): 113–142.

Martin, P., T. Mayer, and M. Thoenig (2008). "Make Trade Not War?" *Review of Economic Studies* 75(3): 865–900.

Marx, K. (1970 [1867]). *Capital*. Vol. 1. Moscow: Progress.

Mason, T. (1968). "The Primacy of Politics: Politics and Economics in National Socialist Germany," in S. J. Woolf (ed.), *The Nature of Fascism*. London: Weidenfeld & Nicolson, pp. 165–195.

Milward, A. S. (1965). *The German Economy at War*. London: Athlone Press.

Mommsen, H. (2005). "The Impact of Compulsory Labor on German Society at War," in R. Chickering, S. Förster, and B. Greiner (eds.), *A World at Total War: Global Conflict and the Politics of Destruction, 1937–1945*. Cambridge University Press, pp. 177–188.

Morgan, T. C. and C. J. Anderson (1999). "Domestic Support and Diversionary External Conflict in Great Britain, 1950–1992," *Journal of Politics* 61(3): 799–814.

Morgan, T. C. and K. N. Bickers (1992). "Domestic Discontent and the External Use of Force," *Journal of Conflict Resolution* 36(1): 25–52.

Münkler, H. (2005). *The New Wars*. Cambridge: Polity.

Murdoch, J. C. and T. Sandler (1984). "Complementarity, Free Riding, and the Military Expenditures of NATO Allies," *Journal of Public Economics* 25(1–2): 83–101.

O'Brien, P. K. (2005). "Fiscal and Financial Preconditions for the Rise of British Naval Hegemony, 1485–1815," Working Paper No. 91/05. London School of Economics, Department of Economic History.

(2011). "The Nature and Historical Evolution of an Exceptional Fiscal State and its Possible Significance for the Precocious Commercialization and Industrialization of the British Economy from Cromwell to Nelson," *Economic History Review* 64(2): 408–446.

Offer, A. (1989). *The First World War: An Agrarian Interpretation*. Oxford: Clarendon Press.

Olson, M. (1982). *The Rise and Decline of Nations: Economic Growth, Stagflation, and Social Rigidities*. New Haven, CT: Yale University Press.

Olson, M. and R. Zeckhauser (1966). "An Economic Theory of Alliances," *Review of Economics and Statistics* 48(3): 266–279.

Overy, R. J. (1994). *War and Economy in the Third Reich*. Oxford University Press.

Pamuk, Ş. (2005). "The Ottoman Economy in World War I," in S. Broadberry and M. Harrison (eds.), *The Economics of World War I*. Cambridge University Press, pp. 112–136.

Pelletière, S. C. (2004). *America's Oil Wars*. London: Praeger.

Pinker, S. (2011). *The Better Angels of our Nature: Why Violence has Declined*. New York: Viking.

Pospelov, P. N., chief ed. (1965). *Istoriia Velikoi Otechestvennoi voiny Sovetskogo Soiuza 1941–1945*. Vol. VI. Moscow: Voenizdat.

Proudhon, P.-J. (1861). *La guerre et la paix: recherches sur le principe et la constitution du droit des gens*. 2 vols. Paris: Collection Hetzel.

Raack, R. C. (1995). *Stalin's Drive to the West, 1938–1941: The Origins of the Cold War*. Stanford University Press.

Ricardo, D. (1971 [1817]). *On the Principles of Political Economy and Taxation*, ed. R. M. Hartwell. London: Pelican.

Ritschl, A. (2002). "Deficit Spending in the Nazi Recovery, 1933–1938: A Critical Reassessment," *Journal of the Japanese and International Economies* 16(4): 559–582.

   (2005). "The Pity of Peace: Germany's Economy at War, 1914–1918 and Beyond," in S. Broadberry and M. Harrison (eds.), *The Economics of World War I.* Cambridge University Press, pp. 41–76.

Robinson, J. (1972). "The Second Crisis of Economic Theory," *American Economic Review* 62 (1–2): 1–10.

Rockoff, H. (1998). "The United States: From Ploughshares to Swords," in M. Harrison (ed.), *The Economics of World War II: Six Great Powers in International Comparison.* Cambridge University Press, pp. 81–121.

   (2012). *America's Economic Way of War: War and the US Economy from the Spanish–American War to the Persian Gulf War.* Cambridge University Press.

Rodrik, D. and A. Subramanian (2005). "From 'Hindu Growth' to Productivity Surge: The Mystery of the Indian Growth Transition," *IMF Staff Papers* 52(2): 193–228.

Rogerson, W. P. (1994). "Economic Incentives and the Defense Procurement Process," *Journal of Economic Perspectives* 8(4): 65–90.

Schulze, M.-S. (2005). "Austria-Hungary's Economy in World War I," in S. Broadberry and M. Harrison (eds.), *The Economics of World War I.* Cambridge University Press, pp. 77–111.

Schweitzer, A. (1964). *Big Business in the Third Reich.* London: Eyre & Spottiswoode.

Shiba, T. (1994). "Business Activities of Japanese Manufacturing Industries During World War II," in J. Sakudo and T. Shiba (eds.), *World War II and the Transformation of Business Systems.* University of Tokyo Press, pp. 1–25.

Simonov, N. (2000). "New Postwar Branches (2): The Nuclear Industry," in J. Barber and M. Harrison (eds.), *The Soviet Defence Industry Complex from Stalin to Khrushchev.* Basingstoke and London: Macmillan Press, pp. 150–172.

Smith, A. (1970 [1776]). *An Inquiry into the Nature and Causes of the Wealth of Nations.* Harmondsworth: Penguin.

Smith, R. P. (1977). "Military Expenditure and Capitalism," *Cambridge Journal of Economics* 1(1): 61–76.

   (2009). *Military Economics: The Interaction of Power and Money.* Basingstoke: Palgrave Macmillan.

Steindl, J. (1952). *Maturity and Stagnation in American Capitalism.* Oxford University Press.

Suvorov (Rezun), V. (1990). *Ice-Breaker: Who Started the Second World War?* London: Hamish Hamilton.

Tilly, C. (1975). "Reflections on the History of European State-Making," in C. Tilly (ed.), *The Formation of National States in Western Europe.* Princeton University Press, pp. 3–83.

Tooze, J. A. (2006). *The Wages of Destruction: The Making and the Breaking of the Nazi Economy.* London: Allen Lane.

Trevor-Roper, H. R., ed. (2000). *Hitler's Table Talk, 1941–1944,* 3rd edn. London: Enigma Books.

Turner, H. A. (1985). *German Big Business and the Rise of Hitler.* Oxford University Press.

Uldricks, T. J. (1999). "The Icebreaker Controversy: Did Stalin Plan to Attack Hitler?" *Slavic Review* 58(3).

Urlanis, B. T. (1994 [1960]). *Istoriia voennykh poter. Voiny i narodonaselenie Evropy. Liudskie poteri vooruzhennykh sil Evropeiskikh stran v voinakh XVII–XX vv. (Istoriko-statisticheskoe issledovanie.)* St. Petersburg: Poligon.

Von Staden, P. W. (2008). *Business–Government Relations in Prewar Japan*. London: Routledge.

Weeks, A. L. (2002). *Stalin's Other War: Soviet Grand Strategy, 1939–1941*. Lanham, MD: Rowman & Littlefield.

Wilson, M. and J. Eloranta (2010). "Thwarting the 'Merchants of Death' Accusation: The Political Economy of Military Procurement in Industrial Democracies before the Second World War," *Essays in Economic and Business History* 28: 91–106.

12

Modern capitalism: enthusiasts, opponents, and reformers

JEFFRY FRIEDEN AND RONALD ROGOWSKI

Since its emergence in the late 1700s, modern capitalism has been the focus of intense controversy. On the one hand, capitalist economic growth has been extraordinary. On the other hand, capitalism has been prone to crisis and is also associated with a striking degree of inequality. Much of the political controversy is driven by conflict between those who have gained or stand to gain from the rapid economic development of capitalism, and those whose fortunes are threatened by capitalist advance and cyclical crises.

On the positive side of the ledger is the extraordinary productive power that modern capitalism has unleashed, combining land, labor, capital, and human capital in ways that have increased output and income at a previously unimaginable pace. Even capitalism's severest critics recognized the great economic advances the system had wrought. As Marx and Engels wrote in the Communist Manifesto, capitalism "has created more massive and more colossal productive forces than have all preceding generations together." In the process, they wrote, capitalism had "rescued a considerable part of the population from the idiocy of rural life."

On the negative side is the undoubted fact that capitalist development can threaten the livelihoods of those who cannot compete with new technologies and new producers. Just as capitalism creates many winners, it also creates losers. Among these have been European craftsmen and farmers, undersold by new factory production and New World farming. The disaffected have also included countries in Latin America, Africa, and Asia, whose production structures proved poorly suited – at least in the first instance – for international competition. And today there are many workers, small businesses, and others, who fear the market and political power of the large corporations that have come to dominate contemporary capitalism.

Another aspect of capitalism that has drawn criticism is its tendency toward periodic crises. This has been a feature of the system since its inception, and although governments seem to have developed more effective measures to mitigate the impact of crises, they certainly have not eliminated them. Critics of the capitalist order point with concern to the expectation that modern capitalist economies will intermittently hit the skids.

In what follows, we survey political responses to the development of capitalism since the late 1700s. Throughout, we focus on the two principal sides of the debate. Capitalism's principal supporters have been those who have benefitted most from its development, or hope to do so. Capitalism's principal opponents have been those who have lost, or expect to lose, as the system progresses. In the middle, often, are reformers who want to salvage what is best about capitalism while smoothing some of its roughest edges. While it is impossible to do justice to every part of the globe, we try to cover both the advanced industrial countries – Europe, North America, Japan – as well as the poorer countries of Africa, Asia, and Latin America.

The mercantilist prelude

Modern capitalism arose out of an international economic order in which Europeans dominated the rest of the world both economically and militarily. From the fifteenth to the eighteenth centuries, Europe's early-capitalist economies were governed by a mercantilist system that limited the operation of markets (O'Brien, Chapter 12 in Volume 1). These restrictions served to empower rulers, and to enrich or protect powerful economic interests. They were very successful at acquiring and exploiting colonial possessions for the benefit of the mother countries, and at channeling the energies of the budding capitalist societies toward the new manufacturing activities.

At the top of the European societies, the main champions of the mercantilist, early-capitalist, social order, apart from the rulers themselves, were the city-dwelling commercial and financial classes, principal beneficiaries of the systematic biases of economic activity. Governments at this early stage typically sanctioned monopolistic control over much economic activity, including overseas trade and access to colonial markets and resources. The monopolists – the Hudson's Bay Company and the Dutch East India Company, for example – naturally backed the system. Some landowning elites gained from the new overseas opportunities – which many sent offspring to exploit. In addition, urban craftsmen and their guilds gained, for mercantilist restrictions on trade stimulated early local manufacturing by turning the terms of trade in favor of the mother country, especially by depressing the price of primary inputs and raising the price of manufactured output. Given its combined military and economic goals, mercantilism was a striking success, associated with Western Europe's rise to global economic and military dominance. Yet it soon gave way to a more modern economic order.

The industrial revolution, 1770–1850

The rise of modern industrial capitalism

Over the course of the 1700s, the new industrialism began to supplant the previous economic order in parts of northern Europe. Cottage industry and the "putting-out" system gave way to the factory system (see Harley on European industrialization, Chapter 16 in Volume I). Skilled craftsmen were replaced by water- and steam-powered machinery, which could be operated by less skilled workers, including children, and which required large amounts of capital. The result was an unprecedented increase in industrial output. But the extraordinary productivity of the new industries caused problems for many existing producers.

As the factory system thrived, it drove many of the earlier manufacturers out of business. Handloom weavers, on the continent as in England, were first pressed by the putting-out system, then by Asian imports, and from the end of the Napoleonic Wars by textiles produced in the British factories that had leapt to the technical forefront. In many weaving-dominated regions, mass unemployment and actual starvation ensued, most notably in Silesia in the 1840s.

In the independent towns and principalities still dominated by guilds, the entry of capitalist modes of production and wider markets presaged a swift demise. The appearance on the European market of inexpensive mass-produced goods – textiles, shoes, apparel, toys, appliances – doomed traditional labor-intensive guild production. If the town admitted cheaper goods (even after paying high tariffs), the traditional craftspeople lost their customers. If mass-produced goods were excluded in an effort to preserve the local market, home-town consumers moved to areas that offered a cheaper and greater variety of goods, services, and occupations, and again the traditional town withered.

Capitalism was more disruptive in many of the craft-based German towns than in England, France, Prussia, and the parts of Germany that the French had occupied under Napoleon, for there the guild system had already been abolished. These regions' petite bourgeoisie was correspondingly less tied to traditional manufacturing for everyday consumption and more to shop-keeping and highly specialized, often luxurious, decorative crafts (furniture, tapestries, jewelry, wine, glass). Even so, in some sectors, notably again spinning and weaving, the impact was catastrophic even in these more "enlightened" regions.

Whether in England or on the continent, the expansion of modern industry – and something recognizably like modern capitalism – gave rise both to movements of enthusiastic supporters and to groups opposed to the new social system.

Enthusiasts

The new manufacturing interests were both the principal protagonists and the most fervent supporters of the new industrialism. The centers of the burgeoning factory system were to be found in the Midlands and the north of England, including such cities as Birmingham and Manchester; in parts of northern France and Wallonia, and in the German states (chiefly Prussia).

Entrepreneurs in the new industrial centers quickly recognized that what Adam Smith called "the mean and malignant expedients of the mercantile system"[1] were impediments to the full development of modern manufacturing. Mercantilist monopolies restricted entry to new economic actors, even (or especially) when they were more efficient. Limits to overseas trade sometimes restricted access to promising foreign markets. Agricultural protection raised the cost of inputs, and – inasmuch as food was a major part of workers' consumption basket – raised employers' labor costs as well. Where modern industrial production took hold, so too did political movements to curtail or eliminate existing controls on the new economic activity.

In Great Britain, the main early incubator of the new industries, two great and interrelated political battles marked the political coming of modern capitalism. The first was the struggle to reform the country's political system to give more representation to the "middle classes," originally defined as those in between the aristocracy and the peasantry, especially the town-dwelling business and professional classes. The notoriously lopsided nature of British parliamentary representation dramatically overweighted the countryside and underweighted the cities. Large landowners not only had their own House of Parliament, the House of Lords, but personally controlled many seats in the House of Commons by means of their influence over the so-called pocket boroughs. Neither Manchester nor Birmingham, by the 1830s cities of over

---

1 Smith (1776), Book IV.

200,000 and 100,000 inhabitants respectively, had a parliamentary representative of its own, while there were dozens of districts ("boroughs") with only a few score residents. The most notorious of the rotten boroughs, such as Old Sarum, had few if any inhabitants: none of the eleven voters in the 1831 election in that borough lived in the area.[2] Another, Dunwich, was literally under water, the sea having encroached on almost all the land of what had once been a flourishing port town.

From the 1760s onward there were scattered attempts to expand the franchise and correct parliamentary mal-apportionment, but – unsurprisingly – they received little support from sitting members of Parliament. The French Revolution hardened the opposition of those concerned that an enlarged franchise would only lead to that sort of catastrophe. But after 1815, pressures for reform grew, and the underrepresented regions roiled with protest and mass demonstrations; some of them met with violent repression. Perhaps even more importantly, the new elites of the manufacturing towns began to mobilize their wealth and influence on behalf of parliamentary reform. Eventually, in 1832 Parliament passed a Reform Act that substantially expanded the franchise (to about 5 percent of the country's population), despite the continued opposition of many elite factions.[3]

Electoral reform, once enacted, provided the opportunity for the strongest business supporters of the new capitalism to make their voices heard more effectively, and they immediately set about attempting to affect policy along these lines. The new representatives of the industrial areas were especially concerned about one of the principal issues of the day, repeal of the Corn Laws. These were tariffs on grain, originally imposed during the Napoleonic Wars, and by the 1820s a major benefit to British farmers. They also, however, raised the cost of food ("the dear loaf," in the working-class propaganda of the day) and thus of wages. Perhaps just as important, supporters of repeal believed that freeing British trade would help open markets abroad. This would happen both because foreigners' enhanced ability to sell to Great

---

2 The standard history of the period is still Woodward 1962: 25–30 and Book I, chap. 1. For a (much) fuller account, see Buttle 2011.

3 Even after the measure had passed the House of Commons, the landlord-dominated House of Lords threatened to reject it; their opposition was overcome only when the King, pressured by the Prime Minister and accommodationist Conservatives, threatened to create enough new peers to assure a majority for the bill in the Lords. The threat did not need to be exercised – once it had been credibly made, the existing Lords gave way – but this constitutional crisis suggested how high the stakes were and how much the balance of power had already shifted.

Britain would increase their incomes, and their demand for British goods; and because they would be moved to reciprocate for British liberalization.

The impact of the protective tariff on the United States was prominently mentioned in the British debates. On the one hand, as manufacturer and free trade activist Richard Cobden noted, the tariffs reduced foreigners' income and encouraged them to produce their own manufactured goods rather than buy from Britain: "We offer [the Americans] no inducement to spread themselves out from the cities – to abandon their premature manufactures – in order to delve, dig, and plough for us." On the other hand, British protectionism reinforced the political position of the American protectionists. Home Secretary James Graham said in 1846, "We convert our natural and best customers, not only into commercial rivals, but into commercial enemies ... They accordingly meet us with hostile tariffs; they impose high duties upon our manufactures."[4]

After over a decade of bitter battles in Parliament, in the press, and in the streets, in 1846 Parliament finally repealed the Corn Laws. Again, the struggle was intense and enduring: the Conservative Party split into Peelite (pro-repeal) and anti-Peelite (anti-repeal) factions, and the breach was not fully healed until the prime ministry of Benjamin Disraeli (earlier the leader of the anti-Peelite faction, but by then resigned to free trade). The repeal of the Corn Laws marked the effective end of the age of mercantilism, and the beginning of an era of trade liberalization that became nearly synonymous with the rise of modern industrial capitalism in the nineteenth century.

In post-revolutionary France (once the Bourbons were finally displaced in 1830), strong elite support for capitalism came to the fore, at both the national and the local level. Pro-capitalist elites dominated both in the Orleanist monarchy (1830–1848) and in the Second Empire (1852–1870). Here, too, the crucial infrastructure for capitalist development was expanded: harbors, canals, railways, sometimes drastic urban renewal (Hausmann's rebuilding of Paris under Louis Napoleon). And in the Second Empire, beginning with the famous Cobden–Chevalier Treaty, France followed Britain in embracing free, or at least much freer, trade. In a particularly farsighted move, the Second Empire significantly advanced one of France's important exports, wine, by imposing a standardized system of ranks and labeling that assured buyers of the origin and quality of the product.[5]

---

4 James and Lake 1989: 18, 20.
5 The phylloxera epidemic, which killed off so many of France's vines, turned out to be only a temporary setback. To oenophiles, America more than repaid its debt to Lafayette by providing root stocks hardy enough to be immune to phylloxera.

Elsewhere on the European continent, nascent capitalists similarly pushed to modernize existing institutions, yet here the prevalence of pre-capitalist modes of production meant that electoral reform or a wider franchise were rarely seen as the answer. While advocates of wider markets, deeper finance, and larger enterprises sought similar policies – an end to local protectionism, the abolition of the remaining guilds, rationalization of agriculture (to free up rural workers for urban industry), and low tariffs on food – continental industrialists often allied with "modernizing autocracies" to achieve those goals.

As early as the eighteenth century, some of the continent's "enlightened despotisms," most notably the Prussia of Frederick the Great and the Austria of Joseph II, had prepared the legal and institutional soil for capitalism, unifying and rationalizing legal codes, guaranteeing judicial independence, weakening or abolishing guilds, and dismantling barriers to internal trade. Politically, the earliest leap toward acceptance came with the founding of the independent kingdom of Belgium in 1830, which welcomed capitalist enterprise more than any other jurisdiction on the continent. In post-Napoleonic Germany, and more particularly in Prussia, capitalist development was spurred by the Stein–Hardenberg reforms (1807–1811), which included abolition of most guild privileges, and by the expansion of the Zollverein, the customs union that embraced not only Prussia but an increasing number of its neighboring states: Mecklenburg, Saxony, Thuringia, Bavaria, Hesse.

Intellectuals, particularly in England, sometimes reinforced the broad evolution of public policies more favorable to modern urban, industrial capitalism. The most direct connection was between new generations of classical British political economists and the new manufacturing interests. Thomas Malthus, James Mill, David Ricardo, and Adam Smith all regarded mercantilism's restrictions as barriers to economic progress, its monopolistic practices as impediments to the advance of modern industry. They preached the value of competition, specialization, and comparative advantage to a receptive audience of dynamic entrepreneurs. Among historians, Thomas Babington Macaulay, the father of "Whig History," emerged as an enthusiastic supporter of the new, capitalist, expansive order. Across the channel, Physiocrats such as Quesnay and Turgot preceded the British political economists in their distaste for mercantilism and enthusiasm about competition and efficiency, although they saw farming, not industry, as the principal source of productive advance. These new philosophical and analytical trends reinforced the broad acceptance of the precepts of modern liberalism, and its general sympathy for modern industrial society.

Opponents

The enthusiasts, for all their energy, faced substantial opposition. Mass sentiment in France seems to have been very skeptical of capitalism. To the peasantry, secure ownership of their small farms was the signal achievement of the Revolution. Peasants were eager neither to mechanize, nor to see their young people drawn away by industry, nor (above all) to accept large imports of grain. The Revolution had also enfranchised French peasants, so that liberalization occurred only under authoritarian regimes (see above). It was peasant support that suppressed the Paris Commune, that later sustained the Third Republic, and that steadily embraced the restrictions on retailing and industry that kept France a nation at best ambivalent about modern capitalism.[6]

Most visibly, in the areas where traditional guilds and artisanal manufactures had dominated, resistance was far stronger than in France or Britain. Handloom weavers and spinners rebelled and smashed machines in many areas of Germany (Augsburg, Silesia, Saxony), emulating but far surpassing the English Luddites. Other crafts joined in, at first demanding enhanced protection by way of the prohibition of imports from outside the locality, or of the revision or abolition of the *Zollverein*. Eventually, they perceived that any effective remedy had to come at a much broader level, and sought in the revolutions of 1848 a unified and democratic Germany. The noble aspirations of the revolutionaries' draft constitution of 1848 should not blind us to the fact that its major backers were the traditional craftspeople and that two of its crucial provisions gave the envisioned national government full authority to enact tariffs and to regulate trade and licensure. Had Germany achieved a democratic national government at this stage, the restrictions on capitalist enterprise would likely have been even more severe than those imposed by the democratic Third French Republic.

Many, if not most, European intellectuals and artists were opposed to, indeed often appalled by, the rapid rise of capitalism around them. Whether in industrializing England, post-revolutionary France, or prerevolutionary Germany, poets, playwrights, painters, novelists, can be counted as overwhelmingly anti-capitalist. In most of its aspects, Romanticism represented – despite its freshness of technique and its fondness for natural language – a

---

6 Note, in Balzac's novels, how few of his striving Parisian characters hope to get rich from industry, or even from commerce; how many from government favors, official appointments, aristocratic patronage, or (curiously, but related to all of the above) artistic success.

visceral yearning for a lost, preindustrial past. William Blake, most famously and most directly, saw "England's pastures green" being displaced by "dark satanic mills." But not by accident did Beethoven's Sixth Symphony, a paean to a countryside untouched by industry or urbanization, rapidly become one of his most popular works. Wordsworth's initial enthusiasm for the French Revolution[7] yielded quickly to the rustic longings of *Tintern Abbey*, and, with his close friend Coleridge, he drew inspiration not from England's cities, harbors, or commerce, but from the pristine Lake District. And even the Impressionists, although capable of lyrical urban scenes, often focussed on the traditional countryside of haystacks and wheat fields, often enough, once one notices, with a threatening, smoke-belching railway looming in the background.

Even more directly, many poets and commentators (foremost among them Heinrich Heine[8]) sided passionately with the displaced Silesian weavers in 1844–1845. Decades later, the Naturalist Gerhard Hauptmann produced a tear-jerking account of their suffering, and of the horrid selfishness and hypocrisy of their capitalist employers, in his 1894 play, *Die Weber* (*The Weavers*).

Unionism

Industrialization, in addition to threatening many traditional economic actors and political and social traditionalists, created an industrial working class. This new working class began to organize itself almost as soon as it arose, and eventually became a significant political force in every industrial society (see Huberman, Chapter 13 in this volume). Its demands ranged from the purely economic to the broadly political, and from the mildly reformist to the openly revolutionary.

British working men began creating expressly political organizations in the 1790s, largely to demand greater rights, but these were mostly suppressed in the general atmosphere of fear that followed the French Revolution. By the 1830s, when agitation picked up again, the character of the working class had changed. Those involved in the movements of the 1790s were largely crafts-men, artisans, and middle-class professionals, while the mobilizations of the

---

7 To be sure, the French Revolution and the experience of Napoleonic conquest hastened the artistic longing for a more orderly and idyllic past; but, with rare exceptions, intellectuals sought a preindustrial, rather than an explicitly prerevolutionary, past.

8 Heine's poem "Die armen Weber," popularly retitled "The Silesian Weavers," first appeared in Karl Marx's newspaper *Vorwärts* in 1844 and was promptly banned in Prussia for its "subversive tendencies."

1830s and 1840s included large numbers of factory workers, a new category born of the previous decades of rapid industrialization.

British working-class hostility to capitalism – or at least to the form it had taken – was most clearly expressed in the Chartist movement. Chartism, organized around the People's Charter of 1838, agitated for universal male suffrage, the secret ballot, and a range of other reforms that would have given the working classes much greater access to the political system. They gathered millions of signatures on two great petitions to Parliament, organized mass meetings around the country, and led strike waves, especially in the industrial north and Scotland. The Chartists were met with hostility and repression by the British government, especially while the revolutions of 1848 swept the European continent. Nonetheless, they directed national attention to the cause of more radical political reform, and to the new-found strength of the working class; and the Chartists arguably smoothed the way for the eventual adoption, over the next thirty years, of most of their proposals.

Early socialism

Other European revolutionary and reformist critics of capitalism were increasingly active in the 1830s and 1840s. This activism culminated, in most countries, in the multifarious revolutions of 1848. In France and the German states, especially, the urban middle and working classes were prominent in demanding a greater role in political life. The revolutionary wave was very disparate, and did not affect some countries, but nonetheless it indicated that there were substantial sectors of modern European societies that were profoundly dissatisfied with the conservative rule that had prevailed. Almost all of the revolutionary onslaughts were resisted, often brutally repressed, and the aftermath of 1848 largely saw a return to autocracy. Nonetheless, a generation of Europeans had seen mass movements in opposition to the reigning political and economic order.

The proliferation of working- and middle-class agitation for political and social change between the 1790s and the 1840s was accompanied by attempts on the part of European reformers to address the glaring and growing inequality they observed as industrialization proceeded. British and French social reformers, in particular, developed both trenchant critiques of the poverty and inequality they observed in the new industrial societies, and suggested more cooperative and egalitarian alternatives.

Most of these reformers – ridiculed by Marx and Engels as "utopian socialists" – pinned their hopes on the establishment of new cooperative communities that would illustrate the possibilities of a more just, but still economically productive, social order. Such French thinkers as Charles Fourier and Henri de Saint-Simon, and such British thinkers as Robert Owen, encouraged the creation of these "utopian" communities. Owen himself took over his father-in-law's factory town of New Lanark, Scotland, and turned it into a showcase of this more humane industrialism. Fourier's followers set up dozens of such communities (among them Brook Farm, Massachusetts, and Corning, Iowa, in the United States). Although New Lanark remained a model town for decades, most of the other utopian settlements lasted only a few years. Nonetheless, they provided reformist thinkers and activists with something of a model of what a different society might look like. So pragmatic a progressive thinker as John Stuart Mill evinced sympathy for Fourierist and other utopian socialists. Yet despite their broader appeal and impact, the movements were too small and isolated to have a profound effect on mass politics.

At the other extreme were anarchist and anarcho-syndicalist thinkers who argued for very radical change. Many of them, such as the Russian Mikhail Bakunin and the Frenchman Pierre-Joseph Proudhon, largely rejected private property and the modern state in favor of self-organized producers' communities grouped in loose federations. The early anarchists, in the 1840s and 1850s, mounted a powerful critique of the autocratic capitalism then prevailing, in favor of their "libertarian socialism." And anarchism appealed to intellectuals and workers in some countries.

In the 1840s, as these socialist currents swirled throughout Europe, Karl Marx and Friedrich Engels began their collaboration. They were leading members of the Communist League, an organization formed just before the 1848 revolutions and made up largely of German workers living in England. Although the Communist League was dissolved in 1852, Marx and Engels continued to work with radical opponents of capitalism around Europe. They became influential among the growing and disparate groups calling themselves socialistic of one variant or another. Yet by 1860 there was no one dominant strand of socialist thought or action. There was, instead, a proliferation of working-class and middle-class reformers who shared a critical view of capitalism as it existed, and a desire to find a different way to organize society.

The heyday of modern industrial capitalism and *laissez-faire*, 1850–1914

The opponents of European capitalism in the 1850s were of the most varied sort, ranging from feudal romantics to fiery communists; but European capitalism itself was gradually converging on a path toward the early British model. In the years after the repeal of the Corn Laws, most of Western Europe moved toward the kind of international economic integration that was the foundation of British economic policy. Two pillars of this model were free trade and the gold standard. With the Corn Laws gone and mercantilism a dead letter, Britain was committed to minimizing barriers to international trade.[9] With the Cobden–Chevalier Treaty of 1860, as already mentioned, France opted for trade liberalization, and over time most Western European countries followed. The Prussians, paradoxically, supported free trade with especial enthusiasm, since the dominant East Prussian landlords were highly successful exporters of grain[10] – a situation that would soon change. Outside Europe, many New World governments also liberalized trade, and integration into world markets was the order of the day. Over the course of the 1800s, the trade of the advanced countries grew twice to three times as fast as their economies; by the end of the century, trade was seven or eight times as large a share of the world's economy as it had been at the beginning of the century.[11]

The international gold standard emerged and solidified along with, and as a facilitator of, trade liberalization. Britain had been on gold since 1717, and as the country cemented its status as the global market leader, it attracted other countries to use the same monetary system. Over the course of the 1870s most major industrial countries joined the gold standard, committing themselves to exchange their currencies for gold at a pre-established rate. By 1879, most of the industrial world had adopted the gold standard.

The classical world economy of the 1850–1914 period, organized around free trade and the gold standard, saw a very high level of international economic integration. In addition to trade, international financial flows grew rapidly – foreign investments, largely in bonds and stocks, accounted for about one-third of the savings of the United Kingdom, one-quarter of France's, one-tenth of Germany's (see James, Chapter 9 in this volume).[12] International migration also grew rapidly, as 50 million Europeans and 50 million Asians left their homelands for new countries overseas. The international economy – and

---

9 John Nye (2007) argues that the extent of British trade liberalization has been exaggerated; while his arguments are interesting, they remain outside the general historical consensus.

10 The East Prussian landlords, as Barrington Moore observed, were at this time the rough equivalent of plantation owners in the US South. Both depended heavily on export markets, and both vehemently rejected protective tariffs.

11 Maddison Historical GDP Data: 38. For an excellent survey of the period see Marsh 1999.

12 O'Rourke and Williamson 1999: 209.

most of the world's nations – grew faster than they ever had. Indeed, the world economy grew more in the 75 years from 1840 to 1914 than it had in the previous 750.[13] This performance may well have merited its common label as a Golden Age of capitalism, or as (from 1815 to 1914) the Hundred Years' Peace,[14] but the spread of capitalism and its development in this period had many critics. There was plenty to complain about – an agrarian crisis in Europe, colonial expansion in Asia and Africa, a Great Depression of prices that lasted nearly twenty-five years,[15] miserable conditions in the world's industrial centers, limited or non-existing democracy – and there were plenty of forms this protest took.

Enthusiasts

The principal supporters of the new order – both internationally and domestically – were again, not surprisingly, its principal beneficiaries. International financial, commercial, and industrial interests were able to take advantage of opportunities around the world, in an environment that largely welcomed global flows of goods, capital, and people. Within most countries, a consensus formed around the orthodoxy of the age. This orthodoxy privileged a country's international economic relations, even at the expense of some national concerns. The consensus included a commitment to the gold standard, to respect for cross-border property rights, to strong involvement in international commerce, and in most cases to free migration of persons. In the developed nations of Europe and North America, this consensus was embraced by most economic and political leaders, as well as by large portions of the middle classes and even among workers, especially ones whose livelihoods were closely tied to international trade and investment.[16] Many European labor movements were, indeed, supportive of trade liberalization – in part because it meant cheaper food, in part because it meant greater access

13 The rapidity of growth is even more impressive on a per-person basis. According to Maddison Historical GDP Data: 264, world per capita GDP grew by barely 50 percent from $435 in 1000 to $667 in 1820, and then more than doubled to $1,510 by 1913. All data are in 1990 international dollars.

14 The sobriquet conveniently overlooks the expansionary wars of Prussia, the bloodshed of the Paris Commune, and the outright slaughter of the US Civil War (in which probably one in every twelve adult males perished); but these events, admittedly, paled in comparison to the butchery of World War 1.

15 This "Great Depression" is more accurately described as a "Great Deflation," as nominal prices declined, especially for primary commodities.

16 The US "realigning" election of 1896 turned largely on fidelity to the gold standard (Populists and most Democrats having rallied behind William Jennings Bryan's advocacy of silver), and most urban workers rejected Bryan and adhered to gold-standard orthodoxy.

to foreign markets for their manufactures, and above all because it steadily raised their real wage.[17]

In the poorer nations of the world – Latin America, parts of Asia, around the Mediterranean – the orthodox consensus was largely restricted to a narrow elite. It also was quite loose with regard to trade liberalization – plenty of business leaders, especially in North and South America, had no problem with protecting industry, even while generally favoring both the gold standard and close commercial and financial ties with Europe. In any event, this internationalist elite typically exercised tight control over their countries' political and economic orders. If there was dissent from below – especially inasmuch as the sacrifices made to sustain a country's foreign commitments were imposed on those with little say in the matter – it was ignored or suppressed.

Nonetheless, the late nineteenth and early twentieth century witnessed a remarkable convergence among the economic and political leaders of most of the world's countries. Almost all accepted that an open international economy was highly desirable; and that it was sensible and advisable for their nations to adjust their economic policies in order to maintain their ties to the international economy. At times this might mean imposing difficult austerity measures on a recalcitrant populace. *In extremis*, even the most internationalist of ruling groups might find themselves forced to go off gold – as southern European and Latin American governments did with some regularity. But the goal remained full participation in the British-led global trading, financial, and monetary order; and this goal was more often achieved than not. As an indication, by the early 1900s, virtually every nation of any economic importance – save only China and Persia – was on the gold standard.

The statist alternative

If most of the world admired and emulated the British model of unfettered capitalism, we must note that quite a different way emerged in this period, one that turned out both to be extremely important and, in some cases, to have a dark underside. This was state-led, or state-stimulated, industrialization: in its extreme form, state capitalism. Conservative leaders who saw the great advantages (not least in military power) that industrialization could bring, yet feared the social disruption it seemed inevitably to unleash, often

---

17 Europe, relative to any other part of the world at that time, was abundant in labor: Central Europe had almost 120 inhabitants per square kilometer, southern Europe 70, northwestern Europe 55; East Asia, the next most densely populated region, had 45 inhabitants per square kilometer (United Nations 1961: 41).

decided to "guide" the process; and strong preexisting states permitted them to do so.

These "conservative modernizers" sharply accelerated the pace of industrial development by accumulating and channeling capital, often through favored banks, using state power to build infrastructure, and working in tandem with leaders of major industrial corporations. At the same time, to contain and defuse opposition in traditional sectors, these leaders pursued a three-pronged strategy: (a) toleration or encouragement of a re-ordered system of guilds; (b) state provision of extensive social insurance benefits; and (c) severe limits on popular participation in politics. In short, the conservative modernizers constructed a powerful state that accelerated capitalist development, sheltered the most threatened traditional sectors, and provided extensive social benefits, but opposed democracy.

The almost ideal-typical example is Wilhelmine Germany (and, before 1867, Prussia) under Otto von Bismarck. Even before Bismarck came to power in 1862, rapid capitalist industrialization had begun in Prussia's Ruhr district: coal, iron and steel, and above all railways developed rapidly from about 1850, the period now often called the *Gründerzeit* (Founding Era). Characteristically, the Prussian state invested heavily in many of the crucial early railways, but they remained under private management. The Ruhr's rapid development intensified the conflicts that had peaked in the 1848 Revolution, and the political threat to the existing order again seemed dire. While the Prussian monarchy had severely limited popular participation by the trick of retaining universal manhood suffrage (granted in 1848) while imposing a "three-class" electoral system that empowered the wealthy,[18] even under that system the parliamentary representation of the mostly liberal Left steadily increased, until a majority of the Prussian state Parliament

18 In each parliamentary district, all adult males were listed in the order of how much direct tax they had paid in the previous year (most to least), and the total amount of direct tax collected in the district was also calculated. Officials then proceeded down the list until one-third of the total direct taxes had been accounted for. These were "voters of the first class," and they were rarely more than 10 percent of the electorate; indeed, in areas dominated by large landowners, sometimes a single person. Proceeding on down the list until the next third of direct taxes had been accounted for, one attained a list of "voters of the second class." The taxpayers who provided the final third of total taxes (almost always the great majority of voters) were "voters of the third class." At the polls, each group voted separately, and not for parliamentary candidates directly, but (among each group) for three members of an "electoral college." After the popular votes were counted, the winning nine "electors" assembled and chose the actual MP. Thus, in practice, the wealthiest minority of voters normally held two-thirds of the votes that really mattered in electing the district's representative.

refused supply: If the monarchy would not concede important powers, especially over the military, no money would be appropriated.

In this crisis, the King summoned Bismarck as Prime Minister. Bismarck simply ignored the constitution, appropriated the money (especially for the military), assured himself of the support of the bankers and industrialists, and won a successful and popular war against tiny Denmark over Schleswig-Holstein. Buoyed by this victory, Bismarck called new elections, won a parliamentary majority, and forced passage of an Indemnity Bill that retro-actively approved all he had done. From that point he never looked back.

The foundation of all Bismarck achieved, including Germany's rapid rise to the very front rank of European powers, was his scheme of state-capitalist industrialization at home. Together with his close friend, the brilliant Jewish banker Gerson Bleichröder[19] – who may fairly be called the "German Hamilton" – Bismarck reorganized German banking into a few large and interlocked conglomerates that could readily finance rapid industrial expansion.[20] Bismarck also involved the Prussian state directly in the leading industrial enterprises (Krupp, Thyssen), worked closely himself with many of the major industrialists, and made sure that government smoothed the path to their further expansion. Perceiving, for example, that the monopolistic freight rates of some of Germany's private railways were impeding industrial development, Bismarck (helped by Bleichröder) nationalized all of Prussia's railroads by 1880 and all of Germany's by 1889. And, of course, the large manufacturers of steel and armaments found much to like in the ever-escalating expansion of German armaments, including – a point at which even Bismarck drew the line – a big navy.

To guard against any repeat of the guild-led insurrections of 1848, and indeed to bind artisans and shop-keepers firmly to the state, Bismarck reversed decades of Prussian policy and re-invigorated those guilds that a modern economy could accommodate. Bakers, pharmacists, grocers, booksellers,

---

19 It cannot have hurt Bismarck's chances that he was largely free of the fashionable anti-Semitism of the era – at least in his actions, if not always in his speech. He made sure that observant Jews were received regularly at court, exchanged home visits and dinner invitations with Jewish friends, sponsored the ennoblement of leading observant Jews (including first of all Bleichröder in 1872), and – perhaps his most daring move – collaborated with Bleichröder and others to develop what is now the Grunewald area of Berlin (then a swamp) as the one *Villenviertel* (villa quarter) of the city that did not discriminate against Jewish buyers and, indeed, by 1933, was about 40 percent Jewish. The Grunewald development turned out to be personally lucrative to Bismarck, who (perhaps typically for the time) was not greatly constrained by conflict-of-interest considerations and had put a substantial part of his own money into it.
20 Stern 1977.

and many other specialties were granted local monopolies by the state and could legally combine to set minimum prices.

The state's guarantee of monopolistic profits extended also to big business: Cartel agreements that divided up the market (e.g., for steel or sugar) and set a common price were legally enforceable in Germany. Protective tariffs, enacted in 1879, shielded both East Prussian estates and West German heavy industry ("rye" and "iron") from import competition. While the system amounted to a consumer tax on the German economy, both Bismarck and Bleichröder were well aware that private wealth generated yet greater private investment; and indeed the titans of German industry plowed their super-profits back into their own industries and into the broader German economy.

The German state also directly subsidized research and development, not least in establishing the world's first entirely research-oriented university system, with a particular emphasis on physics and chemistry. University researchers often worked closely with industrialists, and among the results was Germany's early and almost total dominance of the world markets for synthetic dyes, industrial chemicals, and pharmaceuticals.

Finally, to contain working-class unrest, and, as he believed, to increase productivity, Bismarck enacted the first state systems of sickness, old-age, and disability insurance in Europe, the beginnings of the modern welfare state. These measures had also an ulterior motive, openly recognized even earlier, when Prussia had become the first country in Europe to outlaw child labor in the 1830s: healthier workers made better soldiers, and German officialdom paid close attention to any rise in the rate at which conscripts were rejected for service on grounds of disability or infirmity.

Bismarck's system of state-led capitalism spurred a rapid growth of the German economy. Total real output more than tripled in Germany between 1870 and 1913, against a rough doubling in the same years in France and the United Kingdom. Just before World War I, Germany produced as much steel as the rest of Europe put together, more than 90 percent of the world's output of synthetic dyes, and the world's most advanced and successful pharmaceuticals.

Not surprisingly, other countries tried to imitate Germany's success. Most were at best pale imitations – Cavour in Italy, the tepid efforts (already mentioned) of the Orleanist monarchy and the Second Empire in France – but one came close to succeeding and another overtook and surpassed the German example. In Czarist Russia, Count Sergei Witte, as Minister of Finance with far more absolute powers than Bismarck ever enjoyed, pursued the same path of rapid railway expansion, cartelized industry, protective tariffs, and forced-draft investment (much of it from, or subsidized by, the state). In Japan, the governments of the Meiji Restoration (also uninhibited by parliamentary institutions) imitated Germany even more explicitly, modeling the Constitution of 1889 directly on those of Prussia and Germany,[21] and adopting much of the German Civil Code of 1892 as their own in 1896. Japan also imitated Germany in its state-led industrialization and its strong emphasis on heavy industry and armaments.

Progressives and reformers

On both sides of the Atlantic, some "enlightened" members of the middle class deplored both the inequality and squalor of unbridled capitalism and the threat of working-class revolution. While remaining committed to democracy, and sometimes even embracing direct democracy, they sought answers in regulation of big business and empowerment of the less fortunate. Trusts were to be broken up (the Sherman Act) or constrained (the Interstate Commerce Act, the Food and Drug Act); factories were to be made safer, hours of labor limited, and workers given the tools to shape their own destinies (cooperatives, credit unions, settlement houses, even small garden plots for cultivation and a weekend escape from tenement living). On the European continent, these policies were associated with Left Liberalism: the reformer Schulze-Delitzsch (also a Left Liberal politician) founded producer and consumer cooperatives, while others advocated credit unions for small farmers (*Raiffeisenverbände*) or urban workers (*Sparkassen*) to encourage savings and provide what now would be called "microfinance."

In Europe, Left Liberals (or Progressives; the two names were interchangeable) increasingly found common cause with Socialists, not least on the issues of free trade and more vigorous government regulation. In the US, the movement reached its peak in Theodore Roosevelt's 1912 run for the presidency as an independent Progressive candidate who framed the regulatory solution of the "New Nationalism."

Middle-class reactionaries and proto-fascists

The solutions advocated by the Progressives hardly sufficed for the owners of small farms and businesses, increasingly doomed by capitalism and terrified of socialism. Neither did traditional conservatism nor socialism appeal to these

---

21 A special commission made a world tour to study various possible Western models, including the US, British, Spanish, French, and German systems of government. Not surprisingly, the commission found the Prusso-German model worthiest of emulation.

groups. A substantial part of them turned, especially after 1890, to a virulent and often violent strain of populist politics that rejected market economics and "cosmopolitanism," dreamed of a restoration of the pre-capitalist order, and readily embraced anti-Semitism. To many of these groups, the threat of a new, unfamiliar, and more competitive world, and especially of a world market, could be attributed to one especially "cosmopolitan" group, namely Jews.

To these groups, it somehow followed that making Europe "free of Jews" would resolve all threats from capitalism – or, for that matter, from socialism – and guarantee return to an idyllic and pastoral or small-town past. As the pioneering student of comparative fascism Ernst Nolte first argued, these early anti-Semites and populist reactionaries focused their hatred on Jews as the embodiment of free markets, large-scale finance, and international trade – in short, of a despised modernism.[22]

The strongest such movement, and indeed Europe's first mass anti-Semitic party, was the Viennese Christian-Social Party, which drew on the organizational skills of the Catholic clergy and was led by the ex-Liberal Karl Lueger, who eventually won the post of Mayor of Vienna. Lueger's anti-Semitism was particularly virulent, as in his 1899 insistence that "the Jews here practice a terror as bad as anything that can be imagined."[23] The aspiring young artist Adolf Hitler, then living in Vienna, later confessed his "unreserved admiration" for Lueger and his tactics. In Germany, an organized Anti-Semitic Party (or League) emerged as early as 1879 and struck deep roots in smaller towns, among struggling peasants, and among Berlin artisans.[24] Although it split and re-assembled continually, the movement was united in its opposition to liberalism of all stripes, and especially to Left Liberalism, which it denounced as "Jewified" (verjudet).

Relations between the populist anti-Semites and more traditional conservatives were complicated. In France, the movement called Action Française, inspired directly by the Dreyfus Affair, wobbled between monarchism (albeit for the Orleanist claimant) and simple hatred of the Third Republic, dominated (as they saw it) by "metics" (Jews and foreigners) and characterized by an increasingly sharp distinction between Church and state.

Yet on the eve of World War I, the populist anti-Semites were on the wane, while socialism was steadily rising.[25] Indeed, Lueger won power in Vienna only on the basis of a restricted franchise; the Social Democrats won, and expanded, a majority of the popular vote.

22 Nolte 1963. 23 Geehr 1990.
24 For a close study of one such party, and of the background from which it sprang, see Norda 2009.
25 Levy 1975.

Socialist labor

Karl Marx, who died in 1883, would have been surprised at how quickly and completely the European working-class movements adopted his brand of socialism in the late nineteenth and early twentieth century. Friedrich Engels lived until 1895, and he too would have been amazed at how rapidly Marxist socialism swept through European labor movements, and how quickly the labor movements came to influence European electoral politics.

The modern socialist movement can be dated to an 1864 meeting in London, which established the International Workingmen's Association (often called the First International). The organization eventually came to comprise a wide variety of radicals from around Europe, including trade unionists, republicans, nationalists, and anarchists. While the relationship between the First International and the various national movements was sometimes weak, its activities reflected the gradual rise of a serious, organized movement in opposition to capitalism, one that found substantial support among working-class and middle-class reformers and revolutionaries.

The culminating moment of the First International's epoch was the Paris Commune, which ruled the French capital for a couple of months in spring 1871 in the aftermath of Prussia's humiliating defeat of France in the Franco-Prussian War. The Commune – and similar uprisings in some other French cities – represented a thoroughgoing challenge to the rule of Europe's conservative political and economic elites. Its violent suppression stifled the socialist movement, and the experience contributed to a major split between the followers of Marx and the organization's large anarchist membership. In 1876, the First International disbanded. Despite repression and the end of the International, there was little question that the underlying sources of support for the socialists and related revolutionaries remained.

Over the course of the next few years, socialist parties gradually organized around Western Europe. The most important developments were in Germany, where a merger of existing organizations created the Social Democratic Workers' Party (SDAP) in 1869 and the Socialist Workers' Party (SAP) in 1875. Although Bismarck's anti-socialist laws made the party illegal a few years later,[26] it continued to grow over the next decade. Meanwhile, socialist parties of one sort or another were forming all over Europe – in Denmark in 1876, Belgium in 1885, Norway in 1887, and Austria in 1889. In July

---

26 Despite the ban, socialists continued a vigorous underground existence and even managed to publish newspapers and elect representatives (not so labeled, of course) to the *Reichstag*.

1889, representatives from two dozen countries met in Paris to create a new Socialist (or Second) International. By then, many of the constituent parties were significant political forces in their homelands. Within a year, the newly legal and newly renamed Social Democratic Party of Germany (*Sozialdemokratische Partei Deutschlands* or SPD) was receiving 19.7 percent of the vote in national elections, more than any other party and almost double what it had won in elections only three years earlier.[27]

The movement signaled its sympathy for Marxist ideas by electing Friedrich Engels as its honorary chairman in 1893. Engels returned the favor by accepting, shortly before his death in 1895, that times had changed so much that "We, the 'revolutionaries,' the 'overthrowers' – we are thriving far better on legal methods than on illegal methods and overthrow."[28] The socialists' electoral successes were having much more impact than the illegal and conspiratorial methods of the past. By this point, the socialist parties and movements were primarily concerned to reform the capitalist system, even if many of their leaders and followers believed in the desirability and inevitability of its eventual overthrow. A combination of labor organization and electoral mobilization turned out to be remarkably successful at making the socialists central players in the rapidly democratizing political systems of the late nineteenth and early twentieth centuries. However, socialists and other radicals remained relatively weak in most of the Areas of Recent Settlement, for reasons that probably combined economic, political, and cultural factors.

On the eve of World War I, socialist parties and their related trade unions were among the most powerful political forces in most Western European countries. At their prewar peak, socialist parties were getting between 15 and 25 percent of the vote in France, Italy, and Austria; and 30 to 35 percent of the vote in Belgium, Germany, and Scandinavia.[29] In 1916, Finland's socialists received a remarkable 47 percent of the vote, which gave them a parliamentary majority and allowed them to form the national government as it

---

27 In 1890, the Catholic Center Party came in a close second, at 18.6 percent; the National Liberals and Progressives (Left Liberals) each won about 16 percent; and the rest of the vote went to conservative and regional parties. Already at this point, what would become the dominant "Weimar Coalition" of the First Republic, Socialists, Center, and Left Liberals, commanded a majority of the electorate (about 55 percent).

28 Engels 1895.

29 In the German national elections of 1912, the Socialists received 34.8 percent of the vote, the Left Liberals 12.3 percent, and the Center (Catholics) 16.4 percent. The combined Conservative vote totaled a mere 11.5 percent, and the National Liberals, as the most consistent defenders of untrammeled capitalism, won only a little over one voter in every eight (13.6 percent).

prepared for independence from Russia.[30] Some of the most theoretically consistent, internationally unified, and extreme opponents of the classical capitalist order seemed to have arrived at the gates of the fortress, whose defenders were in any event thinning rapidly and often enough on the verge of panic.

Globalizing capitalism in the rest of the world, 1870–1914

Modern industrial capitalism spread rapidly from its northwestern European origins, finding especially fertile soil in the Areas of Recent Settlement (ARS) (see Allen, Chapter 2 in this volume). These were regions that either had sparse populations when Europeans arrived, or whose populations had been decimated by the arrival of Europeans (purposely or not): the United States, Canada, Australia, New Zealand, the southern cone of Latin America (Argentina, Chile, Uruguay, southern Brazil). There were other regions outside Europe that also took enthusiastically to the new international economic order. Most took advantage of booming European demand for primary products; many tapped the great European financial markets for capital. Some began a rapid route toward industrialization themselves, both by more or less natural means and with the help of protective government policies.

Enthusiasts

There is little mystery in the expansion of modern capitalist economic and political patterns to many of the ARS: they were former or current British colonies and simply replicated British socio-economic and political patterns, adapted to local conditions.

It is a bit more complicated to explain how and why other regions so easily accepted the pillars of the classical international economy, the gold standard, and free trade. In some, such as the southern cone of Latin America, the socio-economic structure was roughly similar to that in the English-speaking ARS. They had ample supplies of fertile temperate land, ideally suited for growing wheat or raising cattle. Once advances in the technologies of transportation (and eventually refrigeration) made it feasible to ship wheat and beef from South America to Europe, production in these regions grew dramatically. In the early 1880s, Argentina exported only 1.6 million bushels of wheat – barely

---

30 Sassoon 1996: 10.

one percent of US exports; on the eve of World War I; less than thirty years later, Argentine wheat exports were 93.6 million bushels, over 85 percent of US exports. The growth in Australian and Canadian wheat exports was comparable.[31] As the economies of these countries were completely reoriented, so too were their political economies largely remade to place the beneficiaries of links to European markets at the centers of power.

In these ARS – whether present or former English colonies, or booming South American temperate resource exporters – national economic and political elites were closely aligned with global economic interests, and closely allied with the centers of the classical world economy, London in particular. The economic policies they favored, and were typically able to have adopted, were aimed at securing access to European markets, European goods, and European capital on the best possible terms. This usually meant adhering to the gold standard, pursuing "reasonable" macroeconomic policies, and maintaining relatively open markets. It did not necessarily mean free trade: Most of these countries had high tariffs on manufactures, for some combination of revenue and special-interest reasons.[32] Nonetheless, there was little question about elite commitment to participation in the global economy.

Along similar lines, there were a number of European colonial possessions for which the golden-age expansion had strong positive effects – at least on powerful local groups. Parts of South and Southeast Asia and West Africa tapped into world markets for tea, rice, and rubber, and for cocoa, groundnuts, and palm oil. Some of the farmers who prospered as a result were European settlers; but in many instances, local elites developed around the lucrative colonial trade.[33]

Another group of reasonably enthusiastic members of the classical club was made up of countries that began the period in a semi-industrial state and wanted to catch up to the European capitalist centers. This included countries on the European periphery – Spain, Russia, Austria-Hungary – as well as some farther afield, such as Japan. While all these countries' governments had some reservations about the way the world economy was ordered – and in particular their relative weakness in that order – they were all eager to join the ranks of the industrialized world.

Japan, as we have already noted, was an especially enthusiastic emulator of the Western model. Horrified by the nearby experience of growing Chinese subjugation to the West, the Meiji leaders regarded rapid economic growth as

---

31 Harley 1980: 218–250.   32 Coatsworth and Williamson 2004: 205–232.
33 E.g., in West Africa. The classical account is Hopkins 1976.

essential to continued Japanese independence. Importing Western technologies, they also funneled state funds into investment; forbidden by treaties to raise tariffs, they subsidized domestic monopolies that taxed domestic consumers to provide yet more capital for investment. Railroads, shipping facilities, steel mills, coal mines all sprang up rapidly. Japan's results also paralleled those of Germany: Between 1870 and 1913, real Japanese total output almost tripled.[34]

Rejectionists

Not all of the developing world was enthusiastic about participation in the classical capitalist world economy. The world's most populous country, China, was particularly reluctant to subordinate its long-standing insularity to the needs of international economic engagement. China's imperial government regarded modern economic growth as a threat to its authority, both because it would create powerful business interests that might challenge the bureaucracy and its landed supporters, and because it would inevitably open the country and its people to foreign influence. The Chinese central government tried continually to limit the impact of foreign powers, and foreign businesses, on Chinese society. While this was often justified on nationalist military grounds, it is hard to see how retarding economic growth did anything but accelerate the country's descent into diplomatic degradation. And even when it came to purely domestic measures to encourage economic growth, the Chinese government lagged seriously – development of the country's railroad system was two or three decades behind that of Japan or India.

India, with rare exceptions, resisted capitalism for the simpler reason that it experienced it in the form of exploitative colonialism. The British East India Company, chartered in 1600 by Elizabeth I and subsequently granted both a monopoly of trade and extensive powers of rule and taxation, had come by 1813 to control, either directly or through vassal princes, all of the subcontinent except the Punjab, Sindh, and Nepal. The Company's exploitation, via unequal terms of trade, heavy land taxes, and a legal regime that privileged the British and their allies, supposedly came to an end in 1858, when Parliament, outraged by the Sepoy Mutiny against the Company's misrule, passed the Government of India Act, nationalized the company, and imposed direct British rule on the whole subcontinent (again, excepting the princely states).[35]

---

34 Maddison Historical GDP Data.   35 See Tomlinson 1993 for an overview.

Direct rule, including the institution of the highly professional Indian Civil Service, was less corrupt and brought significant improvements in infrastructure; yet, as E. J. Hobsbawm put it succinctly, India "was the one part of the British Empire to which *laissez-faire* never applied."[36] Instead, it remained a captive market for British manufactured goods, especially cotton textiles, where the Indian market accounted by the 1880s for over 40 percent of Britain's total exports of such goods.[37] India was also a major revenue source for the Crown via so-called "Home Charges," India's fee for being administered by Britain. Above all, it was a supplier of such raw materials as wheat, cotton, and jute to British industry. A variety of policies discouraged the development of domestic industry. Two results were clear: India's economic growth was much slower (total output increased by only about 60 percent between 1870 and 1914,[38] versus the tripling that Japan experienced in the same period); and India, more than other less developed regions, experienced recurrent large-scale famines, e.g., in 1876–1878, 1896–1897, and 1899–1900.

Capitalism between the wars, 1918–1939

World War I was a turning point in the development of modern capitalism. To be sure, most of the trends that characterized the capitalist world after 1918 were present in 1914; but the war and its aftermath heightened virtually all aspects of the system, including some of the more troubling. Before 1914, the core parties and movements of both Right and Left were oppositional but not radical; there were mainstream movements on both sides that strove to remake capitalism in a different image. But there were few serious supporters of a radical break from the capitalist order, and these few had little influence.

After 1918, all that changed. As the interwar period wore on, it became increasingly evident that the classical capitalist order that had prevailed before World War I could not be restored. Radical movements of both Right and Left developed and grew stronger, in the face of the obvious failures of any semblance of a centrist capitalist consensus. The results were disastrous.

Enthusiasts and their failures

In the aftermath of the wartime breakdown of the world economy, the political and economic leaders of most of the world's principal nations shared an interest in restoring the prewar international economic order. Classical capitalism had worked reasonably well, and there was little reason to abandon

36 Hobsbawm 1968, 148.   37 Ibid, 147.   38 Maddison Historical GDP Data.

it. Elites in virtually every developed society continued to support open trade relations, easy cross-border capital movements, and the monetary stability of the gold standard. And so in the years after World War I, the major powers endeavored to restore the open international order of the pre-1914 era.

And yet every attempt to reconstitute the classical international economy failed. Despite continuing rounds of meetings, conferences, and consultations, the signing of agreements, and the establishment of new international institutions, it seemed impossible to restore international economic stability. The brief return to relative normalcy after 1924 collapsed as soon as recession hit in 1929, with devastating effect.

Many forces led to the failure of interwar capitalism, but there was no real shortage of enthusiasts who favored a restoration of some form of open capitalist system.[39] There were supporters of open trade relations and free capital movements everywhere – and they often dominated the making of economic policy. The same was true of the gold standard. When the United Kingdom returned to gold at the prewar exchange rate in 1925, the overwhelming weight of established opinion around the world saw this as a normal and natural thing to do.[40] However, as Keynes argued at the time, and subsequent analysis has largely confirmed, the commitment to a return to pre-1914 policies ignored the very substantial economic, social, and political changes that the industrial nations had undergone in the interim.[41]

Some of the enthusiasts remained firmly committed to gold-standard orthodoxy, even after the collapse of the 1930s, and indeed blamed the prolonged Depression on the failure to adhere to the gold standard. Others, who came to the fore during the Depression, were strong supporters of open markets at home and abroad but were willing to make compromises to sustain them. The center-right and center-left in Europe – largely Christian Democrats on the one side and Social Democrats on the other – shared the view that capitalism was better than the authoritarian alternatives at either extreme. So too did America's New Dealers and analogous political movements (in or out of government) in Canada, Australia, and New Zealand. And these less orthodox defenders of capitalism tried to navigate a middle ground that maintained or restored some semblance of economic openness, on the one hand, and that permitted a politically desirable degree of government involvement in the economy in times of crisis, on the other.[42] In much of

39 Frieden (2006: chaps 6–10) covers this period in detail.
40 See, e.g. Eichengreen and Temin 2000: 183–207.
41 Eichengreen (1996) is the classic statement of this case.
42 Ruggie (1982) is a well-known statement of the point.

Western Europe and the Anglo-American world, this sort of compromise was reasonably successful – and presaged the post-World War II settlement – but it failed miserably elsewhere.

Rejectionists and their successes

As capitalist orthodoxy failed, and as halting attempts to find another liberal way forward stalled, extreme alternatives came to the fore. From the vantage point of the late 1930s, traditional capitalist forms of economic organization seemed outmoded, and certainly outnumbered. The wave of the future appeared to be semi-autarkic, authoritarian, command-style economies, of the fascist or communist variety.

Fascism

World War I fundamentally re-ordered world capitalism and put its various regions on divergent paths. The United States, Japan, and Latin America, spared from the brunt of the conflict and able to purvey crucial supplies and credit to the belligerent powers, prospered. The United States in fact went from being the world's greatest debtor to its largest creditor. However, the war-ravaged states of Europe were bankrupt, saddled with debts and, in the case of Germany, reparations they could not repay except by destroying their own economies. But these were not their only burdens. Wartime demand had built overcapacity in such armaments-related industries as steel, and had created whole new sectors (synthetic nitrates, for gunpowder and fertilizer) that now lobbied for protection that would preserve their wartime domestic monopolies. Wartime hatreds, sometimes coupled with long-simmering nationalist resentments, amplified the demand for tariff barriers and self-sufficiency. Vast numbers of demobilized troops, many of whom had served at the front for as long as four years, returned home to face unemployment, families they barely knew, societies that had changed fundamentally (or that they had outgrown).[43] A younger generation of males, just short of military age, grew up fatherless – their fathers were either dead or had been perpetually at the front – and obsessed with the propaganda of wartime heroism. At the same time, women moved into non-traditional occupations, particularly in industry, to replace the male conscripts.

Moreover, wartime shortages of labor, regime acquiescence in the growth of trade unions, and the example of the Bolshevik Revolution had radicalized

---

43 It was not only in the US that people asked, in the words of the popular song of the time, "How are you gonna keep them down on the farm, after they've seen Paree?"

the working class, while postwar repudiation of public debts, whether explicit or via inflation, impoverished much of the middle class.

All of this proved an exceedingly toxic brew. First in Italy and Portugal, then in Germany and Austria, still later in Spain and much of Central Europe, the dispossessed middle class and peasantry rallied around movements led by war veterans, staffed in their middle ranks by the men who had been too young to serve, and obsessed with hyper-nationalism, anti-modernism,[44] and (in most cases) anti-Semitism.

The new fascist movements purveyed the machismo and the authoritarian leadership of the wartime front. They were fanatically anti-socialist and anti-communist, seeking national glory and conquest, and (often as a corollary) advocating a rigidly autarkic economic policy. Fascism offered simplistic and seemingly efficient answers to the anxieties of the postwar peasantry and middle class. Replace disorderly democracy with tough and hierarchical leadership, re-establish traditional patriarchy, break trade union power, exclude threatening imports, preserve traditional agriculture, restore national pride, and, if necessary, conquer sources of needed raw materials. These appeals enjoyed a burst of popularity in the immediate postwar chaos (and, indeed, carried fascism to power in Italy in 1922), waned as prosperity and trade partially revived in the mid-1920s, and then again won both popular and elite support as the world economy fell into Depression and autarky after 1929.

While fascist movements were many – they arose even in the United Kingdom and the United States – they achieved the "totalitarian" power they aspired to in only a few countries, most notably Italy, Germany, Spain, and Japan. Only in Germany did fascism originally achieve substantial electoral support, but once in power and able to display significant achievements in foreign and economic policy, fascism often won enthusiastic popular support, particularly of course among its beneficiaries: the peasantry, the traditional middle classes, the military.

Germany is of particular interest because we know, or can reliably infer, much more about who supported fascism – or, more precisely, who did not – at least so long as elections remained free and fair. At both the national and the district level, Catholic and working-class voters remained almost wholly immune to fascist appeals. As economic conditions worsened, many socialist voters shifted to communism, but in very few cases to fascism. German

44 In most cases, this extended to a renunciation of modern (or, as the Nazis called it, "degenerate") art and music. Italy, where the artistic movement of Futurism found a mutual embrace with fascism, was the rare exception.

Catholics, under clerical pressure, remained doggedly loyal to their traditional Center Party. Rather, the Nazi vote rose almost in direct proportion to declines in the traditional middle-class liberal parties, above all the right-liberal German People's Party (DVP) of Stresemann and the left-liberal German Democratic Party (DDP) of Rathenau.[45] Fascism appears also, rather late in the game, to have siphoned off about half of traditional monarchist support (the German National People's Party, or DNVP, which the press lord Hugenberg enthusiastically supported), and to have won some new support from previous non-voters. Those constituencies, however, paled in comparison to the hordes of previous Liberal voters who went over to the Nazis. It was this "treason of the Liberals" that led Seymour Martin Lipset, somewhat misleadingly, to classify fascism as an "extremism of the Center."[46] So far as we can tell, fascism in most other countries drew its strongest support from the traditional Right – albeit, admittedly, mostly from the middle-class supporters of the traditional Right.

Did fascism support, or oppose, capitalism? While it certainly opposed (and expropriated) "Jewish capitalism," fascism readily collaborated with each country's major industrial firms and trusts, especially those crucial to its plans for territorial expansion and aggression: steel, armaments, aircraft, energy, chemicals, and construction. At the same time, the fascist regimes did not hesitate to seize firms that resisted their plans or carried them out too slowly; they frequently founded state-owned firms in sectors they deemed especially important; and, above all, they renounced capitalist orthodoxy about free international trade, ruthlessly pursuing autarky, even when doing so condemned millions to hunger, starvation, or the more "humane" route of extermination.[47] Moreover, in pursuit of their anti-modernist vision of society, the fascists excluded from the industrial workforce, to the extent possible, important segments of the population – especially women and peasants – even when doing so compromised their wartime efficiency.

The fascist efforts at world domination seem, in retrospect, audacious to the point of foolhardiness: taken together, the fascist powers, even at the height of their conquests, had nothing like the industrial capacity of the United States and the British empire or the manpower of the Soviet Union. That said, it

---

45 The DVP traditionally drew its support from big industry and elite professionals; the DDP, from small business and mainstream professionals. As one adage of the time went, academics voted DDP until they received tenure, then shifted to the DVP.

46 Lipset 1960: chap. 5.

47 Tooze (2006) has now become the authoritative study of German economic policy under the Nazis.

must be admitted that they came perilously close to winning, and that such a victory would have altered capitalism to the point of destroying it.

The interwar experience is a striking illustration of how the failures of capitalism, and particularly the wars that disrupt it, can inspire rabid and highly destructive resistance to it (see Harrison, Chapter 11 in this volume). Nonetheless, the complete defeat of fascism by 1945 set the stage for a triumphal revival of world capitalism, this time under US leadership, and indeed for another "Golden Age" of economic growth, social peace, and expansion of the welfare state in most capitalist countries. The darker side of the victory was that capitalism now faced a more effective and determined opponent, Stalinist communism, that dominated almost half of the globe.

Communism

World War I, the Russian Revolution, and the electoral successes of European socialist parties cemented the division in the world socialist movement between socialist (or social democratic) and communist parties. By the 1920s, the former were firmly committed to participation in democratic political processes, and had realized substantial successes. The latter, on the other hand, were dedicated to a twofold mission: defending the Soviet Union, and organizing revolutionary movements in the capitalist world.

The emergence of the Bolshevik wing of the Russian socialist movement as the ruling force in the world's largest country shocked both the capitalist world and the socialist movement. By the early 1920s it was clear to both that the Soviet Union was not a passing aberration. In the advanced industrial countries, the principal implication was that the more extreme elements of the socialist movement were now separate and organized into a disciplined, international force under Soviet direction. This was a new phenomenon: a global radical movement in control both of a large territory and of opposition parties around the world. The emergence of the Soviet Union itself was of somewhat less consequence, as it was economically and militarily weak and played little role in international politics. But the movement organized by the Soviet-led Communist International was a meaningful force in dozens of countries around the world, especially after the Depression magnified the miseries that many identified with capitalism.

Communism was a major political force in only a few industrialized nations, and achieved success in none of them. Foremost among these, however, was Germany, the troubled centerpiece of interwar European politics. In some southern European countries, too, communists inherited some of the support of previously powerful radical socialist and anarchist movements.[48] The strength of the communists helped provoke extreme right-wing reactionary takeovers of government in such countries as Italy and Portugal, and led to a decade of conflict and civil war in Spain, ending in an even more brutal right-wing authoritarianism. And the polarization of German politics certainly contributed to that country's troubled path. Indeed, the rise of right-wing extremism eventually led communists, in Moscow and elsewhere, to move away from insurrection and to search out moderate allies who would cooperate to defend both democracy and the Soviet Union.

In the colonial world, communism had substantially more success. The Soviet Union allied itself with anti-colonial activists almost everywhere. Hostility between the Soviets and other Western powers gave credibility to the communists' anti-imperialist credentials. And the Soviet Union made much of its efforts to create a progressive multinational state out of the tsarist prison-house of nations. For many in the colonial world, the Soviet Union was represented by the new socialist republics in central Asia, among the first regions in the Islamic world to modernize everything from the alphabet to the economy. Soon many of the Soviet Union's supporters were prominent in movements against colonialism, and the Soviet Union itself appeared to be a viable alternative to colonial and semi-colonial patterns of economic and political development.

Communism's appeal remained somewhat limited through the 1930s. The Soviet Union was too weak and isolated, and the communist movements too far from real influence, to have a substantial impact on the political life of the world's major countries.[49] Nonetheless, both the socialist homeland and the communist movement came to represent a clear alternative to traditional capitalism and authoritarian fascism. The true division of the world between Soviet-style socialism and US-style capitalism did not come until after World War II.

Contemporary capitalism

The capitalist world economic order that emerged after World War II was unprecedented on at least two dimensions. First, its broad outlines were

---

48 In Spain, however, the communists often battled the anarchists, to the sole advantage of Franco: Orwell 1952.

49 Nonetheless the Communist Party of Germany (KPD), by refusing all cooperation with the Social Democrats, whom the KPD routinely denounced as "Social Fascists," contributed significantly to bringing the Nazis to power.

negotiated by the major economic powers, largely at meetings held at a resort hotel in Bretton Woods, New Hampshire. The Bretton Woods system represented an organized and planned attempt to reconstitute a functioning, relatively open, international capitalist system. Second, world capitalism was confronted by a full-fledged alternative international economic order, the world socialist camp headed by the Soviet Union. This alternative to capitalism now stretched from central Europe to Korea, included the world's most populous country, and attracted adherents from all over the colonial world.

Enthusiasts: the Bretton Woods compromises

As World War II wound down, the major powers agreed upon the broad contours of the postwar international economy.[50] Although the system as implemented was different from the plans on paper, its general characteristics were roughly as envisioned by Allied policy-makers, led by Harry Dexter White of the United States and John Maynard Keynes of the United Kingdom. The postwar order was a wide-ranging compromise between the classical open economy of the nineteenth and early twentieth centuries and the emerging welfare states of the advanced industrial countries. The arrangements put in place reflected the views of the reformist supporters of capitalism who had come to the political forefront in the 1930s, and who dominated the "centrist consensus" that reigned for decades after the war ended.

The core principles of the Bretton Woods system included general commitments to international economic integration, to multilateral agreements, to international organizations, and to gradualism. The three great Bretton Woods international economic institutions covered trade (the General Agreements on Trade and Tariffs, or GATT, since succeeded by the World Trade Organization or WTO), monetary and financial relations (the International Monetary Fund or IMF), and development (the International Bank for Reconstruction and Development or World Bank).[51]

In trade, the Bretton Woods dedication to trade liberalization was tempered by a recognition that some sectors would be too contentious to allow rapid progress. As a result, barriers to trade in farm goods were explicitly excluded from the liberalization agenda, as was trade in services; developing countries were given wide leeway to pursue protectionist measures. In

---

50 This section relies upon the material in Frieden 2006: chaps 11 and 12, which see for more detailed discussion and references.

51 The GATT was in fact the "interim" solution to the failure of the original treaty establishing the International Trade Organization to meet with the approval of American legislators.

addition, countries were permitted to impose temporary trade barriers in response to "dumping," under circumscribed conditions, and more broadly in times of (ill-defined) economic necessity. This gave governments leeway to use "escape clauses" to avoid or postpone politically difficult measures, which in turn made it easier for them to participate in the liberalizations GATT members were bargaining toward. The reduction in trade barriers was slow but continual, and by the late 1960s trade among the developed countries was roughly as free as it had been in the late nineteenth century – and was growing twice as rapidly as it had then.

The IMF oversaw the construction of a highly modified gold standard, in which the US dollar was pegged to gold and other currencies to the dollar. Again, the compromises involved were substantial. The United States could not alter its exchange rate, but other countries could and did, as permitted in response to (undefined) "fundamental disequilibria." Capital controls were ubiquitous, as Keynes and White had anticipated. The result was a monetary system that provided stability on the foreign exchanges, while allowing governments to pursue their own desired monetary policies and in particular to engage in demand management as they felt necessary. The World Bank, for its part, assisted in rekindling the interest of foreign investors in the developing and newly independent countries. In this atmosphere of monetary and financial stability, world financial markets and foreign investment grew rapidly.

The Bretton Woods system was a great success, as the world economy grew more rapidly than ever before. Yet this very success made the system hard to sustain, based as it was on compromise. The more integrated the international economy became, the harder it got to maintain truly independent national policies. Eventually the contradictions of the system caught up with it. In 1971 the monetary order collapsed, to be replaced by floating exchange rates. More generally, the major compromises of the early postwar period began to come undone as the world economy grew and became ever more tightly integrated. Nonetheless, the enthusiasts for capitalism were firmly in command of the levers of economic policy in developed countries. Things were not so clear in the developing countries, especially among those who had recently freed themselves from their colonial ties.

Skeptics: decolonization and developmentalism

In the less developed countries (LDCs), enthusiasm about classical capitalism faded during the interwar period. To some extent this was due to the sorry record of interwar capitalism itself. From the standpoint of the independent LDCs and of many colonies, the entire period from 1914 until the early 1950s was one in which events in the developed world were largely irrelevant or harmful. The industrialized nations were preoccupied with war and reconstruction for a decade after 1914. After a brief normalization came the Depression of the 1930s, during which international trade and investment collapsed; and then came another decade of preoccupation with war and reconstruction.

For nearly forty years, the developing world had little choice but to rely largely on its own economic resources. Export markets were depressed or cut off by war, while suppliers of manufactured products were often producing for war or reconstruction efforts. Even when foreign manufactures were available, the terms of trade deteriorated so frequently and substantially that they were priced out of local markets. All this created powerful incentives for local entrepreneurs to produce industrial products that had previously been imported, largely from Europe or North America. The result was rapid industrialization in both the independent developing countries, such as the major Latin American nations and Turkey, and in many of the more developed former colonies, such as India.

Decolonization gathered speed from the late 1940s onward, even as world trade and payments revived (see Austin, Chapter 3 in this volume). However, the previous forty years' experience had a powerful impact on the politics of development in both long-independent and newly independent developing countries. There were now significant industrial sectors in many countries, and the enterprises that had grown up more or less immune from foreign competition had little desire to change matters. At the same time, political influence had largely passed from the previously dominant export-oriented groups – farmers, miners, ranchers – to the urbanizing, industrializing segments of local populations. All this was wrapped in a commitment to construct national, and nationalist, identities, often in contradistinction to the now reviled colonial and semi-colonial rulers and their open-economy models.

The result was that virtually every LDC turned away from world trade and toward the protection and subsidization of domestic industry. The new strategy, eventually dubbed "import-substituting industrialization" (ISI), provided support for domestic industry that included import barriers, subsidized credit, tax breaks, and other policies to replace imports with domestic products. Countries whose economies had been strongly oriented toward foreign trade now closed themselves off to many imports, and in some instances, to foreign investment as well. ISI often went together with substantial state involvement in the economy, with government ownership of everything from mines and steel mills to banks and airlines. In many cases, as in India, this inward orientation was associated with Soviet-style planning; in others, it was simply a part of nationalist attempts to develop the local market.

Nationalist economic policies were typically justified with a bitter criticism of the structure of the capitalist international economic order. For some, a new "dependency theory" provided some intellectual justification, arguing that global capitalism was structurally biased against poor countries. Some insisted that the terms of trade of primary producers deteriorated continually, so that following comparative advantage was a dead end. Others complained about a world economy whose rules were written by the rich. Still others saw multinational corporations and international banks as tools of Western imperialism, attempting to continue by economic means the dominance that the colonial powers had been forced to give up. In the early 1970s, the LDCs came together in international forums to demand a New International Economic Order, a reformed international capitalism that served their interests more directly.

Developing-country demands for a reform of international capitalism were largely ignored by the rich nations. Meanwhile, the semi-autarkic policies of the LDCs began to show signs of serious strains. In the early 1980s, a debt crisis hit even the more advanced developing countries and revealed some of the real weaknesses of ISI – in particular, the difficulties countries pursuing ISI faced in stimulating exports in times of difficulty. Over the course of the 1980s, virtually all LDCs jettisoned their previous hostility to exports, to world trade, and to international investment, and came to adopt much more open economic models. The developing-country rejection of Western-style capitalism was largely dead.

Rejectionists: the Soviet bloc

If developing countries were somewhat skeptical about the desirability of global capitalism, the Soviet Union and its allies – including newly communist China – were decidedly hostile. The Soviet-led socialist camp was now much larger – including Eastern and central Europe, China, and increasing numbers of allies in the developing world. And its members denounced capitalism both on principle and in practice. Although the Chinese regime split from the Soviets in the early 1960s, it too embraced a powerful rejection of capitalism.

The Soviet bloc turned to central planning, which attempted to replace the market with strategies devised by the government. Prices were largely divorced from considerations of relative scarcity, and used primarily for accounting purposes. Resources were allocated centrally, or at least by economic ministries and regions that reported to the central government.

Essential consumption goods were significantly underpriced, which made for constant shortages of them. "Luxury" goods, such as electronics and automobiles, were either unavailable or severely rationed. Investment, especially in heavy industry, was favored over expansion of the production of consumer goods. In the Soviet Union and China, in particular, military needs were given priority.

The centrally planned economies achieved rapid growth in the twenty years after World War II, as they drew underutilized resources into production. But Soviet-style planning had many limitations. As was true of the import-substituting economies, the Soviet bloc found that it increasingly needed imports – not only of food, but of technology and precision parts – that it lacked the hard currency to buy. Collectivized agriculture proved massively inefficient, forcing the formerly grain-exporting USSR to expend scarce foreign currency, year after year, on imported cereals. Recurrent campaigns to increase manufactured exports, particularly from the bloc's most advanced economies (e.g., East Germany), brought little success. Only the bloc's raw materials and a few artisanal products found ready purchasers in the West. The absence of incentives gave workers and managers little need to monitor quality, or to innovate either in the production process or with new products. Over time, the industrial plant fell farther and farther behind the technological and quality criteria prevailing in the West, and by the 1980s growth had slowed dramatically. With Western Europe within easy reach of people in the Soviet bloc's central and eastern European nations, it was easy for citizens to see the relative failure of the system.

In 1979, the Chinese and Vietnamese regimes both dropped many of their commitments to planning and endorsed movement toward a market economy, including openness to the rest of the (capitalist) world economy. The Soviet Union and its allies attempted a gradual movement toward economic reform, but after 1989 their governments effectively collapsed, and were replaced by new rulers who largely turned toward global capitalism. Some of the former component parts of the Soviet Union remain reluctant about the capitalist world economy (Belarus and Turkmenistan, for example), as do a few Soviet-style regimes in the developing world (Cuba, North Korea). But by the early 1990s, central planning as an organized, feasible alternative to Western capitalism was of only historical interest.

Globalization: the "Washington Consensus"

While the communist economies stagnated, their capitalist rivals experienced new bursts of innovation, productivity, and growth. The 1971 demise of the

Bretton Woods system signaled also the developed world's abandonment of capital controls, which in any event had come to be widely evaded. Cross-border investment flourished, and the larger and more mobile pool of world capital both encouraged greater risk-taking and, by allowing production to shift easily to other jurisdictions, eroded trade-union power. In the US, deregulation of such ossified sectors as telecommunications, trucking, and airlines stimulated competition, lowered prices, and increased capacity.

At the same time, capitalist economies experienced a spate of innovations that, to contemporary eyes, seemed lifted from science fiction: lasers; fiber optics; microprocessors that packed first thousands, then millions, now billions of transistors onto a single chip;[52] personal computers; the Internet; genetic engineering; and, more mundane but perhaps even more important, containerized shipping.[53] Productivity of labor, land, and intellect all sky-rocketed, aided by the far greater global specialization that cheaper communication and transportation made possible.

As in the nineteenth century, this "second globalization" opened enticing new markets for countries and regions. Chile, Argentina, Mexico, Brazil; Indonesia, Malaysia, China, India; almost all of the former Soviet bloc; and, most recently, rapidly growing parts of Africa – all abandoned earlier paths of import substitution or central planning, now to take their places in the new and ever-changing global division of labor. The combination of opening to trade, specialization, foreign investment, and new technology often produced economic growth that far surpassed what the "first globalization" had achieved. China, the stellar example, saw its GDP per capita grow consistently over thirty years by 8 to 10 percent annually, thus doubling on average every eight years and increasing 10- to 15-fold over the interval from 1980 to 2010 – something like four times the rate of growth achieved by Germany or Japan in the nineteenth century.

And this globalization, like its predecessor, generated and sustained its own orthodoxy: no longer the gold standard, but the "Washington consensus,"[54] a distillation of what the IMF, the World Bank, the US Treasury, and developed-world bankers and officials more generally saw as the magic formula for

---

52 This was the basis of "Moore's Law," according to which the price of computing power is halved roughly every eighteen months.

53 Levinson 2006.

54 The term was coined in 1989 by the economist John Williamson but subsequently developed a somewhat different, and broader, meaning than Williamson had intended. More pejorative terms like "golden straitjacket" and "neoliberalism" are roughly equivalent.

economic growth. The "consensus" prescriptions involved openness to trade and investment, secure property rights, fiscal balance (public debt only to finance productive investment, e.g., in infrastructure), a realistic (perhaps even undervalued) exchange rate, public spending chiefly on investments in human and physical capital, moderate marginal tax rates, privatization of state enterprises, and abolition of stifling regulation (e.g., what Indians called the "permit raj").

As with the gold standard a century earlier, the "consensus" rapidly won the endorsement of elites around the globe. Also as before, some countries adopted mildly heretical versions of the creed: China maintained strict capital controls and massively undervalued its currency; many of the "Asian tigers" protected infant industries; almost everywhere intellectual property remained insecure and agriculture was regarded as a "special case," coddled in some cases (Korea) but exploited in others (Argentina, much of Africa).

Often enough, the new orthodoxy achieved remarkable success, most notably in some of the former ISI or communist states (Brazil, Chile, most of Eastern Europe), while sometimes the "magic" failed or encountered insuperable resistance (Russia under Yeltsin, Mexico in the early years of NAFTA). The failures, like fallen soufflés, invited frenzied inquiries by the leading chefs: Were the cultures incorrigibly anti-capitalist, were the governments or their subjects recalcitrantly authoritarian or corrupt, had there been (as one quip about Russia had it) "too much shock, and too little therapy?" Or even (*sotto voce*) might the "consensus" somehow be mistaken – not, of course, in its main thrust, but in one or another unforeseen detail?

Finally, and again in close parallel with the earlier orthodoxy of the gold standard, the "consensus" spawned zealots: in this case, believers in perfectly efficient markets, perfectly rational actors, deregulation that compromised even prudential supervision of banks or elementary guarantees of public safety. The market could only shower blessings on mankind: there would be rapid and sustained growth, corrupt markets would be shunned in favor of honest ones, earnings exactly equal to marginal product, and – above all – an accurate pricing and allocation of risk, hence a hitherto unknown smoothing of markets. In short, no surprises, no bubbles, no slumps.[55] This time, indeed, was different.[56] Except that it wasn't.

---

55 That theoretical macroeconomists embraced such beliefs need not have occasioned worry. Unfortunately, among the most fervent adherents of this ultraorthodox sect was Federal Reserve Chairman Alan Greenspan. Hence Greenspan took no action to deflate the asset bubble (indeed, dismissed the possibility that one existed).
56 Reinhart and Rogoff 2009.

Globalization and its discontents: the crisis of 2007–

Just as globalization appeared triumphant, disaster struck. In 2007 the US economy ran into trouble. After several years of growth and a particularly striking expansion in real estate and asset markets, housing prices began to fall. This led to distress in an important segment of the country's financial system, the market for mortgage-backed securities and their derivatives. Eventually the weakness spread to the entire American financial system, causing the modern equivalent of a massive system-wide bank run, and it was transmitted immediately to the rest of the world. In early October 2008, it appeared that the whole capitalist world was on the brink of a massive financial collapse, as markets froze in ways not seen since the 1930s and not imagined by the new orthodoxy.[57] As the impact of the financial crisis reverberated throughout the global economy, a Great Recession hit.[58]

In most industrial countries, the Great Recession was longer and deeper than any experienced since the 1930s, and recovery was slower and more halting. Europe, in fact, slid into a second recession in 2012. The problem was a familiar one: dozens of countries had accumulated massive debts, including foreign debts, that could not now be serviced as contracted. This was in fact the consequence of a strange but historically familiar pattern that emerged after 2000, in which one large group of countries came to depend upon foreign financing to fuel their economies, while another large group of countries came to depend on exports as the engine of their economic growth.[59] The first group, those that embarked on a debt-financed consumption boom, included the United States, the United Kingdom, as well as countries on the periphery of the European Union (Ireland, Spain, Portugal, Greece, much of central Europe, the Baltic states). The second group, those whose growth was driven by exports (and lending to the consuming countries), included countries in northern Europe, East Asia, and the oil-producing nations. After several years of increasingly feverish borrowing and asset price growth, the merry-go-round stopped with a crash in fall of 2008.

As recovery lagged and unemployment reached, and stayed at, levels not seen for decades, dissatisfaction spread at this particular turn of events. As the more serious economic problems were in the Organisation for Economic

---

57 Famously, Greenspan confessed later in public testimony that he had regarded the events with "shocked disbelief."
58 For a summary, see Chinn and Frieden 2011.
59 There was an eerie parallel to the 1920s, when the US was the lending nation and postwar Europe (especially Germany) was the borrower.

Co-operation and Development (OECD), most of the political conflict was there as well. On the Right, the long crisis inflamed sentiment against immigration, and in some quarters against components of the welfare state. On the Left, the crisis provoked another round of objections to increasing inequality, and to the alleged inadequacies of government regulation of business and finance. Virtually every government in office in one of the major debtor nations at the time of the crisis was turned out, and in some cases (Greece, Italy) entire political systems were thrown into disarray.

In the aftermath of the crisis, world capitalism once again faces difficult macroeconomic and distributional issues. As there have always been, there will continue to be debates over how best to stimulate and encourage economic recovery and growth. There will continue to be conflict over who should be asked to sacrifice to restore some vigor to economies that have become stagnant. And there will continue to be heated disagreements over the appropriate role of the government in modern capitalist economies.

Conclusion

The downturn that began in 2007, severe as it was, simply reminds us of the two enduring realities of modern capitalism that provoke antagonism to the system: it is prone to recurring crises; and it is associated with a substantial gap between rich and poor. Almost everyone would agree that the benefits of a market economy outweigh the costs of its volatility and of the inequality it can breed. But there is massive disagreement over how significant both the volatility, and the inequality, are, as compared to the creative destruction associated with the capitalist economic order. And there is just as much disagreement over how aggressive governments should be in attempting to address both the cyclical fluctuations, and the income inequality, that characterize capitalism.

These issues have been present since capitalism first arose as an integrated economic order in early modern Europe. Some, whether as utopian socialists or Soviet-style communists, want the state to intervene massively to dampen both fluctuations and inequality – at the expense of capitalism's ability to increase productivity and generate economic expansion. Others, from state capitalists to fascists, also want the state to intervene, albeit not so much to reduce inequality as to squelch dissent and compel investment. Orthodox enthusiasts of modern capitalism express confidence that the system can, and will, largely look after itself. Wherever the truth may lie, there seems little doubt that so long as capitalism is with us, so too will be conflict over whether it should be preserved, and if so, how.

References

Buttle, P. (2011). *England's Rotten Boroughs: A Compendium*. Edinburgh: Amadorn.

Chinn, M. and J. Frieden (2011). *Lost Decades: The Making of America's Debt Crisis and the Long Recovery*. New York: W W Norton

Coatsworth, J. and J. Williamson (2004). "Always Protectionist? Latin American Tariffs from Independence to Great Depression," *Journal of Latin American Studies* 36(2): 205–232.

Eichengreen, B. (1996). *Golden Fetters: The Gold Standard and the Great Depression, 1919–1939*. New York: Oxford University Press.

Eichengreen, B. and P. Temin (2000). "The Gold Standard and the Great Depression," *Contemporary European History* 9(2): 183–207.

Engels, F. (1895). "Introduction to Karl Marx's *The Class Struggles in France 1848–1850*." Available at www.marxists.org/archive/marx/works/1895/03/06.htm (accessed March 12, 2012).

Frieden, J. (2006). *Global Capitalism: Its Fall and Rise in the Twentieth Century*. New York: W W Norton.

Geehr, R. S. (1990). *Karl Lueger: Mayor of Fin de Siècle Vienna*. Detroit, MI: Wayne State University Press.

Harley, C. K. (1980). "Transportation, the World Wheat Trade, and the Kuznets Cycle, 1850–1913," *Explorations in Economic History* 17: 218–250.

Hopkins, A. G. (1976). *Economic History of West Africa*. New York: Columbia University Press.

Hobsbawm, E. J. (1969 [1968]). *Industry and Empire. The Pelican Economic History of Britain*. Vol. III: *From 1750 to the Present Day*. Harmondsworth: Penguin Books.

James, S. and D. Lake (1989). "The Second Face of Hegemony: Britain's Repeal of the Corn Laws and the America Walker Tariff of 1846," *International Organization* 43(1): 18–20.

Levinson, M. (2006). *The Box: How the Shipping Container Made the World Smaller and the World Economy Bigger*. Princeton University Press.

Levy, R. S. (1975). *The Downfall of the Anti-Semitic Political Parties in Imperial Germany*. New Haven, CT: Yale University Press.

Lipset, S. M. (1960). *Political Man: The Social Bases of Politics*. Garden City, NY: Doubleday and Co.

Maddison Historical GDP Data. World Economics. Available at www.worldeconomics. com/Data/MadisonHistoricalGDP/Madison%20Historical%20GDP%20Data.efp.

Marsh, P. T. (1999). *Bargaining on Europe: Britain and the First Common Market, 1860–1892*. New Haven, CT: Yale University Press.

Nolte, E. (1963). *Der Fascismus in seiner Epoche*. (Translated from the German: L. Vennewitz (transl.) (1965). *Three Faces of Fascism*. New York: Holt, Rinehart and Winston.)

Norda, G. (2009). *Die Deutschsoziale Partei (DSP): Entstehung, Aufstieg und Niedergang einer antisemitischen Partei im Deutschen Kaiserreich*. Norderstedt: GRIM Verlag.

Nye, J. (2007). *War, Wine, and Taxes: The Political Economy of Anglo-French Trade, 1689–1900*. Princeton University Press.

O'Rourke, K. H. and J. G. Williamson (1999). *Globalization and History: The Evolution of a Nineteenth-Century Atlantic Economy*. Cambridge, MA: The MIT Press.

Orwell, G. (1980 [1952]). *Homage to Catalonia*. Orlando, FL: Harcourt.

Reinhart, C. and K. Rogoff (2009). *This Time is Different: Eight Centuries of Financial Folly.* Princeton University Press.

Ruggie, J. G. (1982). "International Regimes, Transactions, and Change: Embedded Liberalism in the Postwar Economic Order," *International Organization* 36(2): 379–415.

Sassoon, D. (1996). *One Hundred Years of Socialism: The West European Left in the Twentieth Century.* New York: Tauris Publishers.

Smith, A. (1776). *The Wealth of Nations.*

Stern, F. (1977). *Gold and Iron: Bismarck, Blerichröder, and the Building of the German Empire.* New York: Alfred A. Knopf.

Tomlinson, B. R. (1993). *The Economy of Modern India, 1860–1970.* New York: Cambridge University Press.

Tooze, A. (2006). *The Wages of Destruction: The Making and Breaking of the Nazi Economy.* London: Allen Lane.

United Nations (1961). *Statistical Yearbook*, 13th issue, 41.

Woodward, L. (1962). *The Age of Reform: 1815–1870*, 2nd edn. Oxford: Clarendon Press.

13

Labor movements

MICHAEL HUBERMAN

In 1900, union density of the industrial and industrializing world, consisting of the future members of the Organisation for Economic Co-operation and Development (OECD), was approximately 5 percent. By 2000, global union density stood around 23 percent.[1] While it would be rash to conclude that the twentieth century belonged to labor, these gains were not insignificant. To be sure, some of the achievements attributed to the labor movement, like the declines in hours of work, upgrades in employment conditions, and the elimination of child labor, may simply have been the fruit of economic growth. But the labor movement has had a part in improvements, if only by maintaining workers' share of the gains in productivity, always a constant challenge and ever more so since the 1980s. There was also a geographic dimension to the movement's accomplishments. As Table 13.1 registers, the spread of the labor movement beyond the 'old' industrial core to the far reaches of Africa, Asia, and South America, has had implications for worker well-being everywhere.

These figures certainly underestimate the reach of the labor movement, which, as described in this chapter, consists of a sizeable informal component of unorganized labor, social groups, reformers, and political representatives, operating at the national and international levels, like the International Labor Organization and its predecessors. Eclectic in their goals, the common denominator of these groups was their initial opposition to capitalism; indeed it was labor that first defined its adversary. But despite the truism that capital hires labor, workers came to partake in the system's benefits, although never to the extent that the pioneers of the labor movement prophesied. Indeed, economic growth in the twentieth-century OECD was strongest when the labor movement was also at its peak. As a result, over the last 100 years or so,

---

1 The 1900 and 2000 figures are from Friedman (2008) and Visser (2003), who also give country estimates.

Table 13.1. *World and regional union density rates*

	Union density in 2000	
Region (no. of countries)	Average	Population weighted
EU15	37.4	23.3
Eastern Europe and ex-USSR (13)	46.1	56.4
Oceania and North America (4)	21.1	14.1
South and southeast Asia (14)	15.8	20.5
Middle East (9)	25.6	18.6
Africa (25)	13.7	13.5
Latin America (21)	17.1	20.9
World	24.1	21.7

Source: Visser 2003: 376–399.

opposition has given way to a non-enthusiast's acceptance, a position which may have contributed to the movement's remarkable resilience. Labor movements have outlasted different political, economic, and social epochs, beginning with the liberal order of the late nineteenth century, extending into the interwar era, the Cold War, the Washington Consensus, and beyond. The objective of this chapter is to relate this history as the outcome of domestic and external factors, the relative importance of which has shifted over space and time. My contention is that these forces were both overlapping and interconnected, a seemingly banal observation but one that has been curiously overlooked.

Almost exclusively, the dominant narrative in the history of labor movements has given prominence to domestic concerns. The main contours of this history are familiar. Inspired by the French Revolution, in the century after Waterloo labor organized, formally and informally, to demand better working conditions, to put an end to long hours of work and child labor, and to obtain a share of the gains of industrialization. Following Engels, whose views were later propagated by Eric Hobsbawm (1988), this narrative is written as a chapter in national history, in which the rise of the nation-state is perceived to be the dominant "force of history" over the last two centuries.

Extending this line of argument, the typical comparative study juxtaposes case histories of labor movements based on domestic conditions and institutions, for instance, the share of the labor force in non-agricultural activities, the percentage of workers voting, ethnic fragmentation, political and legal structures, and the general growth in income.[2] These histories give rise to well-known typologies which are almost tautological in reasoning. The labor movement first took hold in Western Europe and its rich offshoots because of its initial conditions which, in turn, were its major realizations. There are exceptions, like the United States, where the development of the labor movement was embedded in a wider ideology of individualism and opportunity. As for poor regions in southern and eastern Europe, in the colonial world, and elsewhere in the periphery, the labor movement was delayed because structural change was slow. But here too the basic pattern was repeated. The labor movement, originating in the manufacturing sector, was an active participant in bringing democracy and often national independence to these regions, benefitting as well from these same social and political currents.

The typical labor history has not ignored completely external influences like the spread of ideas.[3] More commonly, international competition is perceived to have endangered labor power because of commercial rivals' cheap labor costs and unobstructed access to capital. Indeed, the modern labor movement is often cast as a casualty of globalization forces (Tilly 1995).[4] The trouble is that the relation between domestic and external forces was not straightforward. More than a conduit of common shocks, globalization forces altered in a fundamental manner the nature, growth, and direction of labor movements. Globalization was as much a handmaiden to the labor movement as it was a harbinger of its decline.

The divergence of Old and New World industrial relations before 1914 is the centerpiece of my claim that domestic and external forces were entangled. The Old World's technological head start and relative abundance of labor and capital gave rise to a thriving manufacturing sector – the stronghold of the labor movement. By the eve of the war, European labor's opposition to capitalism melded with acceptance. The expansion of foreign markets was a windfall to labor, which came to use its support of trade as a lever to obtain better wage and employment conditions. Trade and the labor movement were thus joined in a virtuous circle. These salutary effects were weaker, and sometimes absent, in much of the New World before 1914 because of its

---

2 See Bain and Elsheikh (1976) for empirical studies of this type.
3 For the transnational turn in labor history, see Van der Linden (2003).
4 Typical is Zolberg (1995: 28): in "post-industrial society the workers to whose struggles we owe the 'rights of labor' are rapidly disappearing and today constitute a residual endangered species."

comparative advantage in resources. Of course, organized labor achieved a toehold in countries seeking to shelter import-competing sectors, but this was an outcome of globalization too, or at least the backlash to it. As the periphery was integrated into the global economy, the exploitation of resources intensified at the expense of indigenous manufacturing, casting a pall on the rise of organized labor. In certain countries, the high concentration of resource ownership exacerbated income inequality. Labor in poorer regions was effectively shut out by international trade forces and by domestic political exclusion.

Comparative advantages were never static. Over the course of the mid to late twentieth century, technology spread outward from the industrial core. The increase in manufacturing employment in the periphery, along the lines of the Krugman–Venables (1995) model of international trade, altered bargaining powers within countries and across regions. For the old core, the displacement of manufacturing resulted in declining union membership (see Table 13.1), forcing established labor movements to seek other channels to defend wages, employment conditions, and social entitlements. As for emerging economies, the labor movement's realizations were conditional on local developments, like the strength of domestic forces behind the demand for wider political representation, but the rise in democracy itself was not independent of globalization forces or their absence (López-Córdova and Meissner 2008). Herein lies the rub. For global capitalism, a weak labor movement everywhere is not a guarantee of its own success. Increasing inequality may push labor's lukewarm acceptance into outright opposition, with unforeseen consequences for the entire system.

I take as my starting point Kevin H. O'Rourke and Jeffrey G. Williamson's chronology of the spread of global capitalism in the introductory chapter to this volume (Chapter 1), and José Luis Cardoso's, and Jeffry Frieden and Ronald Rogowski's description of the intellectual origins of the disparate groups that eventually coalesced into the labor movement (Chapter 18 in Volume 1 and Chapter 12 in this volume, respectively). While I define this movement broadly to encompass formal organizations and informal pressure groups at the national and international levels, I will give attention to organized labor and labor parties, since this part of the movement is more easily recognizable and most often correlated with its other components. The first wave of globalization left an indelible mark on industrial relations for more than a century, and I devote special consideration to the early period before turning to the interwar years and the recent wave of globalization.

Labor movements in the Old World during the first wave of globalization

In the modern age of capitalism, the factory was the crucible in which the labor movement took form. Labor contested the long hours of work, the unhealthy conditions of the mills, the poor and often uncertain remuneration, and the willingness of employers to dismiss and replace workers at their whim. In the heyday and heartland of industrialization, Great Britain, workers' bargaining power was weak, the legal status of unions was undecided, and the distribution of income favored capitalists (Allen 2009). Initially, informal worker organizations opposed capitalism in its entirety, harking back to a moral economy in which they were rewarded by a fair wage for a fair day's work. But in the half-century from the demise of Chartism (1848) to the foundation of the Labour Party (1900), subsequent generations of British labor, while still condemning capitalism and without forsaking alternative models of social and economic organization, were prepared to use collective bargaining and the ballot box to achieve their objectives. The acknowledgment of the fundamental structures of capitalism was implicit. A parallel transition took place on the continent. Militancy, however, was never renounced outright, manifesting itself in punctuated outbursts, like strike waves, or in confrontations, such as the Paris Commune of 1871. These episodes gave the broader labor movement credibility, compelling elites to avoid outright social upheaval by recognizing formal labor movements and acknowledging the place of their representatives in the political sphere (Acemoglu and Robinson 2012).

The conventional history of the labor movement regards big and rich countries, France, Germany, and the United Kingdom, as role models in achieving social reforms. The extension of the vote was both a cause and consequence of labor's escalating voice. In the United Kingdom, the Trades Union Congress spearheaded demands for electoral reform, while in Germany, the electoral success of the socialist party propelled the climb in union membership (Crouch 1993). Workplace reforms were at the top of the agenda. In the decade before 1914, the decline in hours of work across Europe was unmistakable (Huberman and Minns 2007), and in many industrializing countries, as Peter Lindert documents more fully in Chapter 14 in this volume, workers had access to some early forms of social insurance.[5]

---

5 Mares (2003) presents case studies of the relation between the labor movement and the welfare state in Europe.

A competing narrative is that the long-run decline in hours beginning in 1870 or so was the product of the rise in income and fall in the relative cost of leisure (Vandenbroucke 2009). But despite a downward trend almost everywhere, distinctive national and regional patterns of worktime emerged even before 1914. Because hours of work, like labor standards, were a public good to which all workers in the mill or plant adhered, some form of collective-decision-making was mandated (Wright 1987). This process varied across countries even at the same level of development, depending on, among other factors, the gender and ethnic composition, and skill levels of labor forces, technologies in place, and bargaining strengths. To be sure, some groups were inevitably marginalized. For instance, in its early history, organized labor was comprised almost entirely of male skilled workers whose influence was reflected in the nature of the demands to lessen the "evils" of the factory system.[6] The elimination of night work for women would effectively reduce competition in the labor market, thereby raising wages of men, without necessarily improving the social and economic position of women.[7] Nonetheless, the social benefits of reform may have offset these effects. Anticipating the claims of Richard Freeman and James Medoff (1984), organized labor would have given more effort as the menace of dismissal abated. Moreover, the rise in the minimum age of labor, and the subsequent increase in years of schooling, had long-term economic and social benefits.

Even at this juncture, globalization was part of the story. Workers confronting global competition had specific concerns. International integration had made the demand for labor more responsive to changes in its price, with the result that shocks in demand generated much greater fluctuations in both earnings and hours worked than had appeared in the closed economy prevailing in the first half of the nineteenth century (Rodrik 2011). The gold-standard regime exacerbated the effects of trade shocks on wages, because as prices contracted, the burden of adjustment fell on labor (Frieden 2006). This form of structural adjustment was a prelude to the pressures organized labor in developing economies confronted in the decades after 1980. I return to this parallel below.

The demands of labor in tradable sectors to stabilize income and employment overlapped with the long-standing grievances of the domestic reform movement. Labor regulation was a cornerstone of their platforms. Legislation

---

6 Roediger and Foner (1989: vii) report "great unanimity" on demands for a shorter work day.
7 On female workers and organized labor in Britain, see Rose 1992.

restricting labor supply compressed wage distributions, redistributing income as a result, and provided some guarantee against uncertainty and volatility of the world trading order.[8] Labor movements in small countries had heightened concerns because their economies traded more than larger ones and they demanded more direct measures like social entitlements to redress volatility and uncertainty. In Denmark, a small and open economy, labor petitioned for and received social insurance to subsidize relocation from contracting to expanding sectors. Denmark, it should be added, resisted the protectionist backlash of the period, a good example of how the labor movement could draw benefits from increased trade exposure.

A binding constraint on the labor movement was its dependence on political allies to get reform through. The upside was that coalition building secured labor's place in the public sphere. In the framework of Daron Acemoglu and James Robinson (2012), organized labor in Western Europe and its New World offshoots came to be embedded in the pluralistic and inclusive political institutions integral to these countries' economic success. The nature of the early coalitions revealed the interdependence of domestic and external forces. For example, labor-abundant Belgium had in theory good reason to support free trade, and ever more so after the expansion of the rail network in the 1880s, when labor became mobile within its borders.[9] After the extension of the vote in the early 1890s, the Belgian Workers' Party formed a coalition with liberal parties, whose own constituents consisted of manufacturers and commercial interests. In Parliament, labor representatives exchanged their support of lower tariffs for increased labor regulation and improved social entitlements. Concretely, labor took its share of the benefits of globalization in reduced hours and better work environments. The point is that domestic factors were not sufficient to assure demands for social reform, since labor could not by itself dictate the political agenda. Globalization had made possible new coalitions that tilted the balance of political forces toward reform. The outcome was an early variant of The Grand Bargain between European labor, capital, and the state that cohered after World War II.

The trajectories of labor movements in the Old World were certainly not uniform. In the European periphery, informal and formal organizations were constrained because of the preponderant share of workers in agriculture and the negligible number of voters. But one size did not fit all. The Catalan textile

---

8 In Europe, legislation, if only because it was imposed by commercial rivals on their trading partners, affected labor market outcomes. This was not the case in the New World. See below.

9 On the Belgian labor movement and trade, see Huberman 2012.

industry was a hotbed of socialism and anarchism. The labor movement succeeded in pressing for reform, and, by 1914, Spanish hours of work corresponded to those found elsewhere on the continent (Huberman and Minns 2007). In backward economies like Russia, foreign investors, worried about the political and social environment, aligned with the embryonic labor movement to demand improved factory conditions (Gorshkov 2009). The case of small, developing European countries, and even larger ones like Italy, was still different. In certain situations, richer trading partners, concerned about competitors' cheap labor, compelled rivals to adopt factory and employment legislation. Because these episodes were a prelude to recent attempts at the WTO and the International Labor Organization (ILO) to establish minimum labor standards across countries, the level playing field, I describe them more fully below.

Labor movements in settler economies and the colonies

The transplanted and indigenous labor movements in areas of new settlement had occasion to draw on the ideas, experiences, and legislation of the Old World, but labor in the two regions faced different political and economic contexts, and, by 1914, their movements' objectives had diverged. Some have maintained that, despite a larger franchise in settler economies, the federal structures of the New World – labor law was the responsibility of sub-national units, provinces, or states – divided and weakened the nascent reform movement. But the success of Australian labor dispels this argument.[10] In many regards, labor law in the New World was ahead of Europe's. The Mexican constitution of 1857 proclaimed the rights of free labor, whereas in the United Kingdom, until 1875, under the Master and Servant Act workers faced penal sanctions if they abandoned their employment (Suarez-Potts 2012: 38).[11] Another claim is that New World states sided more often with employers and were more disposed to use force to suppress strikes than was the case in the Old World.(Friedman 1998). But this holds mainly for the United States. Following the British model, Canada, after a period of labor militancy, established arbitration boards to bring the parties together and settle disputes (Craven 1980). More fundamentally, at least for the United States and parts of Canada, the embarrassment of opportunities across vast continents, accessible

10 For a review of the effects of federalism on labor movements, see Archer 2007).
11 On the legal status of free labor, see Steinfeld 1991.

because of the high degree of labor mobility, fit well with the seemingly ingrained disposition toward individual responses to the detriment of collectivist action.

International trade caused the divergence of labor's goals and achievements in Old and New Worlds in other ways. In the European core, trade in specialized items was important.[12] If states failed to imitate the legislation of commercial partners, they would have exposed themselves to embargoes on exports and terms of trade shocks. In this fashion, cross-class and cross-border coalitions brought pressure on recalcitrant governments to take seriously demands for better working conditions. The French–Swiss trade war in the early 1890s provides an example of external pressure on domestic agendas. Switzerland was initially reluctant to adopt limits on hours, fearing the loss of export markets if it introduced legislation ahead of major partners. Germany and France did introduce limits on women's work in 1891 and 1892. During the subsequent trade war with France, the Swiss were unable to find alternative outlets for their exports of high-end cotton textiles and silks, clocks, and cheese. In 1894, Switzerland heeded to the demands of French producers, which joined those of the domestic reform movement, and agreed to adopt restrictions on night work and an eleven-hour working day for women.

In the New World, domestic concerns trumped external pressures. Relatively abundant in land, regions of recent settlement mainly exported foods and raw materials whose prices were fixed in world markets. Consequently, governments were not compelled to adopt laws of major partners because threats of market loss were not credible. For instance, Canada's wheat exports did not contract after Germany launched a trade war between 1903 and 1910 to protest Ottawa's preferential agreement with London; in fact, it was British manufacturers and workers that feared collateral damage. This line of argument does not apply perfectly to the United States, which began exporting manufacturing items before 1914, but resources were still a large share of its exports. Anyway, many of its manufacturing exports were of standardized goods, and exporters could shift outlets without severe loss. Much of the labor legislation that was adopted in the United States simply codified existing practice or was the outcome of the general rise in prosperity (Fishback 1998). The end result was a growing divide between social Europe and liberal America.

International migration deepened the wedge between Old and New World social movements. In the Atlantic region, the dependence on slave and

---

12 The next two paragraphs are based on Huberman and Meissner 2010.

contract labor had receded, being replaced by an epoch of unrestricted and non-coerced mass migration. Unskilled immigration from the Old World, which intensified late in the century, exerted a downward force on wages at the lower end of the distribution. Often exploited as strikebreakers, immigrant workers challenged labor's ability to mobilize (Rosenbloom 2002). While skilled New World laborers were to a large extent insulated from these pressures, their organizations were not. Increasingly, heterogeneous groups of workers had difficulty in negotiating collective or public goods.

The Canadian experience is instructive regarding the trade-offs the labor movement made between demands for better working conditions and calls for tighter immigration controls (Goutor 2007). Because labor was relatively scarce, Canadian workers in the manufacturing sector had good reason to support the National Policy of 1879 that remained the framework of Canadian tariff structure into the 1930s. Import substitution promoted the growth of the union movement comprising almost exclusively of skilled male workers. Initially, the state accommodated labor, passing new legislation guaranteeing trade unions' rights. But, as in Belgium, Canadian workers were dependent on a cross-class alliance to satisfy demands for improved labor legislation. Labor's alliance with manufacturers was rapidly undone. Regulation was delayed since it was uncertain whether or not legislation was a federal or provincial jurisdiction (Drummond 1987: 234). More substantially, capital was not prepared to go beyond basic standards limiting children's and women's work, claiming that, in the absence of supplementary tariff changes, they could not pass on to consumers the costs of regulation. Organized labor's attempts to build bridges with rural and export interests were equally unrewarding. Exceptionally for the New World, Australian labor succeeded in forming a coalition with rural interests, but Canadian farmers were less enthusiastic, expressing concern that an earlier round of regulation of the railway trades had increased transport costs; faced by world markets, labor regulation would entail higher input prices in the export sector.[13]

By 1900, the demand for labor regulation took a back seat to calls for immigration quotas. Contrary to its intended effect, tariff protection seems to have tied the fate of workers closer to international economic forces, since foreign workers were attracted by the earnings and employment security Canada's commercial policy guaranteed. Canadian labor would expend much of its political energies in the decade before 1914 demanding an end to the open door policy. Unlike regulation, immigration was a federal jurisdiction, but

13 For a comparison of Australia and the US, see Archer 2007.

coalition building was no easier at this level and labor found few allies in industry and agriculture. In the early 1900s, the Trades and Labour Congress had threatened to withdraw its endorsement of the tariff, deeming it as important to get its voice heard on immigration.

> While the government's assistance to immigration compels the laborer to sell his labor at the lowest price in competition with the whole world, the employers are protected from foreign competition by a tariff often exceeding 50 percent. (cited in Craven 1980: 277)

Canadian manufacturers rejected the link between immigration and the tariff. Rural interests, dependent on seasonal supplies of labor, had no reason to support quotas either. New restrictions on arrivals were imposed in 1910, but like earlier laws they were limited in application and scope, as the state held to its open door policy. Broad-based support for quotas had to wait until the 1920s and emerged mainly in response to US policy (Hatton and Williamson 2005: 177). Any political capital expended on limits on foreign workers translated into fewer resources to demand better labor regulations and social entitlements. Hours of work in Canada in 1914 were pretty much the same as in 1880.

The focal point of European labor lay elsewhere, since intracontinental migration did not seem to have had the same effects on labor market outcomes. Inflows of unskilled labor mapped onto existing factor supplies, leaving the region's comparative advantage in labor-intensive items unaltered. To be sure, certain labor movements in Europe's industrial core were hostile to foreign workers, but this was not at the expense of increased demands for labor regulation and social entitlements. French silk workers rioted in response to the hiring of Italians to replace them, but, by the turn of the century, the labor movement turned its attention to extending social benefits to immigrants. In Britain, while some labor groups stood behind the Aliens Act of 1905 (Hunt 1985: 186), Keir Hardie insisted that immigration did not cause unemployment. Under his authority, the British Labour Party devoted its energies to securing general improvements in working conditions. European states were not impartial to labor's position on immigration, because to preserve their own credibility, they had an incentive to protect the social contract that had been agreed on, and, as I describe below, even to extend it beyond their borders.

Inevitably, the Canadian labor movement resorted to age-old industrial relations' practices of protecting and improving workers' livelihoods. Tellingly, in the pre-1914 period, militancy as measured by the number of strikes was greater in Canada than in continental Europe, the wave of agitation causing a spurt in union membership which tripled from 1902 to 1914 (Huberman and Young 1999). While adversarial relations were integral to continental industrial relations, the nature of disputes diverged between Europe and its offshoots. Conflicts in Canada, as in the United States, concerned wage issues because strikers had a greater probability of success of winning them (Card and Olson 1995); European disputes centered on working conditions. Organizational forms also differed. An irony of the period is that international unions were almost exclusive to North America. Skilled workers across the forty-ninth parallel banded together to match employers' bargaining power, which drew its strength from the threat of capital flight. A union card gave workers comparable mobility. These continental unions were a mainstay of the labor movement for over a century. While capital was equally mobile across European frontiers, international unions were practically unknown on the continent, and those that were established before 1914 did not survive the renewal of nationalism in the interwar years.

Outside the European core and its offshoots, labor made few gains. In Japan, despite the rapid growth of the textile industry, paternalism was the overarching ideology of industrial relations (Hunter and Macnaughtan 2010). In south Asia, the migration of Indians and Chinese was of the same order of magnitude as between Europe and the Americas (McKeown 2004). These groups were effectively banned from the rich Western offshoots in North America and Australia, and so they congregated instead in the commodity-exporting economies in south Asia, Africa, and the Caribbean. With the end of slavery, contract labor or assisted migration comprised a good part of these population flows. Contract labor was effectively immobile, a specific factor seemingly defenseless against price and wage shocks.[14] As for the periphery's indigenous manufacturing sectors, labor lost ground since trade forces had compelled economies to specialize ever more in resource extraction. As deindustrialization gained momentum, any clues of a labor or reform movement in resource economies became progressively difficult to detect. At this juncture, it could be said, the arrested development of the labor movement in the periphery was the flipside of its precocious budding in the core.

There were signs of a reversal before 1914, as export prices of commodities moved downward and manufacturing imports became more expensive. In Brazil, local businesses in urban centers and importing foreign technology

---

14 As a result, swings in wages were much larger in regions of contract labor than in free labor economies (Hatton and Williamson 2005).

established a modern cotton textile industry, which presaged the shifting of comparative advantage of the later twentieth century. Workers began to organize. Again immigration had offsetting effects. New arrivals in the cities displaced the indigenous and former slave populations as the mainstay of the workforce. While many union activists may have had first-hand experience in Old World ideals of social reform, they encountered obstacles in delivering their message.

> Italian labor leaders failed to recognize the special economic plight of the recently arrived Portuguese ... Well into the early twentieth century organizations like the bricklayers' unions in São Paulo had difficulty in keeping non-Italians in the union because the Italian language was used in union assemblies and propaganda. (Maram 1977: 258–259)

These fissures overlapped with ideological conflicts among anarchists, socialists, and liberal reformers (Wolfe 1993). The labor movement would gain strength in the interwar years under different economic and political conditions.

In the absence of voting rights and support of liberals and reformers, and cut off from external pressures of trading partners to adopt better labor standards, workers in the periphery were dependent on extraordinary circumstances to improve their well-being. Mexican workers, seizing the opportunities created by the revolution, successfully challenged workplace authority. Employment conditions in Mexican textile mills improved dramatically after 1910. In line with European norms, working hours contracted from fourteen to eight hours and accident compensation was introduced (Bortz 2000). The revolution abolished debt peonage (Suarez-Potts 2012). These outcomes were exceptional in the periphery.

Empire left a lasting mark on the labor movement and industrial relations. Given the large proportion of workers in agriculture and informal activities, an independent India circa 1900 would have been hard pressed to have adopted any recognizable labor legislation. In colonial India, the first pieces of colonial legislation were in fact directed against workers, penalizing them if they walked out of a job during the period of contract (Hensman 2011: 95–99). The operation of these laws in the plantations was especially brutal. Beginning in the 1880s, legislation began to restrict the unlimited power of employers. The drive behind the first factory acts, and the establishment of the indigenous labor movement, were supported and financed by Lancashire millowners keen to protect their international competitiveness. But there still remained a large gap between Indian and British practices. The act of 1881 prohibited the employment of children under seven years of age – it was eleven years in the United Kingdom – and that of 1891 limited the hours of work of women to eleven per day – it was about nine in the UK (Huberman 2012). Most importantly, large numbers of workers were not covered by the factory acts, a legacy of colonialism which shaped legislation after independence.

The international labor movement in the age of globalization

Even as globalization channeled the demands of labor in Old and New Worlds alike, international economic integration framed its achievements. From the outset, social reformers recognized that global pressures had rendered national labor laws on limits to the workday or child labor toothless. In the 1830s, Robert Owen, a pioneer of the modern British labor movement, proposed the establishment of international guidelines to harmonize working conditions; others on the continent echoed the call, the movement gathering momentum beginning in the 1870s. In many respects, the goals and outcomes of the international movement in the first wave of globalization paralleled those of the second wave of the late twentieth century.

As in 2000, the early reformers had disparate goals, labor organizations, social activists, and European states holding separate conferences. There are a number of possible readings of the meetings organized by labor. One interpretation is that they were driven by the ideal of an international socialist brotherhood described by Frieden and Rogowski in Chapter 12 in this volume; another is that labor acted as spokesperson for various humanitarian groups determined to eliminate child labor and reduce hours of work of women and that international conferences were an occasion to network on how to achieve goals. But a third reading is that workers, conflating national and class interests, recognized that declining transport costs had fundamentally altered the international trading order, and they used international meetings to defend their industry's competitive advantages, which, they perceived, guaranteed those labor regulations and standards, or social contract they had contributed to making.

The last interpretation seems to have been closer to the mark. Labor-sponsored conferences made little headway in harmonizing national standards. Initially, delegates met under the auspices of the Workers' International, but conflicts between adherents of socialist revolution and international liberalism splintered the movement, with the result that labor's representatives began to meet along sectoral or industrial lines after 1890 or so (Donald 2001). Although these groups continued to exchange sermons on the benefits of international brotherhood, the imagined community they proposed did not mask underlying divisions. In a discourse that was remarkably similar to their employers', labor was far more motivated to extract real advantages from their competitors and, ultimately, defend the economic structure in place. In the conflict between ideals and interests, the latter seem to have had the upper hand.

At the industry level, labor convened informally and formally. In 1900, British cotton-textile unions invited representatives of Belgian, French, and German unions to tour Lancashire. In earlier times, textile unions had been in the forefront of demands for universal suffrage and factory regulation, although they began to depend more on collective bargaining than legislation to achieve their goals. By the turn of the century, British hours of work were 20 percent below continental levels, putting the Lancashire industry – it was believed – at a competitive disadvantage since improvements in cotton-spinning technology had increased substitutability between home and foreign-produced goods. The objective was to demonstrate to Europeans the superior organization of Lancashire's factories and its social and moral benefits. If all went according to plan, European workers would put pressure on their bosses and their governments to reduce working hours. The British plan backfired. Upon visiting Lancashire, foreign unions discovered a higher proportion of children at work than in Europe. They would agree to press for a shorter workday if the British unions would push for greater restrictions on youth employment. Fearful of constraining their ever-diminishing overseas markets, British (male) workers balked. Sidney and Beatrice Webb (1902: 868) summarized labor's frustration.

> If, indeed, we could arrive at an International Minimum of education and sanitation, leisure and wages, below which no country would permit any section of its manual workers to be employed in any trade whatsoever, industrial parasitism would be a thing of the past. But internationalism of this sort – a Zollverein based on a Universal Factory Act and Fair Wage clause – is obviously utopian.

In the wake of trade unionists' failure to level the playing field, social activists took control of the reform program. After Brazil abolished the slave trade in 1888, the protection of industrial workers became the calling card of reformers worldwide. By the 1890s, a broad-based movement had taken shape with the goal of harmonizing labor standards internationally. Many of the movement's leaders were Belgians and Swiss, whose small open economies had much to gain from international guidelines. Early meetings in 1897 in Brussels and

Zurich brought together an amalgam of labor representatives, socialists, Catholics, and liberal reformers, but it was quickly evident that labor distrusted the orientation and goals of the movement. At the founding of the International Association for Labor Legislation (IALL) in Paris in 1900, social reformers set the agenda. After the war, the ILO was to borrow heavily from the IALL model.

The IALL was principally an epistemic community whose primary objective was evidence-based policy and advocacy (Van Daele 2005). The IALL depended on national branches to collect standardized information on workplace conditions, which it disseminated across its network. Reformers did not shy from stigmatizing their own country's inferior labor laws and showcasing achievements elsewhere. European interests dominated proceedings. Japan sent delegates but had a marginal role in deliberations, whereas Carroll Wright, the founder of the US Bureau of Labor, was an occasional New World observer. Although the movement had its precedents, the novelty of the IALL was that it placed labor regulation in the context of globalization. Reformers contended that while trade may have increased volatility and risks of employment, labor regulation, properly designed, would secure workers the benefits of economic integration. IALL meetings did not contest globalization; delegates bashed protectionism instead, many of its leading spokespersons embracing free trade.

The IALL meetings were not always harmonious. The concept of "core standards," integral to twenty-first-century debates on international labor codes, was not formally developed. There was bickering over the competitive advantages and disadvantages of projected labor standards and, like the meetings of trade unions, delegates fell back on the rights of countries to legislate as they saw fit. From the outset, activists from Italy and Norway spoke against recommendations to raise the legal age of child labor, arguing, as poor countries do today, that international standards protected market share of rich countries. With regard to night work of women, delegates at the 1905 Berne Conference recommended twelve hours of continuous night rest for women, but Belgium (an original sponsor of the motion) demanded ten hours of rest to protect its export interests. A compromise was reached at eleven hours, which Belgium accepted only after it received the guarantee that the introduction of the new law was to be delayed for four years. Discussions at Berne also concerned occupational safety, an accord being reached on the content of phosphorus in matches. Most countries did adopt the safety measure, but the United States refused, claiming that Japan, its chief competitor, had opted out of the agreement (Huberman 2012).

The lofty goal of harmonizing legislation was resisted. The powers of the IALL, like its successor the ILO, were limited, depending on moral suasion or soft coercion, and there was no procedure in place to ensure ratification. And like today's arrangements, there was no link made between labor standards and market access. Even its leading architects saw the movement as a "chapter full of hope," restricted to the use of "moral force" (Fontaine 1920: 181). The few conventions that were actually signed, according to Stanley Engerman (2003: 37–38), had little to no effect because many of the signatories had introduced these provisions previously. Still, the IALL may have mattered as a purveyor of the reform ideal. In the five years after Berne, Belgium, Italy, Portugal, Spain, and Sweden, all latecomers to the reform movement, prohibited night work of women. National legislation converged on the maximum number of working hours for women and children (Huberman 2012). Attendance at conferences grew in the decade before the outbreak of war, although the commonality of purpose was strongest among countries with comparable factor endowments. Even British delegates took a decisive role in discussions, unlike previous international associations where their contribution was typically phlegmatic (Lyons 1963).

For a pioneer organization, the achievements of the IALL did not go unnoticed. States sending delegates to monitor proceedings came to see that the IALL was not a radical movement, hostage to radical interests. Governments benefitted from the scientific research conducted, since in many countries newly founded Departments of Labor were unprepared to do the necessary groundwork. More importantly, states drew the lesson that multilateral agreements were costly to negotiate and compliance was difficult to enforce. Instead, countries turned increasingly toward bilateral labor accords to harmonize labor standards. Unlike IALL declarations, bilateral accords were successful because they were tied directly to trade.

The France–Italy labor treaty of 1904 provided the template for the reform movement. France and Italy had engaged in a trade war that began in 1886 and effectively lasted into the early 1900s. The war was especially hard on Italy because of its dependence on France for its exports of specialty goods. While Italian silk was a relatively standardized item and producers readily found markets in Switzerland, its specialty wine producers were less fortunate and they had to dump their stock. As part of the agreement ending the trade war, France demanded that Italy raise certain labor standards to international norms, allowing its exporters greater market access. In exchange, France agreed to give Italian migrant workers the same level of benefits that French workers received. It also enticed its trading partner by removing selective commercial duties on Italian imports. Italy was not opposed to the French initiative. Its history of labor legislation was recent and, because the percentage of eligible voters was low, the liberal government exploited the French initiative to circumvent vested interests that opposed social reform. In this regard, Italian labor drew on the support of French capital in a cross-class and cross-border coalition.

In the decade before 1914, European states signed thirty accords based on the French–Italy model.[15] Underlying these agreements was states' desire to guarantee market access for their specialized goods. Thus European governments came to support their labor movements, because when commercial rivals adopted better standards, their own countries' exports became relatively less expensive, and imports more so. The end result was an increase in intra-European trade and a level playing field in labor legislation. Migration of labor and capital would not unleash a race to the bottom. The basic idea behind the bilateral labor agreements has resurfaced, albeit in a different form, in current debates on the inclusion of a social clause in trade agreements. I return to the labor movement's role in these contemporary debates in the conclusion.

Labor movements in the interwar period

The macroeconomic and political upheavals of the interwar years altered the balance of power in labor markets. In the immediate aftermath of the war, labor movements, spurred by the Russian Revolution, sought to exploit the "political capital" workers had justly earned for their patriotism – labor parties supported the war effort – and sacrifices endured as civilians and combatants. The immediate outcome was a global strike wave. The extension of suffrage to women and working-class men changed the rules of the game more fundamentally. In retrospect, the labor movement, broadly defined, was perhaps never stronger than it was in the decades following the conflict and into the Bretton Woods period. The demise of the gold standard was itself, according to Barry Eichengreen (1992), the inevitable outcome of new mass politics. In some countries, union membership stagnated in the 1920s, but the Depression initiated a spurt in mobilization, as workers' desire to join unions increased and employers' resistance declined (Freeman 1998). Organized labor extended its representation to the unskilled and women. This did not necessarily imply a complete break with the past. Labor representatives and legislators leaned heavily on lessons learned from the first wave of

15 Lowe (1935) gives a complete listing of the labor accords.

globalization, and, despite the plurality of responses at the country level, the pre-1914 divisions between Old and New World labor movements were still evident, if not reinforced. In this fashion, domestic and external forces remained entangled even as international trade collapsed.

If the fall in trade costs before 1914 had caused the convergence of world labor markets, the rising tide of economic nationalism in the wake of World War I pulled them apart. The Depression, and the varied responses to it, heightened divisions across national economies. For a good part of the twentieth century, certainly until the recent wave of globalization beginning in the 1970s, the spatial dimension of labor markets was limited by national boundaries. The implication was that different types of social and economic projects, promoted by states, business, and labor, and impervious to international competition, could coexist.

Across the New World, the labor movement's long-standing demand for immigration restrictions was realized, non-Europeans being excluded, and Europeans' entry based on quotas. For instance, the British dominions restricted entry of Commonwealth citizens beginning in the early 1930s. Labor's bargaining advantage was bolstered, taking a larger share of national income as a result. As wage distributions collapsed, ever-greater egalitarianism promoted, along the lines of Peter Lindert's (2004) Robin Hood paradox, further demands for redistributive programs. At least in the interwar years, Milton Friedman's claim (cited in Razin, Sadka, and Suwankiri 2011) that "you cannot simultaneously have free immigration and a welfare state," because of pressures on government finances, was close to the mark in North America.

Developments in the United States were typical of the reversal in fortunes for labor in the New World. The contraction of labor supply owing to the end of mass European migration caused sweeping changes in the functioning of labor markets. Turnover fell, employment durations lengthened, and hiring standards improved. The introduction of human resource departments was a direct response to labor's enhanced bargaining power (Jacoby 1985). By the eve of the depression, the average American worker was older, better educated, and more committed to industrial work (Wright 2006). Subsequently, New Deal legislation preserved and extended workers' gains. The Wagner Act promoted union organization in semi-skilled sectors, union density rates doubling to 21 percent of the nonagricultural labor force between 1928 and 1939. Combined with restrictions on the use of child labor and increases in the compulsory schooling age, earnings increased across the board, but perhaps most notably at the bottom end of the distribution. Because of the new restrictions in the labor market, unemployment in the 1930s did not exercise downward pressure on wages as in principle it ought to have. The labor market changes originating with the New Deal laid the basis to the golden age of American labor which lasted into the early 1970s.

The roadmap in the Old World is more difficult to read because of the variety of national experiments in social and economic policy-making. In Germany, the war marked a major turning point in the history of German capital–labor relations (Kaufman 2004: 475). As occurred elsewhere under the pressure of war mobilization, the German government shifted from a policy of suspicion to cooperation with unions. German defeat unleashed a wave of popular uprisings and revolutionary takeovers of cities and factories. But fearful of relinquishing their hard-fought gains, the major trade unions formed an alliance with business interests, defending representative democracy and preserving the basic outlines of a market economy. Under the Nazis, labor's independence was seriously compromised, but the 1920s alliance constituted the template for what later became the principle of social partnership, an accord which opened up the door for a continued program of social reform and the establishment of work councils, a key component in German industrial relations and determinant of economic growth in the second half of the century.

Where labor parties achieved electoral success, Europe's liberal democracies extended prewar gains in social legislation and entitlements. In the early 1920s, unemployment insurance schemes were revamped. Even though many countries did not ratify the ILO founding convention of an 8-hour day – of which I will say more below – the length of the workweek had generally fallen to about 48 hours by 1929 from close to 56 hours before the war. Moreover, many governments introduced paid vacation days, European workers enjoying about two weeks off by the 1930s. Labor had recourse to the past as well, drawing heavily on blueprints of social reform circulating in the international community before 1914. The European labor movement remained flexible, if not realistic, on immigration issues. The dislocation of population caused by the war was considerable, and in response several states attempted to negotiate agreements along the lines of the French–Italian accord of 1904 guaranteeing market access while extending safety nets, thereby assuring a level playing field. France sought to sign agreements of this type with Poland and Czechoslovakia.

The historic division between Old and New World labor movements persisted. A case in point was their divergent attitudes toward worksharing initiated in the wake of the Depression. Europe had a long tradition of reduced worktime during periods of contracting demand. Initially an informal rule of thumb, worksharing was codified in the revised and extended unemployment insurance schemes of the 1920s that included subsidies for time loss at work. In contrast, the United States had no tradition of job sharing and its experiment with it in the 1930s was bittersweet. Although some jobs may have been saved, many held that managers used the policy arbitrarily, turning one group of workers against another (Moriguchi 2005). At Bethlehem Steel, available work during the Depression was shared only among "efficient and loyal workers" (Jacoby 1985: 212). After the war, US labor contracts avoided worksharing clauses, with layoffs determined by seniority.

While domestic forces may have had the upper hand in the interwar years, international influences were not absent. The interwar period was the heyday of the ILO, a creation of the Treaty of Versailles, whose mission was to promote and enshrine basic human rights in the workplace and equitable conditions of employment for men and women.[16] In contrast to Soviet ideology, the ILO embraced cross-class consultation. Many of the leading figures in the ILO had been active in the IALL. To its founders, the ILO represented a significant move away from liberal economics, or what they referred to as the "commodity approach to labor" (Kaufman 2004: 205), but, paradoxically, its architects were ardent free traders, claiming that international trade was a pathway in transmitting labor standards, or social justice, from the industrial core to periphery. The ILO stood apart from the backlash toward globalization in the interwar period that had emerged among labor's supporters and which was personified by Karl Polanyi's opposition of states – meaning social protection – and markets (Polanyi 1944). Émile Vandervelde, the *patron* of the Belgian Labor Party, a past chairman of the Second International, and active in the formative years of the ILO, warned that as the international trading order contracted, emerging countries would not be able to enact better working conditions. The labor movement in rich and poor economies alike would suffer.

> To shut small nations out from the great markets of the world through customs barriers would condemn them to a cramped and narrow life which would check the development of their industry in every branch, and stifle progress towards the attainment of labour reforms and the high standard of living for workers which is the object of the International Labour Organization. (Vandervelde 1920: 130)

In the face of mounting isolationism in the 1930s, which it condemned, the ILO assumed its role as the preeminent research body in the field of labor policy,

---

16 For an early history of the ILO, see Shotwell (1934); for the interwar years, see Kott (2010).

pursuing both "science building" and "problem solving" (Kaufman 2004: 210). While many countries failed to ratify its recommendations on working hours, vacation times, and health and safety guidelines, they served nonetheless as terms of reference for national labor movements. When international trade collapsed, ideas continued to flow across borders. The *International Labour Review* was a conduit of the organization's research. By the eve of World War II, early and late industrializers alike had standard working times and labor conditions. Ironically, the convergence in hours of work was at no time more apparent than in the anti-global 1930s, the length of the workweek being about the same in the United States, France, and the Soviet Union (Huberman and Minns 2007). It would be difficult to attribute this outcome to mere coincidence. The acceptance of the ideals of harmonization, the fruit of the first wave of globalization, also mattered.

In Latin America, the rise of authoritarian regimes with state-sponsored unions and political incorporation of labor date from the 1930s. But even as isolationism reigned, the ILO carried weight. The Brazilian case is instructive. In the footsteps of Canada and the United States, immigration restrictions were imposed after World War I, the labor movement subsequently gaining in strength. Beginning in the 1920s, the state sought support of key labor unions in the urban sector to maintain social order. Labor policy was imposed in a top-down fashion and embedded in the larger import substitution initiative. But when President Getúlio Vargas assembled existing laws on regulation and social entitlements in the Consolidation of Labor Act, in 1943, he drew extensively on the ILO's recommendations (French 2004). In this period, Brazilians toiled the same hours as workers across the globe.

Even colonial labor relations had traces of the imprint of ILO conventions. The initial impetus for institutionalizing trade unions in Anglophone Africa came from Sidney Webb. Acting in his capacity as Secretary of State for the Colonies, in the early 1930s Webb issued a colonial despatch suggesting to the governors of the respective colonies that British interest would be furthered by enacting protective labor laws, as well as legislation modeled on the British Trade Union Act of 1871. Ever paternalistic, he cautioned the governors to proceed with care, noting that "without sympathetic supervision and guidance the unions . . . might divert their activities to improper and mischievous ends" (Kaufman 2004: 521). Nigeria passed the Trade Union Ordinance in 1938; Kenya adopted an Employment Act in the same year. But a further impetus to these legal initiatives was the pressure the United Kingdom and other colonial powers felt to conform, or at least appear to conform, to the labor standards of the ILO, such as the Forced Labor Convention (1930).

The synergy between domestic and international pressures evolved differently in India. By the 1920s, the demand for contract labor had receded and a local manufacturing industry was established alongside an artisanal sector. Inspired by British law, the Indian Trade Union Act of 1926 required at least seven persons to form a union, and it permitted an unlimited number of unions in each factory. While organized labor made few gains in improving working conditions, an indigenous and militant labor movement demonstrated a capacity and willingness to carry out strikes (Wolcott 2008). In fact, disputes in the subcontinent were more common than in the United Kingdom or the United States during these years.

The arrival of the ILO, one historian remarked, "galvanized Indian workers into life" (Rodgers 2011: 47). In 1928, the ILO opened a branch office in Delhi, and, by 1929, it had already contributed to the Royal Commission on Labour's decision on the centralization of labor law. ILO conventions influenced the adoption of labor legislation beginning in the 1930s (Menon 1956), although this did not imply immediate harmonization with rich countries. The Treaty of Versailles had given colonies and non-metropolitan territories the option of applying lower standards as part of native labor codes (Rodgers et al. 2009: 41–42). At this juncture, Indian textile workers could still count on the support of Lancashire unions and millowners, but faced by the resistance of Indian employers, the ILO recommended a dual framework that recalled previous IALL agreements. For instance, Convention 1 on hours of work specified a general limit of 48 hours per week, but 57 hours for Japan, and 60 for India. During discussions on minimum age of employment, the ILO recommended a "principle of gradualness," so as not to "stifle and hamper" India's developing industrialism (Rodgers 2011: 48). Similar arguments were used about forced labor, even though the ILO's 1930 convention aimed at its eventual elimination. By this date India had ratified eleven of the ILO's twenty-eight conventions.

The concept of a native labor code was abandoned in the period of decolonization after the war. Following independence, the new Indian state rapidly adhered to an amalgam of ILO standards, including freedom of association and collective bargaining, and adopted more than 200 labor laws guaranteeing labor some of the most generous freedoms in the developing world. The employment of contract labor was prohibited and the state imposed restrictive laws on layoffs (Rudra 2008: 112). Tellingly, postcolonial India, despite its early enthusiasm, has had a poor scorecard with international guidelines on working conditions. This reversal reflected the emerging political and economic weight of the developing world that would have repercussions on labor movements everywhere in the second great wave of globalization.

Labor movements under the Bretton Woods regime

On May 1, 1951, Getúlio Vargas addressed Brazilian workers:

> The Labor day celebration has a symbolic importance both for me and for you: it represents a new coming together of workers and the government. It is with deep emotion that we restore this relationship . . . Workers never came to me seeking selfish or private favors. They also spoke in the name of the collectivity to which they belong, for the recognition of their rights, for improvement in their living conditions, for redress of grievances of members of their class, and for the well-being of those sharing these difficulties . . . I need you workers of Brazil . . . as much as you need me.   (cited in Rudra 2008: 200)

Vargas was seemingly speaking for many political leaders in the 1950s; even Presidents Truman and Eisenhower would have addressed American workers in approximately the same way. The immediate post-1945 years saw a spurt in union growth and renewed interest in social change. From its base in manufacturing, organized labor expanded into education, service, and government sectors. More women than ever before became union members. Under the Bretton Woods regime, domestic forces seem to have had the upper hand on the fortunes of the labor movement. The 1970s marked a turning point. The deepening of international economic integration posed a serious challenge everywhere. Overlapping the historic distinction between labor movements in Old and New Worlds was the growing divide between labor in the North and South, as comparative advantage in manufacturing shifted to developing economies.[17]

In the United States, the industrial relations framework of the New Deal had laid the basis for a golden age of labor lasting into the early 1970s, which has been described as a unified high-wage national regime (Rosenbloom and Sundstrom 2011). While the Taft-Hartley Act of 1947 rolled back some of the gains labor had achieved in the 1930s, union density in the United States peaked in the period. Across a broad swathe of the economy, labor served as an effective countervailing power. The imposition of high minimum wages established a pay floor and hours of work declined. In the

---

17 For case studies, see Silver (2003).

flagship automobile sector, worker militancy compelled union representatives and business to negotiate the Treaty of Detroit, whose reach, owing to pattern bargaining, quickly spread to other sectors of activity. Under the settlement, management preserved the right to determine the direction of production, but unions dictated the impact of these decisions on the shop floor. To be clear, minority groups and women were excluded from some of the negotiated benefits, but overall the average worker shared in the economy's productivity gains (Levy and Temin 2011).

In the golden age of labor, the trade content of US GDP was small. Labor movements in Canada and the United States sought to exploit their industry's advantages in foreign markets, as illustrated in their support of the Marshall Plan. In the absence of strong foreign competition, official labor did not oppose increased trade exposure. Because tariffs were initially at a high level, even a small downward movement produced substantial gains in trade and negligible effects on the distribution of income (Rodrik 2011). Labor seems to have been vindicated since wages rose across the board. This was a short-term decision that would be undone as the distributional effects of trade mounted. Similarly, organized labor was not opposed to changes in the US Immigration Act in 1965, which ended the ban on immigrants from Asia and introduced a quota system for the western hemisphere. Again, labor's evolving attitude was the outcome of domestic and foreign factors. It was hard to sustain discriminatory policies against countries that were becoming significant trading partners. Social and political changes in the wake of the Civil Rights movement pushed the labor movement in the same direction.

A paradox of postwar labor-market history is that unions in Europe appear to have been more accommodating in their demands than their North American counterparts. European labor, after the debacle of the interwar years, reaffirmed the role of trade for sustained growth. Workers opted for wage restraint, a strategy that was more feasible in countries with centralized (Germany and Scandinavia) than decentralized bargaining institutions (France and the United Kingdom). With business, workers exchanged wage moderation for reinvestment of profits in enhanced technologies; with the state, workers committed themselves to social peace, because they did not want to jeopardize the extension of unemployment insurance and health and retirement benefits, and promises of more vacation time. As part of the social pact, all parties agreed to greater international exposure that also operated as a disciplinary device. This was a long-term commitment that served Europeans well up to the 1990s. Workers did not demand excessive wages for fear of overpricing themselves, firms upgraded their plant and equipment in the face of stiff import competition, and states guaranteed market access for trading partners to receive in return the benefits of membership in political and commercial unions (Eichengreen 2008). Given the shortage of labor in the core, controlled immigration was part of the equation. Europeans were rewarded for their moderation, hours of work per week gradually falling and vacation days rising, beginning in the 1960s.

The continuity with the past was not lost on contemporaries, and certainly not on trade economists. In 1955, the ILO mandated a commission, chaired by Bertil Ohlin, to report on the "social aspects of problems of European economic cooperation." The commission (ILO 1956: 1) interpreted its terms of reference to investigate whether or not "international differences in labor costs and especially in social charges" constituted an obstacle to economic integration; whether "a freer international market" called for a "greater degree of international consultation and co-operation than at present"; and, lastly, whether the "free international movement of labor" would claw back existing labor standards and entitlements (ILO 1956: 1–4). The responses of the commission combined contemporary theoretical insights and historical observation reaching back to the IALL. To begin, Ohlin and his colleagues claimed that it was natural for varieties of national labor standards to coexist even as trade expanded, because discrepancies in working conditions arose from differences in productivity, itself a result of increased trade between countries. Still, "it may be found desirable to harmonize to some extent action for the improvement in workers' living standards," where wages in any one sector are lower than the economy average, owing perhaps to workers' poor bargaining position (ILO 1956: 61). International pressure may be needed to bring these sectors up to some acceptable norm. "Such measures for harmonization should not be regarded as a prerequisite to the liberalization of trade, but should be undertaken during the period of transition" (ILO 1956: 73). Low-standard countries, Ohlin proceeded, have an incentive to improve employment conditions when they have guarantees of market access, a process that was underway in the first wave of globalization. Similarly, labor mobility did not pose a threat to the social policy of rich countries as long as trade barriers were low. "Countries will come to adopt a more flexible attitude towards the question of admitting foreign workers and we would consider this to be a desirable concomitant to free international trade" (ILO 1956: 75). Again, these types of arrangements had been in operation before 1914.

The Ohlin report served as a blueprint for European labor into the second wave of globalization. External exposure was not seen as antithetical to social protection, even if countries had different labor rules and the playing field was uneven. The strong mutual feedback between labor regulation and trade has implications for the heated debates on the effects of labor and social protection on productivity and employment. To some, labor regulation has created divisions between insiders and outsiders in labor markets. The adoption of employment protection legislation has reduced human capital formation of one group, offsetting any aggregate productivity gains linked to the stable jobs of the other.[18] But in the open economy setting after 1945, as regulation shrank the labor supply and raised its costs, the comparative advantage of European economies shifted toward higher-value, more capital-intensive items. In this way, social protection was revealed in improved terms of trade. Paolo Epifani and Gino Gancia (2009: 630) wrote: "If the price of a Nokia phone partially reflects high domestic taxes, every unit sold to foreigners provides a subsidy to the Finnish welfare state." The extension of the market generated productivity effects in tradable and non-tradable sectors alike. European labor had good reason to remain attached to international trade in the face and because of high degrees of social protection.

The European model did not transfer easily to other contexts and continents, a reflection in part of the demise in the Old World's political influence. The Soviet Union provided an alternative model of industrial relations that became ever more tolerable after it joined the ILO in 1954. The ILO was the only international body created by the Treaty of Versailles in 1919 that had managed to survive into the postwar period, but as it was drawn into debates on competing ideologies and development models, its authority was tested. The Americans sought to fill the void. In 1954, Clark Kerr and John Dunlop, and others, formed the Inter-University Study of Labor Problems in Economic Development project (Kaufman 2004: 307). A motivation behind this group was the conviction that American industrial relations were too insular, and that the horizons of the field could be broadened through a cross-country comparison of labor in the industrialization process. But the group also aimed to bring aspects of the US model of industrial relations to developing and developed countries. The ILO came to play a role in the project, Kerr and his colleagues being received in Egypt, India, and Japan.

It is telling that Kerr made no contacts in Latin America (Kaufman 2004: 537). The region had isolated itself from the forces of trade, but this did not

---

18 Allard and Lindert (2007) found delayed negative effects of two to three decades of employment protection legislation on productivity. The effects of EPL on jobs was smaller. Enflo (2011) reported similar findings.

imply that labor reaped the gains of import substitution as it was promised. In Argentina, Juan Perón, as Minister of Labor, built a coalition with trade unions and the wider labor movement. Initially, labor benefitted from the military coup of 1943 (Acemoglu and Robinson 2012: 330), union density attaining 48 percent by the mid-1950s (Visser 2003: 107). This period marked its peak influence. After the military interventions of 1966 and 1976, labor was effectively marginalized, union density falling to 25 percent by 2000. Nonetheless, the rise of diverse social movements filled the vacuum caused by the decline of organized labor (Atzeni and Ghigliani 2007: 116). A similar portrait held for Chile and Uruguay after 1973.

Labor in Brazil seems to have been ostracized from an earlier date. The state rewarded its constituents in business and in the trade unions. Into the 1990s, Brazil had among the highest levels of tariffs and maintained some of the toughest labor market laws by international standards, and exceptionally for the region, ratified eighty-one ILO conventions, double the number of India, or advanced countries like Canada. This did not imply social peace, however. Rural and low-wage workers, about 50 percent of the labor force (Rudra 2008: 204), were excluded from the state's largesse, and in the organized sector wages lagged behind productivity change. Inequality surged. Eventually, the radicalization of organized labor created a climate of distrust. In the absence of foreign trade operating as a disciplinary device, relations between labor and capital were antagonistic. And while economic growth was strong in the period, fueled by domestic and foreign capital, there was no "golden age" of labor as in Europe (Colistete 2007). With the military dictatorship of 1964, the isolation of labor was nearly complete. In subsequent decades, labor was compelled to revisit its origins, and, as European labor had accomplished a century earlier, promote the (re-)establishment of democracy as a precondition for reform, a struggle that brought together the resources of organized labor and its partners in the larger social movement.

In India, labor relations retained the marks of its colonial origins. While trade unions were at the forefront of the independence movement, the Indian Congress Party was not willing to tolerate an autonomous labor movement. Legislation did not promote collective bargaining, which was effectively taken over by the government. A narrow group of union members occasionally prospered in terms of its influence on the government's import substitution policy (Visser 2003: 387). But by excluding workers in small shops and factories, labor legislation discriminated against informal activities. As a result, the number of establishments and workers in the informal sector expanded. The 1960s, a period of economic stagnation, saw bitter fighting between competing unions for membership, rivalries intensifying because of political allegiances and regional and ethnic cleavages. Union organizations became decentralized, and any influence they had had waned subsequently.

Labor movements and hyper-globalization

The oil shock of 1973, the shift in the ideological landscape, the adoption of information technologies, and, finally, the ramping up of globalization in the 1990s put labor movements everywhere on the defensive. The individual contributions of these factors have been the source of debate. In the United States, the information revolution spurred a strong demand for skilled and educated workers. Since the rate of growth of their supply did not always keep pace with demand, the wage gap between skilled and unskilled widened. The ideological rebalancing that promoted reductions in the real minimum wage and deunionization since the 1980s extinguished definitively the golden age of labor. But the changing international landscape also mattered. Dani Rodrik (2011: 85) relates that the import competition faced by a US shoe machine operator roughly doubled between 1983 and 2002. "It is inconceivable that this change would not have had a substantial impact on his or her wages." Because commercial barriers had fallen significantly since the heyday of Bretton Woods, the realization of further gains in trade came at the expense of changes in the distribution of income. The widening of inequality coincided with the weakening of the labor movement. It may be that in sectors dependent on the new information technology and the employment of skilled labor, the effects of globalization on labor were more imagined than real. But the drive behind investments in the new technology was itself not exogenous to changes in the global trading order. The "bias of the new technologies adopted in manufacturing was shaped by the country's changing comparative advantage niche in the world economy, as opposed to imperatives inherent in the technology itself" (Wright 2006: 152).

The pressures on the labor movement have been ubiquitous, even in its heartland, the industrial core of Europe where labor's political representation remained intact. Across continents, organized labor, according to Gerald Friedman (2008), has atrophied, its defensive and at times lethargic posture caused by the falling off in strike activity and a failure to reorient itself toward sectors of activity and issues outside of its traditional bailiwick. Some of the slack has been picked up by various social movements, including anti-globalizers and anti-Wall Street protesters. Still, the labor movement, even narrowly defined, has appeared to have survived the political upheavals of the last decades of the century. The collapse of the Soviet Union has been a backstop against large declines in world trade union membership. Over 20 million workers belong to unions in the Ukraine, amounting to a density rate of nearly 100 percent (Visser 2003: 380).

In Japan, changes in business organization deterred union militancy. Immediately after World War II, the Trade Union Law, patterned after the US Wagner Act, guaranteed the right of union membership. The response was immediate, between the fall of 1945 and the summer of 1946 union numbers increased at the rate of 500,000 a month, with density peaking in 1949 at 55 percent. Union membership was sustained as long as employment in industrial large firms was unchallenged, because Japanese unions tended not to organize outside this sector. But as international competition mounted, and as employment in large firms ratcheted down, the labor movement was squeezed (Tsuru and Rebitzer 1995). The labor movement in China went through a comparable transition. After the revolution, the sprawling All-Chinese Federation of Trade Unions had widespread control of industrial relations with the aim of mitigating disputes. As long as China opted for autarky, rich and poor countries alike were unaffected by its labor policies. But after the opening up of markets in the 1990s, managerial control has reasserted itself. To the chagrin of China's economic rivals, membership numbers in the foreign investment enterprise sector have remained low, somewhere between one-tenth and one-third of the workforce (Visser 2003: 388). Exceptionally, South Korean workers resisted similar pressures. In the auto sector, attempts by Japanese multinationals and local producers to introduce new automated technologies were met by waves of labor militancy, culminating in a twenty-day general strike in late December 1996 (Silver 2003: 61–64).[19]

In Europe, the expansion of the labor movement into public and service sectors ought to have counteracted the direct effects of globalization, but immigration has become a flashpoint of labor's frustration. This marked a reversal from past periods. For certain EU countries, like Germany, confronting shrinking workforces because of aging populations, immigration would appear to offer a respite against the pending crisis in the delivery of pensions and other social entitlements. But there is a widespread perception that migrants from new EU members have tended to abuse welfare states, even though there is no evidence that they receive more transfers than natives after controlling for education levels and family characteristics (Boeri 2010).

---

19 Capital does not seem to always get its way. Multinationals' strategy of seeking out cheap labor has often proved costly. For a case study of RCA, see Cowie 1999.

Nonetheless, low-skill migrants are particularly attracted to rich countries that have the most extensive welfare states, and this underlies EU citizens' unease. And there is also genuine concern that immigrants in these countries crowd out low-skilled indigenous workers, who themselves have become dependent on social benefits. There are fears that if immigration remains uncontrolled, welfare states, the crowning achievement of the labor movement, will spiral downwards. Echoing Milton Friedman, Hans-Werner Sinn (2007: 269) remarked that in the case of Germany the trilemma of "a policy of wage compression, an expansion of the welfare state, and mass immigration are three things that simply do not fit together."

These pressures have provoked demands for quotas, but these measures have proven ineffectual since restrictions have not impeded illegal immigration. As an alternative, the labor movement has promoted harmonizing labor standards across countries in the EU core and periphery (Boeri 2010). At the same time, European labor has not forsaken its attachment to international trade. History offers guidance to reconciling labor's demands for a level playing field and its attachment to trade. Recall that European welfare states had originally encouraged social inclusion while securing the harmonization of labor standards across trading partners. In the iconic example, France accepted Italian workers as Italy adopted improved labor standards. Market access assured that higher labor costs in Italy did not harm its exports. A rising tide lifted all boats.

For emerging countries, the balance of domestic and external forces shifted to favor the former, a change that mirrored the new world trading order based on low wages, technological adaptation in the South, and the expansion of outsourcing. Into the 1950s, the ILO was the main channel of international transmission of ideas to the region, and political leaders, from Vargas to Nehru, ratified international conventions to appease supporters in the labor movements. As the developing world reduced trade barriers, and became richer, states began challenging the role of the ILO. In contrast to the early period, India since independence has disregarded the ILO, ratifying only 41 of its 189 conventions. Beginning in the 1990s, Brazil rolled back its guarantees of labor protection. President Fernando Henrique Cardoso denounced Brazil's adherence to Convention 158 on the termination of employment, putting in its place flexible short-term contracts. The labor movement, which Vargas and his successors had partitioned between insiders and outsiders, was divided on these and subsequent reforms of the pension system which had favored skilled and public-sector workers (Rudra 2008: 189–203). Unlike in Western Europe, labor has been unsuccessful in coupling increased international exposure and a secure safety net, the ramifications of which are considerable because of the country's long-standing inequality.

The dynamic between internal and external forces in the development of the African labor movement unfolded still differently. Initially, the former seem to have been dominant. Paralleling the history of labor movements in Europe 100 years earlier, African trade unions were active in civil society, a key participant in the transition between colonialism and democratization, and, in the dismantlement of apartheid regimes. In francophone West Africa, labor movements have contributed to the broadening and deepening of popular involvement in the political process (Phelan 2011a: 476). Into the 1980s, democratization led to a rapid proliferation of trade unions. But weak export prices and structural adjustment programs originating with the Washington Consensus restricting the size of the public sector have exacerbated latent social and ethnic divisions and political instability (Phelan 2011b). As a result, trade union density rates have fallen, the labor movement being sidelined by government interference. In francophone West Africa, unions have become dependent on external organizations for support, just as they had relied on French trade unions in the colonial era.

Conclusion

The debate over the adoption of international labor standards at the turn of the twenty-first century revisits many of the themes previously discussed in this chapter. The manufacturing sector in industrialized countries was the foundation stone of the labor movement for a good part of a century, but the recent wave of globalization has challenged the basis of labor's bargaining power. In the 1990s, after the collapse of the Soviet bloc, and as China and India turned their backs on autarky and protectionism, the overall world labor supply in the 1990s, according to one estimate, doubled (Freeman 2005). In certain countries, teachers, nurses, and government workers have become the redoubt of the union movement, which has declined almost everywhere since the 1980s (see Table 13.1).

To workers in the old industrial core, many developing economies have an unfair trade advantage because of their low wages and weak regulatory environments. In response, labor representatives in rich countries have sponsored several options to harmonize the rules of trade and level the playing field. They have sought to attach social clauses in regional trade agreements to compel negligent or refractory commercial partners to upgrade their regulatory environments. On the global stage, rich countries have appealed to the WTO and the ILO to take action against latecomers to the reform movement. However, in developing economies, labor and its spokespersons have seen international guidelines as a conceit, an attempt by richer countries to block trade, which would have had the consequence of delaying the adoption of labor standards in poorer countries because of its harmful effects on income. So-called substandard working conditions in the poor countries were not trade-related, but a domestic problem arising from the side effects of industrialization, similar to what today's OECD economies experienced 100 years earlier (Singh 2003).

The debate pivots on the balance between national sovereignty and international authority. The last 100 years have seen a reversal of the position of labor movements in rich and poor countries with regard to the relative importance of domestic and external forces. To many contemporaries, the strength of the labor movement in the industrial core into the 1970s was pinned down by domestic politics; it was the labor movement in the periphery that was dependent on external influences and references, such as those of colonial powers and the ILO. By 2000, the roles were reversed, workers in rich regions appealing to international organizations to level the playing field, while labor in the poor world opposed this type of intervention.

The meetings of the WTO and the ILO mirrored this tension. The ILO, whose authority had weakened since the 1960s, was reluctant to intervene on behalf of workers in the industrial core. At Seattle in 1999, the United States sponsored a coalition of governments and trade unions, including the AFL-CIO and the International Confederation of Free Trade Unions (ICFTU), which sought to pressure the WTO to append social clauses in trade agreements.[20] But developing countries put paid to the idea. In India, external pressure precipitated an alliance of national trade union federations and government against social clauses (Hensman 2011). In the wake of this failure, and seeking to reassert its leadership on labor matters, the ILO adopted the concept of core standards to reconcile competing interests of member states.[21] The adoption of standards was not tied to trade, however, the ILO tightening its supervision of enforcement instead.

There are some reasons to remain optimistic about the future. The labor movement has withstood the turbulence of the past century. Whereas political regimes, technological revolutions, and social experiments have come and gone, the labor movement has persevered. The geographic scope of the labor

---

20 Deardorff and Stern (2002) have a balanced account of Seattle.

21 These core standards consist of the freedom of association and the elimination of all forms of forced or compulsory labor, the effective abolition of child labor, and the elimination of discrimination in respect of employment and occupation.

movement is wider than it has ever been (see Table 13.1). As manufacturing spread out of the industrial core, the labor movement established itself in the developing world, density rates in Europe only slightly greater than those of Asia. This accomplishment, which is considerable, was the outcome of domestic and external forces that were rarely independent and as likely to be complementary as opposing.

Any optimism needs to be cautioned, however. Since the 1980s, the world trading order has posed a serious challenge to workers, and across countries earnings have not kept up with changes in productivity (ILO 2012). But there are counter-examples. Previous generations of workers exploited globalization to their advantage, extracting better wages and improved working conditions. Throughout this period, labor never abandoned its adversarial role, but capital did not seem to suffer either. A strong labor movement went hand in hand with a robust capitalism. The lesson is that workers need to be at the bargaining table, for their own sake as well as capital's.

References

Acemoglu, D. and J. A. Robinson (2012). *Why Nations Fail: The Origins of Power, Prosperity, and Poverty*. New York: Crown Business.

Allard, G. J. and P. H. Lindert (2007). "Euro-Productivity and Euro-Jobs since the 1960s: Which Institutions Really Mattered," in T. J. Hatton, K. H. O'Rourke, and A. M. Taylor (eds.), *The New Comparative Economic History*. Cambridge, MA: The MIT Press, pp. 365–394.

Allen, R. C. (2009). "Engels' Pause: Technical Change, Capital Accumulation, and Inequality in the British Industrial Revolution," *Explorations in Economic History* 46: 418–435.

Archer, R. (2007). *Why Is There No Labor Party in the United States?* Princeton University Press.

Atzeni, M. and P. Ghigliani (2007). "The Resilience of Traditional Trade Union Practices in the Revitalisation of the Argentine Labour Movement," in C. Phelan (ed.), *Trade Union Revitilisation: Trends and Prospects in 34 Countries*. Oxford: Peter Lang, pp. 105–121.

Bain, G. S. and F. Elsheikh (1976). *Union Growth and the Business Cycle*. Oxford: Blackwell.

Boeri, T. (2010). "Immigration to the Land of Redistribution," *Economica* 77: 651–687.

Bortz, J. (2000). "The Revolution, the Labour Regime, and Conditions of Work in the Cotton Textile Industry in Mexico, 1910–1927," *Journal of Latin American Studies* 32: 671–703.

Card, D. and C. A. Olson (1995). "Bargaining Power, Strike Durations, and Wage Outcomes: An Analysis of Strikes in the 1880s," *Journal of Labor Economics* 13: 32–61.

Colistete, R. P. (2007). "Productivity, Wages, and Labor Politics in Brazil, 1945–1962," *Journal of Economic History* 67: 93–128.

Cowie, J. R. (1999). *Capital Moves: RCA's Seventy-Year Quest for Cheap Labor*. Ithaca, NY: Cornell University Press.

Craven, P. (1980). *"An Impartial Umpire": Industrial Relations and the Canadian State 1900–1911*. University of Toronto Press.

Crouch, C. (1993). *Industrial Relations and European State Traditions*. Oxford: Clarendon.

Deardorff, A. V. and R. M. Stern (2002). "What You Should Know about Globalization and the World Trade Organization," *Review of International Economics* 10: 404–423.

Donald, M. (2001). "Workers of the World Unite? Exploring the Enigma of the Second International," in M. H. Geyer and J. Paulmann (eds.), *The Mechanics of Internationalism: Culture, Society, and Politics from the 1840s to the First World War*. Oxford University Press, pp. 177–204.

Drummond, I. (1987). *Progress Without Planning: The Economic History of Ontario from Confederation to the Second World War*. University of Toronto Press.

Eichengreen, B. (1992). *Golden Fetters: The Gold Standard and the Great Depression, 1919–1939*. New York: Oxford University Press.

(2008). *The European Economy since 1945: Coordinated Capitalism and Beyond*. Princeton University Press.

Enflo, K. (2011). "The Institutional Roots of Post-war European Economic Underperformance: A Regional Approach," *European Review of Economic History* 15: 329–355.

Engerman, S. J. (2003). "The History and Political Economy of International Labor Standards," in K. Basu, H. Horn, L. Roman, and J. Shapiro (eds.), *International Labor Standards: History, Theory, and Policy Options*. Oxford: Blackwell, pp. 9–83.

Epifani, P. and G. Gancia (2009). "Openness, Government Size and the Terms of Trade," *Review of Economic Studies* 76: 629–668.

Fishback, P. (1998). "Operations of 'Unfettered' Labor Markets: Exit and Voice in American Labor Markets at the Turn of the Century," *Journal of Economic Literature* 36: 722–665.

Fontaine, A. (1920). "A Review of International Labour Legislation," in E. J. Solano (ed.), *Labour as an International Problem*. London: Macmillan.

Freeman, R. B. (1998). "Spurts in Union Growth: Defining Moments and Social Process," in M. D. Bordo, C. Goldin, and E. N. White (eds.), *The Defining Moment: The Great Depression and the American Economy in the Twentieth Century*. University of Chicago Press, pp. 265–96.

(2005). "The Great Doubling: Labor Policy in the New Global Economy," Georgia State University, 2005 Usery Lecture in Labor Policy.

Freeman, R. B. and J. Medoff (1984). *What Do Unions Do?* New York: Basic Books.

French, J. D. (2004). *Drowning in Laws: Labor Law and Brazilian Political Culture*. Chapel Hill, NC: University of North Carolina Press.

Frieden, J. A. (2006). *Global Capitalism: Its Fall and Rise in the Twentieth Century*. New York: Norton.

Friedman, G. (1998). *State-Making and Labor Movements: France and the United States, 1876–1914*. Ithaca, NY: Cornell University Press.

(2008). *Reigniting the Labor Movement: Restoring Means to Ends in a Democratic Labor Movement*. New York: Routledge.

Gorshkov, B. B. (2009). *Russia's Factory Children: State, Society, and Law, 1800–1917*. University of Pittsburgh Press.

Goutor, D. (2007). *Guarding the Gates: The Canadian Labour Movement and Immigration, 1872–1934*. Vancouver: UBC Press.

Hatton, T. J. and J. G. Williamson (2005). *Global Migration and the World Economy: Two Centuries of Policy and Performance*. Cambridge, MA: The MIT Press.

Hensman, R. (2011). *Workers, Unions, and Global Capitalism: Lessons from India*. New York: Columbia University Press.

Hobsbawm, E. (1988). "Working Class Internationalism," in F. van Holthoon and M. van der Linden (eds.), *Internationalism in the Labour Movement, 1830–1914*. Leiden: E. J. Brill, pp. 3–16.

Huberman, M. (2012). *Odd Couple: International Trade and Labor Standards in History*. New Haven, CT: Yale University Press.

Huberman, M. and C. M. Meissner (2010). "Riding the Wave of Trade: The Rise of Labor Regulation in the Golden Age of Globalization," *Journal of Economic History* 70: 535–567.

Huberman, M. and C. Minns (2007). "The Times They Are Not Changin': Days and Hours of Work in Old and New Worlds, 1870–2000," *Explorations in Economic History* 44: 538–567.

Huberman, M. and D. Young (1999). "Hope Against Hope: Strike Activity in Canada, 1920–1939," *Explorations in Economic History* 39: 315–354.

Hunt, E. H. (1985). *British Labour History, 1815–1914*. London: Weidenfeld and Nicolson.

Hunter, J. and H. Macnaughtan (2010). "Japan," in L. H. van Voss, E. Hiemstra-Kuperus, and E. van Nederveen Meerkerk (eds.), *The Ashgate Companion to the History of Textile Workers, 1650–2000*. Farnham: Ashgate, pp. 305–332.

International Labor Organization (1956). *Social Aspects of European Economic Co-operation*. Studies and Reports, new series, no. 46. Geneva: ILO.

(2012). *Global Wage Report 2012/2013: Wages and Equitable Growth*. Geneva: ILO.

Jacoby, S. (1985). *Employing Bureaucracy: Managers, Unions, and the Transformation of Work in American Industry, 1900–1945*. New York: Cambridge University Press.

Kaufman, B. (2004). *The Global Evolution of Industrial Relations: Events, Ideas and the IIRA*. Geneva: ILO.

Kott, S. (2010). "Constructing a European Social Model: The Fight for Social Insurance in the Interwar Period," in M. Rodriguez Garcia, J. van Daele, and M. van der Linden (eds.), *ILO Histories: Essays on the International Labour Organization and its Impact on the World During the Twentieth Century*. Berne: Peter Lang, pp. 173–195.

Krugman, P. and A. J. Venables (1995). "Globalization and the Inequality of Nations," *Quarterly Journal of Economics* 110: 857–880.

Levy, F. and P. Temin (2011). "Inequality of Institutions in Twentieth-Century America," in P. W. Rhode, J. L. Rosenbloom, and D. F. Weiman (eds.), *Economic Evolution and Revolution in Historical Time*. Stanford University Press, pp. 357–386.

Lindert, P. H. (2004). *Growing Public: Social Spending and Economic Growth since the Eighteenth Century*. New York: Cambridge University Press.

López-Córdova, J. E. and C. M. Meissner (2008). "The Impact of International Trade on Democracy: A Long-Run Perspective," *World Politics* 60: 539–575.

Lowe, B. E. (1935). *The International Protection of Labor: International Labor Organization, History and Law*. New York: Macmillan.

Lyons, F. S. L. (1963). *Internationalism in Europe, 1815–1914*. Leiden: A.W. Sythoff.

Maram, S. L. (1977). "Labor and the Left in Brazil, 1890–1921: A Movement Aborted," *Hispanic American Historical Review* 57: 254–272.

Mares, I. (2003). *The Politics of Social Risk: Business and Welfare State Development.* New York: Cambridge University Press.

McKeown, A. (2004). "Global Migration, 1846–1940," *Journal of World History* 15: 155–189.

Menon, V. K. R. (1956). "The Influence of International Labour Conventions on Indian Labour Legislation," *International Labour Review* 73: 551–571.

Moriguchi, C. (2005). "Did American Welfare Capitalists Breach Their Implicit Contracts During the Great Depression? Preliminary Findings from Company-level Data," *Industrial and Labor Relations Review* 59: 51–81.

Phelan, C. (2011a). "Trade Unions, Democratic Waves, and Structural Adjustment: The Case of Francophone West Africa," *Labor History* 52: 461–481.

    ed. (2011b). *Trade Unions in West Africa: Historical and Contemporary Perspectives.* Oxford: Peter Lang.

Polanyi, K. (1944). *The Great Transformation: The Political and Economic Origins of Our Time.* Boston, MA: Beacon Press.

Razin, A., E. Sadka, and B. Suwankiri (2011). *Migration and the Welfare State: Political-Economy Policy Formation.* Cambridge: The MIT Press.

Rodgers, G. (2011). "India, the ILO and the Quest for Social Justice since 1919," *Economic & Political Weekly* 46: 45–52.

Rodgers, G., E. Lee, L. Swepston, and J. van Daele (2009). *The International Labor Organization and the Quest for Social Justice.* Ithaca, NY: ILR Press.

Rodrik, D. (2011). *The Globalization Paradox: Democracy and the Future of the World Economy.* New York: W.W. Norton.

Roediger, D. R. and P. S. Foner (1989). *Our Own Time: A History of American Labor and the Working Day.* Westport, CT: Greenwood.

Rose, S. O. (1992). *Limited Livelihoods: Gender and Class in Nineteenth-Century England.* Berkeley, CA: University of California Press.

Rosenbloom, J. L. (2002). *Looking for Work, Searching for Workers.* New York: Cambridge University Press.

Rosenbloom, J. L. and W. A. Sundstrom (2011). "Labor-Market Regimes in US Economic History," in P. W. Rhode, J. L. Rosenbloom, and D. F. Weiman (eds.), *Economic Evolution and Revolution in Historical Time.* Stanford University Press, pp. 277–310.

Rudra, N. (2008). *Globalization and the Race to the Bottom in Developing Countries. Who Really Gets Hurt?* New York: Cambridge University Press.

Shotwell, J. T., ed. (1934). *The Origins of the International Labor Organization.* New York: Columbia University Press.

Silver, B. J. (2003). *Forces of Labor: Workers' Movements and Globalization since 1870.* Cambridge University Press.

Singh, N. (2003). "The Theory of International Trade Standards From an Economic Perspective," in K. Basu, H. Horn, L. Romain, and J. Shapiro (eds.), *International Labor Standards: History, Theory, and Policy Options.* Malden, MA: Blackwell.

Sinn, H.-W. (2007). *Can Germany Be Saved? The Malaise of the World's First Welfare State.* Cambridge, MA: The MIT Press.

Steinfeld, R. J. (1991). *The Invention of Free Labor.* Chapel Hill, NC: University of North Carolina Press.

Suarez-Potts, W. J. (2012). *The Making of Law: The Supreme Court and Labor Legislation in Mexico, 1875–1931*. Stanford University Press.

Tilly, C. (1995). "Globalization Threatens Labor's Rights," *International Labor and Working Class History* 47: 1–23.

Tsuru, T. and J. B. Rebitzer (1995). "The Limits of Enterprise Unionism: Prospects for Continuing Union Decline in Japan," *British Journal of Industrial Relations* 33: 459–492.

Van Daele, J. (2005). "Engineering Social Peace: Networks, Ideas, and the Founding of the International Labour Organization," *International Review of Social History* 50: 435–466.

Van der Linden M., (2003). *Transnational Labor History: Explorations*. Aldershot: Ashgate.

Vandenbroucke, G. (2009). "Trends in Hours: The U.S. from 1900 to 1950," *Journal of Economic Dynamics and Control* 33: 237–249.

Vandervelde, E. (1920). "Labour Reforms in Belgium," in E. J. Solano (ed.), *Labour as an International Problem*. London: Macmillan, pp. 105–131.

Visser, J. (2003). "Unions and Unionism Around the World," in J. T. Addison and C. Schnabel (eds.), *International Handbook of Trade Unions*. Cheltenham: Edward Elgar, pp. 366–413.

Webb, S. and B. Webb (1902). *Industrial Democracy*, new edn in one vol. London: Longmans, Green and Co.

Wolcott, S. (2008). "Strikes in Colonial India," *Industrial and Labor Relations Review* 61: 46–84.

Wolfe, J. (1993). *Working Women, Working Men: São Paulo and the Rise of Brazil's Industrial Working Class, 1900–1955*. Durham, NC: Duke University Press.

Wright, G. (1987). "Labor History and Labor Economcs," in A. J. Field (ed.), *The Future of Economic History*. Boston, MA: Kluwer, pp. 313–347.

   (2006). "Productivity Growth and the American Labor Market: The 1990s in Historical Perspective," in P. Rhode and G. Toniolo (eds.), *The Global Economy in the 1990s: A Long-Run Perspective*. New York: Cambridge University Press, pp. 139–160.

Zolberg, A. (1995). "Response: Working-Class Dissolution," *International Labor and Working Class History* 47: 28–38.

14

Private welfare and the welfare state

PETER H. LINDERT[*]

Overview

The issues

It is natural to wonder how well poverty and economic risk could be reduced by private means, such as charity, private insurance markets, and private capital markets. We know, of course, that the successfully growing countries trended away from relying on private insurance and poor relief solutions, c.1880 to c.1980. Yet over those hundred years, even private social assistance and social insurance rose in all rich countries.

This chapter summarizes what is known about the causes and consequences of the rise in aid, and the prospects for reversing the shift toward public aid in the twenty-first century. These immediate questions must be faced:

- Why did the world do so little giving and insuring until the last hundred years, and why has its recent rise concentrated in the rich industrialized OECD countries? Is the rise likely to continue across the twenty-first century?
- Among sources of funding for giving and insuring, why did tax financing outrun private financing, and will taxation go on rising, as a share of such funding or as a share of GDP?
- Among uses of the funds, why have poverty and need been reduced so much more for the elderly than for the young, and will that continue?
- Are these developments efficient, in the sense of raising something like GDP per capita?[1] If efficient, why were these gains delayed until the last hundred years? If inefficient, why were these changes so widespread?

* The author thanks Larry Neal, Jeffrey Williamson, Madrid conference participants, and audiences at Korea University, Seoul National University, and the World Economic History Congress at Stellenbosch for criticisms and suggestion on an earlier draft.
1 Among the many ways that economists modify GDP to make it a better measure of well-being, one in particular must be borne in mind throughout this chapter. Private individual giving, as distinct from employer-based or tax-based transfers and insurance,

Arriving at answers to these basic long-run questions does not require a particularly long journey, in comparison with some other basic historical quests. It will turn out that plausible but unnoticed answers can be reached, at least in part, by applying common theories and common sense.

Definitions broad and narrow

An initial preparation for the journey, however, is to define the basic subject matter.

(1) *The broader activity: social spending.* This chapter will start with the broad concept that recent authors, including those managing the SOCEXP data sets for the Organisation for Economic Co-operation and Development (OECD), have called "social expenditure" or "social welfare expenditure." Convention has cast the definitional net very broadly, so broadly as to limit its usefulness. The available measures of social welfare expenditures by the OECD and by scholars include any expenditures that cushion people against low levels of – or short-term drops in – health, income, and general well-being.[2] Some measures include educational expenditures, yet others (e.g. the OECD's SOCX series) do not. This chapter sometimes includes education expenditures, especially public ones, and sometimes excludes them, depending on the issue at hand. Remarkably, the broad measures of social spending do not restrict who pays for these expenditures, or who receives them.[3] The payers need not be richer than the recipients. The payers and recipients tend to be persons in different families, but even this tendency has exceptions, as in the "social" pension expenditures that you get from your own previous paycheck contributions.

(2) *The narrower activity: helping the neediest.* This chapter adopts the narrower, but still conventional, focus on expenditures insuring against, or alleviating, extreme need as defined either by living below the poverty line or by

---

is a form of consumption that delivers utility directly to the individual giver. Its monetary component could be counted as part of consumption, though national income accounting considers it a transfer payment rather than a payment for productive services. Donations of volunteer time could also be valued as consumption on the part of the volunteer, though this, too, is omitted in conventional accounting.

2 The official OECD definition of social expenditures is as follows: "The provision by public and private institutions of benefits to, and financial contributions targeted at, households and individuals in order to provide support during circumstances which adversely affect their welfare, provided that the provision of the benefits and financial contributions constitutes neither a direct payment for a particular good or service nor an individual contract or transfer." Adema *et al.* 2011: 90.

3 See the broad inclusive measures offered by Fishback (2010); Garfinkel, Rainwater, and Smeeding (2010); and Adema, Fron, and Ladaique (2011).

suffering incapacities that greatly reduce material well-being even above the poverty line.[4] That is, we emphasize the kinds of social insurance and social assistance that have always generated more controversy because they involve more vertical redistribution of income.[5]

(3) *Defining success and efficiency.* In what follows, private and public institutions will be judged on the basis of their record in lowering poverty rates, lowering physical suffering, lowering income variance for the targeted populations, achieving a high internal rate of social return, and raising GDP.

A preview of findings

This chapter offers the following tentative conclusions:

(1) Private giving seems to have been driven by relatively narrow sentiments. Donations are driven by the giver's own "warm glow" from being a giver, and people tend to give heavily to their own socio-economic group. Private giving rose slightly with rising incomes, though it has never been a large share of the economy.

(2) The rise of public welfare spending has not crowded out private giving, despite a common fear that it might do so. The two actually have a positive correlation over time.

(3) The modern rise of public social spending probably brought considerable gains in efficiency, GDP, and the larger concepts of human welfare quantified in Chapter 15 in this volume by Leandro Prados de la Escosura.[6] These investments in humans were blocked for millennia by weak and rapacious governments, and by a concentration of political power that rejected universal public schooling, family assistance, and public health insurance. Once the spread of voting power opened the doors to large universal social insurance, economies of scale and

---

4 Again, as with the broader social spending concept, the narrower and more targeted concept will either include or exclude expenditures on education, depending on the context.

5 In this chapter we focus on expenditures of money and commodities, and not the donor's time spent. This again allows us to focus on those resource transfers that are more controversial. For global data on the less controversial giving of volunteers' time, see Charities Aid Foundation (2010) and Giving USA (2010).

6 Prados de la Escosura, Chap. 15 in this volume (Figures 15.8 and 15.9) notes the strong, though declining, international correlation between his broad welfare measure and the share of social transfers in GDP. The historical parallels between social spending and conventional measures of well-being are developed more fully in his background paper.

economies of universal coverage brought down the operating costs of tax collections and or social investments.

(4) Yet since about the 1960s, the expansion of public social programs has probably stopped reaping efficiency gains, due to what journalists would call "mission creep." Several countries, most notably Japan, the United States, Italy, and Greece, have drifted away from their original mission of investing in the young, while at the same time maintaining intergenerational transfers in favor of the elderly. This drift did not bring any obvious net loss of GDP in the late twentieth century, but further population aging in the twenty-first century will force reforms that hold support for the elderly within sustainable steady-state limits.

Linking welfare theory and history: some low-hanging fruit

Linking economic theory with the broad historical patterns of social insurance and giving is not difficult. Microeconomists have developed theoretical ideas that seem to have good predictive power, and some have even been tested on data since the 1960s. To deal with the broader sweep of history, one should concentrate on a common-sense procedure that can establish good prima facie explanations while we await more focussed statistical tests. The procedure is a simple qualitative analogue to econometricians' differences in differences technique. Once the overall historical patterns of social insurance and social assistance have been established (in the next section), let us inspect the timing and the geography of differences in each popular explanatory variable, and see how well they correlate with differences in the level of insurance or assistance. We can further judge their likely unit impacts, or coefficients, with the help of other studies.

The popular explanatory variables are arranged schematically in Table 14.1. As one can see by comparing the two columns, the list of theoretical influences is nearly the same for social assistance (right-hand column) as for social insurance (left-hand column). The straightforward reason for this similarity is that the target group for social assistance consists of those who already suffer the poor condition(s) that social insurance was supposed to cover. What affects the one generally affects the other, albeit with different unit impact. Accordingly, the key players are introduced here by going from top to bottom in Table 14.1, discussing social insurance and social assistance at the same time.

Table 14.1. *Theoretical influences on social insurance and social assistance*

Social insurance (outside the family)	Social assistance (grants, tax breaks) for needy
Supply of private insurance services:	*Supply of private philanthropy:*
Transactions costs (−)	Transactions costs, freeriding (−)
Unit operating cost net of taxes (−), reflecting input prices and information	Unit operating cost net of taxes (−), reflecting input prices and information
Private after-tax incomes, net worth (+)	Private after-tax incomes, net worth (+)
	Tastes (warm glow, altruism, social affinity)
Supply of public tax-financed insurance services:	*Supply of public tax-financed assistance:*
Transactions costs, freeriding (−)	Transactions costs, free riding (−)
Operating cost net of taxes (−), reflecting input prices, technology, state fiscal capacity	Operating cost net of taxes (−), reflecting input prices, technology, fiscal capacity
Private after-tax incomes, net worth (+)	Private after-tax incomes, net worth (+)
Groups' demand, or "need" for insurance:	*Groups' demand, or "need" for assistance:*
Efficient need (e.g. capital constraints [−])	Efficient need (e.g. capital constraints [−])
Rising perceptions of risk, due to macro shocks (+) Moene and Wallerstein (2001)	Rising perceptions of risk (+), due to macro shocks (+), income of poorest groups (−)
Groups' political "voice" demanding insurance:	*Groups' political "voice" demanding assistance:*
Changes in franchise, lobbying institutions	Changes in franchise, lobbying institutions
Social affinity (+)	Social affinity (+)

The generosity of either insurance or assistance is shaped by familiar supply and demand forces, such as cost determinants on the supply side and the usual triad of income, prices, and tastes on the demand side.

Transactions costs and freeriding[7]

To set up firms or agencies supplying insurance requires overcoming the transactions costs of getting organized, aligning private ventures with legal institutions, and overcoming opposition from vested interests. A related task is

---

7 On transaction costs and institutional barriers to setting up private businesses and government institutions more broadly, see North (1981, 1990). On the freerider problem and its possible solutions, see Olson (1965), and the textbook summaries in Musgrave and Musgrave (1989), Stiglitz (2000), and especially Gruber (2005: Part II).

to overcome freeriding from consumers and imitating suppliers. The greater the numbers of potential participants, the higher are the hurdles. Economists are not completely pessimistic about the prospects for overcoming trans-actions costs and freeriding. They note that in some cases, the solution can even be privately achieved, as in the textbook case of port dues to pay for a lighthouse. It is time to breathe more history into this issue: When, where, and how were private solutions achieved?

It can be even harder to solve the public good problems of private social assistance than it is for insurance. Many who benefit from having social assistance given to the needy can "freeride," knowing that their contributions will probably not be crucial. In some cases, the problem can be solved by having the supply of potential charity concentrated into a few hands, so that freeriding does not lead to under-provision. In other cases, donors will not freeride, but instead will give simply because they derive a "warm glow" of utility from the very act of giving. In still others, a large prospective donor may win over the otherwise freeriders with a matching-grant approach, as long as their threat to hold back in the absence of matching is a credible one.[8]

Theorists and authors of public finance textbooks typically see a stronger case for having the public sector intervene to make assistance mandatory, the greater is the "freerider" problem that besets attempts to mobilize private demand for assistance as a public good. However, public approaches also face freeridership problems, especially in democracies. Election campaigns are weakened by voters' realization that their individual votes are not likely to be crucial, so that they often fail to vote. Forming a pressure group in favor of a public solution faces the same difficulties as private efforts. In addition, even elected representatives may have freeriding incentives to avoid supporting a public solution they want implemented, in order to avoid the wrath of constituents who oppose it. We therefore need to explore how the hurdles of both private and public provision of social aid have been lowered or raised in history, and how well these changes correlate with changes in the observed level of provision.

Unit operating costs

Obviously, either insurance or assistance will expand if something lowers its unit operating costs, such as administrative costs or the tax deductibility of

8 Karlan and List (2007, 2012) offer experimental evidence of the power of matching grant offers by large donors. They theorize that part of the power might come from small donors' feeling assured that large donors can monitor the charity's behavior more effectively.

insurance and charity. The key questions about such costs are empirical and comparative, not theoretical or conceptual. The empirical record shows clear patterns of difference in the scale and (therefore) the unit operating costs of private and public insurance and giving, as we shall see.

Income effects

Are social insurance and social assistance luxury goods, so that they take a rising share of the economy as incomes advance? The theoretical answer is yes on the giving front. Incomes do not govern the supply of private insurance directly, the way that income shapes consumer demand behavior. Rather, the effect of rising incomes on private insurance supply works indirectly through the tendency of growth and development to cut the cost of capital to insurance firms. We should expect that private social insurance would spread in response to the declining cost of capital that is integral to the growth process.

The supply of private charity has a more direct (and positive) income effect than does the supply of insurance, since charity supply is equivalent to a consumer demand for providing relief, and any consumer demand responds to income.

Should income growth raise the public supply of insurance and assistance? Theory is less clear here than for private giving. Something called "Wagner's Law" posits a rise in the share of all government spending in GDP in response to rising incomes, and it might seem natural to posit the same for the social part of government spending. Yet Wagner's Law is just something imagined about the data, with little theoretical underpinning, rather like the Kuznets curve of inequality and development, or the Philips Curve of macroeconomics in the 1960s.[9] While we shall explore the possible income elasticity of public support, we shall do so without having any clear theoretical presumption to test.

Taste factors (warm glow versus altruism, affinity versus diversity)

The prominent "warm glow" theory of private giving argues that people get direct utility from the act of their own giving. The same desire might be labeled giving for self-respect or, in a religious person, giving for spiritual salvation. As James Andreoni emphasizes, the warm glow theory denies that the well-being of the recipient is a pure public good. If it were, then extra

9 See Bird (1971). The original reference is Adolph Wagner's *Grundlegung der Politischen Ökonomie* (1863).

donations by others would reduce, or "crowd out," one's own donations. The warm glow theory is thus an alternative to an altruistic theory of private giving.[10]

Economists have also devoted considerable attention to positing and testing theories about private individuals' choices of target populations. *To whom* do people choose to give privately – people like themselves, or people in hardship? Both the prevailing theories and recent evidence suggest a stronger willingness to give to one's immediate social and economic peers, and not to distant groups. An immediate implication is that social diversity and economic inequality reduce private giving, for any given price structure.[11]

For public social insurance and public assistance, there is a similar tendency of theory and, especially, empirics to emphasize the role of social affinity between paying groups and recipient groups. Both within and between countries, the evidence seems to show that ethnic and religious diversity has a negative effect on the willingness to allow public programs to target the poor. The more diverse the population, the more the middle and upper income groups seem to resent public transfers and entitlements as redistributions from "us" to "them" through government.[12] A corollary would seem to be that admitting more immigrants of different ethnicity and religion would cut the provision of public aid.

Demand-side "need"

Common intuition and formal theorizing agree that social insurance should experience greater payouts, and social assistance should also be more forthcoming, in bad economic times and in poor places. The operative kind of need is *perception* of need, either in its altruistic variant ("they need our help") or its self-projecting variant ("that could be me") that has often given rise to fundraising campaigns and new insurance programs. Historical data on poverty and the macroeconomy make it relatively easy to test the strength of this pull of need, since perceptions presumably follow the macroeconomic realities.

---

10 See Andreoni (1988, 1990, 2006) and Andreoni and Payne (2011).
11 Rotemberg 2011; Andreoni *et al.* 2011. Of course, the effect of income inequality on private giving can be sensitive to the tax structure. If tax deduction rates for charitable contributions rise steeply enough with income, then greater inequality of pretax income could raise charitable giving.
12 For a theory of political pressures emphasizing social affinity as the basis for redistribution, see Kristov, Lindert, and McClelland (1992). For empirical verification of the negative effects of ethnic fractionalization on public social and infrastructure spending, see Easterly and Levine (1997); Alesina, Baqir, and Easterly (1999); Alesina and Glaeser (2004); Dahlberg, Edmark, and Lundqvist (2012).

The other principal "need" variable is the general severity of capital constraints. Throughout human history, a large share of the population has been trapped by the inability to borrow for investing in its own future productivity, either for human investments such as schooling or non-human investments such as land improvement. And at any phase of development, social insurance and social assistance provide an efficient means of alleviating that constraint and promoting both growth and equality. This kind of efficient gain from social insurance and social assistance would presumably decline in importance as the economy advances.

Political voice

The theories introduced so far have yet to face the question: "Who makes public decisions on social insurance and social assistance?" For that, we must turn to the field of political economy, for a literature recognizing that the political tug-of-war over redistribution depends on the distribution of political voice. As that literature emphasizes, greater lobbying power for wealthy potential taxpayers is a key negative influence on vertically redistributive public tax-transfer programs. On the other side of the same coin, extending voting rights to lower and lower income groups raises the expected value of tax-based social insurance and assistance. Clearly, if we are to make sense of the long global history of social spending, we must take into account the changes in the voting franchise and in the power of elites.

Social spending since the late eighteenth century

To sort out which of these most popular theories help most, and which help least, in explaining the long history of private and public aid, this section begins by charting the global contours of that long history.

Little before the late eighteenth century

Before the late eighteenth century, there was relatively little in the way of social insurance and social help for the needy, despite all the books and articles written about the institutions of early aid. To be sure, some private institutions of mutual aid did insure their members, conforming to the tendency toward social affinity, the exchange of help with one's own social group. To judge from the few data we have, and to conjecture that absence of data tended to betray absence of generous aid, private insurance and mutual aid seemed to have reached their highest levels in the late eighteenth century in England and Wales and the Netherlands, as shown by a few estimates in

Table 14.2. *Church and private charity for the poor, as shares of national product in the eighteenth and nineteenth centuries*

(1) Netherlands 1790, estimated private and Church aid	= 0.67–1.49% of GNP
(2) Churches in France, 1790	≤ 0.17 % of GNP
(3) England and Wales charities 1819–1837	≤ 0.40% of GNP
(4) England and Wales charities 1861–1876	≤ 0.10% of GNP
(5) Charities in Italy 1868	≤ 0.50% of GNP
(6) Church and private charity in France 1880	≤ 0.50% of GNP

Sources: Lindert (1998: 103–108) and the sources cited there.

Table 14.2. Marco van Leeuwen's important recent study of private Dutch insurance pools in the second half of that century shows significant benefits paid out for burial expenses, sickness benefit, medical costs, widowhood, and old age. For those receiving them, pension and old age benefits ranged from 20 to 50 percent of the typical wage. Yet those covered represented a small fringe of society, mainly middle-class members of large craft guilds in the main cities. Their restrictiveness and small size was one means of avoiding adverse selection.[13]

Much harder to find before about 1800 were significant levels of private insurance or assistance to the poor, even if we include aid from religious institutions and even if we confine our search to relatively prosperous Western Europe. Private and Church charity was ubiquitous, elaborate – and negligible. Every country had tens of thousands of individual bequests. Wealthy individuals seeking salvation went beyond almsgiving and set up their own trusts, just as many do today. Most charities were not for the poor, but for supporting general worship, apprenticeships, and general hospitals.

As best we can gather from official inquiries and later historical studies, churches and other private charities gave little to the poor in the eighteenth and nineteenth centuries (again see Table 14.2). In relatively generous England, officially monitored charities gave less than 0.4 percent of national income to all recipients, only some of whom were poor. Granted, these data miss some unrecorded individual gifts. Yet the amounts in the late eighteenth century, and presumably in previous centuries as well, were low by modern standards, even though the totals would have included donations for

13 Van Leeuwen 2000, 2012. The larger guilds also combated the potential problems of adverse selection by compelling members to pay fees that helped finance the insurance pool.

education. In the Catholic countries of Western Europe, the Church aid received by the needy was apparently even lower, presumably less than half a percent of national income.[14]

As of the late eighteenth century, the public sector's most frequent social prop was confined to its own employees, especially the military. Even the military's own pensions and survivor support was not reliable unless the state itself had permanence. The rise of a stable military state created secure pensions for surviving military personnel, both in the Roman empire and in the early modern period. Often the pension was embodied in a gift of land.[15]

Public support for the poor, disabled, and dependent was extremely limited before the late eighteenth century. The literature on Western Europe sometimes dates the rise of poor relief too early by imagining that it became substantial upon the passage of some early law, such as the Elizabethan Poor Laws of 1597 and 1601. In fact, such laws were largely designed to restrict or at least regularize existing practice, without providing any funding for an expansion of aid. Much of the seventeenth- and eighteenth-century legislation was punitive, calling for increasingly harsh treatment of vagabonds. Poor relief did not exceed 1 percent of national income until after 1750, and then only in two countries, the Netherlands and in England-Wales, where it peaked at around 2.5 percent just before the Poor Law Reform of 1834 slashed assistance (Figure 14.1). Even tax-financed public education was notably absent around the world, as it had been for millennia, although some monarchs (e.g. Prussia's Frederick II (the Great) in 1763 and Austria's Maria Theresa in 1775) passed unfunded mandates telling localities that they should educate their children.[16]

The gradual rise, 1800–1945

Even in the nineteenth and early twentieth centuries, support for social insurance and assistance rose only at a modest pace, relative to the ability to pay. The private insurance business continued to do little business with families. As of 1929 in the United States, for example, households paid only $880 million, or less than one percent of GDP on life insurance, and a negligible amount ($2 million) on health insurance. The postwar era brought

---

14 Lindert 2004: vol I, 40–45. Of course, the amounts given would be higher shares of donor incomes than of national incomes. The national income denominator is used here because it is more available, and because shares of national income suggest the limited extent of overall redistribution and of poverty reduction.
15 Clark, Craig, and Wilson 2003: chaps. 2–3.
16 See Lindert 1998 and 2004: vol I, chaps. 1, 3, and 5.

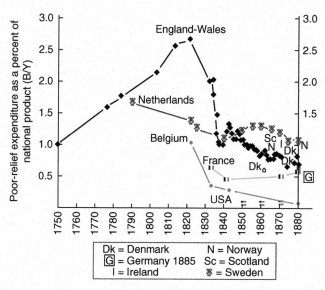

Figure 14.1. Poor-relief expenditures as a share of national product, Europe and United States, 1750–1880

Source: Lindert (2004: Vol I, chap 3).

an acceleration of private purchases of personal insurance, rising by 1999 to a little over 1 percent of GDP for life insurance and personal pension plans and another 0.7 percent of GDP on individual purchases of health insurance, plus the much larger amount of postwar insurance contributions to employer-based plans.[17]

Private philanthropy continued to be modest, and only a small share of it was directed toward the poor and those in bad health. So we conclude from data for the United States, one of the few countries to quantify charitable giving, and perhaps also the country where the most was given privately. Table 14.3 illustrates with estimates of the shares of GDP contributed privately in 1927 and 1970. Even if all philanthropy had gone to "welfare" in 1927, that would have delivered only 1.52 percent of GDP, a lower share than England and Wales local governments gave to their poor a century earlier under the Old Poor Law. As Table 14.3 further reminds us, very little of US philanthropy went, or still goes, to the poor. In 1927, only a tenth of a percent of GDP went to "youth services, welfare, and race relations." The parts of other categories

17 See Carter *et al.* 2006: Series Cd44, Cd48, Cd206, and Cd214.

Table 14.3. *Recipients' philanthropy revenues, United States 1927 and 1970*

	(Percentages of GDP)	
	1927	1970
Total	1.52	1.74
Religious organizations	0.81	0.66
Parochial schools	0.16	0.14
Higher education	0.22	0.24
Youth services, welfare, race relations	0.10	0.20
Hospitals and health	0.06	0.23
Other	0.06	0.27

Source: Professor Ralph L. Nelson's contribution to US Census Bureau (1976), series H398-H411. For slightly different estimates, see US Census Bureau (1973: Table 510).

received by the poor and needy were probably offset by the parts of this category they did not receive. The private contributions to "welfare" were much smaller than the amounts contributed to churches, to parochial schools, and to higher education (e.g. the Ivy League or Stanford).

Another striking pattern from the well-documented US record is revealed by the behavior of private giving after 1927, and after the arrival of huge needs in the Great Depression. Figure 14.2 sketches this history, comparing two different measures of private giving for welfare-type recipients with the time path of public aid to the same target group. Private aid has gone on rising since the 1920s, even though it did not rise as fast as public aid, which jumped twice after having been a tiny share of the nation's income until the Great Depression. During the nation's first jump in public relief under the New Deal, private charity changed little, partly because it was small already and partly because the asset value losses of 1929 to 1933 must have made it more difficult to give to others. The second great rise in public relief spanned the entire postwar period, with temporary accelerations during recessions. Interestingly, private giving also continued its (slower) upward march after the war, judging either from the narrower and more targeted spending on the needy or from a less narrow measure of private welfare services.

For other countries, as well as for the United States, the advance of public social spending accelerated across the twentieth century, as shown in Figure 14.3. Even as late as 1930, no country spent as much as 5 percent of GDP on public social programs, not even in the Nordic states, where it later

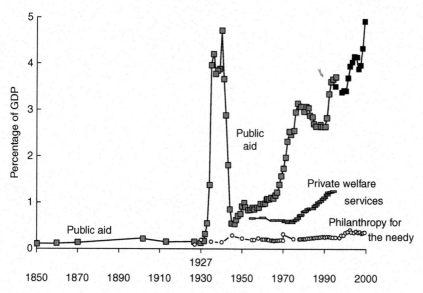

Figure 14.2. Public and private assistance to the needy in the United States, 1850–2009
Notes: *"Public aid"* = Poor relief, 1850–1870: US Superintendent of the Census, *Compendium of the Ninth Census* (1872): 530–537. These figures probably include some public subsidies to private charities.
All public expenditures (federal, state, and local), 1902–1970: *Bicentennial Hist. Stats.*, Series Y533–Y566.
GNP in current prices: Carter *et al.* (2006), Series Ca10, collated by Richard Sutch.
For alternative estimates of public welfare, health-sanitation, and education for 1890, 1902, 1913, and later dates, see Musgrave and Culbertson (1953): 114). The Musgrave-Culbertson estimates were used in Lindert (1994).
Further footnote on public aid 1995–2009 =
The Census Bureau's own footnote explains:
"Consists of federal benefits (food stamp benefits, Supplemental Security Income, direct relief, earned income credit, payments to nonprofit institutions, aid to students, and payment for medical services for retired military personnel and their dependents at nonmilitary facilities) and state benefits (Medicare care, Aid to Families with Dependent Children, Supplemental Security Income, general assistance, energy assistance, emergency assistance, and medical insurance premium payments on behalf of indigents). Financed from state and federal general revenues."
Private philanthropy for the needy, alternative series =
(a) For 1930–1970, featuring "Youth services, welfare, race relations" expenditures: Bicentennial HSUS, Series H405–H411.
For 1955, 1960–2009, the Giving USA series, with these changing series:
(b) "welfare" for 1955, 1960–1962, but not usable for 1963–1967 because it lost health expenditures for the "welfare" population;
(c) "human resources (welfare)" for 1964–1975, now excluding donations to welfare agencies for health spending;
(d) "social welfare" for 1960, 1965, 1970, 1973–1981;
(e) "Human service" and "public/social benefit" for 1970, 1975–2009.
Private welfare services =Private social expenditure, welfare services (*Historical Statistics of the United States*, 2006). Not specifically targeted at those below the poverty line, or those with disabilities.

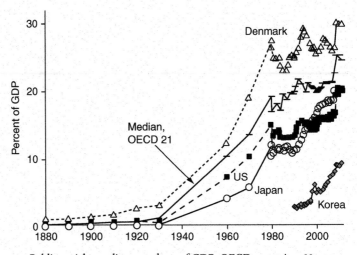

Figure 14.3. Public social spending as a share of GDP, OECD countries 1880–2011
Sources = Lindert (1994), OECD (1985), OECD Social Expenditure Database.
The series excludes expenditures for public education.
The OECD made a series change at 1980, resulting in a drop in the median expenditure
share by 2.2 percent of GDP.

hovered around 30 percent of GDP. We must return to the task of explaining
some glaring historical facts that stand out in Figure 14.3: Why was there no
significant social insurance or social assistance for most of human history, and
why was the eventual rise so unequal among countries?

The postwar welfare state revolution

The real rise of public social spending, and possibly private social spending to a
lesser extent, came after World War II, as shown again in Figures 14.1 and 14.2.
That is, of the major formative episodes highlighted in the introduction to this
volume by Kevin O'Rourke and Jeffrey Williamson,[18] the rise of social
spending accompanied the postwar "spread and deepening" of global capitalism, not the earlier interwar retreat from it. While the trend has stopped after
1980 in the highest-spending welfare states, as illustrated for Denmark in
Figure 14.3, social spending continues to rise as a share of GDP in many
OECD countries. At the core of the dramatic postwar rise of public social
insurance was the switch to universal entitlements, from "means-tested"
support restricted to the poor (those of little "means"). For pensions in

18 Williamson and O'Rourke, Chap 1 in this volume.

particular, support for the middle-income groups became greater than support for the poor in absolute purchasing power, since an individual's pension became greater, the more one had earned at work. Accordingly, the redistribution from rich to poor did not keep pace with the rise in public social spending.[19]

In this setting, and in so many historical settings, the rise of a phenomenon prompts governments to measure and publicize it. The welfare state revolution caused a diffusion of social expenditure data gathering, first among a couple dozen OECD countries and then around the globe. Taking advantage of this diffusion, we can examine intercontinental patterns more clearly, with the help of Table 14.4.

As of 2007, the OECD now has developed a fairly clear snapshot of both private and public social spending, broadly defined. Private social insurance can be mandated by law, as in Switzerland, or overwhelmingly voluntary, as in the United States, or both. The extent of the shift toward public social spending is underlined by contrasting the lowest share among these countries in 2007 – namely, Mexico's 7.2 percent of GDP – with the fact that no country in the world spent such a large share on social services as late as 1930.[20] For twenty countries in Table 14.4, we can now explore the international correlation between public and private social expenditures. That negative correlation (-0.19) suggests that the issue of public programs' "crowding out" private contributions has more potential in the contrast between countries than it does within countries over time.

The fact that lower-income countries still devote lower shares of their incomes to social spending raises the question: Will their social spending shares catch up when their incomes catch up, as Wagner's Law would predict? The answer to the catching-up question, it turns out, varies by world region. Countries of the former Soviet bloc, including those in central Europe, definitely spend a greater share of GDP on social services than did Japan, Sweden, or the United States with comparable income levels in the more distant past. On the other hand, Korea and Singapore and other East Asian countries spend less than income comparisons would have suggested. Among other regions, those from Latin America and the Middle East tended to have larger social budgets than their incomes would have suggested, rather like Chile or Turkey in Table 14.4. By contrast, countries from south Asia spent

19 Reynolds and Smolensky 1977; Baldwin 1990.
20 The one possible exception is the Soviet Union up to 1930, on which we lack sufficient data on social expenditures.

Table 14.4. *Private and public social expenditures as shares of GDP, 2007*

	Private social expenditures		Public social expenditures				
	Mandatory	Voluntary	Total public	Pensions	Working-age income support	Health services	Other
Australia	0.5	3.3	16.0	3.4	4.0	5.7	2.9
Austria	0.8	1.0	26.4	12.3	5.3	6.8	2.1
Belgium	0.0	4.7	26.3	8.9	7.2	7.3	3.0
Canada	..	5.3	16.9	4.2	2.5	7.0	3.2
Chile	1.2	..	10.6	5.2	0.9	3.7	0.9
Czech Rep.	0.2	0.2	18.8	7.4	4.4	5.8	1.2
Denmark	0.2	2.3	26.0	5.5	7.0	6.5	7.0
Estonia	..	0.0	13.0	5.2	3.1	4.0	0.7
Finland	..	1.1	24.9	8.3	6.0	6.1	4.6
France	0.3	2.6	28.4	12.5	4.6	7.5	3.8
Germany	1.1	1.8	25.2	10.7	4.0	7.8	2.7
Greece	..	1.5	21.3	11.9	2.0	5.9	1.6
Hungary	..	0.2	22.9	9.1	5.3	5.2	3.2
Iceland	1.6	3.6	14.6	1.9	3.7	5.7	3.2
Ireland	..	1.5	16.3	3.6	5.3	5.8	1.6
Israel	..	0.5	15.5	4.8	4.0	4.3	2.3
Italy	1.6	0.6	24.9	14.1	2.8	6.6	1.4
Japan	0.6	3.1	18.7	..	..	..	..
Korea	0.6	2.0	7.6	1.7	0.8	3.5	1.5
Luxem.	0.3	0.7	20.6	6.5	5.7	6.4	2.1
Mexico	..	0.2	7.2	1.4	0.9	2.6	2.3
Netherlands	0.6	6.3	20.1	4.7	5.3	6.0	4.1
NZ	..	0.4	18.4	4.3	5.1	7.1	1.9
Norway	1.2	0.8	18.4	4.3	5.1	7.1	1.9
Poland	..	0.0	19.8	10.6	3.5	4.6	1.1
Portugal	0.4	1.5	22.5	10.8	4.0	6.6	1.1
Slovak Rep.	0.1	0.8	15.7	5.8	3.5	5.2	1.1
Slovenia	..	1.0	20.3	9.6	3.9	5.6	1.1
Spain	..	0.5	21.6	8.0	5.1	6.1	2.4
Sweden	0.4	2.5	27.3	7.2	5.6	6.6	8.0
Switz.	7.2	1.1	18.5	6.4	4.3	5.6	2.2
Turkey	..	..	10.5	..	..	..	..
UK	0.8	5.0	20.5	5.4	4.5	6.8	3.8
USA	0.3	10.2	16.2	6.0	2.0	7.2	1.0
OECD	0.6	1.9	19.3	6.9	4.0	5.8	2.5

Source: Adema *et al.* 2011: 21, 24.
Note that this OECD definition excludes expenditures on education.
20-country correlation of total private spending shares with total public = −0.19.

less. We seem to be glimpsing the emergence of a global geography of differences in social spending driven by differences in history. It remains to be seen whether any non-European and non-communist country will develop a welfare state devoting more than, say, 20 percent of GDP to public social spending.[21]

Explaining the delayed rise

Why no take-off in private social spending?

With the broad historical movements in view as fully as the data allow, we can ask whether any simple combination of the theoretically predicted influences can explain the directions and the timing of these movements, beginning with the absence of any known movement over the millennia leading up to the late eighteenth century.

The first question is why private individuals and organizations, including churches, delivered only negligible private aid or insurance, beyond the boundaries of the families and organizations themselves, especially before the nineteenth century. Did the basic variables in Table 14.1 behave differently up through the eighteenth century, or even the nineteenth, from their behavior in the twentieth century, when private giving rose very modestly?

The most obvious difference is that potential donors were poorer in the past. Yet history constrains the likely importance of this income effect. As we have seen, private giving was still less than 1 percent of income in Western Europe by 1800, when incomes of the wealthier classes had already risen considerably, and was similarly low in the much richer United States as late as 1927. The fact that affluent families and organizations were poorer in 1800 than today could not have made a great difference, given that we know of no exogenous rise in the after-tax price of giving or any global shift of tastes away from giving, which could hypothetically have hidden a strongly positive income effect. The income elasticity could not have been very high over the long run.[22]

---

21 The text says "non-European and non-communist" to allow for the exceptional case of Cuba.
22 This argument must remain rough and tentative, of course. The income and price elasticities of private charitable giving are exceedingly hard to identify statistically. Even for the United States today, where we have a rich database, it is hard to extract exogenous measures of income or after-tax price, in part because the income tax deduction for charitable giving is a price effect directly tied to income itself. For a thorough discussion of the difficulty of measuring income and price elasticities of giving see Andreoni (2006: 1233–1258).

History similarly constrains the idea that the after-tax price of private social insurance or giving was higher back before 1800. Granted, the private insurance industry was hobbled by weaker financial and property-rights institutions in the past. Its ability to supply affordable insurance may have improved greatly with subsequent financial developments. Yet, as we have seen, the American experience suggests that private health insurance did not exceed 1 percent of GDP until the postwar era. As for the long-run price history of private charitable giving, it too cannot have changed much, in the general absence of income taxation or of charity-based deductions from it.

If private giving rates and the prices of giving moved little, while incomes rose significantly across the nineteenth and twentieth centuries, we are left with three explanations of the lateness and gradualness of long-run change in private giving as a share of income. Either:

(1) the income effects were in fact large, but their stimulus to giving was largely cancelled by exogenous shifts in tastes away from charity; or

(2) the income effects were in fact large, but the rise of the welfare state crowded out what would have been a large rise in private giving by altruists caring about the total amounts that the needy received (induced shift in tastes); or

(3) the income elasticities were in fact small and the affluent never felt inclined to give much.

Seeing no historical reason why tastes should have shifted away from charity at the same time that incomes accelerated across the nineteenth and twentieth centuries, I tentatively doubt the first explanation. The second option – large income effects were offset by crowding out from the welfare state – would have worked if there had been historical evidence of a rise in private giving during a long period when incomes were growing and there was no welfare state. Yet American experience finds a large rise in per capita income from, say, 1800 to 1927 with no appreciable private giving either at the start or at the end of that period.

Accepting the third explanation fits with that "warm glow" model favored by the present-day microeconomic literature. Over the centuries, people have given privately because they gain utility from the act of giving, and the amounts they gave did not respond much to competing supplies of aid to the targeted group (i.e. no crowding out of altruists). To the "warm glow" theory, this simple reading of history suggests a friendly amendment: The warm glow is achieved by very low levels of giving. Perhaps over the centuries, donors have gained satisfaction by giving at least something, and felt no need to "give until it hurts." That would help to explain why there have always been so many charities, with so little closure of poverty gaps.

Why the delayed arrival of the welfare state

The next interpretive task is to ask why the rise in public social insurance and assistance arrived so late in history, only after World War II, and why it then grew so large in several European democracies. A follow-up set of questions relates to the efficiency of the observed history: Would it have been efficient, in the sense of achieving high rates of return and raised GDP, if the welfare state had arrived earlier; or was the change only efficient under postwar conditions; or was it never efficient? Partial answers are forthcoming, using qualitative contrasts that imitate the econometricians' "differences in differences" approach.

Would today's higher shares of social spending have been efficient anytime before World War II? One's answer must imply, of course, a judgment of what it was that prevented the earlier arrival. The quickest road to an overall tentative answer starts with tax-based public primary education, one of the earliest forms of tax-based social spending. The reason to start with public education is that it is a case with a famously high and positive rate of return, especially in less developed settings, even without reckoning the value of its "externality" benefits. As far as we can tell, there never was a time in the last six or more centuries in which the returns to primary education were low, waiting to be raised by some onset of modernization. Literacy and numeracy paid off, especially for males. Even if access to some occupations, such as government officialdom, was artificially restricted, a young man could apply his literacy and numeracy to unregulated commercial and craft occupations that had a use for them. History's constraint on primary education has always been the inability to solve the capital constraint. Since private capital markets have never solved the problem of universal investments in children's education, to be repaid by their future earnings, primary schooling always needed tax-based support, even in the eyes of Adam Smith, Thomas Jefferson, and Milton Friedman.[23]

The first historical step toward efficient public investment in primary education was to build state fiscal capacity, so that the government could administer public investments with a minimum of mistakes and corruption, while borrowing at a low interest rate reflecting the government's own

---

23 This section's treatment of the history of public primary education draws on Go and Lindert (2010) and Lindert (2009).

credibility. As demonstrated by Mark Dincecco, state fiscal capacity arrived at different times in different countries, as soon as each country's political history cleared the way for limited yet centralized government, as in Britain after the Glorious Revolution of 1688. Dincecco and Gabriel Katz have further shown that the arrival of state fiscal capacity led not just to more military might, but also to investments in education and infrastructure, with a statistically significant and sizeable stimulus to the growth of GDP.[24]

Even after this fiscal barrier had been removed, most governments failed for some additional decades to deliver tax support for universal primary schooling, at an economic cost to the economy as a whole and in some cases a cost even to the government's own budget. As I have quantified elsewhere for two settings, Victorian England and Venezuela from the 1950s to the 1980s (Lindert 2009: Tables 5 and 6), the social rate of return to tax-based investments that were not made in primary education was so high that the government itself could have reaped a competitive rate of return based on the extra tax revenues from adults who had received the tax-based schooling. In the case of England, what we know about interest rates and skilled-wage premia suggests that government and society passed up high rates of return all the way from about 1717 to the implementation of the Fees Act of 1891. Further studies should continue to turn up other historical cases in which prima facie evidence suggests that high returns to public schooling were passed up.

For what other kinds of social investments could the return have been high, and why were the investments not made earlier?

Poor relief was a second kind of social spending that could have yielded a high rate of return in terms of life expectancy, labor supply, and national product. Roderick Floud, Robert Fogel, Bernard Harris, and Sok Chul Hong offer extensive evidence that extra nutrition for the bottom decile or two of English and French society in the eighteenth and early nineteenth centuries would have raised labor supply and productivity. If one further assumes that poor relief brought the extra nutrition it was meant to bring, then the relative generosity of English poor relief before 1834 deserves high marks for feeding the poor and raising their labor supply. Outweighing the famous conservative argument that the poor relief would reduce labor supply, by encouraging laziness and insolence, is the likelihood that labor supply would have been raised overall given the magnitude of the positive survival effects estimated by Floud, Fogel, Harris, and Hong. Unfortunately, England and

24 Dincecco 2011, Dincecco and Katz (in press).

Wales cut poor relief in 1834 and again in 1870, delaying some of the nutrition gains until very late in the nineteenth century.[25] Here too, efficiency seems to have been sacrificed by holding back on social spending.

A third missed opportunity might have been the delay in public health investments, such as urban sanitation. Jeffrey Williamson has argued that Britain's investments in urban sanitation lagged a couple of decades behind the knowledge that cholera and other diseases were waterborne.[26] This third case of temporary underinvestment seems less glaring than the case of primary schooling, since sanitation infrastructure did not lag as long behind the discovery of potential benefits as was true of the long-known gains from schooling.

Why should it be so easy to document historical cases in which high-return social investments failed to receive tax support even though governments had the capacity to finance them? Comparing governments and time periods suggests a clear answer. The key second barrier that had to be removed was the concentration of political power into the hands of elites opposed to taxation for growth-enhancing public investment.[27] The concentration could only be broken up by shifting power toward potential beneficiary groups. Across the nineteenth century and the early twentieth, voting rights finally became more widespread, and the ballot became secret, in one country after another in Europe and North America. Since the earlier restrictions on voting rights favored the wealthy, one impact of spreading the vote was to place fiscal issues more and more into the hands of middle- and lower-income groups. This spread of voice played a clear role in raising public investments in schooling, family assistance, and public health.[28]

---

25 For the evidence linking nutrition with health and labor supply for the poor of England and France, see Floud *et al.* (2011: 125–225). We should add a further pair of links, from poor relief to fertility, and from fertility to labor supply. Boyer (1989) has shown statistically that England's poor relief facilitated fertility, thus further increasing the labor supply in the long run.

26 Williamson 1990: 276–298.

27 The developments sketched here parallel those described as the arrival of "new alternatives to liberal capitalism" in Jeffry Frieden and Ronald Rogowski, Chap. 12 in this volume. That elites with entrenched power, free from political competition, will block innovations and investments enhancing economic growth has long been suspected. For a current theoretical model formalizing this point see Acemoglu and Robinson (2006).

28 For the chronology of the spread of voting rights and voter turnout, see Flora, Kraus, and Pfenning (1983) and Mackie and Rose (1991, 1997). For the issues of public social spending and the taxes to pay for it, the extent of the franchise seems a more useful measure than the oft-used Polity indices of constraints on the executive and interparty competition. On the role of electoral voice in schooling, poor relief, and public health

While these two explanatory forces – the rise of state fiscal capacity and the spread of political voice – deserve to be featured as prime movers in the gradual rise of social spending up to about 1930, they must share the spotlight with several other forces when our historical explanations are to encompass the further acceleration of public spending up to about 1980.

A long-run force tipping in favor of high-budget government social programs has been their efficiency in delivering lower unit operating costs on both the tax side and the expenditure side. Prosperity and democracy have allowed countries to economize on administrative costs by shifting from narrow and expensive taxes and transfers to broad taxes and broad entitlements. On the tax side, history shows steep declines in the administrative cost shares of indirect tax collection across the nineteenth century and the early twentieth, both in the United Kingdom and in the United States, as shown in Figure 14.4. In both countries, the cost of collections dropped from over 4.5 percent of the amounts collected in the mid nineteenth century or earlier to 2 percent or less since the middle of the twentieth century. Economies of scale have cut the costs of bureaucracy, so that the US Internal Revenue Service, for example, costs only half a percent of the amounts collected. To the extent that the same happened in other countries, a part of the history of the rise of public social spending conforms to Mark Dincecco's story of increasing efficiency in government.[29]

On the public social expenditure side, our time series on administrative cost shares do not antedate the 1930s, but we can add comparisons of public and private delivery systems today. These comparisons suggest that shifting from narrow and heavily policed social assistance to broad public entitlements programs have cut costs, through economies of scale and the reduction in monitoring. Back before 1880 Europe's main kind of program was classic poor relief. Societies intent on forcing all the able-bodied to work tried to emphasize "indoor relief" in which one was kept in a poorhouse or workhouse. They never succeeded in getting such "indoor" relief to account for half of their budget, or for half of the recipients covered. Still, to the extent that relief was given indoors, its administrative costs were a high share, often 25 percent, of the total amount spent. The reason was simply that the poor had to be policed and completely provided for. By contrast, once democracy and prosperity and other changes made society more willing to give aid to people in their own

before 1930, see Lindert (2004: chaps 4, 7, 15, and 16); Go and Lindert (2010); and Williamson (1990: 294–298). The same influence of voting power is documented globally for education spending in the postwar era by Ansell (2010).

29 Lindert (2004: vol 1, Figure 12.1 and the accompanying text), and again Dincecco (2011).

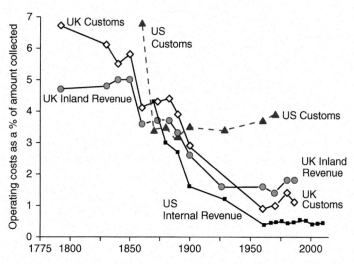

Figure 14.4. Tax collection costs as a percentage of the amounts collected by central government, United States and United Kingdom, 1787/96–2011

Notes: *United States, two main revenue agencies:* The cost percentages up through 1960 are five-year averages calculated from the annual reports of the US Secretary of the Treasury. Those for 1966–2011 are annual figures published in the *IRS Data Book*'s online archive at www.irs.gov/taxstats. I am indebted to Joel Slemrod of the University of Michigan for pointing out this continuation of the IRS series.

United Kingdom, main revenue services: Figures for years before World War I divide the official estimates of collection costs by gross receipts, while those after World War I divide it by what are called "net receipts." The change in official convention matters little, since adding the collection costs themselves to the denominator would change the ratio by only about 1 percent of itself.

For 1787–1796: The figures are calculated from *The Fourth Report* of Great Britain, Select Committee on Finance, 19 July 1797. The collection costs are described only as the "charges of management" on the "collection of revenues," and are compared to gross receipts. For 1830–1860: The main source is a special return in House of Commons, *Sessional Papers*, 1862, vol. xxx, 601. Each figure from this source refers to the single fiscal year starting in the year listed. However, the customs percentages for 1840, 1850, and 1860 are five-year averages centered on that same fiscal year. For 1873–1900: Annual Reports of the Commissioners of Customs and Inland Revenue. The figures for Inland Revenue are again single-year figures for fiscal years starting 1 April, and those for the Customs service are five-year averages centered on that year. The customs figures for years between 1855/6 and 1876/7 had to be adjusted upward, to correct for the temporary exclusion of the Coast Guard costs. For 1926–1986: Single-year figures are calculated from the Annual Reports of the Customs Commissioner and the Commissioner of Inland Revenue.

Figure 14.4 graphs a Customs series and an Inland Revenue series for the United Kingdom as if they were consistently defined throughout. That is, the figure ignores the fact that excises were shifted from the Inland Revenue series to the Customs (and Excise) series between the 1900 data point and the 1926 data point.

homes, with minimal supervision, the administrative costs fell as a share of the amount spent. Stricter regimes are more bureaucratic and more costly.

By the postwar era, program-operating costs have fallen to almost-negligible levels in the high-income OECD countries. So say not only data on programs for the poor, but especially the data on pension programs. International data on pension support programs show that administrative costs are less than 3 percent of the pension-program budget in all high-income countries, and often below 1 percent. As if to re-wind history in a global cross-section, the cost burdens are much higher for the public pension systems of developing countries, partly because they are not universal, but are rather narrow not-so-contributory programs redistributing in favor of the public sector itself.[30]

In the health sector, there is a similar cost contrast, though it shows up as a contrast between two mixed systems, rather than a contrast between purely public and pure private. The best-documented contrast is that the somewhat-more–private health care system of the United States has administrative and overhead (i.e. bureaucratic) costs that are far above those in the universal insurance countries of Canada and Germany, on a per capita basis.[31]

The same relative efficiency of public over private social programs is suggested by today's rough administrative cost shares for private charities, which tend to be higher than the 3 percent for public pensions and broad public assistance programs. For example, in 2010 the administrative cost burden took about 8 percent of current outlays for the American Red Cross, and some large part of the 13.7 percent taken by "Program and administrative expenses" at the Bill and Melinda Gates Foundation. A higher bureaucratic burden seems evident for United Way, given that "general, administrative, and fundraising" support services took 10 percent, and expenses for "Brand Leadership and Campaign and Public Relations" took another 17.2 percent in 2010. Some of these accounting categories might mix some true grant aid in with the administrative burden, but the latter's share would probably still be

---

30 The administrative costs for the US Social Security Administration were 1.6 percent of benefit payments in fiscal year 2012, and are projected as 1.4 percent for fiscal 2013. See www.ssa.gov/budget/FY13Files/2013KeyTables.pdf and similar for 2012. For the late twentieth century, see Estrin (1988). For the slightly higher cost shares of less universal assistance programs in the early twentieth century, see Gordon (1940). For the higher administrative cost ratios in developing countries of Latin America, see K. Lindert, Skoufias, and Shapiro (2006,: pp. 76–78).
31 Woodlander, Campbell, and Himmelstein 2003: especially 771 and Reinhardt 2000.

well above the public programs' cost burden.[32] The most likely reasons for these cost differences are that the more private institutions must invest more in screening applicants, and must operate on a smaller scale because of limitations on donor generosity.

While operating costs were gradually being reduced by the expansion of public social programs, discrete shocks in the twentieth century shifted tastes toward universal social insurance and social assistance. Above all, the two world wars and the Great Depression of the 1930s heightened the public sense of shared downward risk, and promoted new bonds of social affinity. For the United States and for Sweden, the history of the "welfare state" was launched in the peacetime context of the 1930s. Yet for most of Western Europe, the two world wars seemed to have played a bigger role in ushering in the modern welfare state. World War II also brought a revolution in the social thinking of the Roman Catholic Church. Before the war the Church had been a bulwark of conservatism, opposing state intervention into social insurance. After the war, it began to champion welfare state provision to those in need.[33]

While state fiscal capacity, the spread of political voice, the rising efficiency of broad-based social programs, and the shocks of world wars and depression dominate our explanations of *when* public social spending accelerated, other forces must be introduced to explain *where* it accelerated. A frequently noted influence is racial, ethnic, and religious fractionalization. As noted earlier, it makes theoretical sense that whatever erodes social affinity can block the use of the public sector as a means to alleviate hardship. The degree of fractionalization shows statistical power as a negative determinant of public social and infrastructure programs, e.g. among African states, or among states of the United States, or in the contrasts among core OECD countries, once one has controlled for income levels and other variables.[34] Still, its power in explaining differences between countries is not so robust. Consider the contrast between two countries that fail to conform to the usual negative association of ethnic

32 For the American Red Cross expenses in 2010, see www.redcross.org/flash/AnnualReport/2010/AnnualReport.html. For the Bill and Melinda Gates Foundation, see www.gatesfoundation.org/annualreport/2010/Pages/overview.aspx; and for United Way, see www.unitedway.org/pages/2010-annual-report; all accessed April 27, 2012.

33 Lindert 2004: chaps 7, 16, and 17. In Spain, however, this transition began only in the 1960s, in the second phase of the Franco dictatorship. Up to that time the Church was still Franco's ally against large social programs, with a similar alliance to Salazar in Portugal. Still, in countries threatening to vote for communists, as in Italy and France, the Church showed more support for social safety nets.

34 Again see Easterly and Levine (1997), Alesina et al. (1999), and Alesina and Glaeser (2004).

fractionalization with public social spending. Korea has an ethnically homogeneous population, yet makes very little use of the public sector to lift up the poor. Belgium is the opposite kind of outlier, having a bitter and nearly even split between Flemish- and French-speaking populations, yet with a generous welfare state.[35] Such outliers are common enough that history refuses to offer a simple negative correlation between ethnic fractionalization and public social spending. Only when income and other variables are held constant does the negative relationship show up. It is possible that a rise in ethnic divisions caused by rising immigration will erode some countries' political support for universal entitlements.[36]

Gray power, mission shift, and efficiency stagnation

Thus far, the rise of tax-based social insurance and assistance seems like a success story, capturing large gains in GDP as well as greater income security. That success featured different kinds of social spending in different countries. Some, particularly the United States, achieved the growth effects mainly through public education, while European welfare states achieved relatively greater gains through improved public health and safety nets for the poor.

Since about the 1960s, however, the further expansion of government social budgets changed focus, drifting away from the human investments with the greatest GDP gains and toward support for the elderly and the middle classes, with effects on GDP that are more neutral so far. This section charts the mission shift, first viewing the locus of its success, then examining its fingerprints in terms of social expenditure behavior, and finally conjecturing about its efficiency consequences and implications for the future.

Since the 1960s, poverty rates have been reduced much more for the elderly than for children or persons of working age. Figure 14.5 shows this for the United States, and Table 14.5 shows the same for averages over groups of OECD countries. In the United States since the 1960s, poverty declined dramatically for those over 65 but not for children. In larger groupings of OECD countries, we see a clear divide around age 50. All age groups up to 50 years of age experienced an increased poverty share relative to the population as a whole, while those above 50 shifted out of poverty faster than the whole population.

---

35 For an explanation of how Belgium forged a social compact in the early twentieth century, providing for social aid despite its divisions, see Huberman (2008, 2012, and Chap. 13 in this volume).
36 Again see Dahlberg, Edmark, and Lundqvist (2012), showing that the parts of Sweden more exposed to immigrants now express more doubts about the welfare state.

Table 14.5. *Relative risks of poverty, by age of individuals in the OECD, mid 1970s to mid 2000s*

		Poverty rate of the entire population in each year = 100						
		Below 18	18–25	26–40	41–50	51–65	66–75	Above 75
OECD-23	Mid-1980s	110	95	78	70	93	134	190
	Mid-1990s	116	112	83	69	83	115	169
	Mid-2000s	119	127	85	77	80	99	144
OECD-7	Mid-1970s	84	113	61	66	119	180	214
	Mid-1980s	115	120	78	64	87	120	178
	Mid-1990s	116	143	81	61	82	99	149
	Mid-2000s	112	147	86	72	78	95	150

Source: OECD (2008: chap. 5, Figure 5.5), updated 12 September 2008.
OECD-23 is the average of poverty rates across all OECD countries except Australia, Belgium, Iceland, Korea, Poland, the Slovak Republic, and Switzerland.
OECD-7 is the average for Canada, Finland, Greece, the Netherlands, Sweden, the United Kingdom, and the United States. Data for mid-1980s refer to around 1990 for the Czech Republic, Hungary, and Portugal; those for the mid-2000s refer to 2000 for Austria, Belgium, the Czech Republic, Ireland, Portugal, and Spain (where 2005 data are not comparable with those for earlier years). Data based on cash income.

The drift toward lowering poverty rates more for the elderly than for children and those in working age is clearly tied to a bias in expenditure policy, particularly in certain countries. To show this, one needs to avoid just examining social expenditures as shares of GDP, which can be driven by the age group shares of total population. A more telling kind of expenditure measure is a relative support ratio, dividing (social expenditures on the elderly *per elderly person*) by (social expenditures on the young *per young person*). Such a ratio should be above unity, of course, since the average dependency ratio is higher for those over 65 than for younger age groups. We can compare the same ratio across countries to detect outliers. Calculating such ratios takes some work, but fortunately much of the work has been done for us already. Figure 14.6 shows some of Julia Lynch's calculations of such an inter-age-group support ratio, graphed against the overall social spending share.[37] The bulk of countries in Figure 14.6 have similar inter-age-group ratios, whether they are high-budget welfare states like France and Sweden, or lower-budget

37 See Lynch 2001, 2006.

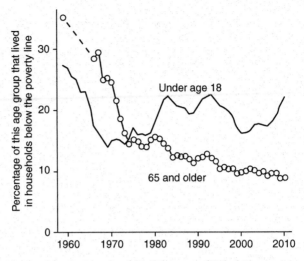

Figure 14.5. Poverty shares among the old and the young, United States 1959–2010
Source: www.census.gov/hhes/www/poverty/data/historical/people.html, accessed December 31, 2011.

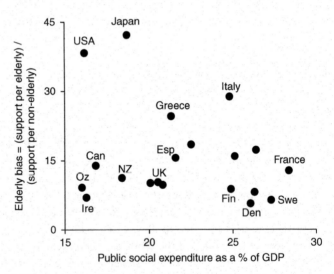

Figure 14.6. Bias toward the elderly in public social spending, 1985–2000
Source: Lynch (2006). For similar figures covering 1980, 1985, and 1993, see Lynch (2001).

states like Australia, Ireland, or Canada. There are four outliers, however, all of them having social expenditures that tilt heavily toward the elderly: Japan, the United States, Italy, and Greece. For the United States one immediately thinks of the fact that Social Security and Medicare, both concentrating on Americans over 65 years in age, are more generous than public support for the poor of working age. Yet the outliers are not extreme in the generosity of their support for the elderly themselves, as defined by (social expenditures on the elderly per elderly person)/ (GDP per capita). Rather they stand out because they give so little to those of working age and to children.

To reinforce the connection between the social expenditure bias measures and degrees of success in curing poverty, let us consider a different data set including additional countries omitted from the Lynch study. Figure 14.7 draws on an OECD study comparing poverty among those of working age with the social expenditures that are specific to working age. Our four outliers from Figure 14.6 – Japan, the United States, Italy, and Greece – again occupy one end of the spectrum, now joined by Mexico, Korea, Turkey, and Canada. This group of countries has the lowest willingness to invest a share of GDP in people of working age, with the result that they have some of the highest poverty rates for that 18–64 age group. Again, their distinguishing fingerprint is their low willingness to invest tax money in the young and the middle-aged, not their treatment of the elderly. A related OECD diagram showing the poverty and spending rates for the elderly shows no revealing differences.[38]

Is the relative underinvestment in those under the age of 65 something costly in terms of GDP? The answer depends on the social-budget counterfactual one chooses to pose. Here are the leading candidates:

Counterfactual A: Take some of the government money spent on the elderly, and shift it toward the leading kinds of social programs for children and those of working age (education, preventive out-patient health care for the children, worker retraining, etc.).
Counterfactual B: Privatize pensions, reducing taxes, and mandating individual savings accounts for old age.

Thus far the text has implied that we are comparing actual practice with Counterfactual A, and for this comparison the answer is clearly yes, the bias in favor of the elderly is clearly costly in terms of GDP. That is evident from the simple fact that investing in human development brings a higher return, the earlier the stage of cognitive and career development. The importance of this

38 OECD 2008.

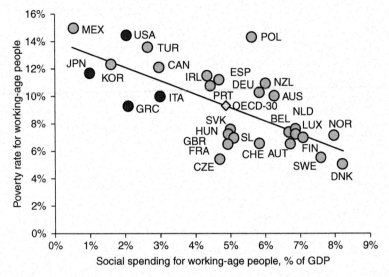

Figure 14.7. Social spending vs. poverty rate, people of working age, c.2005

Source: OECD 2008: 143, using computations from OECD income distribution questionnaire and OECD Social Expenditure database (SOCX).

Note: Poverty rates based on a threshold set at half of median household disposable income. Social spending includes both public and mandatory private spending in cash (i.e. excluding in-kind services). Social spending for people of working age is defined as the sum of outlays for incapacity, family, unemployment, housing, and other (i.e. social assistance) programs; social spending for people of retirement age is the sum of outlays for old-age and survivors benefits. Social spending is expressed in percentage of GDP at factor costs. Data on poverty rates refer to the mid-2000s for all countries; data for social spending refer to 2003 for all countries except Turkey (1999).

From its age-group analysis, the OECD report infers (2008: 143–144) that, "While this pattern reflects the earnings-related nature of old-age pensions in most OECD countries, it also suggests that larger inroads into reducing poverty could be achieved by redirecting spending from pension programmes towards programmes targeted to people of working age and their children at the bottom of the income scale."

point has recently been underlined in the writings of Pedro Carneiro and James Heckman, among others, finding that even among children, the rate of return is higher, the earlier the child age at which parents and society intervene.[39]

By contrast, comparison of actual practice with Counterfactual B suggests no clear difference in GDP. For all we can tell from twentieth-century data, individual saving and tax-financed saving can yield the same GDP result with

39 Carneiro and Heckman (2003), and the sources cited there.

appropriate adjustments of parameters in programs targeting the elderly. One might note that universal programs like Social Security in the United States are administered with lower bureaucratic costs and lower default risk than private pension plans or individual investments. On the other hand, there is reason to fear that the political process would underfund public pensions. Twentieth-century panel data have not allowed us to deny that there is a zero net effect on GDP from choosing public pensions over mandated private individual pensions. Thus the historic drift toward funneling tax money to the elderly either has cost GDP or not, depending on whether one wants to consider Counterfactual A or Counterfactual B.

If there is no clear gain in GDP from shifting social insurance and assistance toward the elderly, why have so many societies done it? The answer seems to be gray power. In the postwar democracies, an ever-greater population share consists of the elderly plus those approaching old age, and the elderly have a relatively high participation rate in politics. They have succeeded in gaining intergenerational transfers, with or without a net effect on GDP.

Yet something has to give in the twenty-first century, as many have long warned. Those over the age of 65 will go on rising as a share of the adult population, just as they have done over recent centuries. The ratios of the elderly to those of working age are rising most ominously in East Asia and Italy, but no country is exempt. The main reason is simply the upward march of senior life expectancy. The natural solution of having people work to later ages, to hold fixed the share of their adult lives spent at work, has been undermined by a decline in the average age of male retirement, though this has historically contributed less to the lengthening of retirement than has the improvement in life expectancy.[40] As some have argued, countries need to devise ways to prevent a rise in taxation on behalf of pensions (and elderly health care) by indexing each cohort's annual pension benefits to its senior life expectancy. Sweden's "notional defined contribution" pension system has that desirable feature, though Sweden – like other OECD countries – is still groping for solutions on the elderly health care front.[41]

---

40 For historical retirement trends from the United States see, for example, Costa (1998) and Lee (1998, 2001). One should also note that the trend toward earlier male retirement has reversed itself in many OECD countries since 2000.
41 On the need for a tax-rate-capping formula linking pension benefits to survival and elderly labor force participation, and on the Swedish 1998 reform, see Lindert 2004: vol. 1, chaps. 9 and 11.

Conclusion

While the history of private and public behavior toward social insurance and social assistance has only begun to be written on the global level, this chapter found it easy to pick some low-hanging fruit, in the form of links between economic theory and an economic history featuring North Atlantic experience. An obvious next task is to break out of the confines of European and North American experience, plunging into the history of non-family social insurance and social assistance in other continents.

Private insurance and charity appear to have advanced slowly to modest levels, helped by the rule of law and income growth. Private giving has not been crowded out by the rise of public aid, because it has always fit the "warm glow" model better than the altruism model of caring about the aggregate conquest of need.

This chapter suggests some tentative summary judgments on the history of efficiency in the provision of social insurance and social assistance. Throughout history, and still today, many opportunities for growth-enhancing provision have been sacrificed by both sectors. Those opportunities are revealed by high rates of marginal return on several fronts, particularly investments in human capital formation. The private sector faces daunting problems of freeriding in assistance, asymmetric information in some voluntary insurance markets, and above all the inability to enforce long-term lending contracts that would repay private lenders for investments in human capital. The public sector faces daunting problems of organization, freeriding, and the concentration of voice into special interest groups whose objectives conflict with maximizing social efficiency.

The rise of public social insurance and assistance was held back for millennia until the arrival of state fiscal capacity plus the spread of mass political voice. Together these opened the door to lower-cost, more efficient, less bureaucratic public provision. The rise of universal tax-based education and health has brought great gains in GDP, and early poor relief may have done so too. Yet from the 1960s on, the further expansion of social spending has wandered away from its pro-growth egalitarian social targets toward relative underemphasis on aid to the young and overemphasis on aid to the elderly. Something has to give in the rapidly aging societies of the twenty-first century.

References

Acemoglu, D. and J. A. Robinson (2006). "Economic Backwardness in Political Perspective," *American Political Science Review* 100(1): 115–131.

Adema, W., P. Fron, and M. Ladaique (2011). "Is the European Welfare State Really More Expensive? Indicators on Social Spending, 1980–2012; and a Manual to the OECD Social Expenditure Database (SOCX)," OECD Social, Employment and Migration Working Papers, No. 124, OECD Publishing. Available at http://dx.doi.org/10.1787/5 kg2d2d4pbfo-en (accessed January 17, 2012).

Alesina, A., R. Baqir, and W. Easterly (1999). "Public Goods and Ethnic Divisions," *Quarterly Journal of Economics* 114(4): 1243–1284.

Alesina, A. and E. Glaeser (2004). *Fighting Poverty in the US and Europe: A World of Difference.* Oxford University Press.

Andreoni, J. (1988). "Privately Provided Public Goods in a Large Economy: The Limits of Altruism," *Journal of Public Economics* 35(1): 57–73.

  (1990). "Impure Altruism and Donations to Public Goods: A Theory of Warm-Glow Giving," *Economic Journal* 100(401): 464–477.

  (2006). "Philanthropy," in S.-C. Koln and J. Mercier Ythier (eds.), *The Handbook of Giving, Reciprocity, and Altruism.* Amsterdam: North-Holland, pp. 1201–1269.

Andreoni, J. and A. Payne (2011). "Crowding-Out Charitable Contributions in Canada: New Knowledge from the North" (November). Available at http://econ.ucsd.edu/~jandreon/research.htm (accessed June 24, 2013).

Andreoni, J., J. Smith, and D. Karp (2011). "Diversity and Donations: The Effect of Religious and Ethnic Diversity on Charitable Giving" (October). Available at http://econ.ucsd.edu/~jandreon/research.htm (accessed June 24, 2013).

Ansell, B. W. (2010). *From the Ballot to the Blackboard: The Redistributive Political Economy of Education.* Cambridge University Press.

Åslund, A. (1997). "Social Problems and Policy in Postcommunist Russia," in E. B. Kapstein and M. Mandelbaum (eds.), *Sustaining the Transition: The Social Safety Net in Postcommunist Europe.* New York: Council on Foreign Relations, 124–146.

Baldwin, P. (1990). *The Politics of Social Solidarity and the Bourgeois Basis of the European Welfare State, 1875–1975.* Cambridge University Press.

Bird, R. M. (1971). "Wagner's 'Law' of Expanding State Activity," *Public Finance/Finances Publiques* 26(2): 1–26.

Boyer, G. R. (1989). "Malthus Was Right after All: Poor Relief and Birth Rates in Southeastern England," *Journal of Political Economy* 97(1): 93–114.

Carneiro, P. and J. Heckman (2003). "Human Capital Policy," in J. Heckman and A. Krueger (eds.), *Inequality in America: What Role for Human Capital Policies?* Cambridge, MA: The MIT Press.

Carter, S., S. S. Gartner, M. R. Haines, A. L. Olmstead, R. Sutch, and G. Wright, eds. (2006). *The Historical Statistics of the United States: Millennial Edition,* 5 vols. Cambridge University Press.

Charities Aid Foundation (2010). *The World Giving Index* Available at www.cafonline.org (accessed June 24, 2013).

Clark, R. L., L. A. Craig, and J. W. Wilson (2003). *A History of Public Sector Pensions in the United States*. Philadelphia, PA: University of Pennsylvania Press.

Costa, D. L. (1998). *The Evolution of Retirement: An American Economic History, 1880–1990*. University of Chicago Press.

Dahlberg, M., K. Edmark, and H. Lundqvist (2012). "Ethnic Diversity and Preferences for Redistribution," *Journal of Political Economy* 120(1): 41–76.

Dincecco, M. (2011). *Political Transformations and Public Finances: Europe, 1650–1913*. Cambridge University Press.

Dincecco, M. and G. Katz. (in press). "State Capacity and Long-Run Performance" *Journal of Economic Growth*.

Easterly, W. and R. Levine (1997). "Africa's Growth Tragedy: Policies and Ethnic Divisions," *Quarterly Journal of Economics* 112(44): 1203–1250.

Espuelas, S. (2012). "Are Dictatorships Less Redistributive? A Comparative Analysis of Social Spending in Europe, 1950–1980," *European Review of Economic History* 16(2): 211–232.

Estrin, A. (1988). "Administrative Costs for Social Security Programs in Selected Countries," *Social Security Bulletin* 51(88): 29–31.

Fishback, P. V. (2010). "Social Welfare Expenditures in the United States and the Nordic Countries, 1900–2003," NBER Working Paper No. 15982 (May).

Fishback, P. V. and M. A. Thomasson (2006). "Social Insurance and Public Assistance," in Carter *et al.* Vol. II, pp. 2-693-2-835.

Flora, P., F. Kraus, and W. Pfenning (1983). *State, Economy and Society in Western Europe, 1815–1975*. Frankfurt: Campus Verlag.

Floud, R., R. W. Fogel, B Harris, and S. C. Hong (2011). *The Changing Body: Health, Nutrition, and Human Development in the Western World since 1700*. Cambridge University Press.

Garfinkel, I., L. Rainwater, and T. Smeeding (2010). *Wealth and Welfare States: Is America a Laggard or a Leader?* Oxford University Press.

Giving USA Foundation (2010). *Giving USA Annual Report 2010*. Glenview: Giving USA Foundation.

Go, S. and P. H. Lindert (2010). "The Uneven Rise of American Public Schools to 1850," *Journal of Economic History* 70(1): 1–26.

Gordon, J. (1940). "Comparative Costs of Administering Public Assistance: An Analysis of the Administrative Expenses of 28 Public Assistance Agencies during 1938–39," *Social Security Bulletin* 3(2): 11–20.

Gruber, J. (2005). *Public Finance and Public Policy*. New York: Worth.

Huberman, M. (2008). "Ticket to Trade: Belgian Workers and Globalization Before 1914," *Economic History Review* 61: 326–359.

(2012). *Odd Couple: International Trade and Labor Standards in History*. New Haven, CT: Yale University Press.

Karlan, D. and J. A. List (2007). "Does Price Matter in Charitable Giving? Evidence from a Large-Scale Natural Field Experiment," *American Economic Review* 97(5): 1774–1793.

(2012). "How Can Bill and Melinda Gates Increase Other People's Donations to Fund Public Goods?" NBER Working Paper No. 17954 (March).

Kramer, M. (1997). "Social Protection Policies and Safety Nets in East-Central Europe: Dilemmas of the Postcommunist Transformation," in E. B. Kapstein and M. Mandelbaum (eds.), *Sustaining the Transition: The Social Safety Net in Postcommunist Europe*. New York: Council on Foreign Relations, pp. 46–123.

Kristov, L., P. Lindert, and R. McClelland (1992). "Pressure Groups and Redistribution," *Journal of Public Economics* 48(2): 135–163.

Lee, C. (1998). "Rise of the Welfare State and Labor Force Participation of Older Males: Evidence from the Pre-Social Security Era," *American Economic Review* 88(2): 222–226.

(2001). "The Expected Length of Male Retirement in the United States, 1850–1990," *Journal of Population Economics* 14(4): 641–650.

Lindert, K. A., E. Skoufias, and J. Shapiro (2006). "Redistributing Income to the Poor and the Rich: Public Transfers in Latin America and the Caribbean," World Bank, SP Discussion Paper 0605 (August).

Lindert, P. H. (1994). "The Rise of Social Spending, 1880–1930," *Explorations in Economic History* 31(1): 1–37.

(1998). "Poor Relief before the Welfare State: Britain versus the Continent, 1780–1880," *European Review of Economic History* 2(2): 101–140.

(2004). *Growing Public: Social Spending and Economic Growth since the Eighteenth Century.* 2 vols. Cambridge University Press.

(2009). "Revealing Failures in the History of School Finance," NBER Working Paper No. 15491 (November).

Lynch, J. (2001). "The Age-Orientation of Social Policy Regimes in OECD Countries," *Journal of Social Policy* 30(3): 411–436.

(2006). *Age in the Welfare State.* Cambridge University Press.

Mackie, T. T. and R. Rose (1991). *The International Almanac of Electoral History,* 3rd edn. London: Macmillan.

(1997). *A Decade of Election Results: Updating the International Almanac.* Glasgow: University of Strathclyde, Centre for the Study of Public Policy.

Moene, K. O. and M. Wallerstein (2001). "Inequality, Social Insurance, and Redistribution," *American Political Science Review* 95: 859–874.

Musgrave, R. and P. B. Musgrave (1989). *Public Finance in Theory and Practice,* 5th edn. New York: McGraw-Hill.

Musgrave, R. A. and J. M. Culbertson (1953). "The Growth of Public Expenditures in the United States," *National Tax Journal* 6(2) 97–115.

North, D. C. (1981). *Structure and Change in Economic History.* New York: W.W. Norton.

(1990). *Institutions, Institutional Change and Economic Performance.* Cambridge University Press.

Organisation for Economic Co-operation and Development (OECD) (1985). *Social Expenditure 1960–1990.* Paris: OECD.

(2008). *Growing Unequal? Income Distribution and Poverty in OECD Countries.* Paris: OECD.

Olson, M. (1965). *The Logic of Collective Action: Public Goods and the Theory of Groups.* Cambridge, MA: Harvard University Press.

Reinhardt, U. E. (2000). "Health Care for the Aging Baby Boom: Lessons from Abroad," *Journal of Economic Perspectives* 14(2): 71–84.

Reynolds, M. and E. Smolensky (1977). *Public Expenditures, Taxes, and the Distribution of Income: The United States, 1950, 1961, 1970.* New York: Academic Press.

Rotemberg, J. J. (2011). "Charitable Giving when Altruism and Similarity Are Linked," NBER Working Paper No. 17585 (November).

Stiglitz, J. E. (2000). *Economics of the Public Sector,* 3rd edn. New York: W.W. Norton.

US Census Bureau (1973). *Statistical Abstract of the United States.*

   (1976). *Historical Statistics of the United States, Bicentennial Edition.*

Van Leeuwen, M. H. D. (2000). *The Logic of Charity: Amsterdam 1800–1850.* Houndmills and New York: Macmillan.

   (2012). "Guilds and Middle-Class Welfare, 1550–1800: Provisions for Burial, Sickness, Old Age, and Widowhood," *Economic History Review* 65(1): 61–90.

Williamson, J. G. (1990). *Coping with City Growth during the British Industrial Revolution.* Cambridge University Press.

Woodlander, S., T. Campbell, and D. U. Himmelstein (2003). "Costs of Health Care Administration in the United States and Canada," *New England Journal of Medicine* 349(8): 768–775.

15

Capitalism and human welfare

LEANDRO PRADOS DE LA ESCOSURA[*]

How has well-being evolved under capitalism during the last one and a half centuries? How do advanced, capitalist nations, that is, Western Europe and the regions of European background plus Japan – (pre-1994) OECD, for short – compare with the rest of the world (the Rest)? Has social spending contributed to human development advancement in the OECD? And if so, how much? How do capitalist and socialist societies compare in terms of well-being at early stages of economic development? These are important questions that require historical answers.

The ambiguity of the concept *capitalism* complicates any assessment of its impact on human welfare, although it has not prevented endless debate (Engerman 1997). The use of the market as the main way of allocating goods and factors of production and the predominance of the private property of resources seem elements of a minimal definition of capitalism (Hartwell and Engerman 2003).[1] The spread of capitalism has been associated with free markets and freedom of contract, that is, with the absence of interference in agents' decisions (or 'negative' economic freedom). However, increasing government intervention during the twentieth century and the emergence of the welfare state contradict such a depiction, adding complexity to any evaluation of capitalism's long-term impact on well-being (Pryor 2010; Frieden 2006; Frieden and Rogowski, Chapter 12 in this volume). The emergence of

[*] I am grateful to participants at a conference on the History of Capitalism, Fundación BBVA, Madrid, November 14–16, 2012, for their comments and, in particular, to my discussants, Jeffry Frieden and Ronald Rogowski. I also want to thank Jeff Williamson for his detailed editorial comments, and his encouragement. Financial support from Fundación Rafael del Pino's "Freedom and Wellbeing in Historical Perspective" research project and the HI-POD Project, Seventh Research Framework Program Contract no. 225342, is gratefully acknowledged.
1 According to Pryor (2010: 8), "Capitalism is an economic system in which goods, labor, land, and financial services are transferred through relatively competitive markets and in which the means of production are primarily owned privately."

command economic regimes after World War I (socialism, fascism) provides a convenient yardstick for the achievements and shortcomings of capitalism in its different forms.

For a long time, economic historians looked at living standards during the British industrial revolution when assessing the impact of capitalism on well-being. A negative appraisal of this early experience of modern economic growth (the so-called 'pessimistic hypothesis'), largely rooted in Marx's immiseration hypothesis, dominates the historical literature (Allen 2007; Feinstein 1998; Hartwell and Engerman 2003). Even the most benign of economic historians' assessments stresses that, despite sustained economic growth since the late eighteenth century, workers' living standards only improved significantly from the 1820s onwards (Lindert and Williamson 1983). Systematic research on real wages has lent support to this pessimistic assessment on a larger geographical scale. Living standards in preindustrial Europe, with the exception of England and the Low Countries, would have remained stagnant until a sustained improvement took place in the early nineteenth-century industrialization, leaving the Rest – and China in particular – way behind (Allen 2001; Allen et al. 2011; Li and Van Zanden 2010; Pomeranz 2000). However, this view is not shared by all (see Broadberry and Gupta 2006 and Maddison 2006).

Along with industrialization, the impact of the integration of commodity and factor markets (namely, globalization) on well-being deserves to be considered. Globalization not only increased economic activity in those countries or regions involved, bringing with it higher per capita income, but it also improved the relative returns of abundant factors that was then raw labor, as in the cases of nineteenth-century Europe and East Asia. Globalization resulted in a decline of income inequality, a trend reinforced by the presence of mass migration (Lindert and Williamson 2003; O'Rourke and Williamson 1999). The comparison between preindustrial and industrial eras shows a significant improvement in welfare across the board, in terms of both average incomes and equity, as a result of globalization and economic growth (O'Rourke and Williamson 2005).

From the early nineteenth century onwards, evidence on well-being and economic progress is available for an increasing number of countries. Real wage rates, for example, have exhibited sustained gains in Western Europe and its offshoots over the last 200 years (Williamson 1995). Improving well-being during the modern era can also be established on the basis of (crude) estimates of real GDP per head (Maddison 2010), which, despite recurrent debate about its measurement of welfare, continues to be widely used (Engerman 1997).

Contradictions between alternative measures of well-being have been highlighted. For example, trends in real wages – that accrue, in principle, to those at the bottom of the income distribution – do not match trends in average real incomes per head.[2] In fact, there is nothing unusual about a low correlation between these two indicators, as they address different aspects of income: the returns to all factors of production (in the case of GDP) and those to a single factor, raw labor (in the case of real wages), and, unless the distribution of income remains unaltered over time, no reason exists for them evolving alongside (Williamson 2002).[3] In fact, long-run trends in income inequality can be crudely measured on the basis of the ratio of real GDP per head or, ideally, per worker, to real wage rates, the so-called Williamson Index. The Williamson Index provides a reasonable proxy for the functional distribution of income and, assuming the dispersion of returns per head within each factor (labor, capital, land) remains basically unaltered, also for interpersonal income distribution. Scattered evidence suggests that the functional distribution of income captures trends in personal income distribution up to the early twentieth century in European countries (Dumke 1988; Prados de la Escosura 2008; Waldenström 2009). The available estimates suggest a long-term decline in income inequality across the board during the twentieth century, with its beginnings ranging from the early to the mid century and ending by the 1980s (Van Zanden et al. 2013).

A welfare adjustment to per capita income, that incorporates income distribution, defined as GDP per head times the degree of equality, was postulated by Amartya Sen (1973) and adopted in early Human Development Reports (see UNDP 1993). Given the dearth of historical estimates of personal income distribution across countries, splicing available estimates of personal income distribution (for example, the Gini coefficient) with the Williamson Index (and, alternatively, with inequality measures derived from data on heights) provides long-run trends in inequality. Thus, on the basis of Maddison's (2010) real per capita GDP and the Gini and pseudo-Gini coefficients (Van Zanden et al., in press), historical estimates of Sen-welfare, or inequality-adjusted income per head (GDP per head times 1 minus the Gini) can be computed for world regions. Figure 15.1 provides long-run

---

2 Beyond conceptual disqualifications of real wage rates (Maddison 2001) and of guess-timates of GDP per head (Williamson 1995) as measures of well-being, attempts have been made at reconciling these indicators (Angeles 2008; Van Zanden 2001).

3 The comparison between Holland and Java carried out by Van Zanden (2001) shows that differences in terms of unskilled wages were closer than in per capita income terms suggesting higher income inequality in the metropolis.

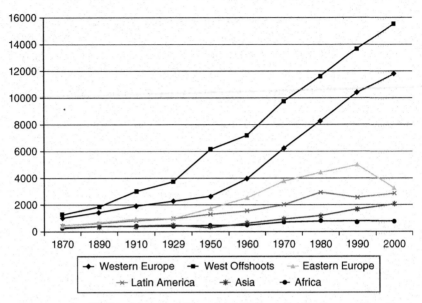

Figure 15.1. Sen-Welfare (inequality-adjusted real GDP per head) across world regions

trends for inequality-adjusted GDP per head across world regions. Although Sen-Welfare levels increased across the board, they grew less than GDP per head (1.2 vs. 1.5 percent per year between 1870 and 2007), a difference with its origin largely in the pre-1950 era. Moreover, when measured with the inequality-adjusted GDP per head, the gap between advanced and developing regions widens further, due to the fact that while inequality declined in OECD countries from the early twentieth century until late in the century, it remained high in developing regions. In fact, while Western Europe tended to close the gap with the Western offshoots in terms of the Sen-welfare index, and while Asia has done the same since the 1970s, Latin America and Africa fell further back. The relative position of Eastern Europe deteriorated after the demise of communism as a combined effect of economic stagnation and increasing inequality.

If a longer-run comparison, encompassing the last half a millennium, is chosen, the evidence suggests that industrialization and globalization had long-term positive effects on well-being, not only because of higher income levels, but because inequality declined. During the early modern period, inequality increased in Europe, declining only in the modern era, particularly, during the twentieth century (Álvarez-Nogal and Prados de la Escosura 2013; Hoffman et al. 2002; O'Rourke and Williamson 2005). The recent research on top income shares confirms a sustained declining trend in inequality through-out the last hundred years in both developed and developing countries, even though a partial reversal was experienced since 1990 (Atkinson, Piketty, and Saez 2011). These findings provide a positive answer to the question of whether living standards were higher after the industrial revolution. However, they do not provide an answer to whether living standards could have been better under alternative regimes.

So far, trends in well-being have been discussed in terms of real wages or real inequality-adjusted GDP per head. Human welfare, however, is widely viewed as a multidimensional phenomenon, in which per capita income (and its distribution) is only one facet. In fact, attempts at providing more compre-hensive measures of living standards go back to the origins of modern national accounts (Engerman 1997). Non-income dimensions such as infant mortality, life expectancy at birth, height, adult literacy, school enrolment, and such have been used either individually or combined in index form (physical quality of life, basic needs, and, more recently, human development) to provide meas-ures of well-being beyond the strait-jacket of GDP. Thus, in the rest of the chapter, a multidimensional approach will be used in which human develop-ment and its health and knowledge dimensions will be examined. Human development has been defined as "a process of enlarging people's choices" (UNDP 1990: 10), namely, enjoying a healthy life, acquiring knowledge, and achieving a decent standard of living, that allows them to lead "lives they have reasons to value" (Sen 1997).

I will start by presenting trends in human development for the world and its main regions. I will explore, then, the differences observed in terms of human development between laissez-faire and regulated capitalism, and between market (capitalist) and command (socialist) societies in their early stages of economic development. Lastly, I will investigate the contribution of each dimension of human development to its overall performance and the extent to which they help understand the observed differences between the West and the Rest.

As regards the time span considered, the 1870s represent an appropriate starting point. The dearth of data for earlier decades is one reason for the choice of that date. Another is that it is when large-scale improvements in health – to which the diffusion of the germ theory of disease contributed significantly after the 1880s (Easterlin 1999; Preston 1975) – and mass education emerged in Western Europe and the European offshoots (Benavot and Riddle 1988; Lindert 2004). It is also in the late nineteenth century that social spending started expanding in Western Europe and its offshoots (Lindert 2004; Riley 2001).

Some findings can be highlighted. Substantial gains in world human development are observed since 1870 – and especially after 1913. Although the gap between advanced capitalist countries (OECD) and the Rest widened in absolute terms, an incomplete catching-up to the OECD took place across the board in developing regions between 1913 and 1970. During the last forty years, the variance in regional performance has been large. Asia, driven by China and India, and, to a lesser extent, Latin America and North Africa, managed to catch up, while central and eastern Europe (including Russia) and sub-Saharan Africa fell behind.

Major gains in human development were achieved in the West during the regulated phase of capitalism, when the public provision of health and education appears to have played a distinctive role in human development advance. In socialist societies, gains in human development matched those of capitalist economies until the late 1960s, which, in some cases, shows socialism's success in raising health and education from initial low levels. This was especially true of the Soviet Union and central and eastern European communist or socialist experiences, and it helps explain the appeal of communism to newly independent nations in mid-twentieth-century Africa and Asia. However, a dramatic divergence appeared after the late 1960s as relative gains in life expectancy and income per head stopped and catching-up gave way to falling behind. Cuba's success in raising longevity and education provides a counterpoint. Is there, then, any conflict between freedom and the delivery of public goods, at least in the early phases of development? The concept of human development precludes, however, this conflict, as agency and freedom are its final goals. Thus, a rigorous definition of human development reduces the achievements in communist (or any other totalitarian) countries to "basic needs."

Education and, to a lesser extent, life expectancy at birth appear to lie behind the periphery's limited catching-up in terms of human development up to 1970. Since then, all world regions in the Rest have fallen behind the OECD in terms of the longevity index. The first health transition involved mainly an improvement in child mortality instead of an increase in life expectancy of the elderly. In the second health transition, life expectancy at birth increased faster in the West and the proportion of healthy years out of the total life span rose. In the Rest, the first health transition is the only period in which substantial gains in longevity were achieved. This largely explains the

Rest's failure to catch up with the West, despite educational expansion and per capita income growth catch-up at the turn of the twentieth century.

Measuring human development

The different dimensions of human development are combined into an index in a reduced form: life expectancy at birth as a proxy for a healthy life, education measures (schooling, literacy) for access to knowledge, and discounted per capita income as a surrogate for other well-being dimensions other than education and health (Anand and Sen 2000; UNDP 2001: 240).

How progress in human development dimensions is measured matters. Usually, the original values of social variables (life expectancy, schooling) are used untransformed (see, for example, Acemoglu and Johnson 2007; Becker, Philipson, and Soares 2005; Lindert 2004). However, since social variables have usually asymptotic limits, a linear transformation was employed to convert its dimensions into index form in the human development index (UNDP 1990). Thus, by reducing the denominator, the range of the index widens. For each dimension, the original values (x) are transformed as indices (I),

$$I = (x - Mo)/(M - Mo), \qquad [1]$$

where Mo and M are the maximum and minimum values, or goalposts. Each dimension ranges, thus, between 0 and 1.[4]

The human development index is, then, derived as a multiplicative combination of the transformed values of each dimension that receives equal weights, as all are considered indispensable. By denoting the non-linearly transformed values of life expectancy at birth and education as LEB and EDU, and the adjusted per capita income as UNY, it can be expressed as,

$$HIHD = LEB^{1/3} EDU^{1/3} UNY^{1/3} \qquad [2]$$

---

4 Goalposts in the so-called 'hybrid' HDI (Gidwitz *et al.* 2010: 3) are employed here (all the data come from Prados de la Escosura 2013b). Upper and lower bounds for life expectancy are fixed at 83.2 and 20 years, respectively. For education (adult literacy and gross primary, secondary, and tertiary enrolment rates), maximum and minimum values of 100 and 0 were combined using two-thirds and one-third weights, respectively. In the case of per capita GDP, the observed maximum and minimum over 1870–2007 were, expressed in Geary-Khamis [G-K] 1990 dollars, \$42,916 and \$206 (Maddison 2010), respectively, transformed into logarithms.

The linear transformation of the social, non-income dimensions employed in the conventional HDI (UNDP 2010) remains a serious obstacle, however, for the comparison of human development levels over space and time. In the linear transformation, a given absolute change in a dimension reflects the same change regardless of its starting level and, thus, its corresponding increase would be larger the lower the initial level, favoring the country with the lower initial level of human development. In fact, it should be the other way around because, to put it in Sen's words (1981: 292), "as ... longevity becomes high, it becomes more of an achievement to raise it further."

The limitations of the linear transformation become clearer when quality is taken into account. Life expectancy at birth, and literacy and schooling rates are just crude proxies for a "long and healthy life" and for access to knowledge, respectively, the actual goals of human development. Unfortunately, information on health-adjusted life expectancy or quality-adjusted education is only available for recent years. Research over the last two decades concludes that healthy life expectancy increases as total life expectancy expands, and as life expectancy rises, disability for the same age-cohort falls (Salomon et al. 2012). Similarly, the quality of education, measured in terms of cognitive skills, grows more than proportionally as the quantity of education (gross rates of literacy and enrolment) increases (Hanushek and Kimko 2000). The bottom line is that more years of life and education imply higher quality of health and education during childhood and adolescence in both the time series and the cross-section.

A practical solution to the problem derived from the linear transformation is provided by Kakwani (1993) who constructed a normalized index from an achievement function in which an increase in the standard of living of a country at a higher level implies a greater achievement than would have been the case had it occurred at a lower level,

$$I = f(x, Mo, M) = (\log(M - Mo) - \log(M - x))/\log(M - Mo), \tag{3}$$
for $\varepsilon = 1$

where x is an indicator of a country's standard of living, M and Mo are the maximum and minimum values, respectively, and log stands for the natural logarithm.

Thus, the original values of the social, non-income dimensions of the index have been transformed, rather than using a linear transformation (expression 1), with a convex achievement function (expression 3), allowing for the more than proportional increase in the quality of non-income dimensions as its quantity rises.[5]

Trends in human development

A long-run upward trend in world human development is observed which increased sixfold between 1870 and 2007, implying a yearly growth rate of 1.3 percent. Three main phases can be distinguished: first, steady and moderate progress up to 1913; second, acceleration (but for World War II) between 1913 and 1970; and third, a deceleration in the 1970s and 1980s before giving way to an expansion from 1990 onwards (Figure 15.2).

Trends in human development do not match closely those observed in real GDP per head (Figure 15.3). More specifically, phases of economic globalization have a dramatic impact on per capita income growth (Lindert and Williamson 2003) but not on the progress of human development. A counterintuitive lack of association is observed between human development and per capita income prior to World War I. Although the

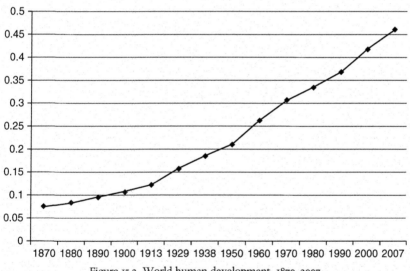

Figure 15.2. World human development, 1870–2007

---

5 A more detailed explanation of the methodology used and of the sources and procedures employed to construct the indices of human development and its main dimensions is provided in Prados de la Escosura 2013b.

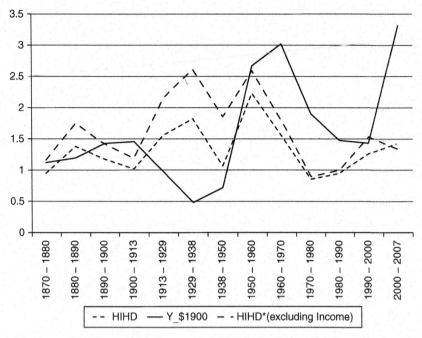

Figure 15.3. World human development and GDP per head growth rates, 1870–2007 (%)

initial large-scale progress in health can be traced back to the late nineteenth century, with the diffusion of the germ theory of disease (Riley 2001), and primary education experienced a significant advance (Benavot and Riddle 1988), in the era of liberal capitalism, the progress in human development dimensions fell short of the economic advancement resulting from global-ization and industrialization. The negative impact of urbanization on life expectancy and the lack of public policies on education and health may account for human development's slower progress in the late nineteenth century (Easterlin 1999; Lindert 2004). More significantly, while real GDP per head stagnated or declined during the globalization backlash of the interwar years, human development progressed steadily. Health and edu-cation practices became increasingly globalized during the economic back-lash of the period 1914 to 1950. Could a delayed impact of economic globalization on human development be, perhaps, hypothesized? Since 1950, advancement in human development has been hand in hand with growth in the world economy, although at a lower pace during the Golden Age (1950–1973) and, again, since 2000.

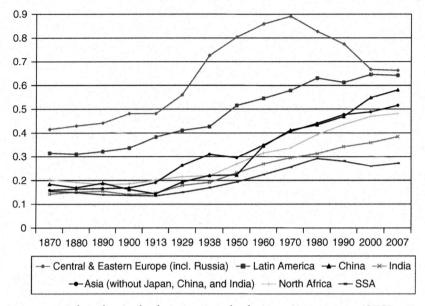

Figure 15.4. Relative human development across developing regions, 1870–2007 (OECD = 1)

A deeper perception of world human development derives from comparing the performance of different regions in absolute terms and relative to OECD (Figures 15.4). Did the gap in human development between the OECD and the Rest deepen over time? The answer is negative. Relative to the OECD, the Rest showed, on average, stability up to 1913 and catching up thereafter, more intense up to 1970 – with the exception of the World War II years – and weaker afterwards. Then, catching up to OECD slowed down dramatically after 1970, and, by 2007, its level still represented only 50 percent of the OECD countries. In general, relative to the core, the periphery performed better in human development than in terms of income per head (Prados de la Escosura 2013b). Thus, by 2007, the Rest's human development had reached the level of OECD in 1950, but only that of 1938 in terms of real per capita GDP.

The long-run behavior of human development in developing regions shows a wide variance. Latin America was catching up to the OECD until 1980, although more intensively during the first half of the twentieth century. In Africa, a sustained improvement and catching-up took place between the 1920s and the 1970s, which, since 1980, slowed down in North Africa and ceased altogether in sub-Saharan Africa. In Asia, starting from low levels, human development improved significantly until 1970 and, again, at the turn of the century. Due to central and eastern Europe's falling behind OECD and Asia's (especially China's) and North Africa's catching-up, a process of convergence between these regions with Latin America has taken place since the 1970s, while sub-Saharan Africa fell behind.

What explains the superior human development performance of rich capitalist economies? It has been argued that systematic market failure required public intervention, as markets would not have contributed to control disease transmission, encourage immunization, nor stimulate medical research (Easterlin 1999). Did growing government intervention, the expansion of social spending, and the introduction of the welfare state, play a crucial role in OECD well-being achievements? Lindert (2004: 20–21, 188; and his Chapter 14 in this volume) associates the increase in the relative size of social spending to globalization, economic growth, democratization, and longevity. The association between globalization and social spending is predicated on the fact that international market integration increases external risks and, hence, the demand of government-led social protection (Rodrik 1997). During the first globalization epoch (1870–1913), increasing exposure to international trade and, thus, uncertainty among European workers, led to demands for social protection and government introduction of "labor compacts" (Huberman and Lewchuk 2003). Thus, to a large extent, globalization and social protection seem to go hand in hand (Huberman 2012; and his Chapter 13 in this volume) while the expansion of free markets is correlated with economic prosperity and democracy.

Did countries with higher levels of social spending achieve longer longevity and more education and, hence, higher human development? Figure 15.5 plots levels of human development against social transfers (that is, all social spending but that in education) expressed in proportion of GDP for a group of OECD countries.[6] The result suggests a positive non-linear association between the expansion of social protection and the improvement in human development that stabilizes above a low threshold of social transfers (as a share of GDP). On the left of the graph, small changes in social transfers are associated with large increases in human development. Then, as we move to the right, we observe that increases in social transfers are associated with

---

6 The data on social transfers as a share of GDP for OECD countries (Australia, Austria, Belgium, Canada, Denmark, Finland, France, Germany, Greece, Ireland, Italy, Japan, Netherlands, New Zealand, Norway, Sweden, Switzerland, UK, and US) at decadal intervals from 1880 to 2000 (except from 1960 when data are for five-year intervals) comes from Lindert (1994) and the Allard–Lindert OECD 1950–2001 Dataset on Peter Lindert's website, http://lindert.econ.ucdavis.edu (accessed on August 18, 2012).

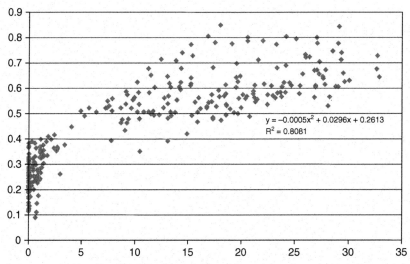

Figure 15.5. Human development (vertical axis) and social transfers (% GDP) (horizontal axis) for a group of OECD countries, 1880–2000

smaller, but still positive, increases in human development. As social transfers reach 25 percent of GDP the curve tends to flatten, suggesting a reversal for levels above 30 percent.

The welfare state expanded in capitalist countries at the same time that socialism emerged as an alternative economic and social system.[7] How do the capitalist and socialist systems compare? It has been frequently argued that it is at low levels of economic development when socialist societies have an advantage over capitalist ones in lifting human well-being and, in particular, its non-income dimensions. A glance at the former Soviet Union shows that substantial gains in human development were obtained between the 1920s and the 1960s, which resulted in an impressive catching-up to the OECD. Since the mid-1960s, however, this progress gave way to stagnation, and relative to OECD, to a dramatic decline up to 2000, of special intensity during the 1990s. The significant achievements in health and education behind human development advance and catching-up in the Soviet Union up to the mid-1960s can be also observed in socialist Central and Eastern Europe since 1950.

---

7 I have chosen to use the term 'socialist' rather than 'communist' as in Marxist thought the latter was the goal to be reached and socialism was the means to reach it. See a discussion in Ivanov and Peleah (2010).

In fact, the success of the Soviet Union in raising longevity and education during the central decades of the twentieth century provided an appealing model for newly independent nations in Asia and Africa after World War II as they were facing the challenge of meeting basic needs (Collier and O'Connell 2008; Ivanov and Peleah 2010). Cuba, the only socialist experience in the Americas, achieved remarkable success following the 1959 revolution, driven exclusively by its non-income dimensions. In Asia, human development improved significantly in China during the first half of the twentieth century, accelerating under socialism up to the 1960s, and, again, in the 1990s, after the introduction of economic reforms. Notwithstanding, social engineering experiences during China's Cultural Revolution and Cambodia's Khmer Rouge era proved disastrous in terms of human development. In Indo-china, socialist experiences were only comparatively successful in the late twentieth century, once institutional reforms liberalizing their economies were introduced. Thus, Vietnam, Laos, and Cambodia caught up to the East Asian average only after 1990. Socialist experiences in sub-Saharan Africa did not succeed in terms of human development as the cases of Benin, Ethiopia, Congo, Angola, and Mozambique reveal. Political-economic distortions, particularly those associated with moving away from market resource allocation, appear inversely related to human development progress in sub-Saharan Africa (Prados de la Escosura 2013a). A preliminary evaluation suggests that, but for Russia during the central decades of the twentieth century and Cuba, socialism has not delivered higher human development for developing countries than capitalism.

The short-cut approach to 'measure' human development that has been used here so far leaves aside agency and freedom. Without agency –that is, the ability to pursue and realize goals a person has reasons to value – and freedom, the human development index becomes a 'basic needs' index (Ivanov and Peleah 2010). Thus, in order to achieve a comprehensive depiction of human development the opportunities individuals have to exercise their political capabilities and influence public decisions also need to be taken into account (Cheibub 2010; Dasgupta and Weale 1992). Human development and democratization are, nonetheless, correlated since 1950 and its association grows stronger as their respective levels get higher (as implied by the positive sign of the quadratic term in the regression (Figure 15.6).[8]

---

8 The index of democratization comes from Vanhanen (2011), normalized by dividing its value by its potential maximum so it ranges between 0 and 1, and becomes comparable to the HIHD.

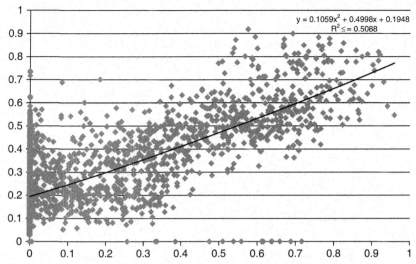

Figure 15.6. Human development (vertical axis) and democratization (horizontal axis) in the world, 1950–2007

This caveat is particularly relevant for the comparison between capitalism and socialism. Strictly speaking, since restrictions of individual choice in socialist countries – such as collectivization, forced industrialization, and political repression – affected negatively agency and freedom, their achievements in health and education could be better depicted as 'basic needs' rather than as human development (Ivanov and Peleah 2010). From this perspective, the demise of socialism after 1989 would have represented an advance in terms of human development (Brainerd 2010a). The same reasoning applies to fascism and other totalitarian regimes under capitalism.

Breakdown of human development growth

Long-run gains in human development mainly result from the progress of its non-income dimensions, longevity and education. Sustained progress in Kakwani indices of life expectancy at birth and education is observed in different world regions. Exceptions are the practical stagnation of life expectancy indices in Central and Eastern Europe from the 1960s onwards and in sub-Saharan Africa since the 1980s. Nonetheless, the improvement in the Rest falls short from that of OECD, and catching up either stops, as it did in the case of life expectancy after 1970, or fails to be complete, as happened in the case of education (Figures 15.7 and 15.8).

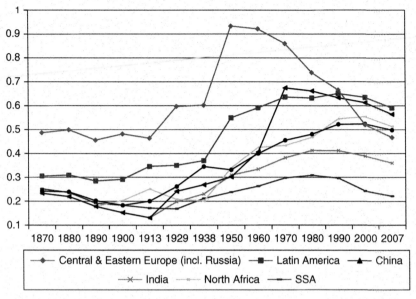

Figure 15.7. Life expectancy Kakwani indices in world regions, 1870–2007 (OECD = 1)

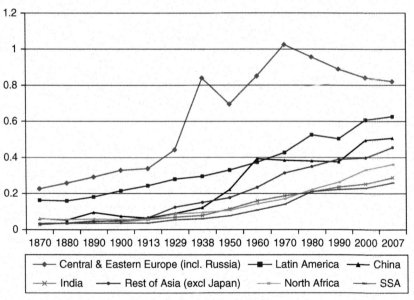

Figure 15.8. Education Kakwani indices in world regions, 1870–2007 (OECD = 1)

The growth of human development (*HIHD*) can be broken down into the contribution of its different dimensions – life expectancy at birth (*LEB*), education (*EDU*), and truncated income (*UNY*)- on the basis of expression [2] above. Using lower case to denote rates of variation:

$$hihd = 1/3leb + 1/3edu + 1/3uny \qquad [5]$$

It appears that social dimensions drove world human development gains over time, with life expectancy representing the leading force during the 1920s and 1940s, while education dominated in the 1930s, 1950s, and 1990s (Figure 15.9).

Gains in life expectancy resulted from the diffusion of preventive methods of disease transmission (Preston 1975; Riley 2005); improvements in nutrition (Fogel 2004); medical technological change (vaccines since the 1890s and sulfa drugs (1930s) and antibiotics (1950s) to cure infectious diseases) (Easterlin 1999; Jayachandran, Lleras-Muney, and Smith 2010); and the public provision of health (Cutler and Miller 2005; Loudon 2000). These elements were crucial in the epidemiological or health transition in which persistent gains in lower mortality and higher survival were achieved as infectious disease gave way to chronic disease as the prevalent form of morbidity and main cause of death (Omran 1971; Riley 2005).

Why does longevity's drive in human development fade away by the mid twentieth century? The contrast between the experiences of the OECD and the Rest is illuminating. In the case of developed countries, improvements in life expectancy have driven human development advance since 1880 (except for the 1960s) (Figure 15.10). The sustained progress in life expectancy during the late twentieth and early twenty-first century is associated with gains in healthy life years that reach 90 percent of the years lived in OECD countries at the turn of the new century.[9] Thus, a second health transition has taken place in the OECD in which mortality falls among the elderly as a result of a better treatment of cardiovascular disease and of better health and nutrition in their early years (Eggleston and Fuchs 2012). These health improvements not only resulted in a longer life but also in more healthy life years (Salomon *et al.* 2012).

In the Rest, the role of life expectancy in human development advance is, despite its very impressive gains between 1913 and 1970, less decisive, especially after 1970, as life expectancy gains appear to have slowed down once the first health transition is completed and when education constitutes the main force underlying long-run progress in human development (Figure 15.11).

9 Cf. www.conferenceboard.ca/hcp/details/health/life-expectancy.aspx#quality.

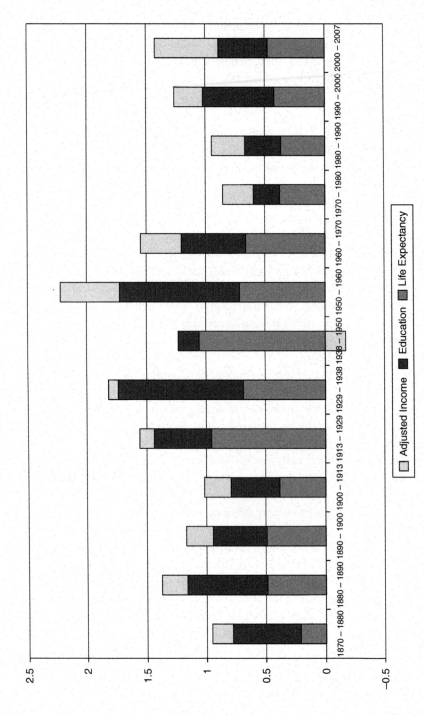

Figure 15.9. Breakdown of human development growth in the world, 1870–2007 (%)

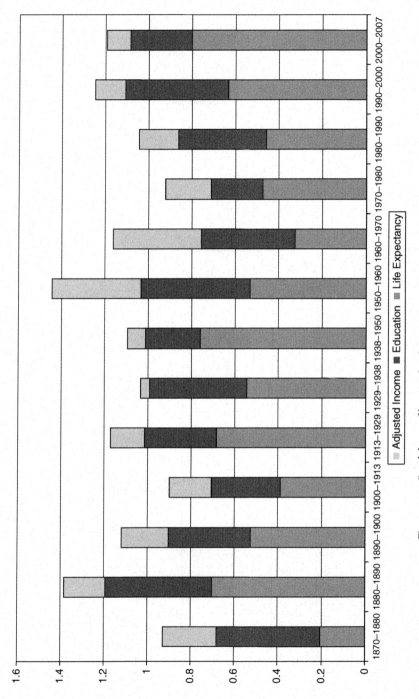

Figure 15.10. Breakdown of human development growth in OECD, 1870–2007 (%)

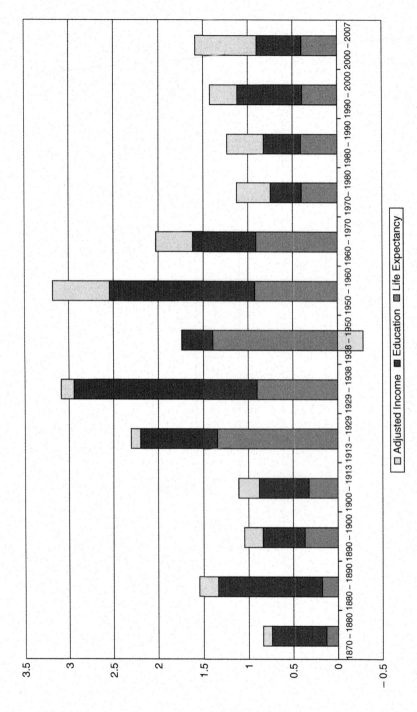

Figure 15.11. Breakdown of human development growth in the Rest, 1870–2007 (%)

Human development catching-up of the Rest on the OECD, concentrates between 1913 and 1970, and more intensely in the interwar decades and the 1950s, years in which a large proportion of the Rest was still under colonial rule. In the sluggish catching-up of the Rest since 1970, life expectancy plays a crucial and negative role, providing support for the view that health inequalities across countries increase as new health technology and knowledge is introduced at a faster pace in developed countries (Cutler, Deaton, and Lleras-Muney 2006: 117). Only after 2000 does income per head constitute the main element behind the Rest's catching up.

A glance at the main regions of the Periphery is illuminating. In eastern and central Europe (Russia included), most improvement in human development took place up to 1970, and more intensely in the 1890s and between the 1920s and 1950s, when catching up to the Core took place. Human development progress collapsed after 1970, falling behind the OECD, only to recover mildly after 2000. Education was the driving force, but for the 1920s and the 1940s, when dramatic life expectancy advances took the lead. Since 2000, income has become the main dimension of human development advancement. A glance at Russia's performance, the dominating country in the region, confirms and accentuates this depiction, although most of its catching-up was restricted to the 1890s and to the period between 1913 and 1950.

In the Soviet Union, the expansion of health care to the whole population was particularly successful in fighting infectious disease and child mortality. Infant mortality fell rapidly between 1940 and 1965 (Brainerd 2010b; Brainerd and Cutler 2005). By the mid-1960s life expectancy at birth had practically converged with Western Europe, after a dramatic improvement over the previous four decades, especially during the 1950s (Mazur 1969). However, life expectancy fell after 1965 as a result of the decline in adult (male) longevity, which Dutton (1979) attributes to diseases of the circulatory system, increasing death rates by accident, suicide, and poisoning, and alcoholism. Increasing infant mortality since 1970 reinforced this declining trend. In the rest of the socialist countries in Eastern Europe, life expectancy gains disappeared after the mid-1960s.

The collapse of socialism in central and eastern Europe and the disintegration of the Soviet Union brought with it a decline in life expectancy, more severe and persistent in the former Soviet Union, in which there has been no complete recovery (Brainerd 2010a; Brainerd and Cutler 2005). In the former socialist countries of central and eastern Europe, however, life expectancy recovered quickly and expanded after the mid-1990s, especially in Czechoslovakia, Poland, and Hungary (Brainerd 2010a; Stillman 2006). The collapse of life expectancy in Russia is associated with an increase in middle age and infant mortality. Alcohol consumption and stress from the transition to a market economy (unemployment uncertainty for mid-age workers, rising inequality), along with worsening of diets and health and material deprivation, appear to be largely responsible for the increase in mortality (Brainerd 2010a; Cutler and Brainerd 2005; Shkolnikov, McKee, and Leon 2001). As regards agency, advances in civil and political liberties have been quite uneven in former socialist Europe, with serious restrictions in the countries of the former Soviet Union, but indisputable progress in Central Europe and the Baltic republics.

In Latin America, human development experienced moderate and steady progress and catching-up between 1880 and 1980. In this region, too, education is the leading dimension in human development, especially during the second half of the twentieth century (but for the 1980s). Life expectancy had a distinguished role during the early twentieth century, especially in the 1940s, when the strongest catching-up on the OECD took place. Interestingly, such an advance did not take place as much as a result of the diffusion of treatment of infectious diseases by sulfa drugs and antibiotics and vaccination because, although available, they were not accessible to the low-income population, as of the diffusion of hygienic practices among the population, as the cases of British Guiana and Jamaica during the early twentieth century demonstrate (Mandle 1970; Riley 2005). In Jamaica, for example, mortality declined sharply between 1920 and 1965, but more intensively during the late 1920s and 1930s while real per capita GDP was relatively stagnant. Low-cost public health measures and diffusion of health knowledge played a major role in eradicating communicable diseases (diarrheal diseases, malaria, and tuberculosis), prior to the introduction of antibiotics (Riley 2005). Latin America's weak convergence with developed countries deserves investigation. In particular, we need to understand better the role that inequality played in restricting access to health and education in the late twentieth century.

Cuba, an exceptional case in the Americas, provides an interesting counterpoint to other socialist experiences. In striking contrast with Cuba's poor economic performance since the 1959 Revolution, an impressive improvement in life expectancy has taken place (Devereux 2010; Ward and Devereux 2010, 2012). Such a tendency built on earlier trends during the first half of the twentieth century, initiated after the US occupation delivered sanitation and public health innovation that resulted in good health services especially for the urban poor (Díaz-Briquets 1981; McGuire and Frankel 2005). Advancement in health care during the early twentieth century implied that, by the eve of the 1959

Revolution, Cuba was above the average Latin American and southern European countries. From 1959 onwards, the success in fighting and eradicating infant mortality is largely the result of the socialist state commitment (Devereux 2010). Thus, the case of Cuba provides an extreme case of contrast between the success in achieving 'basic needs' and the failure to enlarge people's choices as agency and freedom are severely curtailed by a political regime.

Significant progress of human development has taken place in Asia during the last century, although it varied widely across its regions. China has experienced an impressive advancement and catching-up in human development during the last hundred years, with special intensity in the interwar years (1913–1938) and the early Maoist years, during which education and life expectancy led its progress. During the last forty years the income dimension has dominated progress in human development, largely a consequence of the post-1979 economic reforms, while its social components (life expectancy, in particular) played a minor role. The slowdown in health improvements has been regarded as a direct consequence of the new economic policies (Cutler, Deaton, and Lleras-Muney 2006; Drèze and Sen 2002).

India experienced a steady advance in human development since the late nineteenth century, catching up on the OECD over the last century, especially in the 1920s and, again, during the 1940s and 1950s. Education appears as the main contributor to such advancement in the long run, although life expectancy at birth drove it during the early twentieth century (1913–1950). Improvements in sanitation, medical care, and famine prevention – based upon the new transport network, the economy's diversification, and government relief – successfully contributed to reduce the impact of infectious disease like malaria, smallpox, and cholera (McAlpin 1983; Roy 2006: 311–312). These achievements are especially remarkable because they took place during a period of stagnation in real incomes per head (Maddison 2010; Roy 2006: 78). Interestingly, significant gains in well-being were achieved before independence, despite claims of underinvestment and poor health infrastructure (Amrith 2009), raising the issue of how colonial rule affected well-being. In the last three decades, the income dimension played a major role, along with education, in human development progress, a feature associated, as in the case of China, with the economic impact of pro-market reforms. The latter has contributed to the reduction in the absolute extreme poverty rate by half since the early 1970s (Kotwal, Ramaswami, and Wadhwa 2011). As for China, the slowdown in infant mortality reduction occurred at the time when new economic policies were implemented (Drèze and Sen 2002).

In the rest of Asia (excluding Japan), sustained progress in human development has taken place since 1870 and catching-up to OECD can be observed since 1913, especially up to 1938 and during the 1950s and 1960s. Education and health improvements jointly contributed to the advancement of human development in Southeast Asia. As in the case of India, health improvements were achieved before colonial independence: mortality from smallpox, cholera, and plague was reduced through specific public health measures in Indonesia, the Philippines, and Taiwan during the 1920s (Preston 1975).

In Africa, a very distinctive performance is observed between its north and sub-Saharan regions. In North Africa, a steady improvement has taken place in human development, on the basis of both longevity, which experienced a major improvement in the 1940s, and education gains, that allowed the region's catching-up to OECD over the twentieth century, especially in the 1940s and 1950s and in the 1970s. South of the Sahara the period 1913 to 1980 is also the one of human development advancement and catching-up. However, the leading role played by life expectancy is restricted to the 1930s and 1940s, and education provided the main source of progress, especially as economic growth per head collapsed during the last quarter of the twentieth century. The stagnation of life expectancy has been due to the spread of HIV / AIDS and the resilience of malaria, together with arrested growth and the deceleration in the expansion of education. All of these appear to result largely from economic mismanagement, political turmoil, and civil wars. The surge in human development during the 2000s has been helped by the recovery in economic activity and, to a lesser extent, in life expectancy, but education has remained the main force behind its advance.

Conclusion

Human development provides a multidimensional approach to well-being. Reconstructing its trends since 1870 allows us to establish the extent to which progress took place in the era of capitalism. It also gives us a measure of the differences between the advanced capitalist countries of the West and the Rest, and across developing regions, emerged and developed. Furthermore, it highlights the leading dimensions. A substantial but incomplete improvement in world human development has taken place during the last one and a half centuries, although it was the period between World War I and the oil shocks of the 1970s when well-being expanded most intensively and across the board. Thus, a major phase of health and education globalization took place between

1920 and 1950, just at the time of a globalization, resulting in substantial gains in human development.

The last four decades have witnessed a deceleration in human development advancement and a widening of the absolute gap between the OECD and the aggregate Rest. Nonetheless, a large variance in regional behavior is concealed behind the Rest. Progress and catching-up in large areas of Asia, North Africa, and, to a lesser extent, in Latin America, coexisted with the collapse and falling behind of former socialist Europe and sub-Saharan Africa.

Longevity is the key element in the West's forging ahead, not only because of the longer life span enjoyed by its population, but because of the higher quality of life associated with it. Conversely, in the Rest, life expectancy only played a major role in human development progress and catching-up until the central decades of the twentieth century onwards, at the time of the demographic and epidemiological transition. Afterwards, its dynamic role diminished. A second wave of longevity expansion comparable to that of the West has not yet taken place in the Rest. Thus, education carried most of the weight in human development progress during the last four decades, with the income dimension playing a decisive role in catching-up to OECD: positive in China and India, negative in sub-Saharan Africa and Russia and former European socialist countries.

The choice of economic and social system had an important influence on the progress of human development across countries. Socialist and capitalist models implied different health and education policies, as well as different economic policies. The results presented in this chapter suggest that, despite its initial success as provider of "basic needs," socialist experiences failed to sustain the momentum and, but for Cuba, stagnated and fell behind before the demise of communism. Furthermore, its suppression of agency and freedom prevented real achievements in human development.

A research agenda emerges from this review of the evidence. Why do we observe big regime changes in the drivers of human development? In particular, why did life expectancy stop being its driving force after the mid twentieth century? Once the "first" health transition was completed, its leading role faded away. Why hasn't a "second" transition, like the one currently taking place in the OECD, been triggered in the Rest? Is it due to a lack of public policies, or to the inequality-creating nature of the new technologies? Or is it because health and education are high income-elastic goods?

Why are trends in GDP per head and human development only poorly correlated over time when increases in per capita income should contribute to better nutrition, health, and education? Why did the Rest undergo catching up on the OECD in terms of human development, life expectancy, and education, but not in GDP per capita? Is the difference related to public policy – public schooling, public health, and the rise of the welfare state – or to the fact that medical technology is a public good?

References

Acemoglu, D. and S. Johnson (2007). "Disease and Development: The Effects of Life Expectancy on Economic Growth," *Journal of Political Economy* 115: 925–985.

Allen, R. C. (2001). "The Great Divergence in European Wages and Prices from the Middle Ages to the First World War," *Explorations in Economic History* 38: 411–447.

(2007). "Pessimism Preserved: Real Wages in the British Industrial Revolution," Oxford University, Department of Economics, Working Paper No. 314.

Allen, R. C., J.-P. Bassino, D. Ma, C. Moll-Murata, and J. Luiten Van Zanden (2011). "Wages, Prices, and Living Standards in China, 1738–1925: In Comparison with Europe, Japan, and India," *Economic History Review* 64(S1): 8–38.

Álvarez-Nogal, C. and L. Prados de la Escosura (2013). "The Rise and Fall of Spain, 1270–1850," *Economic History Review* 66: 1–37.

Amrith, S. S. (2009). "Health in India since Independence," University of Manchester Brooks World Poverty Institute Working Paper 79.

Anand, S. and A. Sen (2000). "The Income Component of the Human Development Index," *Journal of Human Development* 1: 83–106.

Angeles, L. (2008). "GDP per Capita or Real Wages? Making Sense of Conflicting Views on Preindustrial Europe," *Explorations in Economic History* 45: 147–163.

Atkinson, A. T. P. and E. Saez (2011). "Top Incomes in the Long-run of History," *Journal of Economic Literature* 49: 3–71

Becker, G. S., T. J. Philipson, and R. R. Soares (2005). "The Quantity and Quality of Life and the Evolution of World Inequality," *American Economic Review* 95: 277–291.

Benavot, A. and P. Riddle (1988). "The Expansion of Primary Education, 1870–1940: Trends and Issues," *Sociology of Education* 61: 191–210.

Brainerd, E. (2010a). "Human Development in Eastern Europe and the CIS since 1990," UNDP Human Development Reports Research Paper No. 2010/16.

(2010b). "Reassessing the Standard of Living in the Soviet Union: An Analysis Using Archival and Anthropometric Data," *Journal of Economic History* 70: 83–117.

Brainerd, E. and D. M. Cutler (2005). "Autopsy on an Empire: Understanding Mortality in Russia and the Former Soviet Union," *Journal of Economic Perspectives* 19: 107–130.

Broadberry, S. N. and B. Gupta (2006). "The Early Modern Great Divergence: Wages, Prices and Economic Development in Europe and Asia, 1500–1800," *Economic History Review* 59: 2–31.

Cheibub, J. A. (2010). "How to Include Political Capabilities in the HDI? An Evaluation of Alternatives," UNDP Human Development Reports Research Paper 2010/41.

Collier, P. and S. A. O'Connell (2008). "Opportunities and Choices," in B. J. Ndulu, S. A. O'Connell, J. P. Azam, R. H. Bates, A. K. Fosu, J. W. Gunning, and D. Njinkeu (eds.), *The Political Economy of Economic Growth in Africa, 1960–2000*, 2 vols. Cambridge University Press, Vol. 1, pp. 76–136.

Cutler, D. and G. Miller (2005). "The Role of Public Health Improvements in Health Advance: The Twentieth Century United States," *Demography* 42: 1–22.

Cutler, D., A. Deaton, and A. Lleras-Muney (2006). "The Determinants of Mortality," *Journal of Economic Perspectives* 20: 97–120.

Dasgupta, P. and M. Weale (1992). "On Measuring the Quality of Life," *World Development* 20(1): 119–131.

Devereux, J. (2010). "The Health of the Revolution: Explaining the Cuban Health Care Paradox" (unpublished).

Díaz-Briquets, S. (1981). "Determinants of Mortality Transition in Developing Countries before and after the Second World War: Some Evidence from Cuba," *Population Studies* 35: 399–411.

Drèze, J. and A. K. Sen (2002). *India: Development and Participation*. Delhi: Oxford University Press.

Dumke, R. (1988). "Income Inequality and Industrialization in Germany, 1850–1913: Images, Trends, and Causes of Historical Inequality," *Research in Economic History* 2: 1–47.

Dutton Jr., J. (1979). "Changes in Soviet Mortality Patterns, 1959–77," *Population and Development Review* 5: 267–291.

Easterlin, R. (1999). "How Beneficient is the Market? A Look at the Modern History of Mortality," *European Review of Economic History* 3: 257–294.

Eggleston, K. N. and V. Fuchs (2012). "The New Demographic Transition: Most Gains in Life Expectancy Now Realized Late in Life," *Journal of Economic Perspectives* 26: 137–156.

Engerman, S. L. (1997). "The Standard of Living Debate in International Perspective: Measure and Indicators," in R. H. Steckel and R. Floud (eds.), *Health and Welfare during Industrialization*. University of Chicago Press/NBER, pp. 17–45.

Feinstein, C. (1998). "Pessimism Perpetuated: Real Wages and the Standard of Living in Britain during and after the Industrial Revolution," *Journal of Economic History* 58: 625–658.

Fogel, R. W. (2004). *The Escape from Hunger and Premature Death, 1700–2010: Europe, America and the Third World*. New York: Cambridge University Press.

Frieden, J. (2006). *Global Capitalism: Its Fall and Rise in the Twentieth Century*. New York: Norton.

Gidwitz, Z., M. P. Heger, J. Pineda, and F. Rodríguez (2010). "Understanding Performance in Human Development: A Cross-national Study," UNDP Human Development Reports Research Paper No.2010/42.

Hanushek, E. A. and D. D. Kimko (2000). "Schooling, Labor-Force Quality, and the Growth of Nations," *American Economic Review* 90(5): 1184–1208.

Hartwell, R. M. and S. L. Engerman (2003). "Capitalism," in J. Mokyr (ed.), *The Oxford Encyclopedia of Economic History*, 5 vols. New York: Oxford University Press. Vol. 1, pp. 319–325.

Hoffman, P. T., D. S. Jacks, P. A. Levin, and P. H. Lindert (2002). "Real Inequality in Europe since 1500," *Journal of Economic History* 62: 322–355.

Huberman, M. (2012). *Odd Couple: International Trade and Labor Standards in History*. New Haven, CT: Yale University Press.

Huberman, M. and W. Lewchuk (2003). "European Economic Integration and the Labour Compact, 1850–1913," *European Review of Economic History* 7: 3–41.

Ivanov, A. and M. Peleah (2010). "From Centrally Planned Development to Human Development," UNDP Human Development Reports Research Paper No. 2010/38.

Jayachandran, S., A. Lleras-Muney, and K. V. Smith (2010). "Modern Medicine and the Twentieth Century Decline in Mortality: Evidence on the Impact of Sulfa Drugs," *American Economic Journal: Applied Economics* 2: 118–146.

Kakwani, N. (1993). "Performance in Living Standards: An International Comparison," *Journal of Development Economics* 41: 307–336.

Kotwal, A., B. Ramaswami, and W. Wadhwa (2011). "Economic Liberalization and Indian Economic Growth: What's the Evidence?" *Journal of Economic Literature* 49: 1152–1199.

Li, B. and J. L. Van Zanden (2010). "Before the Great Divergence? Comparing the Yangzi Delta and the Netherlands at the Beginning of the Nineteenth Century," CEPR Discussion Paper No. 8023.

Lindert, P. H. (2004). *Growing Public: Social Spending and Economic Growth since the Eighteenth Century*, 2 vols. Cambridge University Press.

and J. G. Williamson (1983). "English Workers' Living Standards during the Industrial Revolution: A New Look," *Economic History Review* 36: 1–25.

(2003). "Does Globalization Make the World More Unequal?" in M. Bordo, A. M. Taylor, and J. G. Williamson (eds.), *Globalization in Historical Perspective*. University of Chicago Press/NBER, pp. 227–271.

Loudon, I. (2000). "Maternal Mortality in the Past and its Relevance to Developing Countries Today," *American Journal of Clinical Nutrition* 72 (supplement): 241S–246S.

Maddison, A. (2001). *The World Economy: A Millennial Perspective*. Paris: OECD Development Centre.

(2006). *The World Economy*. Paris, OECD Development Centre.

(2010). Statistics on World Population, GDP and Per Capita GDP, 1–2008 AD. Available at www.ggdc.net/maddison/ (accessed June 24, 2013).

Mandle, J. R. (1970). "The Decline of Mortality in British Guiana, 1911–1960," *Demography* 7: 301–315.

Mazur, D. P. (1969). "Expectancy of Life at Birth in 36 Nationalities of the Soviet Union: 1958–60," *Population Studies* 23: 225–246.

McAlpin, M. B. (1983). "Famines, Epidemics, and Population Growth: The Case of India," *Journal of Interdisciplinary History* 14: 351–366.

McGuire, J. W. and L. B. Frankel (2005). "Mortality Decline in Cuba, 1900–1959: Patterns, Comparisons, and Causes," *Latin American Research Review* 40: 83–116.

Omran, A. R. (1971). "The Epidemiological Transition: A Theory of Epidemiology of Population Change," *Milbank Memorial Fund Quarterly* 49: 509–538.

O'Rourke, K. H. and J. G. Williamson (1999). *Globalization and History. The Evolution of a Nineteenth Century Atlantic Economy*, Cambridge, MA: The MIT Press.

(2005). "From Malthus to Ohlin: Trade, Industrialisation and Distribution since 1500," *Journal of Economic Growth* 10: 5–34.

Pomeranz, K. (2000). *The Great Divergence: China, Europe, and the Making of the Modern World Economy*. Princeton University Press.

Prados de la Escosura, L. (2008). "Inequality, Poverty, and the Kuznets Curve in Spain, 1850–2000," *European Review of Economic History* 12: 287–324.

(2013a). "Human Development in Africa: A Long-run Perspective," *Explorations in Economic History* 50: 179–204.

(2013b), "World Human Development, 1870–2007," Universidad Carlos III Working Papers in Economic History 13–01.

Preston, S. H. (1975). "The Changing Relationship between Mortality and Level of Economic Development," *Population Studies* 29: 231–248.

Pryor, F. L. (2010). *Capitalism Reassessed.* New York: Cambridge University Press.

Riley, J. C. (2001). *Rising Life Expectancy: A Global History*, New York: Cambridge University Press.

(2005). *Poverty and Life Expectancy: The Jamaica Paradox*, New York: Cambridge University Press.

Rodrik, D. (1997). "Trade, Social Insurance, and the Limits to Globalization," NBER Working Paper No. 5905.

Roy, T. (2006). *The Economic History of India 1857–1947*, 2nd edn. New Delhi: Oxford University Press.

Salomon, J. A., H. Wang, M. K. Freeman, T. Vos, A. D. Flaxman, A. D. Lopez, and C. J. L. Murray (2012). "Healthy Life Expectancy for 187 Countries, 1990–2010: A Systematic Analysis for the Global Burden Disease Study 2010," *Lancet* 380: 2144–2162.

Sen, A. K. (1973). *On Economic Inequality.* Oxford: Clarendon Press.

(1981). "Public Action and the Quality of Life in Developing Countries," *Oxford Bulletin of Economics and Statistics* 43: 287–319.

(1997). "Human Capital and Human Capability," *World Development* 25: 1959–1961.

Shkolnikov, V., M. McKee, and D. A. Leon (2001). "Changes in Life Expectancy in Russia in the Mid-1990s," *The Lancet* 357: 917–921.

Stillman, S. (2006). "Health and Nutrition in Eastern Europe and the Former Soviet Union during the Decade of Transition: A Review of the Literature," *Economics and Human Biology* 4: 104–146.

United Nations Development Program [UNDP] (1990–2011). *Human Development Report.* New York: Oxford University Press.

Van Zanden, J. L. (2001). "Rich and Poor before the Industrial Revolution: A Comparison between Java and the Netherlands at the Beginning of the 19th Century," *Explorations in Economic History* 40: 1–23.

Van Zanden, J. L., J. Baten, P. Foldvari, and B. van Leeuwen (2013). "The Changing Shape of Global Inequality, 1820–2000: Exploring a New Dataset," *Review of Income and Wealth* 59(4).

Vanhanen, T. (2011), Measures of Democracy 1810–2010 [computer file]. FSD1289, version 5.0 (2011–07–07). Tampere: Finnish Social Science Data Archive. Available at www.fsd. uta.fi/en/data/catalogue/FSD1289/meF1289e.html (accessed July 23, 2012).

Waldenström, D. (2009). *Lifting All Boats? The Evolution of Income and Wealth Inequality over the Path of Development.* Lund: Lund Studies in Economic History.

Ward; M. and J. Devereux (2010). "The Absolution of History: Cuban Living Standards after Fifty Years of Revolutionary Rule" (unpublished).

(2012). "The Road Not Taken: Pre-Revolutionary Cuban Living Standards in Comparative Perspective," *Journal of Economic History* 72: 104–132.

Williamson, J. G. (1995). "The Evolution of Global Labor Markets since 1830: Background Evidence and Hypotheses," *Explorations in Economic History* 32: 141–196.

(2002). "Land, Labor, and Globalization in the Third World, 1870–1940," *Journal of Economic History* 62: 55–85.

16

The future of capitalism

LARRY NEAL AND JEFFREY G. WILLIAMSON

When *The Cambridge History of Capitalism* project was initiated in 2005, it appeared that capitalism was triumphant worldwide. Indeed, economist David Hale wrote an op-ed piece for the *Wall Street Journal*, July 31, 2007, entitled "The Best Economy Ever," and the facts at the time bore him out. More people were alive on the surface of the globe than at any previous moment in history, and with much lower poverty rates than ever before. The average global per capita income was 10,200 in 2006 dollars, also the highest ever recorded. The world's gross domestic product was growing at over 5 percent annually in real terms, raising per capita incomes worldwide at annual rates of 2 to 4 percent, again an unprecedented economic achievement. As events unfolded in the summer of 2007, however, the "best economy ever" began to show some cracks, first in Germany, then in the United States, the United Kingdom, and the Netherlands. These four countries had earlier been celebrated by the International Monetary Fund's (IMF) *World Economic Outlook* in September 2006 as leading the financial changes driven by deregulation and improvements in technology that were transforming the global economy (IMF 2006: chap. 4). Now they were at the forefront of the most serious global financial crisis since the Great Depression of the 1930s.

Thus, as the two volumes of the *Cambridge History of Capitalism* – Volume I on "The Rise of Capitalism" and this Volume II on "The Spread of Capitalism" – neared completion at the end of 2012, the future of capitalism as we know it was very much in doubt. The irony of writing a chapter on "The Future of Capitalism" as the world limped so slowly out of prolonged recession is clear. Some critics of the project even suggested that we move quickly to a third volume, "The Decline and Fall of Capitalism"! But the on-going crisis of the global economy, which has cast a pall over the financial innovations celebrated as late as September 2006, can – in the long sweep of history covered by these two volumes – be viewed simply as the latest of growing pains that have afflicted the development of capitalism from the beginning. It is useful to recall that the year 1848, which we take as the start of the "Spread of Capitalism," was also the year that Marx and Engels published their *Communist Manifesto*. There they predicted the fall of capitalism. As the chapters in this volume demonstrate, capitalism did not fall in the decades leading up to World War I, but rather spread worldwide, eventually creating a truly global economy.[1] At the height of the first globalization boom, Norman Angell discounted the threat of a general European war in his best-selling book, *The Great Illusion* (1913). He argued cogently that the financial linkages that bound together the industrial countries of the world to their mutual benefit made it inconceivable they would disrupt the global economy by going to war with each other. But, of course, they did go to war and suffered not only the *Great War*, as World War I was termed, but also the *Great Depression*, and then the even more horrific costs of World War II (see Harrison, Chapter 11 in this volume, and Broadberry and Harrison 2005). The most eminent US economist in 1929, Irving Fisher, is still remembered for his October 17, 1929 statement, "Stock prices have reached what looks like a permanently high plateau," just before Black Monday, October 28, when the stock prices began their steep decline to lose nearly 90 percent of their value by mid-1932. And, just as the capitalist West's "Golden Age of Economic Growth" was well underway in 1956, Nikita Khrushchev blustered, "We will bury you!," predicting the eventual collapse of the West and the triumph of Soviet communism (*Time* magazine, November 26, 1956).

Rather than risk this kind of humiliation by future economists and historians, here we draw upon the analyses contained in Volume I but mainly in the preceding chapters of this volume to identify the specific challenges that capitalism will have to meet in the future, while noting how they have been met in the past, whether successfully or not. As capitalism spread worldwide in the last quarter of the twentieth century, and as alternative economic systems collapsed, different countries and cultures have fashioned their own varieties of capitalism in response, just as they did in the first surge in global capitalism up to 1914. The different varieties reflect the adaptations made by each country as it entered the international economy at different times and under different local conditions. Each country confronting the challenges of the global economy must decide what aspects of capitalism are most attractive as well as most amenable to assimilation into its existing economic institutions. Looking enviously at the obvious success enjoyed by the most

---

1 In fairness to Marx, he did predict that the energies unleashed by bourgeois capitalism would quickly encompass the entire world, before then collapsing.

prosperous advanced economies throughout history, local politicians have tried to determine what was critical for that success and how it could be imitated, often getting it wrong on the first attempts. Establishing free markets for capital, labor, and goods is difficult to get right. It is especially difficult to get capital markets right. Government access to the capital market is critical, both for initiating the transition and for sustaining the spread of capitalism domestically. Yet, this goal is often difficult to achieve, given the abilities of elite groups to expropriate funds and thus to entrench further their hold on power.

Nevertheless, whenever a country adopted its particular variety of capitalism in the nineteenth century, it also began to experience the onset of modern economic growth. Sustained rises in per capita income followed, at least until World War I, or, in some instances, until the onset of the worldwide Great Depression. The question lurking behind the historical coincidence of capitalism, its financial markets, and modern economic growth is, of course, just how interdependent are these phenomena, whether and how they are causal, and whether they are sustainable. The question remains open, even as capitalism seems finally to have spread to all corners of the world here at the start of the twenty-first century. The end of the twentieth century saw many countries trying to adapt capitalism to their circumstances, thus to achieve already the benefits of modern economic growth that had been achieved by the capitalist economies. A global spread of capitalism had also taken place over the half-century up to 1914, but further advance was stymied during the middle third of the twentieth century (see O'Rourke and Williamson, Chapter 1 in this volume). Will a resurgence of capitalism in the first decade of the twenty-first century lead to continued worldwide economic growth or will the obstacles to growth discussed at the conclusion of this chapter prove the eventual downfall of capitalism, or at least its serious modification? Let's look first at the causes of the resurgence of capitalism after World War II, and some of its problematic legacies.

Economic transitions, the Washington consensus, and the Copenhagen criteria

Prior to World War I, it was conventional wisdom that the key to the success of US capitalism was the continental extent of its domestic market, while the success of UK capitalism was due to the global extent of its market overseas, led by its colonies. Attempts to imitate these models of self-sufficient economic empires by Germany, Japan, and Italy during the interwar period were thwarted by their defeat in World War II. The experience of World War II put an end to the drive for *lebensraum* by Germany and a Greater Asian Co-Prosperity Sphere for Japan, but the postwar developments also put an end to the Belgian, British, Dutch, French, Portuguese, and even the more recent US colonial adventures. It took at least a generation of postwar experience with decolonization by the European powers to make governments in the rest of the world realize that something other than just market size explained the evident success of US and UK capitalism. Postwar nations also came to learn again what had been learned in the late nineteenth century: Small and resource-scarce nations can use world markets to achieve the benefits of size and to offset the absence of natural resource endowments. The resurgence of the capitalist economies after World War II thus coincided with decolonization (see Austin, Chapter 10 in this volume) and a rise in trade volumes. In contrast, the Soviet Union and China remained closed and experimented with colonizing most of the Eurasian landmass under the leadership of central planners and party bosses. The Soviet empire failed, although China's imperialist and capitalist venture appears to be still on-going. This experiment by competing economic systems should suggest that we rethink our conceptions of what drove capitalist development in the past and therefore what will drive it in the future. While foreign markets give industries an opportunity to realize economies of scale, it is clear that the intensity of competition for technological advantages within those markets is probably even more important for sustaining economic growth.

Openness to competition, combined with the ability to finance responses to competitive challenges, were the chief factors that drove continued economic growth and the advance of capitalism during the Golden Age of economic growth for the industrial leaders from 1950 to 1972. By the end of the 1980s, economists in the IMF and the World Bank – the international organizations most concerned with the spread of capitalism after World War II – summarized this experience succinctly by "the Washington consensus," so-called since both organizations were headquartered in Washington, DC. Their recommendation for countries wishing to enjoy the fruits of capitalism was *stabilize, privatize,* and *liberalize.* This was the essence of the conditions that the IMF had set for ensuring repayment of its loans to countries suffering from a debt crisis (mainly Latin America in the 1980s).

These conditions were also applied by international organizations and banks in response to the needs of the transition economies emerging from the collapse of the Soviet Union after 1990 – it put their ideas of what underlay the success of capitalism to the test. They were applied immediately to

Poland, the first country to establish political independence from the Soviet Union and the local Communist Party. The result was a severe shock to a country that was making simultaneous multiple transitions – economic, political, and social. Viewing Polish anguish as it underwent the so-called shock therapy, most other countries giving up central planning and Communist Party rule decided to introduce more gradual transitions. The most successful of the East European countries under Soviet domination, the German Democratic Republic, saw its citizens vote overwhelmingly in April 1990 to join the existing German Federal Republic as five new states. The German reunification was complete by October 1990, less than one year after the fall of the Berlin Wall. The reunification terms were that the former East Germany adopt as quickly as possible all of the institutions as they existed in West Germany, including its currency, the deutschmark. While East German citizens accepted the terms, West German citizens accepted responsibility for paying additional taxes to finance the transition of the East German economy to West German-style capitalist institutions.

The remaining east European, south European, and Baltic countries, who had won independence from the Soviet Union, all desired quick access to the European Union (EU) and on terms as close as possible to those which the East Germans received from West Germany. The reluctance of the EU to take on the expense that West Germany seemed willing to undertake for absorbing East Germany led to a series of accession agreements with each applicant country. The EU leaders agreed on a set of criteria that each applicant would have to meet before accession would be granted – the so-called "Copenhagen criteria," announced at the end of 1993. Essentially, the criteria pose a test of institutional capability for the applicants to make a capitalist economic system work and with popular support. Applicant countries would not have to undergo the shock therapy imposed on Poland, or agree to the strict reunification terms imposed on East Germany. But, they would have to meet EU standards regarding the functioning of their political institutions, the competitiveness of their economic firms, and the capacity of their bureaucracies to transpose effectively the EU's many directives and regulations.

The Washington consensus made macroeconomic stability the first priority for the transition economies. For IMF experts, this meant a balanced budget for the central government and a central bank that was dedicated to maintain price stability through its independent control of the money supply. By contrast, the Copenhagen criteria made a functioning democracy with universal voter franchise, secret ballots, fair elections, the rule of law, and the protection of human rights its first priority. Macroeconomic issues were left to

534

the future, and each country agreed to adopt, at least eventually, the common currency after gaining the approval of the European Central Bank (ECB).

The second priority for the Washington consensus was privatization of state-owned enterprises, with guarantees of property rights so that the new owners would have incentives to use capital and labor more efficiently and to invest in new technology. Given the West German experience in attempting to privatize the farms and firms of East Germany after 1990, the EU Copenhagen criteria softened the second priority to read that the transition economy's firms were expected to compete with those of the existing EU member countries. It would be up to each country to determine how to do this, but subsidies or financing of infrastructure would not be forthcoming from the EU as in the East German case, nor would the EU write off existing debts as had been the case for Poland.

The third and final priority of the Washington consensus was liberalizing markets, thus to allow competitive forces to determine prices and the allocation of capital, labor, and output. By contrast, the third priority of the Copenhagen criteria was to provide effective regulation and oversight of the economy by the administrative apparatus of the country's government, implying that price controls and subsidies for backward regions or agricultural producers could be maintained, but only at levels commonly agreed upon by EU consensus (Neal 2007: chap. 19).

Repeated applications of the Washington consensus prescriptions upon IMF aid recipients – when confronted with a financial crisis during the 1990s – often led to political unrest, continued economic distress, and, eventually, to new thinking about the wisdom of the consensus. The prescriptions imposed on those receiving badly needed IMF financial aid clearly did not always generate the desired outcomes, whether they were better growth performance, reduced unemployment, lower inflation, or all three. For example, Malaysia's policies used to recover from the Asian financial crisis of the late 1990s ignored the IMF by imposing temporary capital controls directly against Singapore banks. To take another example, the Argentine economy rebounded following its massive default in 2000 (after which it was excluded from the international capital markets) and it was spared suffering from the subsequent global financial crisis of 2008, at least for a while. Indonesia, however, continued to play by IMF rules, but economic malaise persisted. These contrasts suggested that other institutional reforms were needed to supplement or even replace the Washington consensus. When economic recovery by those playing by IMF rules was swift, the Washington consensus prescriptions looked good. When aid recipients who played by the rules lapsed into continued political and/or economic malaise, the prescriptions looked bad. They also looked bad when those not playing by IMF rules did well. The Washington consensus clearly needed a reassessment.

The problem with the Copenhagen criteria, on the other hand, was that the process of creating the organizations needed to sustain institutional change takes a very long time. The first entries into the EU came in 2004 after ten years of intensive monitoring and collaboration between EU officials and national civil servants. Moreover, the acceptance of applicants was made more on political than economic grounds – all ten candidate countries were admitted at the same time, despite having widely different institutional capabilities. The last hurdle facing new EU applicants – adopting the euro – largely still remained as of 2013, since the eurozone crisis that began in 2010 made adopting the euro less desirable.

Keeping track of the subsequent transitions to capitalism across the Eurasian continent became one of the functions of the European Bank for Reconstruction and Development (EBRD), and their observations allow us to see how Washington consensus and Copenhagen criteria policies have worked across a wide variety of country conditions. Created in 1990 to deal with the transition economies that had formerly been centrally planned, the EBRD combines the institutional focus of the Copenhagen criteria with the essential economic aspects of the Washington consensus. After twenty years of projects and cooperation with the bank, the EBRD could state in its *Transition Report* of 2012 that those countries with the highest ratings were those that went through the EU vetting process before gaining full membership in 2004 (EBRD 2012: 9, Table 1.1). The first two test cases of transition strategy based on shock therapy – Poland and East Germany – proved to be recovering best from the sub-prime crisis while also weathering the eurozone crisis best. Much of the explanation for their relative success must be due to their longer transition experience rather than just the mandates of the IMF, the World Bank, and the EU. Thus, at least part of their success was due to their total commitment to the transition from the very beginning in 1990, in contrast to the fitful attempts made by other countries spun off from the Soviet Union's deconstruction (Aslund 2002).

The World Bank has broadened the geographical scope of the EBRD's *Transition Report* with its annual *Doing Business*, which started in 2003 and covered 185 countries by 2013. Although *Doing Business* limits its analysis to the laws and regulations imposed by governments on the private sector, it still finds a positive correlation between its index and levels of per capita income. It also reports continuing progress with governments easing regulatory and legal obstacles to starting up new businesses. Most encouraging is the relatively more rapid improvement in the poorest and worst-performing countries, overwhelmingly located in sub-Saharan Africa, as well as the positive regulatory reforms made by countries most affected by the financial crisis in the eurozone (Greece, Italy, Portugal, and Spain). While the world's governments had made transitions to capitalism somewhat easier over the decade, progress was still slow. Coordinating the various aspects of a capitalist economy operating in global markets – especially the financial aspects – takes time to get right, as the history of capitalism has demonstrated time and again.

Sovereign debt and the transition to capitalism

Access to capital was crucial for countries making the transition to capitalism in preindustrial Europe, in the nineteenth-century age of globalization, and in the most recent age of globalization. Sovereign bonds issued by emerging nations on the London and Paris capital markets were the major source of financing for nineteenth-century transition economies (see Michie, Chapter 8 and James, Chapter 9 in this volume). While foreign direct investment by newly emerging multinational companies was also important then, it has proven to be the major source of transition finance in the twenty-first century, as multinational companies increasingly directed their investments overseas to the emerging economies after the 1970s (see Jones, Chapter 6 in this volume).

While international sources of finance for transition, emerging, and developing economies have been private rather than official, their sovereign debt has been used to finance private projects as well as state-owned enterprises and infrastructure. However, the sovereign debt in advanced capitalist economies continues to rise as a share of total GDP as well. Moreover, until the eurozone crisis developed at the beginning of 2010, such debt was increasingly held abroad, the most dramatic case being the amount of US government debt held by China and Japan. The widespread holding of sovereign debt by private interests abroad combined with the low interest rates paid on US and German public debt highlights the critical role played by government bonds in global finance and in both the rise and spread of capitalism.

This had happened before, *long* before. The rise of state finance as well as the establishment of English national debt following the Glorious Revolution of 1688–1689 was associated with the rise of capitalism (Dickson 1967; Neal 1990; North and Weingast 1989). Other European states tried to imitate British success at the conclusion of the Napoleonic Wars, something clearly documented by José Luis Cardoso and Pedro Lains in their *Paying for the Liberal State* (2010). The British model created modern excise taxes on basic consumption goods that could be mass-marketed, something easy to administer by a central government bureaucracy and cheap to collect (see Lindert, Chapter 14 in this volume). Britain then used these taxes to service an ever-growing sovereign debt (see O'Brien, Chapter 12 in Volume I, and Daunton 2010). Servicing long-term debt by stable revenue sources seemed pretty simple to Britain's competitors, but it was not easily imitated. Grasping the essential complementarity between a steady flow of tax revenues dependent upon continuing prosperity for consumers and the attractiveness of public debt held by a prosperous middle class for long-term savings goals did not come easily to the governing elites of Europe. Only the revolutions of 1848 forced even the ruling Junker classes in East Prussia to acknowledge the need to placate the urban labor force of West Prussia by increasing employment opportunities through improved infrastructure, especially the creation of a rail network, all of which required large-scale finance (Spoerer 2010; Tilly 1966).

The ultimate complementarity of market economies and liberal states, therefore, does not rest solely on the protection of private property rights and the impartial enforcement of private contracts, fundamental as they are for efficient markets. And it certainly does not rest on light taxation since capitalist economies have always had higher taxation than traditional ones (see again Lindert, Chapter 14 in this volume). However, it is clear that the complementarity of capitalism and liberal government does require the choice of sovereign debt as a favorite long-term asset held by the public (once again, see O'Brien, Chapter 12 in Volume I, and also Neal 2010 and MacDonald 2003). For both firms and households, government debt provides insurance against the vicissitudes of daily life, while entrepreneurs use it as collateral widely accepted even by distant and unknown investors. Whether the franchise is extended widely or not, widespread holdings of sovereign debt also demonstrates political support for the government. This is as true today as it was in 1848, and even much earlier.

Federations, unions, and finance

As market capitalism expanded in advanced Western economies from the end of World War II to 1973, so did the relative size of government, marked by rising tax revenues and outstanding government debt. While the oil shocks of the 1970s brought "miracle growth" to a halt in the advanced industrial economies, those same shocks actually encouraged the further growth of government debt. Greater global openness, measured by a country's ratio of exports plus imports to gross domestic product, was augmented in response to the first oil shock of 1973. This was a massive and negative terms of trade shock that industrialized, capitalist economies faced when oil-exporting countries, mostly unindustrialized and suspicious of capitalism, colluded to raise the price of crude oil. One impetus for the observed increase in openness for capitalist economies thus came as a result of the increased cost of imports due to a sharp rise in crude oil prices imposed by the Organization of the Petroleum Exporting Countries (OPEC).

Financing this permanent rise in import costs, however, required many adjustments including a new approach to international finance. The capital controls that were accepted as part of the conditions for joining the IMF were first evaded, mainly by recycling petro-dollars earned by OPEC countries through the euro-dollar markets. But by the 1980s, OECD members agreed that capital controls should be eliminated entirely. Maintaining free trade within a customs union comprised of countries all exercising national sovereignty over their currency with each keeping fixed and stable exchange rates was becoming impossible as capital controls were losing their effectiveness in a new world of euro-dollar and petro-dollar markets. The EU solved the problem – called the trilemma – by creating a common currency, the euro. Thus, most EU members agreed to surrender their control over their national money supply. The EU solution to the macroeconomic trilemma then became free movement of capital, irrevocably fixed exchange rates (with each other, but not the rest of the world), and the surrender of monetary independence.

Surrender of monetary independence was not easily done, however, and all countries joining the euro insisted on maintaining fiscal independence over their domestic tax bases and expenditure decisions to compensate for their loss of control over the money supply. A technical aspect of the euro banking system eventually proved to be its downfall. As the EU had no independent taxing authority of its own, it could not issue bonds with any credible backing. Instead of a common EU-bond, there were just the euro-denominated bonds of each member. When lending money short-term to member country banks, however, the ECB accepted sovereign bonds from each member country as though they were just part of a common pool of EU-bonds. The result was to make high-risk bonds from Italy, Greece, Portugal, and Spain equally good as low-risk German, Dutch, or French bonds when posted as collateral for short-term loans throughout the EU. Since banking supervision was still the responsibility of the individual member countries, this optimistic view of the value of member bonds led to excessive bank lending in some countries (Ireland and Spain), and large government deficits in others (Italy, Greece, and Portugal). Low interest rates on their outstanding debt encouraged government spending and rising debt.

How the EU responds to the eurozone crisis will determine the future of the euro within its free trade and integrated labor market area, as well as the future of all members' fiscal autonomy. Likewise, the future of capitalism within the EU hinges on the outcomes of these decisions as they affect the ground rules of international finance. While the future of capitalism in the United States has been assured by the prompt and vigorous response by its Treasury and the Federal Reserve, it, too, depends heavily on the outcome of EU actions. Finance, as the most visible face of modern capitalism, is also the most vulnerable to political pressure (Rajan and Zingales 2004), both from entrenched interests seeking to preserve their positions and from infuriated citizens seeking revenge for their losses from a financial crisis and its bailouts. Yet, two lines of defense have helped maintain the vitality and promise of capitalism, and both have survived the crisis. One has been to allow outside competition to domestic firms through minimum barriers to trade. Another has been to allow inside competition through access to startup finance by new firms.

Looking ahead on the financial front

Regardless of their specific policy challenges, each country should focus on policies that foster the productive use of capital, which increasingly has come to mean that which is embodied in people (human capital), land (exploitable natural resources), or buildings and equipment (physical capital). Moreover, making productive use of the various forms of capital requires repeatedly solving coordination problems over varying time horizons. Initial success, as history has shown again and again, can stall out as capitalists, flushed with success, capture the support of governments persuaded to retain their privileges. Such appeared to be the case worldwide with the great reversal of globalization after World War I (Rajan and Zingales 2004: chap. 9). Initial successes, however, can be sustained if complementary initiatives emerge elsewhere in the economy and become supportive (see Morck and Yeung, Chapter 7 in this volume). Family farms, for example, have provided urban populations with plentiful food more successfully than collective farms or plantations (see Federico, Chapter 3 in this volume and his book *Feeding the World* [2005]).

After decades of providing government aid to developing countries, mainly by former colonial powers and their international agencies, the removal of capital controls in the 1970s allowed private capital flows, initially in the form of foreign direct investment to finance capitalist enterprises in Africa, South America, and Asia. These private capital flows were on a scale that was orders of magnitude larger than were the aid flows from international agencies and government-to-government loans and grants in the early postwar decades. As we have seen in the years since, capitalist enterprises operating on a global scale can sustain repressive governments. This has often been the case with exploitable natural resources at locations that require mining or drilling operations. Large corporations exploiting government controls for natural resource extraction generally had the benefit of finance from impersonal equity and bond markets, starting with the English and Dutch East India Companies of the seventeenth century up to the multinational oil and mining companies of this century. Getting the mix of financing sources right for the benefit of the population at large has to be the responsibility of the state. The state's dilemma is how to finance its response to emergencies created by exogenous shocks, whether caused by war, natural disaster, famine, disease, or financial crisis. The ongoing challenge for governments of capitalist economies in the future will be how to maintain the incentives for capitalist enterprises to continue creating the new products and increasing productivity that has led to higher living standards and popular support. Incentives alone, however, may not suffice.

Growth and the future of capitalism

The future of capitalism in the twenty-first century will be conditioned by maintaining rapid economic growth, peaceful global relationships, and efficient global trade, factor, and financial markets. After 1848, the attraction of capitalism to non-capitalist systems was greatly enhanced by industrialization and rising GDP per capita among the capitalist leaders. The twenty-first century will demand the same. But the first global economy up to 1913 and the second since 1950 have both required wrenching social and economic changes by all participants – whether adapting to the import of new and cheaper products, to vastly more foreign migrants, to new technologies, to complicated financial institutions, or to new distributions of military and political power. These changes produced a wide variety of responses by those who lost and those who gained. These responses took place within and between nations, and they were sometimes violent. Capitalism and globalization in the twenty-first century will require continued change to remain viable, and to the extent that they are public goods, their changes are the responsibility of the state. History should offer some guidance on this score. The contributions of these two volumes provide just such a chronicle of successive challenges and responses, both creative and destructive, as capitalism matured across the nineteenth and twentieth centuries.

Even though global capitalism will always generate struggles between winners and losers (shown so well in this volume in Austin, Chapter 10; Frieden and Rogowski, Chapter 12; Harrison, Chapter 11; Huberman, Chapter 13; and O'Rourke and Williamson, Chapter 1), rapid economic growth is the prize that makes all participants more tolerant of financial crises and competitive adjustment. Members of the European capitalist club were growing faster during the nineteenth century, and more European countries and their overseas offshoots were joining the club. Thus, tolerance, or even enthusiastic acceptance, of capitalism followed. In the interwar period, slow growth and a great depression challenged that view. It appeared that the growth prize could be better achieved by competing economic systems – like communism and fascism, exceeding the performance of capitalism. In the years following World War II, capitalism got the upper hand again. Why? Because it grabbed the growth prize once more. But, as Chapter 14 in this volume by Peter Lindert and Chapter 15 by Leandro Prados de la Escosura demonstrate, capitalist economies initiated welfare programs that were both pro-growth (by improving education, nutrition, and health), and welfare-enhancing (by making life longer, healthier, and creating more opportunities for human enjoyment). The consequence was to maintain the political legitimacy of capitalist institutions while undergoing the sometimes painful changes required to regain rapid economic growth.

So, what about the growth prize in the twenty-first century?

To answer that question, let's start by repeating an observation made at the beginning: At the start of this century, and before the recent great recession, world real GDP was growing at over 5 percent annually, an unprecedented economic achievement. Furthermore, capitalism could take much of the credit for it. Is it likely that this rapid growth rate will continue across the century? The answer is almost certainly, no. The recent rapid world growth rate has been driven largely by "miracle" growth in very large emerging nations like China, India, Indonesia, Brazil, and Russia. All emerging countries tend to record "miraculous" growth as they catch up with the leaders. Neoclassical economics makes that prediction (Barro 1991, 1997; Solow 1956), and the new endogenous growth literature agrees (Helpman 2004; Lucas 1988;

Romer 1986, 1990), as the best technologies, institutions, and policies are transferred to poor countries where they replace old and inefficient ones. The faster poor countries transfer and adapt, the more miraculous their growth. But as the emerging countries catch up, the gap between best practice abroad and traditional practice at home gets narrower, so the "miraculous" growth possibilities diminish.

There is another reason for the slowdown in the emerging countries – demography. As these economies undergo the transition from preindustrial poverty to industrial wealth, they also undergo what is called the demographic transition (Bloom and Williamson 1998; Williamson 2013). As infant mortality rates fall, child cohorts get bigger, and, with a two-decade lag, the working adult share rises, and per capita income growth is fostered. This phase of the demographic transition is also called the demographic dividend. For all three reasons – neoclassical economics, endogenous growth theory, and demography – growth rates soar in emerging countries to "miraculous" rates. But what goes up, then comes down, as these economies finish their transition and seek some mature steady state, much like the industrial leaders. This, of course, will drag down the world growth rate. The only force that might forestall this future Third World slowdown is the addition of new emerging countries to the "miracle" club, like those in sub-Saharan Africa or the Middle East. But as the number of poor, preindustrial countries disappears, a world slowdown becomes increasingly inevitable.

What about the so-called steady state growth among the leaders? Are those rates likely to decline as well? It seems possible, and perhaps even likely. First, the demographic transition is at work for them too, and as the OECD world gets older and older, it puts a drag on per capita income growth. But there are more reasons to expect a slowdown in the rich capitalist world. Robert Gordon (2012) thinks there are five additional reasons for a slowdown among the North American and EU leaders (education, energy/environment, inequality, globalization, and the overhang of consumer and government debt). In addition to demography, we think four of Gordon's five might matter as well. First, education is becoming less a carrier of growth among the leaders, partly because the relative cost of good secondary and tertiary education has soared and will soar further, perhaps placing it out of reach of all but the upper classes. To make matters worse, public investment in schooling seems likely to diminish as retired citizens demand a larger share of the public pie. Second, the rising cost of energy and the demands for better environmental quality (especially in the big emerging and still environmentally "dirty" nations) will contribute further to a growth slowdown. Third, since the 1970s, global capitalism has been consistent with rising inequality within major participants like the United States as a leader and China and Russia as catchers-up. Will the widening gap between the rich at the top, the poor at the bottom, and the middle class squeezed in between create a political crisis and a growth breakdown? No matter what the reader's position is on these issues, world growth rates will fall over this century: they will definitely fall for the catchers-up, and they will probably fall for the current leaders.

True, globalization can offset these diminished-growth forces since it raises living standards worldwide either directly by the improved allocation of labor and capital around the globe, or indirectly by trade and its resulting specialization, or both. But will countries continue to favor free trade, mass migration, and the operation of global capital markets? Perhaps, but we have already seen the contrary between 1914 and 1950 (see O'Rourke and Williamson, Chapter 1 in this volume). We have discussed financial capital markets at length in this concluding chapter, but what about labor markets and trade? Restrictions on immigration in high-wage capitalist countries certainly show no sign of falling, while the new economic powerhouses in Asia have never had an immigration tradition (Hatton and Williamson 2005). Furthermore, many developing countries in Asia, Africa, and Latin America have expressed suspicions about free trade since 1848 (Williamson 2011), and those who went open in the late twentieth century are now having second thoughts.

Of course, growth isn't everything. Capitalist governments can, of course, continue to make the kinds of interventions that Leandro Prados de la Escosura identifies (Chapter 15 in this volume) as having actually increased human welfare during the earlier globalization backlash between 1914 and 1950. The overhang of debt, both personal and government, takes time to work off, but is unlikely to be a long-run impediment to pro-growth policies, provided that governments can exercise the political will required to re-direct resources to education and R&D – especially in bio-medical areas.

Still, if capitalism gets the credit for the secular speed-up in world growth rates since the early nineteenth century, will the world also blame it for any secular growth slowdown in the twenty-first century? If so, will it choose some alternative? Or, will capitalist economies adapt to a possible growth slowdown by introducing policies that continue to ameliorate the human condition?

References

Angell, N. (1913). *The Great Illusion: A Study of the Relation of Military Power to National Advantage*, 4th rev. and enl. edn. London: G. P. Putnam & Sons.

Aslund, A. (2002). *Building Capitalism: The Transformation of the Former Soviet Bloc.* Cambridge University Press.

Bank for International Settlements (2012). *Annual Report.* Basel: BIS.

Barro, R. J. (1991). "Economic Growth in a Cross Section of Countries," *Quarterly Journal of Economics* 106: 407–443.

(1997). *Determinants of Economic Growth.* Cambridge, MA: The MIT Press.

Bloom, D. and J. G. Williamson (1998). "Demographic Transitions and Economic Miracles in Emerging Asia," *World Bank Economic Review* 12(3): 419–455.

Broadberry, S. and M. Harrison, eds. (2005). *The Economics of World War 1.* Cambridge University Press.

Cardoso, J. L. and P. Lains (2011). *Paying for the Liberal State: The Rise of Public Finance in Nineteenth Century Europe.* Cambridge University Press.

Daunton, M. (2010). "The Case of Great Britain," in J. L. Cardoso and P. Lains (eds.), *Paying for the Liberal State: The Rise of Public Finance in Nineteenth Century Europe.* Cambridge University Press, pp. 27–56.

Dickson, P. G. M. (1967). *The Financial Revolution in England, A Study in the Development of Public Credit, 1688–1756.* New York: Macmillan.

European Bank for Reconstruction and Development (2012). *Transition Report, 2012.* London: EBRD.

Federico, G. (2005). *Feeding the World: An Economic History of Agriculture, 1800–2000.* Princeton University Press.

Gordon, R. J. (2012). "Is U.S. Economic Growth Over? Faltering Innovation Confronts the Six Headwinds," Working Paper 18315, Cambridge, MA: National Bureau of Economic Research (August).

Hatton, T. J. and J. G. Williamson (2005). *Global Migration and the World Economy: Two Centuries of Policy and Performance.* Cambridge, MA: The MIT Press.

Helpman, E. (2004). *The Mystery of Economic Growth.* Cambridge, MA: Harvard University Press.

International Monetary Fund (2006). *World Economic Outlook, 2006,* Washington, DC: IMF.

(2012). *Global Financial Stability Report, April 2012,* Washington, DC: IMF.

Lucas, R. E. (1988). "On the Mechanics of Economic Development," *Journal of Monetary Economics* 22: 3–42.

MacDonald, J. (2003). *A Free Nation Deep in Debt: The Financial Roots of Democracy.* New York: Farrar, Straus & Giroux.

Neal, L. (1990). *The Rise of Financial Capitalism: International Capital Movements in the Age of Reason.* Cambridge and New York: Cambridge University Press.

(2007). *The Economics of Europe and the European Union,* Cambridge University Press.

(2010). "The Monetary, Fiscal, and Political Architecture of Europe, 1815–1914," in J. L. Cardoso and P. Lains (eds.), *Paying for the Liberal State: The Rise of Public Finance in Nineteenth-Century Europe.* Cambridge University Press, pp. 279–302.

North, D. C. and B. Weingast (1989). "Constitutions and Commitment: The Evolution of Institutions Governing Public Choice in 17th Century England," *Journal of Economic History* 48(4): 803–832.

Rajan, R. and L. Zingales (2004). *Saving Capitalism from the Capitalists: Unleashing the Power of Financial Markets to Create Wealth and Spread Opportunity.* Princeton University Press.

Romer, P. M. (1986). "Increasing Returns and Long Run Growth," *Journal of Political Economy* 94: 1002–1037.

(1990). "Endogenous Technological Change," *Journal of Political Economy* 98: S71–S102.

Solow, R. M. (1956). "A Contribution to the Theory of Economic Growth," *Quarterly Journal of Economics* 70: 65–94.

Spoerer, M. (2010). "The Evolution of Public Finances in Nineteenth Century Prussia," in J. L. Cardoso and P. Lains (eds.), *Paying for the Liberal State: The Rise of Public Finance in Nineteenth Century Europe.* Cambridge University Press, pp. 103–131.

Tilly, R. (1966). "The Political Economy of Public Finance and the Industrialization of Prussia, 1815–1866," *Journal of Economic History* 4(26): 484–497.

Williamson, J. G. (2011). *Trade and Poverty: When the Third World Fell Behind.* Cambridge, MA: The MIT Press.

(2013). "Demographic Dividends Revisited," *Asian Development Review* 30(3): 1–25.

World Bank (2013). *Doing Business 2013: Smarter Regulations for Small and Medium-Size Enterprises.* Washington, DC: International Finance Corporation and World Bank.

Index

accounting, 250
Acemoglu, Daron, 131, 327–28, 432
Action Française, 402
adversarial legal system, 132
aerospace, 105, 121
Afghanistan, 370
AFL-CIO, 458
Africa: agriculture in, 54, 55, 57, 61, 62, 77, 118, 322, 327, 339, 421; banking in, 244, 325, 337; capitalism rejected in, 13; cloth sales in, 310; colonialism in, 29–30, 177, 303, 304, 307–8, 311, 315, 318–19, 321–22, 327, 396, 406; copper mining in, 182; economic dislocation in, 384; economic reform in, 5, 420, 537; European trade with, 302, 307, 314; export controls in, 324; expropriation in, 186; forced labor in, 316, 318–19; foreign investment in, 541; human development gains in, 504, 506, 514, 524, 525; independence movements in, 313; labor relations in, 426, 447, 457; Latin America contrasted with, 335–36; legal systems in, 152, 160; manufacturing in, 334; migration from, 10; migration to, 437; population growth in, 331; prospects for, 543, 544; rent seeking in, 30, 46; scramble for, 150, 307, 325; uneven growth in, 117, 214, 511, 525; wage labor in, 326–27
agency problems, 208–11, 287
Agnelli family, 218
Agricultural Adjustment Act (1933), 76
agriculture, 25, 75–79; acreage devoted to, 54–55; in Africa, 29; in Asia, 39, 339; beginnings of, 47; in China, 39, 44–45, 50, 54–55, 57, 58, 71, 72, 110; consumer protection and, 72–73; in developing

nations, 176; in Egypt, 35; factory system counterparts in, 64–70; farmers' cooperatives in, 69–70; financing of, 70–72; in India, 29; intensive growth in, 56–60; in Japan, 36; mechanization of, 55, 57, 58, 59, 60, 67–68, 83, 85; in Mexico, 30, 74; nineteenth- and twentieth-century growth of, 48–52; property rights and, 60–64; protection of, 17–18, 387; research and development in, 59–60, 73–75, 77, 96–97, 118, 121, 329, 330; in Russia, 33; slash-and-burn, 57, 61, 62; as source of rents, 355; in Soviet Union, 40, 41; specialization in, 50; types of tenure in, 67; workforce in, 52–53
AIDS, 524
aircraft, 28, 86, 100
airlines, 184, 193, 420
Aitken, Max, 206
Alexander II, Tsar, 32
Alfa-Laval, 112
Algeria, 311, 313, 315, 318
Allen, R. C., 309
Alsace, 111
aluminum, 111
American Red Cross, 488
Amin, Samir, 304
Amsden, Alice, 332
anarchism, 394, 438
Anderson, Christopher, 369
André (grain trader), 182
Andreev, Svetlozar, 374
Andreoni, James, 470–71
Angell, Norman, 352, 356, 531
Anglo-Iranian Oil Company, 180
Angola, 514

Printed by Printforce, United Kingdom